TOWARD THE MEETING OF THE WATERS

TOWARD THE MEETING OF THE WATERS

Currents in the Civil Rights Movement of
South Carolina during the Twentieth Century

Edited by
WINFRED B. MOORE JR.
AND ORVILLE VERNON BURTON

The University of South Carolina Press

© 2008 University of South Carolina
"An 'Ominous Defiance': The Lowman Lynchings of 1926" © 2008 Elizabeth Robeson

Published by the University of South Carolina Press
Columbia, South Carolina 29208

www.sc.edu/uscpress

Manufactured in the United States of America

17 16 15 14 13 12 11 10 09 08   10 9 8 7 6 5 4 3 2 1

Library of Congress Cataloging-in-Publication Data

Toward the meeting of the waters : currents in the civil rights movement of South Carolina
   during the twentieth century / edited by Winfred B. Moore Jr. and Orville Vernon Burton.
      p. cm.
   Includes bibliographical references and index.
   ISBN 978-1-57003-755-9 (cloth : alk. paper)
   1. African Americans—Civil rights—South Carolina—History—20th century. 2. African
Americans—Segregation—South Carolina—History—20th century. 3. Civil rights
movements—South Carolina—History—20th century. 4. African American civil rights
workers—South Carolina—History—20th century. 5. Racism—South Carolina—History—
20th century. 6. Lynching—South Carolina—History—20th century. 7. South Carolina—
Race relations—History—20th century. 8. South Carolina—Politics and government—20th
century. I. Moore, Winfred B., 1949– II. Burton, Orville Vernon.
E185.93.S7T69 2008
323.1196'07307570904—dc22   2008018604

This book has been printed on Glatfelter Natures, a recycled paper with 30 percent postconsumer
waste content.

In honor of Benjamin E. Mays, Lilly Graham, and Catherine, Brother, Pat, and Skip Williams, of Ninety Six, South Carolina, and Nancy and Ed Haywood of Cowpens, South Carolina, mentors in the full meaning of friendship and civil rights

A few years ago I was in Brazil, a thousand miles inland at a place called Manaus. A few miles northwest of Manaus, two rivers converge at a place they call "the meeting of the waters." The Rio Solomos, a clearwater river, flows down out of the mountains and intersects the Rio Negro, a blackwater river like the Waccamaw near my home in South Carolina. At first their waters do not mingle but flow along side by side. I have videotape of myself on a boat going back and forth across that line. But after two or three miles the two rivers flow together, and when they do they become the mightiest river in the world—the Amazon. I see that as a metaphor for the people of our beloved South Carolina.

Charles Joyner

Contents

Illustrations

Foreword

On a chilly day in January 2003 in downtown Columbia, I bumped into a friend who asked if I'd heard about the upcoming civil rights history conference being held at the Citadel in Charleston that March. I said no. A smile crossed his face.

"There's not a lot of publicity about it. I'll send you a copy of the agenda, if you'd like."

A few days later, after scanning a copy of the agenda that had arrived in my mailbox at the newsroom of the *State*, South Carolina's largest newspaper, I uttered a single, unjournalistic word: "Wow."

It was not just that there were more than twenty panels featuring more than seventy civil rights scholars from across the nation and the world. Or that their subjects were such largely forgotten topics as lynching, desegregating South Carolina's universities, the role of the NAACP in South Carolina, the Clarendon County *Briggs v. Elliott* lawsuit (the real linchpin of the U.S. Supreme Court's 1954 landmark *Brown v. Board of Education* decision), and the 1968 Orangeburg Massacre. Presentations would also include scholarly looks at the late, great civil rights activist Septima Clark and the trailblazing U.S. judge Waties Waring of Charleston, also deceased.

What also caught my eye was that some of the aging actors of those dramatic days would be present and speak about their roles—former governor and current U.S. senator Ernest Hollings, a former staunch segregationist who became an equal rights advocate; the brave Harvey Gantt, who as a young black in 1963 risked ostracism and, some felt, death, to desegregate Clemson University; the aristocratic black legal revolutionary and now U.S. judge Matthew Perry; John West, a beloved icon whose 1970 election as governor marked a bright line between the state's old hardline racial ways and the new, more open and inclusive South Carolina; and Cleveland Sellers, a black activist who was shot by highway patrol troopers at a college civil rights demonstration in Orangeburg and who served time in prison for inciting a riot. These days, Sellers has a pardon and teaches African American studies at the University of South Carolina. Leading off the three-day panel was John Hope Franklin, eighty-eight, the legendary Duke historian who as a young NAACP researcher had played a vital role the plaintiff's case in the 1954 U.S. Supreme Court *Brown* decision.

In short, there would be not just scholarship; there would be witnessing. It would be an opening of minds, of hearts, of eyes—the closest thing South Carolina had ever had, and maybe ever would have, to a reconciliation meeting, those psychologically cleansing sessions where they who have done wrong acknowledge their deeds, apologize, and are forgiven. Here, the purpose was not to apologize or explain but simply to reflect that long-ago reality, to tell the truth of about the grip of state-sanctioned racism upon South Carolina, and relate stories of the heroes, black and white, who freed us all.

The conference had its ironies. It was being held at the Citadel,[1] a state-run military college established before the Civil War to "insure domestic tranquility"— in other words, prevent slave uprisings. In 1861 Citadel cadets fired the first shots of that war. A century later its cadets and alumni fought hard (and lost again!) to keep blacks and women from becoming students. The Citadel is in Charleston, where the 1860 secession convention split the Union. It is a city in which for many residents the past is likely to be symbolized by historic homes or the Confederate submarine, the *H. L. Hunley,* pulled from a watery grave off Charleston in 2000. Public inquiries into slavery and civil rights—the issues that have defined South Carolina politically, economically, and socially for hundreds of years—have never ranked high among the Holy City's, or South Carolina's, for that matter, priorities.

I took the conference agenda to the *State*'s top editor, Mark Lett. He saw its significance immediately. In fact, he one-upped me. Where I had envisioned sending a reporter (me) or two to the conference—which would have been far more coverage than we give most scholarly events—Lett's idea was to use the conference as a springboard to produce our own stories on the South Carolina civil rights era. In the days leading up to the conference we would explore, in a series of feature articles, various topics based on those to be presented at the Citadel. Writing these preconference stories would liberate us from solely stenographic coverage of just reporting on the Citadel's sessions. As for the conference itself, we would flood it with reporters, having four or five there each day, with photographers, as well a technology-trained reporter to capture some panels on digital camera for our Internet site.

To us the conference was far more than a news event; it was a chance to educate our readers and ourselves about a story as dramatic as it was untold. For South Carolina's civil rights era, a period roughly between 1940 and 1970, was a time of great battles and their warriors, with no less than the American promise— justice and equal rights versus oppression—hanging in the balance.

We wrote dozens of stories. Supplementing our core team of myself, Claudia Smith Brinson, Carolyn Click, and Roddie Burriss—all veteran reporters—were more than ten other reporters, photographers, editors, and graphics designers. Our technical people shot digital video of some conference sessions and put them on our Internet site. Two months later we produced a twenty-six-page special section, with most of our stories.

We at the *State* felt this was a special project. We were revealing a submerged past and showing how far we had come. Reader reaction was intense and widespread. Most was favorable, but as might be expected, a few complaints surfaced from those who felt the newspaper was just stirring up trouble.

Three years later, I'm still getting calls from people, asking for copies of stories we did back then.

The Citadel conference was about history. But it also made history. To understand that statement it is necessary to know this: for much of the twentieth century most South Carolina newspapers and professors at the state's universities failed to speak out fully, forcefully, and truthfully about the state's racial dilemmas.

This was tragedy of a high order. Journalists and professors are the people who, by their education and choice of profession, might have been expected to be most vocal in providing moral leadership in articulating civil rights matters. The silence of most South Carolina journalists and professors in those times most likely not only prolonged that sad era, it in some ways allowed the state's history to be hijacked by those who would deny history—how else to explain that in 2000, during the debate over whether to fly the Confederate flag atop the statehouse, a group of more than one hundred South Carolina historians felt it necessary to hold a press conference to document that slavery—and not "states' rights," as claimed by flag defenders—was the major cause of the American Civil War!

As I write this in mid-2006, there is still a powerful strain in South Carolina that would quash examinations of the past that might "taint" the ideal of a Confederacy that symbolized anything less than "freedom" or delve too deeply into the wellsprings of injustice that propped up segregation in South Carolina during much of the twentieth century. Only this spring I asked two of South Carolina's most prominent historians, both of whom work for public universities, to comment on historical significance, or lack thereof, of the *H. L. Hunley* submarine. Both historians declined to make public their honestly held opinions for fear of offending powerful neo-Confederates in the state legislature. A third historian reluctantly agreed to comment. Such reticence today on the part of even our finest historians underscores the fact that large patches of South Carolina's historical landscape—from slavery to Reconstruction to lynching—still have "Keep Out" signs posted.

We journalists like to call our stories the "first rough draft of history." When it came to state-supported apartheid in South Carolina, members of my profession in this state wrote a very rough draft indeed. While it is true that events with a racial dimension were covered—lynchings, "colored" gatherings, protests in the twentieth century—these events were often written in a kind of one-dimensional code, written by white journalists for white readers. Nearly all whites—writers and audience alike—believed in the legitimacy of a white-dominated, racially segregated world.

In the 1950s and 1960s the editorial writers at my paper, the *State,* had upheld segregation and criticized anyone, including the federal government, who would pass laws affirming equal rights for black people. In so doing they comforted themselves and their readers with the fiction that their stands were enlightened and part of a southern cultural tradition with sound intellectual underpinnings. They took pride in the nods they made to African Americans as people. Former *State* editor Sam Latimer noted in his 1970 history of the *State* newspaper that it not only had editorialized in favor of compulsory black public education up through the twelfth grade but also (before World War I) "was the second newspaper in the South to capitalize the N in Negro."[2]

William Workman, one of South Carolina's most prominent journalists in the mid–twentieth century and editor of the *State* from 1966 to 1972, likened integration in his 1960 book, *The Case for the South,* to that most hated of ideologies: communism. "What Communism has been to the rest of the nation, so integration is to the South—something so undesirable, so foreign to the domestic way of life, so fraught with danger to present and future generations that it is fought on every front, including the educational."[3]

From the 1920s to the early 1960s the *State*'s editorial pages regularly carried a cartoon featuring Hambone, a shuffling, dialect-speaking black man, the kind of harmless black who dispensed amiable wit but who would never upset folks by asking to vote or sit at a lunch counter. (As the 1960s went on, the *State*'s news coverage improved and its editorial stances moderated. In the crucial 1970 gubernatorial elections, it endorsed the moderate John West, not the race-baiting Albert Watson.)

But segregationist views dominated almost every South Carolina newspaper, sometimes to an extreme. In the 1950s, as he closed out a long career as a noted editor and first dean of the University of South Carolina journalism program, for example, William Watts Ball at the *Charleston News and Courier* wrote "amusing" stories about black lynchings.[4] Many editorial writers adopted a rhetorical technique of segregationist politicians: they would compare the NAACP—which was trying to end legally segregation's injustices—with the Ku Klux Klan, which preached a virulent, sometimes violent brand of racism. Thus, in a few words, journalists of that era routinely smeared the NAACP while decrying Klan excesses.

There were a few exceptions. The *Charlotte Observer*—widely circulated in South Carolina in the 1950s and 1960s—was noted for its "liberal" news and editorial stances (that is, advocacy of simple justice and equal rights for blacks). Just over the North Carolina/South Carolina border, newsman Horace Carter of Tabor City exposed Klan violence in South Carolina, especially in Horry and Marion counties. For this work he won a Pulitzer Prize in 1953. (It is telling that no South Carolina newspaper has ever won a Pulitzer for exposing racial injustice, despite ample opportunity for generations!) In the mid-1950s John O'Dowd, a Citadel graduate and editor of the *Florence Morning News,* wrote editorials after the *Brown* decision in which he said things such as, like it or not, the U.S. Supreme Court is the law of the land. Because of his moderate racial stands, O'Dowd attracted a wide range of enemies and critics, from the Ku Klux Klan to the *News and Courier.* Eventually community pressure forced O'Dowd to leave, a one-man exodus noted by *Time* magazine, which reported that O'Dowd was moving to Chicago and quoted him as saying, "I'm certain the *News* will no longer buck racial feeling."[5]

In the state's universities a parallel universe of self-censorship and lack of freedom of speech also existed. Professors who spoke up for equal rights for black people, or who might dare to defend the legitimacy of the U.S. Supreme Court, were ostracized and in extreme cases forced to leave. The most infamous incident involved University of South Carolina's Chester Travelstead, dean of the School of Education. In 1955 Travelstead wrote a letter to segregationist governor George Bell Timmerman, telling Timmerman he was wrong to try to undermine decisions of the U.S. Supreme Court. Timmerman responded by seeking, and eventually getting, Travelstead's dismissal. "Fear covers South Carolina like the frost. Men are afraid to speak," wrote Camden Episcopal minister Stiles B. Lines.[6]

Inaction based on fear also paralyzed much of the black community. In 1956, under pressure from Governor Timmerman, black officials at all-black South Carolina State College (now University) in Orangeburg halted rallies and expelled students.[7] In his autobiography, *The River of No Return,* South Carolina activist Cleveland Sellers tells how as a young teenager he had been so excited at the spreading sit-ins in the early 1960s that he helped organize protests and rallies in his home town of Denmark until his father ordered him to stop. "I've been working all my life to build something for you," Sellers's father told him. "If you keep on, you're going to destroy everything."[8]

These days it is fashionable for many whites to say, in excusing the conduct of segregationist whites back then, "But everyone did it. That was the custom."

But the examples of men such as Travelstead and O'Dowd show us that not everyone did it. Injustice is injustice, and there are moral choices to be made to speak out in every generation. It was part of the tragedy of South Carolina's civil rights era that so many journalists and professors, people who supposedly dedicate their lives to finding truth and speaking about it, chose silence.

So it was that the Citadel's 2003 gathering of scholars and the *State's* saturation coverage each had its own historical significance. No one in their wildest imagination fifty years earlier would have ever imagined a South Carolina where scholars would gather to talk publicly about civil rights, or where a newspaper would give those scholars such prominence.

Such an event was, as they say, a long time coming.

In addition to the unspoken moral imperatives to have such a conference in South Carolina, along with wide press coverage, another reason was, simply, that these were stories that needed to be told to a new generation.

By 1971, when moderate white John West took office as governor, the great racial battles of the 1940s, 1950s, and 1960s were over. Libraries, public universities, voting booths, many public schools, restaurants, parks, beaches—all mostly closed a few years earlier—were now open to African Americans.

From 1971 on, the legacy of the past's injustices became harder to discern. Racial issues morphed into less definable areas such as single-member city council districts, segregation academies, partisan battles over school board seats, and school vouchers. In time generations of South Carolinians, white and black, forgot the struggle that had shaped today's life.

Moreover few accessible books have been written about South Carolina's racial battles. Although this state had seminal figures and issues (*Briggs v. Elliott*, for example, and Waties Waring), South Carolina had lacked the attention-getting people or events that might have caught the media's attention, such as a Selma or Mississippi civil rights kidnappings. There was no activist of the stature of a Martin Luther King Jr. Without such events and figures, a myth had been created in some quarters that South Carolina had been a kinder, gentler state, a place where all the white folks somehow, one day, had an epiphany and, without much prompting, decided to give the black folks equal rights. (At the Citadel's conference scholar Tony Badger of Cambridge University demolished this myth, saying South Carolina in no way deserves a reputation as a "moderate" state on civil rights issues. "Far from dousing the fire of popular racist sentiment, the leaders of South Carolina sought to fan the flames," Badger said. Only when pushed to the brink by federal authorities and forced to choose between rebellion or compliance did South Carolina's white officials begin to grant rights to blacks, he said.)

Prompted by the attendance of so many historical figures (including pioneer protesters at South Carolina State in the 1950s and blacks who as children integrated Charleston public schools) and the *State*'s landmark coverage, the conference drew hundreds, students and adults, blacks and whites. Even the attorney general of South Carolina, Henry McMaster, dropped down for a morning, and later said he wished he could have stayed longer.[9] The *Charleston Post and Courier* gave the conference front-page coverage. Local television stations aired reports on the nightly news. The Associated Press ran stories about the conference, putting them on the wire. In this way this scholarly conference reached an audience of South Carolinians potentially numbering in the millions.

The conference had many dramatic moments, from former governor West choking back tears when relating how former governor Hollings had shocked the General Assembly when he said the South Carolina was going to obey the law and allow Harvey Gantt to enter Clemson, to Gantt himself describing his first night on the Clemson campus, filled with hostile whites.

As good as the Citadel conference was, however, it represented only a beginning. There is much in South Carolina's past yet to be examined. Entire conferences, for example, could be held on such matters as the Ben Tillman–inspired 1895 Constitutional Convention, in which rights were taken away from South Carolina blacks, or the actions of the South Carolina news media during the 1940s, 1950s, and 1960s. Conferences could be held around missing documents (should they ever be found) from the civil rights era: for example, the State Law Enforcement Division conducted extensive police surveillance of civil rights organizations in the 1950s and 1960s, and its undercover agents, who infiltrated NAACP meetings and, presumably, KKK meetings, wrote reports, a few of which I have in my possession, having stumbled across them in the archives at the Strom Thurmond Institute at Clemson University. But most of these papers are missing, as are the complete records of the Gressette Committee.

But make no mistake: the Citadel conference was a tour de force. It demonstrated that in South Carolina, when it comes to history, there should be no "Keep Out" signs posted anywhere. At the Citadel, for a few shining days, there was only one sign, and it said, "Enter."

JOHN MONK

Notes

1. Charles R. Wilson and William Ferris, *Encyclopedia of Southern Culture* (Chapel Hill: University of North Carolina Press, 1989), 277.

2. S. L. Latimer Jr., *The Story of "The State," 1891–1969, and the Gonzales Brothers* (Columbia, S.C.: *State* Printing, 1970), 221.

3. William D. Workman Jr., *The Case for the South* (New York: Devon-Adair, 1960), 245.

4. Tinsley E. Yarbrough, *A Passion for Justice: J. Waties Waring and Civil Rights* (Cambridge: Oxford University Press, 1987), 190–91.

5. *Time,* July 30, 1956, 50.

6. Henry H. Lesesne, *A History of the University of South Carolina: 1940–2000* (Columbia: University of South Carolina Press, 2001), 124, 125, 127.

7. William C. Hine, "Civil Rights and Campus Wrongs: South Carolina State College Students Protest, 1955–1968," *South Carolina Historical Magazine* 97 (October 1996): 310–31.

8. Cleveland Sellers, with Robert Terrell, *The River of No Return: The Autobiography of a Black Militant and the Life and Death of SNCC* (New York: Morrow, 1973), 29.

9. Henry McMaster, telephone interview with author, July 5, 2006.

Preface

What . . . strikes me now is how much of the painful past we have yet to confront, even when we love one another and think that we know one another. So much of what agonizes and divides us remains unacknowledged. Even more of it simply fades into oblivion. . . . We are runaway slaves from our own past, and only by turning to face the hounds can we find our freedom beyond them.

Timothy B. Tyson, *Blood Done Sign My Name: A True Story*

South Carolina has often been at the center of the American racial drama. As an English colony it was the primary point of entry for African slaves shipped into British North America. Of the original thirteen United States it had the highest percentage of slaves and slave owners. Amid rising national controversy over slavery it led the southern march toward secession and civil war. Of the defeated Confederate states, none underwent a longer or more hotly contested "Reconstruction." And almost as soon as that brief experiment in interracial democracy was overthrown South Carolina blazed a trail into the "Jim Crow" era of racial disfranchisement and segregation. These chapters in the state's history have been extensively examined and are generally well known.

Far less well known is what happened in South Carolina during the long civil rights struggle that followed. In general accounts of the era important people and events in South Carolina are often either invisible or glossed over in favor of more widely publicized happenings in Alabama, Mississippi, and other states. Most of those accounts, for example, remind readers that Governor George Wallace stood in the doorway of the University of Alabama to obstruct racial integration. But few point out that South Carolina's chief executives were more successful in the same effort. Almost every scholarly treatment of the civil rights movement assigns significance to the challenge of the Mississippi Freedom Democratic Party to the regular Mississippi delegation at the national Democratic Convention of 1964. But few mention that black South Carolinians and their Progressive Democratic Party (PDP) had set that precedent at both the 1944 and 1948 national conventions. Most Americans learn that the Supreme

Court's ruling in *Brown v. Board of Education* was a landmark in the fight for equal rights. But hardly any are taught that the case that first raised the issue came not from Kansas but rather from South Carolina, as *Briggs v. Elliott*. Fewer still have heard of Harry Briggs, or John McCray, or Joe De Laine, or Esau Jenkins, or Septima Clark, or the price that they and black South Carolinians like them paid to expand the boundaries of American freedom.

Like their fellow Americans, citizens of the Palmetto State continue, regularly, to grapple with issues that inflame racial passions. Stormy exchanges over the flying of Confederate flags, the funding of rural school districts, and the observance of a holiday in honor of Martin Luther King Jr. are but a few of the best-known recent examples. All are deeply rooted in the state's troubled racial history—a history that many South Carolinians do not know and many others prefer to forget. Public discourse is diminished accordingly. So is the prospect for bringing her people closer together.

A conference on "The Civil Rights Movement in South Carolina" was held at the Citadel in Charleston from March 5–8, 2003. The meeting brought together historians, civil rights leaders, former governors, and members of the community. The scholars presented research papers on a large number of topics within twentieth-century race relations. Those who helped to shape the events of the era shared their memories and perspectives on what happened. Discussions followed among all who were present. Nearly one hundred people were on the program. Approximately two thousand attended at least one of the twenty-two sessions.[1]

This volume is a product of that meeting. It is divided by topic into six sections, all of which, in their separate ways, argue that the struggle within South Carolina was much fiercer and of far greater national significance than is generally recognized. It is our hope that this work will promote a better understanding of the civil rights movement and a more informed and productive discussion of racial issues in the Palmetto State.

The gathering that gave birth to this book would not have been possible without a major grant from the South Carolina Humanities Council, a state program of the National Endowment for the Humanities. Indispensable financial assistance was also provided by the Citadel Foundation and the Citadel Alumni Association, the latter of which generously donated the use of its Holliday Alumni Center for the conference. The Avery Research Center for African American History and Culture hosted one of the plenary sessions and a reception afterward. Sonya Fordham, Committee of Descendants Fund of the Community Foundation, awarded a grant to defray costs of transporting participants to campus and for a plenary luncheon session. The Self Family Foundation provided funds to transcribe oral remarks made at several of the plenary sessions and to secure rights to republish photographs.

Additional contributions were made by the Waccamaw Center for Cultural and Historical Studies, Coastal Carolina University; the South Carolina Historical Society; the University of South Carolina Institute of Southern Studies; the University of South Carolina Press; the University of Georgia Press; the College of Charleston Program in the Carolina Lowcountry and Atlantic World; the College of Charleston School of Humanities and Social Sciences; and the Citadel College of Graduate and Professional Studies.

Heartfelt thanks are also gratefully extended to our colleagues in the history departments at Clemson University, Coastal Carolina University, the College of Charleston, Francis Marion University, Furman University, South Carolina State University, and the University of South Carolina—all of whom, at a time of fiscal contraction, shared their scarce resources with us to make this a statewide initiative of the South Carolina higher education network.

Beyond financial contributions, numerous people provided important assistance to this undertaking. Sherry Moon transcribed, from videotaped recordings, the oral remarks made at several of the plenary sessions. Elizabeth Brooks handled the secretarial work of the conference. Rachel Carr skillfully performed the secretarial, and no small amount of the editorial, work for this volume. Randy Akers, Chaz Joyner, Jack Bass, Marvin Dulaney, Bernie Powers, Sherman Pyatt, and Tom Kuehn provided much appreciated encouragement and support throughout the process. Harry Carter, the provost of the Citadel, generously helped, on more than one occasion, to solve unexpected problems. So, too, did Kyle Sinisi and Marc Cox of the Citadel's Department of History. Simon Appleford provided invaluable research assistance. All the while, Alex Moore, our editor at the University of South Carolina Press, has been a model of patience and good humor when we deserved neither.

Finally we offer special thanks to the *State* and to the *Charleston Post and Courier,* South Carolina's most widely read newspapers. The *State* devoted eight consecutive days of front-page coverage, along with a companion Web site and a special supplement, to the meeting.[2] The *Post and Courier* contributed four days of extensive reporting. This rare, if not unprecedented, level of attention to an academic gathering made the history of the civil rights movement a topic of conversation throughout much of the state and encouraged a broad cross-section of South Carolinians to turn, for a few days at least, and "face the hounds." These and the large number of other folks who helped to make the conference a success deserve most of the credit for this volume. Its shortcomings are ours alone.

Notes

1. Nearly one hundred separate presentations were made. The plenary sessions were videotaped. An outline of the entire conference, and its related activities, is available online at http://www.citadel.edu/civilrights/.

2. The *State*'s coverage began on Sunday, March 2, 2003, with background pieces on the civil rights movement and the upcoming conference. It ended the following Monday with an editorial on the current state of race relations in South Carolina. Much of the coverage may be found at http://www.thestateonline.com/civilrights/. The *Post and Courier* published a couple of brief pieces in the weeks prior to the conference and provided continuous coverage of the events from March 6 through March 9.

Part 1 ⟿ Governors

The interpretive framework of the volume is set forth in part 1. In its principal essay, "From Defiance to Moderation: South Carolina Governors and Racial Change," Tony Badger places the state's response to the civil rights movement into a regional context. He challenges the conventional wisdom that the Palmetto State's elected leaders did not share the ingrained racism of the state's white voters, that they exercised commendable restraint on racial matters, and that they were powerless to prevent massive resistance to reform. Rather, he argues, from J. Strom Thurmond and James F. Byrnes to George B. Timmerman and Ernest F. Hollings, they led an impassioned, aggressive, and effective defiance of racial change right up to the brink of disaster in 1963.

By then, in the aftermath of widespread and well-reported incidents of white violence against blacks throughout the Deep South, the political climate of the nation had changed. And it was becoming increasingly apparent that South Carolina would either have to change with it or suffer the same level of national condemnation that was then being directed toward Mississippi and Alabama. At that point, responding finally to ever-rising pressure from black Carolinians and from a belatedly committed federal government, South Carolina's governors halted their march and charted—in comparison to their counterparts in other states of the Deep South—a more balanced course. But even it, Badger laments, all too often was marred by white actions to minimize additional gains in civil rights.

Two of the governors discussed in Badger's essay, Ernest F. Hollings and John C. West, were present when he read it at the civil rights conference. Afterward, they commented on his analysis of their gubernatorial leadership. They also fielded questions from the audience about the state's celebration of the

Civil War centennial, the integration of Clemson University, the Orangeburg Massacre, and current racial issues. Transcripts of those comments and discussions complete the first section and are offered to provide insights into the ways that race relations in South Carolina have, and have not, changed during the intervening years.

From Defiance to Moderation

South Carolina Governors and Racial Change

Tony Badger

It is a great privilege to share the platform tonight with two of the men, Senator Hollings and Governor West, who did most among South Carolina's white leadership to guide the state into an acceptance of the end of segregation and the embrace of dynamic and diversified economic growth, to lead the state's move from defiance to moderation. It is also a daunting task, as I am not a historian of South Carolina, although I have done some work on the state's congressmen and the Southern Manifesto. I am not attempting tonight to add freshly researched material to the wonderfully nuanced studies of South Carolina's response to racial change by Marcia Synnott and John G. Sproat, the comprehensive dissertation on 1963 by Ron Cox, the overview by Walter Edgar in his remarkable *South Carolina: A History,* or the fine study by Gordon Harvey of New South governors and education that features John West.[1] What I believe the organizers want me to do, instead, is to put the established narrative of white South Carolina's response to racial change into a regional context, to see what was distinctive and what was not about the state's reaction.

1

It may be a measure of British provincialism, but South Carolina unfortunately does not feature in the news in Britain very often. Even the hundredth birthday of Senator Thurmond might not have broken that pattern of neglect. But the BBC's Washington correspondent, Nick Bryant, was a Cambridge historian who went to Oxford to write a rather good Ph.D. dissertation on the Kennedy administration and civil rights. He was also a great admirer of Dan Carter's biography of George Wallace. So, well before the furor over Trent Lott's comments, British viewers and listeners had the benefit of listening to Professor Carter give his views at some length on the then senior senator. At the same time the *Economist* reminded its British readers of Olin Johnston's comment, handed on by Harry Ashmore, when listening to one of Senator Thurmond's diatribes on the subject of civil rights: "Listen to ol' Strom. He really believes all that shit."[2]

Johnston's implication that South Carolinian politicians, unlike Thurmond, did not believe their segregationist rhetoric has been widely accepted. Johnston himself warned a young Dick Riley that segregation was on its way out—and should be. William Jennings Bryan Dorn later claimed, "We did not really believe what we said back then." For that matter, Thurmond himself always denied that the Dixiecrat movement was about race. Leading political figures told John Sproat, off the record in the early 1980s, that they had known from the start that segregation was doomed. The argument was that the forces of popular mass white racism were so powerful that no politician could challenge them and be reelected. Harriet Keyserling, from a later generation of reformers, accepted that argument in her memoirs. The linked argument was that precipitate desegregation would unleash a tidal force of white violence and pave the way for racial demagoguery of the Tillman and Cole Blease variety. Rembert Dennis argued that the Gressette School Committee, the legal fountain spring of South Carolina's massive resistance legislation, "was more of a delaying procedure, a maneuver because of the finance involved than it was any real effort to forever thwart it [desegregation]. Everybody recognized it couldn't be done. It was just a delaying proposition, until the state could take on the full responsibility, principally in education, of full integration."[3]

These views are not merely the comfortable efforts of veteran politicians to reassure themselves. They link closely to two important strands in current historiography. The first is Michael Klarman's argument that the *Brown* decision "temporarily destroyed racial moderation in the South and it halted the incipient amelioration of Jim Crow practices that had been occurring in much of the South in the late 1940s and early 1950s." It propelled "southern politics towards racial fanaticism" because it "decreed that racial change take place first in an area of life, grade school education, where white southerners were certain to be most resistant." Numan Bartley similarly argues that the civil rights movement was wrong to target education: it should have targeted voting rights, where resistance would have been less. Bartley also blames national liberals and the Truman administration, in the same terms as Olin Johnston, for substituting a moralistic concern for symbolic opportunity and the elimination of de jure segregation for the substance of a drive to tackle the economic problems of lower-income blacks and whites.[4]

These views constitute what I would call the self-exculpatory model of massive resistance in South Carolina, in which the responsibility for massive resistance lies with everybody except the white political leaders of the state. The blame is instead placed on racist white workers in the state, the NAACP, the Supreme Court, and northern liberals. In the face of the obstacles placed on them by these irresponsible forces, the leadership of the state acted with as much restraint as it could.

If the model of South Carolina in the 1950s is self-exculpatory, the model of the state in the 1960s is self-congratulatory. From the peaceful integration of Clemson in 1963, anticipated and orchestrated by Governor Hollings, to the collapse of "freedom of choice" schemes and the acceptance of substantial school integration under the watchful eye of Governors McNair and West, South Carolina surprised observers by the peaceful nature of racial change in the state, in stark contrast to the violent confrontations that wracked Alabama and Mississippi. The state's responsible leadership received high praise from the Kennedy administration, its governors attracted national media attention and commendation, and historians have concurred. The titles themselves convey the essence: "Firm Flexibility," "Integration with Dignity," "Pragmatic Conservatism," "Calm and Exemplary."

What had happened? Gordon Harvey saw John West as one in "a long line of moderate governors who have steered [South Carolina] to safety through the swirling waters of Civil Rights without major violence." According to Walter Edgar, following an argument originally made by Numan Bartley, the new, growth-oriented metropolitan elites had triumphed over the old, traditional county elites. They did so by "championing 'moderation and social stability'" and thus used "an old and venerated South Carolina tradition." These elites and the governors of the 1960s had realized that order and harmony were crucial to economic growth, and that was more important than preserving the racial status quo.[5]

There is some force to the self-exculpatory model of defiance and the self-congratulatory model of moderation. But let me try to tease them out a little and ask some questions about the context to make explicit the implicit comparisons that often underpin them.

2

The self-exculpatory account of the years of defiance up to 1963 plays down the coherence and proactive quality of the massive resistance strategy that existed in South Carolina and underestimates just how pioneering and successful the strategy was in a regional context.

Fritz Hollings and John West were together here at the Citadel before World War II—a formative experience for both men, as it was for many Americans. As West recalls, "We spent four years in public service of a very special but very demanding kind. And we realized that there were satisfactions in public service. The four years that we spent many of us had opportunities—Fritz Hollings for example in North Africa, I in the Pacific, including Japan with the occupation forces [and] you were then on a mission that was an unselfish mission in terms of you weren't working for yourself. You were working for a bigger cause, a cause that transcended any selfish motives. The only selfish motive was trying to survive, of course. So, I think that our class, and I look back at the group that came into our university law school in 1946, many of them entered public service, and a lot of political people: Jim Mann, Hugo Sims in the Congress, innumerable people in the legislature and, of course, Hollings himself."[6]

Throughout the South, white veterans returned home determined to construct a better South. They went to law school under the GI Bill; they dominated the legislatures of, for example, Texas in 1946 and Mississippi in 1948; they organized GI revolts against local political machines and rings; they supported candidates for statewide office who were putting together coalitions of lower-income whites and the small but increasing black electorates, candidates who promised the long-overdue investment in public services that had been denied by conservative elites, candidates such as war hero Sid McMath in Arkansas.[7]

In South Carolina such a candidate was Strom Thurmond, war hero, injured when his glider crashed behind enemy lines on D day. When Thurmond ran for governor in 1946 and promised a "progressive outlook, a progressive program, a progressive leadership," when he called in his inaugural speech for greater attention to African American education and equal rights to women, he sounded like so many of the New Deal–style southern liberals elected in the late 1940s. When he claimed "the solution of our economic problems" would cause racial problems to disappear, he sounded like Hodding Carter or Frank Smith. When he explicitly equated ridding the state of the influence of the Barnwell ring with ridding Europe of the Nazis—"I was willing to stamp out such gangs in Europe"—he sounded exactly like Sid McMath in Arkansas or Delesseps Morrison in New Orleans.[8]

But as with fellow veteran Herman Talmadge in Georgia, Thurmond argued that the freedom he had fought for in Europe was the freedom to fight for traditional patterns of race relations. Thurmond took the state not down the liberal GI route but the Dixiecrat route. Whatever he claimed later, race was at the core of the Dixiecrat challenge. It was important to tell the nation that "there's not enough troops in the army to force the southern people to break down segregation and admit the Negro race into our theaters, into our swimming pools, into our homes, and into our churches."[9]

Thurmond's presidential run in 1948 may have been a quixotic gesture, born of opportunism and ambition. But it was fundamentally a preemptive strike against civil rights legislation. As such, it had the overwhelming support of most of South Carolina's political establishment, especially the congressional delegation in the House, if not Senator Johnston. It was, as the *Spartanburg Herald* complained, a "top-heavy organization." If the national Democrats were competing for the black vote, then the independence of the South manifested by the revolt in 1948 would either put a Republican in the White House or would force the Democrats to make concessions in the future. The convoluted stance of the national Democrats on civil rights and party loyalty in 1952 and 1956 suggests

1. A gathering of governors: James F. Byrnes, J. Strom Thurmond, and John C. West in Camden, 1964. Courtesy of the John Carl West Papers, South Carolina Political Collections, University of South Carolina

that this tactic did have an effect. Thurmond's successor in the governor's mansion in Columbia, his local friend James F. Byrnes, "knew that third parties were never going anywhere." Instead, he adapted Thurmond's strategy into, first, attempts to mobilize regional solidarity in the Democratic Party, to reinstitute Calhoun's doctrine of a concurrent majority so that the South could thwart federal civil rights initiatives, and second, into support for Republicans for Eisenhower in 1952 and later for Richard Nixon.[10]

Byrnes returned to South Carolina as governor with immense prestige with both the traditional county and the new metropolitan elites in the state. He came back with unparalleled international exposure and experience in the highest echelons of the country's legislative, executive, and judicial branches. No one was better placed to lead South Carolina into a realistic acceptance of racial change. As future superintendent of education C. B. Busbee recalled, "whatever the problem was," the universal assumption was that Byrnes "could solve it."[11]

Byrnes instead took the lead in masterminding the region's resistance to racial change. Byrnes and attorney Robert Figg first conceded that the schools in Clarendon County, the subject of the *Briggs v. Elliott* case, were not equal. Then he put before the legislature a massive school equalization program and secured the passage of a three-cent sales tax to fund it. The aim was to render "separate but equal" genuinely equal and to forestall court-ordered desegregation. No other state mounted such a massive program. It was a remarkable achievement and had short-term success in persuading the local federal court, over Judge Waring's passionate objection, to give the state time to make good its commitment to equalization. The dramatic improvement in black schools may possibly have lessened the African American leadership's desire to push school desegregation cases in the state. It is also important to stress that this preemptive strategy meant that conservatives had the only coherent strategy on offer in the region in the years before the *Brown* decision. Southern liberals, as I have argued elsewhere, may have espoused the necessity for gradual racial change, but they did not lay out a strategy for achieving that change. Liberals may have believed that eventual desegregation was inevitable, but they did not share that insight with the voters. The Byrnes strategy instead had the field to itself before 1954.[12]

The second strand of Byrnes's strategy was to take charge of the legal defense in the school desegregation cases: to persuade legendary lawyer John W. Davis to take the Brown case; then to lobby his old Supreme Court colleagues Fred Vinson and Felix Frankfurter to persuade his political ally, Dwight Eisenhower, to prevent the Justice Department filing an amicus curiae brief on behalf of the plaintiffs; and finally to persuade the attorney general of Kansas, a state in which facilities were genuinely equal, to join the case. This personal tour de force, of course, came to naught, to Byrnes's bitter disappointment and surprise. But his efforts did make an important contribution to the short-term success of massive resistance. His warnings of bloodshed and demagoguery in the event of precipitate desegregation may not have finally swayed the justices in the first *Brown* decision, but the warnings, and Byrnes's reputation among the judges and with the president, did influence the implementation decree the following year. They also shaped Eisenhower's refusal to put his massive personal authority behind the *Brown* decision and the Court's subsequent reluctance in the 1950s to assert its authority in school desegregation cases.

As the Court bent over backward to accommodate the South, the argument of moderates and liberals that white southerners had no alternative but to comply with the law of the land was undercut. It was patently obvious that the Court could be defied. The Clarendon County case highlighted that result. After *Brown II*, Judge Parker ruled that the decision did not mandate integration, only nonsegregation, paving the way for pupil placement laws. The NAACP did not commit resources to appeal that decision because they feared that the Supreme Court, influenced by its faith in the reasonableness of southerners such as Jimmy Byrnes, would formally accept that the Parker interpretation was adequate.[13]

Byrnes had spurned the opportunity to provide moderate regional leadership before 1954, but in that year there was another opportunity. He might have led South Carolina into accepting *Brown* as the law of the land and mediated the state's transition to some form of gradual compliance with the decision. That prospect was held out to Byrnes by historian Arthur Schlesinger, who communicated with Byrnes via Ben Cohen, the old New Dealer who had worked with Byrnes at the State Department. For Schlesinger, the "greatest challenge to constructive statesmanship that we have had in this country" was for responsible southerners to bring forward plans that fully took into account local conditions but "honestly directed to the abolition of segregation in the schools" provided "responsible northerners" did "not insist on abrupt or precipitate changes." Might, Schlesinger asked Cohen, Byrnes "now accept the inevitable and dedicate these last years to an earnest attempt to work the thing out?"[14]

Schlesinger's query reflected how much prestige Byrnes enjoyed in the North. One can only speculate on what might have happened if Byrnes, who had so much political power and prestige in rural and metropolitan South Carolina, who was as comfortable with farmers as with business giants, and Eisenhower, with his immense status as a military hero in the South and his reputation particularly among southern businessmen, had invested their prestige in making it clear to white southerners that the Supreme Court had to be obeyed. One reason why Eisenhower would not was because of the respect he had for Byrnes. What Byrnes and other conservatives in the South failed to realize was just how much understanding and leeway that northerners, including Americans for Democratic Action (ADA) liberals such as Schlesinger, were prepared to show the South. As Walter Jackson has shown, northern liberals were as gradualist as their southern counterparts. They accepted the southern argument that precipitate change would lead to violence and demagoguery. They were no more anxious to secure speedy compliance than white southerners.[15]

Instead of compliance, the General Assembly, under the grim leadership of George Bell Timmerman, passed just about every massive resistance measure known to man. Timmerman himself was determined that "segregation would not end in a 1000 years." By the time that the Gressette Committee had done its work, the state had deleted its constitutional provision for public schools, taken the power to withdraw state funds from any schools to and from which courts had ordered a student transferred, given local school board rules the force of law, screened library books, investigated the NAACP at South Carolina State College, banned NAACP members from government employment, closed Edisto State Beach, and reaffirmed bus segregation. In 1956, in Howard Quint's words, the General Assembly passed segregation measures at a mass production rate.[16]

South Carolina's version of massive resistance worked. It created a society just as closed as Mississippi, in which dissent was not tolerated. Fear, said an Episcopal minister, covered the state like a frost. Dissenting academics both black and white at the University of South Carolina, Benedict College, Allen University, and South Carolina State College were fired. Dissenting clergy were driven out by their congregations. Jack O'Dowd from the *Florence Morning News* left the state. What happened to Will Campbell and Hazel Brannon

Smith in Mississippi happened to their counterparts in South Carolina. Public advocacy of moderation was restricted to the publication, organized by Episcopalian ministers, of *South Carolinians Speak: A Moderate Approach to Race Relations,* itself a tortured and defensive volume; to the occasional church resolution; to the few chapters of the South Carolina Council for Human Relations led by the redoubtable Alice Norwood Spearman; and to the defense of public schools by women's clubs.[17]

This climate of conformity was not created simply by persuasion or even social ostracism. It was created by blatant economic pressure and by violence. One of the abiding impressions of this conference in both papers and personal testimony is the countless examples of violence and economic intimidation, often unacknowledged in the records, directed especially at African Americans. Black plaintiffs such as Harry Briggs and his wife were fired. Other black activists, such as Joseph De Laine, were fired on and his church burned. An African American candidate for the Gaffney City Council in 1952 withdrew because of death threats. Whites who helped blacks were flogged and beaten. The Klan revived in the Piedmont in 1957, and as Tim Tyson has vividly described, Klansmen on three occasions attempted to dynamite the house of Claudia Thomas Sanders, who had contributed one of the less tortured essays to *South Carolinians Speak* and was consequently ostracized by her friends and extended family. As Tyson concluded, "No public figure of any stature uttered one public word against either the attempt to kill Claudia Sanders and her family or the acquittal of her assailants. The silence was louder than the dynamite."[18]

Defiance in South Carolina, then, was not a restrained response by a leadership anxious to channel popular white supremacist thought into safe channels until an accommodation with inevitable change could be worked out. If there were politicians who saw the writing on the wall, they were silent. As a black minister once wryly observed to Calvin Trillin in 1960, if all the white politicians who said they were working backstage for racial justice actually were, "it must be pretty crowded there behind the scenes." What white leaders were concerned about was not that whites in the state or the region were too fired up on the race issue; rather they worried that they were too quiescent and resigned. Conservative journalist W. D. Workman bemoaned a "blight of submissiveness," the "cry of surrender." Citizens Council leader Farley Smith complained of "the apathy of the average white citizen." Alice Spearman described the committee of fifty-two leading clergy, businessmen, and professionals, who called for maintaining segregation and interposition, as a "revolt in high places." When the South Carolina Association of Citizens Councils gathered to hear James Eastland in early 1956, the entire political leadership of the state was on the platform. When Strom Thurmond drafted the Southern Manifesto, his aim was not to assuage popular racism but to stir up popular segregationist feeling by convincing wavering politicians and their constituents that the Supreme Court could, and should, be defied. Defiance in South Carolina was a top-down phenomenon.[19]

Would the defiance have been any less if the NAACP had not made education its primary target? The immediate postwar violence in response to any signs of black assertiveness does not suggest that an alternative strategy would have provoked less opposition. If the NAACP had concentrated on voting, progress would not have been quick. The hysterical reaction to the end of the white primary, and the fact that only ten thousand additional blacks were able to register in the fifteen years between 1946 and 1961, did not suggest a calm reaction to an emphasis on voting. As in the rest of the South, violence was as likely to be the response to voter registration as it was to school desegregation drives.[20] In short, South Carolina's leaders united for the long haul to defend segregation and white supremacy.

Thurmond and Byrnes, in particular in 1948, 1950, and 1954, had separate opportunities to lead their state in a different direction. They chose not to. Instead the leaders worked to convince white South Carolinians that the Supreme Court could be defied. These leaders did nothing to disabuse ordinary South Carolinians of that notion. White South Carolinians, like their leaders, saw no reason voluntarily to give up the privileges of whiteness, even if they had doubts about segregation, if they did not have to. And South Carolina's leaders were telling them that they did not have to.

3

Fritz Hollings, as a member of the General Assembly and as lieutenant governor, had been part of the inner circle masterminding South Carolina's strategy of defiance. He believed that most blacks favored segregation: "If there's one thing against our way of life in the South, it's the NAACP. And if the U.S. Supreme Court can declare certain organizations as subversive, I believe South Carolina can declare the NAACP both subversive and illegal." The NAACP was part of a conspiracy with the CIO and New England politicians to "cut off the flow of industry to the South." When he ran for governor in 1958 he race-baited his opponent, Donald Russell. Hollings maintained that he was the candidate best qualified to "defend the southern way of life," in contrast to his opponent, who had been prepared to entertain the possibility of integration at the University of South Carolina. Hollings promised to "resist the demands of a power-hungry federal government." Hollings's supporters would race-bait Russell again in the senate race in 1966, distributing among textile mill workers photographs of Russell shaking hands with black civil rights leader Deke Newman at his integrated inauguration.[21]

But the context of that latter incident is revealing. The Hollings supporters had the photograph because black leader Newman himself had given it to them, anxious to help Hollings win. Hollings had from the late 1940s spoken passionately about the appalling state of South Carolina schools. He had made it clear

that "it's foolish to even consider for a moment that abolishing public education is the solution. We can never abandon our public school system." South
Carolina needed jobs, and to get jobs it needed an educated workforce, both
black and white. Hollings brought in John West and other powerful legislators
to strengthen the State Development Board and jump-start the industrial
recruitment program. He continued spending on school education, attempted
to turn the state universities into the equivalent of the North Carolina Research Triangle (a move thwarted by the lack of imagination of the University
of South Carolina leadership), and instituted a major program of technical
institutes that would provide the necessary skilled workforce. Fifty-seven thousand new jobs came in four years. The economic progress Hollings and his
allies sought would eventually come into conflict with the requirements of
white supremacy and segregation.[22]

But first, Hollings had to confront the civil rights demonstrations of 1960. It
has been suggested that a moderate civil rights leadership in South Carolina
tended to eschew direct action protest and that this helped moderate white leadership in the state. Whether or not this was true, that is certainly not how
Hollings experienced it. "We had the first cases. I was on the scene. I was either
out in front of Trinity Church, I was either out down the hill, I was over in
Sumter, there was a competition thing. CORE would demonstrate in Charleston,
time you got down there the NAACP had demonstrated in Columbia, then you
came back to Columbia, then they'd break out with CORE in Rock Hill, and time
you'd turn up at Rock Hill they'd try to put one down in Sumter."

What has not been much commented on is how Hollings handled these
demonstrations in order to avoid violence. Just as Laurie Pritchett realized that
police and mob violence in 1961–62 in Albany, Georgia, would give great leverage to the black protesters, so Hollings worked to avoid violence and prided himself that no one got hurt at the South Carolina demonstrations. He understood
that badly trained local police would make mistakes. Instead he brought in black
deputies from SLED and black policemen from Columbia, Charleston, and the
State College campus and used them to police the demonstrations: "We had
black policemen policing the streets and the incidents, and when one of them
[the demonstrators] stepped out of line there was a black policeman leading him
to the paddy wagon and they then put away their cameras. They said this isn't
what we wanted. So they started in this state but they didn't get the news story
and the impact that they thought was necessary and we just stayed out there
ahead of them every time."

Hollings believed that black leaders understood that he was enforcing the law
impartially for blacks and whites. At the same time J. P. Strom, head of SLED,
who did a "magnificent job" according to Hollings, was infiltrating the Klan and
controlling white extremists. Hollings, like his contemporary and fellow World

War II veteran, and ally in the Kennedy campaign of 1960, Terry Sanford, also kept open lines of communication with the black leadership.[23]

But it is important to remember that a corollary of the Laurie Pritchett approach was an uncompromising refusal to negotiate with the protesters. Similarly Hollings's strategy made possible mass arrests and enabled local communities to refuse to negotiate with the sit-in demonstrators. As a result communities in South Carolina did not make the concessions on the desegregation of lunch counters and public accommodations in 1960 and 1961 that cities in the North Carolina and Tennessee Piedmont did.[24] When Hollings toured the state in 1961, he recalled, "People thought I ought to have some magic to stop the monster that was about to gobble us up, or else they expected me to go to jail. It looked to me like it was high time that we started sobering people up, before it turned out to be too late." One might note in parenthesis that it was the South Carolina leadership that had given people the drinks in the first place.[25]

Hollings set about to educate people in 1962 that change would have to come. He told newspaper editors that they should prepare their readership for eventual defeat in the courts, that legal defenses would fall "like a house of cards," and that inevitable desegregation would follow. Benjamin Muse, traveling the state for the Southern Regional Council in 1961 and 1962, detected a note of change. All over the South, southern businessmen had the dreadful warning of what had happened at Little Rock and the loss of investment that had followed the violence and the school closings there. Representatives of the Little Rock Chamber of Commerce had made it their business to travel around the South warning communities not to go down the Little Rock route. Atlanta businessmen had taken that warning to heart in 1961 and paved the way for the desegregation of the University of Georgia and Atlanta schools. Alabama businessmen had started to react after the violence inflicted on the Freedom Riders in May 1961. Mississippi businessmen would respond more slowly. It would be the Ole Miss crisis that in retrospect convinced them that they were "whistling in the wind," "fighting a cannon with a pea shooter." In South Carolina in 1961 and 1962, construction magnate Charles Daniel and Textile Manufacturers Association chief executive John Cauthen were working to convince businessmen that they needed to support compliance with eventual court decisions.[26]

It was the handling of the integration of Clemson at the start of 1963, the peaceful admission of Harvey Gantt, that really showed that South Carolina might avoid the violence that bedeviled other massive resistance states. "The conspiracy for peace" involved in that incident has been amply documented, and is the subject of a splendid paper at this conference. But I just want to make three observations about the crisis. First, the actual admission of Gantt took place on Governor Russell's watch, and Russell and his staff always claimed that "Hollings had little to do with it," that there was "no big planning," and that Russell never talked to Hollings about it. "People may have drawn up a plan," said Russell, "but

I don't think any particular plan like that was followed." This interpretation clearly flies in the face of all the evidence from the meetings of businessmen, newspapermen, and the Clemson administration that took place in the twelve months preceding desegregation. It also ignores the importance of Hollings's farewell address to the General Assembly, when he told them that *Brown* was "the fact of the land," that "South Carolina was running out of courts," that they operated under a "government of laws," that "law and order would be maintained," and that the state would conduct itself with "dignity." As John West recalls: "The legislature was all white of course. It was very tense. If Hollings had said 'Go to War' the legislature would have done just that. They had all sorts of ideas of massive resistance. Then he departed from his text. He said to Pete Strom of SLED, 'Pete, you make sure nothing happens up there.' Well, that was a turning point and it was a stupid political move for the immediate situation, because there was no black voting in those days. It was really one of the most courageous and one of the most dramatic things I've seen in public life. And that speech simply deflated the strong pro-segregationist sentiment."[27]

Second, it has been argued that South Carolina would have complied with the courts irrespective of what had happened at Ole Miss in the fall of 1962. Certainly the planning and university and government acceptance that they would have to comply with the courts were already there. But Ole Miss clearly concentrated minds. Hollings refused to send a motorcade in support of Barnett. Instead, he sent Pete Strom to observe the situation, and that visit informed the detailed plan for Clemson they drafted: law enforcement control of the entire area around the university and, particularly, careful management of the press, giving them defined access and information on a controlled basis but not allowing a free-for-all "so they wouldn't roam around for a week ahead of time."[28]

Third, the Kennedy administration was as anxious to avoid another Little Rock as were South Carolina businessmen, and as Marcia Synnott notes, harried federal officials fretting over crises in states such as Alabama and Mississippi must have been relieved to see responsible leadership in South Carolina and were clearly prepared to cut the state a good deal of slack. John Seigenthaler, assistant to Bobby Kennedy, confirmed that faith in responsible local leaders for me last week (February 2003). He recalled that there were three southern states where the administration believed "there was a comfort level with the leadership": Oklahoma, North Carolina, and South Carolina. In each state there was a governor—Howard Edmondson, Terry Sanford, and Fritz Hollings, respectively—who had worked for the Kennedy campaign in 1960. "But you had the feeling that Fritz and Howard and Terry had a handle on the politics of their own state. And that didn't mean they wouldn't whistle Dixie, it just means that they were going to make sure that progress was made." These were the responsible local leaders that the Kennedy executive civil rights strategy relied on. After Ole Miss, an understandably nervous administration was reluctant to trust southern assurances that troops would not be needed to enforce court orders, but they were, in the end, prepared to trust assurances they received from South Carolina: from William Jennings Bryan Dorn and the congressional delegation and from Governors Hollings and Russell.[29]

As Ron Cox has shown, Clemson was the model for the desegregation of the University of South Carolina and the desegregation of Charleston schools in 1963. In both cases the state appealed court decisions as far as it could in order to demonstrate that all avenues of protest had been exhausted. Meanwhile, the governor, university officials, and the local officials made careful plans for peaceful desegregation.[30]

If Ole Miss had concentrated the minds of South Carolina's business and political leaders, so the violence in Birmingham in May 1963 concentrated the minds of local leaders as they confronted the planned demonstrations and sit-ins to desegregate public accommodations held in eight cities in June 1963. They had seen the appalling national publicity that Bull Connor's dogs had provoked. What happened in South Carolina was instead what had happened earlier in cities in the upper South in 1960. Local business leaders worked feverishly to establish biracial committees that would negotiate a peaceful desegregation of public facilities. It was often a tortuous process. It involved riots and mass arrests in Charleston, and no progress was made in Orangeburg and Sumter, which both had to wait for the 1964 Civil Rights Act to compel the desegregation of local facilities. But, on the whole, urban South Carolina desegregated in 1963.[31]

Despite his integrated inauguration, Governor Donald Russell was as grudging a mediator of racial change as one might expect a protégé of the unrepentant and bitter Jimmy Byrnes to be. But his successor, Robert McNair, worked much harder to ensure that the industrial development drive would not be derailed by racial violence. McNair had to confront the initial token-compliance desegregation of most South Carolina school systems, the effects of the 1964 and 1965 civil rights acts, a new generation of more assertive African American leaders, and the eventual impatience of the courts with the slow pace of desegregation under freedom-of-choice plans and the requirement for full-scale integration. McNair worked tirelessly to keep lines of communications open with black leaders and developed an informal alliance with Deke Newman. He set up a fifteen-man advisory board that worked with community leaders and businessmen to facilitate peaceful school desegregation, and like Hollings, he made it clear that "when we run out of courts, then we must adapt to the circumstances"—at all costs law and order must be maintained. His hands-on approach generally enabled him to exercise control over events. Although his attention strayed disastrously at Orangeburg in 1968, he generally played a very similar role to that played by Bob Scott in North Carolina at a time when other states were in the hands of good ol' boy segregationists such as Governor Wallace, Claude Kirk, and Lester Maddox.[32]

In 1970 mobs overturned two school buses, crowded with schoolchildren, in Lamar while a Republican gubernatorial candidate ran a white backlash campaign. Randy Sanders described this campaign memorably this morning (March 5, 2003). Stirred by this violence, suburban Republican whites and an overwhelming percentage of black voters put Lieutenant Governor John West in the state house. West had stood up to the Klan in the 1950s after the beating of a white Camden band teacher. West's response to the death threats, on J. P. Strom's advice, was to carry a gun for two or three years. His wife's response was to go around to the local Klan leader and promise that if any harm came to her husband she would personally kill him. Although West "probably couldn't hit anything at ten feet," his wife was an excellent shot. West was part of the Hollings industrial development team, and as lieutenant governor he had arranged for the grievances of Orangeburg students to be published in the *Senate Journal* and to investigate those grievances.[33]

In his inaugural speech he promised a "color-blind" administration, and like other New South governors elected in 1970, he received favorable national media attention. He liked to think that "the election of 1970 hopefully will be the last in which race was the dominant factor." West worked to ensure that the massive school integration that came to Deep South states after 1970 worked smoothly at the local level. To that end, and to eliminate discrimination in government agencies, he established the Human Affairs Commission. He recalled with pride, "I guess, if I had to single out any one thing for which I've gotten the most satisfaction [it] is the race relations thing. That was a crucial area when I was elected we passed the Human Affairs Commission and I like to think that we broke those color blinders. It's disturbing to see the polarization of the states now, black and white. At least in a fairly critical period we made a transition and changed a lot of attitudes."

He explained how the commission worked: "We selected the blacks as the problem spotters and the whites as the problem solvers. That meant we got a lot of the very active, almost militant blacks who could spot the problems, and who had the support with the blacks who weren't militant. The whites were establishment people who had judgment and concern, and who could change public attitudes and change things that ought to be changed." West was not, however, without his critics. Hayes Mizell complained that his emphasis on "quality education" was a sop to law-and-order whites. But he managed palpably to lessen racial tensions and to secure general black and white support for the process of change.[34]

At the same time his drive to secure outside investment was spectacularly successful, bringing in more than forty thousand new jobs in two years. African Americans benefitted. First, the booming textile industry integrated. In 1964 only 5 percent of mill workers in South Carolina were black; by 1976 one third were. Second, international investors brought industry below the fall line. More than 10 percent of all foreign investment in 1972 was made in South Carolina. Firms from outside the United States did not share the stereotypes of American managers, northern and southern, that African American workers were lazy, uneducable, and militant unionists. Overseas investors were prepared to locate industries in areas of high black populations. What the investors were interested in was not that the workforce might be black but that it was nonunion and well-educated in the technical institutes that Fritz Hollings had established. Most dramatically, Koyosako located in Orangeburg because their managers were impressed by the good race relations that now existed in the community that had been so wracked by racial tension from 1955 until after the Orangeburg Massacre.[35]

Self-congratulation seems therefore to be justified in no small measure. The state at the heart of defiance of the federal government had responded to court decisions, legislation, and the opportunities of economic growth by desegregating without the turmoil of other massive resistance states. But nagging doubts remain about this model. First, defiance continued. No sooner than Clemson had integrated than Governor Russell called for the provision of tuition grants to enable children to go to private schools and circumvent court-ordered segregation. Private schools flourished and, as the executive director of the South Carolina Independent Schools Association admitted, "everyone knew that our purpose was to set up segregated schools." The state's reaction to the Voting Rights Act was to be the first to test its constitutionality. Its second response, inspired by segregationist diehards such as Micah Jenkins, was to introduce at-large elections in many areas to dilute the black vote. The state's textile industry was one of the most resistant of all southern industries to integration. Tim Minchin has shown that it did not integrate voluntarily or because of a labor shortage; it integrated because of the pressure imposed before 1964 by the federal government in return for government contracts and after 1964 under the mandate of the EEOC (Equal Employment Opportunity Commission) and the pressure mounted by the NAACP's Textile Employment and Advancement for Minorities initiative. Even then, countless EEOC suits indicate the continued discrimination prevalent in the industry, especially against black men.[36]

Second, the emphasis on a peaceful transition can lead us, Vernon Burton warns, to "understate the occasional horrors and the daily indignities with which African Americans lived." There may not have been the state-sanctioned terrorism that took place in Alabama and Mississippi or the lawlessness there of the agencies that were supposed to be upholding the law. But there were mass arrests, fire hoses, and countless examples of black activists fleeing for their lives. It is salutary to remember that more protesters were killed in Orangeburg than at Ole Miss, Birmingham, or Selma. There was no incident in the entire South in 1970 to compare with the overturning of the school buses at Lamar.[37]

Third, racial change did not come to South Carolina through the efforts of South Carolina's whites. It did not come gradually or through the inevitable effects of economic modernization. It came through the legal and legislative crises created by white intransigence on the one hand and the combined efforts of the civil rights movement and the federal government on the other. How much congratulation is due to a white leadership for eventually and belatedly complying with the law? Finally, how much credit is due the white leadership for averting the threat of violence, a threat that the leadership had unleashed in the first place?

4

We may rightly talk of the limitations of today's biracial politics in South Carolina, and of the state's racial polarization, and of the persistence of discrimination and African American poverty. Nevertheless, the collapse of segregation, the end of malapportionment, and the end of black disfranchisement constituted a remarkable transformation in the daily lives of white and black southerners that few in the late 1940s could have predicted. Historians have started to take segregationist leaders seriously. They are rescuing them from the massive condescension of posterity. The leaders of South Carolina in the massive resistance years were able and conscientious men. It should not surprise us that they were reluctant to relinquish the privileges of white supremacy. Even moderate and liberal white southerners found it difficult to envisage the dismantling of segregation and were certainly reluctant to lay out a strategy for achieving gradual change. It is all too easy for historians, and especially from the safe distance of three thousand miles, to second-guess politicians who failed to take a stand in favor of civil rights or school desegregation. But to understand the leaders of South Carolina is not to absolve them of responsibility in the way that the self-exculpatory model of the defiance years does. The strategy of defiance was not a holding operation designed to allow racial passions to cool. It was a strategy in which the leadership invested vast resources and energy to try to preserve their own traditional way of life. Far from dousing the fire of popular racist sentiment, the leaders of South Carolina sought to fan the flames. It had chilling consequences for black and white dissenters and for a generation of black schoolchildren and students. It is possible that the policy did in the end act as a safety valve, that exhausting all the means of resistance meant that leaders could demonstrate that there was no alternative but to comply with the courts and legislation in the 1960s, thus undercutting the appeal of a rabid Red Bethea or a John Long. But that argument ignores the fact that it was the leaders of the state who had been remorselessly telling white South Carolinians that segregation could be preserved and who then had to tell them otherwise. South Carolina leaders marched their followers to the brink. It is to their credit that, having got there, they looked into the abyss and turned around. They had the good fortune to be able to see in Little Rock, at Ole Miss, and in Birmingham what dire economic and social consequences would follow from continued defiance. They started the slow process of persuading their followers to straggle back. The energy that had been invested in defiance was now invested in moderation. In that situation it took no little courage and no little political skill to reorient the state toward economic development and peaceful racial change. Fritz Hollings, Robert McNair, and John West deserve their measure of self-congratulation.

Notes

1. Marcia G. Synnott, "Desegregation in South Carolina, 1950–1963: Sometime between 'Now' and 'Never,'" in *Looking South: Chapters in the Story of an American Region,* ed. Winfred B. Moore Jr. and Joseph F. Tripp (New York: Greenwood Press, 1989), 51–64; Synnott, "Federalism Vindicated: University Desegregation in South Carolina and Alabama, 1962–63," *Journal of Policy History* 1, no. 3 (1989): 292–318; John G. Sproat, "'Firm Flexibility': Perspectives on Desegregation in South Carolina," in *New Perspectives on Race and Slavery in America: Essays in Honor of Kenneth M. Stampp,* ed. Robert H. Abzug and Stephen E. Maizlish (Lexington: University Press of Kentucky, 1986), 164–84; Sproat, "'Pragmatic Conservatism' and Desegregation in South Carolina" (unpublished paper kindly provided to the author by Professor Sproat); Maxie Myron Cox Jr., "1963—The Year of Decision: Desegregation in South Carolina" (Ph.D. dissertation, University of South Carolina, 1996); Walter B. Edgar, *South Carolina: A History* (Columbia: University of South Carolina Press, 1998), chap. 22; Gordon E. Harvey, *A Question of Justice: New South Governors and Education, 1968–1976* (Tuscaloosa: University of Alabama Press, 2002).

2. *Economist,* November 30, 2002.

3. Charles Joyner, communication with the author, February 20, 2003; Dan T. Carter, communication with the author, June 17, 1985; Strom Thurmond, interview with James Banks, July 1978, Southern Historical Collection, University of North Carolina, Chapel Hill; Sproat, "Firm Flexibility," 182; Harriet Keyserling, *Against the Tide: One Woman's Political Struggle* (Columbia: University of South Carolina Press, 1998), 111; Rembert Dennis, interview with Jack Bass, March 4, 1975, Southern Historical Collection, and South Caroliniana Library, University of South Carolina.

4. Michael Klarman, "How Brown Changed Race Relations: The Backlash Thesis," *Journal of American History* 81 (1994): 81–118; Numan Bartley, *The New South, 1945–1980* (Baton Rouge: Louisiana State University Press, 1995), 70, 73; Bartley, comment, Fortieth Anniversary of Little Rock Conference, September 27, 1997.

5. Harvey, *Question of Justice,* 8; Edgar, *South Carolina,* 552.

6. John Carl West, interview with Herbert J. Hartsook, 1997, Oral History Project, South Carolina Political Collections, University of South Carolina. I am extremely grateful to Governor West for allowing me to consult this interview.

7. Tony Badger, "Whatever Happened to Roosevelt's New Generation of Southerners?," in *The Roosevelt Years: New Essays on the United States, 1933–45,* ed. Robert A. Garson and Stuart Kidd (Edinburgh: Edinburgh University Press, 1999), 122–38; Jennifer Brooks, "From Fighting Nazism to Bossism: Southern World War II Veterans and the Assault on Southern Political Tradition" (unpublished paper in the author's possession).

8. Nadine Cohodas, *Strom Thurmond and the Politics of Southern Change* (New York: Simon & Schuster, 1993), 89, 96, 132.

9. Ibid., 177.

10. Kari Frederickson, *The Dixiecrat Revolt and the End of the Solid South, 1932–1968* (Chapel Hill: University of North Carolina Press, 2001), 180; David W. Robertson, *Sly and Able: A Political Biography of James F. Byrnes* (New York: Norton, 1994), 496, 501–2, 511–12.

11. Sproat, "Firm Flexibility," 166.

12. Robertson, *Sly and Able,* 507–10; Synnott, "Federalism Vindicated," 299; Tony Badger, "Closet Moderates: Why White Liberals Failed, 1940–1970," in *The Role of Ideas in the Civil Rights South,* ed. Ted Ownby (Jackson: University Press of Mississippi, 2002), 97–98.

13. Robertson, *Sly and Able,* 513–20; Raymond Wolters, *The Burden of Brown: Thirty Years of School Desegregation* (Knoxville: University of Tennessee Press, 1984).

14. Robertson, *Sly and Able,* 520–21.

15. Walter Jackson, "Northern White Liberals and Civil Rights, 1955–1965," in *The Making of Martin Luther King and the Civil Rights Movement,* ed. Brian Ward and Tony Badger (Washington Square, N.Y.: New York University Press, 1996).

16. Howard H. Quint, *Profile in Black and White: A Frank Portrait of South Carolina* (Washington, D.C.: Public Affairs Press, 1958), 101–4.

17. Quint, *Profile in Black and White,* 35, 101, 117–28; Edgar, *South Carolina,* 524–30.

18. Timothy Tyson, "Dynamite and 'The Silent South': A Story from the Second Reconstruction in South Carolina," in *Jumpin' Jim Crow: Southern Politics from Civil War to Civil Rights,* ed. Jane Dailey, Glenda Elizabeth Gilmore, and Bryant Simon (Princeton, N.J.: Princeton University Press, 2000), 275–97.

19. Calvin Trillin, "Reflections: Remembrances of Moderates Past," *New Yorker,* March 21, 1977, 85–99; Quint, *Profile in Black and White,* 35, 46; Marcia G. Synnott, "Alice Norwood Spearman: Civil Rights Apostle to South Carolinians," in *Beyond Image and Convention: Explorations in Southern Women's History,* ed. Janet L Coryell, Martha H. Swain, Sandra Gioia Treadway, and Elizabeth Hayes Turner (Columbia: University of Missouri Press, 1998), 184; Tony Badger, "The Southern Manifesto of 1956," paper delivered at the Southern Historical Association meeting, 1993 (copy in the author's possession).

20. Orville Vernon Burton, Terence R. Finnegan, Peyton McCrary, and James W. Lowen, "South Carolina," in *Quiet Revolution in the South: The Impact of the Voting Rights Act, 1965–1990,* ed. Chandler Davidson and Bernard Grofman (Princeton, N.J.: Princeton University Press, 1984), 195.

21. Quint, *Profile in Black and White,* 86, 163; Earl Black, *Southern Governors and Civil Rights: Race, Segregation and Campaign Issues in the Second Reconstruction* (Cambridge, Mass.: Harvard University Press, 1976), 82–83; West interview, 1997.

22. West interview, 1997; Quint, *Profile in Black and White,* 97; Cohodas, *Strom Thurmond,* 231–32.

23. Ernest F. Hollings, interview with Marcia G. Synnott, 1980, South Carolina Political Collections, University of South Carolina; Synnott, "Desegregation in South Carolina," 59–60; Synnott, "Federalism Vindicated," 302.

24. Synnott, "Federalism Vindicated," 302.

25. Sproat, "Firm Flexibility," 170.

26. Elizabeth Jacoway and David R. Colburn, eds., *Southern Businessmen and Desegregation* (Baton Rouge: Louisiana State University Press, 1982); James C. Cobb, *The Selling of the South: The Southern Crusade for Industrial Development, 1936–1980* (Baton Rouge: Louisiana State University Press, 1982).

27. Donald Russell, interview, July 6, 1992, Oral History Project, South Carolina Political Collections, University of South Carolina; George McMillan, "Integration with Dignity: The Inside Story of How South Carolina Kept the Peace," *Saturday Evening Post,* March 16, 1963, 16–21; Joseph C. Ellers, *Getting to Know Clemson University Is Quite an Education: Determination Makes Dreams Come True* (Clemson, S.C.: Blueridge, 1987), 48–58; West interview, 1997.

28. Synnott, "Federalism Vindicated," 293; Hollings interview, 1980.

29. Synnott, "Federalism Vindicated," 311; John Seigenthaler, interview with the author, February 27, 2003.

30. Cox, "1963—The Year of Decision," 84–85, 171; Henry H. Lesesne, *A History of the University of South Carolina, 1940–2000* (Columbia: University of South Carolina Press, 2002), 137–50.

31. Cox, "1963—The Year of Decision," 345–469; Paul Lofton, "Calm and Exemplary: Desegregation in Columbia, South Carolina," in *Southern Businessmen and Desegregation,* ed. Elizabeth Jacoway and David R. Colburn (Baton Rouge: Louisiana State University Press, 1982), 70–81.

32. Edgar, *South Carolina,* 543–45; Sproat, "Pragmatic Conservatism," 21–22, 24–27; Harvey, *Question of Justice,* 118–19.

33. West interview, 1997; John C. West, interview with Jack Bass and Walter DeVries, 1974, Southern Historical Collection, University of North Carolina at Chapel Hill.

34. West interview, 1997; West interview, 1974; Harvey, *Question of Justice,* 123–40.

35. Timothy J. Minchin, *Hiring the Black Worker: The Racial Integration of the Southern Textile Industry, 1960–1980* (Chapel Hill: University of North Carolina Press, 1999), 3; West interview, 1997; West interview, 1974.

36. Cox, "1963—The Year of Decision," 219–58; Burton et al., "South Carolina," 200–203; Minchin, *Hiring the Black Worker,* chaps. 1–2.

37. Vernon Burton, in "'A Monumental Labor': Four Scholars Assess Walter Edgar's *South Carolina: A History,*" *South Carolina Historical Magazine* 100 (1999): 264.

Comments

Ernest F. Hollings

Thank you very much, Professor Carter, my friend, Governor West; Professor Badger, you covered it extremely well. You've said everything that needs to be said about civil rights in South Carolina, only I haven't had a chance to say it. It's sort of hard. I've been looking at that program. I just got in, and you folks have really covered the waterfront and said everything that possibly could be said of interest on civil rights and its development in the South. I feel very much like

2. Governor Ernest F. Hollings (right) greeting Senator John F. Kennedy at the Columbia airport, May 1960. Photograph by Cecil J. Williams

Elizabeth Taylor's seventh husband, who on the wedding night said, "I know what I'm supposed to do, but it's going to be difficult to make it interesting." And Elizabeth Taylor said, "Don't worry I'm not going to keep you long."

I have a few heroes—Matthew Perry, as you well know, is one of them—but I met the son of a real hero of civil rights, Reverend Joseph A. De Laine. I was just a sort of sideline part of that *Briggs-Elliott* case, and when I saw Reverend De Laine Jr. as I came in let me hearken a few comments about it.

What happened was when I got elected in 1948, there was a superintendent of education who is ninety-eight years of age and out at Bishop Gadsden: Allen G. Craton Frampton. I got elected on a Tuesday and Friday, he said, "Fritz, I want to take you and show you something." So we went across the Cooper River Bridge, down the Mathis Ferry Road, on about a mile and a half, and over on the right-hand side was Freedom School. I'll never forget it. It was just a one-story, block, room-like. It was cold November, of course, and they had a potbellied stove in the middle, a class in one corner, a class in another corner, another corner and another corner. They had four classes and one teacher and that was black education in South Carolina. And Craton said, "We're going to have to do something about it." That there shocked me. You see, we had come back—I say we, young veterans—when we got into the legislature, one of the first things was that women couldn't vote. The [South Carolina] Constitution said "white male electors." We repealed that in the Constitution. We had—it took us a couple of years—but I put in the Anti-Lynch Bill. We had the Willie Earle case mount up in Greenville and we had no schools at all with respect to our minority population and it wasn't easy.

I put in the [3 percent] sales tax. They talk about regressive. Regressive? That's the most progressive thing I've ever done, but you've got to mind . . . we were poor. At that time, the top dean in a university was paid nine thousand. The governor was paid only fifteen thousand. We had no money and we had no white or black schools at that particular time, but we put that [sales tax] in. And as Senator Legare in the back there, who's joining us, we couldn't get the Senate to go along with us in a joint committee. I'll never forget going up to Mr. Hunter, the clerk of the house, and asking "Mr. Jim, can you have just a house committee?" "No, no, you can't do that." And about two nights later he did like that to me [come here]. He said, "I've been studying that thing." He said, "You ought to go ahead and do it." We did, and we worked with the Federation of Tax Administrators, we worked with the directors of the tax in Ohio and California, the best laws. This has never been reversed or really elaborated upon in any court proceeding since that time when we passed it in 1951. We got together with Governor Byrnes when he got elected, and I'll never forget in the Ways and Means Room we sat down, our little six-man house committee, and explained the term, and he said, "I never heard of this thing." He said, "Let me study it." Over Christmas he did, and the first part of January he called me, and he said, "I've been looking at that thing. I think I'll go along with it." And he did. And right to the point, you've got to give him credit because I wouldn't have had any authority to do it. In any event we got that passed, and when the *Briggs-Elliott* case came along, separate but equal was the issue. And Governor Byrnes had been an associate justice on the United States Supreme Court. He got the best of the best. The outstanding lawyer at the time was John W. Davis as a constitutional lawyer. He was the most respected before the court. He persuaded Davis to represent us. Later Dean Robert McC. Figg, Bob Figg, really had handled all the cases with— the case with Thurgood Marshall representing Briggs, Harry Briggs at Summerton. And right till a few days before, we went up there, I didn't know I was going, but the governor said, I'm appointing you. I want you to be sure, 'cause I knew intimately the equalization, whether it was a teacher's pay or transportation or construction or whatever.

We got up on that Saturday morning in [December] 1952 . . . before the Monday arguments and Figg, Dean Figg, and I walked in to get breakfast at the railroad station there, and in came Thurgood Marshall and he sat down and was eating breakfast with us. He said, "Now—." By the way, Figg and Marshall were intimate friends. Later Figg had been recommended for a federal district court judgeship and was endorsed by Thurgood Marshall and the NAACP. They passed him over, but that wasn't the reason. It was thought at the time that since he was the lawyer for South Carolina that had handled these cases that that was the reason, but that was not the reason. They admired each other, and Thurgood tried his best to help. But I'll never forget and to give you a flavor of the times, Marshall turned to Figg and he said, "Now, Bob," he says, "you know that black family in Cicero"—up in Cicero, Illinois, a black family had moved into the white neighborhood, and there were all kinds of demonstrations and . . . violence and what have you—and he said, "now don't say anything 'cause it will ruin me," but he said, "I got down to Springfield and I told Governor [Adlai] Stevenson that we had to send that family for safekeeping back to Mississippi." And we sent them down there for a little while until things cooled, but he said, "For heaven sakes, don't tell anybody that, that will ruin me." I said, "Thurgood, don't tell anybody that I'm eating breakfast with you, that'll ruin me. I'll never get elected to a damn thing anymore. I can tell you that." Incidentally, Justice Marshall used to get me with his friend Justice [William] Brennan over at Kronheimers in Washington to tell that story time and again. But another thing, he said, "Bob, let's assume you've won—we won the case. How long do you think before there will be any integration? That's what we're all assembled about." And Figg hesitated and talked along and what have you, and he said, "It will take twenty-five years, Thurgood, I'll tell you right now it's going to take a long time." Marshall turned to him, and he said, "You're wrong. It will take fifty years." And it's just at fifty years and we still have got—well, the record will show what happened.

We went before the court and another thing you should understand is why it's called Brown against the Board. . . . The State of Kansas had about seventeen counties segregated, but they had twenty-three counties integrated. And they didn't have a particular interest [in defending segregation], 'cause they were moving forward with integration in the State of Kansas. They had elected not even . . . to participate in the oral arguments [although Kansas had filed a brief]. And Roy Wilkins was clever, 'cause he knew the solicitor general, and he went to the solicitor general and he got the Kansas case moved up ahead of the main case, which was Thurgood Marshall's Briggs against Elliott down in South Carolina. On that Saturday, we were on the phone with Governor Byrnes and he was on with the Kansas governor and arguing and fussing with him and everything else like that, and Sunday we went out and I picked up [Paul E.] Wilson, the deputy attorney general [of Kansas]. You couldn't get the attorney general or anybody else, and we went to Waterman Park going over the case until about two or three in the morning on the Monday morning when at ten o'clock we started arguments. Wilson, instead of tripping up, knocked the ball over the back fence. That surprised everyone at that time. We were the second to argue. The best arguments made at that particular time we all agreed [were made by] Attorney General [H. Albert] Young of Delaware. But I had been told by Governor Byrnes that we were going to win that case. He had been on the court, he knew the judges and everything else of that kind, and Fred Vinson was the chief justice at the time and I can still hear them all arguing, Sweatt against Painter. The decision, formative decision, that Chief Justice Vinson had written in the Oklahoma case that the value association what have you. And fortuitously Vinson died and Earl Warren was appointed chief justice, and he told us to get on out and don't argue separate but equal, argue that segregation in and of itself was unconstitutional.

The decision came down on May 17, 1954, with the key phrase "in all deliberate speed,"[1] and Wilkins and Marshall and Figg and Emory Rogers of Summerton . . . all got together, and to a person they agreed what we ought to do is integrate the first grade the first year and in the second year the first grade and the second grade. And then the third year, the first, second, and third grades and we'll have a deliberate, orderly, peaceful integration and respond with the court. But the chief counsel of the NAACP in New York, [Jack] Greenberg. She said, "We will not be given our constitutional rights on the installment plan." And as a result, as Professor Badger has pointed out, White Citizens' Council and all these other movements took over until I guess the time came with Martin Luther King, and they found out that they couldn't get any rights except in the streets of America. "Burn Baby, Burn!" and everybody came running then the governor, and Congress and all that they weren't paying any attention. But that set us back.

There isn't any question that the schools [are still a problem in South Carolina]. We had 13 private schools on May 17, 1954. I think . . . we've got 436 private schools in South Carolina now. And [there's] a struggle about vouchers and tax credits, charter schools—anything to take the money away. And the movement has become national. That kind of movement has been institutionalized with the southern strategy of the Republican Party with Harry Dent from South Carolina and Senator [J. Strom] Thurmond particularly, and Richard Nixon's race in 1968 to become president. That was the southern strategy. I don't see that in any of these papers [at the conference], but y'all are not getting to the reality of it. Why do you think they've got two Republican senators in Alabama, Mississippi, Tennessee, Kentucky, Virginia? You go all around, and they are ready to get rid of me this next year, but we keep fighting them, but what have you.

But the truth of it is that it's been institutionalized and it's been set back in large measure now in that regard because as long as that persists with that southern strategy and it's institutionalized in the leading and winning political party and leadership that we've got in this country, you're not going to get any real progress as I see it. It's very difficult. Particularly with the number-one issue where I think both the white leadership and the black leadership on affirmative action is just as wrong as they can be. I know all about diversity, and we work on all the programs to get diversity, whether it's Head Start, Women's, Infants, and Children Feeding, Title IX of the Disadvantaged, Community Health Centers—I can go on: Trio Program, program after program—but the Constitution says. . . citizens cannot be denied the equal protection of laws because of race, and it doesn't say except for diversity. . . . I have to confront that charge. . . . [People say to me:] "See that fellow over there, I've been here five years, but he just got in here, but they were looking for an African American and he got the promotion."

I hear that at the police station, in the city hall, all going around [the state] and everything else like that, and yet you see all of these coming along with the Michigan case in affirmative action saying you can't eliminate discrimination with discrimination. I think that case—it'll be a five-four decision I think—Sandra Day O'Connor will write it and maybe we can get by that. And if we get by that, then we can begin to make some progress.

Note

1. *Editor's note:* The famous "with all deliberate speed" dictum was issued not in the initial *Brown* decision of 1954 but in the *Brown II* decision of 1955.

Comments

JOHN C. WEST

I'd like to give a few observations, two or three, and a couple of anecdotes. First of all I want to say, Tony, you have done a magnificent job in this paper you have presented. Reading it, as you were kind enough to give me an advance copy, it told me things about myself that I didn't realize. And made me think and that provocative question that you put at the end: "How much credit do these white leaders have for doing what the federal government and the pressures of the NAACP made them do?" How much credit?

Well, I want to go back though and make one observation. It's impossible for those who were not living at the time to understand the emotions that were aroused by the Civil Rights Act and particularly *Brown v. Board of Education*. The emotions were absolutely unbelievable. I'll give you one example. I was just out of the war, and I went to the local county Democratic convention in 1948 and the then state senator proposed a motion to condemn the Civil Rights Act. Well, there was a new Episcopal preacher, his name has been mentioned, Stiles Lines, who rose up and said, "Mr. Chairman, has anybody here ever read the Civil Rights Act?" It so infuriated the senator that he ruled him out of order, went back the next day, resigned from the church, and refused to be buried in the Episcopal faith with that church. That was 1948, and yet there were some compensations. There were some—and I like to think there was a basic goodness that we like to think we enjoy in South Carolina. You mentioned it in the paper there, Tony. Fritz, you mentioned it.

When the sit-ins came, that was the early manifestation of the Civil Rights Movement. The young blacks would come and picket the various areas for various reasons. One of the stories that I remember made an impression on me and throughout the state because a group of these young blacks came to Charleston and picketed, and among the places they picketed was the law office of Allan Legare who's here tonight, the senator. The senator at that time was the boss of the county, and Allan went out on a hot summer day, invited them in and gave them a Coca-Cola. Now that was evidence of a humaneness and so on.

Now that brings us to the question of did we move soon enough and should we have moved quicker or could we have moved quicker? And I come to a question of leadership, and I want to tell this story. It's in the paper that Tony gave, but I want to give you the full version.

The most dramatic and the most meaningful speech that I have ever heard in my public life was given in January 1963, by Fritz Hollings here. Harvey Gantt had applied, and a federal decree had come down ordering him admitted, to Clemson. Now at one time there was an act in the General Assembly, fortunately it didn't pass, that said if any black student is admitted by federal court order, that college will close and the state college at Orangeburg will also close. And I remember sitting with Bob Edwards, the president of Clemson, when that act was pending, and he said, "If we close Clemson for one day, we're ruined forever." But anyhow in came this court order, and again the political background is interesting. Fritz had just run for the United States Senate against Olin Johnston and "Rollin with Olin" had rolled Fritz over. He had won one county, and his successor was Donald Russell, who he had defeated four years before in a very bitter race in which there were a lot of personalities exchanged and so on. And so virtually all of Fritz's advisers said, "Well, Harvey won't go to Clemson until Donald comes in. Leave it to him. It's a no-win situation." Well, Fritz has been known since our Citadel days as the "bull-headed Dutchman." And he doesn't often listen to advice, sometimes to Peatsy [Mrs. Ernest F. Hollings], and at any rate he said, no, I'm going to speak to the legislature, give them a farewell address. I was a member of that legislature. I was in the Senate. At that time, [Governor George Wallace of Alabama] was standing in the courthouse door. Wallace was defying. There were all sorts of ideas. There was interposition, which was a legal idea that had been advanced. There was the option of closing Clemson. The tension in that legislature was as high as I have ever seen, because few people knew what Fritz was going to say. And when he said, "We've run out of courts. We've run out of time. Clemson will be integrated. Harvey Gantt will be admitted. Pete Strom make damn sure there is no trouble." The whole state changed on that one speech. If he had said differently, it would have changed a whole generation of South Carolinians. And to me it is the best example I've ever seen of raw political courage.

Now ending up with a personal note. People ask me how I became a flaming liberal, and I said, "Easy, let the Ku Klux Klan threaten you and your wife and it's like Saul on the road to Damascus. You get a conversion."

So thank you, Tony. Thank you, Dan [Carter], and I'll be glad to try to answer any questions.

Questions and Answers

Unknown Speaker: On the thirty-fifth anniversary of the Orangeburg Massacre recently, the incumbent governor issued an apology for the first time for what happened in '68. Since both of you were in office in that period, of course not in office at the time, I wonder if you would agree with that apology or have a comment on whether Governor [Robert] McNair should make his own apology or at least address it after all of these years.

John C. West: I'm delighted to answer that question because I think Bob McNair has gotten a bad rap on the reputation that he's gotten from the Orangeburg situation. It was a most unfortunate thing, but I credit it, and maybe I have a prejudiced hindsight that it was . . . a riot where we didn't have sufficiently trained people to handle it and it was an isolated incident. Bob McNair—I give him great credit because during his term, the private schools took off. We were afraid, he was afraid, and I shared his concern . . . because of the integration in the lower grades and . . . the four hundred and some odd private schools that sprung up—all of the affluent citizens virtually were supporting the private schools. The public school system was in jeopardy, and I give Bob McNair major credit for saving the public school system and I think the blame he gets or the—sure it doesn't hurt to apologize. Jim Hodges, Mark Sanford, if it helps anybody an apology is certainly not inappropriate, but I think McNair has been unfortunately stigmatized with this.

Ernest F. Hollings: Let me agree with this 100 percent. John has really described it to you. You've got to understand that I had had until that time, or South Carolina had had, the best record. There was serious injury and loss of life in Georgia, Florida, North Carolina, Tennessee, all around [the South], and I had prided myself after the fours years of being out there like Bedford Forrest, "firstest with the mostest." I spent over half of my time as governor out in the streets with Pete Strom and a fellow named Harry Walker and right to the point, Orangeburg was a failure of law enforcement. Now you are the Chief Law Enforcement Officer, I wouldn't let crowds get out of hand; namely, I was up there with Reverend [Cecil Augustus] Ivory in Rock Hill, where Martin Luther King started and the CORE [Congress of Racial Equality] group started, both. And they came 'cause they could stay at the Barringer Hotel, which was integrated, and come over into South Carolina, and that's where I had all the black law enforcement officers, but Reverend Ivory would bring these twelve little innocent children. They'd sit at the lunch counter and these white punks, ducktail haircuts with the peg-leg britches, would pile in behind them, and the poor little child would get up to go to the bathroom and they would dive for the seat. There was the physical contact, the fight, the injury, and in Greensboro and up in Tennessee they were killed. And I said, "No, I'm not going to allow, but twelve in and twelve out." And they called me from New York, and I said, "Send Earl Warren down. I'm the chief law enforcement officer, I'll lock him up. I'm *Salus Populi Suprema Lex.*" The twelfth roman cannon. It's the safety of the people, the supreme law. Now Governor McNair did an outstanding job. What had happened on that third day, they were relying a lot on highway patrolmen. They weren't taught to handle crowds and everything else out there. Yes, a patrolman or otherwise I was not there in '68, I was up in Washington at that time, but somehow one of the law enforcement officers, whether it was a SLED officer or not, we only had incidentally 34 SLED officers when I was the chief law enforcement officer. We didn't even have one a county. They've got 485 today. As you've got an idea about handling crowds and law enforcement, that's a growth industry along with health. But right to the point, he couldn't be there day and night, and it was in the evening that that thing happened, and I think it was a highway patrolman, they didn't know how to handle crowds and when one got hit with a brick and fell, they started firing. But Governor McNair, no, he's been given a bad rap.

Robin Morris: I'm Robin Morris from the Levine Museum of the New South, and Senator Hollings, I'm wondering how, in addition to leading the state through the civil rights movement, you were also the governor through the Civil War centennial, and I was wondering if you could comment on leading the state through both of these times in the state's history at the same time.

Hollings: I was governor in 1961. John Amasa May, but we call him John Amazinly from Aiken, frankly, I came down to the Fort Sumter Hotel, and we reenacted on that April Day the beginning of the Civil War, the firing by the Citadel cadets on Fort Sumter. Amasa May, he said, "The devil with that. They're trying to make fun of us down here. We're going to celebrate our hundredth anniversary too." You know that there little image and cartoon, 'Forget Hell,' and all that kind of stuff, he manufactured, fashioned them. A Confederate uniform came down there and stood on the Battery and every-thing else of that kind, put in a concurrent resolution to put the flag up, the Confederate Flag up. It wasn't signed by me as the governor. I had to answer this question back in the '80s and in the '92 race. The flag is still an issue in 2002, but I said, "Take it down." I'm still trying to find the *State* newspaper, because they had an editorial story to the effect it was temporarily taken down to put back up, but it didn't have any significance. Nobody was think-ing of that. Just like you asking now about an apology and everything else. . . . We've got to move forward. Is there a particular phase of that or some-thing like I was running civil rights at that time? I wasn't even thinking about it to tell you the truth. Literally, no, in 1968 I was writing a book on hunger. I. D. Newman he was the head of the [South Carolina] NAACP, and he and I have had our struggles since then, but he won out. When [John F.] Kennedy died, I went up and I was—Bobby [Kennedy] and I were two of the ten [Junior Chamber of Commerce] men of the year—he met me and wanted me to come with the family and everything else. I said no. I stood in line all night long. I got my ticket, went to the St. Matthews Church. I'll never forget it and I was doing pretty well. I had a seat on the thirty-fifth row, but there comes I. D., Reverend I. D. Newman, he had on spats. He had on striped pants and a swallow-tail coat and that by-gosh bowtie and a derby and everything else, and when he walked up to the church they said, "Mr. Ambassador, come right this way." They sat him up on the second row. Naw, in '68 I can tell you—any specific thing you're asking about, I'll be glad to try to respond.

Yeah, the Confederate War centennial, I don't remember anything other than that firing when Frank Blair came down on NBC on the *Today Show*, yeah.

Jack Bass: Let me just say a couple of things. I accompanied Senator Hollings on all of his hunger tours, I think, and he not only saved the food stamp program, he greatly expanded it, and I think that's one of the things he deserves great credit for. I also covered Governor West during his full term as governor, and I think what he said both in terms of the impact of Senator Hollings's statement at the end of his term is accurate and also [State] Senator West. Great, tremendous leadership after Orangeburg in establishing the Human Affairs Commission deserves great credit, but I do have a couple of questions. And Senator, I would like to correct, though, that the shooting at Orangeburg did not—it was more than five minutes that elapsed after the patrolman was hit before the firing began, a small detail, but I think an important one. And I was glad to hear Governor West say perhaps an apology might be useful. Now I would like everybody in the audience to know we're going to discuss Orangeburg tomorrow morning. There will be a video in which eight of the people who got shot will be telling their story of what happened that night, and I would like to ask them this question. If either of you had been governor at the time, one—the first real question is—would you have authorized the use of buckshot in the shotguns on a college campus for the highway patrol? And two, after thirty-five years, do either of you believe if three students had been killed, three white students on the campus of Clemson University and twenty-seven others wounded, do you believe after thirty-five years there would never have been a state investigation and report of what happened and that there would be no restitution for those who were shot?

Hollings: I didn't realize Jack Bass was here; he wrote the book on it so he knows. He was a Neiman fellow from Harvard, and Jack is an authority on this particular event. To compare—no, you wouldn't have buckshot; that was the whole idea. In fact, I was embarrassed, and I continue with embarrassment with my good friend Congressman [James] Clyburn when he was a student at Orangeburg and I was the governor. I was headed down to Orangeburg, and it was a cold winter and they didn't use buckshot, Fisher was the name of the Fire Chief, he hosed them down, and when I got there you had about two hundred students. I said, "Man, you can't leave them out there all wringing wet in the cold like that." [And Fisher replied,] "Yeah, we've got them charged." We got them into a theater, got them warm and dried and everything else like that, and I talked to the magistrate and we threw out the particular charges, but no, you wouldn't have buckshot. On the other hand, you know about the patrolmen and everything. I didn't realize you were in the audience, but don't compare it to—just because they were black. Come on, that's not a proper question—Clemson or something. Why don't you say the Citadel? If we had three white students—. Look here this crowd, I lost all the Citadel vote in the '92 race backing that young lady here as a cadet. You don't realize—I congratulate Professor Moore and General Grinalds on holding this on my campus, I'll tell you that right now. You just don't know the feeling that's still out there. Yeah, go ahead. You can clean it up.

West: Well, my hope is that we can put Orangeburg behind us and one of the more satisfying events during my term as governor, I believe it was '74. We were locating a plant at Orangeburg, a Japanese plant, it's still in existence there. The chief executive officer came over from Japan for the dedication, and in talking to him I said, "Why did you select Orangeburg?" And his answer was this: He said, "You know, we're still sensitive to discrimination because of our role in World War II, and we looked all over the state and we found that there was no discrimination or no feeling in Orangeburg." The announcement that day took place in the hall built in honor of those three black students. So I like to think the healing process has been going on, maybe it isn't finished. I don't see any state investigation or anything like that that would help the healing process, but I think it's time to move forward.

Unknown Speaker: The question is, it's like the lynchings that occurred all over this country since there were no arrest and no investigation, the healing can't start. So could there be someone with the courage to say that an investi—at least an investigation letting the family members know what happened that night.

West: Is that a question? Well, of course it would have been inappropriate and probably could not, an investigation could not have happened until after the highway patrolmen were tried. You know it was a federal indictment and there was an investigation, and until that case was decided it would certainly have been inappropriate to have an investigation. I think the hope then after the decision was that that was closure. Obviously it has not been adequate at least for some of the family members and I sympathize with them, but I think it would be a useless and nonproductive exercise to try after these thirty years to go back—and nearly forty years I guess now—and try to unearth any facts or any information that would really be meaningful.

Robert Black: Senator Hollings, I'm also in the audience, Robert Black, and represented the young lady whom you just referenced in her effort to get in the Citadel. Her name was Shannon Faulkner.

Hollings: That was it. I was right.

Black: And while I am here I would also like to say on the case, just less than fewer than ten years after the U.S. marshals left the very spot we're standing in actually on campus, but for Governor West, one of the hardest things I had to do in the case was to convince one of our witnesses for the plaintiff for Shannon, Bob Edwards, that you were actually a witness for the defense.

Paul Gaston: Paul Gaston, the University of Virginia. I want to make two statements and then lead to a question for Senator Hollings. First, I would like to say as a historian confined to the colonies that I've never heard such a brilliant speech, and we're grateful to you and the mother country for bringing it to us, Tony. Second, my very good friend Lenwood Holton sends his wishes to the governor, New South governor, West. And Lenwood and I were talking recently about the time in 1970, he took the hand of one of his children and his wife, Jenks, took the hand of the other and while governors in the Deep South, my home state of Alabama, neighboring state of Mississippi, for which you always said "Thank God it existed" compared to Alabama, took their children to the integrated schools in Richmond, Virginia. They didn't have to do that. It was one of the greatest stands ever made by a governor in a southern state, and he is the only Republican I ever voted for. And then the Republican Party eliminated his influence, and that leads to my question to you, Senator Hollings. You talked about the southern strategy that began about this time. And I think the way Lenwood was treated was sort of strong evidence that the Republican Party was going to adopt that kind of strategy. So I have a very simple question for you, sir. How do we defeat that? Your comments? How do we turn that around in the South? A very easy question for you to answer, sir.

Hollings: We're losing out more and more every day. I've had again good authoritative friends that have come to me and said, "Look if you just changed to being a Republican, you won't have to worry about getting the money or getting the vote, or having any opposition. You've got a shoo-in, so don't give us this talk about not running next year and everything else." The Republican Party is growing, and the Democratic Party is losing out. We've got a Republican house, senate, and governor, and you've got Max Cleland, he got beat down there in Georgia, and all that's the move that's still afoot. That's why I'm saying on the racism part when I came in on inaugural day and I made my talk. And incidentally we didn't talk about segregation and integration or race in anybody in that inaugural address. Look at it. I was very careful about it because I had taken stands all the way down the line integrating the school board right in this county. Asked a minute ago about lynching. I introduced the Anti-lynch Bill and I worked with Morris Dees [of the Southern Poverty Law Center] on this recent lynching case that we had against the Klan when we got a $35 million verdict in South Carolina, but we just had a dickens of a time with the party in trying to build it and everything else. I've tried every way in the world and the best way I know that we hold and to make any progress is to get with the programs. Yes, I worked with Bob Dole, a Republican senator, up there. He helped us save food stamps. They were about to get rid of it. The same with Kit Bond and I last year. He'll help me, the Senator, Republican from Missouri, but, no, they are orchestrated, organized. They pick the candidates from the White House, they get the money. I mean, money talks, and I don't know how you get a stronger Democratic Party other than to take the stands that we're doing, and I think they're the right stands. We are for government. We're for public education and everything else, and we're not going to move forward in this state unless we get better public education. But there is no silver bullet or thing that we're doing particularly wrong in the Democratic Party, it's just that that thing is more predominant. When Oklahoma was blasted, I called up 'cause I had infiltrated the Klan when I was governor. What I had done when I got sworn in, I came back at my desk and had a gold embossed envelope there, a lifetime membership in the Grand Klavern of the Klan, and I had never heard of all that. And I called in Pete Strom and I said, "We've got the Klan that organized in this state?" He said, "Yeah, we got 1,867 members." I said, "Gosh, you've got to count them." He said, "Yeah, and I can get rid of them if you help me." I said, "I'll help you. What are we going to do?" Get me a little help, we can get a few agents. We get the word around that they're meeting right outside of Hemingway. The first illuminated field was not a football field, it was the Klan down in South Carolina. I'll show it to you. The post is still there. They would come out of Whiteville, North Carolina, and that was a big meeting that they had. And wherever they worked, they got the words to go into those kinds of meetings and it wouldn't help their business, and the next thing you know by the time we integrated Harvey at Clemson, I was calling the meetings. Then when Oklahoma was blasted up, we had less than 300 members in 1963, January. He told me this was just a few years ago they had at least 35,000. That's why that fellow [David] Duke from Louisiana came and talked in Spartanburg County. We've still got them in Lexington County and everything else. I don't know how many they've got now. You can ask these reporters.

Dan Carter: We're running close on time, but I have one more question here if we could.

Unknown Speaker: A short question for Dr. Badger. Your knowledge of South Carolina for someone so far away is truly amazing. My question is, is it true that Senator Byrnes, who was the majority leader in the 1930s, agreed with Roosevelt that he would push the New Deal through the Senate if Roosevelt would agree not to push for civil rights? And if so, should it have been a surprise in the 1950s when Byrnes didn't do what you said he could have done?

Anthony Badger: I don't think there is any evidence that Roosevelt made anything as explicit as an agreement as that. It was simply that Roosevelt himself had no intention of pushing the civil rights legislation through. He believed that there was a new generation of Southerners coming and you know they had to be patient, and getting economic legislation through was more important. And that was certainly what his position was in the 1930s, and in a sense all of my work has been to see what happened to that new generation of Southerners and was he right to be patient.

Carter: One last—okay, this is my friend. I'll let Armand ask one more question here.

Armand Derfner: I don't want to go out on a limb, but I have to say this. Senator and Governor, you both are good friends of mine. I've worked hard with you and supported you and still do and plan to support you every time you run. In fact, Senator Hollings, I was one of your greatest supporters in your race for president back when I was living in Washington, D.C., temporarily. But I do have to say that I think there are probably a lot of people in this audience who would take issue with you in your views of, for example, the Orangeburg Massacre. Because I think there are a lot of people here who believe that that has not been laid to rest, but a lot of other things have not been laid to rest and that we can't really move forward adequately as a society of white and black unless we lay to rest the things in the past that are still festering.

Part 2 ⇆ Aggressors

The essays in part 2, "Aggressors," return to the early years of the Jim Crow era in South Carolina to trace the efforts of white South Carolinians to forestall African American attempts to improve their situation. Collectively these essays demonstrate the continuity of the violence that underpinned white supremacy in the Palmetto State.

In "Lynching in the Outer Coastal Plain Region of South Carolina and the Origins of African American Collective Action, 1901–1910," Terence Finnegan documents that those eastern counties spawned more racial murders than any other part of the South during the first decade of the twentieth century. A typical lynching in this region, the author shows, occurred as a consequence of some alleged affront against whites on the part of the African American victim. Finnegan argues that these murders were so barbaric and the amount of bloodshed so great that they, ironically, stimulated the very sort of organized black resistance that whites sought to forestall. This new cadre of African American leaders lobbied white politicians and, indeed, persuaded some of them to denounce mob violence and to make efforts to ensure that those who participated in it felt some repercussions. African American reformers also worked hard to create a united front against the violence—holding caucuses, petitioning for the removal of the most racist white officials, refusing to bury the bodies of victims, and even demonstrating that they could exert significant economic pressure on the perpetrators—efforts that were to become more refined and effective during the later civil rights movement.

Less than a decade later, similar ironies accompanied white efforts to prevent blacks from participating in Woodrow Wilson's crusade to "make the world safe for democracy"—as Janet G. Hudson demonstrates in her essay,

"Conflicting Expectations: White and Black Anticipations of Opportunities in World War I–Era South Carolina." The coming of war was greeted by white and black South Carolinians as an opportunity for change. The former looked to the increased economic opportunities that would result from ever-rising demand for the state's cotton. The latter saw a "catalyst for change from the previous decades of oppression and dismal prospects for an improved standard of living" and actively sought opportunities to fight for their country in the hope of maneuvering future economic and political gains. Many whites, however, were concerned that, by becoming soldiers, African Americans would come into contact with different social values, leading them to challenge the South's existing racial order and undermine the principles of segregation. Others believed that African Americans should indeed be sent to Europe, if only to prevent the deaths of more white South Carolinians in the fighting. They also worried that the increased wages that workers could demand as a result of the war-induced labor shortages would give African Americans more economic opportunities and facilitate their resistance to the Jim Crow system. Hudson argues that war mobilization, therefore, challenged white supremacist ideals, creating a central dichotomy over what role African Americans should play in the war effort that many whites found impossible to reconcile. But African American hopes about the potentially dramatic gains to be made from the Great War were soon dashed. Although white resistance to racial change was a contributing factor, it was the success of the Allied forces in France in bringing the war to an unexpectedly early victory that precipitated the failure of African Americans to make real progress against South Carolina's racial structures.

Despite disappointments, many African American soldiers returned home to South Carolina determined to improve not only their own prospects, but also those of their families and neighbors. In "An 'Ominous Defiance': The Lowman Lynchings of 1926," Elizabeth Robeson shows that fear of the "New Negro" who returned from the war kept racial tensions high and helped to produce in Aiken, South Carolina, one of the most brazen, widely publicized, and conspicuously unpunished, acts of white mob violence in the nation. The plot was evocative of *To Kill a Mockingbird*—with the exception that there was no Atticus Finch.

The Lowman lynchings reveal many of the complexities of life in the New South for both African Americans and whites. Sam Lowman was the son of slaves and had successfully created a comfortable life of economic independence for himself and his family; all his children were educated, and two of his sons were among those who had fought in World War I and, on their return to the United States, had left South Carolina for the greater economic opportunities available in northern cities. At the same time, many previously affluent whites were encountering economic hardships, and the success of the Lowman household clearly threatened their notion that African Americans were fundamentally inferior to whites. The Lowmans thus became an obvious target for their retribution.

A generation later, in the wake of another world war, a similar case in Greenville—richly described in "The Civil Right Not to Be Lynched: Law, Government and Citizen Response to the Killing of Willie Earle (1947)" by William Gravely—suggests that little had changed in white South Carolina's seemingly instinctive response to black-on-white violence. As the author points out, the dictum "an eye for an eye" still held sway at every level of the state. The reaction of African Americans to this incident reveals that the seeds of resistance evident following the Lowman lynchings had continued to develop, and the early roots of South Carolina's civil rights movement can clearly be seen in the response of some African American groups, which successfully organized student protests, petitioned state and federal officials, and even launched a boycott of the local taxi companies that employed many of Earle's killers. That the forces unleashed by World War II were eroding some of the old racial barriers is evident from the unprecedented number of whites from across the country who protested Willie Earle's murder and his assailants' subsequent acquittal. Many of these outraged citizens wrote to Governor Strom Thurmond objecting to the state's handling of the case, in many instances echoing the rhetoric of the recent war by expressing their belief that if nothing was done to rectify the racial inequities of the state then "even White Protestant Americans will not be safe if this [violence] is not checked."

A further sign that interracial attitudes were beginning to change across the state appeared along the "Grand Strand" of Myrtle Beach, where black and white teenagers attracted to each other's music came together at Charlie's Place to create a new dance that came to be known as the shag. Set against the backdrop of the racially charged battle for the Democratic nomination for the United States Senate between Olin D. Johnston and Strom Thurmond, journalist Frank Beacham's "This Magic Moment: When the Ku Klux Klan Tried to Kill Rhythm and Blues Music in South Carolina" explores the fusion of cultures evident at Myrtle Beach and the threat that it posed to the existing order. Like Sam Lowman before him, Charlie Fitzgerald, the owner of Charlie's Place, was an African American who, in the eyes of the white community, had clearly risen above his station. Not only was he a successful businessman, he also openly flaunted the social norms of the South, refusing to make concessions to segregation and operating his business in the same manner. This was a uniquely integrated environment, in which white teenagers knowingly and willingly violated many of the underpinnings of the Jim Crow South; they used the same facilities as African Americans, attended their churches, and even danced with them without regard to each other's color. The white establishment of Myrtle Beach inevitably frowned upon these activities, and the Ku Klux Klan targeted Fitzgerald for reprisals, launching an attack on him and his establishment in the summer of 1950. In the aftermath of the Klan's unpunished assault on Charlie's Place, a half century after that part of the Palmetto State became infamous for racial violence, it became apparent that, despite some small progress, white promises of justice continued to have no real meaning.

Lynching in the Outer Coastal Plain Region of South Carolina and the Origins of African American Collective Action, 1901–1910

Terence R. Finnegan

At first glance, the opening decade of the twentieth century might not seem like an especially important period in the formation of the civil rights movement. Segregation was entrenched; racial violence was rampant; African Americans were politically impotent; and the accommodationist policies of Booker T. Washington were in vogue. In the opinion of one recent scholar, African Americans in the early twentieth century found themselves in "a miserable situation being deprived of their political rights, being segregated in social life and being in a generally subordinate position."[1] Yet by the end of the same decade, the NAACP, arguably the most important civil rights organization of the twentieth century, had been founded. The crucible of humiliation and oppression that African Americans endured early in the twentieth century was the catalyst for the mass movement that developed later in the century.[2] During the early-twentieth-century struggle against lynching, African Americans tentatively and sporadically developed strategies of protest that would be used to greater effect during the civil rights movement.[3]

The opening decade of the twentieth century was a period of prolonged brutality in terms of racial violence throughout the South and especially in the outer coastal plain region of South Carolina. From 1901 through 1910 the seven counties in the outer coastal plain endured nearly 60 percent of the lynchings that occurred in the region from 1881 to 1940, making this the worst decade for lynching (in percentage terms) for any region in the state's history. The tide of racial violence that covered South Carolina after the turn of the century prompted white leaders, especially progressive governor Duncan C. Heyward, to denounce extralegal violence vigorously. African Americans also protested against lynching, and the collective efforts of African Americans had a tangible impact on whites, contributing to a precipitous decline in lynching during the 1910s and 1920s.

The first twentieth-century lynching that occurred in the outer coastal plain region happened at Port Royal in Beaufort County and involved an African American sailor named William Cornish. Whites lynched Cornish for allegedly attempting to rape several white women, but the charges were unsubstantiated at best. Local African Americans reportedly launched an energetic search for Cornish's body, and rumors spread about a retaliation plot among African Americans.[4]

The next lynching incident in the outer coastal plain took place in June 1902, when three black men (and possibly four) were lynched in Colleton County for allegedly killing a white woman during a robbery the previous month. A mob took one of the lynching victims from police custody before tying the man to a pine tree and shooting him to death. After the lynching rumors of a race riot circulated, but the most dramatic consequence of the lynching was in fact the resignation of George Koester, the founder of the *Columbia Record,* from his position as collector of internal revenue for South Carolina.

Koester's fall was largely the work of African American activist Edmund Deas, also known as the "Duke of Darlington," who was chairman of the South Carolina Republican Party and was such an outspoken advocate for the rights of African Americans that he had been physically assaulted by supporters of Benjamin Tillman.[5] Deas had been lobbying the Roosevelt administration for Koester's removal since his appointment in October 1901, and he had enlisted the aid of Booker T. Washington to the cause.[6] Koester claimed that Deas and other black politicians had joined with Koester's journalistic rivals at the *State* newspaper and falsely accused him of participating in a triple lynching at Gaston in 1893. Koester denied the charge and insisted that he had only been present at the lynching as a reporter. He went on to claim that he had personally captured one of the victims, Tom Preston, and that he had forced the mob to shoot Preston instead of burning him to death by threatening "to blow out his [Preston's] brains the moment a match was applied to the rosin." Contemporary accounts make no mention of Koester's "heroics," but he insisted that President Theodore Roosevelt believed his story. Deas and the *State,* however, organized a massive letter-writing campaign against Koester's appointment.[7] In the aftermath of the multiple lynching at Colleton, the Roosevelt administration apparently agreed with Booker T. Washington that "it would clear the atmosphere wonderfully and serve as the greatest encouragement to our race if it could be understood that this man lost his position because of having taken part in a lynching."[8] The African American community was still smarting from the tepid response of the McKinley administration to the 1898 lynching of U.S. Postmaster Frazier Baker in Lake City, South Carolina, and the Roosevelt administration probably saw little risk in sacrificing a "Gold Democrat" such as Koester to satisfy the demands of Republican activists that the administration take a strong stand against lynching. (Gold Democrats opposed expanding the supply of currency.)

About fourteen months after the resignation of Koester, and partially in response to a lynching that occurred in the inner coastal plain region, African Americans organized a statewide conference on lynching in Columbia, sponsored by the African American Ministerial Union and held at Bethel Church in Columbia on August 25, 1903.[9] About 150 people attended, including ministers, teachers, and political officials, and the major newspapers in the state sent reporters to cover the proceedings. White newspapers attempted to downplay the political implications of the speeches, but several speakers directly addressed the connection between human rights and lynching. Charleston minister G. C. Rowe, for instance, argued that lynching "cheapened human life" and that it represented the "rape of the public conscience." Lynching, said Rowe, was not punishment for an unspeakable crime but rather the "self-imposed degradation and condemnation of a so-called superior people!" Whites lynched, according to Rowe, mainly to "degrade the negro," and the only effective remedy was the elimination of "race distinctions" that were clearly wrong.

Former U.S. representative George Murray connected lynchings to the "narrow, bigoted spirit of slavery," which bred violence and hatred between the races. Murray claimed that, if the unjust economic and social disparities that existed between blacks and whites were removed, then lynchings would cease.[10] The summary statement from the conference condemned the racial bigotry of U.S. Senator Benjamin Tillman, called for judicial equality between whites and blacks, and requested more educational assistance for African Americans, which the signatories believed was an indispensable aid to the improvement of race relations. In commenting on the conference, the *Charleston News and Courier* condemned Rowe for arguing that "the existence of the gorilla negro" was not "the chief cause of lynching." The "better class of whites," said the paper, wanted African Americans to be "useful and happy in due subordination to the superior race," but the radical opinions of leaders such as Rowe and Murray were a hindrance, not a help, to solving the lynching problem.

During the fall after the conference, South Carolina suffered no further lynching, but during the winter of 1903–1904, two black men were lynched in Dorchester County in separate incidents. Not surprisingly, both lynchings allegedly involved attempted assaults on white women, and the second lynching prompted Governor Heyward to ask the state legislature for more money to combat lynching and to pass legislation that would make it easier to arrest suspected members of a mob.[11] About five weeks later, the outer coastal plain region endured another lynching; this one occurred in Berkeley County and involved a disorderly man named Robert Williams, who may have been shot with the active cooperation of a local law enforcement official.[12]

Five months later Berkeley County was the site of the depraved lynching of Kitt Bookard, an event that seemingly confirmed the opinions of African American leaders such as Rowe and Murray about the causes of lynchings.[13] Bookard was a twenty-one-year-old black tenant farmer, who in mid-July 1904 went fishing with five white men: three brothers, Benny, Andrew, and Piney Martin, and two other white tenants, Henry Edwards and Adgar Butler, all of whom worked on the farm of Lewis Martin, father of the Martin brothers. On the trip home an argument ensued in which Bookard threatened to "spank" Henry Edwards, whom the African American tenants on the Martin farm apparently did not like. The same day Edwards had Bookard arrested and fined five dollars. When Bookard could not pay the fine, he was sentenced to fifteen days in jail.

Four days later six white men—Edwards, town marshal John Palmer, constable S. A. Eadons (who was married to Lewis Martin's sister), Adgar Butler (who was a son-in-law of Lewis Martin), Penny Martin (a nephew of Lewis Martin), and Benny Martin—took Bookard from the Eutawville calaboose supposedly intent on whipping him. When the men reached the Santee River, however, they told Bookard that he had reached the banks of the River Jordan and that they were going to kill him. After tying Bookard's limbs and stuffing cotton in his mouth to muffle his screams, the six men proceeded to torture Bookard in a heinous manner. The lynchers scalped him, cut off his genitals and ears, removed his eyes and tongue, and inflicted numerous knife wounds on his body. Following the torture the men tied Bookard to a grate bar and threw him into the river. The body was found a week later. Outraged about Bookard's lynching, a thousand African Americans from the surrounding area attended the coroner's inquest.

Whites in the area feared that a race war might erupt unless authorities made some arrests. Governor Heyward told the press that he was "utterly disgusted" with the lynching, and he quietly used his own money to employ a Pinkerton detective to investigate the murder. For weeks nothing appeared to happen in the case, but whites from Eutawville became so paranoid about undercover detectives that they banned traveling salesmen from the town.

In early August 1904, Aaron P. Prioleau, a prominent African American politician from Berkeley County and perennial candidate for Congress, attempted to generate some progress in the case by writing a letter that suggested that African Americans had lost patience with waiting for the law to provide protection from such outrages. The *Columbia Record* opined that Prioleau's threatening words would "doubtless be remembered" by any future jury "even though they are sworn to find a verdict according to the law and evidence." The *Charleston News and Courier* condemned Prioleau and "his ignorant and viciously inclined friends" and worried that his letter might be "an excuse" for a jury to acquit anyone charged with Bookard's murder.[14]

In late October authorities finally arrested six white men for Bookard's lynching, shocking the Eutawville community. At a preliminary hearing in December, Bookard's wife, Mamie, revealed reluctantly that the animosity between her husband and Benny Martin stemmed from Martin having coerced sexual relations with Bookard's sister, Eliza. The state's major witness was Henry Edwards, who admitted that the men had been drinking before the murder. Edwards claimed that Palmer and Eadons had actually killed Bookard. When asked about the condition of the body, however, Edwards maintained that the men had not tortured Bookard in any way. Instead, Edwards conjectured that predatory fish had probably removed the various body parts. Such ridiculous testimony did not help the state's case. State senator E. J. Dennis conducted the defense and portrayed the defendants as devoted family men whom the system had abused, in contrast to the cowardly and traitorous Edwards. The jury deliberated for only sixteen minutes before acquitting the defendants.

The state's inability to obtain a conviction in the Bookard lynching chagrined Governor Heyward, not only because he had spent his own money to bring the lynchers to justice, but also because he was a rice planter from nearby Colleton County and wanton violence undoubtedly offended his paternalistic sensibilities. When the state's next potential lynching crisis occurred in August 1906, Heyward decided to risk his personal reputation to prevent a lynching from actually taking place.

Bob "Snowball" Davis was a husky day laborer and former convict from Greenwood County, whose dark complexion and sullen, sickly features elicited trepidation among whites.[15] About thirteen years earlier, in 1893, a mixed mob of whites and blacks from around the town of Ninety-Six had lynched Davis's brother Jake, supposedly for raping the wife of a white farmer.[16] Bob Davis allegedly attempted to rape Jennie Brooks, the twenty-year-old daughter of a prosperous farmer from the Mount Moriah section of Greenwood County. Davis purportedly assaulted the young woman in the family's country store and inflicted severe cuts to her hand and throat before he fled when a white patron drove by and heard Brooks's screams. A two-day manhunt ensued, which involved approximately one thousand searchers, and sentiment was strong to burn Davis at the stake. Heyward wanted to avoid this atrocity at all costs and contemplated sending troops to protect Davis from the mob. When Davis was finally captured, Heyward decided not to use the militia, because he worried that a mob would lynch Davis as soon as his plan became known. Instead, he resolved to make a personal appeal on behalf of the law. Although Heyward arrived at the Brooks home before Davis could be identified by the victim, those present informed the governor that "there was no earthly chance" that Davis could be saved from a lynching. When Heyward told the Brooks family that he did not want Davis lynched, the victim's father retorted that he wanted Davis burned and the Brooks women responded that "they would act as men if need be."

After Davis had been brought to the farm and Jennie Brooks identified him as her assailant, Heyward mounted a makeshift platform on the front-yard fence and made his plea for the law. Heyward's effort was doomed from the start because the mob knew that Davis could not be executed for attempted rape and assault, but he nevertheless assured the crowd that he understood how they felt living isolated in the country, and he implored the "manhood of Greenwood County" to let this "brute be punished as the law dictates." To bolster the chances of avoiding a lynching, the authorities apparently convinced an African American woman to accuse Davis of assaulting her niece, and after Heyward's speech the same woman made a staged identification and pleaded that she be allowed the privilege of shooting Davis first. Heyward promised the mob that if Davis was convicted of a capital crime, he would personally preside at the legal execution. Heyward reminded the crowd of the negative consequences that the Phoenix riot of 1898 had had for the region, and he warned that the propensity of mobs to take the law into their own hands was an ominous cloud on the state's horizon. The governor admitted that he could do little to stop the mob from lynching Davis but begged his listeners "in God's name do not put another stain on the name of your State." Finally, "fagged out and hopeless," Heyward descended the makeshift platform in defeat.

After attempting to elicit a full confession from Davis and rejecting Mr. Brooks's plea to burn the victim, a horde of armed men tied Davis to a pine tree and shot him to pieces during a ten-minute fusillade that could be heard as far away as Greenwood. Throughout the night onlookers came to observe the mob's macabre handiwork. The more ghoulish among the passersby periodically fired a round into the body, and the usual "souvenirs" were removed from the corpse. African Americans refused to bury Davis in the graveyard at Mount Moriah, so the authorities interred the body in a neighboring farmer's field. Heyward recognized that any attempt to prosecute the hundreds of men involved would be futile, and he dejectedly returned to Columbia, knowing that his "manly effort" had done nothing to protect the "fair name of South Carolina" from the vengeance of the mob.

Heyward probably believed that the state's reputation for grisly vengeance could suffer no further, but a week later, a Dorchester County mob proved him wrong. The lynching of Willie Spain, which involved the active collaboration of the county sheriff, was, according to Heyward, "about as much as folks ought to be asked to accept."[17] The immediate circumstances surrounding the lynching of Spain were strikingly similar to those present in the Davis lynching. Spain was in his early twenties and was described as a "sullen, worthless negro" who had recently migrated to the state from North Carolina. He occasionally found work at the Dorchester Lumber Company, where he ostensibly tried to break into the house of the company manager, S. L. Connor. The screams of Connor's eleven-year-old daughter, however, supposedly frightened Spain away, and after a brief altercation with Connor, he fled the scene. Within two hours, a posse had apprehended Spain and turned him over to the county sheriff, M. M. Limehouse. Spain was in jail for all of a half hour before a mob came to lynch him. The pusillanimous Limehouse allowed the mob to take Spain from the jail without resistance before he wired Heyward for assistance.[18] After a perfunctory identification by the Connor girl, the mob hanged Spain and riddled his body with so many bullets that it was beyond recognition. Limehouse later claimed that he thought the men only wanted to interrogate Spain for attempting to break into Connor's house.

African Americans in the area were infuriated over the lynching and began expressing their dissatisfaction at the coroner's inquest, at which they organized a "caucus" to prevent other blacks from helping to bury Spain. They also began to construct a plan to punish the coroner, S. E. Kizer, whom they blamed for not doing enough to investigate the lynching. In order to ease racial tensions, Heyward called a special term of court to prosecute Limehouse and to indict some of the lynchers. In October 1906 Limehouse became the first sheriff in South Carolina indicted for malfeasance in office under a provision of the 1895 constitution. He was subsequently tried in Orangeburg County and acquitted in 1907.

Kizer became sheriff upon the removal of the cowardly Limehouse, but his troubles were hardly over. Kizer was one of the wealthiest and most influential cotton planters in the area, and he had apparently ordered some of his African American laborers to bury Spain's body. Local African American leaders deeply resented Kizer's actions, which ran contrary to the sentiments that they had expressed at the inquest. African Americans often refused to bury the remains of lynching victims, not only because they were unwilling to bear the expense, but also because they wanted to emphasize that lynching was an affront to the human rights of all African Americans. By requiring that whites bury the victims of mob violence, African Americans were subtly forcing them to acknowledge the humanity of persons that white supremacists claimed were thought of as inhuman and therefore outside of the law.

To Kizer's amazement, African American leaders organized a boycott of his plantation, and he later complained of constant threats and the loss of thousands of dollars of income because he could not hire enough workers to pick his cotton. Other whites suspected of being involved in the lynching faced similar threats and boycotts. The economic pressure placed on Kizer forced him to use the courts to strike back against the suspected leaders of the protest. He secured indictments against four African Americans who had allegedly organized the labor boycott, and this presumably ended his labor problems, at least in the short term. Chastened by the experience, Kizer resigned as sheriff, and few whites seemed to want to replace him.[19]

The direct action protests that African Americans organized in response to the killing of Spain did not end lynching in the region, but racial violence and terrorism was afterward on the wane. The outer coastal plain and the southern Pee Dee regions were the only two areas of the state where lynchings ceased before 1920. The response of African Americans to the lynching plague was sporadic and cautious, but it convinced whites that racial terrorism would not intimidate blacks into submission. African Americans vigorously rejected white claims that lynchings were about crime and law and order rather than the human and political rights of blacks. African American political leaders used the limited influence that they had on the national and state level to remind whites that lynchings could have negative repercussions for white officials. At the local level African Americans frequently arrived en masse at the coroner's inquest to express their outrage over a lynching, and they usually refused to bury the victim's corpse. In the case of the Spain lynching, they courageously organized boycotts and protests to convince whites that if they supported a lynching, their own economic interests might suffer. It would take another couple of generations before African Americans possessed the grassroots organizations necessary to sustain these kinds of protests on a state and national level, but the fight against lynching helped lay the groundwork for the broader struggle for political and civil rights of the mid-twentieth century.

Notes

1. Zhang Aimen, *The Origins of the African American Civil Rights Movement, 1865–1956* (New York: Routledge, 2002), 10.

2. Ibid., 15.

3. On a national scale and in a broader context of violence, Herbert Shapiro has made much the same point. See Shapiro, *White Violence and Black Response: From Reconstruction to Montgomery* (Amherst: University of Massachusetts Press, 1988), chap. 4. Earlier interpretations of this period emphasized the "wretched degradation" that African Americans endured during the early twentieth century and argued that the roots of the civil rights movement could be found no earlier than the New Deal era. See, for example, Edwin D. Hoffman, "The Genesis of the Modern Movement for Equal Rights in South Carolina, 1930–1939," *Journal of Negro History* 44 (October 1959): 346–69.

4. See *Charleston News and Courier,* July 24, 1901, and Jack Simpson Mullins, "Lynching in South Carolina, 1900–1914" (M.A. thesis, University of South Carolina, 1961), 133.

5. *Washington Bee,* July 19. 1902.

6. Louis Harlan and Raymond Smock, eds., *Booker T. Washington Papers,* vol. 6, *1901–1902* (Urbana: University of Illinois Press, 1977), 414–15.

7. *Charleston News and Courier,* June 29, 1902. Details concerning the infamous lynching at Gaston, which African Americans accused Koester of being involved in, can be found in *Charleston News and Courier,* July 27–31, 1893, and August 1–3, 1893.

8. Harland and Smock, *Booker T. Washington Papers,* 6:289.

9. For details concerning the antilynching conference, see *Charleston News and Courier,* August 26–27, 1903; and Mullins, "Lynchings in South Carolina," 105–6.

10. Murray, incidentally, had been Koester's choice as deputy collector of internal revenue. See Harland and Smock, *Booker T. Washington Papers,* 6:310–11.

11. See *Charleston News and Courier,* November 29–30, 1903, and January 16, 17, 20–21, 1904.

12. *Charleston News and Courier,* March 3, 1904, and Mullins, "Lynching in South Carolina," 49–50.

13. The details concerning the Bookard lynching can be found in the *Charleston News and Courier,* July 18, 21, 22, 23, 25, 1904; August 5, 8, 1904; October 20, 1904; December 3, 9, 1904; May 10, 11, 1905; and in Mullins, "Lynching in South Carolina," 24–33.

14. *Charleston News and Courier,* August 5, 8, 1904.

15. For details on the Bob Davis lynching, see *Charleston News and Courier,* August 15–18, 1906.

16. *Charleston News and Courier,* August 22–23, 1893.

17. For details of the Spain lynching and its aftermath, see *Charleston News and Courier,* August 24, 25, 26, 31, 1906; September 5, 12, 1906; October 18, 21, 1906; also see Mullins, "Lynching in South Carolina," 55–57.

18. Limehouse's conduct met with some scorn even among whites. Some local ruffians apparently took delight in chiding Limehouse for his cowardice. Thomas Harley, for instance, who had been tried and convicted in absentia for assault because Limehouse had refused to arrest him, informed the *Dorchester Eagle* that he would have surrendered but was afraid "that I would have been lynched by a mob as others have been while in the custody of Limehouse." See Mullins, "Lynching in South Carolina," 55–57.

19. *Charleston News and Courier,* October 25, 30, 1906; November 22, 1906.

Conflicting Expectations

White and Black Anticipations of Opportunities in World War I–Era South Carolina

JANET G. HUDSON

Historians are often drawn to watershed epochs, periods when an unusual confluence of circumstances, events, and people produces significant change. Despite its importance in world and United States history, World War I has seldom been identified as an important watershed in southern history because it did not trigger substantial change in the South's economic, political, and social order. In 1917, however, many southerners saw their world poised on the brink of momentous change. From that vantage point they could not foresee that the opportunities presented by the war would be short-lived, that an agricultural depression would follow on the heels of the armistice and continue for two decades, or that the Jim Crow social order would remain firmly in place well beyond mid-century. South Carolina's African American majority instead welcomed the war as a catalyst for change from the previous decades of oppression and dismal prospects for an improved standard of living. Leaders in the state quickly envisioned increased postwar opportunities for African Americans as a reward for military service and other war-related, patriotic expressions to their country in time of need. Anticipating that their support of the nation's war effort would leverage future economic and political opportunities, African Americans readily looked for chances to serve.[1]

Not only did South Carolina's African American majority anticipate that the Great War would offer positive change, but white South Carolinians, especially reformers, also welcomed the war as an economic opportunity. Between 1917 and early 1920 cotton prices rose to all-time highs, enabling the cotton-dependent state to pay off debts and anticipate a brighter tomorrow. The textile industry also had its most successful years of the new century during the war. In addition to windfall profits for owners and investors, textile mill operatives enjoyed wage increases. Thus, World War I brought the region and the state new economic opportunities and a glimpse at prosperity that reformers envisioned would be sustained and would affect permanent change in South Carolina. "It is possible, indeed likely, . . . that the South Carolina and the South that we have known will be, on account of this war, unrecognizable in the course of a few years," the *State*'s editor, William Watts Ball, declared.[2] Yet the vision of South Carolina's white ruling elite directly conflicted with the aspirations of the state's black majority. All segments of South Carolina society seized on World War I mobilization as a potential agent for desired change, but they did not share a common vision, and the eventual outcome disappointed everyone. This essay will examine the conflicting aspirations between black and white South Carolinians exemplified in the debate over the appropriate role for African Americans in the war effort.[3]

While Congress debated President Woodrow Wilson's plea for a declaration of war against Germany, prominent African Americans in South Carolina took preemptive action by calling a meeting of black South Carolinians to Columbia. During this April 4, 1917, meeting, held at First Calvary Baptist Church, participants discussed the issue of allowing African American men to serve as soldiers. The Columbia forum drafted a resolution to Richard I. Manning, South Carolina's wartime governor, and President Wilson expressing the following sentiment: "It is the sense of this meeting that the government, State or national, should provide at once for military training and instruction of those members of our race who are ready to enlist, that they may be able to render good and efficient service."[4] Moreover, Rev. Richard Carroll, a prominent Baptist minister who advocated reform in the tradition of Booker T. Washington, urged that African Americans be allowed to serve in all ranks of the military from major on down. "We've had jim crow cars; jim crow street cars; jim crow cemeteries, churches and schools. Now let us have a jim crow regiment, surgeons and hospital corps," Carroll implored. Twelve men from this meeting—which included J. J. Durham, pastor of Second Calvary Baptist Church; N. J. Frederick, attorney and principal of Howard School; R. W. Mance, president of Allen University; and Columbia businessman I. S. Leevy—personally delivered this resolution to Governor Manning, who summarily dismissed their plea for inclusion in military service, telling them that their services were needed in capacities other than as soldiers. "Stay on the farm and work," Manning retorted.[5]

Despite Manning's rejection, African Americans persisted in their petition. Within days Beaufort's African American community responded with a public resolution pledging their commitment to military service. The resolution boldly declared the loyalty of Beaufort's African American population: "in spite of the discriminations, injustice and lack of protection under the laws, both local and national, we feel that we are still citizens of this great country." Furthermore, the resolution reminded its audience that African Americans had fought and died in every war since the American Revolution, and they offered the same commitment to the current conflict even while "we feel keenly the ill-treatment of the Negro by our State and national governments."[6]

Archdeacon E. L. Baskervill of Charleston penned a letter to the *News and Courier* reiterating the Columbia committee's request. "In this crisis I hope that the federal and state governments will authorize the organization of a negro regiment in this state and give the young men of my race in South Carolina an opportunity for military service against the enemy," Baskervill implored.[7] Another prominent African American leader followed with a similar demand. Thomas E. Miller, former Republican congressman from South Carolina and former president of State Agriculture College in Orangeburg, made a specific offer to both President Wilson and Governor Manning in a letter addressed to both executives:

> I come to you in this hour of our nation's calamity, offering you the patriotic service of 30,000 American negroes of my native state to serve in the regular army and navy of our nation. . . .
>
> I come you to bring no treasures from my people, for they are poor, but . . . in their name to offer to their country their fidelity, patriotism, devoted service and courage.
>
> I bring their manhood for service or for sacrifice upon the alter of a nation "conceived in liberty and dedicated to the principle that all men are created equal."[8]

As clergy, educators, lawyers, and entrepreneurs, African American leadership in South Carolina had long worked to create opportunities, improve the standard of living, and ameliorate some of the harsher realities of poverty for the majority of black South Carolinians. Yet, as evidenced by Manning's reaction, African Americans faced formidable difficulties when they called for just and equal treatment, because African Americans lacked political and economic power, essential tools for producing significant change in South Carolina society. They fully understood white southerners' incontrovertible commitment to white supremacy and the oppressive consequences that tenacious ideal had on black South Carolinians. Yet within these constraints, black leaders worked constantly to capitalize on the contradictions that emerged from the peculiar political, economic, and social structure white supremacy helped create in their state. While white southerners feared the difficulties of permitting African Americans to serve in the military, black southerners recognized the potential opportunities for economic and social improvement that military service might provide them, and many were anxious to afford African Americans the opportunity to join the United States military. Moreover, they were anxious to exploit the contradiction of privilege and responsibility associated with military service.[9]

Clearly South Carolina's white leadership did not readily embrace African Americans' call to arms. Military induction centers in South Carolina routinely rejected African American volunteers until the federal government ordered the state to accept black recruits.[10] When the U.S. military's need for rapid deployment of five hundred thousand troops sparked a national debate about the possibility of enacting a draft, white southerners anguished over the notion, since a national draft would not make any racial distinctions. Rhetorically South Carolinians revered military service as honorable, sacrificial, and worthy of admiration. Fighting for one's country had often been depicted as the highest form of patriotism. Consequently whites felt conflicted about the prospect that blacks would be drafted just like whites, trained alongside whites, and eventually serve on the battlefield with whites. This implication of equality was not only repugnant to white southerners but also in direct opposition to the imperative of their white supremacy creed, which insisted that African Americans were inferior and should be segregated from whites.[11] Opposition to including African Americans in the military prevailed when whites contemplated the rhetorical glories of war. One South Carolinian, who privately expressed reservations about African Americans serving in Europe as soldiers, indicated that southerners should not consent to using black soldiers. "We should cling to the notion that arms is a gentleman's profession, therefore, a white man's profession!"[12] Governor Manning exhibited this attitude through his initial efforts both to limit the privilege of military service to white South Carolinians and to quell the enthusiasm African Americans expressed for becoming soldiers. Their anxiety exposed the inherent contradictions between the rhetoric of American patriotism and the reality of military service.

Governor Manning's suggestions that African Americans could best serve their country as civilians, and more specifically as laborers, persisted. The Commission for Civic Preparedness, chaired by prominent white reformer David R. Coker, organized much of the early war preparation efforts by encouraging South Carolinians to plant gardens, assist the Red Cross, buy bonds, and "be loyal." After rejecting African American offers to serve as soldiers, Manning quickly appointed a committee of eight black men to assist Coker with the African American counterpart to the preparedness commission. Consistent with other southern institutions, all aspects of civic war preparation were segregated, even patriotic rallies and parades.[13] By channeling African Americans into the domestic side of the war effort, white Carolinians hoped to prevent them from experiencing social relations elsewhere that might conflict with the South's peculiar racial mores. Moreover, whites feared African Americans later returning to South Carolina with attitudes and expectations that would have been incompatible with the South's racial order.

Rather than concerns about rhetorical allusions to the grandeur of military service or potential challenges to the culture's future racial hierarchy, constituents' communication to Congressman A. Frank Lever often relayed practical arguments against using African Americans as soldiers. Distressed about labor shortages that would result from a military draft, J. Harry Foster told Lever he supported conscripting African Americans, but as agricultural laborers and not as soldiers. Foster argued that farmers would find it increasingly difficult to secure an adequate supply of labor unless labor could be compelled. The crisis of war, Foster argued, should justify labor conscription.[14] Charles L. Rhame of Sumter acknowledged familiarity with the antagonism white southerners expressed about using black troops. An investigation into this hostility, Rhame asserted, would reveal that "large land owners who are not planting grains . . . but mostly cotton and merchants who expect to do a big business in cotton traffic after the war" were fomenting this opposition against allowing African Americans to serve in the military.[15] Fundamentally, the large landowners and merchants were protecting their cotton investment and feared labor shortages that threatened their financial interests. Rhame's testimony revealed how easily white elites could exploit white supremacy to mask their economic self-interest.

Despite implications of social equality and fears of labor shortages, white South Carolinians' resistance to African American men serving as soldiers was tempered by the harsh reality of military service, a risky endeavor often relegated to the poor. Whites quickly realized that if African Americans did not serve in the military a larger proportion of whites would be compelled to go to Europe, thus increasing the probability that more whites would lose their lives. Because a majority of South Carolinians were African American, white men would have been particularly burdened to meet the state's recruitment quota if black men were prohibited from serving. When white southerners considered the real hardships of war, their posture more closely resembled insistence that African Americans not be allowed to escape the ordeal young white men faced. In a letter to the editor of the *State* S. L. Kransnoff indicated he would not want to see the "white flower of manhood sacrificed upon the battlefields for democracy without the negroes contributing their share."[16] Several business leaders from Columbia told Congressman Lever that they believed African American men should be drafted if the state hoped to benefit any from their labor, since, they argued, the great "quantity of negroes leaving this section daily for the north, unless they are conscripted also for the army, will do us no good."[17]

Others supported conscripting African American men on the grounds of defending public safety. Consistent with whites' fears that African Americans posed an inherent danger to whites if inadequately supervised, M. M. Mann, clerk of South Carolina Senate, suggested that if only white men went to war and left black men at home, those left behind, especially women, could be in great danger.[18] A Rock Hill attorney reiterated this same concern that the federal government should ensure the protection of white South Carolinians who stayed home: "The negro situation, at home would have to be made secure before you and other good men left our homes. We could not leave our wives and babies here even with the negro women. These things cannot well be talked, but we people of the South realize the situation."[19]

Those African Americans who recognized this attitude showed less enthusiasm for insisting on the opportunity for exploitation. Just as white South Carolinians differed in their views on this issue, black opinions in the Palmetto State also varied. At the April 4 meeting in Columbia, the prevailing sentiment insisted that black men have the opportunity to serve as soldiers, but a minority of those attending strongly disagreed. One dissenter boldly declared, "The white folks have the Winchesters, and you haven't even a little popgun. They'll not ask you whether you want to enlist. They'll just take you out and shoot you, if you don't." Shocked and dismayed by this utterance, dozens of participants protested the comment. Pandemonium prevailed momentarily, and the crowd's adamant disapproval prevented the speaker from continuing his impassioned outburst. The public suggestion of white violence against blacks and whites' complete control over blacks no doubt offended many present at the meeting. The disapproving tone of Richard Carroll, presiding minister, suggests, however, that some of the crowd's disapproval was not just from disagreement about African Americans' role in the war, but rather it stemmed from fear of offending whites by too boldly criticizing white supremacy. As the resolution indicated, African American leaders were willing to beseech the governor and make requests of white political leaders that encroached upon areas forbidden by white supremacy, but there were clear limits on their collective willingness to challenge whites' most fundamental values.[20]

Once Congress passed the Selective Service Act in May 1917, which made no racial distinction, South Carolinians' reservations about African Americans' military service became moot. Yet, the national draft debate forced white South Carolinians to confront the competing meanings of military service. They wanted compulsory military service for blacks, but they wanted it devoid of any connotation, even rhetorical, of equality. African Americans welcomed the opportunity for military service and seized the patriotic rhetoric, desperately seeking to link their actions with broad heroic meanings.[21] Black South Carolinians responded as required and often with eagerness. Robert Moorman, chairman of Columbia's draft board, reported that African Americans requested exemptions less often than white registrants and that "negroes were keenly disappointed when they were rejected." Moorman attributed African Americans' enthusiasm for military service to the racial differential in job opportunities and pay scales, noting that "$30 a month, clothing and sustenance is far beyond what many of them can expect in civil employment." The majority of registrants in South Carolina were black men, and African American draftees exceeded whites by 7,500, the highest differential of any state. At times white South Carolinians had trouble meeting their quotas because of the uneven racial distribution of the population across the state. Lowcountry counties, whose black populations exceeded 70 percent, could not meet their white quotas set by the state. Therefore, more whites had to be drafted from counties with a higher density of whites to satisfy the overall state quota for white soldiers. Thus an ironic consequence of whites' demand for segregated mobilization was the drafting of more Piedmont whites.[22]

Seemingly comfortable with drafting African American men, white southerners soon faced another challenge to white supremacy. The War Department, as it prepared for mobilizing young draftees, announced in August its intention for biracial military training in southern camps. The Wilson administration's failure to organize military training according to the white southern axiom of racial segregation egregiously offended white South Carolinians.[23] South Carolina had aggressively sought and experienced a substantial boost from three new military training facilities—Camp Jackson, a permanent army base in Columbia; Camp Sevier in Greenville; and Camp Wadsworth in Spartanburg. State officials thought the Wilson administration would honor their preemptive pleas for separate training camps for black solders outside the South, thus averting yet another public debate that placed them in the awkward position of having to defend the South's racial hierarchy during a national crisis that stressed common efforts to defend democratic principles. Yet, in August, when white South Carolinians learned that Washington planned to send all recruits from South Carolina, North Carolina, Florida, and Puerto Rico, regardless of race, to Columbia's Camp Jackson, they responded with outrage. They also quickly realized their defense of segregation would have to be both public and determined.[24] Ironically, the training camp, which South Carolina's progressive reformers had first diligently sought and later rejoiced in receiving, became the source of a critical problem. The irony of the training camp controversy again revealed the persistent difficulty reformers faced when seeking economic development while struggling to maintain white supremacy. Economic progress often introduced unwelcome threats to the existing racial order.

Governor Manning lodged a vigorous protest with President Wilson's secretary of war, Newton Baker. Manning opposed training African American troops in South Carolina or anywhere in the South and argued that allowing large numbers of blacks, who had been furnished with guns, to train as soldiers in areas with large civilian African American populations presented "dangers" to the white community. South Carolina whites also feared that allowing northern blacks, unfamiliar with the South's Jim Crow mores, to train with southern blacks would undermine the entire system.[25] The War Department sent strong signals that it was uninterested in capitulating to southern racial protocol and planned to stick by its decision to train in the South African Americans who lived in the South. An army being raised to spread democracy to the rest of the world, the War Department reasoned, could not sanction racial distinctions in its own ranks.[26]

White South Carolinians responded with dismay and frustration when the Democratic administration suggested an arrangement that was clearly inconsistent with prevailing white supremacy beliefs. Moreover, news of training African American soldiers in the same camps with white recruits galvanized white South Carolinians to defend their ideals and resist the War Department's order. Prominent citizens confronted Governor Manning and expressed their emphatic disapproval of Washington's order.[27] Consequently, Manning organized a trip to Washington to meet the South Carolina congressional delegation and lodge a personal protest against Secretary Baker's order. Accompanying Manning on his trip were agribusiness leader and chairman of the state's Council of Defense, David R. Coker; business leader and banker R. G. Rhett of Charleston; and George Baker, J. W. Lillard, and William Clio of the Columbia Chamber of Commerce. This prestigious delegation of South Carolinians represented key business and agricultural interests in the state.[28] The *Charleston News and Courier* suggested that Washington's decision for biracial military training in Columbia had caused "utter astonishment" in South Carolina. "The authorities in Washington can not afford to forget that in the South the problem of the relations between the white people and the negroes underlies and overshadows nearly every other problem." The newspaper argued that biracial military training directly conflicted with the policy of the state, "a policy which has become fixed through the process of years and which is accepted today by the people of both races."[29]

Not all South Carolinians agreed. Isaac Edwards, for example, made a paternalistic plea in favor of training black soldiers in South Carolina. "God has placed these creatures in our care," Edwards contended, "and it becomes our duty to give him that training for this duty that the South alone can give him." As long as the troops were segregated during their training, Edwards believed, white southerners should provide a place for black soldiers at Camp Jackson.[30] Secretary Baker's response resembled Edwards's. Baker insisted that African American troops would be trained in South Carolina, but he accepted the condition of segregating the troops. An undercurrent in this swirling debate about where and with whom black soldiers should be trained was an internal political struggle between reformers and their leading political nemesis, the Bleaseite faction. Bleaseite Fred Dominick, representative of the Third Congressional District, articulated his complaint about the War Department's decision to train black soldiers in the South to Manning with the following telegram: "It is an outrage on decency that negro troops should be placed in the same camp with our white troops and it is hardly conceivable that such action should be even considered by a Democratic administration. Such action on the part of the government and the placing of negro troops by the side of white troops in our armies will undo the half century efforts of our people to prevent social equality of the races. South Carolina can well afford to lose all cantonments, camps and favors rather than suffer such disgraceful conditions within her borders."[31]

Dominick—law partner and avid supporter of Cole Blease in state politics—had joined Blease as a vocal critic of Wilson's administration and U.S. involvement in the war. Although Dominick's opposition to the war diminished his popularity, he hoped to vindicate his criticism of Wilson by capitalizing on the administration's even more unpopular decision to train black troops in the South. By linking both the Wilson administration and South Carolina reformers, including Manning, to an attack on white supremacy, Dominick hoped to discredit the anti-Bleaseite faction in state politics. Cognizant of this Bleaseite strategy, Manning minimized his association with the Wilson administration's decision concerning the training of African American soldiers and then forcefully opposed the decision by defending white supremacy. Manning revealed his concern about the consequences of this issue on state politics in a note reading: "I am not overstating it when I say there are persons in South Carolina who would not be above exciting race troubles if they occur to throw the responsibility on the Administration."[32] Each political faction used white supremacy as a shield to disguise its own class and factional interests and a sword to attack its opponents.

Woven throughout the debates about African Americans serving as soldiers and training at southern bases were references to yet another challenge posed to white supremacy by the war effort: the threat to its cheap labor supply. South Carolina's labor-intensive economy, both agricultural and manufacturing, depended heavily on cheap labor. The military's need for soldiers, the demand for labor generated by new industrial jobs in the North, and increased demand for agricultural products created labor shortages that either made laborers scarce or raised their wages. Because African Americans composed the majority of the state's agricultural labor, black laborers often found themselves snared in the middle of conflicts between agricultural interests and war demands. White leaders regularly complained to Congressman Lever about the state's labor shortages.[33] The agricultural extension service's white leadership entertained ideas about legal ways to coerce black laborers, such as a Saturday Service League, which would require African Americans to work all day Saturday during the busy farm season. Lever suggested that local communities in South Carolina demand that sheriff, magistrates, and other local law enforcement officers "enforce rigidly the vagrancy law and let the construction of that law be rather unlimited. There are a lot of darkies hanging around towns and cities, and on farms even, that should be put to work either on the farms and in places where they are needed or on the public works of the State."[34]

South Carolina's whites resented the leverage that war-induced labor shortages gave African American laborers. Julia Seldon of Spartanburg communicated to David Coker her frustrations with the unusual prerogative she perceived the war afforded black South Carolinians. Seldon complained that African Americans had "plenty of money now" and that they "take a pride in seeing how wastefully they can spend it." She asked Coker if "anything can be done about the negroes with their unskilled labor carrying from $60 to $100 a month. When the white men are giving up professions and offering their lives for $30? Is it possible to fight the high prices paid the laborers? It is a sinful waste of the money people have sacrificed."[35] Seldon's attitude further illustrates the irony of white southerners who relished market forces when they kept labor cheap but abhorred the capricious power of market forces when they drove the costs of labor up, especially labor they deemed inferior.

While Seldon complained that white soldiers, risking their lives for their country, were underpaid, another South Carolinian argued that black soldiers' pay was exorbitant. R. Charlton Thomas, president of Thomas Company in Ridgeway, insisted that the federal government paid dependents of enlisted black soldiers in the South too much. Thomas argued not only that the government spent "vast sums of money unwisely," but also that these payments were "demoralizing what little labor is left in the country." Thomas blamed federal government interference for hindering the ability of white southerners to control and compel black labor, as he believed they were entitled to do. No doubt Thomas also perceived that these payments drove up the price of labor he hoped to hire. Asserting that many African Americans who received payments were not actually dependent on the absent soldiers, Thomas advised authorities to review all soldiers' applications and cull the list of dependents to only the "truly dependent."[36]

The greatest opportunity the war afforded many African Americans was not the chance to improve the state's conditions but the chance to leave South Carolina. Between 1910 and 1920 approximately 74,500 African Americans migrated from South Carolina, and those numbers peaked during the war.[37] T. J. Wise, an African American from Greenwood, told a white readership in 1917 what he claimed most would not. Blacks leave South Carolina, Wise reported, because "they say they are tired of hearing continually, 'This is a white man's country.'... They say they are tired of their ignorance; not even getting the amount of school tax for their enlightenment they are forced to pay.... They say they are tired of being pointed out in court houses as scullions by barristers who might not win their cause without this cheap appeal to prejudice." Wise continued his list of grievances against the white-dominated social order by recounting African Americans' frustration at being used as a scapegoat for all the South's ills. Politicians become popular, Wise lamented, with their "unabridged vocabulary for abusing negroes." The most obvious reason African Americans migrated north, he reiterated, was that they wanted better wages. Ultimately, Wise surmised, a black man leaves the South because "he wants something of this world, since his Father created it. It's natural to seek."[38] The simple act of leaving made black southerners agents of change that immediately put whites in a defensive and uncomfortable position. They were reacting to rather than initiating change.

Migration fundamentally challenged white supremacy because it enhanced African Americans' independence and opportunities for escape from white control. Collectively whites shared a desire to regain control of the situation, to assert their authority, and to restore the "appropriate" social hierarchy, but whites' differing economic interests caused disagreement on precisely how to do this.[39]

South Carolina's African American leaders seized the unique opportunities that war mobilization needs presented, but they experienced criticism and obstacles at every turn. Black South Carolinians, like their white counterparts, remained loyal to the nation, expressed their patriotism, provided military service, died fighting the enemy, worked in war industry, raised money, participated in civil preparedness, held rallies, marched in parades, but their world was not made over when peace commenced. Why did the mobilization surrounding the Great War not fulfill the expectations of South Carolinians—black and white? Fundamentally for African Americans in the Palmetto State, the restraints imposed by white supremacy ideals and practices prevailed against the short-lived war-related opportunities and challenges. The success of the Expeditionary Forces in France enabled a quick end to the war, limiting the duration of the mobilization effort and stopping the momentum that first signaled significant change. Not only did the war's end halt the necessary momentum, but the vital dynamics that would forge legal challenges to segregation and stimulate direct-action campaigns against Jim Crow were still in a fledgling stage of development. The NAACP had just organized its first South Carolina chapters during the war, located in Charleston, Columbia, Darlington, Orangeburg, Beaufort, Aiken, Anderson, and Florence.[40] Time still awaited the maturation of a sizable black middle class under de jure segregation. The Great Migration that would create an economic, social, and political base of African American support outside the South had only just begun. Later in the century, the federal government would become an important partner for African Americans in the civil rights revolution. Yet in 1919, with *Plessy v. Ferguson* as the existing precedent and with the Wilson administration firmly allied with white southern Democrats, the federal government was not an ally for African Americans. Demagogues and lynching mobs still intimidated, and not as distant memories. The dashed hopes of World War I–era African Americans in South Carolina stand as a testament to the vulnerability of the disfranchised. Without measurable political power or influence, African Americans did not have the tools to alter the economic, political, and social structure. Not only could they not craft legislation, but without the ballot they also could not partner with others seeking political change. Although white allies would be limited in the future, they were almost nonexistent at this time.

Across the economic and social spectrum, white South Carolinians' shared commitment to maintaining the ideals of white supremacy effectively suppressed many African American aspirations. Yet these uniting ideals also

3. W. E. B. Du Bois (standing at center) with members of the Charleston chapter of the NAACP, March 1917. Photograph courtesy of the Avery Research Center for African American History and Culture at the College of Charleston

complicated white reformers' agenda. Reformers soon discovered that war mobilization—the catalyst for economic prosperity—although welcomed in many respects, frequently challenged white supremacy, the organizing principle that all development formulas had to honor. South Carolina reformers found that controlling change during the World War I era was difficult because many agents of change lay outside the region, as either the invisible hand of the market economy that stimulated demand, the federal government, or African Americans themselves. Ultimately white reformers' commitment to maintaining a segregated society, characterized by oppression and racial hierarchies, squandered valuable time and energy that might have been expended in more productive pursuits. First, the draft revived the issue of racial equality or, at least, how to defend inequality to the rest of the nation. Second, the issue of training African American soldiers on southern bases threatened the newly fixed principles of segregation that had earned consensus as a day-to-day institutionalization of white supremacy. Training raised white South Carolinians' concerns both by threatening integration on military bases and by threatening to bring in African Americans from outside the region who were unaccustomed to formal segregation and its peculiar "etiquette." Third, and perhaps most fundamental, the war effort threatened South Carolina's abundant supply of cheap labor, a necessary component in the state's economy in the minds of many. White South Carolinians' reaction to black migration out of the state revealed even more directly the preoccupation with preserving their cheap labor. Finally the economic changes induced by war mobilization—benefits and threats— were all viewed through the prism of white supremacy but not perceived in precisely the same way by all whites. In the absence of this white supremacy prism to refract these questions at peculiarly southern angles, it is hard to imagine that anyone would have seen problems rather than merely benefits in these wartime developments.

Notes

1. For more on Woodrow Wilson and World War I, see Robert H. Ferrill, *Woodrow Wilson and World War I, 1917–1921* (New York: Harper and Row, 1985); for more of World War I's effect on the home front, see David M. Kennedy, *Over Here: The First World War and American Society* (New York: Oxford University Press, 1980); for more on African American aspirations and experiences, see I. A. Newby, *Black Carolinians: A History of Blacks in South Carolina from 1895 to 1968* (Columbia: University of South Carolina Press, 1973).

2. For labor data, see *Eleventh Annual Report of the Commissioner of Agriculture, Commerce, and Industries, Labor Division, 1919* (Columbia, S.C.: Gonzales and Bryan, 1920), 4–12; "On the Brink of Change" (editorial), *State,* May 26, 1917. William Watts Ball, editor for the *State,* was a vocal proponent for reform during this era. Although Ball is often remembered in South Carolina history for his reactionary opposition to the New Deal, in this era he very much accepted and promoted the reform agenda. For more on Ball, see John Stark, *Damned Upcountryman: William Watts Ball; A Study in American Conservatism* (Durham, N.C.: Duke University Press, 1968); see Jack Temple Kirby, *Rural Worlds Lost: The American South, 1920–1960* (Baton Rouge: Louisiana State University Press, 1987), for the economic depression that followed the war.

3. This essay draws extensively from my dissertation research. For a more thorough discussion, see Janet Goodrum Hudson, "Maintaining White Supremacy: Race, Class, and Reform in South Carolina, 1917–1924" (Ph.D. dissertation, University of South Carolina, 1996).

4. *State,* April 5, 1917.

5. *State,* April 5, 6, 7, 1917; *Charleston News and Courier,* April 7, 1917.

6. *Charleston News and Courier,* April 18, 1917.

7. E. L. Baskervill to *Charleston News and Courier,* April 8, 1917.

8. Thomas E. Miller to Governor Richard I. Manning and President Woodrow Wilson in *Charleston News and Courier,* April 9, 1917.

9. See Newby, *Black Carolinians,* and Theodore Hemmingway, "Beneath the Yoke of Bondage: A History of Black Folks in South Carolina, 1900–1940" (Ph.D. dissertation, University of South Carolina, 1976), for a discussion of the African American leadership in South Carolina; see August Meier, *Negro Thought in America, 1880–1915* (Ann Arbor: University of Michigan Press, 1963), for general analysis of African Americans' struggles in this era.

10. *State,* April 11, 12, 15, 1917.

11. See George M. Fredrickson, *White Supremacy: A Comparative Study in American and South African History* (New York: Oxford University Press, 1981); Fredrickson, "Social Origins of American Racism," in his *The Arrogance of Race: Historical Perspectives on Slavery, Racism, and Social Inequality* (Middletown, Conn.: Wesleyan University Press, 1988), 189–93; Hudson, "Maintaining White Supremacy," 7–33.

12. W. W. Ball Diary, book 3, January 13, 1918, Williams Watts Ball Papers, Manuscripts Division, Perkins Library, Duke University (hereinafter cited as DU).

13. *State,* April 11, 12, 15, 1917; Reed Smith to David R. Coker, November 22, 1917, David R. Coker Papers, Manuscripts Division, South Caroliniana Library, University of South Carolina (hereinafter cited as SCL). The Commission for Civic Preparedness was the forerunner to the South Carolina State Council for Defense, formed later in 1917. Accounts in the *State* throughout 1917–1919 refer to the segregated African American war preparation organizations. For more on David Coker, see James A. Rogers, *Mr. D.R.: A Biography of David R. Coker* (Hartsville, S.C.: Coker College Press, 1994).

14. J. Harry Foster to A. Frank Lever, May 2, 1917, Congressional Series, Asbury Frank Lever Papers, Special Collections, Strom Thurmond Institute, Clemson University (hereinafter cited as CU).

15. Charles L. Rhame to A. Frank Lever, May 16, 1917, Congressional Series, Lever Papers, CU.

16. S. L. Kransnoff to the *State,* September 2, 1917.

17. Frank S. Terry, W. M. Lesley, and M. Brabhau to A. Frank Lever, April 25, 1917, Congressional Series, Lever Papers, CU.

18. M. M. Mann to A. Frank Lever, April 28, 1917, Congressional Series, Lever Papers, CU.

19. Foster to Lever, May 2, 1917.

20. *State,* April 5, 1917; another meeting was held on April 11 at Second Calvary Baptist Church in Waverly.

21. See Theodore Hemmingway, "Prelude to Change: Black Carolinians in the War Years, 1914–1920," *Journal of Negro History* 65 (Summer 1980): 212–27, for a more complete discussion of African Americans' contribution to the war effort. For African Americans' role in the war as soldiers, see Arthur E. Barbeau and Florette Henri, *The Unknown Soldiers: African-American Troops in World War I* (Philadelphia: Temple University Press, 1974); W. Allison Sweeney, *History of the American Negro in the Great World War* (New York: Negro Universities Press, 1919); Emmett J. Scott, *Scott's Official History of the American Negro in the World War* (Chicago: Homewood, 1919); Chester D. Heywood, *Negro Combat Troops in the World War: The Story of the 371st Infantry* (Worcester, Mass.: Commonwealth, 1928). The 371st Infantry was organized in Columbia, and many black South Carolinians served in this unit. W. J. Megginson, "Black South Carolinians in World War I: The Official Roster as a Resource for Local History, Mobility, and African-American History," *South Carolina Historical Magazine* 96 (1995): 153–73.

22. *State,* August 9, 1917; Barbeau and Henri, *Unknown Soldiers,* 36; *State,* September 11, 1917.

23. *State,* August 5, 12, 1917; December 17, 1918; South Carolina State Council of Defense, *The South Carolina Handbook of the War* (Columbia: State Co., 1917), reveals the reformers' enthusiasm for the war. Although located in Georgia, the training camp at Augusta, Camp Gordon, also helped South Carolina's economy because of its close proximity to the state's border. Moreover, as a result of wartime needs, the Marine base at Port Royal, near Charleston, was greatly expanded. Construction of the cantonments brought new jobs and new capital to the state. Once completed, the camps brought soldiers to the state.

24. *Charleston News and Courier,* August 18–19, 1917; Richard I. Manning to S. L. Kransnoff, August 20, 1917, Richard I. Manning Papers, SCL; account of a conversation between Fitz McMaster and Leonard Woods reported by William Watts Ball, W. W. Ball Diary, book 3, June 9, 1917, Ball Papers, DU.

25. *Charleston News and Courier,* August 19, 1917; *State,* August 22, 1917; Richard I. Manning to Acting Secretary of War, September 12, 1918, "Washington U.S. Officials and Congressmen Manning and Cooper" Section, Robert A. Cooper Papers, South Carolina Department of Archives and History, Columbia (hereinafter cited as SCDAH); *State,* August 1, 1917.

26. *State,* August 21, 1917.

27. Manning to Kransnoff, August 20, 1917; Richard I. Manning to Judge Thos. E. Richardson, August 24, 1917, Richard I. Manning Papers, SCL. These letters were Manning's responses to the correspondents' complaints.

28. Manning to Acting Secretary of War, September 12, 1918.

29. *Charleston News and Courier,* August 20, 1917.

30. *State,* August 23, 1917.

31. *State,* August 21, 1917.

32. Undated manuscript, cited in Robert Milton Burts, *Richard Irvine Manning and the Progressive Movement in South Carolina* (Columbia: University of South Carolina Press, 1974), 161.

33. A. Frank Lever to J. Harry Foster, May 5, 1917, Congressional Series, Lever Papers, CU.

34. J. F. Duggan (Alabama Extension Service) to W. W. Long, who forwarded the letter with his own letter to David R. Coker, May 30, 1918, Coker Papers, SCL; Lever to Foster, May 5, 1917.

35. E. Julia Seldon, Spartanburg, to David R. Coker, April 1, 1918, Coker Papers, SCL.

36. R. Charlton Thomas to David R. Coker, June 14, 1918, Coker Papers, SCL.

37. The migration figures were derived from the intercensal estimation of net internal migration, which is based on the survival-rate method of estimating, which subtracts the enumerated population at the end of the decennial period from the estimated survivors at the beginning of the decade. Intercensal estimation for both decades are found in United States Bureau of the Census, *Historical Statistics of the United States, Colonial Times to 1970* (Washington, D.C.: U.S. Department of Commerce, Bureau of the Census, 1975), 1:87, 95. For a more complete discussion of migration in South Carolina from Reconstruction to the Great Depression, see George Alfred Devlin, "South Carolina and Black Migration 1865–1930 in Search of the Promised Land" (Ph.D. dissertation, University of South Carolina, 1984); Newby, *Black Carolinians;* James R. Grossman, *Land of Hope: Chicago, Black Southerners, and the Great Migration* (Chicago: University of Chicago Press, 1989); Joe William Trotter Jr., ed., *The Great Migration in Historical Perspective: New Dimensions of Race, Class, and Gender* (Bloomington: Indiana University Press, 1991).

38. T. S. Wise to the *State,* April 15, 1917.

39. For a thorough discussion of the diverse and conflicting response of white South Carolinians to the out-migration of African Americans, see Hudson, "Maintaining White Supremacy," 118–57.

40. The order is indicative of the chapter sizes, from five hundred Charleston members to one hundred in Florence. *Crisis,* August 1920, 181.

An "Ominous Defiance"

The Lowman Lynchings of 1926

ELIZABETH ROBESON

On Friday morning, October 8, 1926, the *Aiken Standard* trumpeted a bold headline: "Three Lowman Negroes Lynched This Morning." The report stated that after severing electricity to half the town, a "mob of men" had stormed the county jail between 3:00 and 4:00 A.M., "overwhelmed" the sheriff and jailer, and whisked away Bertha, Damon, and Clarence Lowman in cars filled with passengers to an outlying woods, where their bodies were "riddled with bullets." Provocatively, the account included information that the *Standard*'s publisher, Walter E. Duncan, a former comptroller general of South Carolina and secretary to two governors, could have secured only from an eyewitness to the abductions: "On the way from the jail to the scene of the lynching, one of the negroes, supposedly Demmond [*sic*] Lowman, *according to report* [emphasis added], jumped from the moving automobile in which he was being driven to the death scene, and attempted to make his escape. The men in the car quickly overtook him with bullets, wounding him. He was placed back in the car and the determined party drove on to the pine thicket." Duncan's reportage is just as remarkable for its omissions. At the time of their deaths, the Lowmans were on trial for a second time by order of the South Carolina Supreme Court for the 1925 murder of Aiken County Sheriff Henry H. Howard, a fact that rendered the jailbreak and killings a brazen usurpation of the high court's prerogative. Instead of condemning this act of vigilantism, as was his habit, publisher Duncan cast a steely pall over his announcement by emphasizing the mob's efficiency and resolve: "The negroes were not swung up. Their bodies fell where they stood. . . . They were all shot from the front." The most peculiar aspect of Duncan's account is that it exists at all. As a small-town weekly newspaper, the *Standard* was not in the habit of breaking news. The exigencies of production meant that its regular Friday issue rarely carried items dated later than the prior Wednesday morning. Given the predawn Friday hour of the Lowman murders and the power outage in Aiken, it seems implausible that, without advance notice, Duncan could have managed everything required to print a new run of the *Standard* in time to scoop the *Augusta Chronicle* and the *State* in Columbia, the much larger morning dailies read in Aiken County. But he did.[1]

When the *Columbia Record* appeared later that afternoon, its front-page, boxed editorial decried the lynchings as "a challenge to the law-abiding people of South Carolina. . . . It is a startling and ominous defiance!" Reminding his readers of the state's record-breaking rates of homicide, editor R. Charlton Wright asked, "Have things come to such a pass in this State that individuals and mobs can snap their fingers in the face of the law and the courts with impunity?" Wright characterized the Lowman lynchings as a crime against the state's sovereignty and presciently warned that unless Governor Thomas G. McLeod and the "constituted officers" of Aiken County swiftly brought its perpetrators to justice, South Carolinians would "deserve the contempt of the law-abiding people of the world."[2]

Astonishing to the studied reader, the *Record*'s accompanying news article is littered with peculiar and conflicting details that implicate the same "constituted officers" appealed to by Wright. If the Lowmans' killers were truly unknown, how could the town's assistant police chief state unequivocally that they wore no masks? By all accounts the only two officials in the jail at the time of its storming were Aiken County Sheriff Nollie Robinson and the jail superintendent, Rupert Taylor, both of whom stated that the mob *did* wear masks and disguised their voices. Who other than a member of the mob could relay to the *Record* that Bertha Lowman's mouth was stuffed with a handkerchief as she was taken from her cell and that the cars waiting outside left Aiken by way of Chesterfield Street? Sheriff Robinson, who necessarily figured at the center of the drama, told the *Record* that he had been disarmed and waylaid on the floor of the jailer's kitchen (through which adjacent door the prisoners were accessible), but after composing himself he "followed the mob part of the way toward the scene of the lynching." Robinson said the pack's "high-powered cars" outdistanced him, so he "turned back near the city limits." The next morning's editions of the *State* and *Augusta Chronicle*, however, reported that Robinson went straight to the killing grounds, arriving after the mob had departed. How did he know where to go? According to the *State*'s terse account, "About two miles from town [Robinson] met the returning automobiles and discovered the three Negroes dead." If Robinson suspected the returning cars to be carrying the lynching party, why didn't he follow them back to town? The *Chronicle* provided a more elaborate account, having been filed by Aiken resident and *Chronicle* "bureau chief" James Edward Kerr. Here Robinson said that when he left the jail, he heard a gun fired from the direction of the Catholic church. Going there and not finding anyone, he headed out of town—without an inkling about which road the mob had taken. Perhaps Robinson was simply lucky; having chosen U.S. 1 north, he saw coming toward him "25 or 30 men returning from the direction of the lynching ground but they kept the lights of their automobiles glaring and he could not recognize any of them." Proceeding to the precise spot in the dense pine woods where the Lowmans were executed, described as having been some seventy-five to one hundred yards off the pitch-black highway, Robinson "saw the bodies of the three negroes stretched out on the ground. The clothing of the woman he said was afire but whether an attempt was made to burn the body, or the clothing caught ablaze from the gunfire he could not state. The sheriff said that he had extinguished the flames, which had already consumed *most of the clothing* [emphasis added]." How could Robinson have arrived before Bertha Lowman's thin nightgown had completely burned but after the mob had absconded?[3]

Whether southern journalists eschewed precision or Robinson's myriad accounts are a reflection of his hubris, the controversy that ensued was both national and sustained, placing South Carolina's Jim Crow regime under a glaring spotlight. For one of the few times in their postbellum experience, the "better sort" of white Carolinians were forced as a group to publicly confront, albeit without repentance, their complicity in the deaths of vigilante victims. Largely forgotten today, the Lowman lynchings marked a significant event in the long struggle for the African American's civil rights in South Carolina.

South Carolina's Reconstruction legislature established Aiken County in 1871, drawing it in large part from territory that had lain previously within the old Edgefield District, a region long associated with a tradition of extreme violence. It was South Carolina's antebellum U.S. senator, James Henry Hammond, whose Aiken County plantation is now a state park, who said, "You have to say but 'nigger' to the South to set it on fire," and who lectured his colleagues in 1858 that black slaves were "the very mud-sill of southern society." In 1876 guerrilla bands of Democrats, the self-styled "Red Shirts," dismantled through bloody force the Reconstruction government of South Carolina; the two most pivotal encounters with "radical" blacks occurred in the Aiken County communities of Hamburg and Ellenton. One of those Red Shirts, Aiken attorney D.L. Henderson, went on in the 1880s to help draft the notorious "eight box ballot" law, the first of many schemes designed to rob black men of their suffrage. Over the next four decades, Benjamin R. Tillman and his protégé, Coleman Livingston Blease, found some of their staunchest supporters in Aiken County. As governors and U.S. senators, both men spoke in raw, highly publicized language to the nation at large about the imperative of lynching as a white man's prerogative that superseded the Constitution.[4]

The Tillman-Blease stronghold was located in Horse Creek Valley in the westernmost section of Aiken County, where William Gregg had established the first southern cotton mill at Graniteville before the Civil War. By the early 1920s the valley had matured into a corridor of segregated mill towns close to the Georgia border, where in Graniteville, Langley, Vaucluse, and Warrenville ill-tempered white men garnered a notorious reputation—once described by the

Charleston News and Courier as "a largely ruffian element . . . continually breaking into crime." Animated by the prickly code of southern honor, which, after the
loss of the Civil War, metamorphosed into an overwrought anger with African
Americans, these men took refuge from their miserly lives in the righteous violence of the Ku Klux Klan. The valley's concentration of white men boded por-
tentously for all Aiken County residents: holding the electoral balance of power,
the valley controlled the office of sheriff, which reigned supreme in the management of local affairs.[5]

In 1920 a slim majority of Aiken County residents was black. A smattering of
black professionals and landowners could be found among their number, but
most of these men and women worked as tenant farmers, sharecroppers, and day
laborers in the fields and homes of white landowners to the south and east of
Horse Creek Valley. Complicating this juxtaposition of the white mill worker and
black farm laborer, the county seat of Aiken was, in the provenance of the Gilded
Age, a "winter colony" treasured by the Whitneys, Vanderbilts, and Rockefellers
for its "irresistible, tempting, alluring" climate, making it what one promotional
pamphlet called "the ideal wintertime playground." Beginning in December,
America's wealthiest families repaired to their castle-sized "cottages" in Aiken,
where they staged polo tournaments and thoroughbred horse races and attended
evening concerts by the likes of Pablo Casals. Such a peculiar place was Aiken
County by the middle of the 1920s that one could read in the *Standard* about a
party at the Vanderbilt home, a Friday afternoon Klan rally, evangelical revivals,
the reminiscences of an aged Confederate veteran, gunplay on noonday streets,
a labor strike, all manner of whippings and homicides, a smallpox outbreak, or
as happened in April 1925, the shotgun death of the Aiken County sheriff at the
hands of some "bad nigger" bootleggers.[6]

April 25, 1925, a Saturday, began routinely in the household of Sam Lowman.
The family stirred, as usual, with the sun. The day before had been unseasonably
hot, reaching 94 degrees and setting a new state record. By eight o'clock that
morning, Lowman, a middle-aged black man, had left home, taking corn to a
gristmill in nearby Monetta, a village situated in the northeastern corner of
Aiken County. His wife, Annie, stood over a fire behind the house making soap.
Their pregnant daughter, Bertha, twenty-seven, and thirteen-year-old niece
Naomi swept the backyard. Another niece, Eleanora, eighteen, scoured the back
porch. Damon Lowman, the twenty-one-year-old son of Sam and Annie, and his
teenaged cousin Clarence each ran a plow in the field directly across the road
from their rented house. As Damon's wife, Rosa, started to prepare the midday
meal, his sister Bridie, eighteen, gave a bottle to his and Rosa's month-old baby
girl. It was a busy but unremarkable Saturday morning.[7]

Sometime between 9:00 and 9:30, Damon recalled, "We had gotten through
[plowing] and was going to get some more plows and go to another field, and we

were coming to the house." As he and Clarence approached the road with their mules in tow, two cars pulled over, each carrying two white men, one of whom asked Damon if Sam Lowman lived in the house there. Unbeknownst to Damon, the man speaking to him was Aiken County deputy sheriff Nollie Robinson, riding in an unmarked car driven by Sheriff Henry Hampton Howard. None of the men identified themselves to Damon, nor did they wear uniforms or display badges. Perhaps uneasily, Damon acknowledged to Robinson that yes, his father, Sam Lowman, did live there. Having answered Robinson's query, Damon recalled, "He broke on to the house."[8]

Sheriff Howard and his three deputies—Robinson, Arthur D. Sheppard, and Robert L. McElhaney—turned into the Lowmans' yard and bolted out of their vehicles. Howard and Robinson ran up the right side of the house to the back, where the frightened Annie and Bertha screamed and headed for the door at the back porch. Eleanora and Naomi ran away from the house altogether. Hearing the upset from inside, Rosa snatched her baby from Bridie, and the three of them exited the house from a side door on the left, just as Deputy Sheppard was poised to enter. Later Bridie said, "I don't run off every time anyone comes. . . . I saw the pistols in their pockets and that is why I ran." Meanwhile, Deputy McElhaney came through the Lowmans' front door and, hearing the disturbance out back, started toward the kitchen. On the back porch he found Sheriff Howard and Deputy Robinson scuffling with Annie and Bertha Lowman, who verbally contested their right to enter the house. McElhaney was distracted by the sound of Damon, who had followed him through the front door and grabbed a .45 Colt revolver from a cupboard. The two began to skirmish. Coming to McElhaney's aid, Robinson left Sheriff Howard on the back porch; while the two deputies fought Damon in the front room, they alleged that shots were fired "in the rear of the house." No one except Deputy Sheppard claimed to have seen Clarence inside or near the house, and his testimony on this crucial point is inconsistent.[9]

A bloody frenzy ensued. The sequence of events as the participants later swore to them is in conflict, but all confirmed the terror and lightning duration of the encounter. The mother, Annie Lowman, was shot above her left eye by Deputy Sheppard and died immediately. Pregnant Bertha Lowman was pistol-whipped around the head and shot in the abdomen, right breast, and arms several times by Nollie Robinson. Damon Lowman, at one time exchanging gunfire with all three deputies in the front room before tumbling off the porch and running three miles in the direction of his mother's cousins' home, suffered a gunshot wound in the shoulder. Deputies Robinson and Sheppard shot Clarence Lowman in the shoulder and legs several times as he ran into the woods behind the house. Remarkably none of the lawmen sustained any injuries except for Robinson, whose face had been scratched by Bertha Lowman.

During the melee, as Damon and Bertha were inside the house battling the deputies, Sheriff Howard was shot at close range. Apparently he never entered the house, but died in either the back yard or on the right side of the house. No one admitted to having witnessed the shooting. A few hours after the incident, Deputy Robinson told G. A. Buchanan Jr., a reporter for the *State,* in what sounds suspiciously apocryphal, that he heard Howard cry out, "O, Lord, they've killed me!" According to Buchanan's initial report:

> Aiken folk had been stunned by the news [of Howard's death], which had spread—frequently exaggerated—throughout the county. Automobiles literally filled the road to Monetta: fully 1,000 men gathered at the Lowman farm and after a time dispersed, only to make way for others from Aiken, Graniteville, Lexington, Columbia, etc. There was talk of lynching and about the courthouse and jail [in Aiken] there was mustered in the early afternoon some hundred or more citizens—men who had known and admired the slain officer. It was considered advisable that the two Negroes—Clarence and "Son" [Damon]—be moved to [the state penitentiary in] Columbia to avert probable mob violence. . . . Deputy Sheriff Robinson secured the group's attention. "I have lost the best friend I had," he said. . . . If Sheriff Howard were here he would say, "Let the law take its course. We must protect these men; we are sworn to do so."

Meanwhile, Bertha, who was thought to be near death, had been rushed to an infirmary in Leesville, where her fetus perished but she miraculously recovered.[10]

At nine o'clock on Sunday morning, a hearse escorted by one hundred members of the Ku Klux Klan in full regalia transferred Sheriff Howard's flower-laden casket from the George Funeral Home in Aiken to the county courthouse for viewing. As the *State* described the scene, "A large group of hooded members of the Ku Klux Klan suddenly appeared to march solemnly and silently down the street to the courthouse and silently and suddenly to disappear." The local klavern deposited a "large, floral offering in the shape of a cross" beside the open casket, while the American Legion draped a silk flag at its head. Citizens filed past the bier for much of the day. At four o'clock that afternoon, a capacity crowd of 1,600 people overflowed the Aiken Baptist Church, where Governor McLeod paid homage to Howard as "a man of great humanity." According to the *Standard,* "All that was mortal of Sheriff Henry H. Howard was laid to rest beside the bodies of his mother and father in the Graniteville cemetery Sunday afternoon. The funeral cortege was one of the largest ever witnessed in this section." Five days later, in the Aiken County Court of General Sessions, Clarence, Damon, Bertha, Rosa, and Bridie Lowman were all indicted for the murder of Sheriff Howard.[11]

The question naturally arises: What prompted the sheriff to take his full contingent of deputies that Saturday morning and drive twenty-five miles to the Lowman house? McElhaney told the county coroner just after the incident, "Our business up here at Monetta was raiding for whiskey." In subsequent affidavits and court testimony, however, the deputies admitted that no whiskey or distilling operation had been found in or around the Lowman house. On Monday, April 27, Clint Fallaw, Monetta constable, "found" two jars of corn whiskey "behind the [Lowman] chicken house buried in the ground." On his word alone, and with such "evidence" found at a crime scene trampled on by hundreds of people, Sam Lowman received an unprecedented two-year sentence of hard labor on the county chain gang. It was the first time he had ever been in trouble with the law.[12]

Damon later explained that he had taken a defensive posture with the sheriff and his deputies because "a couple of Sundays before a man had run me away from the house." As this cryptic reference suggests, there was more happening in the Lowmans' lives than met the public eye. Months later an investigative reporter for the *New York World* revealed that sources in Horse Creek Valley had confided that an unnamed disgruntled white man, unable to repay a loan to Will Hartley, the Lowmans' landlord, sought revenge against him for a mule that Hartley had foreclosed on and sold to Sam Lowman. Robinson, by this time sheriff of Aiken County, refused to disclose the nature or source of the complaint that led to the fateful raid but confirmed to the *World* that a "prominent" white man lodged it, alleging that the Lowmans supplied liquor to rowdy "hot suppers" and "negro frolics" held in the community's African American churches. Pieced together with the Sunday incident alluded to by Damon, one might reasonably suspect that the Lowmans were guilty, in the peculiar social world of the New South, of demonstrating too much "independence," that prized and increasingly elusive status deemed to be the white man's alone.[13]

An examination of public records suggests that Sam Lowman and his family were hardly lowdown, but instead the unwitting victims of a grudge match between white men, one that lays bare the complex and precarious world inhabited by rural black southerners in the age of Jim Crow. Contrary to newspaper accounts that described him as a sharecropper living in a "grim four room shack" with "rotting floors saturated with liquor," Sam Lowman had been a self-sufficient farmer since at least 1897, paying property taxes on an estate worth several hundred dollars (and sometimes more) over the span of twenty-five years. In 1906 he purchased a 146-acre tract of land near Monetta from Elijah Coleman, which he then sold in 1913 to D. L. Cato, Monetta's mayor, merchant, and banker, from whom Lowman simultaneously bought a 100-acre tract. In 1918 Lowman sold this land for $900 to J. C. Burton of Monetta. Chattel mortgage books portray Lowman as a man of impressive accomplishment and material wealth: livestock, horses, mules, wagons, furniture, sewing machine, a 1924 Ford touring car, and bales of cotton. Born in November 1869 to former slaves, he could read and write, and reported to the census takers in 1900 and 1910 that all eight of his children attended school. Until 1923 Lowman paid his poll tax annually. Nothing is amiss in the reconstructed facts of Lowman's life except for the migration of his two oldest sons, Dozier, twenty-nine, and Lester, thirty-one, to Philadelphia in 1923 and 1924, respectively. The Lowman brothers had served in the U.S. Army during World War I—Lester as a corporal with the American Expeditionary Forces in France—and returned home to Monetta in 1919, undoubtedly changed men. Migrating when they did, at the height of the postwar African American exodus from South Carolina, Dozier and Lester Lowman served stark notice to Monetta's white landowners that the vexing "New Negro" lived in their midst.[14]

Just as the *New York World* hinted, public records also confirm that in late 1920, Sam Lowman's landlord, Will Hartley, lent one thousand dollars to Chester Swearingen of Monetta, a landless tenant farmer and nephew-in-law of Mayor Cato, a rival in wealth and influence to Hartley in the Monetta section. A chattel mortgage drawn up between Hartley and Swearingen included, among numerous items, a four-year-old black mare mule named Queen. In September 1921 Hartley took action in the Aiken County Court of Common Pleas to collect the principal and interest on Swearingen's promissory note; his complaint stated that the "property in said chattel mortgage has been exhausted and the same is not now of any value so far as being available for credit on this said note." Hartley continued to pursue the matter as late as June 1924, the debt not being discharged until 1931. Meanwhile, Sam Lowman executed a chattel mortgage in December 1923 with the Farmers and Merchants Bank of Aiken, offering the mule Queen as collateral.[15]

The Lowmans' trial for the murder of Sheriff Howard got underway at noon on May 12, 1925, a hot Tuesday, and as depicted by newspaper coverage is evocative of the tense scene drawn by Harper Lee in *To Kill a Mockingbird*. The *State* described a crowded courtroom into which the five defendants were escorted under heavy guard and placed in an anteroom where they could not be seen until the proceedings began. Sheriff Howard's widow and seven children, reported the *Columbia Record,* "took reserved seats within the railed enclosure." Going into the trial, the community evinced special prejudice toward young Clarence, who, reported the *State,* "officers are convinced . . . is to be held responsible for the sheriff's death." This opinion was based on nothing more than the inconsistent allegations of Deputy Sheppard, the only one of the raid's eight surviving participants who claimed to have seen Clarence in or near the house with a gun.[16]

In his opening remarks Aiken County solicitor Berte D. Carter told the jury that the Lowmans had conspired to kill Sheriff Howard, knowing full well who he was and why he had come to their home. Not one of the Lowmans' five court-appointed attorneys challenged the prosecutor's assumption, nor did they ask any of the deputies to defend the propriety of the raid's aggressive execution. Prior to the trial both Damon and Clarence had stated independently that Annie

4. *Spotlight on South Carolina: an editorial cartoon from the* New York World, *November 18, 1926*

Lowman likely killed Howard since a shotgun was kept in the kitchen just inside the door to the back porch where she had scuffled with him and Robinson. In the trial, however, and under direct questioning by his court-appointed attorney, Damon swore that Clarence had confessed the night before to killing Sheriff Howard, after the cousins had been reunited in the Aiken County jail for the first time since April 25.

> Do you know who shot the Sheriff?
>
> That boy there is the only one that could have shot him. They said he did. Nobody else had a shot gun. I didn't see him shoot him.

I am going to be frank with you, these twelve men are to pass on your case, and it is up to those men to say whether you are going to the electric chair or whether you are going to the penitentiary for life . . . and you cannot get off by trying to tell those men any lies . . .

I am telling the truth.

Who shot Sheriff Howard?

That boy there shot him.

Clarence's attorney then cross-examined Damon, asking repeatedly whether he actually *saw* Clarence shoot the sheriff, to which Damon replied that he had not.

You don't know whether or not he [Clarence] killed him?

Yes, sir; he killed him. . . .

Didn't you tell Mr. Kneece that your mother killed the Sheriff?

I told you once I said so.

Now, you say that Clarence killed him?

Yes sir; I say that. . . .

You don't know who killed the Sheriff?

No, sir; but he did it.

You don't know of your own knowledge who killed him?

He did it.

Damon's panic is evident, a chilling illustration of Jim Crow's vise. He had been ruled out as Howard's shooter, having been present in the front of the house for the duration of the gun battle. If his mother, Annie, had killed Howard, her death was not tribute enough, nor would such accomplishment reflect well on the sheriff's manhood. Damon knew that death loomed for someone else in his family and wagered that an offering of his fourteen-year-old cousin's life might save his along with Bertha, Bridie, and Rosa.[17]

As the trial drew to a close the following afternoon, Judge Hayne Faust Rice, a judge of South Carolina's Second Circuit Court who made his home in Aiken, charged the jury with these opening remarks: "Some person might be so foolish as to condemn these attorneys for undertaking the defense of these defendants. But I want to say that they were appointed by the Court—none of them wanted to do it—but it was their duty. . . . All that they were required to do was to see that their clients got a fair and impartial trial. . . . Now, it has been said by those who don't like us here in the South that a Negro don't [*sic*] get a fair trial in our

Courts. . . . I have no patience with those statements. If there is any place in the world where a Negro can get a fair trial it is before a jury of South Carolina white men." In what would have been understood by Aiken's white community as evidence of his judiciousness, Rice directed verdicts of not guilty for Rosa and Bridie Lowman, both of whom had fled the house before the shooting began. He then continued to instruct the jurors in the laws of self-defense and conspiracy, reminding them ipso facto that "there is no dispute that the Sheriff had a search warrant to search the house for contraband whiskey, and that he had with him his Deputies, and having a search warrant it was his duty under the law to go and search that house, and it was the business of every person in that house to submit to it." Judge Rice skirted the question of whether Howard and his deputies had properly identified themselves or executed the warrant, implying instead that their mere presence usurped the family's right to self-defense. Spoon-feeding the jury its verdict, he ascribed omniscient powers to the Lowmans, while glossing over the absence of liquor: "Now, if there was a plan or concert among these defendants that when the officers came to search the house, that they were going to shoot them, and that when they got there they did oppose the officers and start the row with the officers and try to prevent it, and in the resulting fight that took place the Sheriff was killed; then, Mr. Foreman and Gentlemen, if one is guilty, then all that took part in that are guilty."[18]

Eighty minutes ticked by. Shortly after 5:00 P.M. on May 12, 1925, the jury declared Clarence, Damon, and Bertha Lowman guilty of murder. The next morning Judge Rice sentenced Clarence and Damon to die in the electric chair at the state penitentiary on June 12, 1925, and Bertha to life imprisonment there. That evening Sheriff Nollie Robinson drove the Lowmans to Columbia, where, according to the *State,* Clarence and Damon "were immediately placed in the death house to await consummation of their sentence." Not one of the five court-appointed attorneys filed an appeal.[19]

Fifty-five miles away, B. F. Wiley, a black resident of Orangeburg, sent newspaper clippings to Walter White, the assistant secretary of the National Association for the Advancement of Colored People (NAACP) in New York, asking him to look into the matter. Another black citizen of Columbia also wrote to White, imploring that he "see if we cannot get these boys commuted to life in prison." This anonymous writer stated that Annie Lowman had indeed shot and killed Sheriff Howard before Damon got to the house, and that it was in retribution that the deputies attempted to "wipe out the family." The letter continued, "Like many other dastardly cases of this kind against the negro of this state, this old man [Sam Lowman] owned his own home, and was getting along to [*sic*] nicely to suit some of these officers." White contacted C. C. Johnson, M.D., of Aiken, a grand master of South Carolina's black Masons and president of the moribund local chapter of the NAACP, asking for his opinion. In a foreshadowing of the intransigence that led to the Lowmans' deaths, Dr. Johnson advised White that "it would be useless as well as impracticable and possibly imprudent" for the NAACP to get involved. He added, "Personally I knew well and very favorably Mr. Howard, and I assure you that I do not know of any man of any race who was at heart more fair and true.... Colored people who knew him feel that they have lost a real friend." Convinced that the Lowmans had not been "unjustly prosecuted . . . for their color," White let the matter drop. Meanwhile, N. J. Frederick, a black attorney in Columbia, filed an appeal with the South Carolina Supreme Court.[20]

A native of Orangeburg, Nathaniel Jerome Frederick (or N. J., as he always signed his name) is one of the most accomplished black Carolinians to have come of age during Jim Crow and a forgotten pioneer of the modern civil rights movement in the Palmetto State. Frederick's father, Benjamin Glenn Frederick, was a reputed black Red Shirt, a Methodist minister, and a Democratic member of the South Carolina General Assembly in the years immediately following the violent overthrow of Reconstruction. These facts make for interesting contemplation in light of the younger Frederick's career. He held bachelor's and master's degrees from Claflin College in Orangeburg and a second master's from Columbia's Benedict College. In 1899 Frederick entered the University of Wisconsin at Madison, where he studied American history, almost certainly under the tutelage of the venerable Frederick Jackson Turner. As part of the requirements for the Wisconsin baccalaureate, Frederick prepared a thesis on the origins of the Freedmen's Bureau, a manuscript that regrettably has not survived. He returned to South Carolina in 1901 as principal of the Howard School in Columbia, the only public institution for many years to provide the capital city's African Americans with a secondary education. While so employed and involved in the state's African American education and fraternal organizations, Frederick "read" law with what his obituary described as "some of the best legal minds of the state bar." In 1913 he established his private law practice in downtown Columbia at 1119 Washington Street, and when he died twenty-five years later, he was the only black member of the Richland County Bar Association.[21]

Active in the World War I–era Capital City Civic League, which aimed to register the city's qualified black electors, Frederick helped organize the Columbia branch of the NAACP in 1917 while editing the *Southern Indicator.* In 1925 he cofounded and edited the *Palmetto Leader,* a progressive weekly known for blunt editorializing. Active in the Republican Party, Frederick attended the Republican national conventions as a South Carolina delegate in 1924, 1928, and 1932. In 1932 he accepted appointment to the NAACP's National Legal Committee (a forerunner to the Legal Defense Fund), a tribute to his standing as one of three black attorneys active in civil rights work throughout the entire South. From 1915 until his death in 1938, Frederick argued an astonishing thirty-three cases before the state supreme court, including those that challenged the barring of black jurors from South Carolina courtrooms and two explosive cases of alleged rape of white women by black men. In 1928 he ruminated in a letter to the NAACP's Walter White: "Some how, it seems that I am destined to be involved in cases where human rights (black) [*sic*] are at a low discount. Though financially they mean a loss to me . . . I get quite a 'kick' out of trying to help the poor and unfortunate, especially since I belong to the group which comes under that classification, and is always the victim."[22]

Suffice it to say that N. J. Frederick was a singular black man in South Carolina in 1925, formally trained and willing to challenge the machinery of the Jim Crow state. He later wrote that the press coverage of the Lowman case demonstrated to him that "justice was far from that Court House during the trial of those people." In his appeal, which he argued before the high court in November 1925, Frederick set up seven exceptions to the original trial, the most significant of which asked the court to review Judge Rice's instructions to the Lowmans' jury. He wrote, "His Honor charged fully the duty resting on citizens to subject themselves to legal process, but not one word as to the duty resting on officers in the serving of process." Hence the Lowmans had acted in self-defense when confronted by Howard and his deputies because the aggressive officers failed to identify themselves or make known the purpose of their visit. Frederick went on to pick apart the illogical assumptions underlying Judge Rice's charge of conspiracy: "So far as the record discloses, there is an absolute want of reason for a conspiracy. There was no liquor in their dwelling, and none was found. There being no liquor, there was no reason to expect officers; and having no reason to expect officers, there certainly could be no reason to form a conspiracy. . . . There then can be no conspiracy inferred from any action on their part. And especially since they were ignorant of the character and purpose of the officers, who would not or did not put them on notice." Frederick characterized Rice's apology to the Aiken court for appointing counsel for the Lowmans as "highly prejudicial to the rights of the appellants" and proof that the trial took place in an emotionally charged and biased venue.[23]

The high court agreed. Upholding six of Frederick's seven exceptions to the original trial, the South Carolina Supreme Court voted unanimously on May 27, 1926, to grant the Lowmans a new trial. Written by Associate Justice Robert O. Purdy, a former Sumter mayor, circuit court judge, and ardent anti-Tillmanite, the high court's opinion stated unequivocally that, under the circumstances, the Lowmans had the right to defend themselves.

> It is manifest from the nature of the case, that, if the judgments against the defendants are to stand, there must have been a conspiracy on the part of the defendants to attack the officers. . . . From the nature of the testimony it will not be amiss to say that *a conspiracy could not have been formed by all of the defendants to attack the officers after the officers arrived upon the*

premises, and the testimony given by the witnesses does not disclose that a conspiracy existed before the visit of the officers. . . . The defendants were at their home where they had a right to be. . . . *It does not appear that any of the defendants knew that the sheriff and his deputies were officers;* certainly not before the disturbance commenced, and the testimony on that point throughout the case is of a doubtful character as to imparting this knowledge to the defendants. *The defendants had a right to use so much force as was necessary in keeping the officers from entering the house, or in expelling them from it and protecting themselves in their home, until the authority of the officers was made known* . . . [emphasis added throughout].[24]

The Supreme Court's decision created a dilemma for the likes of Judge Rice and, indeed, the late honorable sheriff of Aiken County. Not only was it a rebuke of each man's professionalism, but also a cautionary tale suggesting that the state's highest court would check excesses in local jurisdictions, even at the behest of a black attorney. In a *Palmetto Leader* editorial dated June 5, 1926, Frederick wrote exultantly, "Whatever may be said of the administration of justice in the South in so far as colored citizens are concerned it cannot be said that they do not receive justice when their cause is before the Supreme Court of South Carolina. . . . One of the chief reasons for setting the [Lowman] convictions aside was because the defendants had not received a fair and impartial trial as contemplated by the law of the State. But this is not an isolated case. This same court has rendered other decisions where justice to the colored defendants were [*sic*] not given in the lower courts."[25]

While awaiting their second trial, Clarence, Damon, and Bertha remained lodged at the state penitentiary in Columbia, a facility Governor McLeod described in his January 1925 message to the legislature as "an antiquated dungeon incapable of being remodeled." South Carolina's enlightened citizens had long decried the languishing prison, a complex of dilapidated lean-tos built in 1866 along the banks of the Congaree River, a mile west of the capitol building. In May 1922, after guards killed one prisoner and injured a dozen others, a legislative probe depicted the state penitentiary as the domain of a sadistic captain of the guard visited occasionally by its superintendent and board of directors. The investigation catalogued a gruesome array of routine punishments, including flogging, manacling, and chaining prisoners. "There is no limit, as far as we can find, to any of these punishments," the investigators wrote. "Their severity is left entirely to the will of the Captain of the Guard." Noting that among the female prison population only black women received whippings, the commission reported that all prisoners so punished were stripped naked and lashed between twenty-five and forty times with a strap of "smooth, pliable harness leather about a quarter of an inch thick, two inches wide and twenty inches long." (The captain of the guard disingenuously assured investigators that "the skin is not broken.") Governor McLeod took office in January 1923, just as this report surfaced publicly. His inaugural address committed his administration to altering the penitentiary to "reflect the civilization of our people," but three years later, fire hazards, vermin, insufficient heat and ventilation, poor nutrition, violence, illness, and "unspeakable immoralities" still prevailed. The inmates continued to wallow in conditions described by yet another commission as "so obsolete, so inadequate, so unsafe and so unsanitary that one cannot view [the prison] except as an expression of another age." The Lowmans endured this draconian netherworld for the better part of seventeen months while awaiting their retrial. On Monday evening, October 4, 1926, Sheriff Robinson and State Constable J. P. Hart arrived at the penitentiary to take them back to Aiken. A special term of the Aiken County Court of General Sessions convened the following morning.[26]

The court reporter's notes have not survived, leaving us the spare coverage in the Columbia, Aiken, and Augusta newspapers as narrow portals through which to glimpse the Lowmans' last days. Special judge Samuel Tucker Lanham, master in equity of Spartanburg County, presided, having been appointed by Governor McLeod. Jury selection consumed most of the proceedings on Tuesday, it being difficult to find white men in Aiken County of no stated opinion about the circumstances surrounding the death of Sheriff Howard. "Contrary to expectations," reported the *State*, "no motion was made by attorneys for the defendants for a change of venue." This was indeed odd, but in the absence of surviving documents, we cannot discern Frederick's strategy, which did include the engagement of a white attorney, Lawrence Geddings Southard, also from Spartanburg, as the Lowmans' chief trial counsel. The first and only witness to appear on Tuesday was Dr. Benjamin F. Wyman, the physician who transported Bertha to the Leesville hospital after the raid. He described for the court the number and type of wounds sustained by Sheriff Howard.[27]

On Wednesday morning, in a cross-examination of Arthur D. Sheppard (who killed Annie Lowman), Southard asked the deputy to produce the original warrant that authorized the April 25 raid, and Sheppard complied. Southard immediately declared it "an illegal paper." In the first place, he stated, the warrant only bore the name of Sam Lowman. Contrary to section 857 of the S.C. Criminal Code, a search warrant must "contain a statement setting forth the sources of information, and the facts and grounds of belief upon which the affiant bases his belief." Second, the affidavit portion of the warrant had been written by Sheriff Howard and simply stated that "a reliable source" accused Lowman of storing liquor at his home. Southard cited the state supreme court's recent unanimous decision in *State v. Dupre*, a case from Florence County, which held that a warrant issued to an officer who both swore the affidavit and served the paper to be a nullity. In that opinion the court had stated adamantly: "There should be a strict compliance with the law before a magistrate should issue a warrant to search a person's house. Rich, poor, and humble are equal in law. The poorest and humblest are entitled under the law to equal protection." Southard consequently motioned that Judge Lanham throw the warrant out as admissible evidence. "The move of Attorney Southard," reported the *Record*, "caused a big surprise in court," indicating to those present that this native white South Carolinian intended to provide his black clients with a committed defense. Attorney Julian B. Salley, assisting prosecutor Carter in the retrial, hotly objected to Southard's motion, arguing that "even if the warrant was defective it showed the legal intention of the officers and that they were not trespassers." In the late morning Lanham recessed the agitated courtroom to consider the arguments; reconvening at two o'clock, he declared the warrant would stand as admissible evidence. During the afternoon Howard's former deputies all testified that the Lowmans had put up a "strong fight" to their attempted search of the house.[28]

At 11:00 A.M. on Thursday morning, October 7, 1926, in a courtroom "filled with spectators," the state rested its case. Southard rose and motioned that Judge Lanham direct a verdict of not guilty for the Lowmans, hammering away again at the "illegally drawn" warrant carried by Sheriff Howard. Because the Lowmans did not know the identities of the four officers—a fact that the state's highest court had affirmed—Southard insisted that the Lowmans had acted perforce in self-defense, particularly given the menacing haste with which the officers approached the house. "Not even the governor of the state could keep even the humblest Negro away from his own home!" he declared, referring specifically to the instincts of Annie, Bertha, and Damon to rush to the house and resist the armed men. Southard's motion set off a "vigorous contest" with the prosecution that lasted well into the afternoon. At the close of the day and after "long and heated debate," reported the *Record*, "the trial of the three Lowman negroes took a rather unexpected turn." Lanham directed a verdict of not guilty for Damon Lowman and recessed the court until nine o'clock the next morning.[29]

N. J. Frederick later wrote that Lanham's decision indicated to him that Bertha and Clarence too would be exonerated, but instead of liberating the Lowmans, Lanham's ruling prefigured catastrophe. Damon was rearrested immediately on the lesser charge of assault and battery with intent to kill the deputies on April 25, 1925, thus ensuring that all three Lowmans would be locked in the Aiken County jail that night. No precautions were taken to ensure their safety. Governor McLeod, a timid, pious man, had kept abreast of the trial's developments through his state constable, J. P. Hart, and Sheriff Robinson, who assured him by telephone on Thursday evening that Aiken was calm. One of Aiken's most venerated citizens, however, intuited that trouble was brewing when he perceived the mood of a group of "petty officers and courtroom loungers" who abruptly left upon hearing of Damon Lowman's acquittal. Colonel Claude Epanimandus Sawyer, an aging attorney, celebrated Red Shirt, and surviving member of the legendary Wallace House (the contested Democratic slate elected to the General Assembly in 1876) voiced his concern about the Lowmans' safety to Lanham and prosecutor Carter after court adjourned, only to be shunned. According to an account published weeks later in the *New York World,* "Col. Sawyer says he stopped Mr. Carter on the sidewalk and said, 'There's a lynching in the air.' Mr. Carter, according to this version, sniffed, looked about him sarcastically as if searching for something, and replied, 'Hush, I don't see it,' and thereupon turned on his heel and strode off."[30]

Sometime between three and four o'clock on the morning of Friday, October 8, a group of men, including Hart; Robinson; his deputies Sheppard and McElhaney; Marion Bell, the county chain gang superintendent; John B. Salley, Aiken County traffic officer; and Taylor, Robinson's handpicked jailer, came noisily into the Aiken jail with flashlights. They unlocked the Lowmans' cells, then herded them past those of other prisoners—including Sam Lowman, still an inmate on the county chain gang—and down the stairs to the street. According to numerous jailed witnesses, Clarence and Damon were removed first and placed in two of three waiting cars. Chain gang inmate Cliff Robertson, a black man, later swore in an affidavit: "When they went in the Lowman boys cell Mr. Sheppard reached and got one of the boys and Hart got the other and they brought them on out of the door and Mr. Sheppard locked the cell door, and as they came on out the oldest Lowman had a little cigar box under his arm and State Constable Hart knocked it out from under his arm saying, 'You won't need that any more throw that Dam [*sic*] thing down.' It was knocked from his arm and fell to the floor and the Vaseline and things spilled on the floor." Having deposited their male prisoners, Sheriff Robinson led the group back upstairs to Bertha Lowman's cell. Clad only in a thin cotton nightgown, she attempted to dress, but was told it wasn't necessary because she would be taken straight home. One prisoner swore that Bertha began to "holler, 'Lord have mercy, what you all going to do with me?'" As she was jostled roughly from her cell, said another prisoner, Bertha heard "her brother hollering from the outside [and] she just began crying and screaming. Just as she started downstairs somebody hollered up to her to shut her G__D__ mouth or they would kill her there on the spot." Robertson, the chain gang inmate, recalled: "I heard the woman scream, and Sheriff Robinson spoke, as I recognized his voice, saying to her 'Shut up your God dam mouth' and then two shots were made in the jail, then all of them [prisoners] started to hollering 'MURDER' 'MURDER' 'MURDER' as they were being carried out. Mrs. Taylor screamed up stairs and Mr. Taylor the jailer said to her, 'Hush Sugar, No one is going to hurt you.'"[31]

The Lowmans were driven out U.S. 1 to the blanket of pines that lay beyond Aiken. Ordered out of their vehicles, they were shot execution-style, although various accounts (including Walter White's sensational treatment in *Rope and Faggot: A Biography of Judge Lynch*) stated that, having been told to run, the

Lowmans were shot in their backs as they attempted escape. As happened in the April 1925 raid, Bertha seems to have been particularly tortured. The *New York World* reported that she "had been shot once but had not died promptly and had crawled amongst the crowd beseeching them not to kill her, so that, terrified, they had shot her through the head with a pistol and through the body with a shotgun, the shotgun bullets setting her dress afire." According to the county coroner, Clarence Lowman died from a shotgun wound to the throat; Damon Lowman died from a .38 caliber revolver shot in the chest; and Bertha Lowman had been shot two inches above the left ear, also with a revolver. There were powder burns on her left shoulder blade as well.[32]

Hours after the Lowmans were killed, Judge Lanham convened his courtroom. Having first received the jury's verdict of "not guilty" for Damon Lowman, he announced the deaths of the three prisoners and adjourned the session. He called the Aiken County grand jury to meet at noon, charging it to conduct a "thorough and complete investigation." Lanham's resignation is palpable in the *State*'s account as he pleaded with the jurors: "I wish that you could understand that nothing threatens white supremacy unless it is the failure of white men to govern themselves and their failure to direct government which is entirely in their hands." A county truck delivered the Lowmans' corpses the next morning to Monetta, where local black residents lodged what constituted their protest. According to the *Record,* "The negroes of the Monetta section refused to have anything to do with the burial, and the county convicts were compelled to bury them. They were placed in one large grave."[33]

Within forty-eight hours of the Lowmans' deaths, actions taken by disparate parties soon culminated in a national cause célèbre. James L. Quinby Jr., a vindictive Graniteville eccentric and former grand cyclops of the Aiken County Ku Klux Klan (whose motives were driven by vendetta and not an aversion to lynching per se) initiated the most far-reaching of these by writing to James Weldon Johnson, the NAACP executive secretary, alleging that the Lowman murders had been carried out by the Klan, an entity indistinguishable from Aiken County's constituted authorities. Johnson handed the letter over to Walter White, who in turn contacted Will W. Alexander, head of the Atlanta-based Committee on Interracial Cooperation (CIC), asking for his input. Alexander consulted with CIC board member G. Croft Williams, an Episcopal minister and sociology professor at the University of South Carolina (and, coincidentally, the son of one of Aiken's most prominent citizens), who replied that the Aiken Klan was indeed "in the hands of a most dangerous element." At White's behest, Herbert Bayard Swope, editor of Joseph Pulitzer's *New York World,* provided a letter of introduction identifying him as a *World* investigator. Credentials in hand, White, who could pass as a Caucasian, arrived in Aiken on October 24. He met with Quinby at his Graniteville home, a building surrounded by loaded shotguns and searchlights, while his host, armed with a .38 revolver and two .45s, por-trayed Nollie Robinson and his deputies as Klan leaders who ran the local organ-ization as "a dirty, corrupt whiskey and political ring." According to Quinby, the Klan, whose membership had included Sheriff Howard, orchestrated the bogus raid on the Lowman home in April 1925 and planned the lynchings in the Aiken law offices of John Edwin Stansfield, Quinby's own first cousin, immediately after Damon's acquittal. (Stansfield had been Damon's court-appointed attorney in the first trial and was elected to the South Carolina General Assembly weeks after the lynchings.) Colonel Sawyer and Austin H. Johnson, a Southern Railway clerk in Warrenville, vouchsafed Quinby's information to White, who returned to New York and lobbied Swope to dispatch an investigative reporter to South Carolina. On October 28, White prepared a bold, six-page letter to Governor McLeod that named thirty-three Aiken County men as accomplices or witnesses to the lynchings, including three of McLeod's second cousins, one of whom owned Aiken's Chevrolet dealership. "I am placing these facts before you at such great length that you may have the benefit of my investigation," White explained, "and that you and the state of South Carolina may take such steps as you feel dis-posed to take to apprehend the lynchers. . . . " Not having an answer from McLeod, White forwarded copies of the letter on November 4 to the editors of South Carolina's largest newspapers.[34]

By the end of October it had become apparent that the grand jury would not bring any indictments and that Governor McLeod would not attempt to remove Nollie Robinson from office. On Halloween Day, Oliver H. P. Garrett, a star *New York World* reporter, arrived in South Carolina; six days later the first of his twenty-nine sequential reports appeared. They read like a Dashiell Hammett novel and gripped contemporary America in their unfolding. In spite of the per-sistent urging of South Carolina's most prominent newspaper editors, it was Garrett's series that forced Governor McLeod to make good on his pledge to launch a serious investigation. He assigned the task to W. W. Rogers, a small, one-eyed state constable lauded as the cleanest and most competent detective in the state. As he worked Rogers leaked his findings to Garrett, who in turn splashed them on the *World*'s front pages, from whence newspapers across the country promptly copied them.

Nollie Robinson emerged as the villain in extremis, a "tall, raw-boned man of 41 years" with pale blue eyes who, Garrett hinted, may have killed Howard himself as part of an internecine Klan struggle for control of Aiken County's bootleg liquor traffic. Lucy Mooney, a young white prisoner in the Aiken County jail on the night of the lynchings, told Garrett, "I was looking right at Sheriff Robinson," who she knew personally from his visits to her stepfather. Mooney said that on Saturday morning, October 9, Robinson came to her cell "and asked me if I knew anything about the lynching. I told him I recognized him; he turned deathly pale and denied that he was with them. He turned and walked away."

When Garrett asked Robinson about *his* investigation of the lynchings, the sheriff "shoved his black felt 'Cole Blease' hat from his matted, gray hair, and said: 'I ain't got no idea at all who done it. If I had I would sure enough swear out a warrant for 'em an' don't you mistake.'" To Garrett's questions about the allegations of Mooney and other prisoners that he led the jailbreak, Robinson, a deacon in the Graniteville Baptist Church, lost his temper: "G__d__ it, man! I wouldn't do a thing like that. I'm going to heaven; nobody's goin' ter meet me in hell. And I haven't the blood of them Lowmans on my hands."[35]

The twists and turns and revelations of Garrett's reportage cannot be treated here except to say that it drew a shocking portrait of Aiken County (and by inference, the entire state) as a miasma of Klan ignorance and blood feuds, an anarchistic backwater where hapless black people died for the incessant quarrels between white men. Amid this national humiliation, "the better sort" of white South Carolinians, while seconding the *World*'s denunciation of the "lawless class" of poor whites blamed for the Lowmans' deaths, exposed themselves as the impotent leaders they were and had been for decades. Causing them further embarrassment, U.S. Senator Coleman Blease jumped into the fracas with his highly publicized bluster to defend pro bono anyone the grand jury might indict, while the Ku Klux Klan burned a thirty-five-foot cross at Sheriff Howard's grave, drawing a thousand spectators. As captured in the editorial pages and letters to the editors of South Carolina's newspapers, a consensus emerged among the "intelligent minority" that their state lay in peril if its chronic, pernicious violence continued unabated. Virtually no expression of remorse for the Lowmans can be found in these discussions; most white Carolinians continued to believe that the family had wantonly murdered Sheriff Howard. Rather, these citizens insisted that "law and order" must prevail through the workings of the courts, never minding the injustices enshrined therein.

In the wake of the Lowman lynchings, the concerns of South Carolina's gentility swirled around four tangled preoccupations: the restoration of their beloved state's honor through the arrest, trial, and conviction of the murderers (which never occurred); the dreaded possibility of congressional intervention, whether in the form of a federal remedy for lynching or a renewed discussion of the Force Bill; the goading by demagogues of the poor whites' vicious antipathy for African Americans; and the escalating number of black laborers migrating to points north and west. The solution, these citizens naively agreed, required an intensified effort to promote charity toward black Carolinians while reining in the excesses visited upon them by the lower classes, but how? In short, they harkened back to the idealized benevolence of Wade Hampton, unwilling to acknowledge that his authority had rested on massive violence and that the threat of force secured white supremacy for them in the present moment. The propinquity of the Lowman lynchings to the fiftieth-anniversary celebration of Hampton's "Liberation" in December 1926 led the editor of the *Columbia Record* to compose a remarkable editorial that unconsciously limned the irony: "What have the people of South Carolina done, what are they doing, to justify the labors of the men of 1876? Hero-worship is a very desirable thing, but without emulation . . . it is the most barren of lip-service and mockery. . . . it is sheer hypocrisy to commemorate them with a flag in one hand and the assassin's knife or pistol in the other. In this year of our jubilee, what more notable act have we published to the world than the murder of three Negroes by a mob in Aiken county?" A Confederate flag and the assassin's weapons were *exactly* the proper images to be used in a commemoration of 1876, just as the Lowmans' recent deaths—in Aiken County no less—were fitting symbols of what white supremacy had wrought over the past fifty years. Violence against African Americans gave birth to and sustained the postbellum South such that lynching was but a continuation of tactics used during Reconstruction and the period of its undoing. Yet the uncoupling of Wade Hampton from the terror of his Red Shirts, embalmed among his devotees for generations, absolved the Hamptonites personally of having mistreated black Carolinians, while fostering the belief that a peaceable social order could spring from an oxymoronic program of benign repression. The general had carefully cultivated the myth by his refusal to participate in the nasty work required to quash "Negro thralldom" and elevate him to power. The set piece of Hampton entering a village astride his spirited horse, cheered by throngs of white women and children and respectful colored persons—the local radicals having been swept by advance teams of Red Shirts—exercised potent influence over the conservatives' romantic conception of leadership, captured in their many encomiums to Hampton's genius for "bloodless" revolution. Long after Ben Tillman grabbed power in 1890, the Hamptonites continued to delude themselves that he and his band of wool-hat boys had irrevocably destroyed a biracial utopia well on its way to fruitful cultivation. Since 1890 they had done little more than carp from the sidelines, but black southerners and demagogues knew better. William Pickens, the Yale-educated son of South Carolina slaves, offered this incisive delineation of realpolitik in the postbellum era: "It is hard really for even the best white people to tell just exactly what position they do want the Negro to occupy. But this seems true: that the majority want him down and under, but do not wish to brutally mistreat him in any other way,—they would not hang and burn him without law. They fail to see, however, that brutality and murder are the necessary sequel to their own finer forms of repression: if the better whites keep the Negro down, the inferior whites will take care of the hanging and burning."[36]

Notwithstanding the conservatives' blinding ambivalence, their repugnance for vigilantism dovetailed with the NAACP's modus operandi: by holding a mirror to middle-class America of its rabid mobs and mutilated victims, lynching could be extinguished. Robert L. Zangrando has correctly perceived that the urgency and drama of the organization's antilynching campaign "became the wedge by which the NAACP insinuated itself into the public conscience," thus clearing a space in which the modern civil rights movement could take root. Prefiguring later events, prominent white Carolinians, including editors, attorneys, clergymen, and academics, allied themselves and openly communicated with the NAACP and the *New York World* in 1926–1927, a remarkable group of bedfellows for the time.[37]

The deaths of the Lowmans did bear tangible fruit: Nollie Robinson lost his 1928 bid for reelection as Aiken County sheriff, and no more lynchings occurred in South Carolina until 1930, when a flurry of mob violence broke out upstate during Coleman Blease's last Senate campaign. Stumping in Union that July, Blease ridiculed Governor John G. Richards for having called out the National Guard two weeks earlier to prevent, unsuccessfully, the lynching of Dan Jenkins. "When I was governor of South Carolina you did not hear of me calling out the militia of the State to protect negro assaulters," he bellowed. In an opinion representative of editors across the state, the *Charleston News and Courier* swiftly responded, "The people cannot reelect Mr. Blease without endorsing lynching." James F. Byrnes, future U.S. secretary of state, defeated Blease in the primary, a victory seen by contemporary observers as South Carolina's repudiation of mob violence.[38]

Social conditions for black Carolinians did not improve qualitatively for decades, and show trials and legal executions surely continued the de facto work of the mob, but the furor unleashed by the *World*'s campaign revealed that many white South Carolinians were fatigued by what Charlton Wright, editor of the *Columbia Record,* called the "Nigger-baiting type that disgrace the South," even as they were hardly of one mind about where to draw the boundaries of white supremacy. That these same white people did not forge ahead with a solution to South Carolina's "Negro problem" in late 1926 is not surprising, yet the ugly revelations of the *New York World* gave them pause for a much-needed reckoning with the disposition of their society. Until historians excavate more of South Carolina's early-twentieth-century past, it is difficult to gauge the full impact of the Lowman affair. Aiken County's black population decreased by 10 percent between 1920 and 1930; how many abandoned the county after the Lowman murders is unknown. The sources do confirm that many South Carolinians, black and white alike, recognized that something momentous had occurred, even as they were uncertain about its implications. Editor Wright, who emerged during the Lowman crisis as the most outspoken critic of South Carolina's social pathology, ventured his own analysis: "If the white man still believes his race, alone, can impose inequitable *ex parte* judgments, without reference to the Negro's interests, he is kidding himself."[39]

Notes

1. "Three Lowmans Lynched This Morning," *Aiken Standard,* October 8, 1926 (all quotations). In the extensive media and manuscript documentation related to the Lowman murders, the name is given as "Demon" and occasionally, "Demmond" Lowman. Family members have told me that the name was Damon, which may have been spelled colloquially as Demon, but which also carries the subliminal connotation of evil. For that reason I have chosen to use the modern spelling of the name. This essay is an elaboration of the original presentation made to the Citadel Conference on the Civil Rights Movement in South Carolina in Charleston, March 6, 2003. I wish to acknowledge the critical assistance and friendship of three fellow South Carolinians·who have pushed me to examine my assumptions and without whom I could not have succeeded with this project: W. Lewis Burke, professor of law, University of South Carolina; Marion Chandler, archivist emeritus, South Carolina Department of History and Archives; and William D. Duncan of Aiken. Meeting Bill Duncan and drawing on his well of knowledge and patience have been the most rewarding aspect of this project. For their indispensable and generous assistance, I am also indebted to Marsha Trowbridge Ardila of the South Carolina Law Enforcement Officers Hall of Fame; Janet Meyer, librarian at the Supreme Court of South Carolina; David Moore, formerly with the Interlibrary Loan Office at Butler Library, Columbia University; Pete Peters of the Aiken-Barnwell Genealogical Society; and the following persons at the University of South Carolina: Robin Copp, Brian J. Cuthrell, and Henry Fulmer, all of the South Caroliniana Library, and Michael Mounter of the Law Library.

2. "Aiken Challenges South Carolina!," *Columbia Record,* October 8, 1926.

3. "2 Men and Woman Killed by Aiken Mob Early Today," *Columbia Record,* October 8, 1926 (first through third quotations); "Negro Prisoners Lynched at Aiken," *State,* October 9, 1926 (fourth quotation); "Slayers of Lowman Negroes Denounced by Aiken Officials," *Augusta Chronicle,* October 9, 1926 (fifth and sixth quotations).

4. Quotations are from Fox Butterfield, *All God's Children: The Bosket Family and the American Tradition of Violence* (New York: Knopf, 1995), 33 (first), and Carol Bleser, ed., *Secret and Sacred: The Diaries of James Henry Hammond, a Southern Slaveholder* (New York: Oxford University Press, 1988), 273 (second). Act 420 of the South Carolina General Assembly established Aiken County on March 10, 1871. For readings in the violent social history and cultural milieu of "Bloody Edgefield," see Richard Maxwell Brown, *Strain of Violence: Historical Studies of American Violence and Vigilantism* (New York: Oxford University Press, 1975), 67–89; Orville Vernon Burton, *In My Father's House Are Many Mansions: Family and Community in Edgefield, South Carolina* (Chapel Hill: University of North Carolina Press, 1985); Butterfield, *All God's Children,* 3–67; Jack Kenny Williams, *Vogues in Villainy: Crime and Retribution in Ante-Bellum South Carolina* (Columbia: University of South Carolina Press, 1959), 3–5. For readings about the violence in South Carolina during Reconstruction, see Hyman Rubin III, *South Carolina Scalawags* (Columbia: University of South Carolina Press, 2006); Joel Williamson, *After Slavery: The Negro in South Carolina during Reconstruction, 1861–1877* (Hanover, N.H.: University Press of New England, 1990); and Richard Zuczek, *State of Rebellion: Reconstruction in South Carolina* (Columbia, S.C.: University of South Carolina Press, 1996). The state's postbellum violence is treated in John Hammond Moore, *Carnival of Violence: Dueling, Lynching, and Murder in South Carolina, 1880–1920* (Columbia: University of South Carolina Press, 2006). Benjamin R. Tillman (1847–1918) served as governor of South Carolina from 1890 to 1894 and as U.S. senator from 1895 to 1918. Coleman Livingston Blease (1868–1942) held the same offices, respectively, in 1911–1915 and 1924–1930.

5. Quotation is cited in Tom E. Terrill, "Murder in Graniteville," in *Toward a New South? Studies in Post–Civil War Southern Communities,* ed. Orville Vernon Burton and Robert C.

McMath (Westport, Conn.: Greenwood Press, 1982), 211. The strength of Horse Creek Valley as a political constituency can be measured by the fact that in 1914 one of every seven South Carolina Democrats was a mill operative. Horse Creek Valley was home to one of the largest and most militant mill districts in the state, comprising one third of the Aiken County electorate. See Bryant Simon, *A Fabric of Defeat: The Politics of South Carolina Millhands, 1910–1948* (Chapel Hill: University of North Carolina Press, 1998), 4. For the history of Horse Creek Valley, see David L. Carlton, *Mill and Town in South Carolina, 1880–1920* (Baton Rouge: Louisiana State University Press, 1982); Pat Conroy, "Horses Don't Eat Moon Pies," in *Faces of South Carolina: Essays on South Carolina in Transition,* ed. Franklin Ashley (Columbia, S.C., 1974), 47–56; Thomas M. Downey, "Riparian Rights and Manufacturing in Antebellum South Carolina: William Gregg and the Origins of the 'Industrial Mind,'" *Journal of Southern History* 65 (February 1999): 77–108; Simon, *Fabric of Defeat;* Terrill, "Murder in Graniteville"; and W. E. Woodward, "A Cotton Mill Village in the 1880s," in *The Way Our People Lived: An Intimate American History* (New York: Dutton, 1944), pp. 319–58. Conroy describes Horse Creek Valley as "the nasty little secret of Aiken County" (52).

6. According to the 1920 federal manuscript census, the population of Aiken County was 45,571 persons, of whom 23,988 were black and 21,583 were white. The descriptions of Aiken are taken from a promotional pamphlet titled *Queen of Winter Resorts: Aiken, South Carolina* (Aiken, S.C., 1921). The Lowmans were described as "bad niggers" in several instances; see for example "South Carolina Whispers Names of Most Killers," *New York World,* November 6, 1926; "South Carolina Governor Moved by Girl's Story," *New York World,* November 8, 1926; and "Lynching Inquiry Shows Life but Real Action Is Doubtful," *New York World,* November 10, 1926.

7. The activities of the Lowman family on April 25, 1925, are delineated in the extensive legal files relating to *State v. Lowman,* 134 S.C. 485, 133 S.E. 457 (1926), including the trial testimony found in the "Transcript of Record," Library of the Supreme Court of South Carolina, Columbia (hereafter "Transcript of Record"); Aiken County Court of General Sessions Journal, no. 4; Aiken County Coroner's Inquisitions, J-T, box 2; Aiken County Coroner's Inquests Book and Inquests, 1923–1929; Aiken County Coroner's Inquests, box 2; Aiken County Indictments, bundle 208, all housed at the South Carolina Department of Archives and History in Columbia (hereafter SCDAH).

8. "Transcript of Record," 58 (first quotation) and 59 (second quotation). During this period, sheriffs in South Carolina generally wore dark suits, string or bow ties, and fedora hats. They drove their own vehicles and carried their personal firearms. In trial testimony Clarence Lowman described the group as "one man with leggings [*sic*] and one with a blue suit." See ibid., 50. In this time and place of primitive print and visual media, it is conceivable that no member of the Lowman family recognized Sheriff Howard and his deputies. Straddling the border of Saluda and Aiken counties, and only a stone's throw from the Lexington County line, Monetta is roughly twenty-three miles northeast of Aiken, the county seat; residents in this part of Aiken County tended to do business in the nearby Lexington County towns of Batesburg and Leesville or in Saluda, county seat of Saluda County.

9. Quotation is from the affidavit of Bridie Lowman before the coroner's jury, SCDAH.

10. Quotations are from "Sheriff of Aiken Killed by Negro," *State,* April 26, 1925.

11. "Aiken Folk Pay Howard Tribute," *State,* April 27, 1925 (first and third quotations); "Sheriff Howard Killed in Performance of His Duty," *Aiken Standard,* May 1, 1925 (second and fourth quotations). Howard had served as sheriff of Aiken County since his election to the office in 1912.

12. McElhaney affidavit before the coroner's jury, SCDAH (first quotation); "Transcript of Record," 100 (second quotation).

13. "Transcript of Record," 64 (first quotation). On May 15, 1925, the *Aiken Standard* reported that the raid on the Lowman home had been precipitated "on the strength of a letter from a prominent white man of the section, who said that there would be liquor sold by the Lowmans at a big social affair to take place at a negro church on the Saturday of the killing." See its article "Two to Die for Murder of Sheriff Howard; Another to Serve Life Imprisonment."

14. Quotation is from "Mob Gathers, Negroes Rushed to Pen," *Sunday Record,* April 26, 1925. The composite of Sam Lowman's economic history is drawn from examination of the following: Records of Saluda County Treasurer, Tax Duplicate Books, 1897–1923; Records of Aiken County Auditor, Tax Duplicate Books, 1913–1914; Records of Aiken County Treasurer, Tax Duplicate Books, 1921–1924; Aiken County Court of Common Pleas, Grantor Index, 1913–1967; Aiken County Agricultural Lien Abstracts, 1900–1909; Aiken County Title Books, 1913–1918; Saluda County Chattel Mortgage Index; U.S. Census, 1900, Lexington County, S.C.; U.S. Census 1900, Saluda County, S.C. (Soundex); Selective Service System, World War I Draft Registration, Saluda County, S.C., all SCDAH. See also *The Official Roster of South Carolina Soldiers, Sailors and Marines in the World War, 1917–1919,* vol. 2 (Columbia: Joint Committee on Printing, General Assembly of S.C., 1929), 1496. Governor McLeod's miscellaneous correspondence files contain numerous letters from Aiken County landowners asking that he put an end to the migration of black laborers. Publicly, McLeod downplayed the exodus, telling the *Manufacturers Record* in September 1923, "The stuff that is appearing in the Northern and Eastern Press as to the causes for negroes leaving the South is all sentimental and psychological rot, for the negroes know they have no reason to fear the Ku Klux, and ninety-nine out of every hundred have no desire for social equality. They are going North and East simply because they can get more wages in those sections than our people can afford to pay." See "Governor McLeod of South Carolina on Negro Migration," *Manufacturers Record,* September 20, 1923. Governor McLeod failed to mention that the legislature of South Carolina, like those of North Carolina and Georgia, had deemed it a crime to transport or otherwise "entice" black laborers out of the state. The effects of the Great Migration in the Palmetto State can be measured by the fact that the white residents of South Carolina obtained a numerical majority in 1926 for the first time since 1810. Of this development the *Columbia Record* opined, "In every respect we think the migration of the negro to the North and West is a splendid move. It is good for the negro and the white race as well. It solves to a nationwide degree the race question and it distributes the negro around so that ultimately each State will have approximately the same number." See "Negrotide Sweeping North," *Columbia Record,* October 2, 1926.

15. Chester Swearingen and W. M. Hartley, October 6, 1921, Aiken County Chattel Mortgage Books; *William Hartley v. C. M. Swearingen,* Aiken County Court of Common Pleas, Plaintiff's Index to Judgments, 1873–1949; Sam Lowman and Farmers and Merchants Bank, December 19, 1923, Aiken County Chattel Mortgage Books. The Aiken County Chattel Mortgage Books are in the possession of the Aiken-Barnwell Genealogical Society. D. L. Cato was likely the "prominent white man" who lodged the bootlegging complaint against Lowman, with whom, it will be recalled, he had made a simultaneous sale and purchase of land in 1913. Swearingen's wife was the daughter of Cato's dead brother.

16. "Trial of Lowman Family Started," *Columbia Record,* May 12, 1925 (first quotation); "Aiken Folk Pay Howard Tribute" (second quotation).

17. "Transcript of Record," 62–64 (first blocked quotation) and 65–66 (second blocked quotation). The line of questioning used with Damon by John Edwin Stansfield, his attorney, is typical of the court-appointed attorney representing black defendants during the age of segregation. As an anonymous black citizen wrote to Walter F. White of the NAACP

about the Lowman trial, "Appointing lawyers in cases of this kind is nothing more nor [*sic*] less than a slow death penalty." See unsigned letter to White, May 18, 1925, Papers of the National Association for the Advancement of Colored People, Washington, D.C. (hereafter NAACP Papers).

18. For Judge Rice's charge to the jury, see "Transcript of Record," 100–109.

19. "Lowman Negroes Sentenced to Die," *State*, May 15, 1926.

20. Unsigned letter to Walter F. White, May 18, 1925 (first, second, and third quotations); C. C. Johnson to White, May 16, 1925 (fourth and fifth quotations); White to Johnson, May 19, 1925 (sixth quotation), all NAACP Papers. Contrary to the anonymous writer's claim, Sam Lowman did not own the house that he and his family occupied. It belonged to his landlord, Will Hartley.

21. The quotation is from "Atty. N. J. Frederick, a Lawyer and Newspaper Editor Passes," unidentified clipping, n.d., Frederick Vertical File, South Caroliniana Library (hereafter SCL), University of South Carolina. The *State* wrote of Frederick, "He is a son of Clint [*sic*] Frederick, a noted Red Shirt Negro, and a Democrat," in its article "Directs Not Guilty for Demon [*sic*] Lowman," October 8, 1926. No direct evidence for this allegation has surfaced thus far, but if true, we might discern the deep-seated nature of Frederick's unwavering commitment to the overthrow of white supremacy in South Carolina. For Frederick's father's terms of service in the South Carolina General Assembly, see George Brown Tindall, *South Carolina Negroes, 1877–1900* (rpt., Baton Rouge: Louisiana State University Press, 1966), appendix, 309–10. For a treatment of black Democrats in Reconstruction South Carolina, see Edmund L. Drago, *Hurrah for Hampton! Black Red Shirts in South Carolina during Reconstruction* (Fayetteville: University of Arkansas Press, 1998). I must thank William L. Van Deburg and Stanlie James, Department of History; David Null, reference librarian; and Jerry Pellowski, student archivist, all at the University of Wisconsin at Madison, for their enthusiastic assistance regarding Frederick's tenure there from 1899 to 1901. I am also indebted to Hemphill P. Pride II, Esq., of Columbia, S.C., for a memorable lunch and conversation at the Summit Club in August 2002. Thanks to Pride, the Richland County Bar Association recognized N. J. Frederick as the association's first black member at a ceremony several years ago. It must be noted that Frederick was not the only black attorney practicing in Columbia during the years of his legal career. Green Jackson and Butler Nance were also engaged in the work of civil rights until 1929 and 1923, respectively. Frederick was the sole black lawyer in Columbia after 1929 and until his death in 1938. Lewis Burke, whose important work is concerned with the work of black lawyers in South Carolina during Jim Crow, generously provided this information.

22. Quotation is from N. J. Frederick to Walter White, August 4, 1928, NAACP papers. The biographical information is culled from the Frederick Vertical File, SCL. Michael Mounter at the University of South Carolina Law School provided the tally of Frederick's appearances before the state supreme court and much other helpful contextual information relating to the supreme court's adjudication of Jim Crow legal cases.

23. See "Unfinished Statement by N. J. Frederick, Columbia, S.C.," 1, SCL (first quotation); "Transcript of Record," 4 (second quotation) and 8–9 (third quotation). Frederick's argument may be found in "Brief of Appellants," *Supreme Court of South Carolina Cases Heard and Submitted, October and November 1925*, vol. 12, case no. 205, 1–11. The fifth quotation is from his brief, 8–9.

24. The opinion of the state supreme court may be found in *Supreme Court of South Carolina Cases Heard and Submitted*, October and November 1925, vol. 12, case no. 205, 485–93. Quotations are located on 488 (first) and 491–92 (second). For biographical information on Justice Purdy, see David Duncan Wallace, ed., *The History of South Carolina*, vol. 4 (New York: American Historical Society, 1934), 796.

25. "A New Trial for the Lowmans," *Palmetto Leader,* June 5, 1926, SCL.

26. "Inaugural Address of Thomas G. McLeod, Governor, to the General Assembly of South Carolina," in *Reports of State Officers, Boards, and Committees to the General Assembly of the State of South Carolina* (Regular Session Commencing January 13, 1925), 1:8 (first quotation); "Report of the Special Joint Legislative Committee to Investigate Conditions at the State Penitentiary," in *Reports of State Officers, Boards, and Committees to the General Assembly of the State of South Carolina* (Regular Session Commencing January 9, 1923), 2:46 (second and third quotations); "Governor Tells Needs of State," *State,* January 17, 1923 (fourth quotation); "State Penitentiary Is a Medieval Prison out of Place in Present Day," *Aiken Standard,* August 14, 1925 (fifth quotation); "Report of the Joint Legislative Committee to Investigate the State Penitentiary," in *Reports of State Officers, Boards, and Committees to the General Assembly of the State of South Carolina* (Regular Session Commencing January 12, 1926), 2:5 (sixth quotation). For the early history of the South Carolina state penitentiary, see Henry Douglas Kamerling, "'Too Much Time for the Crime I Done': Race, Ethnicity, and the Politics of Punishment in South Carolina and Illinois, 1865 to 1900" (Ph.D. dissertation, University of Illinois at Urbana, 1998) and Albert D. Oliphant, *The Evolution of the Penal System of South Carolina from 1866 to 1916* (Columbia, S.C.: State Co., 1916). A comparison of the whippings administered in twentieth-century South Carolina with those given eighty years earlier to slaves is instructive. James Henry Hammond, one of South Carolina's largest slaveholders, used a one-inch-wide whip on recalcitrant slaves. "In general," he wrote, "15 to 20 lashes will be a sufficient flogging." See Drew Gilpin Faust, *James Henry Hammond and the Old South: A Design for Mastery* (Baton Rouge: Louisiana State University Press, 1982), 100.

27. Quotation is from "New Trial Opens in Lowman Case," *State,* October 6, 1926. More research is required to determine the nature of Frederick's acquaintance with Southard, a devout Baptist and graduate of Clemson College and the University of North Carolina. In his "Unfinished Statement," Frederick wrote that Southard was known as "able and conscientious," 1. The only hint of irregularity, as it were, is that Southard's father was a native of Brooklyn, New York. See Wallace, *History,* 4:56.

28. "Lowman Trial Pauses a While," *State,* October 7, 1926 (first quotation); S.C. Code of 1922 ß857 (criminal code) (second quotation); "Surprise Comes in Lowman Trial," *Columbia Record,* October 6, 1926 (third, fifth, and sixth quotations); *State v. Du Pre,* 134 S.C. 268, 131 S.E. 419 (1925), 271 (fourth quotation); "Tells Shooting in Lowman Case," *Columbia Record,* October 7, 1926 (seventh quotation).

29. "Tells Shooting" (first quotation); "Surprise Comes" (second quotation); "Directs Not Guilty" (third and fourth quotations); "Directed Verdict for One," *Columbia Record,* October 8, 1926 (fifth and sixth quotations).

30. "South Carolina Governor Moved" (first quotation); "Lynching Inquiry Shows Life" (second quotation). Frederick wrote to James Weldon Johnson on October 11, 1926, "There was every indication that we would have cleared the THREE [*sic*], a directed verdict of not guilty had already been obtained before the lynching. That is what precipitated the whole thing. Evidently it was believed that none would be found guilty" (NAACP Papers). Southard did not venture so boldly, but told the *State* that his vigorous objections to the search warrant "seemed to create uneasiness on the part of a few that perhaps the defendants, if convicted, had the opportunity to get a new trial on appeal." See "Attorney Gives Full Resume of Trial," *State,* October 9, 1926. Interestingly, Judge Lanham took a more conservative view. In remarks made before the grand jury at 3:00 P.M. on Friday, October 8, he said, "In all human probability the trial would have resulted in the conviction of the other two and the majesty of the law upheld." See "Negro Prisoners Lynched."

31. Affidavit of Cliff Robertson, November 11, 1926, 2 (first and fourth quotations); affidavit of Charley Chamberlain, November 11, 1926, 1 (second quotation); "Sheriff Is Accused of Complicity with the Lynchers of 3," *New York World,* November 5, 1926 (third quotation). The affidavits are all housed in the papers of Governor McLeod, SCL.

32. Quotation is from "South Carolina Whispers." For the official causes of the Lowmans' deaths, see "Report of Testimony Taken at the Coroner's Inquest on October 8, 1926," SCDAH. There were conflicting reports on how many times the Lowmans had been shot. Walter White, who sensationalized the Aiken lynchings for public relations purposes, maintained that the Lowmans were told to run when they were turned out of the cars in the woods: "Off they started—and a volley of bullets was pumped into their backs." See his *Rope and Faggot: A Biography of Judge Lynch* (New York: Knopf, 1929), 31. The *Columbia Record* reported on October 8, 1926, "The bodies were found twenty feet apart[;] their clothing was untorn and each body was shot about a dozen times and each one in the forehead." See "Directed Verdict for One." Elsewhere the same edition of the newspaper stated, "The bodies of the negroes show wounds in front but none in the back. Sheriff Robinson refused to let photographs be taken of the bodies." See "Probe Lowman Lynching." The *Augusta Chronicle* stated that Clarence had "received a load of No. 6 shot in the back," suggesting "that the lynchers made him die . . as the slain officer [Howard] was killed." See "Lowmans Killed by Unknown Parties Is Jury's Verdict," October 10, 1926.

33. "Negro Prisoners Lynched" (first and second quotations); "Another Lowman Will Be Brought to State Prison," *Columbia Record,* October 11, 1926 (third quotation).

34. Walter White to Herbert Bayard Swope, October 14, 1926 (first quotation); James L. Quinby to James Weldon Johnson, April 15, 1927 (second quotation); White to Governor Thomas G. McLeod, October 28, 1926 (third quotation). White sent copies of his October 28 letter to McLeod to W. E. Gonzales of the *State;* Charles O. Hearon of the *Spartanburg Herald;* J. C. Hemphill of the *Spartanburg Journal;* Robert Lathan of the *Charleston News and Courier;* T. R. Waring of the *Charleston Post;* and R. Charlton Wright of the *Columbia Record* on November 4, 1926. All citations in this note are found in the NAACP papers.

35. "Sheriff Is Accused" (first, second, third, and fifth quotations); "South Carolina Whispers" (fourth quotation).

36. "After Fifty Years," *Columbia Record,* October 31, 1926 (first quotation); William Pickens, *The New Negro: His Political, Civil and Mental Status and Related Essays* (rpt., New York: AMS, 1969), 193 (second quotation).

37. Quotation is from Robert L. Zangrando, *The NAACP Crusade against Lynching, 1909–1950* (Philadelphia: Temple University Press, 1980), 18.

38. Arthur F. Raper, *The Tragedy of Lynching* (rpt., Mineola, N.Y.: Dover, 2003), 293 (first and second quotations). The history of lynching in South Carolina has been only superficially catalogued and analyzed. See Terence Robert Finnegan, "'At the Hands of Parties Unknown': Lynching in Mississippi and South Carolina, 1881–1940" (Ph.D. dissertation, University of Illinois at Urbana-Champaign, 1993); Susan Page Garris, "The Decline of Lynching in South Carolina, 1915–1947" (master's essay, University of South Carolina, 1973); and Jack Simpson Mullins, "Lynching in South Carolina, 1900–1914" (master's thesis, University of South Carolina, 1961).

39. R. Charlton Wright, letter to the editor, *New York World,* November 19, 1926 (first quotation); and Wright, "The Southern White Man and the Negro," *Virginia Quarterly Review* 9 (1933): 191 (second quotation).

The Civil Right Not to Be Lynched

State Law, Government, and Citizen Response to the Killing of Willie Earle (1947)

WILLIAM GRAVELY

Virtually every detailed scholarly analysis of particular lynchings or averted lynchings . . . powerfully reiterates the central role of law, either as a deterrent before or after the fact of mob formation or as a deliberate or inadvertent facilitator of vigilante hopes.

Larry J. Griffin, Paula Clark, Joanne C. Sandberg,
"Narrative and Event: Lynching and Historical Sociology"

The story of lynching should first tell us that our history never "caused" us to be violent.

Christopher Waldrep, *The Many Faces of Judge Lynch*

The standard version of the lynching of Willie Earle, who was taken from the county jail in Pickens, South Carolina, in 1947, and of the highly publicized trial of his murderers the following May has often been repeated.[1] The events began on a Saturday evening, February 15, when Thomas Watson Brown, a white, forty-eight-year-old taxi driver, picked up a fare at the corner of Markley and Calhoun streets in Greenville, South Carolina. At about ten o'clock that night, a local farmer, Hubert Newell, found Brown alive but bleeding on the ground near his cab outside Liberty—nearly twenty miles from where the fare had begun. The following afternoon, Pickens County and Liberty city authorities arrested Willie Earle, a twenty-four-year-old black laborer who had been living and working in Greenville but who was visiting his widowed mother in Liberty, a small farm and mill town. With some friends Earle had hired Walter Cary Gravely's local taxi to drink and socialize at the Beverly rock quarry two miles from Liberty. As the officers took him from the cab, Earle denied that he had been Brown's assailant.

Before daybreak on Monday morning, February 17, a vigilante mob from Greenville that was made up of at least thirty men, twenty-seven of them cab-drivers, abducted Earle from the Pickens County jail. Jailer J. Ed Gilstrap, who lived with his family in the jail, made no effort to stop the lynchers, who took Earle from Pickens through Easley and then into Greenville County. Outside West Greenville they interrogated, stabbed, and beat him and finally shot him twice, blowing away most of his face. Brown died later that morning in Greenville's St. Francis Hospital.[2] By Friday evening, thirty-one men—not including Gravely, who was held but later released—had been charged. On Sat-urday morning, February 22, pictures of thirty of the accused assailants were printed in the *Greenville News*. Despite hearing twenty-six signed confessions, however, a Greenville coroner's jury on March 4 refused to charge any specific man, saying only that "parties of a mob" killed Earle. A state grand jury never-theless returned a true bill of indictment eight days later. Solicitor Robert Ash-more, aided by Sam Watt as special state prosecutor appointed by newly elected Governor J. Strom Thurmond and his attorney general, John M. Daniel, made the state's case. Lasting for nine days in May 1947, the largest lynching trial in southern—perhaps in American—history unfolded in state circuit court in the Greenville County courthouse. After Judge J. Robert Martin dropped charges against five defendants and then ruled that the confessions could only apply to the men who made them and thus not as witness statements, an all-white, all-male jury acquitted the remainder.[3]

Of contemporary accounts of these events, none achieved the attention of Rebecca West's essay "Opera in Greenville," published in the *New Yorker* three weeks after the trial ended.[4] New attention to the story has emerged over the last decade in the works of historians Christopher Waldrep, Kari Frederickson, Bryant Simon, and John Egerton; of biographers of Jesse Jackson (South Caro-lina native Marshall Frady) and of Strom Thurmond (Nadine Cohodas, Jack Bass, and Marilyn W. Thompson); and in a memoir by Thurmond's African American daughter.[5] Briefer presentations of the story occur in A. V. Huff's his-tory of Greenville, Walter Edgar's survey of South Carolina, Piper Peters Aheron's photographic volume, and Leon Litwack's introduction to the exhibi-tion volume of pictures of lynching, *Without Sanctuary*.[6] Between 1982 and 1992, there were five other contributions to public memory of this lynching. The first was by historian E. Donald Herd Jr., who in 1947 was a fifteen-year-old pho-tographer for the weekly *Easley Progress* taking pictures at the death scene.[7] Another account is a ghost story written by Nancy Roberts, who was teaching World War II veterans in Greenville in 1947.[8] Three Greenville natives have pre-sented other perspectives: a theological reflection by Will Willimon, chaplain at Duke University; a section in a history of Greenville by Nancy Vance Ashmore

Cooper (daughter of the prosecutor in the case); and a novel by the late Bennie Lee Sinclair, the state's poet laureate.[9] Dan Hoover's 2003 retrospective piece in the *Greenville News* embellished, but did not probe beneath, the official story.[10]

In none of these works has anyone systematically examined the applicable state laws or the decisions made to implement or evade those laws in this case. Taken together they explain the failures of law enforcement to protect Willie Earle from being lynched and of the courts to convict his killers. When one examines the various levels of decisions, some surprising new links appear, especially about motivation and behavior. Always keeping in mind that "events . . . are inherently contingent because they did not have to happen as they did," one purpose of this essay is to explore these links from the state's perspective—essentially bracketing out federal aspects of this case.[11] Besides examining the volitional grounds of collective violence and of how state law was applied, a second purpose is to recount the actions of those South Carolinians who protested the lynching and the acquittal of Earle's murderers, thus upholding the principle of the civil right not to be lynched.

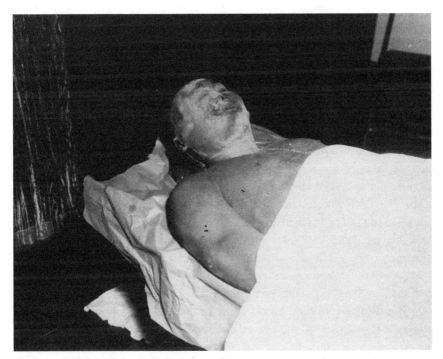

5. *The body of Willie Earle in the Greenville County morgue. Courtesy of the South Caroliniana Library, University of South Carolina, Columbia*

1

There was a single section in South Carolina's Constitution of 1895 acknowledging that lynching required some legal remedy. Titled "Prisoner lynched through negligence of officer—penalty on officer—county liable for damages," this section stated that when prisoners were taken from jail or from law enforcement, the state was exempted from liability for any subsequent violence. Sole responsibility instead rested with county officials, thereby making the county vulnerable to civil action for damages.[12] The 1942 State Code of Laws had three separate sections designed to implement this constitutional provision, two of which were relevant in the Earle case. One section (3041) made the county liable for damages for lynching but also gave it authority to recover costs from guilty parties. The other (1128) detailed the "Penalty upon officer from whom prisoner is taken." Facing potential liability at the state level, not to mention federal issues, it is no wonder that Pickens Sheriff Waymon Mauldin and his jailer, Gilstrap, for whom the sheriff was responsible, were under fire within hours of the lynching.[13]

Despite the fact that South Carolina, like the federal government, had no specific antilynching statute defining a mob and setting consequences for perpetrators, the legal framework was in place for a successful prosecution on charges of murder, accessory before and after the fact of murder, and conspiracy.[14] But the trial jurors in 1947 decided that the evidence in the case was insufficient, despite the twenty-six signed confessions presented by prosecutors.[15] They could not even agree to convict anyone on the lesser charge of conspiracy, which the confessions clearly demonstrated and Martin's charge explained.[16]

The defense attorneys were carefully chosen to represent their constituents. Thomas Wofford was a former federal attorney and Harvard Law graduate. Bradley Morrah, a cousin of John Marchant—the son of a mill owner and one of the defendants—was a state legislator. John Bolt Culbertson was a labor activist, and Ben Bolt a local attorney who meticulously tended to details. They decided not to present any witnesses, instead daring the twelve white jurors from Greenville County to convict any one white man, much less thirty-one of them, for the death of one black man, Willie Earle.[17] Their strategy, which initially featured having Brown's widow, Emma, sitting at their defense table, was to ground the case on the widely shared assumption that Earle was Brown's assailant. The presence of the defendants and their family members sitting together and occupying a considerable portion of the downstairs white section of the courtroom was already a powerful force for the defense. The lawyers also sought to undermine the involvement of the Federal Bureau of Investigation in the case, to link its role to unwarranted federal intervention in local and southern affairs, and thus to invoke sectional rhetoric dating back to antebellum days and renewed in the overthrow of Reconstruction. They asked for, and received, the help of

United States Senator Olin D. Johnston in obtaining a transcript of Walter Winchell's radio broadcast critical of the handling of the case and of the southern propensity of tolerating lynching.[18]

Several factors complicated the state's case against the thirty-one men. Indeed, special state prosecutor Watt, speaking before bar associations after the trial, contended that the prosecution's case had been botched before he even became involved just prior to the coroner's jury proceedings about Earle's death.[19] He might have had in mind the problem, which the defense team exploited, of the various ways in which the signed and witnessed confessions were obtained, especially the fact that they were not sworn to before Judge George B. Greene as part of individual indictments with attorneys for the defendants present. To build the entire case on them, moreover, was a huge risk. Judges had discretion as to whether the statements could be simultaneously confessions and witness testimonies. As an assistant solicitor in 1934 Ashmore had seen a Ku Klux Klan lynching case collapse when aggressive defense attorneys challenged the validity of statements by two defendants against six others. As in 1947, the judge ruled against the state, and all eleven Klansmen were freed.[20]

The special state prosecutor most certainly had in mind the move by Greenville Sheriff Homer Bearden—with prosecutor Ashmore's consent—to release the thirty-second defendant, Cary Gravely, from Liberty on February 25, two days before Watt assumed his role. This cousin of mine, who was of my father's generation, was connected to the conspiracy that led to the lynching. After telling two Liberty cabdrivers about Earle's arrest, Gravely went to Greenville and met local taxi men who were discussing revenge for Brown's stabbing. Since Gravely, whose brother-in-law was Pickens jailer Ed Gilstrap, knew where Earle had been taken, he told the Yellow Cab dispatcher.[21] These facts and relationships might have led investigators to explore events at the jail more thoroughly, if not to uncover possible foreknowledge of the emerging conspiracy, at least to prove inaction, as Waldrep has argued in discussing the federal issues in the case.[22]

However crucial we may consider these decisions—remembering the motif we are pursuing that people made choices all along the way—Ashmore, like much of the general public, also accepted the jailer's story of being unarmed and overwhelmed by the intruders. The sixty-two-year-old Gilstrap put on an impressive performance for the media to solidify his narrative of justification for not protecting Earle's safety. His choice not to be a hero seemed more convincing than did the mandate to do his duty. His oblique statement—"I guess you boys know what you are doing," while warning the mob not to use profanity since his family was nearby—captured his passivity.[23] But Ashmore, Governor Thurmond, and Attorney General Daniel also made choices. Although it would have been a most difficult act, state authorities could have removed Gilstrap, Mauldin, or both. They had the constitutional power to depose them, and Ashmore, as "the prosecuting Attorney," to charge and try "any officer, State, County or municipal" who lost a prisoner through "negligence, permission or connivance" to "a mob or other unlawful assemblage of persons."[24] Instead the focus shifted to the impressive manhunt involving fifty-nine federal, state, county, and city law officers, the speed with which the perpetrators were arrested and implicated, and the possibility of a successful trial against such a blatant lynching.

From the start Ashmore was caught in the crosshairs of the case. The morning of the lynching, he was due in Pickens to open the February term of court, where he would be working closely with Mauldin's office. He anticipated that he would later be called upon to prosecute a case with many potential defendants, and that, as he told Jim Blessing of the *Anderson Independent*, this would be the toughest job of his fifteen-year career. He recognized the "street talk" predicting "that the state will never get a conviction in the lynch case," but was mustering all the courage he had to see that justice was done.[25] Ashmore was aware that it was common knowledge that the lynching was planned around the Yellow Cab office within twenty-five yards of the courthouse that housed the circuit judge's chambers above and the Greenville sheriff's office on the bottom floor.

Some of the defendants recounted in their confessions how they discussed with Bearden's on-duty deputies Brown's stabbing and medical condition and the need for revenge against his attacker. Milford Forrester, a new deputy, and Clark M. Maxwell, a veteran in the department, had heard one driver's drunken account of the lynching plan but dismissed it as hearsay.[26] A potential federal case for "inaction" was initially brewing within the Department of Justice, and thus there emerged the possibility that both counties might be implicated, as they could have been within state law, for not being alert to the dangers to Earle's safety. The issue became hypothetical when the FBI and federal attorney Oscar Doyle from Anderson withdrew and left the case with the state, but that did not lessen the challenge Ashmore faced. Interviewing more than 150 taxi drivers in Greenville, he and the arresting officers had to decide who to indict and who to free and how to handle evidence and try so many men in the face of mounting public sympathy in the defendants' favor.

It was in Pickens County that the first official legal action shaped the course of subsequent developments. Less than thirty hours after Earle's corpse was found, and three days prior to having his death certificate signed, a jury of inquest, which Pickens Coroner Dennis Rampey impaneled, named Earle posthumously as Brown's murderer.[27] The six male jurors first heard Pickens Deputy Sheriff Wayne Garrett submit an autopsy report on Brown. Garrett, who had arrested Earle once before in 1944, presented the circumstantial evidence that led him and Liberty policeman Eugene Merck to conclude that Earle had gone on Saturday night to his mother's house after attacking Brown. Earle had remained in Liberty until the next afternoon, when Chief of Police D. B.

Owens, Garrett, and Merck arrested him and turned him over to Sheriff Mauldin in Pickens.[28]

In the Tuesday afternoon hearing in Pickens there was no effort to make blood type matches between Brown and stains allegedly found on a jacket at Tessie Earle's house or on a Boy Scout knife taken from Earle. There was no testimony from her or the other children. The proceeding seemed hastened in order to protect Pickens County and its sheriff and jailer from liability in a future lawsuit.[29] The most prominent figures in the audience were Brown's brothers, who were asked to take the three dollars from six fifty-cent stipends given to the jurors back to their sister-in-law.[30] The coroner's decision to hold the hearing so soon in the highly charged atmosphere, the deputy's presentation of inadequately analyzed circumstantial evidence, the jurors' sympathy for the grieving Brown family—these moves taken together set in motion the most essential feature for rationalizing the outcome of everything that came afterward. Whatever the intent, the coroner's jury functionally provided the lynchers with essential elements of their later narratives of justification to which the purported confessions further substantiated. These confessions in turn became not admissions of guilt but self-justifying explanations.

The precipitating cause of the lynching of Willie Earle, of course, was the attack on Brown that led to his death. Someone, if not Earle, stabbed the cabdriver, causing his death a day and a half later. The twenty-six confessional statements—even though they were not available to the Pickens coroner's jurors—solidified the perception of Earle's guilt. Fourteen confessors stated that Earle, upon their interrogation at an initial stop on the lynching journey, acknowledged that he had stabbed Brown.[31] Earle's words, despite significant inconsistencies between the statements, were presented as factual and as though they were not being reported by men who were themselves accused of murder. His purported admission, rather than the sources from which it originated, became the essential feature of subsequent stories used to rationalize folk justice.

The confessions also contain four references by cabdrivers asserting that two men were picked up for Brown's Saturday night fare in Greenville.[32] The official story would state that Earle was a single fare, but again someone made a decision to ignore any contradictory evidence. There was no investigative follow-up about who the alleged second rider was and what happened to that person. That omission did not escape attention at the time. South Carolina NAACP and state Progressive Democratic Party (PDP) leader, newsman John H. McCray, was aware of it and of other contradictory aspects of the accounts accepted by much of the public. Writing privately to protest Columbia radio commentator Brim Rykard's May 28 broadcast about the lynching and trial, McCray described his own "dispassionate, impartial and careful" detective work back in February and concluded: "I doubt seriously that Willie Earle, ill as he was, was guilty. Furthermore no effort has been made to locate the second passenger Brown picked up with Earle in Greenville. The Pickens Coroner's jury indicted the dead Earle on the flimsiest information, evidence less than one tenth that the Greenville jury had before it."[33]

Other than Earle's own words of denial to arresting officers and to Sheriff Mauldin at the jail, three accounts of these events exist that differ from the official narrative, which never included a positive identification by Brown of who had assaulted him, and raise questions about Earle's alleged guilt.[34] First, following McCray's reasoning and recalling the four confessions, there was the possibility that Earle, if in Brown's cab, either had an accomplice who was never found or was an innocent bystander, with the unidentified second fare being the violent party who escaped. Second, Tessie Earle insisted to reporters from the African American press of the period that Willie Earle never came to Liberty that night in a cab, but was on a through bus that made an unexpected stop. If her account, which I wrote about in the *South Carolina Review* at Clemson in 1997, was more than a mother's loyalty to her son, then Earle was set up by someone to take the fall for Brown's death.[35] That possibility would help explain why Earle had made no attempt to hide or run away, as might be expected of a murderer. A Clemson University student interviewing Faith Clayton from Pickens County for his master's thesis on the lynching raised a third possible sequence of events. Clayton reported that she had turned Earle away from the welfare office in Liberty that Saturday morning because he was intoxicated.[36] None of these alternative recollections establish proof to confirm Earle's innocence or guilt, such as we would have today with DNA and other forensic tests, but they do suggest reasons to question the official accounts.

The decision of the Pickens coroner's jury effectively transformed the lynchers into law enforcers—the prosecutors, the judges, and the jurors of Willie Earle.[37] Thereafter stories favorable to the jurors could assume, if not assert, that they acted under the Hebrew biblical logic of an eye for an eye. That ancient code sought to approximate equal justice and to provide a hedge against revenge: that is to say, not two eyes for one eye. The vigilantes took no other person from the racially segregated jail. Raymond Robinson, for example, was next to Earle in the cellblock.[38] No other random white-on-black violence occurred in reaction to Brown's demise, although it did surface briefly during and in the aftermath of the trial.[39] It became, therefore, a simple matter to correlate the death of Brown to the death of Earle and conclude, before there was any trial, that an equilibrium of sorts had been achieved. After the lynching occurred, of course, the question of Earle's guilt or innocence was not really the issue. The violation of his rights to a trial by a jury, to a defense attorney, and to protection while imprisoned was clear for all to see.

Most of the general public, right up to Governor Thurmond, however, accepted the view that Earle was guilty. The head of the FBI investigating team, J. C. Bills from Charlotte, apparently also came to this same conclusion, leaking to the press on February 28 that members of the lynching party had attested to Earle's confession. That same day Governor Thurmond sent a letter to the Pickens sheriff commending him and his deputies "for your quick apprehenstion [*sic*] of the murderer of Mr. T. W. Brown of Greenville, S. C." The governor continued, "I deeply regret that the arrest was followed by a lynching of a prisoner," but then praised Mauldin for his work on the investigation of Earle's killers.[40] Mauldin's coordination with state constables, the FBI, and Greenville law enforcement effectively countered any move against him for negligence. His public response was to explain that he had instructed the jailer not to let anyone into the upstairs cellblock. More candidly, he as much as admitted that the idea of a break-in at the jail had crossed his mind, when according to a report in the press he said, "I didn't think they would try it."[41]

Revenge ruled in this story, first when the mob punished a single black man for the ultimately fatal attack on a white man and again when no one was found guilty for the lynching. It was also present in the historical foreground of Valentine's Day weekend in 1947 in Greenville County. Among local historians, another narrative of justification for the lynchers emerged, which even contained a rape story—the motif most often associated with the rhetorical defense for lynching, even though statistically and historically it was rarely the cause.[42] The mob, this account goes, intended to avenge the state's execution in 1945 of another of their own—a white cabdriver, Charles Gilstrap, from Pickens County, who had been convicted of raping a twelve-year-old white girl in Greenville in 1944. The case, ironically, still elicited racial ramifications.[43]

Though he admitted that he took sexual liberties with the pre-teenager, Gilstrap denied that he had raped her. He and his court-appointed attorney, John M. Schofield, failed to convince the jury that the victim had, by hanging out around cabstands, provoked his loss of control. Gilstrap was executed on February 9, 1945, his twenty-ninth birthday. He was initially scheduled to die the previous June 22—the date that George Junius Stinney Jr., a fourteen-year-old black adolescent, went to the electric chair.[44] What prompted the later execution date was an appeal by Schofield seeking to overturn the original verdict and capital sentence handed down by Judge Martin, who was himself trying his first case in circuit court. The appeal claimed that Solicitor W. A. Bull had violated Gilstrap's rights to a fair trial in challenging the all-white, all-male jury to convict in three respects, and especially by playing what today would be called the race card. "If this boy's color were black it wouldn't take you fifteen minutes to return a verdict of guilty, and he is not entitled to any more consideration than if his color were black," the defense charged Bull with saying.[45]

The sentiment that Gilstrap's punishment represented an unjust outcome persisted in his family and among his fellow cabdrivers. Some of their anger targeted Judge Martin. The assault on T. W. Brown in 1947 occurred the week of the second anniversary of Gilstrap's electrocution. The Greenville lynch mob, therefore, not only reacted in vengeance against Earle but also against the legal system itself, which Martin represented, and against the violation of the code of white supremacy, which Bull had committed. That code assumed that the intent of the state in making rape a capital crime was to discourage lynchings as a response and to substitute legal trials against perpetrators. It was further assumed that this change was meant primarily for black perpetrators, and thus the law was misapplied in this case. Swift capital punishment was the norm in 1947 South Carolina, so if Earle had been tried and convicted, he would have been electrocuted.[46] The cabdrivers knew that was the case, and that fact forces an exploration into a more complicated mixture of motivations. In the early morning of February 17, 1947, when selecting the final site for Earle's execution, although such a detail is in none of the confessions, the lynchers found a location near the Martin family property off old Bramlett Road outside West Greenville to deliver a symbolic, if covert, message. That choice prompted the Martin family to make their own investigation of the killing.[47]

In his presiding role for the sensational trial in general sessions court in 1947, Martin earned the praise of a wide range of editors, lawyers, other judges, local community leaders, and citizens across the country that had taken the trouble to write him.[48] As widely reported in the press, his last act on May 21 was to turn his back on the jurors and leave without the customary expression of thanks for their service. Generally interpreted as displaying disdain that all defendants had been acquitted, the judge's gesture had a more personal dimension to it than most observers of the time could have realized. Its significance was not lost on some of the defendants even as they celebrated wildly their escape from judgment. Their victory represented a further computation of an eye for an eye. To pay back the judge for Charles Gilstrap's electrocution and be freed from being punished for killing Earle at the same time was sweet victory indeed. That was especially true for those, in February 1945, who had served as honorary pallbearers at Gilstrap's funeral and who had noted that the electrocution eerily burned his body into a dark caricature of itself.[49]

On March 6, 1947, Governor Thurmond wrote to Mauldin and to all other sheriffs in the state, declaring, "The State cannot afford to have a repetition of the Greenville-Pickens lynching case." He offered to have the chief of the state constabulary to come to any county upon request where there was a need to safeguard "any person in your custody whose safety is endangered." He concluded, "The guarantee of such security in your County is your responsibility."[50] That correspondence wrapped up the primary role of the governor in the case, even though his policy statement on protecting prisoners was repeated in a press release after the trial.[51] By the time he had thanked the FBI, the State Constabulary, the Pickens and Greenville County sheriff departments, and the Greenville chief of police for their work, the courts had taken over and Thurmond's responsibilities ended.[52]

In future years Thurmond would consider his role in this case to have contributed to progress in race relations in the state.[53] As a former trial judge who had sentenced men to the electric chair, he certainly knew murder when he saw it. Of course Thurmond's law and order stance in this instance did not mean that he had been persuaded to join the civil rights campaigns against lynching or for black voting rights and an end to segregation. Over the next year he emerged as the leader of the Dixiecrat movement intent on opposing President Truman's civil rights program. He nonetheless understood that if the state was to retain control over these issues and not be subject to federal pressure, it had to stop lynching.

Until the state legislature adopted a new statute defining and setting punishments for lynching, the most important events in South Carolina in the aftermath of the trial were two civil court cases. Backed by the NAACP Legal Defense Fund, with Columbia attorney Harold Boulware doing the major work, Tessie Earle Robinson in 1948 sued both Pickens and Greenville counties. After the state supreme court decided in 1949 that Greenville was liable, she won a $3,000 claim in a settlement with the county early in 1950. A countersuit by Emma D. Brown held up distribution of the funds until 1956, when Circuit Judge J. Woodrow Lewis, explaining the intent of the state law, released the award to Mrs. Robinson and her family. Pickens County astutely avoided liability, but in a limited sense her success in court against the county from which the lynchers hailed vindicated her son's civil right not to have been lynched.[54]

Those South Carolinians who backed the lynchers also had their turn at bat when in April 1950, the Pickens jailer who had avoided being charged with neglect or complicity in not defending Earle got his revenge against his critics. In 1949 Frederick Philbrick in a textbook on forensics and rhetoric discussed the Willie Earle lynching trial, and mistakenly referred to Ed Gilstrap as "the jailer, himself a Negro." Gilstrap sued for libel and asked for $150,000 in damages, even though the book referred only to him by his position and not by name. The case was argued in federal court, but it was premised on a state statute prohibiting a white man from being called a "Negro." Macmillan publishers and the author settled the suit, and the jailer retired from his post and moved into the county near where Charles W. Gilstrap was buried at Crossroads Baptist Church.[55]

2

Of the vital forces in American democracy, the media and citizen activism often succeed where the legal and political systems fail in keeping alive such principles as the right to a trial by jury. These sectors of American life in 1947 were the most consistent defenders of the civil right not to be lynched. Such politics of advocacy had varied venues in 1947 from individual expressions of moral outrage sent to Governor Thurmond to group protests at the local level to coordination with civil rights organizations of the time.

Two dozen residents of the state or expatriate South Carolinians and more than a dozen locally based groups in the state contacted Thurmond between February and May 1947 to express their support for authorization of state assistance to the prosecution. They often gave a religious cast to their objections to the lynching and wrote about being offended or shamed by the subsequent acquittals. The crime of lynching was "heinous before God and repulsive to man in a free society," a Presbyterian pastor in Conway, Hubert G. Wardlaw, declared. A Baptist college professor in North Carolina spoke of clearing "my home state . . . of this shame," and an Episcopal priest in Spartanburg, in an open letter to the governor, "deplore[d] this cowardly violation of Justice."[56] The writers included a woman in Due West slated to begin missionary work in India that fall, an Episcopal priest in Summerville, the pastor of Second Presbyterian Church in Charleston, a female teacher at the Methodist Church's Mather Academy in Camden, another woman who was student counselor for Presbyterians at Winthrop College campus in Rock Hill, an Episcopal church worker in Clearwater, a professor at Furman University, and a South Carolina native who taught at the Southern Baptist Theological Seminary in Kentucky.[57] Both a Methodist pastor and an educator in Greenville alerted the governor to the low odds for a conviction. A ministerial student at Emory University feared that if this "murder" went "unpunished," more lynchings would occur.[58]

On the day of the lynching Columbia resident Gennie Seideman, as "an American of Jewish Ancestry," wrote to the governor about how "real and personal" the issues raised by the case were to her. "I am made aware how slight is my margin of safety in a land where race hatred is rampant."[59] Seideman called for "the full force of our government . . . against such crime." Echoing German pastor Martin Niemoller as the Nazis imprisoned him, she warned: "even White Protestant Americans will not be safe if this is not checked. Witness Germany, first the Jews, then all the people were involved in senseless blood and death. I pray that you will be strong."[60] Making another European comparison from Belgium, Sumter native, black military veteran, and PDP candidate for the United States Senate in 1944, Osceola E. McKaine, also praised Thurmond's action. The expatriate claimed that public opinion abroad would notice that the nation "and even South Carolina, seeks to practice at home the respect for the rights of minorities she seeks to impose on the rest of the world."[61]

Governor Thurmond also heard from citizen groups—from the state conference and the Cheraw branch of the NAACP to the executive board of the Charleston Young Women's Christian Association and the public affairs committee of the same organization in Greenville.[62] Appropriate to its origins following the Leo Frank lynching in Georgia thirty-two years earlier, the American Civil Liberties Union alerted its South Carolinian members to a $1,000 reward for information leading to the arrest, conviction, and imprisonment of any member of the mob.[63] The Business and Professional Women's Club of

Greenville damned "the mob rule exhibited" in the case as "contrary to the principles of Christian democracy on which is founded the American standard of justice for all through due process of law."[64] A group of "Negro Teachers of Pickens County" collectively commended Thurmond for his stand and appealed to him to use his office to bring "these criminals to justice." Likewise, one white and two black ministerial associations offered appreciation for his forceful leadership.[65]

Besides the persistent work of the NAACP in matters of social justice, there were other agencies and movements for change whose representatives spoke out in 1947. In February two union organizations with locals in South Carolina—the Congress of Industrial Organizations and the Textile Workers Union of America—and John B. Isom, the pastor of the pro-union Saxon Baptist Church in Spartanburg, weighed in to support Thurmond's stance.[66] The newly formed (in 1944) interracial civil rights organization based in Atlanta, the Southern Regional Council (SRC), had both a South Carolina division headed by lawyer Marion Wright from Conway (who also wrote Thurmond personally) and a Richland County committee.[67] The Columbia-based branch worried that the Greenville verdict would deal "a serious blow to good racial relations" in the state, and the interfaith "Resolutions Committee" appealed to the governor to provide better protection to prisoners.[68] A future president of the SRC, Presbyterian layman, former Coker College professor, and writer James McBride Dabbs, wrote Thurmond five days after the lynching to warn "that the quick confessions . . . indicate that the murderers expect to get off without punishment." He hoped that Thurmond represented "progressive government" in the state against the forces of "a reactionary political machine" and "the resistance of a few bitter-enders."[69]

There were also courageous citizens in the center of events willing to protest the lynching and subsequent controversy. In Pickens the editor of the weekly paper and a local Baptist layman, Gary Hiott Sr., immediately condemned the violation of Earle's right to a trial. In a front-page editorial of the *Pickens Sentinel* titled "Does a Man-Made Boundary Remove a Responsibility?" Hiott called the lynching "this blackest of all physical crimes" and predicted that the county and the state would undergo "humiliation" and "shame" over "the next few years" as a result of it. He especially emphasized how violated was "the feeling of a Christian people who tried to provide the protection that a human being has a right to expect," and he concluded that "men have not yet learned the teachings of the principles of America." In a letter to the paper a week later, his pastor at the First Baptist Church, E. R. Eller, praised "the splendid editorial," regretting "in shame that such a blot should be placed on South Carolina."[70]

In the same *Sentinel* issue as Hiott's condemnation and in a neighboring town's *Easley Progress* appeared an invitation urging "public spirited citizens, both men and women" to attend a meeting on Thursday evening at Pickens High School "to discuss and draft a statement in regard to the mob violence" that had invaded the county seat. The instigator for the protest meeting was twenty-seven-year-old South Carolinian Hawley Lynn, who had been pastor of Grace Methodist Church in Pickens for two years.[71] Lynn invited well-known local civic leaders to preside—a Presbyterian churchman, J. T. Black; a Baptist deacon, O. T. Hinton Sr.; and his parishioner who was the widow of a judge, Mrs. J. T. "Queen" Mauldin.[72]

Unfortunately Lynn's invitation attracted persons to the meeting who defended the lynching. These speakers came from the Dacusville area near where Charles Gilstrap was buried and where the last lynching in the county had occurred in 1912. The victim in that case was a seventeen-year-old African American named Brooks Gordon. Retelling that thirty-five-year-old event, which had already been brought to public attention in the daily papers in Greenville and Anderson and in that week's *Sentinel*, squelched the protest effort.[73] Facing the possibility that a motion to approve the lynching might prevail, Lynn and his sympathizers adjourned the meeting without being able to defend the reputation of Pickens.

But Lynn did not let the outcome of the protest meeting silence his conscience. Ten days later, on Sunday, March 2, he preached a powerful sermon to his congregation, which met weekly in the local high school since its church building had burned in October 1945. Titled "Who Lynched Willie Earle?" and subtitled "The Religious Roots of Democracy," Lynn's sermon courageously condemned the sentiments the pastor kept hearing around town. The preacher warned that those who "trample the rights of human beings underfoot" end up committing "a lynching in their hearts." He also composed "A Prayer for the Sin of Lynching" and published it in the Methodist weekly in Columbia, the *Southern Christian Advocate*. Editor Hiott later reprinted it for *Sentinel* readers.[74] Lynn also confronted the owner of a local meat market for collecting money for the lynchers' defense fund. Finally in May, as the trial opened, he praised Judge Martin for refusing motions to delay the case.[75]

In a *Sentinel* editorial titled "Civilization Has a Long Way to Go," Hiott reflected the response that many Pickens residents had to the verdicts in the Greenville trial. A future Pickens resident who would later succeed Eller as pastor of the Baptist church there had a similar reaction. A pre-ministerial student at all-white Furman University in Greenville, Lloyd Batson gave a satirical speech at his school damning the acquittals. In the speech, titled "America, the Land of the Free and the Home of the Brave, 1947 Style," Batson attacked "lily-white justice" and condemned "race-hating, prejudiced people who tolerate and uphold the murder of one."[76]

Batson's student voice coincided with a protest suggestive of later civil rights activities. About fifty students from the then segregated and all-male Wofford College in Spartanburg assembled the night when the verdict became known.[77] Holding up a sign reading "Was Justice Triumphant?," Charles Crenshaw led the students from the newspaper office in downtown Spartanburg to Morgan Square to condemn the outcome. Not accustomed to this kind of student activism and perhaps responding to critics, some faculty and administrators at the college questioned how to respond to the students. Retired professor and Methodist preacher A. M. Trawick came to the students' defense, and the faculty meeting adjourned without action against them.[78]

In Greenville another kind of protest emerged in the African American community. The confessional statements, which appeared in the press, identified the cab companies from which the lynchers had come. Alert black readers or those who sat in the segregated balcony of the courthouse with the reporters of the national African American press knew as well that some taxi drivers refused to join the lynch party. One of them was U. G. Fowler, the state's lone witness among local taxi drivers against the defendants. His stance later earned him a beating and his picture in *Life* magazine.[79] Yellow, Greenville, Commercial, Blue-bird, and American were the offending cab companies, and they became the targets of a boycott from black riders and any white patrons who chose to honor it. Eventually the companies offered free rides on Sunday to church services for black Greenvillians in an attempt to regain the lost business.

Down in Columbia, civil rights activist Modjeska M. Simkins heard about the Wofford protest, and it became for her one of "three pencils of light" to "penetrate the darkness" of depression after she heard the decision of the Greenville jury. Writing in the *Norfolk Journal and Guide,* Simkins described how "stunned and nauseated" she felt. "I am confident I am not alone in saying that I trust I shall never live through another 24 hours during which my heart could generate so much hate."[80] No South Carolinian at that time participated in such a broad network of social activist organizations as Simkins.[81] Her role in the state NAACP was the most relevant connection to another section of her "Palmetto State" column. There Simkins reported that Thurgood Marshall and Robert L. Carter from the Legal Defense Fund were in Columbia planning the lawsuits against the University of South Carolina School of Law for refusing to admit black applicant John Wrighten of Charleston and against "the 'white supremacy' primary," which George Elmore had undertaken. A cabdriver in Columbia and photographer for John H. McCray's *Lighthouse and Informer* weekly newspaper, Elmore also had direct experience of the Earle lynching. In February, four days prior to filing the eventually successful lawsuit to expand voting rights in the state, he shot the widely reprinted picture for the wire photo of Earle's corpse after facial reconstruction.[82]

Although many of the goals of the civil rights movement would not come to fruition in the state for another two decades, the lynching of Willie Earle touched later activists in the NAACP and PDP such as A. J. Whittenberg in Greenville, who filed the lawsuit for local desegregation of public schools in 1963. Whittenberg had viewed Earle's corpse at the S. C. Franks Funeral Home, but he lived to see the same Judge Martin from the federal bench rule favorably in behalf of his daughter's right to integrated education.[83] On occasion someone from the other side in 1947 switched roles. A defense attorney in the lynching trial, John Bolt Culbertson, became the most visible white member of the NAACP in the state, and he assisted Tessie Earle Robinson to free the civil award legally granted to her family.[84]

Four years after the Earle lynching the state got its first statute criminalizing lynching when Representative Ernest Hollings introduced House Bill 1198 in February 1951.[85] After it won General Assembly approval the governor signed it into law. It defined lynching resulting in death as a first-degree violation and made mob violence not resulting in death a second-degree offense. It set punishments of death or with recommendation of mercy of a penitentiary sentence. A lynch mob in the statute became "the assemblage of two or more persons" unlawfully and with "premeditated purpose . . . and intent" to commit violence on another. Its members could be prosecuted for aiding and abetting "the crime and shall be guilty as principals." The county sheriffs and solicitors were duty bound "to act as speedily as possible to apprehend and identify the members of the mob and bring them to trial." Solicitors were given "summary power to conduct any investigation," including subpoena power and taking of testimony under oath. The new legislation retained the civil liability of members of mobs and of "political subdivisions," a provision still on the books today more than a century after its original enactment (1896) and still defining "exemplary charges of not less than two thousand dollars." In 1962 the code added the Earle case to the "application" section of notes citing the 1949 state supreme court case and settlement.[86]

Along with many other factors, this legislative achievement has served in South Carolina to deter classic spectacle lynchings involving large mobs. Prosecutors still employ the statute to deal with small group violence, including murder, against an individual. Ironically, as a 2003 Associated Press story pointed out, those charged a half century later are more often African American than white Carolinians.[87] In itself, the presence in 1947 of an explicit antilynching statute may not have prevented the killing of Willie Earle. It is clear, however, that the failures in this case confirmed the need for legal principles and constitutional guarantees to triumph over all the rationalizations for lynching. Thereby justice, not revenge, can more nearly be approximated. It is also clear that capital punishment does not necessarily deter violence. Unequal and unfair capital punishment systems cynically encourage new rounds of violence, as the associates of Charles Gilstrap demonstrated. And it is finally clear that a vital democracy depends on the courage of people—like those who defended Earle's right not to be lynched—who are willing to go against the grain.[88]

Notes

1. The Harry Frank Guggenheim Foundation (1988–90) and University of Denver Faculty Research Fund (1982–2001) supported this research. The University of South Carolina's Institute for Southern Studies provided an important residency in the spring of 1985, as did the Hambidge Center for the Arts and Humanities in Rabun Gap, Georgia, in 1992, 1993, and 1996. All taped oral history interviews have required permission according to protocols of the Internal Review Board for the Protection of Human Subjects at the University of Denver. A summary of my project is in my essay "Race, Truth, and Reconciliation: Reflections on Desmond Tutu's Proposal," *Journal of Religion and Society* 3 (2001): 1–20, especially 9–11.

2. Death certificates for Thomas Watson Brown, signed by Dr. Thomas Ross, February 21, 1947 (State File no. 01567); for Willie Earle, signed by Dr. Joseph Converse, February 17, 1947 (State File no. C1568), Greenville County Department of Health.

3. This summary distills accounts in the *Greenville News,* February 18–22 and March 5, 12, and 13, 1947; and the *Greenville Piedmont,* February 17–22 and March 4–5 and 12–13, 1947. The official FBI record includes the summary report compiled by Agent James A. Cannon and signed by Charlotte chief John C. Bills, originally file no. 44–73, obtained through the Freedom of Information Act and listed now as Willie Earle File 44–1565. It took me fifteen years and the efforts of two attorneys to receive the file in unredacted form. *Life,* June 2, 1947, 27–31, claimed that this trial was history-making for the South. On Watt's appointment, see Daniel to Watt, February 27, 1947, in the attorney general's annual report in *Reports and Resolutions of South Carolina to the General Assembly of the State of South Carolina* (Regular Session Commencing January 13, 1948), 1:221–22.

4. Rebecca West, "Opera in Greenville," *New Yorker,* June 14, 1947, 31–65, first reappeared with a new concluding paragraph in her anthology *A Train of Powder* (New York: Viking, 1955), 75–114, which is still in print. Ernest M. Lander Jr. and Robert Ackerman, eds., *Perspectives in South Carolina History: The First 300 Years* (Columbia: University of South Carolina Press, 1973), 361–67, republished parts, and all of "Opera" was reprinted in Christopher Waldrep, ed., *Racial Violence on Trial: A Handbook of Cases, Laws, and Documents* (Santa Barbara, Cal.: ABC-CLIO, 2001), 203–38, and in Jay Mecham, ed., *Voices in Our Blood: America's Best on the Civil Rights Movement* (New York: Random House, 2001), 10–11, 75–101. Waldrep excerpted it and the text of one confessional statement in his *Lynching in America: A History in Documents* (New York: New York University Press, 2006), 249–54.

5. Christopher Waldrep, *The Many Faces of Judge Lynch: Extralegal Violence and Punishment in America* (New York: Palgrave Macmillan, 2002), 174–76, and *Racial Violence,* 85, 94, 104; Kari Frederickson, "'The Slowest State' and 'Most Backward Community': Racial Violence in South Carolina and Federal Civil-Rights Legislation, 1946–48," *South Carolina Historical Magazine* 98 (April 1997): 177–202, and *The Dixiecrat Revolt and the End of the Solid South, 1932–1968* (Chapel Hill: University of North Carolina Press, 2001), 58–65; Bryant Simon, "Race Reactions: African-American Organizing Liberalism and White Working-Class Politics in Post-War South Carolina," in *Jumpin' Jim Crow: Southern Politics from the Civil War to Civil Rights,* ed. Jane Dailey, Glenda Elizabeth Gilmore, and Bryant Simon (Princeton, N.J.: Princeton University Press, 2000), 245–47, 249; John Egerton, *Speak Now against the Day: The Generation before the Civil Rights Movement in the South* (Chapel Hill: University of North Carolina Press, 1995), 371–73; Marshall Frady, *Jesse: The Life and Pilgrimage of Jesse Jackson* (New York: Random House, 1996), 96–97, and Nadine Cohodas, *Strom Thurmond and the Politics of Southern Change* (New York: Simon & Schuster, 1993), 99–100, 111–12, 151, 204, 281, 383. Jack Bass and Marilyn W. Thompson coauthored *Ol'*

Strom: An Unauthorized Biography of Strom Thurmond (Atlanta: Longstreet, 1998), 84–85, 98, and updated it in *Strom: The Complicated Personal and Political Life of Strom Thurmond* (New York: Public Affairs Press, 2005), 82–84, 96, 103. Essie Mae Washington-Williams, with William Stadiem, wrote of the Earle lynching in *Dear Senator: A Memoir of the Daughter of Strom Thurmond* (New York: Regan Books, 2005), 121–28, 189.

6. Archie Vernon Huff, *Greenville: A History of the City and County in the South Carolina Piedmont* (Columbia: University of South Carolina Press, 1995), 399–401; Walter B. Edgar, *South Carolina: A History* (Columbia: University of South Carolina Press, 1998), 518; Piper Peters Aheron, *Images of America: Greenville* (Charleston, S.C.: Arcadia, 1999), 114; Leon F. Litwack, "Hellhounds," in James Allen et al., *Without Sanctuary: Lynching Photography in America* (Santa Fe: Twin Palms, 2000), 32.

7. E. Don Herd, "Lynching in the Upcountry, 1784–1980," in *The South Carolina Upcountry, 1540–1980: Historical and Biographical Sketches* (Greenwood, S.C.: Attic, 1982), 498–546 (Earle lynching, 537–46). Authorities confiscated Herd's negatives.

8. Nancy Roberts, "The Specter of the Slaughter Yards," in *South Carolina Ghosts: From the Coast to the Mountains* (Columbia: University of South Carolina Press, 1983), 81–92, 145–46.

9. William H. Willimon, "Paradise Lost," in *Sighing for Eden: Sin, Evil and the Christian Faith* (Nashville: Abingdon, 1985), 11–15; Nancy Vance Ashmore Cooper, *Greenville: Woven from the Past* (Northridge, Cal.: Windsor, 1986), 157–58, 160–61; Bennie Lee Sinclair, *The Lynching* (New York: Walker, 1992).

10. Dan Hoover, *Greenville News,* March 15, 2003. Having access to the Willie Earle file 44–1565 and its FBI summary report and photos from the Greenville Law Enforcement Center (LEC) file enriched his piece.

11. Larry J. Griffin, Paula Clark, and Joanne C. Sandberg, "Narrative and Event: Lynching and Historical Sociology," in *Under Sentence of Death: Lynchings in the South,* ed. W. Fitzhugh Brundage (Chapel Hill: University of North Carolina Press, 1997), 30–31. Their essay focuses on "historical counterexamples" of prevented lynchings to argue that motivation and behavior are not to be seen as inevitable or the results of forces beyond human choice.

12. S.C. Const. of 1895, art. VI, sec. 6.

13. *Code of Laws of South Carolina 1942* (Clinton, S.C.: Jacobs, 1942): Criminal Code, 1:775–76; Civil Code, 2:700–701. Since Earle's killers made no effort to hide their identities, sec. 1131 (Criminal Code), which forbade "Assault, etc. by masked persons," did not apply. Other sections of the code on the responsibilities of sheriffs and of jailers reinforced the constitutional and legislative norms. The FBI summary report contains a paragraph about agents' interview with Sheriff Mauldin (13) and the signed statement by Jailer Gilstrap (20–24). Elsewhere in the Willie Earle file 44–1565 there is an intraoffice memorandum from J. K. Mumford to D. M. Ladd about the bureau's entrance into the case. It reports the conversation of South Carolina federal attorney Oscar Doyle with Lamar Caudle of the Justice Department that "the jailer immediately turned over the man to the mob upon demand and apparently without any force being exerted, and therefore, in his opinion, it was a clear-cut case for the Bureau." See also telegrams from J. C. Bills to J. Edgar Hoover, February 17, 1947, 8:00 P.M., and February 18, 1947, 4:42 P.M., stating that "indications [that] Jailor and Sheriff had talked matter over prior to interview by agents" and that "attitude of Jailor is believed to be improving and this may reflect improving attitude on part of Sheriff W. H. Mauldin of Pickens." The jailer also had in Pickens County the power "to assist the rural police in the enforcement of the law." Criminal Code, sec. 1960–8, *SC Code 1942,* 1:1082.

14. *SC Code 1942:* Criminal Code on murder (sec. 1101), accessories before and after the fact (sec. 1021–22, 1936–37) and conspiracy (sec. 1380–81), 1:704, 748, 857, and 1070–71.

15. Prosecutors read the confessions at the Greenville coroner's inquest and in the grand jury proceedings. The local press and wire services printed excerpts from the statements. See *Greenville News,* March 12 and 13, 1947; May 14–17, 1947; *Greenville Piedmont,* March 5, 12 and 13, 1947; May 14–17, 1947. The text of each confession is in the FBI summary report and in the Greenville LEC file on the case.

16. The eighteen-page text of Martin's charge to the jury typed on the letterhead of the court reporter for the Thirteenth Circuit is the only surviving item as a transcript from the trial. The general indictment and individual warrants are in the General Sessions Court records of Greenville County at the South Carolina Department of Archives and History, Columbia. Martin's charge is in the Olin D. Johnston Papers, South Carolina Political Collections, University of South Carolina.

17. For Culbertson's earlier involvement in social change, see Egerton, *Speak Now against the Day,* 187, 373.

18. Winchell's national broadcast was on March 2, 1947. See Olin D. Johnston to American Broadcasting Co., April 24, 1947; John T. Madigan, national news editor, American Broadcasting Company, Inc., April 29, 1947, to Johnston; Johnston to John Bolt Culbertson, May 1, 1947, in the Johnston Papers.

19. As soon as his role was official, Watt managed to delay an inquest for Earle until he was updated on what had transpired thus far. See Daniel to Watt, February 27, 1947, cited in note 5. Emmett Walsh, interview with the author, Spartanburg, S.C., December 18, 1982. Early in his own career Walsh was Watt's law clerk. The FBI was aware of Ashmore's timidity concerning the case, as Bills put it to Hoover in an office memorandum on May 10, 1947 (Willie Earle file 44–1565), just before the trial began: "It has been apparent that the State Solicitor was not going to prosecute this matter aggressively. . . . Mr. ASHMORE apparently has been trying to feel the public pulse in each move he has made in connection with the prosecution."

20. On November 16, 1933, Klansmen broke into George Green's rented house in Taylors and shot and killed the aging black tenant farmer. A Klan meeting room operated openly in Greenville at the time, where members held "court" to decide on night-riding activity. The owner of the rental house, C. F. James, allegedly asked Andrew Monk to get the Klan to force Green to move, even though the tenant's contract ran until the first of the next year. State constable Fred Newman took statements from the two defendants, who became state's witnesses, but their testimonies were not admitted as evidence. See Tuskegee University Lynching Clippings file for South Carolina (1933); *Greenville News,* November 18, 20–21, 23–24, 28, 30, 1933; December 1–2, 6–8, 1933; November 3–4, 1934; and *Green v. Greenville County,* no. 14088, 180 S.E. 471 (S.C. Sup. Ct. 1935).

21. *Greenville Piedmont,* February 26, 1947; *Greenville News,* February 28, 1947. The two Liberty cabdrivers he told were Eugene Durham and Cleo Garrett (FBI summary report, 139–40, 208–9). Gravely claimed that he did not come to Greenville explicitly to inform the cabdrivers but to bring back to the city a girlfriend named Teat (the names Jackie and Katie both occur in the summary report). He said that he did not want that information shared with his wife. "After considerable questioning," Gravely admitted to state constable Bill Gaines, FBI agent P. B. Beachum, and Sheriff Mauldin what he did but denied other rumors: that if he had only known what Earle had done he would have taken him to Greenville right away in his "fast" Chevrolet before officers could arrest his passenger or that he informed the mob planning the lynching where he could be reached to join them. On Ashmore's

decision to release Gravely, see J. C. Bills to J. Edgar Hoover, March 17, 1947, Willie Earle file 44–1565.

22. "The Taxi-cab Lynching: Mob Law, State Law, and National Law, or How 32 White Men Got Away with Murdering One Black Man in 1947," paper for "The Civil Rights Movement in South Carolina" conference at the Citadel, March 2003. He discloses the failed federal effort to reopen the case after the acquittals in May, not by retrying the same defendants on grounds of violation of Earle's civil rights but by focusing on Gilstrap's "inaction." Though Waldrep does not discuss it, two of the defendants, Perry Murrell and Walter Towers Crawford, received a six-month penitentiary sentence each for having admitted being at the scene of a crime while on federal parole. *Greenville News,* June 7, 1947, and July 2, 1947.

23. After interviewing Gilstrap and his wife in May, Rebecca West quoted what he said to the local press back in February and sympathetically retold his story in "Opera in Greenville," *New Yorker,* 34–35. Just before the lynching trial three prisoners, while trying to escape, hit Gilstrap over the head with a yard-long pipe. Carrying a pistol after being criticized for not being armed in February, he shot and killed one—Albert Finley. *Pickens Sentinel,* May 8, 1947, and June 5, 1947. When he testified in the lynching trial, therefore, he bore the marks of this attack and thus reinforced his public persona of holding a dangerous job. His behavior contrasts radically with the tragic heroism of Sheriff J. L. Thomas seventeen years earlier in neighboring Oconee County. On April 24, 1930, he was overpowered by a mob apparently led by the mayor of the town of Walhalla and its night policeman. The lawman suffered a fractured skull when he refused to turn over his pistol in trying to protect Allen Green. A paroled black convict and formerly a hero for having saved Walhalla's buildings during a fire, Green was held on a false charge of rape. His death by the mob was a gruesome spectacle lynching. See Tuskegee University Lynching Clipping files for South Carolina (1930) and Arthur Raper, *The Tragedy of Lynching* (1933; rpt., Montclair, N.J.: Patterson Smith, 1969), 261–85.

24. S.C. Const. of 1895, art. VI, sec. 6.

25. *Anderson Independent,* March 2, 1947. Robert Ashmore, interviews with the author, Greenville, December 22, 1982, and November 11, 1988. He did not recall Cary Gravely's connection to the case or his relation to the jailer, but he vividly remembered the threats that he and his family received for his role. The post–World War II context in southern race relations, it is important to note, featured "an epidemic of random murder and mayhem [which] was sweeping like a fever through the region." There were frequent atrocities against African Americans. See Egerton, *Speak Now against the Day,* 359–75.

26. Forrester (misidentified as Malford and Winfred in the FBI summary report) and Maxwell were vulnerable to the same charges of inaction as were under consideration for the Pickens sheriff and jailer. The duty of deputies in the state code (sec. 3492) to patrol the county "to prevent or detect crime" was clear. Among a dozen examples of what to monitor is listed "lynching." *SC Code 1942,* 2:858. Neither Forrrester nor Maxwell officially participated in the arrests, while one city policeman, L. E. Duncan, adamantly refused to work the investigation. Erwin Hosteltler (Irving Woodrow Hosteller in the report) was the intoxicated cabdriver. FBI summary report, 34, 37, 39; J. C. Bills, telegrams to J. Edgar Hoover, February 19, 20, 1947; Bills, memorandum to Hoover, March 17, 1947; Hoover, memoranda to Lamar Caudle, February 19, 20, 24, 1947; J. K. Munford to D. M. Ladd, February 20, 1947, in Willie Earle file 44–1565.

27. *Pickens Sentinel,* February 20, 1947. Manuel Rogers called the decision a "posthumous charge of murder" in *Greenville News,* February 19, 1947. See also *Greenville Piedmont,* February 19, 1947. Minutes of the County Coroner, State of South Carolina, County of Pickens, book 4, 331–34, recorded on February 20, 1947, at the Pickens County Courthouse. The

coroner's jury was made up of a Jewish businessman from Pickens, Herman Sperling; two other Pickens city residents, Ted R. Morrison and W. I. Irwin; and three county residents, Hugh Ellenberg, E. C. Porter, and Taylor Batson.

28. *Anderson Independent,* February 19, 1947. Pickens Jail Book records show Earle's arrest on February 16, with an entry that he had been released on February 17 shown to me on August 20, 1984, by Sheriff David Stone in the Pickens County Law Enforcement Center. It is not clear why Merck and Garrett in arresting Earle in December 1944 put up bond for him or what the charge was against him (Jail Book, 156). In Greenville Earle had two arrests in 1946, March 6 and September 16, for damage to property and drunkenness. Greenville LEC file 13948. I can find no record to confirm West's charge in "Opera" (34) that Earle had served time in a penitentiary for having assaulted a supervisor on a job.

29. The South Carolina statute about that potential liability was cited in a notice inserted in *Anderson Independent,* February 18, 1947—the morning before the afternoon hearing. On the role of the coroner in 1947, which included the power to replace or arrest the sheriff, to issue warrants and have the sheriff hold persons in the coroner's custody, to enforce dueling and gaming laws, and to hold inquests over the dead, see *SC Code 1942:* Code of Criminal Procedure, 1:734–42; Civil Code, 1:887–90 and 2:854; Criminal Code, 1:1074. Either the Pickens or Greenville coroner could have done Brown's inquest, under sec. 1020 of the Code of Criminal Procedure, *SC Code 1942,* 1:703–4. During the May trial defense attorney Wofford mistakenly claimed that coroner J. O. Turner was legally required to hold the hearing on Brown's death in Greenville County. See *Greenville News,* May 13, 1947.

30. *Greenville News,* February 19, 1947.

31. FBI summary report in Willie Earle file 44–1565: 41, 45, 54, 67, 72, 75, 80–81, 86, 99, 107, 113, 126, 131, 134.

32. Ibid., 86, 108, 121, 134.

33. John H. McCray to Brim Rykard, May 29, 1947, John H. McCray Papers, South Caroliniana Library, University of South Carolina. McCray and state NAACP president James M. Hinton had come to Pickens and Greenville on Tuesday, February 18, to meet with Tessie Earle. There were reports in the press that Earle was epileptic, and members of his family, including his mother, confirmed to me that he was taking medication for the condition.

34. Minutes of Pickens County Coroner, inquest for Brown; *Greenville News,* February 19, 1947; *Greenville Piedmont,* February 19, 1947; *Pickens Sentinel,* February 20, 1947. The arresting officers who testified at the coroner's hearing said that Brown gave a description that they believed fit Earle but that he did not name Earle or otherwise identify him. Garrett and Merck admitted that Earle denied stabbing Brown. Greenville investigating officers who interviewed Brown in the hospital reported his attacker as being "a large black negro," which did not fit his death certificate or the Greenville City Police Record on Earle (Greenville LEC file 13948) from the two 1946 arrests, where he was listed as 5'9" and weighing 150 pounds. Dan Hoover uses the "large black negro" description of Earle in his article, *Greenville News,* March 15, 2003. See report of officers R. R. Dunn and J. R. Duncan, Greenville LEC files, serial no. 47-OJ-61, February 15, 1947, at 11:45 P.M., which also records only a single fare for Brown originating in Greenville.

35. Her account of his saying that he came by bus is in *Atlanta Daily World,* February 28, 1947, and Sheriff Mauldin told the press that Earle had made the same claim to him, *Anderson Independent,* February 18, 1947; *Greenville News,* February 18, 1947. Earle's mother in December 1982 remembered that the bus stopped in Liberty that Saturday and that when she got home from work at a local restaurant, Willie said he had come on it. See Gravely, "Reliving South Carolina's Last Lynching: The Witness of Tessie Earle Robinson," *South Carolina Review* 29 (Spring 1997): 4–17.

36. David Redekop, "The Lynching of Willie Earle" (master's thesis, Clemson University, 1987), 37n77.

37. Paraphrasing an editorial in the *Pickens Sentinel,* May 29, 1947.

38. See Robinson's statement in the FBI summary file (where his name is spelled *Robertson;* 29–30) and Gilstrap's statement (22) reporting that he told the lynchers that Robinson had nothing to do with Brown's stabbing but had been in jail for a bad check charge. Willie Earle file 44–1565.

39. Early in the May trial, a state highway patrolman, M. J. Floyd, slapped a twenty-six-year-old, black truck driver, Woodrow Drummonds, whose truck had grazed the fender of Floyd's patrol car. Blacks and whites lined opposite sides of the driveway where the accident occurred, but ten white men offered to be witnesses for Drummonds, and a juvenile court judge, Richard Foster, assisted him in filing charges to end the fray. In the interest of "community welfare" the driver later withdrew charges. *Pittsburgh Courier,* May 17, 1947. Also while the Greenville trial was in session Pickens deputy Wayne Garrett shot and killed a thirty-five-year-old African American named Simpson who had set some woodland on fire in the Ruhamah community near Liberty. It is not clear what provoked Simpson to engage in arson, but he apparently threatened Garrett with a knife when the officer sought to arrest him. See the *Pickens Sentinel,* May 22, 1947, where Simpson's first name was given as Furman, while the *Greenville News* account (May 17, 1947) called him James Simpson. Hendrix Rector, one of the freed defendants, was arrested June 3 for harassing a carload of four black Greenvillians by shooting the car's spare tire. *Greenville News,* June 7, 11, 1947.

40. Bills's statement is in *Greenville Piedmont,* February 28, 1947. Thurmond to Sheriff W. H. Mauldin, February 28, 1947, carbon copy of original in Gubernatorial Papers, J. Strom Thurmond Papers, Clemson University. At a press conference on February 25, Thurmond had made a point to offer condolences to Mrs. Thomas Watson Brown, saying, "I would have been just as zealous to bring to the bar of justice the man who killed Brown, as I am to bring to justice the men who lynched Earle. I am against lawlessness of any sort." *Greenville Piedmont,* February 26, 1947. He apparently offered no public or private sympathy to Tessie Earle.

41. *Greenville Piedmont,* February 17, 1947. This double-edged statement is somewhat different from the interview the FBI summarized with Mauldin, in which he is reported to have said that "no suspicion of mob action entered his mind." FBI summary report, page 13, in Willie Earle File 44–1565. The jailer, however, did anticipate the possibility of a lynching attempt, according to Pickens night watchman Ben Looper. He remembered such a hypothetical discussion down at the jail that Sunday evening. Gilstrap first called Looper rather than his superior, Mauldin, to report the abduction. Looper conversation with Will Gravely, Pickens, September 7, 1999.

42. Waldrep, *Judge Lynch,* 109–10, 138.

43. South Carolina's law for the capital crime of rape was based in the S.C. Constitution, art. III, sec. 33, and in the Criminal Code (sec. 1109–10). There was provision to suspend execution with a recommendation by the jury for mercy and have the sentence reduced to penitentiary incarceration. A separate section (1111) titled "Carnal Knowledge of Woman Child" defined the age of consent and provided that if the child was over the age of ten a jury might also alter the punishment to a penitentiary sentence. SC *Code 1942,* 1:765–77. In a conversation with me in July 1981 the late John McCravy of Easley, former state legislator and local historian, cited Gilstrap's case to illustrate the unfair pardon and parole policies of Governor Ransome J. Williams's administration.

44. Stinney's story is the subject of David Stout's novel *Carolina Skeletons* (New York: Mysterious Press, 1988), which became a made-for-television film; see also the *State,* June 23, 1944.

45. *Greenville News*, February 5–6, 1944; March 14, 17–18, 1944; April 30, 1944; May 1–3, 1944; June 17, 1944; February 10, 1945; *State*, February 10, 1945; *Pickens Sentinel*, February 15, 1945; *State v. Gilstrap*, case no. 2542, S.C. Sup. Ct. 15690 (1944), 412–23, at South Carolina Department of Archives and History, case file *State v. Gilstrap*. Bull remembered his statement to the jury in different terms: "Gentlemen, in my opinion, if this were a negro I don't believe the jury would be out long, fifteen or twenty minutes, in arriving at a just verdict in this case."

46. On the move in several states to make rape a capital crime in order "to forestall 'lynching,'" see Waldrep, *Judge Lynch*, 152. One Greenville county example fifteen months earlier in Travelers Rest moved in less than ninety days from incident—a rape on September 26—to African American George Carter's execution on December 14, 1945. *Greenville News*, September 27, 1945; October 20, 31, 1945; November 1, 1945; December 15, 1945.

47. The site for Earle's murder was near a slaughterhouse, the B. P. Crenshaw Packing Company plant, near where Mrs. James Horace Arial and her husband rented "a two room house on the old Railroad cut." She heard the shotgun blasts that killed Earle. The FBI was curious why J. Robert Martin (the agents did not specify whether it was the senior Martin, who was also an attorney, or the judge) had visited his renter to ask what she knew about the case, but she said to him what she later told J. D. Bigham of the Greenville City Police and FBI agents J. M. Cole and Fred R. Mackenzie on February 18. See FBI summary report, page 15, in Willie Earle file 44–1565, and Greenville LEC File, Crime Master Sheet, Case No. 1650 (unnumbered item 15), Serial No. 47–130, signed by Bigham three weeks later, on March 12, 1947.

48. See papers of Judge J. Robert Martin Jr., South Carolina Legal History Collection, University of South Carolina Law School.

49. Gilstrap's obituary is in the *Pickens Sentinel*, February 15, 1945. Grace Norris, wife of one of the 1947 defendants, attended the funeral, at which drivers for the Bluebird and the Commercial Cab companies were honorary pallbearers. She described the corpse in a telephone conversation on December 14, 1989.

50. Strom Thurmond to Sheriff Chester Fleming, Abbeville, S.C., March 6, 1947, carbon copy in the Thurmond Papers. Note at the bottom: "This letter was sent to all sheriffs in South Carolina" alphabetically by county.

51. *Greenville News*, June 8, 1947.

52. See his letter dated May 28 to Arthur E. Kelly of Columbia in the Thurmond Papers. "I cannot influence juries to convict, but I can continue to investigate and apprehend those suspected. This I intend to do." That spring, however, Thurmond was mending fences with the white electorate by visiting the upstate twice. He spoke twice on May 5, a week before the trial opened, first at the church where Brown's funeral had been held in Greenville and then at Fairview Church in Pickens County. At the end of May he gave the Liberty High School commencement address to one thousand people. *Pickens Sentinel*, May 8, 1947; *Greenville News*, May 3, 1947; *Anderson Independent*, May 29, 1947; and Rev. Earl Paulk, pastor of Brown's church, to Thurmond, May 7, 1947, Thurmond Papers.

53. Senator Thurmond's reply, April 24, 1964, to my letter urging him to vote for the Civil Rights Bill of 1964 listed what he thought were his progressive moves. Then he wrote: "You may also recall that I prosecuted a number of cab drivers for the lynching of a young Negro named Earle. I was much criticized for this action, but I felt that justice should be administered." Letters in possession of the author.

54. See papers in the Judge of Probate Office in Pickens County under Willie Earle's estate, and Lewis's order in Pickens County Court of Common Pleas, December 21, 1956. The state supreme court case is *Earle v. Greenville County*, 215 SC539, 54 SE2d 348 (1949),

along with printed versions in the South Carolina Supreme Court Library of the Transcript of Record: Appeal from Greenville County Argument of J. D. Todd Jr. and Argument of Julien D. Wyatt, and Memorandum on Behalf of Respondent. *Greenville News,* March 25, 1948; February 2, 1949; April 1, 29, 1949; May 7, 1949; October 2, 15, 1949; November 13, 1949. There is a collection of relevant papers beginning with a retainer agreement of September 6, 1947, between Tessie Earle and the Legal Defense Fund and running through January 7, 1952, in the NAACP Papers, Library of Congress.

55. Frederick Philbrick, *Language and the Law: The Semantics of Forensic English,* 2nd printing (New York: Macmillan, 1950), 19–21. In a third printing in 1951 University of Chicago Professor Philbrick revised the paragraph referring to Gilstrap and reissued the book. *Greenville News,* April 8, 1950. *Gilstrap v. Macmillan,* Civil Action no. 2486 in the U.S. District Court for the Eastern District of South Carolina, Columbia, Division, April 7, 1950; May 22, 29, 1950; January 9, 1951. On racial references as libel, see *West's South Carolina Digest 1783 to Date,* vol. 13 (St. Paul, Minn.: West, 1950), 118.

56. Hubert Golden Wardlaw, February 22, 1947; L. E. M. Freeman, February 22, 1947; Capers Satterlee, "An Open Letter to Governor Thurmond," March 4, 1947, and follow-up letter, March 10, 1947, all to Strom Thurmond, Thurmond Papers.

57. Sarah H. Pressly, May 26, 1947; James A. McElroy, February 25, 1947; Frank P. Anderson, May 22, 1947; Alma Metcalfe, February 19, 1947; Marjorie Patterson, May 26, 1947; Elizabeth I. Brown, March 6, 1947; Laura Smith Ebaugh, June 3, 1947; Edward A. McDowell, May 23, 1947, all to Strom Thurmond, Thurmond Papers.

58. J. Owen Smith, March 11, 1947; Louise B. Wykes, February 25, 1947; Claude R. Harper, February 19, 1947, all to Strom Thurmond, Thurmond Papers.

59. In correspondence in the Thomas Wofford scrapbook, privately held, the Thurmond Papers at Clemson, and the President's Committee on Civil Rights at the Harry S. Truman Presidential Library there are numerous examples of anti-Semitism often tied to antiblack racism triggered by the Earle case.

60. Gennie Seideman to Strom Thurmond, February 17, 1947, Thurmond Papers.

61. Osceola E. McKaine to Strom Thurmond, March 12, 1947, Thurmond Papers. See Miles S. Richards, "The Eminent Lieutenant McKaine," *Carologue: Bulletin of the South Carolina Historical Society* 7 (Autumn 1991): 6–7, 14–17.

62. J. M. Hinton, February 17, 1947; Levi G. Byrd, February 18, 1947; Opal Kelly Hesse, July 7, 1947; Margaret Keith, May 5, 1947, all to Strom Thurmond, Thurmond Papers.

63. Telegram from ACLU, New York, February 19, 1947, to Strom Thurmond; R. B. Herbert to Strom Thurmond, February 22, 1947, enclosing carbon of Herbert to Arthur Garfield Hays, February 22, 1947, Thurmond Papers.

64. Gurtie Floyd for the Business and Professional Women's Club to the *Greenville News* and the *Greenville Piedmont,* April 17, 1947, with copies to Strom Thurmond, Police Chief J. H. Jennings, Sheriff R. H. Bearden, Chief Joel Townsend (of the State Constabulary), John Bills (FBI), Solicitor Robert Ashmore, Solicitor Sam Watt, Thurmond Papers.

65. Negro Teachers of Pickens County, February 25, 1947; S. A. Tinkler of York A. R. Presbyterian Church, February 26, 1947; W. E. Richardson and H. P. Billups for the Ministerial Alliance of Marion, Mullins, and Latta, March 6, 1947; C. B. Freeman and twenty-two others for the Baptist Ministers Union of Columbia and Richland County, February 18, 1947, all to Strom Thurmond, Thurmond Papers.

66. J. B. Finley, February 17, 1947; John B. Isom, February 18, 1947; telegram from L. E. McGurty, Local 15 FTA CIO Charleston, February 21, 1947; Franz E. Daniel of the Textile Workers Union of America, February 24, 1947, all to Strom Thurmond, Thurmond Papers. Isom's sermon "They Lynched Him," preached at Saxon Baptist the evening of February 23,

1947, is in the private possession of Mary-Elizabeth Isom of Tucson, Arizona. The bulletin of the church for that service is in the James M. Dabbs Papers, South Caroliniana Library, University of South Carolina. An excellent study of union activism in the area, including the role of Saxon Baptist Church, is G. C. Waldrep III's *Southern Workers and the Search for Community: Spartanburg County, South Carolina* (Urbana: University of Illinois Press, 2000).

67. The executive director of the SRC, Guy B. Johnson, wrote a supportive letter to Thurmond, March 11, 1947, in which he also explained the mission of the interracial organization. It and South Carolina division chairman Marion A. Wright's letter of February 22, 1947, to Strom Thurmond are in the Thurmond Papers.

68. A carbon copy of the resolutions of the Richland County committee of the SRC, no date but received by the governor's office on March 31, 1947, is in the Thurmond Papers. The document is signed by F. Clyde Helms, a Baptist pastor and social activist; Rabbi Sidney Ballon; R. Beverley Herbert; Mrs. H. H. Hickman; and Modjeska Simkins. On Helms, see Egerton, *Speak Now against the Day*, 186.

69. J. M. Dabbs to Thurmond, February 22, 1947, Thurmond Papers. See Thomas L. Johnson, "James McBride Dabbs: A Life Story" (Ph.D. dissertation, University of South Carolina, 1980).

70. Gary Hiott Sr., "Does a Man-Made Boundary Remove a Responsibility?," *Pickens Sentinel*, February 20, 1947; February 27, 1947.

71. See Gravely, ed., "'. . . A Man Lynched in Inhuman Lawlessness': South Carolina Methodist Hawley Lynn Condemns the Killing of Willie Earle (1947)," *Methodist History* 35 (January 1997): 71–80.

72. Hawley Lynn, interview with the author, Easley, S.C., June 28, 1983; W. Marvin Gravely, interview with the author, Pickens, S.C., February 16, 1987; F. G. Lindsay, conversation with the author, Over-55 Club, Pickens, S.C., June 28, 1989.

73. *Greenville News*, February 18, 1947; *Anderson Independent*, February 19, 1947; *Pickens Sentinel*, February 20, 1947.

74. *Southern Christian Advocate*, March 6, 1947; *Pickens Sentinel*, March 27, 1947. Lynn republished the sermon under its subtitle in the *Pulpit*, February 1950, 28–30.

75. Lynn interview; Lynn to Judge Robert J. [J. Robert] Martin Jr., May 8, 1947, in the Martin Papers. A contribution envelope for the cabdrivers' defense fund is in the Greenville LEC files.

76. Gary Hiott Sr., "Civilization Has a Long Way to Go," *Pickens Sentinel*, May 29, 1947. Talk in possession of Dr. Lloyd Batson of Easley, with typed copy of the text provided to the author.

77. The *Pittsburgh Courier* account, May 31, 1947, claimed that the students met Watt when he returned after his defeat in the Greenville trial. See *Spartanburg Herald*, May 22, 1947; *Southern Christian Advocate*, May 29, 1947. In publicizing the protest columnist John Temple Graves stated, "The opinion of South Carolina is represented by the marchers at Spartanburg." *Charleston News and Courier*, May 28, 1947.

78. Charles Crenshaw, conversation with the author, Atlanta, November 5, 1988. Professor Lewis Jones, who was at the faculty meeting, recollected the Trawick story to the author on December 7, 1982.

79. Fowler's picture was in *Life*, June 2, 1947, 28. The African American reporters were John H. McCray of Columbia, A. M. Rivera from North Carolina for the *Pittsburgh Courier*, and Albert Hinton for the *Norfolk Journal and Guide*.

80. Modjeska Simkins, *Norfolk Journal and Guide*, May 31, 1947.

81. Besides being state conference secretary for the NAACP, Simkins was on the board of directors of the Southern Conference of Human Welfare and its successor organization, the

Southern Conference Education Fund; the key organizer of the Southern Negro Youth Congress convention in Columbia; an activist with the United Negro and Allied Veterans of America and in the SRC; and a liaison for the Civil Rights Congress. She was also associate editor of McCray's *Lighthouse and Informer* weekly and a correspondent for the Associated Negro Press organization. See Barbara Woods Aba-Mecha, "Black Woman Activist in Twentieth Century South Carolina: Modjeska Monteith Simkins" (Ph.D. thesis, Emory University, 1978); Frank T. Adams, *James A. Dombroski: An American Heretic, 1897–1983* (Knoxville: University of Tennessee Press, 1992), 176, 196–201; and Egerton, *Speak Now against the Day,* 228, 428, 440.

82. John H. McCray, interview with the author, Talladega, Ala., June 10, 1983. On *Elmore v. Rice,* see Aba-Mecha, "Black Woman Activist," 197–207. Elmore's photo of Earle's corpse in the McCray papers appeared in several newspapers, for example, the *Baltimore Afro-American,* May 24, 1947. The Wrighten case led to a separate law school at South Carolina State; see Cohodas, *Strom Thurmond,* 104–5, 112–14, 123.

83. Whittenberg interview, 1982; *Greenville Piedmont,* March 15, 16, 1972.

84. Culbertson's conversion to NAACP activism occurred after Ernest Stokes, one of the defendants from 1947, physically attacked him at a political rally in 1950 in Travelers Rest. He had received threatening phone calls for having voted his progressive conscience when he was in the state legislature. See letters to the NAACP office in New York beginning June 1953, particularly the carbon copy of a letter for Greenville sheriff R. V. Chandler, March 17, 1954, sent to U.S. Attorney General Herbert Brownell and copied to NAACP leader Walter White, describing Stokes's assault, in the NAACP Papers. On Culbertson's help to Tessie Earle Robinson, see *Greenville Piedmont,* March 16, 1972.

85. An Associated Press story emphasized Hollings's motive as a states' rights move, while a United Press story quoted his goal as "to call a lynching what it is." See *Montgomery Advertiser,* March 15, 1951; *Atlanta Constitution,* March 15, 1951, both from the Tuskegee University Lynching files. Eighty-ninth South Carolina General Assembly, 1st sess., 1951, *Journal of the House of Representatives* (N.p.: State Budget and Control Board, n.d.), 389, 488, 525, 540–42, 555, 1354; *Journal of the Senate* (N.p.: Joint Committee on Printing, General Assembly of South Carolina, n.d.), 356, 916, 954, 995, 1153.

86. South Carolina General Assembly, *Acts and Joint Resolutions, Regular Session of 1951. Statutes at Large,* vol. 47, pt. 1 (N.p.: Joint Committee on Printing, General Assembly of South Carolina, n.d.), nos. 166, 233–34; *Code of Laws of South Carolina 1952* (Charlottesville: Michie, 1952), 2:750–51 (art. 2. sec. 16–57, 16–58, 16–59). See *Code of Laws of South Carolina 1976, Annotated* (Rochester, N.Y.: Lawyers Co-operative, 1976), 7:808–10 (art. III, sec. 15–51–210. Liability of a County for Lynching).

87. For an abridged version of AP writer Allen Breed's story, which ran nationally, see the *Denver Post,* May 18, 2003. Tracing definitions of lynching from the Revolutionary era, when both Charles Lynch and William Lynch of Virginia were associated with the term's origins, down to the Clarence Thomas confirmation hearings, Waldrep argues that one must be precise about what the term means in a particular historical period. On Revolutionary War veteran and emigrant from Virginia William Lynch (1742–1820), who is buried in upper Pickens County, see Waldrep, *Judge Lynch,* 19–22, 25, 197nn40–41.

88. Anthony Dunbar's book on white southern activists captures such courage. See *Against the Grain: Southern Radicals and Prophets, 1929–1959* (Charlottesville: University Press of Virginia, 1981).

This Magic Moment

When the Ku Klux Klan Tried to Kill Rhythm
and Blues Music in South Carolina

FRANK BEACHAM

The old saying goes that when Billie Holiday sang on the outdoor patio at Charlie's Place, the pine trees above—fanned by a gentle ocean breeze—whispered along with the music. To this day, that patch of trees on Carver Street is called Whispering Pines.[1]

Whispering Pines

Whispering Pines is on "the Hill," a black neighborhood only a stone's throw from the noisy, neon-lit oceanfront pavilion and amusement park that now dominates the tourist district in Myrtle Beach. Yet, as I drive down this modest street, with its scattered homes and businesses, there's little to reveal an illustrious past when hundreds of music lovers came to hear the likes of Louis Jordan, Billy Eckstein, Count Basie, Ray Charles, Duke Ellington, Lena Horne, and virtually every significant "race music" artist of the 1940s and 1950s.

Charlie's Place at Whispering Pines was run by Charlie Fitzgerald, a stylish black entrepreneur who, from the late 1930s until his death in 1955, operated nightclubs, a motel, a cab company, and—according to some—the beach resort's most notorious brothel. I had been gradually introduced to the Fitzgerald legend in a series of informal interviews I conducted with dancers credited with inventing the shag. All were on the Carolina beaches in the years following World War II, and I wanted them to tell me how the dance was created. As Harry Driver, George Lineberry, Betty Kirkpatrick, Chick Hedrick, Billy Jeffers, and others independently told their stories, the name Charlie Fitzgerald repeatedly came up. One by one, the dancers cited Fitzgerald as a significant cultural influence in the post–World War II years. His name was always spoken with reverence, mystery, and a sense of awe. It was as if Charlie's old nightclub had been some kind of secret hideout that held the keys to a forbidden world. And each of these dancers, through good fortune, had gained admission.

There is no mention of Charlie Fitzgerald's name in South Carolina's modern history books. His contribution to his state's music and dance has been ignored, and now, more than fifty years after his death, he is essentially a forgotten figure. To learn his story an outsider needs to ask a fast-dwindling group of friends who still live and work in the old neighborhood and a handful of music lovers—both black and white—who visited his club as teenagers. One dancer suggested I talk with Dino Thompson, a beach music lover and lifelong restaurateur who had hung out at Charlie's Place as a kid. I found him at Cagney's Old Place, his restaurant on the highway 17 tourist strip in Myrtle Beach. "Charlie was one slick dude. He had an aura about him. He could have been the doorman at the Cotton Club," Thompson told me as he warmed to old memories. He had visited Charlie's Place as a youngster to hear musicians he could find nowhere else. "In 1952, Little Richard came to the Hill. He wasn't allowed to sing in the white clubs here. I begged my father to let the cook and two dishwashers in our restaurant take me. They sat me right up on the stage and I saw Little Richard in his blue suede shoes."

Dino Thompson was not the only southern white kid who pined to hear black performers. In segregated South Carolina, where a prominent local radio station proudly advertised that it played "no jungle music," the provocative and sometimes raunchy mix of black gospel, jazz, and blues was taboo. Labeled "race

6. *Impresarios of the shag: Charlie Fitzgerald (second from right) and the staff of Charlie's Place. Photograph* © *Jack Thompson*

music," it was forbidden fruit that was rarely heard on mainstream southern radio stations or sold in local record stores. By 1950, however, the genie was beginning to come out of the bottle. A young *Billboard* magazine writer, Jerry Wexler (later to head Atlantic Records), published an article arguing that race music was more aptly called "rhythm and blues." The name stuck.

When WLAC, a 50,000-watt AM radio station in Nashville, switched to a black R&B format each night, it started reaching many white teenagers throughout the South. Disc jockeys Gene Nobles and John R became the first major links connecting black music to a white southern audience. In fact, John R was a white South Carolinian and former actor who used his deep voice and hepcat banter to convince many in the listening audience that he was a black man. To facilitate the distribution of the hard-to-find black music, one of WLAC's savvy sponsors, Randy's Record Shop of Gallatin, Tennessee, sold it via mail order, delivering the disks to white customers in discreet, unmarked packages.

Randy's modern-day equivalent is Marion Carter, a white fan of black music who grew up to become one of South Carolina's top R&B record promoters. I spent half a day driving through remote countryside to his Repete Records operation in the tiny South Carolina town of Elliott. From a barnlike structure that seems more likely to house a small farming operation, Carter's employees ship hundreds of R&B recordings to music lovers and record stores each day. "This was the devil's music—you just didn't listen to it in the average white southern home," Carter told me. "White teenagers like myself were relegated to sneaking around to hear the music. We'd listen to WLAC at night out in the car or hide a portable radio under our pillow. What I have found as I've grown up and talked to people is there were tens of thousands of us all doing the very same thing in order to hear this music."

At the Myrtle Beach Pavilion, less than half a mile from Charlie's Place, white nightlife—as it was in other towns throughout the United States—was centered around the jitterbug, a strenuous, acrobatic dance usually performed to quick-tempo swing or jazz. The dance supported a subculture of fashionable, young, creative dancers known as "jitterbugs." The men were instantly recognized by their long, blonde, peroxided hair and custom-tailored, draped peg pants, T-shirts, penny loafers, and swirling gold chains. The women, favoring a simpler look, wore pedal pushers, angora sweaters, and flowing scarves. These dance floor elites ruled beach society in the years following World War II.

By eight o'clock on most summer nights, hundreds of tourists gathered around the balconies and dance floor at the Pavilion. The star jitterbugs—known to the crowd by such names as Rubber Legs, Chicken, Bunk, the Roach, and Little Robin—appeared one by one to show off their latest moves. Just as the streets in the Old West cleared when a known gunslinger appeared, the dance floor emptied for the kings and queens of the night.

One of the undisputed greats was Leon Williams, who was nicknamed "Rubber Legs" after he perfected a technique where he crossed his legs while standing and then began rocking from side to side, eventually sliding into a squat. "He was like a snake on the dance floor," an admirer proudly told me. "Nobody did it but Leon." What few in the white Pavilion crowd realized was that Williams, along with a handful of other dancers on the beach, was adapting the jitterbug with tricks picked up from the black dancers in clubs such as Charlie's Place. "The black dancers had a huge influence on us. They had rhythm and they interpreted the music," recalled Williams. "It still fascinates me how they felt the music so well."

Though Williams and his fellow dancers lived in a racially segregated community, they ignored the repeated warnings against associating with blacks that came from South Carolina's political and social establishment. "The colored girls danced with white boys and the colored boys danced with white girls," said Williams. "We hugged each other's neck. If you had been at the beach in that period of time you'd thought segregation didn't exist." The white dancers' fascination with black music and culture even extended beyond the nightclubs. "We used to go to colored churches on Sunday because we loved the gospel music," said Williams. "We wanted to hear our friends clap their hands and sing. They really got into it and that impressed me. We realized early on that you can dance to gospel music."

Partially due to the passion of another talented young dancer, George Lineberry, R&B was finding its way onto the jukeboxes in the white dance halls and pavilions along the Carolina coast. "Big George," as he was nicknamed, installed records on the coin-operated machines for a local amusements company. He took it upon himself to move the most popular records from the jukeboxes in the black clubs, including Charlie's Place, to the white dance halls. Big George, who died in 1999, was an immensely popular fixture at the beach and was often slipped a few bucks by concerned parents to dance with a daughter who needed a boost in self-esteem. With great ceremony, he made it a point to "test" each new record installation with a personal spin on the dance floor. In South Carolina the R&B that could be heard only at the beach joints became known as "beach music."

In the 1940s young dancers found the beaches a liberating place. For many it was the first time in their lives that they were in a community where no one knew them or their family. "There was a special freedom in that," disc jockey John Hook mused one night as he spun records at a crowded beach dance club. "That meant they could let it hang loose and do stuff they'd never dare do at home." This precious anonymity, Hook shouted over the club's roaring decibel level, also gave the young white men and women a chance to escape the pressures of a segregated society and to emulate what they liked best about their contemporaries in the black community. "There was a certain sensuality, a certain

7. A "magic moment": Leon "Rubber Legs" Williams and partner on the
Grand Strand. Photograph © Jack Thompson

sexuality that put it all out on the edge," he said. "The guys knew when they went out on the dance floor that a hundred women were watching them right at that moment and that each would give anything to be their partner. Man, that's some heady, heady power. Imagine the confidence that produces in you. Imagine what happens to your body when you know—you absolutely know for sure—that you're gonna score tonight." The best of the young male dancers, said Hook, concentrated on their female partner. "The great dancers never danced to the crowd. They gave their whole attention to the woman. They fired on her with great subtlety, sophistication and eloquence. It was not a dance about doing steps, but a dance of moving with her. It was a mating dance. It didn't always lead to sex, but it led to intimacy."

The War Years

It was in the summer of 1945—the waning days of World War II—that the lure of black music began to take hold among white dancers. Until that time artists such as Stan Kenton, Gene Krupa, Tommy Dorsey, Lionel Hampton, and Glenn Miller drove a dance culture based on big-band swing and jazz. However, an unlikely convergence of events on the Carolina coast was to broaden the southern dance repertoire.

One sprang from the logistics of war. Though most of the beach dancers were too young or, for one reason or another, had received deferments from military service, the war still had a huge impact on their daily lives. An inconvenience that would later prove to have a significant effect on the dance was the government-imposed ban on bright lights along the coastline. "You couldn't have lights on the beach at night because they could be seen by enemy submarines off the coast," explained Harry Driver, one of the top beach dancers, in a conversation before his death in 1998. "All the windows and the top half of car headlights had to be painted black until the summer of 1945. If they blew a siren, it was a warning that a submarine was off the coast and all lights had to be turned off." The lighting restrictions temporarily drove beach nightlife 125 miles inland to the resort area of White Lake, North Carolina. It was here, at hangouts such as the Crystal Club and the Hayloft, that the dancers met a continuing stream of soldiers preparing for war at nearby Fort Bragg and Camp Lejeune.

"During the war years our dance styles were influenced at White Lake," recalled Driver. "Soldiers came to that area from all over the world. I met great dancers from Chicago, New York, and California. It was at White Lake that I learned from those soldiers a lot of the steps that have long been attributed to me. It was a real melting pot of dance."

But the same war that brought these regional dancers together was also decimating the big bands that produced their favorite music. Depleted of musicians gone to combat and hindered by increasingly high costs, large traveling orchestras virtually disappeared in the war years, replaced by small combos of six to eight musicians. The musical experience was not the same. "When big bands went out of vogue, there were many more black musicians left to perform in their place. I think that opening for the black performers had a lot to do with the crossover of black music to white audiences," said Chick Hedrick, a beach dancer who later operated the popular Chick Hedrick's Domino Lounge in Atlanta.

That black music was essentially banned in the segregated Carolinas did not hurt either, added Driver. "They called it 'suggestive music.' You've got to understand," he said, "when we were growing up, 'Sixty Minute Man' implied that you could last sixty minutes doing the big trick. A white southern society was not going to listen to that. The music was parental repulsive. Lyrics like 'Sock it to me, baby, one more time' or 'I'm gonna smoke you all night long' made the parents go crazy and left the teenagers wanting to hear more. Plus it had the tempo we liked to dance to."

Chicken Hicks, a charismatic beach legend who emerged from another dance hot spot, Carolina Beach, North Carolina, noted a clear distinction between the raw beach music of the 1950s and the sanitized "bubblegum beach" that emerged as a popular southern party music during the 1960s. "The new crap from bands like the Embers is not beach music. It's college bop. The [original] beach music was race music," said Hicks. "Bull Moose Jackson had a song called 'Bow Legged Woman Just Fine.' 'Old legs built like barrels / wide in the middle / jump start / slamming the straddle.' You didn't hear that kind of stuff on white jukeboxes." Most of the top white dancers agree that it was a mix of jazz, blues, and gospel music that fueled the transition of the jitterbug to the popular slower, smoother dance that is known in the South today as the shag. Spanning the popularity of both the jitterbug and the shag was Bill Pinkney, an original member of the Drifters and a 1988 inductee into the Rock and Roll Hall of Fame. "The only thing that separates the shag from swing and the jitterbug is the movement, the rhythm of the body and the footwork," said Pinkney, sitting at his kitchen table in Sumter, South Carolina. "I can shag at my age [then seventy-six], believe it or not."

Though there is continuing disagreement over the exact origins of South Carolina's state dance, those who created it gave major credit to the black dancers of the era, many of whom did an erotic dance known as the "dirty shag" that mimicked the act of copulation. In fact, the modern definition of the word *shag*, according to the *Oxford Dictionary of Modern Slang*, is "to have sex with." It appears, however, that the slang term did not come into common use in America until years after the dance became popular in the Carolinas.

"I first heard the term *shag* at Charlie's Place," said Big George Lineberry, who left the beach in 1948. "They called it the shag on the Hill. I think the shag and dirty shag came out of Charlie's nightclub." Henry "Pork Chop" Hemingway, who eventually became the first black policeman in Myrtle Beach, was a close friend of Fitzgerald and the official chaplain at the club during its heyday. He now runs a taxi company on Carver Street, a few steps away from where the club once stood. Hemingway watched the dance evolve over many years and emphasizes there is a clear difference between the dirty shag and the dance now called the shag: "The dirty shag was basically a bump and grind type of thing," Hemingway said. "The shag was altogether different. It was a smooth dance. The first person I ever saw do it was a girl from Elloree, South Carolina. She did it so well they nicknamed her 'Shag.' That's where the word came from. It was a girl's name."

That girl, Cynthia Harrol, waited tables and worked behind the bar at Charlie's Place, said her aunt, Dora Lee Goings. Possessed of a friendly, outgoing personality, Harrol lived to dance. She made repeated trips to New York City, where she tore up the dance floors of Harlem's top nightclubs. Everyone, Goings said, wanted to dance with Shag.

The modern version of the shag probably was born in the black clubs, agreed Dino Thompson. "The jitterbug is just an offshoot of the lindy hop. When you throw in some really acrobatic stuff and some flamboyant moves from the lindy hop to the triple-time swing, you've got the jitterbug. The blacks took it to another level with their creativeness and flexibility. The shag is the jitterbug on quaaludes . . . the jitterbug slowed down." Harry Driver, an early member of the

Shag Hall of Fame, said, "The jitterbug was done by a bunch of footloose, fancy-free zoot-suiters—both black and white—from Chicago, New York, and all over the South. I recall seeing a lot of the dancers who would bring the girl in, swing her over their shoulders and never miss a beat." The jitterbug took on a different meaning for Driver in 1946, however, when he saw two dancers come together and then do a very smooth, 360-degree pivotal rotation on the dance floor. "It set me on fire because I saw so much more to the dance than acrobatics." Driver would later perfect the pivot, earning a reputation for his smooth, effortless execution on the dance floor.

Black dancers, said Driver, brought a rhythm that was largely missing in white dancers. "It was the beat—the way they moved. They had a history of African tribal dance. What we learned from the blacks was their rhythm and tempo—the moves. You watch a white person do a syncopated walk and then watch a black do it. The blacks put more into it than you can imagine. We emulated what they did. Everybody claims to have started the shag. Nobody started it. It evolved from one dance to another in a big melting pot." Fitzgerald stirred that melting pot. "When I came to Charlie's club he'd say 'Little Dancin' Harry, come on in, man! You ain't gotta pay!' Charlie was as nice to me as any white guy has ever been on any beach I've ever worked on," Driver remembered. "I loved the guy because he loved me and we both loved dancing." Love of dance and a welcome atmosphere is also what brought Betty Kirkpatrick, a Shag Hall of Fame dancer from Carolina Beach, to Charlie's club. "It was the music and dance that drove us. It had nothing to do with color."

Lineberry had warm memories of his nights at the Hill—many ending at daylight. "Charlie once told me, 'George, you got a little black in you.' I knew the black music had a better beat. It would turn me on a little more. I was the best at the belly roll and the dirty shag. I could lay it on them." For young Thompson, the belly roll—or "vertical sex" as it was also called—was the ultimate shag step, a move that had been perfected by dancers at Charlie's Place. In his personal memoir, *Greek Boy,* Thompson offers a description of the belly roll: "Boy pulls girl close enough to touch belly buttons. Then, in rhythm, they throw one leg out together, then the other. Slick and sexy."[2] The belly roll and a ten-cent song on the jukebox, recalled Thompson, was "your license for romance. Pick out the girl of your dreams, lead her out to the dance floor, ease her out of a fast sweaty pivot into a tight belly roll and bruise your excited private parts all up against hers. Then, right as the lyrics get down and dirty, burn her down with your Tyrone Power eyes."

As I gathered bits and pieces of Charlie's story from those who knew him in his old neighborhood, it became evident that his unique, take-charge persona served to elevate his image within the community. Not only did his nightclub patrons see him as exceptionally stylish, but he was a man who commanded their respect. Hedrick, who would later own and operate his own nightclub, remembered being impressed with how well Charlie managed his place. "He wore a pistol on his side. Nobody bothered anybody there. He didn't need that gun to keep the peace, though. He wore the gun because he was the boss. He was the law there and everybody knew it."

In fact, it was Fitzgerald's aura of control and gangster style that is still most remembered in his old neighborhood. At night he often wore striped suits, round-collared white shirts, kitty bow ties, suspenders, and Stacy Adams lace-up boots. Sometimes he would wear hats, usually a round Stetson derby or an Al Capone–style fedora. By day he would put on denim overalls with his white shirts. "Not just overalls, but starched, clean overalls. The man was a cat . . . sharp, slick," recalled Leroy Brunson, who grew up in the Whispering Pines neighborhood and now lives directly across the street from the vacant grove of trees that was once Charlie's Place. Under those clothes, however, everyone knew that Fitzgerald packed weapons. "He carried a .45 and a .38 all the time. He had holsters that ran around his shoulders," said Brunson. "Charlie was a man of few words. He didn't talk much. But when he told you something, he meant what he said." Then Brunson paused, as if to reconsider his hardball take on Fitzgerald. "Charlie was a bluffer, though. He'd scare a lot of people by pulling a gun out and firing it into the floor or in the air. He'd do this during fights or if he wanted somebody to leave and they didn't want to go."

As a rebellious teenager, Henry Hemingway learned the hard way that Charlie was boss. "Back in those days, I loved to fight. I'd go up to Charlie's Place at night and turn the place out—just raise hell. He'd say 'Boy, you got to quit this! You got to quit this!' One night I went there and stepped on a guy's foot, and he asked, 'What did you step on my foot for?' I hit him." Hemingway said he would never forget what happened next. "Charlie put his nickel-plated shotgun in my mouth and said, 'Son, hell has overtook you.' I was scared outta my mind, and that was the last big fight I ever had." When he was a little older and wiser, Hemingway experienced another side of Fitzgerald. After spending several years playing trumpet in his college band, Hemingway returned home to Myrtle Beach unable to afford his own horn. "Charlie bought me a trumpet. 'Here, boy,' he said; 'maybe you'll make something out of yourself.' He would do things like that for kids. He was a good man."

South Carolina, circa 1950

During the years following the war, the white beach dancers forged their own unique counterculture along the Carolina coast. Some supported themselves as lifeguards, bingo callers, or dishwashers, while others proudly lived off the continuing flow of young female tourists who visited the beach in the summer. "You've heard of tennis bums? I was a dance bum," Chicken Hicks told me over breakfast in an Ocean Drive coffee shop. "I'd get a little money off the girls. I didn't work much. The girls liked to dance with the beach crowd. I'd put the

8. *King and queen of the shag: Harry Driver and Cynthia Harrol. Photographs*
© *Jack Thompson*

poor mouth on. Tell them I was a little bit down. I'd get names, and hell—in the wintertime—I'd travel around to these different towns (to visit the girls at home). I just didn't work. I was sorry as hell."

Jo-Jo Putnam, another Shag Hall of Fame dancer and sometime professional pool player, recalled a beach lifestyle in the 1940s and 1950s that he claims put Jack Kerouac and the Beat Generation to shame. "We were hip, we were first, and we were real. While the Beats drove a car across the country, we stole the car. We laughed at those phony motherfuckers. We encompassed all walks of life, from bank presidents to bank robbers." Putnam apparently felt the need to prove to me, even though he was over sixty, that his survival skills were undiminished. Just outside a packed Columbia dance hall, he abruptly stopped our interview, jumped out of his chair, and ran behind me. Within seconds he was wielding his long switchblade knife firmly against my neck. From that point on, I left his assertions unchallenged.

It was not so much the dancers' carefree ways that bothered the powers that be in South Carolina, but their disregard for the state's social rule that the races should not mix. Even in Myrtle Beach, a frontier town always more forgiving in matters of sin than the rest of the state, the jitterbugs constantly flirted with the edge of the law. "There were always policemen looking to lock somebody up on the beach," remembered Driver. The charge might be dirty dancing, having too much to drink, or swearing in front of an officer of the law. "I got arrested one night for saying, 'No damn kidding, I better get a beer before they close.' The cop reached over and grabbed me and said 'You're going to jail.' I said, 'For what?' He said for using loud and profane language in a place of business. I said all I said was 'damn.' He said, 'You're still going to jail, kid.' But before he could book me they had taken up a collection at the Pavilion for my bail. This happened to everybody from time to time. All they wanted was a fine. They only wanted the money."

Money, everyone knew, was the mother's milk of law enforcement in the beach community. Fitzgerald, as a successful black entrepreneur operating in a segregated town controlled by whites, followed the rule that to survive he had to pay for protection. "I saw Charlie with a cigarette carton—one of those tall boxes that cigarette packs come in—jammed full of money, nothing but bills to go to some law enforcer," said Hemingway. "I can't prove anything today, but law enforcement got mighty rich back in those days."

Even if the eyes of the law looked the other way from his various business enterprises, Fitzgerald's coziness with whites was out of sync with the time and place. Racial tensions in South Carolina began escalating after a federal judge opened the state's Democratic primary to black voters in 1948. It was to the chagrin of many southern whites that blacks began to assume a few positions of power. "To the surprise of a great many 'traditional' Southerners, there is a Negro alderman in Winston-Salem, North Carolina. Richmond, Virginia has a Negro city councilman and a Negro state representative," reported Bem Price of the Associated Press in June 1950. "Even here [Columbia, South Carolina], headquarters for the States Rights Democrats, a Negro undertaker was in the race for city council. Another is running for the council in Chattanooga. Two reportedly may enter the race in Nashville."[3]

The political awakening of the South's black citizens was at the core of the racially charged 1950 Democratic U.S. Senate campaign in South Carolina. The incumbent senator, Olin D. Johnston, entered the summer campaign bolstered by a successful attempt by southern state senators to block the establishment of a permanent Fair Employment Practices Commission (FEPC), a federal agency that would investigate racial discrimination in employment practices. In bombastic southern oratory, the earthy Johnston—his arms flailing wildly—railed in a speech on the floor of the Senate that it would be "a blow to Christianity" to require equal treatment of whites and blacks in hiring. "A responsibility has been placed on mankind to keep his race pure," argued Johnston. "Mongrelization of the races is the greatest destroyer of civilization and Christianity." In his deep baritone voice Johnston decried "persistent agitation, designed to cause all colored people to have such a group consciousness as to carry continuously a chip on their shoulders," and warned his fellow senators "not to mine the road ahead with dynamite that is certain to explode with great destruction when these opposite viewpoints collide."

Back home in South Carolina, anxious to exploit the race issue to the maximum in his campaign for reelection, Johnston stumped the state's forty-six counties in a series of verbal slugging matches with his opponent, incumbent governor Strom Thurmond. It turned into quite a show. In the towns along the campaign trail, the political rallies leading up to the July 11 Democratic primary were considered top-flight summer entertainment. Boisterous crowds of up to four thousand turned out for the carnival-like stump speeches, demanding that the candidates mix it up with an exchange of barbs and insults. For the first time newly empowered black voters joined the mostly white crowds. It did not matter to either candidate that the rising black constituency would witness the most openly racist political campaign in the state's modern history.

The two candidates worked hard to outdo each other with caustic race-baiting rhetoric. Thurmond accused Johnston of being soft on racial segregation and promised if elected to the Senate that he "will not sit with folded arms and my tongue cleaved to the roof of my mouth" when a federal court makes a civil rights ruling that attacks the southern way of life. "Any man that says I am for mixing of the races is a low-down, contemptible liar," rebutted Johnston in a speech at Georgetown. In another appearance at Charleston, the senator—loudly booed by blacks in the crowd—shouted to his hosts, "Make those niggers quit!"

At two stops a day in the grueling campaign, the candidates hammered each other on race. Thurmond was accused by Johnston of inviting the governor of the Virgin Islands, a black man, to the South Carolina governor's mansion. Thurmond was irate. "No Negro will ever be a guest at the governor's mansion so long as I am governor," he shouted to a chorus of boos from blacks at a rally in Columbia. At a rally in Spartanburg, Thurmond chided Johnston for his tenure on the Senate's District of Columbia Committee. "If he's got so much influence, why does he let the Negroes swim in the same pools with white people?" Thurmond barked.[4]

When they were not berating each other on race, the candidates were using paid political ads to polarize South Carolina's electorate. In a newspaper ad for his candidacy, Thurmond urged President Truman to forget about "minority blocs" of voters and withdraw his program to break down segregation in the armed forces. He warned that Truman's desegregation plan would "compel Southern white boys to serve, eat, and sleep together with Negro troops and also use the same recreational facilities."

The governor even published an attack on Paul Robeson, the celebrated black singer and actor who, Thurmond charged, "has been going all over the country demanding that we abolish segregation, and to show his contempt for our way of life in the South, he married his son off to a white girl." Robeson, one of the most talented and politically active black performers of his time, had toured the South in 1948 on behalf of progressive presidential candidate Henry Wallace. Thurmond, presidential candidate of the segregationist Dixiecrat party that year, represented everything Robeson abhorred, especially since he was a black man Thurmond could not intimidate, and the popular singer knew how to get under the governor's skin. Risking life and limb to sing his way through the South, Robeson attacked the Thurmond-led Dixiecrats as "powerful reactionaries who hope to stamp out the militant struggle of the Negro for complete freedom, equality and civil rights [and who] hope to keep all the wealth for themselves."

Framing the "black belt of the South" as the area that would decide whether African Americans "survive or perish," Robeson spoke with a level of public candor then uncommon in South Carolina. "For as long as any boy or girl can be denied opportunity in Alabama, Georgia, South Carolina and Mississippi—so long as one can be lynched as he or she goes to vote—so long as the precious land does not belong to the people of that area (and with the land, the wealth that flows there from in agriculture and in industry)—so long as they do not have the full opportunity to develop and enrich their cultural heritage and their lives—so long are the whole Negro people not free."[5] To the South's white establishment, those were fighting words.

The Ku Klux Klan Attacks

As racial passions flared in the Senate campaign during the summer of 1950, the Ku Klux Klan, whose local members had kept a low profile for many years in Myrtle Beach and surrounding Horry County, sprang back to life. Led by Grand Dragon Thomas L. Hamilton, a Leesville grocer, Klan members in South Carolina were emboldened by the racially explosive political climate.[6] At a July rally attended by two thousand people in Wagner, South Carolina, Hamilton railed about a wide assortment of the Klan's enemies, a grab bag that included blacks, Jews, Catholics, communists, congress, newspapers, radio, and the United Nations. He prayed in public and sought the help of God in the Klan's crusade against "evil." It was about this time that Klan members took it upon themselves to punish those citizens in the community they considered moral deviants. Beatings and cross burnings became rampant in North and South Carolina. Unmarried couples were awakened in the night and flogged with buggy whips. A cross was carved into the head of a pregnant black woman. Dozens of men and women were severely beaten and left naked miles from their homes.

In midsummer the Klan turned its attention to Charlie Fitzgerald. To them Fitzgerald was a black man breaking all the rules. He was wealthy, successful, and fearless. "He went where a lot of black people couldn't go," recalled Brunson. "When we went down to the Cozy Corner to order a hot dog, we'd have to stay outside. When Charlie wanted something, he'd just walk right in the door and sit down. When Charlie went to the movies he went right to where the whites sat. He didn't go upstairs with the blacks." The reason he got away with all of this, Brunson mused, was that Fitzgerald defied the stereotypes that whites had of blacks at the time. "He was a real light-skinned man. People looked at him differently because he was dressed nice, he always drove a brand new convertible car, and he'd wear those hats." With the escalated racial tensions of

1950, however, Fitzgerald's luck ran out. In an intimidating visit to his nightclub, Klan members demanded that white patrons no longer be admitted. "They told Charlie they didn't want the white kids there listening to music," said Hemingway. "Charlie told them to go to hell. They warned him they were coming back." It was a warning that Fitzgerald kept to himself. "He had his gun ready, but few others knew about it," said Hemingway. "If Charlie had told the general public about the threat, there would have been a bloodbath. 'Cause everybody would have tried to help him."

At 9:00 P.M. on Saturday, August 26, the Klan staged a motorcade through the streets of Myrtle Beach. Scores of night riders, outfitted in white KKK regalia, cruised the town in more than two dozen convertibles. The lead car had a fiery cross, made up of glowing red electric light bulbs, mounted on its left fender. Local police provided traffic control. "All of a sudden everything got quiet . . . an eerie quiet," recalled Harry Driver, who was at the Myrtle Beach Pavilion at the time. "We turned around to see what was happening, and we saw all these convertibles coming down Ocean Boulevard. They had on white sheets and cone hats. I get cold chills right now just thinking about it." Betty Kirkpatrick, a white dancer, watched the caravan—announced by blaring sirens—from nearby highway 17. "It was the most frightening thing I have ever seen," she said. "It's not pleasant to talk about."

The Klan motorcade snaked slowly through the black neighborhoods of Myrtle Beach. Eventually it reached Carver Street, the automobile-lined roadway used by club goers for parking during visits to Charlie's Place. As the intimidating convoy passed his crowded establishment, Fitzgerald became enraged. He picked up the phone and called the Myrtle Beach Police Department, warning that if the Klan returned, there would be bloodshed. Instead of providing the club with protection, police passed Fitzgerald's message directly to Klan members, who took it as a dare. "Ladies and gentlemen, we being white Americans could not ignore that dare from a Negro," Hamilton, an organizer of the parade, recalled at a later Klan gathering.

Just before midnight, about sixty Klansmen in twenty-five vehicles—this time with sirens silenced—made a return trip to Charlie's Place. Fifty-nine-year-old Fitzgerald waited defiantly for the white-sheeted mob outside the club. He was 6′3″ tall, 190 pounds, balding, with a thin mustache. In each hand he gripped a pearl-handled pistol.

The arrival of the night riders was swift and violent. A furious rush of ghost-like men streamed from the cars, immediately striking Fitzgerald in the face and seizing his weapons. Overwhelmed, he was thrown into the trunk of a Klansman's car. There, locked in darkness, he listened helplessly as windows were smashed, tables and chairs overturned, and a volley of more than five hundred rounds of ammunition was sprayed into the wooden building that held his friends and customers. "People were screaming, hollering, running everywhere.

And the police were nowhere to be seen," said Brunson, who witnessed the attack as an eight-year-old boy.

Suddenly, in the midst of the fury, the music stopped. The club's jukebox—the most powerful symbol of the cultural fusion that had united young blacks and whites in the postwar years—skipped, sputtered, and went silent as it was riddled by a hail of bullets. "From the way some Negroes left with window panes around their necks and in a hurry, it would seem something was going on inside," Hamilton said sarcastically, as he described the attack to Klan supporters a few weeks later at a public rally.

After wrecking the club, the Klan members—with Fitzgerald still locked in the trunk of a car—quickly left the scene. Gene Nichols, who operated another nightclub on the Hill, was shot in the foot. Clubgoer Charlie Vance sustained internal injuries from a beating he received at the hands of several Klansmen. Cynthia Harrol, the dancer nicknamed Shag, suffered an injured back after being beaten and had her fingers crushed in the cash register drawer as she tried to secure the club's money.

A Klansman, left behind by his cohorts, lay bleeding on the ground and was driven to a local hospital by a bystander. When doctors lifted his blood-soaked sheet, it was revealed that the man was wearing a police uniform. James D. Johnston, age forty-two, an off-duty police officer from neighboring Conway, died

9. *A South Carolina Klan rally near Lexington, 1950. William D. Workman Jr. Papers, South Carolina Political Collections, University of South Carolina*

within an hour from a .38 caliber bullet wound. The coroner said he was shot in the back. His assailant was unknown.[7] As Johnston lay dying, his fellow Klan members viciously whipped and beat Fitzgerald on a deserted road near a local sawmill. A Klansman used his knife to slice off a piece of each of Fitzgerald's ears. Bleeding and nearly senseless, he was left on the road to die.

It was not to be. A defiant Fitzgerald pulled himself up and staggered slowly to highway 17, the main inland business thoroughfare along the Carolina coast. There he was picked up by a motorist and taken back to his nightclub.

At 3:00 A.M., Sheriff C. Ernest Sasser drove to the nightclub and arrested Fitzgerald. Rather than take him to a local hospital for medical treatment, Sasser quickly transported Fitzgerald to an undisclosed jail three hours away in Columbia. The sheriff then took a public stance of silence, revealing no information about the arrest—including what Fitzgerald had been charged with and why he was taken so far away from Myrtle Beach. Newspapers speculated that he was taken to the prison hospital at the state penitentiary. However, no public records exist that even document that Fitzgerald was arrested.

The attack on Charlie's Place shocked both white and black Myrtle Beach residents, many of whom were surprised by the viciousness of the Klan's actions. For a significant number of local blacks, it was cause to leave town. "The aftermath of the terrorizing visit of the Klan to the Hill was the loss of colored employees by hotels and guest houses here at the beach," reported the *Myrtle Beach Sun*. "Many colored waitresses and maids, fearful of a return visit of the Klan, left town Sunday and Monday and this week a number of hotel operators have reported they were without domestic help of any kind."[8]

After publicly denouncing the violence at the nightclub, Myrtle Beach mayor J. N. Ramsey offered a tepid explanation for what triggered the attack. "Some of the conditions that probably caused the Klan to parade through this particular area of Myrtle Beach, namely white people patronizing colored business establishments or visiting in colored sections for amusement purposes, are not approved by the Southern people generally, but they are absolutely legal," the mayor said in a written statement after the shooting.

Five days later Sheriff Sasser made a live radio address that was carried by stations in Myrtle Beach and Conway. In it he cleared Fitzgerald, who was still in jail, of committing any crime related to the attack and said he found no evidence that any black had fired a gun in the fracas. Sasser, as had other law enforcement officers, speculated that James Johnston, the Conway policeman, had been shot in the back and killed by a fellow Klan member. In his radio address the sheriff placed full blame on Klansmen "who left him on the ground to die." Earlier, the Associated Press quoted an unidentified state law enforcement official who contended that Johnston was shot and killed "in a bout with robed and masked men." No one speculated as to why the Klan would kill its own man.

*10. Charlie Fitzgerald after
his encounter with the Klan.
Photograph © Jack Thompson*

The sheriff denied a widespread rumor that Charlie's Place had been attacked because Fitzgerald "was keeping a white woman for immoral purposes." He did suggest, however, that the young white dancers who frequented the night-club had influenced the Klan's actions. "To my knowledge some white men and women do go to this place on special occasions to hear the orchestra and watch the colored people dance," the sheriff said. "I have on many occasions told them it was not a good policy."

The sheriff ended his address by attempting to convey the extremist nature of the Klan's activities while acknowledging that the organization still had strong community support. Sasser told listeners that the Myrtle Beach radio station on which he spoke had been warned that if it carried any information about the Klan it would be blown up. But then he quickly added: "I happen to know a few men that are members. Some are from good families. They were led into this unfortunate thing with no intention of committing a crime."[9]

Just before Sasser went on the air, his department began arresting a handful of Klan members for the attack on Fitzgerald's nightclub. Grand Dragon Hamilton was the first—picked up as he was driving alone to the nearby town of Florence—but was soon released on $5,000 bond. As the night wore on, others were arrested. R. L. Sims Jr., a beer truck driver, was rousted from his bed in the middle of the night. Dr. A. J. Gore, a Conway optician; Clyde Creel, a service station operator; and June Cartrette, a farmer, joined the list. By the following day ten Klansmen were under arrest, and lawmen said they were looking for one hundred more, though that number was never apprehended. All those arrested were charged with conspiracy to incite mob violence.[10]

Meanwhile, Fitzgerald—charged with no crime—remained in an unknown jail. Why? Perhaps to protect him from attack by Klan members working in law enforcement, speculated Henry Hemingway with a quiet chuckle. "You see, Sasser and Charlie were actually good friends. The general feeling was that Charlie was making a lot of money for Sasser. But there were certain things with Sasser being white that he couldn't do or say. On the inside, though, he would help Charlie." About two weeks after the attack, Fitzgerald was finally released from jail under a $300 bond as a material witness, but he was promptly arrested again during a taxi ride in Columbia, charged with possession of a weapon and an obscene motion picture. He was fined $76 and released.[11]

In a rare interview after the proceeding in city recorder's court, Fitzgerald told a reporter he had been holding an automatic pistol on the seat next to him for protection. "I know it was against the law to have that gun, but it was right in my conscience because my life has been threatened and I am still in danger." The film, Fitzgerald added, was collateral for a three-dollar loan he had made to a friend who was short of cash. The club owner went on to confirm that he had been held in three jails since the attack but would not say where. His mood was conciliatory, and he said he had been treated well while in custody. He praised Sasser, saying, "I've never known a straighter white man in my life." In a parting comment, though, Fitzgerald displayed the street smarts that had made him a survivor. "I'm a free man—and I'm not a free man," he declared. "I don't know who is or who isn't a member of Klan."

The Aftermath

After the Klan arrests, Grand Dragon Hamilton began campaigning for public sympathy. "When a Negro fires at a Klansman, we will fire back," he said. "Whenever a Negro tells me to stay away, there'll be trouble." The Klan leader also vigorously denied that Officer Johnston had been killed by a Klan member at the shootout.

The emboldened Klan organization in the Carolinas broke with tradition and did not mask their faces in parades and demonstrations. "The traditional Klan robe includes the hood that covers the face, but no member of this organization whatsoever covers his face," Hamilton said. The reason, he explained, is that the Carolina area Klan members are "white gentlemen" who are neither afraid nor ashamed to be recognized in their regalia.

Hamilton's boast came from a genuine confidence that the Ku Klux Klan enjoyed significant support in the white beach community. After all, Klan rhetoric had carefully targeted the moral sensibilities of the region's conservative Baptist churchgoers. Race was a red-hot political issue, and President Truman's attempts to bring racial reforms to government and private institutions had been unpopular throughout the South. It was perhaps no coincidence that just after the sheriff had made his well-publicized Klan arrests, the Broadway Theater in downtown Myrtle Beach offered the movie *Masked Raiders* to its patrons.

On October 5, the Horry County grand jury supported the sentiments of many of the area's white residents. Even with substantial proof of their involvement, five Klan members, including Hamilton, were cleared of all charges relating to the attack on Fitzgerald and his nightclub. The white grand jurors refused to indict the men on charges of conspiracy to commit mob violence. A strong plea to the grand jurors by Judge E. H. Henderson that "no group or organization, by whatever name or style, has the right to set at naught the laws of our state" fell on deaf ears. All other Klansmen charged in the case had been released after an earlier preliminary hearing found no probable cause for their arrest warrants. A coroner's jury ruled that unknown persons caused Officer Johnston's death. His murder was never solved. Two of the beach community's local newspapers, the *Myrtle Beach News* and the *Horry Herald,* had little to say about the release of the Klan members. Neither felt it significant enough to report the grand jury's action on their front page.

Within weeks of the shooting, the U.S. attorney general directed the FBI to investigate the Klan attack. M. W. McFarlin, special agent in charge of the FBI's Savannah, Georgia, office at the time, permanently stonewalled the press, however, refusing to discuss what he called "the Fitzgerald case." There is no evidence an investigation ever took place.[12]

In November a feisty Hamilton—wearing a bright green cloak—spoke from the back of a truck to a crowd of eight thousand gathered at a Klan rally in a tobacco field near Myrtle Beach. Backed by a twenty-foot-high flaming cross and flanked by a handful of men and women wearing red Klan uniforms, the grand dragon railed against Sheriff Sasser for his arrest. "I have affidavits showing that some people are having to pay law enforcement officers for the privilege of doing business," Hamilton bellowed to the crowd. On his lectern an American flag was draped over a Bible. At his feet more than a hundred white-sheeted men stood guard, acting as a buffer from the assembled masses.[13]

To the Klan's accusations of graft, Sasser responded to the press after the rally: "Enemies stop at nothing; they say I accept graft. Well, I have one thousand dollars to give to anyone who can prove from reliable information that I ever took a dishonest dollar." The proof never came, but it did not matter. Sasser's arrests of Klan members eventually cost him his job. In 1952 the Klan flexed its political muscle and worked to defeat the sheriff in his bid for reelection.

The loss was overwhelming, with Sasser carrying only four precincts in the entire county. One of those he did carry was the "Race Path" precinct that included the Hill area of Myrtle Beach. The precinct's black residents voted 343 to 6 for Sasser's reelection. The man who beat the sheriff, John T. Henry, was sympathetic to the Klan and accused of being a member. Although his Klan connection was never proven, Henry's police force was later charged with violating the civil rights of blacks.

Olin D. Johnston was reelected to the United States Senate in 1950, beating Strom Thurmond for the Democratic nomination in the primary. He served until his death in 1965. Thurmond got another chance to run for a Senate seat and was elected as a write-in candidate in 1954 eventually becoming the longest-serving member in the Senate's history.

"No one can say with certainty that the recent political campaign in South Carolina contributed to the outbreak of violence there," wrote John Lofton of the attack on Charlie's Place in the September 5, 1950, edition of the *Arkansas Gazette*. "But it was obvious that both candidates in the United States senatorial contest were inflaming racial antagonism."[14]

Fitzgerald eventually recovered from his injuries and returned to his night-club. Some whites still came to hear the music, but many were now afraid to visit the Hill. The days of innocence were over. "I never went back there after that because I knew it would not be safe," Harry Driver lamented. "They would hate me because I was white, even though I had nothing to do with it." Young Dino Thompson is one who did return, making the mistake one night of allowing Fitzgerald to catch him staring at his now legendary ears, whose healed scars were faintly visible. "I thought the Klan had put Ks in his ears, and I would kinda peek at them," remembered Thompson. "Charlie saw me staring and said, 'You trying to look at my ears, boy.' I said, 'No sir, no sir.'" Hemingway said that after the Klan attack Fitzgerald was "basically the same guy, but a little meaner."

What Hemingway and others remember is that while all the Klan members went free, Fitzgerald ended up going back to jail, even though I could find no court records or press clippings to document it or explain why. "Charlie went back to jail in less than ninety days for something related to the shooting," Hemingway recalled. Though he does not remember the charge, Hemingway estimated Fitzgerald remained in jail for a year or more. This was confirmed by Leroy Brunson; his brother, Henry; and Elijah "Kidnapper" Goings, all close friends of Fitzgerald at the time. "They put Charlie in prison," said Leroy Brunson. "They were trying to blame him for shooting the Klansman even though they never found any evidence." A now-deceased Hill resident, said Brunson, was beaten by police and threatened with drowning in an attempt to get him to implicate Fitzgerald in the killing. The man refused.

"More or less, they wanted to get Charlie out of the way," said Hemingway of the white establishment that ran South Carolina at the time. "If they had left him alone, Charlie would have been one of the first real rich black men ever to come out of Myrtle Beach."

The lack of records documenting Fitzgerald's return to jail does not surprise Hemingway, who in 1955 joined the police force as Myrtle Beach's first black officer. "Back then, black people had no voice whatsoever. None. You'd be surprised how many things would come down from the state to a little place like

Myrtle Beach in those days. After thirty-two years that I have as a policeman, I've seen so many crooked things in law enforcement it makes me puke."

Hemingway remained Charlie's friend until the club owner's death from cancer on July 4, 1955. "It was the only time I ever saw him break down—he was in his bed sick—and I started praying for him," said Hemingway. "I remember part of the prayer was 'God, if it's your will that Charlie must leave us, prepare his soul. We are not worried about how long he stays here, but where he goes hereafter.' At that point, Charlie broke down. He died a little after that."

Though Fitzgerald's contributions are virtually unknown to the thousands of white shaggers who keep the dance alive more than a half century later, the influence of his club—and the crossover of black music to a white audience—are repeatedly cited by the pioneers credited with inventing South Carolina's state dance. "Black music influenced us from the start, and the only good place to hear it was on the Hill," said Billy Jeffers, a popular jitterbug—and Shag Hall of Fame member—who began working at the Carolina beaches in the summer of 1938. "We learned to smooth it out and do more with just a little bit of music. Being there made you think you were at the best place in the world." Added Harry Driver: "We had integration twenty-five years before Martin Luther King came on the scene. We were totally integrated because the blacks and whites had nothing in our minds that made us think we were different. We loved music, we loved dancing, and that was the common bond between us."

Fast-Forward a Half Century

In late September 1998 the beachside streets of Ocean Drive in North Myrtle Beach are packed with more than twelve thousand middle-aged white shaggers as they barhop between dance clubs such as Fat Harold's, Ducks, Pirate's Cove, the Barrel, the Spanish Galleon, the Boulevard Grill, and the Ocean Drive Pavilion. This ten-day festival of shag is the annual Fall Migration of the Society of Stranders (SOS). (A similar annual spring festival is called the Spring Safari.)

Shagging is big business in Ocean Drive, a small resort community about twenty miles north of where Charlie Fitzgerald's club once stood. On Main Street, Judy's House of Oldies sells hard-to-find beach music records and instructional shag videos, while Beach Memories caters to coastal nostalgia with lithographs, clothing, coffee mugs, and bric-a-brac that commemorate legendary South Carolina beach hangouts such as the Pad and Roberts Pavilion. The best of the white beach dancers are memorialized in a Hollywood-style Walk of Fame along Ocean Drive's sidewalks. Storefront windows display a mountain of shagging kitsch, from T-shirts, cheap watches, and beer bottle covers to specialty ship cruises organized for shag dancers.

Though the music played by the elite group of disc jockeys in these thriving beach clubs is still mostly R&B, there is rarely a black face to be found among the affluent group of mostly fifty-something couples who keep the shag alive. On the Carolina coast the unique biracial collaboration that created the dance a half century ago has all but disappeared. These days the aging white dancers find their beach excursions—with all the boozing and social camaraderie—a pipeline to their youth and a release from the pressures of the modern world. "For many people this is an outlet. It's like a drug. They get high on the music—the energy of the show," said General Johnson, a veteran black singer-songwriter whose group, Chairman of the Board, has long been a staple of the Carolina beach music scene.

Another enduring beach music act on the southern club circuit is Maurice Williams and the Zodiacs, whose recording of "Stay" has long been a beach classic. "Shaggers want the nitty-gritty real thing," said Williams, who is black, noting that he grew up with his white audience, most of whom are now in their forties and fifties. "The beginning of beach music was predominantly rhythm and blues," said Williams, "but today if you say to a young black man, 'Come on, let's go and listen to a beach music show,' he'll say, 'I ain't going to that white music.' The average black kid in his twenties or thirties doesn't know what this is all about. They see a beach music festival and think it's all white music. It's strange. They haven't studied the history of their music and the guys who recorded it enough to know what beach music is all about. They just don't know any better."

Leroy Brunson, still an avid dancer in his mid-fifties, avoids the white shagging scene at nearby Ocean Drive. "I watch the shaggers now on TV and sometimes I have to laugh," he said. "They are doing this shag and beach music now, but we invented it. They just kind of took it away. They just claimed it."

If the blacks lost part of their culture, southern whites gained something precious from their brief creative fling with race music and dirty dancing in the 1940s and 1950s. "Beach music and shagging was a celebration of life that was new for Caucasians," said John Hook. "It was an emulation of what white people thought they were seeing in the black community. Beach music isn't the music or the dance or the attitude, it's all of those married together and what it has become over time. Lots of people listen to this music today and don't know why they like it. They just know that something was missing in their life."

Notes

1. This essay, largely based on recorded interviews conducted with the participants, is based on an edited excerpt from the personal memoir *Whitewash: A Southern Journey through Music, Mayhem and Murder,* by Frank Beacham (New York: Beacham, 2002).

The author learned the story of Charlie Fitzgerald's nightclub after hearing Fitzgerald's name repeatedly mentioned in recorded interviews with the men and women credited with inventing what was to become the shag, South Carolina's official state dance. Interviews and frequent conversations with Shag Hall of Fame dancers Harry Driver and "Big George" Lineberry were essential in describing the creative collaboration that had occurred between young black and white dancers in Fitzgerald's long-forgotten club. In addition to

Driver and Lineberry, both now deceased, the following pioneering dancers contributed to this work with their personal stories: Billy Jeffers, Leon Williams, Clarice Reavis, Jean Ferguson, Chick Hedrick, Betty Kirkpatrick, Jo-Jo Putnam, and Chicken Hicks.

For their valuable help, the author also thanks Lance Benishek, William Holliday, Phil Sawyer, Gene Laughter, Harold Bessent, Norfleet Jones, Hoyt Bellamy, Bo Bryan, Sam McCuen, Miles Richards, Ed Riley, Charles Joyner, W. Horace Carter, Randall Mullins, Jerry Peeler, Leighton Grantham, Jeff Roberts, and Paul Robeson Jr. Some important musicians, disc jockeys, and music industry executives contributed to this work: Bill Pinkney, Jerry Wexler, Jerry Butler, General Norman Johnson, Maurice Williams, Marion Carter, Hoss Allen, John Hook, Eddie Weiss, Ray Whitley, Bill Lowery, Willis and Linda Blume, Charles Pope, Robert Smith, Jackie Gore, Jimbo Doares, Gary Barker, Barry Duke, and John McElrath.

Finally the author owes a special thanks to those who were friends and acquaintances of Charlie Fitzgerald: Henry "Pork Chop" Hemingway Jr., Leroy Brunson, Dino Thompson, Elijah and Dora Lee Goings, and Jerome Thomas. They were there, and their recollections were essential to preserving an important piece of southern musical history. I'd also like to express my appreciation to veteran Myrtle Beach photographer Jack Thompson, who graciously searched his files to help locate the only available photograph of Charlie Fitzgerald. My appreciation also to Marc Smimoff and the staff of the *Oxford American,* the fine magazine of southern writing, which published my first article about Charlie's Place.

2. Dino Thompson, *Greek Boy: Growing Up Southern* (Myrtle Beach, S.C.: Snug Press, 2000).

3. *Sumter Daily Item,* June 16, 1950. A copy of the speech is in the Olin D. Johnston Manuscripts, South Caroliniana Library. It was published in the *Sumter Daily Item,* July 13, 1950.

4. *Sumter Daily Item,* July 7 and June 30, 1950.

5. Interview with Paul Robeson, Jr., Schomberg Center for Research in Black Culture, New York, New York.

6. *Myrtle Beach Sun,* September 1, 1950. In February 1952 Hamilton was named imperial wizard of the Ku Klux Klans of North Carolina, South Carolina, and Georgia. Associated Press, Feb. 7, 1952.

7. *Sumter Daily Item,* August 28, 1950; Associated Press, August 29, 1950.

8. *Myrtle Beach Sun,* September 1, 1950.

9. Ibid., October 6, 1950.

10. Associated Press, September 1, 1950.

11. Ibid., September 8, 1950.

12. *Myrtle Beach Sun,* September 3, 1950.

13. Ibid., November 17, 1950.

14. *Arkansas Gazette,* September 5, 1950.

Part 3 ᗄ Reformers

The people who always spearheaded the movement for meaningful change—
and pushed politicians and others further than they would otherwise have been
willing to go in response to racial inequities—were African Americans. Part 3 of
this book, "Reformers," examines some of their stories.

In "Mr. NAACP: Levi G. Byrd and the Remaking of the NAACP in State
and Nation, 1917–1960," Peter F. Lau shows how an ordinary black plumber in
Cheraw responded to a wave of violence in his hometown during the early
1930s by clandestinely organizing a local chapter of the NAACP, then championed a statewide conference that reinvigorated the organization's activities in
South Carolina and, by 1946, was one of the most important in the country.
That chapter spawned pivotal, but still under-recognized, leaders such as Modjeska Simkins, James Hinton, John McCray, Osceola McKaine, and I. DeQuincy
Newman, who collectively won pathbreaking victories against the state's white
Democratic primary, discriminatory pay for black teachers, and segregation of
public schools.

The prevailing historiography of the state's response to civil rights, initially
set forth in I. A. Newby's *Black Carolinians*, suggests that black activism under
these leaders was largely passive and ineffective. Newby portrayed the successes
of the 1960s movement in South Carolina as being principally the result of
white moderation. This model is rejected by Wim Roefs in his essay "The
Impact of 1940s Civil Rights Activism on the State's 1960s Civil Rights Scene:
A Hypothesis and Historiographical Discussion." Roefs argues that the movement's early legalistic approach to civil rights in fact influenced the tactics of
leaders from both sides during the 1960s, setting the stage for much of what
was to happen in the state—and to no small extent the nation—for the rest

of the era. By establishing a largely successful approach to reform that was careful to stay within the law, the leaders of the movement in the 1940s ultimately conditioned white politicians to accept that a moderate response to civil rights reform was possible. At the same time these tactics enabled the leadership of the 1960s civil rights movement to balance the instincts of the younger generation of activists with a measured response that was in the tradition of the earlier reformers.

Most of the writing on the civil rights movement has emphasized urban experiences such as bus boycotts or lunch counter sit-ins, but South Carolina's rural Clarendon County can legitimately claim to have initiated the modern civil rights movement. Primarily because of the activism of the Reverend Joseph A. De Laine and a small group of African American parents whose children were subjected to some of the worst inequalities of the Jim Crow South, in May 1951 Charleston judge J. Waties Waring put forth the first known opinion by a federal judge that segregation was unconstitutional. With the help of the NAACP Legal Defense Fund, the *Briggs v. Elliott* school desegregation case laid the foundation for and eventually became part of *Brown v. Board of Education of Topeka, Kansas,* which overturned *Plessy v. Ferguson* in 1954, ending the legal justification for segregation of public schools. Yet the sad story of segregated schools continues in Clarendon County today. The *Brown* decision is mentioned in every U.S. history textbook, but the story of Harry Briggs and the other parents in Clarendon County and their struggle for justice has largely been forgotten. In "Seeds in Unlikely Soil: The *Briggs v. Elliott* School Desegregation Case," Vernon Burton, Beatrice Burton, and Simon Appleford trace the course of this story, using the words of Reverend De Laine to provide a unique perspective on this important chapter in South Carolina and United States history.

Not all civil rights activists in South Carolina, however, were content to wait on the NAACP leadership's legal challenges to Jim Crow, leading to an increasing number of direct action protests that revealed that many white South Carolinians remained firmly committed to their white supremacist beliefs. In "Five Days in May: Freedom Riding in the Carolinas," Ray Arsenault chronicles one of those protests. He shows how the journey of Tom Gaither, Joe Perkins, and their bus-mates through the Palmetto State in 1961 not only served as a prelude to the better-known confrontations in Alabama but also "elicited a mixture of hostility and restraint" that, within the spectrum of white southern response, placed South Carolina at "the crossroads of racial progress and reaction."

Of the Carolinians who blended legal with direct action, perhaps none did so more effectively than Charleston's Septima Clark. In "The Developmental Leadership of Septima Clark," Stephen Preskill tells the story of how his subject, an exceptional public school teacher with a forty-year career behind her, was in 1956 fired from her job—with attendant loss of state pension—for her active membership in the NAACP. Clark was immediately hired by the Highlander School in Tennessee, a unique institution that had been established to "help the least privileged members of society work more effectively to battle economic and social oppression and to secure their constitutionally guaranteed rights." Under its auspices she developed a united local action program to launch "citizenship schools" (essentially literacy and civics programs aimed at winning voting rights) on the sea islands of South Carolina for those who desperately needed them. The program was so successful in improving African American literacy, and by extension their ability to exercise their right to vote under the weight of the numerous voting tests that whites imposed, that activists within the Southern Christian Leadership Conference were soon trained to spread that type of "developmental leadership" into uncounted other communities throughout the Deep South. When Martin Luther King Jr. traveled to Stockholm to receive the Nobel Prize for Peace in 1964, he insisted that Clark accompany him in recognition of the critical role that she had played in his work.

Mr. NAACP

Levi G. Byrd and the Remaking of the NAACP
in State and Nation, 1917–1960

Peter F. Lau

This essay is, in its broadest application, a history of the ways in which those on the margins of history and the periphery of power have fundamentally shaped the course of history in South Carolina, the United States, and the larger world. More specifically, it is a history of the ways in which the NAACP in South Carolina was transformed from a small, urban-based organization predominantly representing the interests of a small class of black professionals to a mass organization representing the needs and interests of a broad cross-section of black South Carolinians across lines of geography, gender, and economic status. It is, moreover, a history of the ways in which the NAACP in South Carolina shaped the larger African American struggle for civil rights and equality during the peak years of the NAACP's national influence. What I will argue is that it was precisely the ability of the NAACP to incorporate and champion the interests of a diverse African American population that allowed it to achieve an increasing amount of power and influence that it wielded between 1917 and 1960, most notably in the years between 1943 and 1957.

To make my case I want to highlight the life and activist career of Levi G. Byrd, a man known to many older NAACP activists, but someone who is seldom included in the pantheon of South Carolina's civil rights notables or other prominent figures in the history of the African American struggle for civil rights. In an important way Byrd's life and activism reflect the trajectory of the black civil rights struggle in South Carolina in the twentieth century. But in a more important sense, Byrd's life and activism profoundly shaped the course of the struggle's trajectory, demonstrating the power of individual will and the possibilities that flow from collective human action.

To begin let me set the stage for Byrd's involvement in the South Carolina civil rights struggle and the history of the NAACP in particular. The first branches of the NAACP in South Carolina were chartered in Charleston and Columbia in the early months of 1917. The creation of these two branches was part of the effort of James Weldon Johnson, the NAACP's first black field secretary, to extend the reach of the somewhat stodgy, northern-based organization into communities across the South. By the end of World War I, in fact, the NAACP would transition from an organization funded and led by a predominantly white and board-dominated organization in the North to one funded, led by, and responsive to the needs of a black membership base, one increasingly based in the South. South Carolina was a leader in this transformation. And although the NAACP in South Carolina began in the state's two leading urban areas and, initially at least, drew its membership from these cities' black urban professional classes, the organization quickly expanded its reach, with six additional branches being formed in 1918 and 1919 in Aiken, Anderson, Darlington, Florence, Orangeburg, and Beaufort.

As the NAACP pursued access to better schools and jobs in military facilities (including the Charleston Navy Yard) and led efforts to register black voters, the organization captured the imaginations and loyalties of black South Carolinians from all walks of life. The NAACP's World War I–era success in South Carolina led to a period of rising expectations. Edwin "Teddy" Harleston of the Charleston NAACP even imagined the possibility of "holding over the heads of the white voters the possibility of a black primary." Allen University president Bishop W. D. Chappelle similarly envisioned the possibility that black voters could wield the balance of power in statewide political races, potentially dividing and splitting the all-white Democratic Party. In the 1920s black South Carolinians continued to form NAACP branches as a means of securing their rights and improving their lives, despite (or perhaps because of) increasingly trying circumstances. Between 1917 and 1929 twelve South Carolina communities chartered NAACP branches, and as many as nine others attempted to do likewise (the most dramatic example taking place in Calhoun County). By the opening years of the 1930s, and mimicking large regional and national trends, however, the NAACP had become a defunct organization in the Palmetto State. Violence, economic hardship, out-migration, natural disaster, and ineffective local leadership all played roles in the organization's demise. Officially only Charleston and Columbia maintained branches in 1930, but they largely collected membership dues and did little to advance the cause of black civil rights or equality.[1]

Levi G. Byrd arrived in South Carolina at the precise moment that the NAACP in the state and nation entered into a period of troubling decline. Nationally the organization was virtually bankrupt by the opening years of the 1930s. By mid-decade the organization would become embroiled in internal debates, leading to the departure of W. E. B. Du Bois, its leading propagandist, and threatening the survival of the civil rights organization. Reflecting a larger organizational pattern, as the NAACP's membership base expanded, its responsiveness to grassroots concerns and its overall effectiveness improved. But as membership dwindled, the organization tended toward a more top-down and autocratic approach to achieving civil rights for African Americans. This was the case in the early 1930s and was made manifest by the organization's public relations disaster surrounding its timid nonresponse to the wholly false accusation and prosecution of nine African American youths on charges of raping two white women in Scottsboro, Alabama, in 1931. To be sure, Byrd arrived in South Carolina with little apparent intent or desire to forge a career as an NAACP activist, or activist of any sort. He made the move to South Carolina, in large measure, to find work.

Byrd was the eldest of nine children born to Alfred D. Byrd and Pinkie Hancock Byrd in January 1891. He was reared on a tobacco farm in Anson County, North Carolina, near the town of Lilesville. In 1911 Byrd married and spent two years farming before he and his wife moved to Hamlet, North Carolina, where he took a job as a freight handler for the Seaboard Air Line railroad company. Following the death of his wife seven years later, Byrd continued the strenuous lifting work required by his railroad job, until, as the story is told, he noticed some writing on the inside of a boxcar. "In 1918 I was trucking in Hamlet, N.C.," Byrd remembered. "I was carrying boxes into a boxcar and on one end it was written, 'What is your life?' And on the other end it said, 'Your life is what you make of it.'" Shortly thereafter, the story continues, Byrd resolved to do something with his life, to do something more than work all day and return home at night with little hope for a better future. After leaving behind the railroad work, he spent several years in a number of North Carolina towns before he made the decision to move to Cheraw—a Chesterfield County, South Carolina, town on the Pee Dee River, the birthplace of Dizzy Gillespie, some thirty miles from Byrd's place of birth in North Carolina. In Cheraw a cousin named Annie Hancock graciously provided him with a place to stay until he found work, which he did, as a plumber's assistant to an aging white man named C. F. Pendleton. Byrd would soon marry Mary Ann Love, a neighbor of his cousin, and become an active member of the Pee Dee Union Baptist Church.[2]

By 1931 Byrd and his wife had begun a family, and he soon became the only plumber in Cheraw. Had Jim Crow and white supremacy not maintained such a tight grip on life in South Carolina, the forty-year-old's newfound monopoly on the plumbing needs of the small Pee Dee River town might well have signaled a passage to middle-class security. But in the early part of 1933, less than a year after the birth of his second son, Alfred, Byrd became a victim of racial violence, an event that launched his activist career. From that point forward his struggle for economic security and human dignity would be waged in and through a battle for racial justice.

As the Great Depression swept South Carolina in the early 1930s, racial violence permeated Chesterfield County. In 1933 Bill McNeil, a trombone player in the future jazz great John Birks "Dizzy" Gillespie's first makeshift band, vanished. Although the exact cause of this disappearance was not known, Gillespie and his cohorts understood it as a clear signal to "get the hell out of Cheraw."[3] On a Saturday afternoon in early June of the same year, as he attempted to investigate the mistreatment of black residents in Cheraw's small downtown business district, Byrd was severely beaten by a group of white men. For Byrd the event revealed, in no uncertain terms, the limits imposed on the life he had carved out for himself and his family. "When Daddy was hit," recalled his son Alfred D. Byrd Jr., "that was the turning, there."[4]

Byrd's beating was only one of a series of brutal beatings meted out to black residents of Cheraw in the early part of 1933. Thereafter, Byrd resolved to put an end to the ongoing violence and began efforts to organize a branch of the NAACP. Beginning in June 1933, in a series of roughly typed and handwritten letters reflecting his lack of formal schooling and poor typing skills, Byrd began what would become a virtually continuous correspondence with the NAACP national office that would last well into the 1950s. Rare among NAACP branch file correspondence for their regularity and detailed accountings of black life and organizing efforts in a small rural town, Byrd's letters began to crack the regional isolation of a black community that lacked legal protection and political representation and was regularly brutalized by white residents. "Thir has been so miny out rages cormited own our race hear in Cheraw latly," Byrd wrote Walter White. "We are wishing to form a branch of the N.A.A.C.P. hear to fight the Brutal way thay doin our Race hear for the last 6 are 8 Months we Had 5 are 6 Brutal Beaten hear in town bye the whites and there has not one of them bee eaven arrested for it we have no propten [*sic*] hear when it comes to law." Only two weeks later Byrd wrote the national office to inform them that "the Police Beat up A Woman of our Race hear in Cheraw Saturday June 24 and is Getting worse Each Day." "We are treated as Slaves hear in Cheraw," he explained; "they have no law hear to protect our race at all. So you see how we feel about it."[5]

For Byrd the organization of an NAACP branch represented an important first step toward the amelioration of what he described as the slavelike conditions under which black people lived in Chesterfield County. But organizing a branch of the NAACP in a small town such as Cheraw and a rural county such as Chesterfield was anything but an easy task. Cheraw was a town where everybody knew everybody and where leading white residents prided themselves on what they perceived as their close, even familial, ties to the town's black residents. Any violation of these real and imagined ties could, to be sure, provoke a violent response.[6]

Just as significantly, black residents of Cheraw were anything but a monolithic group. "It's very interesting," Dizzy Gillespie later recalled, "how the blacks became divided over religion in Cheraw." At the top of the social pyramid were those who attended the Second Presbyterian Church, also home to the Coulter Memorial Academy. At the bottom were those members of the Sanctified

Church, where, Gillespie remembered, "everyone knew that the whole congregation shouted."[7]

Organizing in such a context was hard work, but Byrd's in-between social status in black Cheraw made him ideally placed to organize the community. As the town's only plumber, he occupied a position of relative economic privilege in black Cheraw and represented the values of hard work and thrift required for middle-class respectability. He was a member of the Pee Dee Union Baptist Church and a man with little formal education, making him neither a member of Cheraw's black elite nor a member of its lowest-ranking social classes. His work as a regional agent for a number of black newspapers had also made Byrd a well-known figure among black residents of Cheraw and Chesterfield County by the early 1930s. Every Saturday morning Byrd, who never learned to drive a car, toted a small red wagon through Cheraw's black neighborhoods and hand-delivered copies of the *Pittsburgh Courier,* the *Norfolk Journal and Guide,* and the *Baltimore Afro-American* to subscribers. On those same afternoons, as black people from the surrounding countryside made their way into town to shop and socialize, Byrd stood near McBride's Market and sold papers to all those interested, allowing him to become a visible presence in the town and acquainted with people from across the county.[8]

Through hard work and strategic insight, Byrd managed to recruit members to the branch from across Chesterfield County's diverse African American community. In the late 1930s, when the organization and its membership, by necessity, remained underground, Byrd took to wearing an NAACP button in public, becoming the only recognizable member of the organization in Cheraw.[9] For a time black people avoided Byrd on the streets of Cheraw, crossing the street when he approached and bypassing the corner where he sold newspapers on Saturdays. But his public demonstration of fearlessness and his assertion of independence made a powerful case for joining the organization. If Byrd could "step out" and risk his own economic well-being and personal safety in the interest of racial justice, perhaps others could do the same.[10]

Finally after years of organizing, on May 19, 1939, seventy men and women met and chartered the Cheraw and Chesterfield County NAACP branch. Its membership included teachers from Coulter Memorial Academy and the pastors of the Wesley ME Church, Pee Dee Union Baptist Church, AME Zion Church, and the Sanctified Church. Four domestic workers added their names to the charter, as did two barbers, a hairdresser, a midwife, four brick masons, five farmers, an undertaker, two merchants, and fifteen men who listed their occupations as common laborers. Four of its members were also members of the Addie H. Pickens Club, which was an affiliate of the South Carolina Federation of Colored Women's Clubs and the National Association of Colored Women's Clubs. Teachers occupied the positions of president, vice president, and secretary, while Byrd held the formal title of treasurer and the informal position of corresponding secretary. "Because," he explained, "I have worked this part in the past and understand more about that part." As would remain his practice in the years ahead, Byrd pushed members of the more "articulate" classes to assume the organization's formal leadership roles even as he remained the key leader in the day-to-day operations of the organization.[11]

Byrd did not, however, cease his organizational efforts with the creation of an NAACP branch in Cheraw. Increasingly he viewed the dearth of NAACP activity elsewhere in the state as an impediment to the success of his own locally rooted organizing efforts, and he began to search for ways to energize the NAACP across the state. "We wont to Farm A State Conference so as to try to Keep all Branches alive and Keep Them are Get Them to Work," he wrote the national office. "Will you Send me the Names of Each Branch President and his Address," he asked, "so that we May get in Turch With of them so we mayget to gether own that. Would you not think that a good way to living those Dead Branche up."[12]

With a list of officers of the state's nominally active branches in hand, Byrd began a letter-writing campaign to urge the formation of an NAACP State Conference. By September he had secured positive responses from branch leaders in Florence, Georgetown, Greenville, Sumter, and Charleston. But the recently elected president of the Columbia branch, the Reverend James M. Hinton (also a new resident of the capital city), refused to lend the support of the Columbia organization. "It is our responsibility," Hinton explained in 1940, "to supply the material and money" to the national office while "the folks up North have got to stick their necks out for us." "Our branch was not entirely sold on the State Conference," he wrote the national office that same year, "for we felt that it would be just another drain on our funds, which you know are limited."[13]

Byrd realized, though, that the support of black Columbians would be critical to the power and success of a state organization. So he searched for a way around Hinton. The key person in his efforts would prove to be the Reverend Arthur Jerome Wright, the father of the future civil rights attorney and Children's Defense Fund founder, Marian Wright Edelman. Wright lived in the town of Bennettsville, located just across the Pee Dee River from Cheraw in neighboring Marlboro County. Wright had become the full-time pastor of Bennettsville's Shiloh Baptist Church in 1930 when the Reverend J. J. Starks, who at the time was the president of Morris College in Sumter, relinquished his responsibilities there to become the first African American president of Columbia's Benedict College. Starks was Wright's mentor and a close friend of the family, and, as the president of Benedict, was Byrd's entrée to Columbia. By mid-October 1939 Byrd had managed to convince Starks to lend his support to the state conference. Generally regarded as a racial moderate, even an "accommodationist," Starks offered Byrd a way to circumvent Hinton's leadership. Starks also allowed the organization to hold its founding meeting on the Benedict campus, providing the fledgling state conference with an air of legitimacy at a critical juncture in its history.[14]

On the weekend of November 10, 1939, twenty-nine representatives from branches in Florence, Georgetown, Sumter, Cheraw, Greenville, Charleston, and Columbia attended the founding meeting of the South Carolina NAACP State Conference of Branches in the library of Benedict College. For the first time since Edwin Harleston imagined the creation of a "black primary" and W. D. Chappelle imagined an organized statewide challenge to the political exclusion of black South Carolinians, the makings of an institutional challenge to Jim Crow and legalized disfranchisement were in the works on a statewide scale. In this case, however, the call for a collective challenge to Jim Crow and political exclusion emanated from a small town, in a rural county, stretching the organization well beyond the urban confines of Columbia and Charleston and setting it on a new, more inclusive trajectory. Indeed, it is unclear whether or not Hinton even attended the founding meeting of the state conference, and it appears from the documentary record that the participation of the Columbia branch remained in doubt until the last minute. What can be known for certain is that the Cheraw delegation took the lead at the November 10 meeting, helping to elect the pastor of Cheraw's Wesley ME Church, the Reverend Alonzo W. Wright, to the position of president and the head of the Robert Small School's Adult Education program, Maggie B. Robinson, to the position of secretary.[15]

Indeed, the virtually moribund Columbia branch continued to withhold its support from the state conference for more than a year.[16] Nevertheless, Byrd continued to press Hinton and the Columbia branch to support the state organization. After much prodding and negotiation, Hinton agreed to take an active role in the state conference, but not without exacting a price for his participation: "I'll go along with you," Hinton told Byrd, "but if I can't run it, I'll tear it up." For Byrd this was a price worth paying. In June 1941 Hinton was elected president of the state conference, effectively transferring the formal reins of power from Cheraw to Columbia. Robinson would stay on for an additional year as secretary, until Modjeska Monteith Simkins agreed to serve as her replacement.[17]

In the ensuing years Hinton would prove his mettle as state conference president, and the irascible Modjeska Simkins would prove an untiring champion of black civil rights and equality across the state. Between 1943 and 1946 the NAACP expanded from fifteen to forty-nine branches. Membership topped the ten thousand mark in 1945. And the number of branches continued to increase, peaking at better than eighty-four branches in 1955. By the late 1940s, with the hiring of Eugene Montgomery as the state organization's first full-time and paid executive secretary, the state conference had quite literally achieved a presence in the backwoods, cotton fields, and rural churches across South Carolina. During the 1940s the organization provided the crucial infrastructure for an assault on the all-white Democratic primary. It issued the first challenges to the gross disparities of the doctrine of "separate, but equal." And when the organization stretched into rural Clarendon County, it took the legal and cultural moorings of Jim Crow segregation head on. As was so often the case, when those on the edges of power took the initiative and the NAACP accepted their challenge, the organization achieved its most profound successes.

Success in South Carolina was not, however, easily accomplished, and the forward march of racial progress never moved in a straight line. The white backlash to *Brown* and the NAACP, in the mid-1950s, in particular, proved devastating. By 1957 the NAACP had lost more than fifty branches across the state, and total membership plummeted. But black South Carolinians did not halt their struggle for civil rights or equality. James T. McCain, a founding member and president of the Sumter NAACP, used his NAACP connections in the late 1950s to organize for CORE in South Carolina, continuing the struggle for black voting rights and empowerment. The Reverend C. A. Ivory in Rock Hill, the Reverend I. DeQuincy Newman, the attorney Matthew Perry, Bernice Robinson, and Septima Clark, all members of the NAACP, would find ways to push the struggle forward.

Despite this period of upheaval for the state organization, Levi Byrd's activism continued, and he remained active in the NAACP, battling into the 1970s to achieve the integration of public schools in Cheraw.

Notes

1. On the history of the NAACP in these years, see Peter F. Lau, *Democracy Rising: South Carolina and the Fight for Black Equality since 1865* (Lexington: University Press of Kentucky, 2006). Harleston quotation on page 47. Perhaps the best example of the hope inspired by the NAACP in the 1920s and the difficulties facing the organization were demonstrated in Calhoun County. In this rural, cotton-producing county, bordered by the Congaree and Santee rivers to the north and east, Orangeburg County to the south, and the state's Sandhills region to the west, black residents chartered an NAACP branch in 1925. Forty-four farmers, a clerk, four merchants, one teacher, four students, and a minister signed their names to the charter. Half of the members were women. The Calhoun branch was a demonstration of the extent to which the NAACP had reached into the backwoods and rural counties of South Carolina and begun providing a means for ordinary men and women to participate in a larger fight for civil rights and liberation. But revolutionary change was not to come in the 1920s. In September 1928 a major hurricane hit the coast of South Carolina and destroyed Calhoun County's cotton crop. "We are very sorry that [the] Calhoun County Branch has not been able to pay her full quota," wrote the branch's secretary to the national office of the NAACP. "We very much desired to pay out quota but as the September hurricane and floods destroyed all the crops raised in the community it could not be done. . . . Just give us a little time. We are deeply interested in the great work you are doing. . . . " By the following year many of the branch's members had migrated out of Calhoun County in search of better economic opportunity. The branch, like so many others, disappeared from the scene. *Democracy Rising*, 66–67.

2. Byrd quoted in the *Cheraw Chronicle,* December 23, 1971. His biography is drawn from the *Cheraw Chronicle,* September 28, 1972, in Black History File, Cheraw Town Hall, Cheraw, South Carolina; *Cheraw Chronicle,* September 12, 1985; *Cheraw Chronicle,* January 23, 1986; funeral services for Levi G. Byrd, September 12, 1985, from the personal files of Alfred D. Byrd, Hampton, Va.; Alfred D. Byrd, interview with the author, Hampton, Virginia, March 1, 2000; Bernice S. Robinson, interview with the author, Cheraw, S.C., August 3, 1999.

3. Dizzy Gillespie with Al Fraser, *To Be, or Not . . . to BOP: Memoirs* (Garden City, N.Y.: Doubleday, 1979), 30.

4. Lucille Black to Levi G. Byrd, June 14, 1933, Cheraw Branch File, I-G-196, NAACP Papers, Manuscripts Division, Library of Congress, Washington, D.C. (hereafter Cheraw Branch File); Alfred D. Byrd, interview.

5. Levi G. Byrd to Walter White, June 16, 1933, Cheraw Branch File; Levi G. Byrd to National Office, June 27, 1933, Cheraw Branch File. Byrd's writings (typed and handwritten) reflect his lack of formal schooling and the immediacy with which he wrote the national office. I do my best to quote him verbatim.

6. On Gillespie, see *Democracy Rising,* 67–70.

7. Gillespie, *To Be, or not . . . to BOP,* 30–31.

8. *Cheraw Chronicle,* September 28, 1972; Levi G. Byrd to National Office, June 16, 1933, Cheraw Branch File; Alfred D. Byrd, interview; Robinson, interview.

9. Alfred D. Byrd, interview; Robinson, interview. The button was likely from the NAACP's 1937 antilynching campaign. See Robert L. Zangrando, *The NAACP Crusade against Lynching, 1909–1950* (Philadelphia: Temple University Press, 1980), 139–65.

10. Alfred D. Byrd, interview; Robinson, interview.

11. Application for Charter, Cheraw and Chesterfield County, South Carolina, May 19, 1939, Cheraw Branch File; Fortieth Anniversary Program Guide, S.C. Federation of Colored Women's Clubs, part 1, reel 22, Records of the National Association of Colored Women's Clubs, microfilm; Levi G. Byrd to National Office, May 23, 1939, Cheraw Branch File; Hoffman, "Genesis of the Modern Movement," 367.

12. Levi G. Byrd to William Pickens, July 9, 1939, Cheraw Branch File.

13. William Pickens to Levi G. Byrd, July 10, 1939, Cheraw Branch File; Levi G. Byrd to Pickens, July 26, 1939, Cheraw Branch File; Levi G. Byrd to Pickens, September 18, 1939, Cheraw Branch File; Levi G. Byrd to National Office, October 16, 1939, Cheraw Branch File; Hinton quoted in Wilhelmina Jackson, Columbia Memorandum, 1940, box 36, folder 2, Ralph J. Bunche Papers, Schomburg Center for Research in Black Culture, New York; James M. Hinton to William Pickens, June 13, 1940, Columbia Branch File, II-C-177, NAACP Papers (hereafter Columbia Branch File). On the Columbia branch's reluctance to join because of financial concerns, also see William Pickens to R. W. Jackson, November 20, 1939, part 12, series G, reel 18, NAACP Papers.

14. Levi G. Byrd to William Pickens, September 18, 1939, Cheraw Branch File; Levi G. Byrd to National Office, October 16, 1939, Cheraw Branch File. On Reverend Arthur Jerome Wright, see Marian Wright Edelman, *Lanterns: A Memoir of Mentors* (Boston: Beacon, 1999), 1–9, 175. On Reverend J. J. Starks, see I. A. Newby, *Black Carolinians: A History of Blacks in South Carolina from 1865 to 1968* (Columbia: University of South Carolina Press, 1973), 230.

15. Drawing on oral history interviews with Modjeska Simkins and historical sketches from South Carolina State Conference of NAACP Branches annual convention program guides, Barbara Woods has concluded that the founding meeting of the state conference was held on October 10, 1939, and that both Reverend Hinton and Modjeska Simkins

were present. See Barbara Woods Aba-Mecha, "Black Woman Activist in Twentieth Century South Carolina: Modjeska Montieth Simkins" (Ph.D. thesis, Emory University, 1978), 166–67; Barbara A. Woods, "Modjeska Simkins and the South Carolina Conference of the NAACP, 1939–1957," in *Women in the Civil Rights Movement: Trailblazers and Torchbearers, 1941–1965*, ed. Vicki L. Crawford, Jacqueline Anne Rouse, and Woods (Bloomington: Indiana University Press, 1993), 106. Documentary evidence from the NAACP Papers not cited by Woods contradicts this version of the story, as does Byrd's own rendering of the history in an oral history interview conducted in 1956. See Levi G. Byrd to William Pickens, November 10, 1939, S.C. State Conference File, I-G-196, NAACP Papers, which also can be found in part 12, series G, reel 18, NAACP Papers; Report of Election, South Carolina Branch, November 10, 1939, Cheraw Branch File; Lucille Black, Memorandum to the *Crisis*, November 14, 1939; J. A. Johnson to William Pickens, October 21, 1939; Pickens to Johnson, October 26, 1939; A. W. Wright to Pickens, November 12, 1939; Pickens to Levi G. Byrd, November 14, 1939—all part 12, series G, reel 18, NAACP Papers. Byrd's version is recounted in Hoffman's "Genesis of the Modern Movement," 368. Although members of the Columbia branch ultimately came to play a central role in the state conference, it was not until after 1941 that they did so. Their prominence in the organization from that point forward and their power within the organization to record its history is likely the cause of the hazy rendering of the organization's founding.

16. R. W. Jackson to William Pickens, February 8, 1940, Columbia Branch File; Wilhelmina Jackson, Columbia Memorandum, 1940, box 36, folder 2, Bunche Papers.

17. Aba-Mecha, "Black Woman Activist," 167–69. Byrd quoted in note 36. See also Reverend James M. Hinton to Levi G. Byrd, May 31, 1962, from personal files of Levi G. Byrd in possession of his son, Alfred D. Byrd, Hampton, Virginia; Levi G. Byrd to Walter White, December 22, 1941, State Conference File, II-C-181, NAACP Papers; Official Program of the First Annual Conference of the South Carolina Conference of Branches N.A.A.C.P., May 17, 1940, State Conference File; Program guide from the Second Annual Conference, South Carolina Branches, National Association for the Advancement of Colored People, June 15 and 16, 1941, State Conference File; Program, Third Annual Conference of South Carolina Branches of the National Association for the Advancement of Colored People, June 14 and June 15, 1942, State Conference File. Reverend Wright stepped down for health reasons and time constraints. Robinson, who ran the National Youth Administration Center for Negro Girls in Cheraw, was convicted of illegally soliciting funds from NYA participants to make repairs to the NYA Center in 1942 and sentenced to sixty days in the state penitentiary in Lexington County. According to Byrd, after learning about Robinson's involvement with the state conference and the local NAACP, the trial judge denounced the NAACP in court and sentenced Robinson to a jail term rather than ordering her to pay a fine. Levi G. Byrd to Walter White, April 29, 1942, Cheraw Branch File; Levi G. Byrd to Thurgood Marshall, June 6, 1942, Cheraw Branch File; Memorandum to Mr. Marshall from Mr. White, June 10, 1942, Cheraw Branch File.

The Impact of 1940s Civil Rights Activism on the State's 1960s Civil Rights Scene

A Hypothesis and Historiographical Discussion

Wim Roefs

This chapter proposes the hypothesis that the approach and success of 1940s civil rights activism in South Carolina helped shape the fight over desegregation in the state during the 1960s and that this period's leadership was influenced, conditioned, and given opportunities by what happened in the battle for civil rights two decades earlier. By implication the paper finds the standard explanation for the moderation and relative absence of violent confrontation during South Carolina's 1960s desegregation battle lacking in that it ignores the influence of the 1940s. The standard narrative for the 1960s instead focuses above all on the levelheadedness and moderation of the state's white leadership. Furthermore, this interpretation often reduces the black dimension to proclamations of black conservatism and especially the accommodationist attitude of the period's foremost black leader, Isaiah DeQuincey Newman.[1]

This emphasis on moderate white leaders is unsatisfactory in that the phenomenon itself is in need of an explanation, especially since this moderation is usually portrayed as exceptional. Notions about the political conservatism of the state's African Americans are based on little more than historian I. A. Newby's contentions on the matter and suffer from his poor use of sources and dubious historical points of reference. Simply defining Newman as an accommodationist without a thorough assessment of his reasons and motives denies him much deliberateness, which is problematic. Newman was no Uncle Tom; he wanted results in the fight to desegregate South Carolina, not just the appeasement of whites by "going slow," which was just one element of an approach that was most likely informed by what Newman thought would yield results.

The first section of this chapter argues that the behavior in the 1960s of both moderate white leaders and Newman should at least in part be explained by their experience with the state's civil rights activism of the 1940s and early 1950s. It furthermore argues that the strength of the 1940s South Carolina NAACP allowed the organization to dominate the state's civil rights field, even in decades to come, facilitating a relatively restrained approach to desegregation. The second section of the chapter analyzes why the link between the 1940s and 1960s civil rights scene in South Carolina generally has been absent from the historiography. Civil rights historiography has suffered from longtime neglect of pre-*Brown* activism, but the analysis here will focus on the influence on this issue of I. A. Newby's book *Black Carolinians*.[2]

South Carolina's Moderate White Leadership

The notion of the relatively moderate nature and levelheadedness of South Carolina's white leadership in the 1960s is well established. These leaders did not encourage violent resistance to desegregation and mostly insisted that the state and its residents adhere to the law. This created an atmosphere in which violent opposition was frowned upon and limited. White leadership included state and local politicians, school administrators, and the state's metropolitan business elite. Together these groups managed in 1963 a late but peaceful desegregation of Clemson University and the University of South Carolina. Other colleges, as well as several public facilities and businesses across the state, also desegregated without much violent opposition, but often with substantial white resistance. Although the relative peacefulness should not be confused with an absence of violence altogether, as it often is, South Carolina certainly compared favorably to the likes of Mississippi and Alabama.[3]

None of this means that South Carolina's political leadership was not reactionary. It was. Its commitment was to white supremacy, not to desegregation. Desegregation was at best an acquired taste force-fed by black activism and federal law, forces largely beyond the control of South Carolina's political establishment. Even as the state leaders went about being moderate by some standards, they initially closed South Carolina's state parks rather than desegregate them. Several cities did not desegregate their restaurants and other public accommodations until the federal Civil Rights Act passed in 1964. Governor Fritz Hollings was a lieutenant governor committed to segregation during the fiercely repressive 1950s regime of George Bell Timmerman; he maintained that attitude for several years after becoming governor in 1958. His successor, Donald Russell, even in 1963 claimed personally to be against desegregation. Senator Marion Gressette chaired the Gressette Committee, charged in 1951 by the state legislature to propose ways to prevent desegregation, and became known as "Mr. Segregation." Robert McNair, Russell's successor in 1967, rose politically as part of the country elite that generally was less progressive on race than the new moderates.[4]

These men came of age politically, or were already active, in the 1940s and 1950s, when the state of South Carolina opposed black equality and desegregation as vehemently as other southern states. The opposition included at least the threat of violence by state leaders, as when Governor Olin Johnston in 1944 declared the state would stop integrated Democratic primaries by all means necessary. South Carolina led the South in opposition to blacks voting in the Democratic primary after the Supreme Court, in *Smith v. Allwright,* declared that the whites-only Texas Democratic primary was unconstitutional. It also led the opposition to the desegregation of public education. It harassed the NAACP and intimidated teachers and state workers who joined that organization or contributed to it. It put one black leader, newspaper publisher John McCray, on a chain gang on concocted charges.[5]

This opposition to racial equality intensified in the second half of the 1950s, after the *Brown* decision, in the period immediately prior to the era of moderation. Governor George Bell Timmerman Jr. used all means possible to stop desegregation, including intimidation, persecuting the NAACP and its members, closing a state park rather than desegregating it, and having college professors who favored desegregation fired.[6] Timmerman, Sproat has written, "very nearly took the state down the road Alabama and Mississippi were traveling at the time to ultimate civil disorder."

The state's intimidation of the NAACP and its members certainly did not create an atmosphere of law and order among whites. Since the 1940s black leaders such as McCray had received threats against their lives. Gunmen shot at state NAACP president James Hinton's home and state NAACP treasurer Modjeska Simkins's motel. Economic boycotts by whites squeezed several local NAACP leaders out of business.[7]

Still, in the early 1960s several white leaders, including Hollings, advocated moderation and spoke out for law and order and against violent resistance to desegregation. They did so despite their segregationist convictions. Historians have typically noted rather than explained this turn toward moderation, except to mention two factors. First, there is the influence on politics of the state's business elite, which was looking after its economic interests. Still, if businessmen elsewhere in the South did not have such an influence, the attitude of those in South Carolina would have to be explained. If businessmen had this impact in other southern states as well—and there are indications they did—this factor does not set South Carolina apart, and the turn toward relative moderation by the state's political leaders would need further explanation.[8]

Second, historians have observed that South Carolina's politicians learned from disturbances elsewhere in the South, such as those surrounding the desegregation of Little Rock Central High in 1957 and the University of Mississippi in 1962. They did not want such confrontations in South Carolina.[9] Although the effect of those events on South Carolina appears to be beyond doubt, they would require, it seems, a receptive audience. After all, not all southern leaders learned that same lesson from Little Rock and Oxford. George Wallace in Alabama did not, nor did the authorities in Birmingham and Selma. In other southern states,

11. NAACP leaders in Columbia, 1957: From left: Modjeska Simkins, national secretary Roy Wilkins, James Hinton, and John McCray. Courtesy of South Caroliniana
Library, University of South Carolina

especially Mississippi and Alabama, the white political leadership did not create
an atmosphere that prevented widespread violence, including the killing of voter
registration workers and other civil rights activists.[10]

The reactionary impulse of South Carolina's white political leaders was in
fact modified by their particular collective and individual experience with civil
rights activism. Because of that experience, they were susceptible to moderation
and eventually acted with relative moderation. Their experience with civil rights
activism had put them on the defensive since the early 1940s. It had conditioned
them to take South Carolina's civil rights leaders and their demands seriously, as,
for instance, Lofton has pointed out for Columbia.[11] Such conditioning by itself
may have modified white leaders' behavior. Beyond that, these experiences may
have instilled some genuine respect for the black leaders, which would have made
more difficult an extreme reaction to black demands that were squarely in line
with developments elsewhere in the South. The white establishment had, in any
case, been confronted since the early 1940s with forceful, sustained, and militant

civil rights agitation that favored court action and political pressure and as such had been careful to stay within the law. Fighting civil rights battles through politics and the courts had become the norm in South Carolina well before white politicians decided on that approach. It had done so because the state's black leaders had made it the norm.[12]

What had also become the norm was victory for South Carolina's civil rights activists and defeat for the white political establishment. Especially in a world in which the days of legal segregation were clearly numbered, familiarity with defeat may have conditioned South Carolina's white leaders to expect further defeat, which may in turn have undermined their segregationist resolve. When by the early 1960s the serious push for desegregation came to the state and could no longer be sidestepped, the white leaders' hearts may have been with segregation, but they would only go so far opposing what they now likely saw as inevitable.[13]

During the 1940s and early 1950s black activists beat the state of South Carolina and the state Democratic Party in the courts on three major issues. They first forced the state to pay salaries to black teachers equal to those of their white colleagues. Next, with the nation's post–*Smith v. Allwright* eyes upon them, South Carolina's white leaders lost the fight over the whites-only Democratic primary after several embarrassing knee-jerk reactions that led to as many defeats in the courts. Finally came *Brown v. Board of Education,* a combination of several cases, for which South Carolina's blacks had provided the earliest one, *Briggs v. Elliott.*

Much of the civil rights activists' court action was accompanied by political pressure. Throughout the 1940s the state's white establishment had to endure one of the strongest and fastest-growing NAACP organizations in the country. The state's white Democrats were the first to face a black-led alternative Democratic Party, the South Carolina Progressive Democratic Party (PDP), established in 1944. They also were the first to be challenged by an all-black delegation for seating at the National Democratic Convention, in 1944, 1948, and 1956. And they were the first in the South since Reconstruction to face a challenge, albeit nominal, from a black candidate for a major statewide office when the PDP's Osceola McKaine ran against Governor Olin Johnston for the United States Senate in 1944. Also, South Carolina's blacks organized massive, successful voter-registration campaigns in the 1940s among African Americans well before such campaigns became common throughout the South.[14]

South Carolina's white elites were not immune to black pressure, either. The PDP's Democratic convention challenge in 1944 and John McCray's letter-writing campaign to gain support from leading black Democrats in the North were surely not encouraging to James Byrnes. Byrnes lost the nomination to become Franklin Roosevelt's vice president at the convention because of opposition from labor leaders and northern black Democrats, an event that ultimately cost Byrnes the presidency. Byrnes certainly had a bone to pick with McCray, the editor of the state's largest black weekly, the militant *Lighthouse and Informer.* The suspicion of McCray and others was that Byrnes personally had ordered McCray's arrest and subsequent stint on a chain gang in 1952 after dubious charges and a conviction. Byrnes resented the editor's refusal to give up his support for the *Briggs v. Elliott* suit and his opposition to Byrnes's 1950s gubernatorial campaign. Byrnes, who led "Democrats for Eisenhower," also resented that McCray campaigned for Democratic presidential nominee Adlai Stevenson.[15]

Strom Thurmond, too, suffered a loss at the hands of South Carolina's civil rights establishment when his opponent in the 1950 race for the United States Senate, Olin Johnston, courted the black vote. Johnston himself had suffered a loss as the aggressive leader in South Carolina's attempt to keep blacks out of the Democratic primary. Now, in the 1950 election, he was forced to ask favors from black leaders. In return for his promise not to play the race card during the campaign, they delivered the black vote to him, providing his margin of victory. When Thurmond accused Johnston of being soft on race, Johnston asked permission from the black leadership to answer Thurmond in one speech with racial overtones. In short, by the early 1950s, even before the *Brown* decision came down, it had become clear that South Carolina's whites would have to accommodate the state's black leaders.[16]

Still, in the second half of the 1950s South Carolina's civil rights establishment lost the initiative to the white backlash against the *Brown* decision, led by the Timmerman administration. Given the enormous resentment among whites over the prospect of integrated schools, this may have been inevitable. This was not specifically a South Carolinian development but was in fact a regional one. The loss of initiative, in any case, was to be only temporary. It is significant that it took place not just because of the white political establishment's backlash but because South Carolina civil rights activism itself had lost a step. Several factors played a role. For different reasons, the state's three most important black leaders, McCray, Simkins, and Hinton, became less involved with or even left the movement. The second half of the 1950s was a period of generational change within some important local NAACP branches in the state. Furthermore, the state and national NAACP after *Brown,* probably at the urging of Thurgood Marshall and in reaction to the state threatening to close public schools, did not push petitions to desegregate schools but decided on a wait-and-see attitude.[17] In doing so the NAACP relinquished the initiative, killing its momentum but avoiding an even fiercer white backlash. This relative inactivity created controversy among civil rights activists in the state, which further weakened the movement as a whole.[18]

Decreased energy and action at the state NAACP level left various local attempts by black South Carolinians to desegregate schools and a state park relatively isolated. It also provided space for the Timmerman regime to act. Despite this, South Carolina's government did not achieve much beyond pettiness and ugliness for its own sake; it certainly did not manage to roll back civil rights victories or otherwise turn back the trend toward desegregation. Instead of truly regaining the initiative, the Timmerman administration's actions appeared to be merely a final segregationist spasm. Once DeQuincey Newman took charge of the state NAACP and put it back on course, the initiative returned to the levels of the 1940s and early 1950s.[19]

Isaiah DeQuincey Newman

DeQuincey Newman had been active in South Carolina's civil rights struggle since the early 1940s, and in 1943 he helped organize the Orangeburg chapter of the NAACP. He held various other positions in civil rights organizations throughout the 1940s and 1950s before becoming in 1957 the NAACP's state president, then secretary and, in 1960, field director. Newman, who was born in 1911, had experienced the dominant civil rights tactics of the1940s and their success. His first step after taking over the leadership of the state NAACP was, therefore, not surprising, but certainly significant. He immediately established the NAACP Legal Committee in South Carolina and asked attorney Matthew Perry to become its chair. At the end of the 1950s Perry and the Legal Committee filed lawsuits to desegregate a golf course in Charleston and the waiting rooms at Greenville's airport. Those cases were followed in the 1960s with, in John Sproat's words, "a battery of suits against every bastion of segregation in South Carolina, from the state parks to the most remote school district. Perry assembled a team of lawyers that easily matched the Gressette Committee's legal staff. Understanding that the momentum of events nationally was in their favor, they pressed the offensive with a confidence that was unnerving to some of the white defenders."[20]

In initiating the Legal Committee, Newman picked up where the previous generation of state NAACP leaders had left off. The 1940s successes, Sproat has suggested, convinced Newman and other black leaders that the most effective strategy in South Carolina involved politics and the courts, "the traditional strongholds of white conservatism."[21] Still, in the 1960s, with frustrated black youths initiating demonstrations, sit-ins, and other direct action, Newman expanded the arsenal of the state NAACP. He led demonstrations and marches and engaged in civil disobedience, including a "wade-in" at a state park. In 1963 he criticized the slow pace of desegregation in Columbia. During desegregation battles in Charleston that year he kept up the pressure through continued demonstrations rather than agreeing to a cooling-off period for negotiations. Newman's activism led him to be arrested five times. But direct action in his hands was a means to aid political negotiations, which remained a main part of his approach. Newman also insisted that direct action be nonviolent.[22]

Newman did not represent the conservative wing of the state's civil rights activists in the 1960s. He clearly navigated the tactical waters between militant young activists and conservative older blacks in a movement that was more massive and less homogeneous than that of the 1940s. "His emphasis on nonviolent, persuasive tactics," Sproat has written, "doubtless undercut the demands of more militant and younger activists in the movement for direct action. Some even saw him as an Uncle Tom and criticized him bitterly for 'turning white.'" At the same time, older conservative black leaders, as well as some relatively liberal whites, condemned sit-ins and other direct action. In Columbia, when the demonstrative desegregation movement began to pick up steam in the early 1960s, 1940s militants McCray and James Hinton were among the hand-picked black leaders to whom Columbia's mayor, Lester Bates, was prepared to talk. Newman was not, nor was Simkins. Hinton had ceased to be active in the movement and was then considered a moderate, and McCray did not care for the sit-ins in Columbia. He thought they were improper and that merely negotiating with Columbia's white leadership would do the trick.[23]

Newman surely had the temperament for combining a wide range of tactics and applying restraint at all times. He was, by all accounts, mild-mannered and a born diplomat and persuader. He was also persistent, determined, and tough in pushing for change.[24] These personal qualities enabled Newman to chart a course that was informed by what worked in South Carolina in the 1940s and 1950s and by what was necessary for success in the political climate of the 1960s.

Unlike McCray, for instance, Newman realized that the new era not only demanded additional tactics but allowed for tactics that would have been unfit for the 1940s. Unlike younger militants, Newman did not conclude from the lack of progress on desegregation in the late 1950s that politics and the courts were no longer viable arenas for civil rights agitation. His experience since the 1940s convinced him that they were crucial in South Carolina, despite the stagnation evident in the late 1950s. He was probably less frustrated than the younger activists because he had historical perspective and knew the reasons for that stagnation—reasons that could be overcome. Newman's deliberateness suggests that it misses the point to argue that his restraint and "accommodationism" was defined by basic conservatism. Although Newman's personality may have facilitated his course of action, it was informed by his earlier experiences and by what he thought would get results.

The South Carolina NAACP

The tactics and successes of South Carolina's 1940s movement did not have an impact on the 1960s civil rights scene just because of its influence on key players in the later decade. The strength of the 1940s movement, especially that of the state NAACP, also facilitated the relative restraint with which 1960s developments played themselves out. That strength was not only evident in its prominent position on a national level, but was also clear in the way the state NAACP dominated its home turf, to the extent that other civil rights groups never established much of a presence in South Carolina. The Southern Conference of Human Welfare (SCHW), the Congress of Industrial Organization's Political Action Committee (CIO-PAC), and the American Communist Party did some organizing in the 1940s in South Carolina. In the 1960s both the Congress of Racial Equality (CORE) and the Student Nonviolent Coordinating Committee (SNCC) had some presence in South Carolina. But more so than in other southern states, the South Carolina NAACP and organizations associated with it dominated the field. Certainly on an organizational level, this was still true in the 1960s.[25]

NAACP dominance was an important reason why the state's white leadership had the opportunity to learn from the desegregation disasters in Mississippi and Alabama. Stagnation in the push for desegregation in the late 1950s bought white leaders time to learn from developments elsewhere, and that stagnation was in large part due to the activity, or rather inactivity, of the state NAACP. On the one hand the organization took a wait-and-see attitude toward desegregation, waiting to see what the state of South Carolina would do. On the other the state NAACP went through a transition, with a change in leadership and internal dissent, which may have affected its ability to initiate a forceful desegregation campaign. But because the NAACP's domination was so strong among state civil rights activists, no other organization was ready to fill the temporary civil rights leadership vacuum in South Carolina.

Next, in the 1960s the state NAACP's dominance did two things. First, as before, the strength of the state NAACP kept other organizations on the margins of organized civil rights activism in South Carolina. These other organizations would have been groups such as CORE and SNCC, groups that employed more militant tactics than the NAACP. Second, because of a lack of proliferation of other strong civil rights organizations, there was not the kind of intragroup competition that by itself could have had a radicalizing effect on tactics. All these factors facilitated the relatively restrained process in South Carolina in the 1960s and were the result of the foundations laid in the 1940s.

Historians and the 1940s Movement

Unlike the impact of white moderation, the impact of South Carolina's 1940s civil rights activism on 1960s desegregation has received little attention in the historiography. Those who did make the connection between the two decades misconstrued it to different degrees. I. A. Newby, in his classic book *Black Carolinians,* pointed out that perhaps black rather than white moderation in tone and approach was the key factor in the 1960s. He also traced that black moderation to the 1940s and 1950s. Even though Newby linked the two decades, he defined the link in terms of conservatism only. The 1940s black leadership had been conservative and lacked militancy and resolve, Newby argued, which rubbed off on the 1960s black leadership.[26] Newby was right about the link between the decades, but for the wrong reasons. In the process, by defining away the scope and importance of 1940s activism, he implied this activism was not worth much attention.

Sproat made the connection between the 1940s and 1960s in more precise and analytically more meaningful terms when he argued that the legal and political successes of the 1940s movement may have been the impetus for the approach of 1960s black leaders, especially Newman. But Sproat, too, in Newby-like fashion, defined both the 1940s and 1960s movement largely in terms of conservatism and accommodationism. The 1940s leadership, he added, may have been too cautious. Moreover, Sproat made the meaningful part of his link between the two decades in a 1987 conference paper that was not distributed widely. In an earlier, frequently cited, published chapter, he had not done so.[27]

The longtime lack of appreciation for South Carolina's 1940s civil rights activism is surely a major reason why its influence on the 1960s remains unexplored. Not until recently has the state's 1940s movement been portrayed as politically mature, militant, well-organized, successful, and even a national vanguard whose actions had implications beyond South Carolina. This relatively new view comes largely from two groups of historians. There are those, such as Patricia Sullivan and John Egerton in the 1990s, who have studied the South Carolina movement within a regional or national context and as such judged it to be of great importance. Others have conducted research specifically on the state's 1940s activism. They include most recently Miles Richards, Peter Lau, and the current author. Much earlier, in 1978, Barbara Woods conducted important research.[28]

But until well into the 1990s, Newby ruled the historical roost regarding 1940s black activism. When *Black Carolinians* was published in 1973, it provided the first extensive treatment of black life and politics in the 1940s. In many ways the book was invaluable. Newby provided an overview of socioeconomic and educational developments within black South Carolina. He did so with great empathy for the state's African American population, while confronting head-on the state's white supremacist and racist traditions. But despite his clear sympathies, Newby showed a poor understanding of 1940s black political activism in the state. He ignored some earlier, admittedly brief and scattered treatments of the issue that placed 1940s activism within a national context and deemed it more worthwhile than Newby would. He did not ignore an unpublished study of the end of the state's whites-only Democratic primary, but he did ignore the study's portrayal of an active 1940s movement.[29]

After Newby, several studies dealt with aspects of 1940s black activism, often adding insights that contradicted Newby without, however, developing a reinterpretation.[30] Many studies of South Carolina in the 1940s and 1950s, including those on civil rights developments, focused mostly on the white establishment. Some of these studies looked at the reactions of whites to civil rights developments.[31] Others studied civil rights developments without paying much attention to African Americans or black politics.[32] That neglect of civil rights activism was, before and after Newby, also noteworthy in many biographical and autobiographical books about or by relevant white leaders.[33]

The most important exception was Woods's 1978 dissertation on Modjeska Simkins, which was a forceful reinterpretation of Newby's portrayal of 1940s black activism. Woods not only showed and discussed the initiatives and successes of the 1940s struggle, she also stated its importance in explicit terms. "During the early stages of the civil rights movement of the last two decades," she began her dissertation, "South Carolina did not capture the attention of the national media as did other southern states which experienced a wave of bombing of churches and homes, sensational murders and other outbursts of lawlessness. Yet, if South Carolina can claim a period of moderation in race relations, fewer deaths during the civil rights movement, and less violence in integration of public facilities, the credit must be given to the well-organized, strong and aggressive cadre of black leaders who controlled organizations that paved the way for the change in public life by disseminating information, by working for reform legislation and by undertaking mass registration campaigns long before the decade of the sixties."

The black leadership of South Carolina in the 1940s and 1950s, Woods continued, "was in many ways in the vanguard of the civil rights movement in the South." Many of the leaders were, she wrote, "militant, outspoken and charismatic." Woods's dissertation has not been published as a book and consequently did not gain similar influence as Newby's book, which was published five years earlier, nor did an article by Woods published in 1981.[34]

Sproat's conference paper showed the sustained influence of Newby's book. By heralding black activism's legal and political success in the 1940s, Sproat correctly attached to it a level of substance and achievement that Newby denied. Despite that, he endorsed Newby's judgment of the 1940s black leadership as passive and conservative. Referring to Newby, Sproat wrote that African American leaders in the 1940s had failed "to mobilize the masses" and were perhaps "overly cautious and concerned about jeopardizing their own relatively comfortable, yet still precarious, positions." Newby had shown this, Sproat wrote.[35] But Newby had shown no such thing, even though he made claims to that effect. In reality, black leaders in the 1940s did mobilize the masses, not for street demonstrations but through successful NAACP-membership and voter-registration drives. Also, McCray, Simkins, Hinton, and McKaine and other leaders were not "overly cautious," nor did they all live in comfort or fail to jeopardize their positions.

Newby's treatment of black activism in the 1940s and first half of the 1950s is long on rather arbitrary characterizations but short on actual description and analysis, except for the struggle over the all-white state Democratic primary.

Newby discussed the victory in the Clarendon County school desegregation case, too, but not as a political victory for blacks. He discussed it as a factor in the improvement of the quality of segregated black schools as the state of South Carolina tried to hold off desegregation by making separate less unequal. It is within that context, the improvement of black schools, that Newby also mentions briefly the successful 1940s teacher salary campaign.[36]

Overall, the problems with Newby are problems of omission and of interpretation and definition. The omissions, in part the result of dubious interpretations, exist on two levels. First, he failed to report many of the important activities and achievements of the state's early civil rights struggle. Second, what he did mention was stripped of what often defined the effort: extreme difficulties that could only be overcome with dedication, persistence, and strategic and tactical maturity. In other words, in Newby's version, those achievements did not seem all that hard to come by. The omissions result in a picture of activism that was barely worthy of the term.

For instance there is no mention that the South Carolina NAACP was one of the fastest-growing state NAACPs in the country. In Newby's book the organization is merely the dominant civil rights organization in the state.[37] The difficult and involved fight for equal salaries for black teachers does not exist in Newby's book, either. Instead, he relates that, "under pressure from" black South Carolinians, "white authorities gave serious attention to the problem," after which, at some stage, "the state accepted the principle of salary equalization." Newby does not mention that the NAACP had to go to court twice to achieve salary equalization, and that the national NAACP sent its chief lawyer, Thurgood Marshall, to do so. There is no reference to the difficulties of finding plaintiffs or even support from black teachers because of the widespread fear of repercussions, nor of the years of organizing and fund-raising that preceded the 1944 court cases. In short, what was a hard-fought battle was reduced by Newby to a matter of simply applying some undetermined amount of undefined pressure.[38]

Something similar applies to the decisive 1947 and 1948 court cases that gave black South Carolinians access to the state Democratic primaries. In Newby's version they just happen and are without much importance. In reality they took years of preparation and required arduous fund-raising efforts that were made difficult because many blacks feared being punished for supporting the NAACP. These court cases had national implications, as they made South Carolina the primary battleground for the enforcement of the U.S. Supreme Court's *Smith v. Allwright* decision regarding the Texas primaries.[39]

The PDP was a major part of the successful primary fight, but the party was, in Newby's tale, not much of a success. Newby judged its level of success exclusively on whether the party managed in 1944, at its first attempt, to force the national and state Democratic Party into allowing blacks to participate in its primaries. By that narrow test the PDP did indeed fail, but the party conducted highly successful voter-registration drives, ran a candidate for the U.S. Senate in 1944, and made the difference in the 1950s race for the U.S. Senate between Olin Johnston and Strom Thurmond. Newby ignored all that and claimed that it was not until the 1960 presidential race that South Carolina's blacks "determined the outcome of a statewide contest."[40]

Likewise, Newby ignored the national implications of the PDP's 1944 challenge of the state Democratic Party delegation's seating at the National Democratic Convention. It was the first such challenge by an all-black delegation and, in John Egerton's words, made the PDP "a vehicle to force open the political process in [the] state and in the nation." The PDP, Sullivan wrote, "threatened to explode the uneasy accommodation that the national Democratic Party had maintained between its northern black constituency and its white supremacist southern wing."[41]

Newby's problems of definition and interpretation are evident in how he uses concepts such as "success," "moderate" and "radical," or "active" and "passive." Regarding "success," Newby not only entertained a rather narrow definition with respect to the PDP; the glaring omissions in his book suggest that he did not think much of what later historians considered successful activities. Newby also had a peculiar notion of what makes for an "active" or "passive" movement. It was not until the early 1960s, he wrote, that "black Carolinians were swapping a largely passive role in race relations for a far more active one."[42] Newby seemed to define "active" and "passive" not by what was done or even by the immediate and potential impact on what was done. He defined it by the amount of outward excitement and instant, visible consternation—the noise level, in other words—that actions caused and perhaps by the number of people involved.

The demonstrations and sit-ins of the late 1950s and 1960s are in such a scenario "active" activities. The court cases, political pressure, NAACP membership drives, and voter registration of the 1940s and early 1950s are, on the other hand, "passive" activities. In this interpretation the movement's activities in the 1940s were just "a gentle breeze," which in 1950 "assumed the dimensions of a threatening storm," and in the 1960s "mounted to hurricane force."[43] But to Johnston and other white Democrats of the 1940s, there was nothing gentle about efforts by black South Carolinians. And to Hinton, McCray, McKaine, and Simkins there was nothing passive about it, either.

Newby's mind-set toward pre-1960s activism is revealed by how he cited and quoted historian Erwin Hoffman about the 1930s. Hoffman wrote, according to Newby, that prominent black Carolinians of the 1930s recalled the decade for its lethargy and inaction among blacks. Newby failed to include what Hoffman added. "But upon reflection," Hoffman wrote, the prominent black South Carolinians of the 1930s "remembered enough incidents of organization and struggle in the pre-war decade to suggest that the seeds of revolt were germinating and sometimes sprouting in the earlier years." Newby then ignored Hoffman's characterization of the 1940s and 1950s: "One of the South's most dynamic and successful movements for Negro rights flourished in South Carolina during World War II and the postwar decade," Hoffman wrote. "Striking victories were won by a complex of aggressive organizations which were deeply rooted in both the cities and countryside of the Palmetto state."[44]

In Newby's book these black organizations were not aggressive at all. He found them "moderate" as opposed to "radical" in nature. He found blacks so moderate that he thought it fortunate that they, according to him, did not realize clearly that the "piecemeal change" they fought for could "eventually have revolutionary consequences." Had they known, Newby implies, black leaders might have refrained from demanding even "moderate" reforms. But more recent research provides no reason to believe that black leaders of the 1940s did not know they were chipping away at segregation and contributing to an end to discrimination. McCray's editorials in the *Lighthouse and Informer* certainly did not suggest that his militancy depended on him being too dumb to realize what the sum of his demands would be.[45]

For his "moderates" judgment, Newby used several points of reference, none of them very fruitful. First, he leaned heavily on conservative black sources. To show the moderate nature of black attitudes he quoted a black Republican not closely linked to the movement, as well as the *Palmetto Leader,* a conservative black weekly with only marginal involvement with civil rights activity. Second, Newby compared South Carolina's black leaders to the state's white politicians of the 1940s and 1950s and found Thurmond, Byrnes, Johnston, and Timmerman much more extreme and irresponsible than, say, Hinton and Simkins. That observation is correct, unlike Newby's subsequent implication that, therefore, 1940s black leaders lacked militancy and persistence.[46]

Newby's third and perhaps most important point of reference was the 1960s. To him, engaging in court action and political pressure while obeying the law was moderate on its face. Such a view suggests that the norm for radicalism is confrontational action with a willingness to break laws, as happened in the 1960s. But arguing means are not radical when they are effective is akin to complaining that spices are not hot enough when the dish is. Complaining about moderate means only makes sense if the implication is that more radical means were viable and needed, and that is not a case Newby makes. A 1960s standard also applied when Newby called the early movement's goals moderate simply because not all of them involved demands for desegregation.[47]

Newby's emphasis on the early movement's "moderate" nature may reveal a lack of historical perspective. Taking historical setting into consideration, a vanguard is by definition at least somewhat militant since it is ahead of the pack. When the early movement demanded equal pay for black teachers, it was a vanguard within a South Carolina context, as the lack of active support from teachers themselves indicated. When black leaders of the 1940s rapidly built the South Carolina NAACP, they built an organization that many blacks did not dare belong to and that even in the second half of the 1950s was the target of specifically designed, suppressive state laws. When black leaders demanded access to the Democratic primaries, they were on the cutting edge nationally. In the process they demanded desegregation, one of Newby's standards for radicalism. Newby, however, applied a narrow, provincial perspective. Unlike Hoffman before him and other historians later, he made no attempt to study the 1940s struggle within a regional or national context. Newby even defined the importance of *Briggs v. Elliott* in strictly local terms.[48]

Both Newby's problems of omission and definition indicate a lack of intimate knowledge of 1940s black activism in South Carolina. For one, Newby was a victim of his sources. In addition to using dubious sources for his claims about black conservatism, he mostly used newspaper reports from white dailies to chart political developments within black South Carolina. But the mainstream dailies mostly ignored blacks and were, in any case, rather selective in what they reported.[49] Newby did not use sources closely related to the state's civil rights scene or its leaders, nor did he interview them. Later historians who used such sources and interviews were more impressed with 1940s black activism in the state.

Epilogue

During the 1968 Orangeburg Massacre, state police shot dozens of demonstrators trying to desegregate a bowling alley, killing three students. South Carolina, despite the relative lack of violent confrontation until then, would not escape some of the excesses that had plagued other southern states. The episode showed that South Carolina's white political leadership was indeed capable of acting like its less-heralded equivalents in states such as Alabama and Mississippi. In Orangeburg, Sproat wrote, the state's authorities for weeks failed to take effective steps to defuse the crisis. Moreover, "they fell into the mode of the Wallaces and Faubuses by seeing the crisis only as a plot by 'outside agitators' to disrupt the 'felicitous relations' of blacks and whites in South Carolina."[50]

The Orangeburg episode was part of what underscored Marcia Synnott's 1989 conclusion that for South Carolina "the meaning and viability of 'moderation' in terms of black aspirations and white compromises" await "final assessment."[51] This is true even in 2004. The meaning of black moderation in the state remains ill-defined in the historiography and badly applied to different periods. For the 1940s the term does not define black activism well. For the 1960s the term is useful more as a description of certain elements of black activism than as an explanation; black moderation was a tactical device at times but certainly not a straightforward indication of black conservatism. For the state's white political establishment of the 1960s, *moderation* describes part of its activities, but only explains so much. It does not address how deeply felt or tenuous or even voluntary white attitudes were, nor what their origins were.

A better understanding of 1940s black activism in South Carolina and its long-term impact could provide a better understanding of both black and white moderation in the 1960s. Without considering the range, approach, and success of 1940s activism, the 1960s movement led by DeQuincey Newman is stripped of much of its rationale and, consequently, its deliberate nature. And without an understanding of the successful modus operandi developed by 1940s black activists, the explanation for the historically surprising white moderation in the 1960s has to rely too much on unsatisfactory notions about the innately peaceful nature of South Carolina's white leadership.

Notes

1. For studies presenting, citing, or reflecting this narrative or parts thereof, see, for instance, George McMillan, "Integration with Dignity," in *Perspectives in South Carolina History: The First Three Hundred Years,* ed. Ernest M. Lander Jr. and Robert K. Ackerman (Columbia: University of South Carolina Press, 1973), 381–91 (reprint *Saturday Evening Post,* March 16, 1963, 16–21); John G. Sproat, "'Firm Flexibility': Perspectives on Desegregation in South Carolina," in *New Perspectives on Race and Slavery in America: Essays in Honor of Kenneth M. Stampp,* ed. Robert H. Abzug and Stephen E. Maizlish (Lexington: University Press of Kentucky, 1986), 164–84; Sproat, "The Limits of Moderation in South Carolina," paper presented at the Annual Meeting of the Organization of American Historians, 1987; Sproat, "Newman, Isaiah DeQuincey (1911–1985)," in *The South Carolina Encyclopedia,* ed. Walter B. Edgar (Columbia: University of South Carolina Press, 2006; the Newman entry is available at http://www.scencyclopedia.org/newman.htm); William Hine, "Civil Rights and Campus Wrongs: South Carolina State College Students Protest, 1955–1968," *South Carolina Historical Magazine* 97 (1996): 310–31; Edgar, *South Carolina: A History* (Columbia: University of South Carolina Press, 1998), chap. 22; Maxie Myron Cox Jr., "1963—The Year of Decision: Desegregation in South Carolina" (Ph.D. dissertation, University of South Carolina, 1996).

2. I. A. Newby, *Black Carolinians: A History of Blacks in South Carolina from 1895 to 1968* (Columbia: University of South Carolina Press, 1973).

3. See note 1. Also James S. Lofton Jr, "Calm and Exemplary: Desegregation in Columbia, South Carolina," in *Southern Businessmen and Desegregation,* ed. Elizabeth Jacoway and David R. Colburn (Baton Rouge: Louisiana State University Press, 1982), 70–81. On white-on-black racial violence in South Carolina, see, for instance, Orville Vernon Burton, "'The Black Squint of the Law': Racism in South Carolina," in *The Meaning of South Carolina History: Essays in Honor of George C. Rogers, Jr.,* ed. David R. Chesnutt and Clyde N. Wilson (Columbia: University of South Carolina Press, 1991), 161–85.

4. Edgar, *South Carolina,* 523, 538, 543; Cox, "1963—The Year of Decision," 151–55, 178, chap. 3, 470; Sproat, "Firm Flexibility," 170; Timothy D. Renick, "Solomon Black: 'A Segregationist in Moderation?,'" *Proceedings of the South Carolina Historical Association* (1991): 61–68; Burton, "Black Squint," 175

5. The information in this paper about South Carolina's civil rights struggle in the 1940s and early 1950s comes from Barbara Woods Aba-Mecha, "Black Woman Activist in Twentieth Century South Carolina: Modjeska Monteith Simkins" (Ph.D. thesis, Emory University, 1978), esp. chaps. 3 and 4; Miles Richards, "Osceola E. McKaine and the Struggle for

Black Civil Rights: 1917–1946" (Ph.D. dissertation, University of South Carolina, 1994), especially chaps. 6–9; Patricia Sullivan, *Days of Hope: Race and Democracy in the New Deal Era* (Chapel Hill: University of North Carolina Press, 1996), esp. chaps. 5 and 6; Peter Lau, "Freedom Territory: The Politics of Civil Rights Struggle in South Carolina During the Jim Crow Era" (Ph.D. dissertation, Rutgers University, 2002), esp. chaps. 4–6; and Wim Roefs, "Leading the Civil Rights Vanguard in South Carolina: John McCray and the *Lighthouse and Informer,* 1939–1954," in *Time Longer Than Rope: A Century of African-American Activism,* ed. Adam Green and Charles Payne (New York City: New York University Press, 2003), 462–91. For the current paragraph, see also Sproat, "Firm Flexibility," 165.

6. Howard Quint documented much of Timmerman's abuse in his book about the post-*Brown* reaction of white South Carolina. Howard H. Quint, *Profile in Black and White: A Frank Portrait of South Carolina* (Washington, D.C.: Public Affairs Press, 1958); also Edgar, *South Carolina,* 528; Marcia G. Synnott, "Desegregation in South Carolina, 1950–1963: Sometime between 'Now' and 'Never,'" in *Looking South: Chapters in the Story of an American Region,* ed. Winfred B. Moore Jr. and Joseph F. Tripp (New York: Greenwood Press, 1989), 58; Hine, "Civil Rights and Campus Wrongs," 318–19.

7. Aba-Mecha, "Black Woman Activist," chap. 4; Hine, "Civil Rights and Campus Wrongs," 310–20; Sproat, "Firm Flexibility," 170; Cox, "1963—The Year of Decision," 71–78, 238, chap. 3.

8. On the role of businessmen see, for instance, Cox, "1963—The Year of Decision," ch. 4; Lofton, "Calm and Exemplary"; Edgar, *South Carolina,* chap. 22; Sproat, "Limits of Moderation"; Sproat, "Firm Flexibility," 177–82.

9. See, for instance, Cox, "1963—The Year of Decision," 11; Sproat, "Limits of Moderation"; Edgar, *South Carolina,* 537–40.

10. South Carolina's political leadership may from, say, 1962 onward not have been more moderate than those in most other southern states, then. Perhaps the likes of Mississippi and Alabama were, in negative fashion, at that stage the true exceptions. A systematic comparison between southern states could be instructive. That comparison should focus not on the general attitude of white political leaders after the *Brown* decision; it should make the comparisons for specific moments, specific years. The comparison should go beyond, for instance, measuring how white leaders handled desegregation in education in their particular state. Instead, it should measure white southern politicians' attitude toward such desegregation at any given moment. If South Carolina's politicians applauded Arkansas governor Orval Faubus's 1957 position regarding school desegregation but took a different approach when desegregation was forced on them, the earlier violence elsewhere may indeed have been a factor in the way South Carolina acted. That would suggest they learned the lessons historians say they learned. It would still not explain, of course, why South Carolina's leaders—and perhaps those of several other southern states—had learned that lesson by 1962 while those in Mississippi and Alabama did not. In other words, the specific factors that made white politicians in certain states but not in others learn from such experiences need to be explored.

11. Lofton, "Calm and Exemplary," 79.

12. In addition to the sources in note 5 for the 1940s and early 1950s, see also Sproat, "Limits of Moderation."

13. On the inevitability of desegregation, see also Sproat, "Firm Flexibility," 169–71.

14. See note 5.

15. Roefs, "John McCray," 474–76; David W. Robertson, *Sly and Able: A Political Biography of James F. Byrnes* (New York: Norton, 1994), chap. 13, passim.

16. Nadine Cohodas, *Strom Thurmond and the Politics of Southern Change* (Macon, Ga.: Mercer University Press, 1993), 206–216; Sproat, "Limits of Moderation"; Roefs, "John McCray," 479–81.

17. Synnott, "Desegregation in South Carolina," 52–53, 57–79.

18. Ibid., 55, 58; Cox, "1963—The Year of Decision," 71–78, 238; William D. Smyth, "Segregation in Charleston in the 1950s: A Decade of Transition," *South Carolina Historical Magazine* 92, no. 2 (April 1991): 99–123.

19. Sproat, "Firm Flexibility," 170; Hine, "Civil Rights and Campus Wrongs," 310–20; Cox, "1963—The Year of Decision," 346–47.

20. Sproat, "Limits of Moderation"; Sproat, "Newman, Isaiah DeQuincey"; Cox, "1963— The Year of Decision," chap. 3; Kristie Porter, "The Legal Committee of the South Carolina NAACP and the Struggle for Civil Rights in the 1960s" (B.A. thesis., University of South Carolina, 1990), passim.

21. Sproat, "Limits of Moderation."

22. Ibid.; Cox, "1963—The Year of Decision," 348, 386, 411–12.

23. Sproat, "Limits of Moderation"; Sproat, "Firm Flexibility," 171–73; Newby, *Black Carolinians,* 328–29; Lofton, "Calm and Exemplary," 78; Aba-Mecha, "Black Woman Activist," chap. 4.; Cox, "1963—The Year of Decision," 354–55, 362, 376–77, 382–88, 411–12.

24. Sproat, "Limits of Moderation"; Sproat, "Newman, Isaiah DeQuincey."

25. August Meier, "Epilogue: Toward a Synthesis of Civil Rights Activism," in *New Directions in Civil Rights Studies,* ed. Armstead L. Robinson and Patricia Sullivan (Charlottesville: University Press of Virginia, 1991), 221; Adam Fairclough, *Race and Democracy: The Civil Rights Struggle in Louisiana, 1915–1972* (Athens: University of Georgia Press, 1995), xiv–xv; Sproat, "Firm Flexibility," 173, 180; Cox, "1963—The Year of Decision," 350, 456–57; Roefs, "John McCray," 477–79.

26. Newby, *Black Carolinians,* 279–80.

27. Sproat, "Limits of Moderation"; Sproat, "Firm Flexibility."

28. John Egerton, *Speak Now against the Day: The Generation before the Civil Rights Movement in the South* (New York: Knopf, 1994); for the other references, see note 5.

29. Alexander Heard, *A Two-Party South?* (Chapel Hill: University of North Carolina Press, 1952); William Robinson Sr., "Democracy's Frontiers," *Journal of Human Relations* 2 (Spring 1954): 63–71; Hanes Walton Jr., *Black Political Parties: An Historical and Political Analysis* (New York: Free Press, 1972); James O. Farmer Jr., "The End of the White Primary in South Carolina: A Southern State's Fight to Keep Its Politics White" (master's thesis, University of South Carolina, 1969).

30. Richard Kluger, *Simple Justice: The History of* Brown v. Board of Education *and Black America's Struggle for Equality* (1975; rpt., New York City: Vintage, 1997); Julie Magruder Lochbaum. "The Word Made Flesh: The Desegregation Leadership of the Rev. J. A. DeLaine" (Ph.D. dissertation, University of South Carolina, 1993); Luther Brady Faggart, "Defending the Faith: The 1950 U.S. Senate Race in South Carolina" (master's thesis, University of South Carolina, 1992); Cohodas, *Strom Thurmond;* Jack Bass and Marilyn W. Thompson, *Ol' Strom: An Unauthorized Biography of Strom Thurmond* (Atlanta: Longstreet, 1998); Lofton, "Calm and Exemplary," 73; Robert Lewis Terry, "J. Waties Waring: Spokesman for Racial Justice in the New South" (Ph.D. dissertation, University of Utah, 1970); Tinsley E. Yarbrough, *Passion for Justice: J. Waties Waring and Civil Rights* (New York: Oxford University Press, 1987). David Southern's 1981 article about Waring is in this respect less productive: David W. Southern, "Beyond Jim Crow Liberalism: Judge Waring's Fight against Segregation in South Carolina, 1942–1952," *Journal of Negro History* 66 (1981): 209–27.

31. Andrew McDowd Secrest, "In Black and White: Press Opinion and Race Relations in South Carolina, 1954–1964" (Ph.D. dissertation, Duke University, 1972); Dora Thomas Martin, "The Attitude of the Spartanburg, South Carolina, Press toward the 1954 Supreme Court Decision, 1954–1959" (master's thesis, Atlanta University, 1961); John Bartlow Martin, *The Deep South Says "Never"* (New York: Ballantine, 1957), 43–79; Stephen O'Neill, "To Endure, but Not Accept: The *News and Courier* and School Desegregation," *Proceedings of the South Carolina Historical Association* (1990): 87–94; Joyce Johnston, "Communism vs. Segregation: Evolution of the Committee to Investigate Communist Activities in South Carolina," *Proceedings of the South Carolina Historical Association* (1993): 19–29; Kari Frederickson, "'The Slowest State' and 'Most Backward Community': Racial Violence in South Carolina and Federal Civil-Rights Legislation, 1946–1948," *South Carolina Historical Magazine* 98, no. 2 (1997): 177–202.

32. Henry Cooper Ellenberg, "The Congress of Industrial Organizations in South Carolina" (master's thesis, University of South Carolina, 1951); Alex Peter Lamis, "The Disruption of a Solidly Democratic State: Civil Rights and South Carolina Electoral Change, 1948–1972," *Journal of Political Science* 5 (Fall 1977): 55–72; David G. Blick, "Beyond 'the Politics of Color': Opposition to South Carolina's 1952 Constitutional Amendment to Abolish the Public School System," *Proceedings of the South Carolina Historical Association* (1995): 21–30.

33. John E. Huss, *Senator for the South: A Biography of Olin D. Johnston* (Garden City, N.Y.: Doubleday, 1961); Roger P. Leemhuis, "Olin D. Johnston Runs for the Senate, 1938–1962," *Proceedings of the South Carolina Historical Association* (1986): 57–69; Alberta Morel Lachicotte, *Rebel Senator: Strom Thurmond of South Carolina* (New York: Devin-Adair, 1966); Robert Sherrill, *Gothic Politics in the Deep South: Start of the New Confederacy* (New York: Grossman, 1968), 235–54; Thomas L. Johnson, "James McBride Dabbs: A Life Story" (Ph.D. dissertation, University of South Carolina, 1980); Robertson, *Sly and Able*; James F. Byrnes, *All in One Lifetime* (New York: Harper, 1958).

34. Aba-Mecha, "Black Woman Activist," 1, 211; Barbara A. Woods, "South Carolina Conference of NAACP: Origin and Major Accomplishments, 1939–1954," *Proceedings of the South Carolina Historical Association* (1981): 3; Woods, "Modjeska Simkins and the South Carolina Conference of the NAACP, 1939–1957," in *Women in the Civil Rights Movement: Trailblazers and Torchbearers, 1941–1965*, ed. Vicki L. Crawford, Jacqueline Anne Rouse, and Woods (Brooklyn, N.Y.: Carlson, 1990), 99–120.

35. Sproat, "Limits of Moderation."

36. Newby, *Black Carolinians*, chap. 7.

37. Ibid., 278–79.

38. Ibid., p. 303–4; Aba-Mecha, "Black Woman Activist," 176–94; Richards, "Osceola E. McKaine," chaps. 6 and 7

39. Aba-Mecha, "Black Woman Activist," 195–208; Richards, "Osceola E. McKaine," chap. 7; Walton, *Black Political Parties*, 71; Sullivan, *Days of Hope*, 143.

40. Aba-Mecha, "Black Woman Activist," 202, 210; Richards, "Osceola E. McKaine," 170–76, 193; Walton, *Black Political Parties*, 69–74; Sullivan, *Days of Hope*, 170, 190; Newby, *Black Carolinians*, 291; John McCray, "The Way It Was," *Charleston Chronicle*, November 29, 1980; Cohodas, *Strom Thurmond*, 206–16; Faggart, "Defending the Faith," chap. 5; Sproat, "Limits of Moderation"; James G. Banks, "Strom Thurmond and the Revolt against Modernity" (Ph.D. dissertation, Kent State University, 1970), 226.

41. Walton, *Black Political Parties*, 74–77; Egerton, *Speak Now against the Day*, 227; Sullivan, *Days of Hope*, 170; Richards, "Osceola E. McKaine," chap. 7.

42. Newby, *Black Carolinians*, 278.

43. Ibid., 274.

44. Ibid., 229; Erwin D. Hoffman, "The Genesis of the Modern Movement for Equal Rights in South Carolina, 1930–1939," *Journal of Negro History* 44 (1959): 346.

45. See, for instance, McCray's editorials in the *Lighthouse and Informer,* October 19, 1941; January 10, 1943; and February 6, 1944.

46. Newby, *Black Carolinians,* 277–80, 288. For the level of moderation and militancy of the *Palmetto Leader* and the *Lighthouse and Informer,* see Wim Roefs, "Expanding the Media Landscape for African Americans: South Carolina's *The Lighthouse and Informer* in the 1940s," paper presented at the American Journalism Historians Association Annual Convention, Pittsburgh, October 2000.

47. Newby, *Black Carolinians,* 278–79.

48. Ibid., 305.

49. For the coverage in white South Carolina newspapers of black life and politics, see Roefs, "Expanding the Media Landscape."

50. Sproat, "Limits of Moderation"; for the Orangeburg Massacre, see Jack Bass and Jack Nelson, *The Orangeburg Massacre* (New York: World, 1970).

51. Synnott, "Desegregation in South Carolina," 61.

Seeds in Unlikely Soil

The Briggs v. Elliott *School Segregation Case*

ORVILLE VERNON BURTON, BEATRICE BURTON,

AND SIMON APPLEFORD

The people and state of South Carolina have twice had a revolutionary impact on the history of the United States. In 1861 South Carolina fired the first shots in a war they hoped would preserve a society built upon the subjugation of one race by another, but which instead brought about the end of slavery. Almost ninety years later the actions of an extraordinary group of African Americans from rural South Carolina precipitated an immense growth of democracy in American society when they initiated the first in a series of lawsuits that the Supreme Court ultimately ruled as *Brown v. Board of Education.* It is arguably the most famous and important decision the Supreme Court made in the twentieth century and one that, despite its potential inadequacies, fundamentally changed the history of the United States. Little is remembered, however, of the dramatic story of how this community of African Americans risked their homes, their livelihoods, and even their lives in pursuit of the rights of their children to have a decent education. The result of their efforts would end legal segregation and the Jim Crow era in the United States. Indeed, just as South Carolina ultimately began the Civil War, it can be said that the Palmetto State began the modern civil rights movement.

The driving force of this movement was the Reverend Joseph Armstrong De Laine, who led the African American community of Clarendon County in the fight. Twenty years after the beginning of the court cases, De Laine wrote a series of articles in the *AME Christian Recorder* recounting the events. Although Clarendon County and *Briggs v. Elliott* has received more attention in the years since the fiftieth anniversary of *Brown,* "Seeds in Unlikely Soil" offers a unique perspective of events using De Laine's own words. Rather than white South Carolinians' retelling of the story, this essay uses the voice of the leader of the black community. This story deserves to be heard, for in its telling it reveals not only the depths that a people can sink in defense of a way of life that depends on the daily subjugation of a segment of society, but also the heroism of a people intent on claiming their right and the right of their children to be treated as fully equal citizens in the eyes of the law.

Rural Clarendon County was among the poorest counties in South Carolina, which made it among the most underdeveloped in the United States. African Americans comprised roughly 70 percent of the population, and most worked on land almost 85 percent of which was owned by whites. The segregated public schools of Clarendon County had an enrollment of 6,531 African American and 2,375 white students in 1951. Yet total expenditures for white students exceeded that for blacks by $112,379—some 300 percent per pupil—leaving the African American schools in appalling conditions and lacking basic facilities. One school used "two-by-eights . . . propped up by two fifty-five gallon cans" for seating; another required that the boys be responsible for maintaining the fire that heated the school while the girls did the cleaning; yet another, serving some 600 black students, had only two outdoor toilets, and students had to carry drinking water in a bucket from a neighbor's home.[1] Delores Ragin Jones, one of the *Briggs v. Elliott* plaintiffs, later described how students at Scott's Branch High School in Summerton had overcrowded classrooms and lacked such basic facilities as a science lab and indoor gymnasium. In 1964, before the South Carolina Advisory Committee for Commission on Civil Rights, she went on to testify that students at her school lacked "sufficient background in English," while the mathematics curriculum was so inadequate that it did not include such core elements as algebra.[2] Students were not taught mathematics, and the standard of teaching other disciplines such as English remained far below the state-mandated levels of adequacy. So bad was the situation that in his history of the desegregation cases, Richard Kluger described Clarendon County as "the place in America in the year 1947 where life among black folk had changed least since the end of slavery."[3] Despite the county's poverty and outward appearances, however, the 1940s marked a decade of remarkable transition for Clarendon. This was spurred largely by the return of veterans from World War II, who joined an increasingly confident group of African American activists in demanding an end to the area's Jim Crow hierarchy.

White leaders of Clarendon County justified these inequalities by blaming the region's general poverty. The state only provided funding to pay for teachers' salaries, while the maintenance of facilities and provision of equipment was all privately funded from other sources.[4] Many also pointed to the number of African American parents who left their children in South Carolina while they lived and worked in northern cities such as Chicago and New York, arguing that South Carolinian taxpayers "have no moral responsibility to educate somebody else's children when they have left them behind" and did not pay taxes in South Carolina.[5] According to whites, therefore, African Americans could blame only themselves for any discrepancies in the segregated school system. Of course, they overlooked that two-thirds of African American households in Clarendon had

12. For blacks only: Clarendon County's Liberty Hill Elementary School, 1946. Photograph by Cecil J. Williams

an annual income of less than $1,000 and that, despite a 1940 court ruling demanding equal pay for teachers regardless of race, white teachers typically earned a salary two-thirds greater than did African Americans.[6] Nor did this argument explain why African American teachers had to teach, on average, classes with almost twenty more students in them than those of their white counterparts; nor why such substantial gaps in the curriculum at African American schools persisted. Moreover, African Americans did pay sales taxes just as whites did, and the 37 percent that owned the land they lived on paid taxes on their property, not an insignificant amount given their economic standing in the community.[7]

Most African American parents found especially distressing the county's decision to provide a total of thirty buses to transport white students to school while refusing to do likewise for all children, resulting in many African American children being forced to walk many miles each day regardless of weather conditions. Eugene A. R. Montgomery, later field secretary for the South Carolina branch of the NAACP, recounted the situation of a pair of six-year-old twins who had to walk eight miles each way to get to school: "They used to leave in the morning; in the winter, in the morning, they used to leave about sun-up to get to school on time; and when they got back, it was almost night."[8]

Furthermore, the waters behind the Santee Hydro-Electrical Dam, completed in 1941, frequently flooded the old Santee Road, cutting off children from their schools. Whereas the county provided the "two or three" white students affected by these waters with buses to transport them to their schools, African American children received no such provisions—forcing them to take a rowboat across.[9] A young man drowned while crossing the newly formed lake in the same rowboat routinely used to carry the young African American children on their way to school. The parents grew acutely aware of the dangers their children faced.[10]

Reverend De Laine, pastor of Grove Circuit, which included Society Hill AME Christian Church, wrote, "Negro children had to risk their lives crossing the water in the mornings and afternoons, while a large yellow school bus would go and take the white children to a comfortable school where they could be well trained in the principles of America and the deceased confederacy."[11] De Laine's son, Joe, later described how these white students "would throw Coke caps at black children walking or would spit."[12] A committee, which included the Reverend De Laine, formed to discuss transportation; they wrote county officials, local trustees, road supervisors, the Dam Authority, the attorney general, senators, and congressmen, but none responded to their requests for a bus. Finally the community banded together and bought an old, secondhand bus from the school district, which they themselves operated so that African American children could more easily get to school. Even with the black community running their own bus service for the schoolchildren, the school district refused to supply them with gas for the bus, even though they "paid all of the bills for the transportation of the white children."[13]

Although a self-confessed "conformist" who strove "hard to conform to the law even when it was unfair," Joseph Armstrong De Laine was in fact a lifelong activist in the fight for equal rights.[14] Born in Clarendon County in 1898, De Laine was himself the son of a minister and grew up amid the worst that Jim Crow society could offer. Nevertheless, he persevered, and through years of hard work, he found himself at the age of thirty-three principal of a school in Orangeburg County, South Carolina, where he earned a total of $60 per month. His wife, Mattie, worked as a teacher at the same school, raising their combined monthly salary to $110—not an insignificant amount for a household in the area at the time, whether white or African American, and one that provoked some resentment among the white community.[15] The young family soon returned to Clarendon County, where De Laine became pastor at Pine Grove Church and, like many other pastors, quickly became the acknowledged spokesman and leader of the African American community in the eyes of both blacks and of whites. Unlike many others in similar circumstances, however, De Laine became an active campaigner in the fight to end the inequities he encountered on a daily basis. In 1943, for example, he became a founding member of the

Clarendon branch of the National Association for the Advancement of Colored People and spearheaded local efforts in the statewide campaign to bring an end to the all-white South Carolina primary system.[16]

In 1947 De Laine attended a summer class titled Race and Culture at Allen University, an AME university in Columbia, South Carolina, where he heard Dr. James Hinton, the president of the state's branch of the NAACP, speak about the need to "test the discriminatory practices of the school bus transportation." Although the Palmetto Teachers Association had the money needed to pursue such a case, Hinton implied that South Carolina did not have a teacher or preacher with enough "Damn Guts" to find a plaintiff to file a case to challenge inequality. "These words sunk deep into my thinking," De Laine later recalled, and he realized that this was "the opportunity to extend the exhausted efforts which we had been working for in vain. This was the challenge which I was longing for, so I wasted no time." He told Dr. Hinton "to look for me to bring a client next week."[17]

Upon his return to Summerton, De Laine and his son, Joe, met with Hammitt and Levi Pearson, two brothers in the area, to discuss the idea of suing the school board to provide a bus for their children. At first the brothers hesitated, because they did not have the money to hire a lawyer, and these rural African Americans did not trust attorneys or the law. With De Laine's assurances, however, Hammitt agreed to sue for the buses. Rethinking, De Laine realized that Levi's levelheadedness might be more suitable for the struggles ahead and advised that his be the name on the suit. Levi agreed, saying, "Yes, I'll sue if you will get the money to run the case."[18] Aware that the white establishment would be sure to "play every dirty trick imaginable" in their effort to prevent the success of their suit, Pearson "grimly accepted that he would go all the way, even if it cost his life."[19]

The next week De Laine and Levi Pearson went to Columbia and met with James Hinton; A. T. Butler, the Palmetto Teachers executive secretary; and attorney Harold Boulware, the first African American lawyer in Columbia in several years, who would be taking their case.[20] Pearson's petition was filed with the board of trustees of District 26 on March 16, 1948, and declared that the school district should furnish, maintain, and operate a school transportation system for use by African American children in the district.[21] Shortly before the *Levi Pearson v. Clarendon County and School District No. 26* case commenced, however, white defendants discovered that Pearson's property straddled two districts—his children went to a school less than half a mile from his home, located in District 26, where the suit had been filed, while Pearson paid his taxes to District 5. The NAACP consequently determined that they could not pursue the case, and on June 8, 1948, Thurgood Marshall, who was assisting Boulware, requested that the court dismiss the suit. Upon learning this, the state senator from Clarendon County laughed, saying, "The n____r don't even know what district he is in."

Although the African American community of Clarendon County felt disheartened about time and money lost, they did not give up. De Laine later wrote, "I cannot account for what caused me to continue except dogged determination."[22]

The following spring, De Laine received a letter from Boulware inviting him to a meeting at the Palmetto Teachers Building in Columbia and asking him to bring people from Clarendon County. The meeting, which took place on March 12, 1949, included the NAACP legal staff, Palmetto Teachers Association officers, officers of state NAACP branches, and representatives from Clarendon County. NAACP attorney Thurgood Marshall announced that the NAACP planned on pulling out of the Clarendon case because it had only one plaintiff. The organization had invested too much money to risk when white supremacists could easily "liquidate" such a small group "in order to defeat the case of asking for 'Equal Everything.'"[23] Although De Laine pointed out to Marshall that the NAACP had originally asked for only one plaintiff and that abandoning the community would invite white retribution, Marshall was adamant: the NAACP would only continue to fight the case in Clarendon if they could secure at least twenty families to sign a petition demanding equalization.[24] Determined not to abandon their cause, De Laine and the other attendees from Clarendon hosted a number of meetings across the community to persuade people to sign the petition.[25] Eugene Montgomery and Lester Banks, executive secretary of the Virginia state branch of the NAACP, also attended the meetings, convincing De Laine that the court case should focus on Manning High School and Elementary School in District 9 or Scott's Branch combined Elementary and High School in District 22.[26] The rationale behind this change was simple: both District 26 and District 5 already had considerable support for equalization but contained no schools for white students. Both District 9 and 22, on the other hand, "had good [white] High Schools . . . and the comparison was easy." Despite enthusiastic moral support from the communities of these districts, however, the threat of losing white patronage proved too much for most to contemplate joining a lawsuit—in District 22, for example, only two people stepped forward.[27]

Although their parents hesitated because of the consequences of joining an equalization case, the 1949 Scott's Branch High School graduating class had their own concerns. That year they did not have any math. They paid rent for inadequate books. Each child had to pay for the fuel needed to heat the school. Students who lived more than three miles from the school had to pay a twenty-seven-dollar fee because they lived outside the district.[28] Parents held a fund-raiser to pay for basic school supplies, but their money was not used for the purpose for which it had been raised. According to De Laine, I. S. Benson, the newly installed African American principal of Scott's Branch, told the students that what he did with the school's money did not concern them: "If I take it and buy liquor with it, it's none of your business."[29] Mattie De Laine, the assistant principal at Scott's Branch, told her husband, "If those children had anybody to lead them they would straighten up some of the injustices which are going on in Scott's Branch School."[30]

Led by Reverend De Laine, students from the class of 1949 wrote up their grievances and sent copies to the principal, the district superintendent of education, and the county superintendent of education.[31] They organized a meeting for the night of June 8, 1949, exactly one year to the day after the withdrawal of the original bus case, to which they invited school officials to respond to the allegations. Although neither the principal nor any white school official, invited or otherwise, attended the meeting, approximately three hundred outraged parents did.[32] As part of a deliberate attempt "to shift the site of the struggle from District 26 to District 22," the African American community's leaders had prearranged that De Laine would accept the chairmanship of a new Parent Committee on Action, but only after nominating several others from District 26. When they declined the position—usually with the sentiment that they could not talk with the white authorities—De Laine would accept.[33] In accepting the nomination, De Laine told the assembly that the path would be long and hard. The whites would make everything difficult and would ignore and decline their demands, but he would not cease. The African American community would continue appealing their case, he prophetically proclaimed, all the way to the Supreme Court if necessary. Two days later, the white school board unceremoniously fired De Laine from his position of principal of Liberty Hill Elementary School, of which he later wrote, "It was rather funny to me since it came more than a year later than I expected."[34] This meeting came to mark a turning point in the story of school desegregation, for at it the African American community of Clarendon County rallied together, determined to do whatever was necessary to ensure their children's equal treatment. The commitment of Clarendon's children, however, proved even more significant. They recognized they were being denied the same rights granted to their white counterparts and demanded that something be done about it, even though it left them vulnerable to the same reprisals that their parents faced.

At the initial hearing on June 28, with De Laine, three African American farmers, the county superintendent of education, the superintendent of Summerton High School District, an agricultural teacher, and three white trustees of the school district in attendance, whites "tried to brush us off with the old stuff of how good Negroes and whites have been getting along together," and because this was a school matter rather than a church matter, they questioned the legitimacy of De·Laine's role as representative of the students and parents.[35] The NAACP legal staff, however, had coached De Laine on his rights and what he could expect to get out of the meeting. Therefore he quoted with some authority the Fourteenth Amendment to bolster his case. In response the white authorities told him that "that thing don't apply here" and that the school principal had the right to do the things he did. The trustees refused to take any action in the matter. De Laine later wrote, "Well, I couldn't swallow that because I once had it in me that I was a first class citizen. What they were doing was reducing us to third class."[36]

Despite the refusal of the school trustees to take action, De Laine and the parents would not give any ground and determined to have meetings every other Wednesday until they got results. They appealed to the county board of education, who redirected them back to the school trustees and told them their complaints were unfounded because someone who wanted the principal's job made them. They fired any teacher they thought had sympathetic leanings to the students' grievances. Even after De Laine presented seven affidavits from seven teachers to the State Department of Education, the trustees would still not dismiss the principal. After months of petitioning for a new hearing, in mid-September the superintendent of education finally granted the request, setting a date of Saturday, October 1, 1949.[37]

After the hearing district superintendent H. B. Betchman invited De Laine to a private meeting, at which he asked what he needed to do in order to stop the case. De Laine told him that Principal Benson must be dismissed and that the teachers that had been fired must be reinstated.[38] Betchman then offered De Laine the position of principal of Scott's Branch School, but on the condition that "he stop the fight" for improving conditions at the African American schools. De Laine declined the position, stating that he would not sell out those who looked to his leadership.[39] At the next parents' meeting he announced that Principal Benson had been fired and that, in an effort to placate the parents, Betchman had appointed De Laine's wife, Mattie, as acting principal of Scott's Branch, which satisfied many of the parents. De Laine, however, was not fooled by this tactic, pointing out that "next year Mrs. De Laine will be fired and never again will we get anything going as good as it is going now." The parents agreed and refused to give any money to the school other than book rent. Of the four fired teachers, the superintendent rehired two, and they returned to the school.[40] Although Mrs. De Laine held Scott's Branch in good hands for the moment, educational facilities in the school district remained far from equal. The parents' group decided to keep their momentum going by continuing their lawsuit against the state.

Throughout the maneuvering over Scott's Branch, the original issue of school inequality remained unresolved. The NAACP required twenty signatures on a petition before they would continue their support of an equalization lawsuit. After months of waiting, on November 11, 1949, De Laine received a large package from the NAACP, which he had to sign for at the post office, where he could not easily conceal it from the white people who hated the NAACP.[41] His lawyers had advised De Laine against having people sign the petition at a large public meeting, so he approached Harry and Eliza Briggs about having it signed at their house; they agreed, and that night became the first to put their names on the petition. Clarendon County's African Americans finally began their lawsuit, seeking "Equal Education Opportunities and Facilities for Negro School Children" in their community. According to De Laine, that night "there were happiness and wonder mingled together. We knew that there would be much treacherous doings. We had anticipated that the cost would be great but we resolved to set in motion an 'Education Revolution.'" The signed petition was filed with the Clarendon County School Board, chaired by Roderick W. Elliott, while a copy was forwarded to the *Manning Times News*, which published it the next morning. One hundred and four names were on the petition: twenty-nine adults and seventy-five children.[42] One name conspicuously absent from the petition, however, was that of Joseph A. De Laine, whom a concerned Boulware had advised that if he signed, he would become a target, singled out and ruined, and that it would be all but impossible to find another strong leader to see the movement through to the end.[43]

The document itself articulated the grievances of the African American community: Clarendon County's public school system was "maintained on a separate, segregated basis," but was far from equal. "The facilities, physical condition, sanitation and protection from the elements . . . [of] the only schools to which Negro pupils are permitted to attend, are inadequate and unhealthy, the buildings and schools are old and over-crowded and in a dilapidated condition," all of which was in stark contrast to the "modern, safe, sanitary, well equipped, lighted and healthy" facilities provided to the district's white students. African American students were furthermore denied sufficient teachers, classroom space, teaching supplies, and "bus transportation to carry them to and from school." These inadequacies, the petition concluded, were a direct consequence of the African American children of Clarendon County "being discriminated against solely because of their race and color" and were in direct "violation of their rights to equal protection of the laws provided by the 14th amendment."[44] It is important to note that the petition did not seek to integrate Clarendon's schools, as some whites claimed—a charge that De Laine himself denounced as a "malicious lie"—instead asking only for equalization.[45]

The reaction of official white Clarendon County was initially to ignore the petition and delay for as long as possible a public acknowledgment of it in the assumption that the complaints of the African American community would eventually subside. Activists such as De Laine, however, continued to press the district for a response, which they finally received in February 1950. District 22's board of trustees admitted that their school system was "maintained on a separate and segregated basis as required by the Constitution and Laws of the State of South Carolina" but denied that African Americans were being discriminated against on the basis of their race. Indeed, the trustees claimed that any perceived inequalities were the result misinformation—the claim that whites were provided with bus transportation and blacks were not was wrong, they said, because

13. *Plaintiffs in* Briggs v. Elliott *at St. Mark AME Church in Summerton, 1949. Photograph by Cecil J. Williams*

the district in fact provided buses for neither group—that a "cursory inspection . . . [would] reveal that the facilities, condition, equipment, safety, and protection from the elements are accordingly better with the negro schools than the whites," and that they were making every possible effort to ensure any remaining inequalities—such as insufficient teachers—were rectified.[46] The petition consequently did little to improve the situation in Clarendon, but it did raise awareness of the state of public education in Clarendon County, and De Laine recalled that "Scott's Branch became a shrine of public interest" almost overnight and that "cars started pouring in as tourists" came to see the conditions for themselves.[47] Although some whites were sympathetic to the complaints, they feared the consequences of supporting the petitioners and did little to prevent the repercussions suffered by their African American neighbors for their temerity in challenging one of the tenets of white supremacist South Carolina.[48]

Harry Briggs, father of five children—whose profile was higher than most because he was the first to sign the petition, which was therefore named after him—was an illustrative example of the increased discrimination faced by the community, eventually being forced by "economic pressure" to stay "in Summerton by name only."[49] Briggs, who had served in the Navy during World War II, was fired from his job of fourteen years in late November 1949 and was subsequently denied the opportunity of enrolling at Scott's Branch High School as a veteran. Even so, Eliza Briggs told her husband that "if you take your name off that Petition, I'll quit you."[50] Briggs never did remove his name from the petition but found it impossible to find employment in South Carolina and finally left in order to support his wife and children, who remained in Summerton. He lived in Miami for twelve years before moving with his wife to New York in 1961, where the NAACP helped him relocate in appreciation for "his courageous stand during the famous Clarendon County School Segregation Case against South Carolina."[51]

As leader of the petitioners, De Laine came under special pressure. Immediately following the filing of the petition with the school district, he began to receive threats from the Ku Klux Klan, warning him of dire consequences if he continued to lead the movement.[52] At a meeting on December 12, 1949, however, De Laine publicly challenged the Klan. He later wrote, "I sounded the alarm of danger to anybody walking on the side of the street, after dark, near my house. It was made plain that this applied to both colored and white. 'Any animal like a man must call his name as he approached the area of my house or I'll shoot and then ask who's that?'"[53] Whites' violence showed that they were weak and scared, De Laine told his congregation. "You empowered me to speak for all of you and I now declare there will be no retreat nor surrender."[54] He had received warnings that some whites in the community were out to harm him, De Laine continued, but "these warnings instead of frightening me, made me more determined and angry. However, I tried to let my better judgment suppress my anger."[55] De Laine's reaction to the Klan's threats showed whites that the African American community would not bow to their intimidation while simultaneously reassuring the petitioners that they could stand up against the strictures of white supremacy, but it also placed him in considerable danger. On December 15, 1949, he went to the post office around 10:30 A.M. as usual. He left his pistol in the car but had his pocketknife with him. Six white men were standing across the street, but De Laine did not think anything of it until one of the men crossed the street and said, "Me or you going to go to hell today." De Laine responded, "What do you want to go to hell for? I'm not going," and he stuck the man with his pocketknife. The white man thought he was shot and became terror-stricken. Just then, James Brown, one of the signers of the petition, drove up in a truck, blocking the view of the five remaining white men and allowing a relieved De Laine to reach his car and drive to the Brown residence.[56]

De Laine was subjected to a different form of intimidation in January 1950, when District 22's board of trustees persuaded I. S. Benson, the former principal of Scott's Branch, to sue him for $20,000 for slander on the grounds that De Laine had orchestrated the campaign to have Benson removed.[57] Although this was clearly an attempt to discredit De Laine, and by extension the equalization movement, the NAACP was reluctant to take on the case because the plaintiff was himself an African American; De Laine was therefore forced to find his own representation. To make matters worse, De Laine fell ill shortly before the case was to be heard and went to Columbia for several weeks to recuperate. Taking advantage of his absence, whites from Summerton wrote De Laine a threatening letter that was signed by the Ku Klux Klan, which they used to inflame white sentiment against him, promising to burn him in effigy. The NAACP, however, sent copies of the letter to "every law enforcement officer [they] knew, from President Eisenhower [*sic*] on down," and so when a large crowd of whites gathered in Manning to witness the spectacle, they discovered that the area was swarming with federal officers, who held a blanket warrant to search all the houses in the vicinity.[58] At the superintendent's house the officers found the mimeograph used to reproduce the letter sent to De Laine with the original stencil still in it.[59] In the meantime, the slander case against De Laine was heard before an all-white jury, which found for the plaintiff, awarding the former principal $4,200 in damages, although the amount was later reduced to $2,700.[60]

In reaction to these continued threats, Bishop Frank M. Reid, De Laine's prelate in the South Carolina AME Church, encouraged him to move to Lake City, South Carolina, for his own sake. De Laine, however, was reluctant to leave, believing that he still had work to do in Clarendon and remembering his father's stories of Lake City's first African American postmaster, who was murdered in 1898 by Klan members after he ran from his burning home; under the justice system operating in the turn-of-the-century South, and despite national attention and a fourteen-month federal investigation, the killers, inevitably, went free. Reid, however, assured De Laine that his work at Summerton was done—the case was in the NAACP's hands and would soon be filed in federal court—and that it was God's will that he move on.[61] After consulting with several friends, all of whom feared that he would be murdered if he stayed in Summerton, De Laine was finally persuaded that his family should leave. De Laine told his wife of his decision and that the school trustees would fire her from her job the following year, anyway, as indeed they did. Mattie De Laine supported her husband's decision, declaring that "if they move you or fire me, we will make it somewhere, anyhow."[62]

In May 1950, shortly after De Laine left Clarendon, Harold Boulware and Thurgood Marshall filed *Briggs v. Elliott* in the Eastern Circuit of Federal Court in Charleston, South Carolina. The complaint was scheduled to be heard on November 17, 1950, by federal judge J. Waties Waring, a white Charlestonian who had made several important rulings challenging South Carolina's segregationist policies. In the meantime, however, the Supreme Court handed down decisions in the cases of *Sweatt v. Painter, McLaurin v. Oklahoma Board of Regents,* and *Henderson v. United States* that together challenged, without overturning, the fallacy of the "separate but equal" doctrine in public education and transportation. In the wake of these important equalization decisions, the NAACP determined that it would pursue only desegregation, and not equalization, cases. This left the future of *Briggs v. Elliott* in some doubt; considerable time, effort, and resources had been invested in the case, but it would most likely only result in an order for District 22 to ensure the equality of their separate educational systems. In pretrial hearings, however, Judge Waring forced the NAACP's hand by living up to his reputation as a radical on racial matters and unexpectedly declaring that there had been enough cases about equalization. He instructed Marshall to challenge explicitly *Plessy v. Ferguson* and the very institution of segregation. Somewhat taken aback, Marshall agreed, and the equalization case was summarily dismissed without prejudice.[63]

On December 18, 1950, Boulware and Marshall gathered the plaintiffs together and asked them to sign a new petition, one that explicitly attacked South Carolina's 1895 constitution and by extension *Plessy v. Ferguson* with its doctrine of separate but equal. Twenty families signed (nine fewer than had signed the equalization petition), again headed by Harry Briggs, and the new petition was filed in federal court on December 22, 1950. Because the new case attacked the state constitution, however, it would be heard not before the sympathetic Waring alone, but before a three-judge panel, which in conservative South Carolina was a serious obstacle to its chances of success, and on appeal would be sent directly to the Supreme Court for a definitive ruling on the legality of segregation under the Fourteenth Amendment.[64] Up until this point whites had seen equalization as a local concern. This case, if successful, would be transformed into one of national import, heralding a fundamental shift in law affecting all seventeen states that operated segregated schools.

Briggs v. Elliott was heard on May 28, 1951, in Charleston, South Carolina, before Waring, Chief Judge John Parker, and Judge George Bell Timmerman Sr. The African American plaintiffs from Clarendon County met at the St. Mark AME Church in Summerton and rode to Charleston to attend the hearings. De Laine remarked on their enthusiasm, determination, and resilience. After all the white community had done to deter their efforts, they were finally to receive their day in court. "This was one of the most stinging back sets which the racest [*sic*] element of the white people had ever had." People from other states came as well. The courtroom was overflowing; many African Americans could not get into the room. As De Laine recalled, "Not over twelve white people were there but many Negroes were there who couldn't even look inside of the little court house door." Judge Parker was unable to get order in the courtroom and was forced to request that Marshall ask the African Americans to settle down.[65]

Thurgood Marshall and Harold Boulware were again counsel for the plaintiffs. Citing *Missouri ex rel. Raines v. Canada, Sweatt v. Painter, McLaurin v. Oklahoma Board of Regents,* and *Henderson v. United States* as his precedents, Marshall argued that the schools in Clarendon's District 22 were unequivocally inferior to their white counterparts. Their condition made it clear that "there is not just segregation involved; there is exclusion."[66] He continued, "You are made to go to an inferior school—not that you go to a Negro school, but Negro and inferior. . . . Segregation means inferior."[67] Representing the defense was Robert Figg Jr., a renowned lawyer from Charleston and active fund-raiser for Strom Thurmond, and S. Emory Rogers, a local attorney from Summerton. Their tactic was startling: rather than denying that Clarendon's schools were not equal, they openly admitted as such and instead requested that the state be given time to equalize facilities—indeed, under the leadership of Governor James F. Byrnes, South Carolina was already in the process of raising $75 million with the express intent of ensuring that equal educational opportunities could be provided for members of each race. Figg furthermore argued that the courts had continuously upheld the "separate but equal" doctrine, as recently as in the decisions of *Sweatt, McLaurin,* and *Henderson,* and that if the history of segregation were examined it had existed in the North before the Civil War. He went on to claim that the protections of the Fourteenth Amendment did not apply to schools, and looked to Washington, D.C., to prove his point: "The same congress which submitted the 14th amendment to the states of the country also enacted legislations providing for separate schools for the two races in the District of Columbia."[68]

When the decision was handed down, the majority of Parker and Timmerman ruled against desegregation but ordered equalization, arguing that the cited cases involving graduate education did not apply to the lower school levels under question in this case. They furthermore stressed the Supreme Court's continued upholding of *Plessy v. Ferguson* and "separate but equal," writing that it was "for the Supreme Court, not us, to overrule its decisions."[69] Waring, however, penned a scathing dissent: "If segregation is wrong, then the place to stop it is in the first grade and not in graduate schools. . . . I am of the opinion, that all of the legal guideposts, expert testimony, common sense and reason point unerringly to the conclusion that the system of segregation in education adopted and practiced in the state of South Carolina must go and must go now. Segregation is per se inequality."[70] This was the first time that a federal judge had made such a ruling against segregation.

Despite this setback, whites continued to agitate against those involved in desegregation movement; in retaliation for his leadership in the case, De Laine's parsonage was burned down while he attended the AME annual conference, but the police never arrested any suspects. The fire did not surprise De Laine; he had become used to such threats. Whenever anything happened, he immediately reported it to the FBI, who ignored him, and Waring; after Waring retired, De Laine passed the information on to federal judge Ashton Williams of Lake City.[71] Members of local churches took up a collection to help De Laine rebuild his home.[72]

As anticipated, the NAACP appealed the district court's ruling to the Supreme Court, where it ultimately became one of five cases being heard by the Court that challenged segregation in public schools. These five cases combined to become *Brown v. Board of Education.* Yet it is only as a result of an

14. Thurgood Marshall arriving in Charleston for the hearing of Briggs v. Elliott *before the U.S. district court, 1951. Photograph by Cecil J. Williams*

accident of history that we know it by that name. Indeed, the reasons behind the decision to hear these cases under the banner of *Brown* rather than *Briggs,* which preceded the other cases both alphabetically and in terms of when it was initially filed with the Court, is one that remains confused. *Briggs* was the first of the cases to be filed, but only reached the discovery phase before being returned to the district court on January 28, 1952, with instructions to rule on the county's equalization report. Meanwhile the Kansas case had been appealed to the Supreme Court, and as of January 28 *Brown* was the only one of the cases pending before the Supreme Court. The others (including *Briggs* on its way back up) subsequently joined it and were placed under *Brown.* By such a quirk of fate, Linda Brown and Topeka became famous, and Harry Briggs and Clarendon, South Carolina, did not. It seems that the original suggestion to have the case be named for *Brown* rather than *Briggs* came from Associate Justice Tom Clark, "so that people would not view this as a southern issue." Still, this standard explanation ignores the substantial influence that James F. Byrnes still wielded with his former colleagues in the Supreme Court and the Senate. According to Byrnes's biographer, it was South Carolina's governor who maneuvered the court filings in such a way as to ensure that *Brown* appeared on the court docket ahead of the one from his own state. If any man had the power to achieve this, it was the affable Jimmy Byrnes, who had himself served on the Supreme Court from 1941 to 1942; five of the nine justices from Byrnes's tenure remained in the Warren Court in 1951.[73]

After hearing arguments from Thurgood Marshall and Emory Rogers, the Supreme Court justices wanted more information, adjourning the Court until December 1953.[74] The hearing went for three days as the two sides argued their cases.[75] Finally, on May 17, 1954, word came through that the Court was ready to announce its findings. For De Laine, "The long awaited Supreme Court's Decision, which kept us in a high tension, from the eagerness for a favorable decision and the insults and reprisals which we had undergone for at least six years," was a defining moment.[76] The decision was unanimous. Chief Justice Earl Warren read, "In the field of public education, the doctrine of 'separate but equal' has no place. Separate educational facilities are inherently unequal. Therefore, we hold that the plaintiffs and others similarly situated for whom the actions have been brought here are, by reason of the segregation complained of, deprived of the equal protection of the laws guaranteed by the Fourteenth Amendment. This disposition makes unnecessary any discussion whether such segregation also violates Due Process Clause of the Fourteenth Amendment."[77]

Spirits were high among Clarendon County's African American community. De Laine wrote, "For the 20 family Plaintiffs and the rest of us who were envolved [*sic*] it was a victory equal to that of Ulysses Grant over General Lee's Army when they surrendered at Appomattox Court House at the end of the Civil War. We were abused, we were marked as communists, [and] we were mistreated by those who were in and also those who were not in responsible positions. Fortunately we endured hardness as good soldiers until the end came which was only the beginning of a larger struggle which would be taken up others who had either condemned us or wished us well."[78] De Laine reflected on those who had sacrificed their lives for this cause and wrote, "They did not enjoy the fruit of their labors but they had the satisfaction that their labor was not in vain."[79]

Briggs v. Elliott was duly returned to South Carolina's district court for enforcement. Thurgood Marshall, looking to Kansas's immediate desegregation as an example, argued that South Carolina should also desegregate quickly; Emory Rogers, once again arguing on behalf of the defendants, countered by pointing out that South Carolina had been segregated for two hundred years and that it would take time to develop a plan. Figg said the district had to be given time to accept the idea. On May 31, 1955, however, the Supreme Court gave South Carolina that time by issuing its second ruling in the *Brown* case, stating that desegregation must proceed "with all deliberate speed."[80]

The Supreme Court had given its decree, but court procedure required that the cases go back to their states of origin for enforcement. On July 15, 1955, the

Fourth Federal Circuit Court of Appeals met in Columbia, South Carolina, to rule on how desegregation would be achieved in the state. In a ruling that became known as the "*Briggs* dictum," Chief Justice Parker declared that although the Supreme Court had determined segregation to be unconstitutional, it did not state that the races had to mix or indeed require that children attend racially diverse schools. In fact, according to Parker's ruling, a school could be racially homogeneous, so long as the state did nothing to prevent students of any race from enrolling there. As a result of this misrepresentation of the spirit of *Brown*, desegregation was to be delayed in Summerton for a further twelve years.[81]

African Americans in South Carolina, and across the South, soon discovered that "all deliberate speed" in fact meant never, and the unfortunately vague wording of the decision soon became a de facto victory for the segregationists, as it allowed them to defy indefinitely the Supreme Court's intent. Furthermore, the end of the court case did not mean the end of the terror. "All over the South the die-harders were trying to whip in line all law abiding white or Negro Citizens."[82] De Laine remained in the public consciousness as the leader of the desegregationists, placing him in greater risk than others, yet he remained defiant; when he received a threatening letter identifying him as the leader of the desegregation case, he responded, "The above letter was a high compliment to me to know that several hundred folks recognized the power of my teaching."[83] When he was warned that he should leave town for the sake of his wife and children, he replied, "Thank God that I lived to see all my children large enough to run for themselves if necessary and I trust that my wife will be able to take care of herself."[84] On September 3, 1955, shots were fired at the Lake City parsonage. De Laine and his youngest son got the license plate number of the car, which was occupied by five young white men. When they gave the plate number to Lake City's chief of police, Maxie Hines, it was discovered that it was a dealer's number, so they could not identify the culprits. Hines told De Laine to mark the car next time so it could be identified.[85]

Bishop Reid tried his best to convince De Laine to move out of Lake City, but De Laine refused, telling him that when Reid sent him to Lake City, he had said it was God's will that De Laine be there. Now he would not leave unless he received word from God to go.[86] On October 10, 1955, a little after midnight, shots were again fired at the house from a passing car. As Hines had instructed him, De Laine fired at the automobile, which sped off, and "Marked the Car in Jesus Name."[87] De Laine waited for police to come, as they would have heard the shots at the nearby station, but no one came. Finally De Laine recalled, "In my quiet reflection, the Lord said until me, 'Its time for you to leave here.'"[88]

Realizing he would have to flee South Carolina, De Laine drove to Florence and from there flew to Washington, D.C.[89] Taking a limo from the airport, he was joined by several white men, one of whom asked another if he had heard about the African American in South Carolina who shot the white men. None of the passengers knew the details, only that the white men had come to his house because of his role in the segregation cases. One passenger said he had every right to fire at people who came to his house after midnight to cause trouble. De Laine wrote, "While this conversation was going on I was sitting on the front seat too proud to look around. When they got out at the hotels, I said, 'Thank God.' But I did not say it where the driver could hear."[90] From Washington, D.C., De Laine went to New Jersey, where he stayed in hiding for several months, and from there he eventually relocated to New York, where the rest of his family joined him. He remained there until his retirement in 1974, when he moved to Charlotte, North Carolina, which was as close to his home state as he could get because the warrant for his arrest in South Carolina remained in effect until long after his death on August 3, 1974.[91] De Laine was not bitter, however, later commenting that "it's worth some suffering—it's even worth a man's life, if he can start something that will lead to a little more justice for people."[92]

De Laine was not the only African American in the community to suffer. When first organizing *Briggs v. Elliott,* Thurgood Marshall and De Laine did not allow the most vulnerable members of the community, such as sharecroppers, to sign the petitions, because they knew the plaintiffs would suffer. They had no idea to what extent. As the court cases progressed, the full array of Jim Crow terror and repression played out in rural Clarendon County. All forty rural, black, unacknowledged heroes of Clarendon County, having challenged the South's racial codes, suffered. Whatever elements of white paternalism or leniency had existed quickly faded. Long-standing debts, an everyday occurrence in southern agriculture economy, were called in, and whites refused to sell black plaintiffs seeds or supplies. Equipment usually loaned willingly to help African Americans with harvests or plowing was refused; crops rotted in the fields.[93]

The nephew of the white superintendent of schools owned several farms that black tenants rented; the owner made activism synonymous with economic hardship. Every black person who signed a petition to improve conditions lost a job, was denied the ability to trade for necessary agricultural goods, or was threatened with physical violence.[94] William Ragin, one of the original petitioners, stated, "In town they cut us all off from anything; a few of my good white folks [did] stand by me, but they couldn't let it be known." Ragin was a cotton farmer with approximately eighty acres of land, but after signing the petition was no longer able to buy oil in Summerton; the store refused to sell to him, even though he did not owe any money.[95] Another signer of the petition, Thelmaer Berthune, testified, "I signed the petition so that my children could get a better education than I had." She was denied loans, and whites she thought were her friends pressured her to take her name off the petition. But Berthune "told them I couldn't take it down."[96]

White employers openly bragged about what they would do to their employees, who were shocked "to learn some of the things done by persons who we had respected so long."[97] Many of those who signed the petition lost their jobs, while others had their credit immediately withdrawn and mortgages foreclosed. William "Bo" Stukes, father of five children and a veteran of World War II, for example, was fired from his job as a mechanic in early December 1949. To supplement his income he began working on cars in his yard, but he did not have the proper equipment. A little over a year later, in January 1951, while working on a car, it fell on top of him and killed him at the age of thirty-two; although there was no evidence supporting such an assertion, many African Americans believed that it was no accident and that Stukes had been murdered.[98] Teachers suspected of being members of the NAACP were summarily fired and African American veterans refused benefits afforded to whites of the same status.[99] Some paid an even heavier price: in April 1950 James M. McKnight was murdered when he stopped his car at the side of the road in order to relieve himself. With his family waiting in their car, the white driver of a passing car stopped, turned around, and killed McKnight; an all-white coroner's jury later exonerated the murderer. That McKnight had not even signed the petition did not seem to matter to the perpetrator, who, according to private statements from the coroner, killed McKnight because of his anger over the protests and because McKnight was an African American.[100] Such measures hurt the African American community financially or worse, but they also inspired them when they met together, and those who were less dependent on whites did what they could to help those that were more dependent.[101]

Beatrice Brown Rivers, who signed the first petition in November 1949 and whose parents were named on both, was thirteen when these events began to unfold. While Clarendon was in turmoil, her parents "did everything they could to protect us from the craziness that was going on." Rivers also explained the parents' drive in bringing about *Briggs v. Elliott*: "These were basically uneducated people who knew why they were denied an education. They also knew that their parents had been denied the opportunity to get an education. Therefore, they knew that if they did not take a stand we would be relegated to an inferior education or no education at all. I thank God that our parents were our heroes who fought to make life better for us."[102]

Others took inspiration from the courage displayed in Clarendon. Rosa Parks thought of Clarendon County when she would not give up her seat on the bus, according to Billie Fleming of the Clarendon County branch of the NAACP.[103] In 1951 Modjeska Simkins, the NAACP's state conference secretary, spoke at a tribute to the parents and students involved in the court cases, telling them, "You have made Clarendon County Hallowed Ground; you have made it historic ground, for whenever the history of this country and state are written and studied, the Clarendon, South Carolina, case must be discussed. You have become a part of the great world movement of all men, especially those of color everywhere, to be free and walk with dignity."[104]

Although Africans Americans in Clarendon County won the 1954 Supreme Court decision, separate schools were maintained there until 1965, when Harvey Gantt successfully sued Clemson College and the state to grant him admission. Then the state subsequently allowed students to select the schools they would attend, and four black students enrolled in Clarendon County's white school in fall 1965. In reaction whites established a private academy, Clarendon Hall, and in 1969 only 281 white students were left in the Summerton public school system. One year later, when the schools officially desegregated, the number had fallen to 16. Summerton typifies rural "black belt" schools in that white students withdrew after desegregation.[105]

The situation has yet to improve. Although the *New York Times* reported in an article on Summerton written in 1991 that "whites and blacks coexist with an easy surface sociability that is far more amiable than can be found in many Northern cities," as recently as 2004, of the approximately 1,200 students in what is now known as Clarendon County School District 1, only about two dozen were white; of the 275 students at Clarendon Hall, 5 were African American.[106] Until as recently as December 2005, when circuit judge Thomas W. Cooper Jr. ruled that it denied students "the opportunity to receive a minimally adequate education," funding at South Carolina's schools was tied to local property taxes, an initiative that mostly affected poor rural areas with predominantly African American populations.[107] Clearly the work started by Joseph De Laine, Levi Pearson, Harry Briggs, and so many others continues today.

Judge Waties Waring once credited "one man's tenacity" with the court case's arrival to the Supreme Court: Rev. J. A. De Laine.[108] Journalist John Egerton has said, "I found myself wishing the title had been . . . *De Laine v. Clarendon County* in honor of the Rev. Joseph A. De Laine of Summerton, South Carolina, the one individual above all others most responsible for bringing this first of the five cases to court."[109] The impact that De Laine and his followers had on the history of the United States is finally being recognized not only by scholars of the civil rights movement, but also by policy-makers in Washington; in December 2003 the Reverend Joseph A. De Laine, Harry and Eliza Briggs, and Levi Pearson were awarded congressional gold medals in "recognition of their contributions to the Nation as pioneers in the effort to desegregate public schools that led directly to the landmark desegregation case of *Brown v. Board of Education*."[110]

At the time this article was being written, however, there was no acknowledgment of these accomplishments in the state of their birth. The statehouse grounds in South Carolina fly the flag of the Confederacy and are adorned with statues celebrating Confederate heroes and leaders of the illegal, paramilitary overturning of Reconstruction. Public memory of the Lost Cause is held dear in South Carolina, but what of the memory of this extraordinary group of African Americans who initiated the first lawsuit that would ultimately end legal segregation and Jim Crow in the United States? There are no public memorials to the

Briggs v. Elliott plaintiffs in Clarendon County, let alone South Carolina, and no permanent exhibits or museums dedicated to the case. The Clarendon County Chamber of Commerce's Web site mentions that De Laine and Briggs were born in the region, but does so after celebrating that the 1958 winner of the Miss America pageant also hailed from Clarendon and makes no mention of why they are so important, describing them merely as "civil rights leaders."[111] The time surely has come for South Carolina to acknowledge and celebrate a revolution that benefitted not only the state, but the United States as a whole, and began in the rural county of Clarendon.

Notes

1. Eugene A. R. Montgomery and Mattie De Laine quoted in Southern Regional Council, *Will the Circle Be Unbroken: A Personal History of the Civil Rights Movement in Five Southern Communities; Episode 3: Under Color of Law,* Radio Program, 1997, transcript available online at http://unbrokencircle.org/scripts03.htm (accessed July 30, 2006); Orville Vernon Burton, "Rural Race Relations since World War II," in *The Rural South since World War II,* ed. R. Douglas Hurt (Baton Rouge: Louisiana State University Press, 1998), 30.

2. South Carolina Advisory Committee for Commission on Civil Rights, Transcript of Proceedings, Manning, South Carolina, May 22, 1964, 11.

3. Richard Kluger, *Simple Justice: The History of* Brown v. Board of Education *and Black America's Struggle for Equality* (New York: Vintage, 1977), 4.

4. Raymond Wolters, *The Burden of* Brown: *Thirty Years of School Desegregation* (Knoxville: University of Tennessee Press, 1984), 131–32.

5. South Carolina Advisory Committee for Commission on Civil Rights, Transcript of Proceedings, 105–6.

6. Kluger, *Simple Justice,* 13–14.

7. 1940 census data as given by the University of Virginia website: http://fisher.lib .virginia.edu/collections/stats/histcensus (accessed July 15, 2006).

8. South Carolina Advisory Committee for Commission on Civil Rights, Transcript of Proceedings, 7–8.

9. *AME Christian Recorder,* January 3, 1967.

10. Brumit B. De Laine and Ophelia De Laine Gona, *Briggs v. Elliott: Clarendon County's Quest for Equality, A Brief History* (Pine Brook, N.J.: O. Gona, 2002), 14.

11. *AME Christian Recorder,* January 10, 1967.

12. Joseph De Laine Jr., interviews by Orville Vernon Burton, March 5 and 6, 2003, Charleston, S.C.; April 2, 2004, Urbana, Ill.; April 22, 2004, Columbia, S.C. See also "Courage: The Carolina Story That Changed America" (exhibit at the Levine Museum of the New South, Charlotte, N.C., January 30–August 15, 2004; hereafter referred to as Levine Exhibit). Information about this exhibit is available online at http://www.museumofthenewsouth.org/ exhibits/detail/?ExhibitId=9 (accessed July 31, 2006).

13. *AME Christian Recorder,* January 3, 1967.

14. *AME Christian Recorder,* August 30, 1966; probably dating back to Richard Kluger's *Simple Justice,* many accounts mistakenly refer to De Laine's middle name as "Albert," rather than "Armstrong."

15. Kluger, *Simple Justice,* 9–11.

16. Julie Magruder Lochbaum, *The Word Made Flesh: The Desegregation Leadership of the Rev. J. A. De Laine* (Pine Brook, N.J.: O. Gona, 2003), 54–56; *AME Christian Recorder,* October 11, 1966.

17. *AME Christian Recorder,* January 3, 1967; *AME Christian Recorder,* January 17, 1967.

18. *AME Christian Recorder,* January 3, 1967.

19. *AME Christian Recorder,* January 17, 1967.

20. W. Lewis Burke and William C. Hine, "The South Carolina State College Law School: Its Roots, Creation, and Legacy," in *Matthew J. Perry: The Man, His Times, and His Legacy,* ed. W. Lewis Burke and Belinda F. Gergel (Columbia: University of South Carolina Press, 2004), 29.

21. *AME Christian Recorder,* January 24, 1967; Kluger, *Simple Justice,* 16.

22. *AME Christian Recorder,* January 24, 1967.

23. Ibid.

24. The Clarendon County School Segregation Case, in the papers of Joseph A. De Laine, South Caroliniana Library, University of South Carolina, Columbia (hereafter De Laine Papers), Folder 6, 9625, 3; *AME Christian Recorder,* January 24, 1967.

25. *AME Christian Recorder,* January 31, 1967.

26. Ibid.

27. Ibid.; Clarendon County School Segregation Case, De Laine Papers.

28. The state law stated that students should attend the nearest high school to their district.

29. Report on Education, October 16, 1952, De Laine Papers, Folder 5, 9625, 3; *AME Christian Recorder,* February 7, 1967.

30. *AME Christian Recorder,* February 7, 1967.

31. Ibid.

32. Kluger, *Simple Justice,* 20.

33. Clarendon County School Segregation Case, De Laine Papers, Folder 6, 9625, 4; *AME Christian Recorder,* February 14, 1967.

34. *AME Christian Recorder,* February 21, 1967; February 28, 1967.

35. *AME Christian Recorder,* March 3, 1967.

36. *AME Christian Recorder,* March 14, 1967.

37. *AME Christian Recorder,* March 21, 1967.

38. *AME Christian Recorder,* April 11, 1967.

39. *AME Christian Recorder,* April 18, 1967.

40. *AME Christian Recorder,* April 25, 1967.

41. *AME Christian Recorder,* May 2, 1967.

42. *AME Christian Recorder,* May 9, 1967.

43. *AME Christian Recorder,* May 16, 1967.

44. Petition of Harry Briggs et al. to the Board of Trustees for School District No. 22, November 11, 1949, available online at http://www.sefatl.org/pdf/Briggs-petition.pdf (accessed January 14, 2008).

45. "An Open Letter: A Summary of Incidents in the Summerton School Affair," De Laine Papers, Folder 5, 9625, 1.

46. Decision of Board of Trustees of School District No. 22 to Harry Briggs et al., letter, February 20, 1950, available online at http://www.sefatl.org/pdf/reply%20to%20Briggs %20petition.pdf (accessed July 31, 2006).

47. *AME Christian Recorder,* May 23, 1967.

48. Harry Briggs's wife, for example, was forced out of her job because of pressure placed on her employer by the white establishment. See Kluger, *Simple Justice,* 23–24.

49. Harry Briggs's name was not, however, the first alphabetically on the petition filed in November 1949; James Hercules Bennett's was. Because Bennett did not sign the first, qualification, petition, the second, desegregation, petition retained Briggs's name as that of the first-named plaintiff.

50. *AME Christian Recorder,* June 20, 1967.

51. *AME Christian Recorder,* August 29, 1967; "Eliza and Harry Briggs Seek Refuge in N.Y. after S.C. 'Economic Pressure,'" *Afro-American,* January 13, 1962.

52. *AME Christian Recorder,* June 13, 1967.

53. *AME Christian Recorder,* June 20, 1967. De Laine's children later recalled that long before Martin Luther King and the nonviolent civil rights movement of the 1960s, their father, living in what amounted a terrorist society, strategically hid several firearms throughout town to protect himself and his family.

54. *AME Christian Recorder,* June 20, 1967.

55. *AME Christian Recorder,* June 13, 1967.

56. Brown had in fact come to tell De Laine that he and his son Thomas had just been fired from the local Esso filling station, where he had worked for nineteen years. The owner had not wanted to fire them, but a group of whites threatened to boycott the store if he did not. None of the Browns were able to find work in Clarendon County after that, and they were forced to move to Detroit, Michigan. *AME Christian Recorder,* August 1, 1967.

57. J. A. De Laine, *The Clarendon County School Segregation Case,* De Laine Papers, Folder 6, 9625, 1.

58. *AME Christian Recorder,* September 12, 1967. De Laine was, of course, mistaken in this statement, as Eisenhower was not elected until 1952; two years after the events he is describing.

59. Ibid. The Ku Klux Klan took offense at the use of their organization's name in a location that they did not have a presence and sued the town and the superintendent for $3,000.

60. *AME Christian Recorder,* September 26, 1967.

61. *AME Christian Recorder,* October 3, 1967.

62. *AME Christian Recorder,* October 10, 1967; October 17, 1967.

63. *AME Christian Recorder,* November 28, 1967.

64. Ibid.

65. *AME Christian Recorder,* December 26, 1967.

66. *AME Christian Recorder,* January 2, 1968.

67. *AME Christian Recorder,* January 9, 1968.

68. *AME Christian Recorder,* January 16, 1968.

69. *Briggs v. Elliott,* 98 F. Supp. 529 (U.S. Dist. Ct. 1951)

70. Waring's dissent, *Briggs v. Elliott,* 98 F. Supp. 529 (U.S. Dist. Ct. 1951).

71. *AME Christian Recorder,* June 25, 1968.

72. *AME Christian Recorder,* July 16, 1968.

73. David W. Robertson, *Sly and Able: A Political Biography of James F. Byrnes* (New York: Norton, 1994), 515–16. The five justices were Robert Jackson, Stanley Reed, Hugo Black (who had also served in the Senate with Byrnes before they served in the Supreme Court), and Felix Frankfurter. In addition Sherman Minton, who was appointed after Byrnes left the Supreme Court, served in the United States Senate at the same time as Byrnes.

74. *AME Christian Recorder,* September 3, 1968.

75. *AME Christian Recorder,* September 10, 1968.

76. *AME Christian Recorder,* September 17, 1968.

77. *Brown v. the Board of Education of Topeka, Kansas,* 347 U.S. 483, 495 (1954).

78. *AME Christian Recorder,* September 24, 1968.

79. *AME Christian Recorder,* October 8, 1968.

80. *Briggs v. Elliott,* 132 F. Supp. 776 (U.S. Dist. Ct. 1955).

81. *AME Christian Recorder,* December 3, 1968.

82. *AME Christian Recorder,* February 25, 1969.

83. *AME Christian Recorder,* June 10, 1969.

84. *AME Christian Recorder,* August 26, 1969.

85. *AME Christian Recorder,* January 7, 1969.

86. *AME Christian Recorder,* January 13, 1970.

87. *AME Christian Recorder,* date unknown.

88. *AME Christian Recorder,* January 20, 1970.

89. *AME Christian Recorder,* date unknown.

90. *AME Christian Recorder,* date unknown.

91. Levine Exhibit; Joe De Laine Jr., speaking at "The Civil Rights Movement in South Carolina," conference at the Citadel, Charleston, S.C., March 5, 2003. See the transcript of his remarks reprinted in this volume.

92. Charles Joyner, "One People: Creating an Integrated Culture in a Segregated Society, 1526–1990," in *The Meaning of South Carolina History: Essays in Honor of George C. Rogers, Jr,* ed. David R. Chesnutt and Clyde N. Wilson (Columbia: University of South Carolina Press, 1991), 227.

93. Orville Vernon Burton, "Rural Race Relations since World War II," 33.

94. Ibid.

95. South Carolina Advisory Committee for Commission on Civil Rights, Transcript of Proceedings, 36.

96. Ibid., 47.

97. *AME Christian Recorder,* May 23, 1967.

98. *AME Christian Recorder,* August 29, 1967; Dennis C. Dickerson, "Reverend J. A. DeLaine, Civil Rights, and African Methodism," *AME Church Review* (July–September 2003): 55. See also South Carolina's death index, available online at http://www.scdhec .gov/vr/di/asp/vrlist.asp?c=s&pagenum=191 (accessed July 31, 2006).

99. *AME Christian Recorder,* May 23, 1967; Things That Happened Since Nov. 11, 1949, De Laine Papers, Folder 5, 13439.

100. *AME Christian Recorder,* May 30, 1967. See also South Carolina's death index, available online at http://www.scdhec.gov/vr/di/asp/vrlist.asp?c=m&pagenum=102 (accessed July 31, 2006).

101. *AME Christian Recorder,* 23 May 1967.

102. Beatrice Brown Rivers, speaking at "The Civil Rights Movement in South Carolina," March 5, 2003. See the transcript of her remarks reprinted in this volume.

103. Billie Fleming, quoted in "Courage: The Carolina Story That Changed America."

104. *AME Christian Recorder,* March 5, 1968.

105. Raymond Wolters, *The Burden of Brown: Thirty Years of School Desegregation* (Knoxville: University of Tennessee Press, 1984), 129–74; Jeff Miller, "What Tomorrow Can Bring," *Southern Exposure* 22 (Summer 1994): 16–23.

106. *New York Times,* April 21, 1991. Alan Richard, "The Heat of Summerton," *Nation,* May 3, 2004, available online at http://www.thenation.com/doc/20040503/richard.

107. *Abbeville County School District, et al., v. The State of South Carolina, et al.,* no. 93–CP-31–0169 (Lee, S.C., Court of Common Pleas, December 29, 2005), 160; available online at http://www.scschoolcase.com/Abbeville-County-Order.pdf.

108. *AME Christian Recorder,* May 27, 1969.

109. John Egerton, *Speak Now against the Day: The Generation before the Civil Rights Movement in the South* (Chapel Hill: University of North Carolina Press, 1995), 589.

110. *A Bill to Award Congressional Gold Medals Posthumously on Behalf of Reverend Joseph A. DeLaine, Harry and Eliza Briggs, and Levi Pearson in Recognition of Their Contributions to the Nation as Pioneers in the Effort to Desegregate Public Schools That Led Directly to the Landmark Desegregation Case of* Brown et al. v. the Board of Education of Topeka et al. (P.L. 108–180, December 15, 2003).

111. "History," *Clarendon County, South Carolina,* http://www.clarendoncounty.com/history.html (accessed July 31, 2006).

Five Days in May

Freedom Riding in the Carolinas

RAYMOND ARSENAULT

In 1961, during the first year of John F. Kennedy's presidency, more than four hundred Americans participated in a dangerous experiment designed to awaken the conscience of a complacent nation. Inspired by visions of social revolution and moral regeneration, these self-proclaimed Freedom Riders challenged the mores of a racially segregated society by performing a disarmingly simple act. Traveling together in small interracial groups, they sat where they pleased on buses and trains and demanded unrestricted access to terminal restaurants and waiting rooms, even in areas of the Deep South where such behavior was forbidden by law and custom. Patterned after a 1947 Congress of Racial Equality (CORE) project known as the Journey of Reconciliation, the Freedom Rides began in early May with a single group of thirteen riders recruited and trained by CORE's national staff. But by early summer the rides had evolved into a broad-based movement involving hundreds of activists representing a number of allied local, regional, and national civil rights organizations. Attracting a diverse assortment of volunteers—black and white, young and old, male and female, religious and secular, northern and southern—the Freedom Rider movement transcended the traditional legalistic approach to civil rights, taking the struggle out of the courtroom and into the streets and jails of the Jim Crow South.

Empowered by two United States Supreme Court decisions mandating the desegregation of interstate travel facilities, *Morgan v. Virginia* (1946) and *Boynton v. Virginia* (1960), the Freedom Riders brazenly flouted state and local segregation statutes, all but daring southern officials to arrest them.[1] Deliberately provoking a crisis of authority, they challenged federal officials to enforce the law and uphold their constitutional right to travel without being subjected to degrading and humiliating racial restrictions. Most amazingly, they did so knowing that their actions would almost certainly provoke a savage and violent response from militant white supremacists. Invoking the philosophy of nonviolent direct action, they willingly put their bodies on the line for the cause of racial justice. Openly defying the social conventions of a security-conscious society, they appeared to court martyrdom with a reckless disregard for personal safety or civic order. None of the obstacles placed in their path—not widespread censure, not political and financial pressure, not arrest and imprisonment, not even the threat of death—seemed to weaken their commitment to nonviolent struggle. On the contrary, the hardships and suffering imposed upon them appeared to stiffen their resolve, confounding their white supremacist antagonists and testing the patience of even those who sympathized with their cause. Time and again, the riders seemed on the verge of defeat, but in every instance they found a way to sustain and expand their challenge to Jim Crow segregation. After marauding Alabama Klansmen used bombs and mob violence to disrupt and disband the original CORE Freedom Ride, students from the Nashville chapter of the Student Nonviolent Coordinating Committee (SNCC) stepped forward to organize a ride of their own, forcing federal officials to intervene on their behalf. And later, when Mississippi officials placed hundreds of Freedom Riders in prison and imposed bond payments that threatened the financial solvency of CORE, the net effect was to strengthen rather than to weaken the nonviolent movement. On these and countless other occasions, attempts to intimidate the Freedom Riders and their supporters backfired, reinvigorating and prolonging a crisis that would not go away.[2]

It is little wonder, then, that the Freedom Rides sent shock waves through U.S. society. In the mid-1950s, the Montgomery Bus Boycott and its Gandhian leader, the Reverend Martin Luther King Jr., familiarized Americans with the tactics and philosophy of nonviolent resistance. And in 1960 the sit-in movement conducted by black college students in Greensboro, North Carolina, and scores of other southern cities introduced the country to direct action on a mass scale. Nothing in the recent past, however, had fully prepared the American public for the Freedom Riders' interracial "invasion" of the segregated South. With the Freedom Rides, the civil rights struggle reached a new level of intensity, evoking fears of widespread social disorder, racial polarization, and a messy constitutional crisis. By the end of the original CORE Freedom Ride, in mid-May, photographic images of burning buses and bloodied riders were seared in the public mind, both at home and abroad. Deeply embarrassed by the news reports from the Deep South, Kennedy administration officials engaged in a cold war struggle with the Soviet Union took extraordinary measures to quell the crisis. In late May, Attorney General Robert Kennedy urged the Interstate Commerce Commission to issue a sweeping transit desegregation order that would implement the Supreme Court's earlier rulings, and in September the commission responded with just such an order. By the end of 1961 interstate transit facilities were a fact of life throughout most of the South, though compliance was grudging and incomplete in a significant portion of the Deep South. Over the next year the last vestiges of resistance on the issue gave way, bringing the civil rights movement one of its first victories in the war against de jure segregation. Setting the stage for the escalating demands and rising expectations of the mid-1960s, the Freedom Rides accelerated the maturation and nationalization of a broad-based freedom struggle.[3]

Much of the drama, and almost all of the violent resistance, that accompanied the Freedom Rides took place in the Deep South states of Alabama, Mississippi, and Louisiana. Nevertheless, it is important to remember that, directly or indirectly, the rides touched virtually every corner of the South, including North and South Carolina. Situated along the route of the original CORE Freedom Ride, Carolinians, both black and white, were among the first southerners to encounter this new form of civil rights activism. Their responses—varying from enthusiastic endorsement to indifference to outright resistance—helped to shape the first week of the Freedom Ride. The experiences that the riders accumulated during their five days in North and South Carolina constituted an important prelude to the crisis-laden events that would soon put Alabama and Mississippi in the headlines. More specifically, the obstacles and resistance that the Freedom Riders encountered in Charlotte, Rock Hill, and Winnsboro represented a harbinger of things to come. And yet the history of the first week of the Freedom Rides was strikingly different from the dark saga of the second. Indeed, the fact that the confrontations in North and South Carolina did not involve violence on a mass scale—that the full-blown crisis occurred in Alabama and not in the Carolinas—suggests significant subregional differences in white supremacist behavior and political context. For this reason alone it is worth recalling the details of the five days in May 1961 (as well as a brief subsequent drama in June), when the Freedom Riders elicited a mixture of hostility and restraint in two southeastern states standing at the crossroads of racial progress and reaction. Though overshadowed by events in Alabama and Mississippi, this largely forgotten episode in the civil rights history of the Carolinas underscores the complexity of the 1960s freedom struggle. As historians are only now beginning to appreciate, each state—indeed, each community—had its own peculiarities where matters of race and segregation were concerned. For the Freedom Riders themselves, this revelation was not altogether reassuring, since it suggested that the struggle would have to be waged in a bewildering array of settings. But for them, as for us, the variability of Jim Crow culture and the multiple contingencies affecting the pace of change were important historical realities that should not be dismissed or overlooked.

For most Carolinians in the spring of 1961, the Freedom Rides were a shocking development that seemingly came out of nowhere. Unknown to all but a small number of movement activists and public officials in North and South Carolina, CORE's plan called for a two-week Freedom Ride, beginning in Washington on May 4 and ending in New Orleans on May 17, the seventh anniversary of the *Brown* school desegregation decision. Divided into two groups, one traveling on Trailways and one on Greyhound, the Freedom Riders would test compliance to the *Boynton* decision in more than a score of southern bus terminals, stopping for overnight stays in Richmond, Petersburg, and Lynchburg, Virginia; Greensboro and Charlotte, North Carolina; Rock Hill and Sumter, South Carolina; Augusta and Atlanta, Georgia; Birmingham and Montgomery, Alabama; and Jackson, Mississippi. Before setting out on the two-week journey, thirteen Freedom Riders—seven blacks and six whites—gathered in Washington on May 1 for three days of intensive training in nonviolent activism. Four of the riders—national director Jim Farmer, *CORE-lator* editor and Journey of Reconciliation veteran Jim Peck, and field secretaries Genevieve Hughes and Joe Perkins—were CORE staff members; the other nine were carefully selected volunteers representing varied backgrounds and organizations. The five black volunteers were John Lewis, a student activist from the American Baptist Theological Seminary in Nashville, Tennessee; Charles Person, a freshman at Morehouse College in Atlanta; Hank Thomas, a Howard University student active in the Washington area's Nonviolent Action Group (NAG); the Reverend Benjamin Elton Cox of High Point, North Carolina; and Jimmy McDonald, a musician from New York City. The white volunteers included Albert Bigelow, an architect and peace activist from Cos Cob, Connecticut; Ed Blankenheim, a carpenter from Tucson, Arizona; and Walter and Frances Bergman, two retired educators from Detroit, Michigan.

Accompanied by two black journalists and one white magazine writer, the Freedom Riders left Washington on Thursday morning, May 4, with only a limited sense of what to expect. All were experienced and committed nonviolent activists, but several were traveling to the Deep South for the first time. In the pre-trip briefing, they were told that the first few days of the Freedom Ride would almost certainly be the easiest part of the journey, and the uneventful and largely successful compliance tests in Richmond, Petersburg, and Lynchburg confirmed this prediction.[4] Things would get tougher as they traveled farther south, they were told, a truth that began to unfold on the fourth day of the journey when the Riders arrived in Danville, Virginia, a mill town sixty-five miles south of Lynchburg. Here for the first time the Riders encountered open hostility and resistance. At the combined Greyhound-Trailways station, a black waiter refused to serve Blankenheim when he insisted on sitting at the "colored counter." After several minutes of waiting and after the waiter explained that his white boss had promised to fire him if he served a white Freedom Rider on the wrong side of the color line, Blankenheim gave up and reboarded the bus. But, an hour or so later, three other white riders—Peck, Genevieve Hughes, and Walter Bergman—renewed the challenge. Following a curt refusal and a brief standoff, Peck convinced the station manager to relent. The seeming irrationality of insisting on eating at an inferior facility must have puzzled the manager and the rest of the white staff, but the Freedom Riders knew they had won a small but significant victory.[5]

By mid-Sunday afternoon, both buses had crossed the North Carolina border, leaving proud but perplexed Virginia to its own devices. The day's final destination was Greensboro, the birthplace of the 1960 sit-in movement. Prior to the sit-ins, Greensboro had been one of the first communities in the South to initiate voluntary compliance with *Brown,* and local white leaders had taken great pride in the city's reputation for progressive politics and enlightened paternalism. But more than a year of militant civil rights agitation had shaken the white community, which had great difficulty coping with Greensboro's new image as a center of the southern freedom struggle. By the time the Freedom Riders arrived, the city's "civil" approach to racial accommodation had long since given way to the politics of racial polarization and white backlash. Although a few local white leaders continued to push for moderate gradualism, the dominant mood was anything but conciliatory. The result was a curious mix of lingering moderation and rising defiance. This confusion was obvious at the Greensboro Trailways station, where the riders encountered huge signs pointing to a "colored" lunch counter that had been closed down earlier in the week. One local black told Peck that "he was amazed when upon entering the colored lunch room one day, he was advised to walk around to the formerly white restaurant." Two years earlier this same restaurant had refused to serve Joseph McNeil, one of the four students who later initiated the Greensboro sit-ins. Some friends even speculated that the episode, which followed a long bus ride from New York, had triggered McNeil's decision to join the sit-in.

Still enrolled at North Carolina A&T, McNeil was among those who escorted the Freedom Riders to Bennett College for an afternoon meeting with student leaders and later to Shiloh Baptist Church for an eight o'clock mass meeting. This was the same church that had welcomed CORE riders in 1947, following the beatings at Chapel Hill. Shiloh's pastor, the Reverend Otis Hairston, was a fearless activist who had spearheaded a local NAACP membership drive in 1959 and who had turned his church into an unofficial command center during the early stages of the sit-in movement. He was proud that two of the four students who participated in the original February 1, 1960, sit-in were Shiloh members, and he was equally pleased to host the Freedom Riders. After a rousing invocation he turned the meeting over to Dr. George Simkins Jr., the NAACP leader who had urged CORE to become involved in the Greensboro sit-ins. Perhaps more than any other NAACP official, Simkins had been an active supporter of the Freedom Ride, beginning with his insistence to CORE field secretary Tom Gaither (who scouted the route in April 1961) that the riders spend at least one night in Greensboro. He could hardly contain himself as he introduced the riders to an overflowing crowd of well-wishers. Nothing, not even the mass meeting in Petersburg, had prepared the riders for the warm reception they received at Shiloh.

When Farmer expressed both his fear that the desegregation fight had lost some of its "steam" and his determination to make segregation "so costly the South can't afford it," the sanctuary reverberated with *amens* and other words of encouragement. "Life is not so dear and sweet," Farmer added, "that we must passively accept Jim Crow and segregation. . . . If our parents had gone to jail we wouldn't have to go through the ordeal now. Our nation cannot afford segregation. Overseas it gives Uncle Sam a black eye. Future generations will thank us for what we have done." On and on he went, crying out for a resurgence of the spirit that had nurtured and sustained the city's famous sit-ins. By the end of the evening both Farmer and his audience were emotionally spent. But as the Freedom Riders and their hosts filed out of the sanctuary, the dual message of empowerment and responsibility was clear. Before they could hope to redeem the white South, Farmer and the Freedom Riders felt they had to embolden the black South, to stir things up to a point where a critical mass of activists demanded fundamental change. Although they realized that mobilizing and sustaining such a critical mass would not be easy, the warm welcome that the riders received in Greensboro suggested that at least one local movement was poised to take an unequivocal stand for freedom.[6]

The upper North Carolina Piedmont was as far south as CORE's 1947 Journey of Reconciliation had dared to go. So when the Freedom Riders headed down Highway 29 on Monday morning, May 8, they were entering uncharted territory. Gaither's scouting report—and in a few cases their own experiences—gave the riders some sense of what to expect. But they were understandably apprehensive about the dangerous days ahead. In Salisbury, sixty miles southwest of Greensboro, the riders encountered Jim Crow signs at both bus terminals but were able to desegregate the restrooms and lunch counters without incident. Even more encouraging was the unexpected bravado of two black women, both regular passengers on the bus, who followed the riders' example of demanding service at the white counter. They, too, received prompt and reasonably courteous service, which was more than the riders had expected from a town that had once housed one of the Confederacy's most notorious prison camps. Elton Cox, who had spent three years at Salisbury's Livingstone College in the mid-1950s and who had vivid memories of the town's rigid color line, was as surprised as anyone.[7]

From Salisbury, the buses continued southward, through Rowan Mill, China Grove, and Kannapolis, and on to Charlotte. The largest city in the Carolina Piedmont, Charlotte was a banking and textile center with a flair for New South commercialism. The Queen City, as North Carolinians often called it, was 28 percent black and almost 100 percent segregated in 1961. As in Greensboro, city leaders cultivated an image of moderation and urbane paternalism. But they did so with the expectation that all local citizens, black and white, knew their place. The immutability of racial segregation, even in the most mundane aspects of life,

15. *Thomas Gaither of Claflin College, leader of sit-ins and freedom rides,*
wearing a "Jim Crow Must Go" tie, March 1960. Photograph by Cecil J. Williams

was a given, and anyone who crossed the color line in Charlotte or Mecklenburg
County was asking for trouble. Charles Person discovered just how true this was
when he tried to get a shoeshine in Charlotte's Union Station. As he later told
Peck, the young Atlanta student "didn't even think of it as a test. He simply
looked at his shoes and thought he needed a shine." But after being rebuffed he
decided to remain in the whites-only shoeshine chair until someone either
changed the policy or arrested him. Within minutes a policeman arrived and
threatened to handcuff him and haul him off the jail if he did not move. At this
point Person decided to avoid arrest and scurried back to tell the other riders
what had happened.

After an impromptu strategy session the riders designated Joe Perkins as
the group's official shoeshine segregation tester. The whole scene carried a
touch of the absurd—the riders later referred to the incident as the South's

first "shoe-in"—but Perkins agreed to sit in the shoeshine chair until somebody came and arrested him. A few minutes later the young CORE field secretary became the first Freedom Rider to be arrested. The formal charge was trespassing, and bail was set at fifty dollars. Ed Blankenheim, the designated observer in Charlotte, was on hand with the required bail money, but Perkins bravely chose to spend two nights in jail instead. On Monday evening, while the rest of the riders were meeting with Charles Jones and other student activists at Johnson C. Smith University (including twenty-year-old Gus Griffin of Tampa, Florida, who volunteered to replace Perkins on the Tuesday morning Freedom Ride to Rock Hill, South Carolina), Perkins was at the city jail, and he remained there until his trial on Wednesday morning. With Blankenheim looking on, he went before Judge Howard B. Arbuckle expecting the worst. But to his surprise, and to the amazement of his NAACP attorney Thomas Wyche, Arbuckle promptly rendered an acquittal based on the *Boynton* decision. Elated, Perkins and Blankenheim left the courthouse and headed for Union Station. But as they were leaving, they encountered the same police officer who had arrested Perkins on Monday. Advising them "to get the hell out of town," he warned that he was not about "to let no New York nigger come down here and make trouble for us and our good nigras." Though tempted to argue the point, Perkins and Blankenheim decided to let the comment pass and proceeded on to the terminal, where they caught an early afternoon bus to Rock Hill. Arriving in the South Carolina mill town too late to rejoin the other riders, who had already headed southward, they traveled on to Sumter, where they finally caught up with their colleagues on Wednesday evening. Separated from the other riders for two days, the two castaways soon discovered that a great deal had happened during their absence.[8]

Rock Hill, which had been seething with racial tension since the celebrated jail-in three months earlier, turned out to be the first serious trouble spot for the Freedom Ride. Gaither, who had spent considerable time there, both in and out of jail, warned the riders that the town was literally crawling with Klansmen and other hard-line white supremacists. But the relative ease of the journey through Virginia and North Carolina left many of the riders unprepared for the rude welcome that they encountered during their first stop in South Carolina. A cotton mill town with a chip on its shoulder, Rock Hill harbored a large contingent of what Senator Ben Tillman once called "the damned factory trash," displaced farmers who had been pushed off the land by declining cotton prices and a brutal crop-lien system. Over the years their economic and cultural grievances spawned a hardy tradition of racial scapegoating that sustained political demagogues such as Cole Blease and "Cotton Ed" Smith. The fact that the local white elite continued to tolerate all-black Friendship Junior College suggested that Rock Hill may not have been the most "Negrophobic" town in South Carolina. But it was still a tough place to discuss the fine points of constitutional law. As Lewis, who had traveled to Rock Hill earlier in the year to visit his jailed SNCC colleagues, put it, "I could tell we were in trouble as soon as I stepped off the bus."[9]

In his 1998 memoir *Walking with the Wind*, Lewis reconstructed the disturbingly simple origins of what turned out to be the first of many assaults against nonviolent Freedom Riders:

> As Al Bigelow and I approached the "WHITE" waiting room in the Rock Hill Greyhound terminal, I noticed a large number of young white guys hanging around the pinball machines in the lobby. Two of these guys were leaning by the door jamb to the waiting room. They wore leather jackets, had those ducktail haircuts and were each smoking a cigarette.
>
> "Other side, nigger," one of the two said, stepping in my way as I began to walk through the door. He pointed to a door down the way with a sign that said "COLORED."
>
> I did not feel nervous at all. I really did not feel afraid.
>
> "I have a right to go in there," I said, speaking carefully and clearly, "on the grounds of the Supreme Court decision in the *Boynton* case."
>
> I don't think either of these guys had ever heard of the *Boynton* case. Not that it would have mattered.
>
> "Shit on that," one of them said.
>
> The next thing I knew, a fist smashed the right side of my head. Then another hit me square in the face. As I fell to the floor I could feel feet kicking me hard in the sides. I could taste blood in my mouth.
>
> At that point Al Bigelow stepped in, placing his body between mine and these men, standing square with his arms at his sides.
>
> It had to look strange to these guys to see a big, strong white man putting himself in the middle of a fistfight like this, not looking at all as if he was ready to throw a punch, but not looking frightened either.
>
> They hesitated for an instant. Then they attacked Bigelow, who did not raise a finger as these young men began punching him. It took several blows to drop him to one knee.
>
> At that point several of the white guys by the pinball machines moved over to join in. Genevieve Hughes stepped in their way and was knocked to the floor.

Whether out of chivalry or just plain common sense, a white police officer who had witnessed the entire assault finally intervened and grabbed one of the assailants. "All right, boys," he stated with some authority, "Y'all've done about enough now. Get on home." After a few parting epithets, the boys retreated to the street, leaving the Freedom Riders and the policeman to wait for several other officers who had been called to the scene. To Lewis's surprise, one of the officers appeared to be sympathetic to the injured riders and asked them if they wanted to file charges against their attackers. But they declined the offer. Though still shaken and bleeding, Lewis, Bigelow, and Hughes then staggered into the terminal restaurant to join the rest of the riders. Lewis, who had suffered bruised ribs and severe cuts around his eyes and mouth, was in need of medical attention, but he stubbornly insisted on remaining at the restaurant until he finished his hard-earned cup of coffee. Several hours later, after someone at Friendship Junior College fetched a first-aid kit, he allowed a friend to place band-aids over the wounds on his face. But throughout the whole ordeal he downplayed his injuries; no bones had been broken, he insisted, displaying the quiet courage for which he would later become famous. Most importantly, he pointed out, no pledges had been violated: despite violent provocation, the Freedom Riders had passed their first test, refusing to strike back against the blows of tyranny and ignorance.

The Trailways riders who arrived later in the afternoon faced a similarly threatening situation but were able to avoid a violent confrontation, thanks to the intervention of the Reverend C. A. Ivory, the leader of the Rock Hill movement. Upon their arrival the Trailways group discovered that the Rock Hill terminal was locked shut and that the terminal's restaurant had been closed for weeks, a casualty of the Friendship Junior College students's sit-in campaign. As the riders stepped off the bus, Ivory and a welcoming committee of drivers rushed up to inform them about the assault on the Greyhound group—and to protect them from essentially the same gang of white "thugs" responsible for the earlier attack. Across the street was a line of cars filled with tough-looking young white men hoping for a second shot at the outside agitators who had dared to invade their town. Several of the men shouted epithets and motioned menacingly at the riders, but Ivory told the riders not to worry, that he was not afraid of these cowardly "hoodlums." He soon proved his point by glaring at the whites as he and the rest of the welcoming committee hustled the riders into several waiting cars. As they drove to Friendship Junior College, where the riders were scheduled to spend the night, the threatening whites followed for a few blocks but eventually turned off without attacking their prey. Later in the evening, both groups of riders gathered at Ivory's home to share the details of what had happened earlier in the day. While they all had stories to tell, the gashes in John Lewis's forehead drew most of the attention. From the outset the riders had known that violent resistance to the Freedom Ride was almost inevitable. But as Lewis quietly told and retold the story of his confrontation with the young toughs, the dangers of challenging Jim Crow—and the responsibilities of nonviolent protest—took on a new and unsettling specificity.

At the mass meeting held at the college that night, the Reverend Ivory and others praised the courage and restraint of the bloodied but unbowed Freedom Riders. Confined to a wheelchair and in poor health, Ivory himself was no stranger to threats of violence or acts of courage. For four years—ever since he had led a successful boycott of Rock Hill's local bus company—the outspoken minister had been a primary target of militant segregationists, who hoped to drive him out the community. But nothing seemed to faze him—not hate mail, not death threats, not even a recent phone call that pledged to bomb his home and family. "The other night the person on the other end threatened to plant a bomb under my house," he told the riders. "'Why don't you plant two while you're at it?' I asked. Nothing ever came of it." Six months later Ivory would die of natural causes, but those who knew him well placed part of the blame on the extraordinary burden that he selflessly had agreed to bear.

Ivory's eloquent tribute to the injured riders touched everyone in the hall, and Jimmy McDonald, joined by nine veterans of the Rock Hill jail-in, capped off the evening with a joyous round of freedom songs. The exuberance of the students was just what Lewis and the Freedom Riders had hoped to discover in the recesses of the Deep South, though Lewis himself had other things to think about that night. Within minutes of his arrival at the college, he had received a telegram from the American Friends Service Committee (AFSC) notifying him that he had been selected as a finalist for a two-year foreign service internship—the same internship that his mentor Jim Lawson had held in the mid-1950s. It had taken the AFSC some time to track him down, but there was still enough time for him to make the required final interview in Philadelphia. Accompanying the telegram was a money order that would buy him a plane ticket, but if he wanted to pursue the internship he would have to leave the Freedom Ride almost immediately. Following a long night of soul-searching, Lewis decided to fly to Philadelphia for three days, after which he planned to rejoin the ride. Barring any unforeseen problems, he would be back on the bus by Monday, May 15, the day the riders were scheduled to leave Birmingham.

The next morning, as the rest of the riders prepared to head south toward Chester and Winnsboro, a Friendship Junior College student drove Lewis to the Charlotte airport, where he caught a plane to Philadelphia. Before leaving Rock Hill, the remaining riders desegregated the waiting rooms in both bus terminals without incident. As a relieved Peck put it, "the hoodlums did not stage a repeat performance," though as the riders left the scene of their first violent confrontation they had no illusions about the hard road to freedom in towns such as Rock Hill. Just how hard this road could be became increasingly obvious as the day progressed. The riders had planned to stop for lunch in Chester, a mill town and county seat twenty-three miles southwest of Rock Hill. Chester's closest brush with notoriety had occurred in 1807, when former vice president Aaron Burr, while under arrest for acts of treason, momentarily escaped from his guards while passing through the town. But the riders did not get the chance to stay long enough to see the famous rock from which Burr "harangued a curious crowd before he was recaptured." Having learned that troublemakers were on their way, local officials had locked the doors of the Chester bus terminal. Over the doors several makeshift signs announced that the terminal was "closed" until further notice. Shaking off this lapse in southern hospitality, the Trailways and Greyhound drivers changed the lunch stop to Winnsboro, twenty-eight miles farther down the road.[10]

The seat of hilly Fairfield County, Winnsboro was a conservative community with a deep Confederate heritage. On his march north from the capital city of Columbia in February 1865, General William Tecumseh Sherman had stopped in Winnsboro just long enough to burn most of the town, an act that was not soon forgotten. Later in the nineteenth century local patriots constructed one of the state's largest Confederate monuments, which stood guard against any transgressions of the "Southern way of life." Nearly 60 percent black in 1961, Winnsboro had earned a reputation as an ultra-segregationist stronghold, a place where the local White Citizens' Council invariably got its way. Challenging the white supremacist traditions of Winnsboro would have been dangerous under any circumstances, but in the wake of the Rock Hill incident it was especially so. As the Freedom Riders rolled into the sand hills of central South Carolina on the morning of May 10—which happened to be Confederate Memorial Day—newspapers all across the nation ran a wire story describing the beatings of the previous day. Thanks in part to the hoopla surrounding Alan Shepard's recent space flight, the Rock Hill story generally appeared on the back pages far removed from the front-page limelight. But much of South Carolina, not to mention the rest of the South, now knew that riders were coming their way, which helped to explain the locked doors in Chester. Officially CORE welcomed the publicity, but from this point on the riders would have to deal with an awakened white South. Suddenly the potential for confrontation had ratcheted upward.

In Winnsboro the first sign of trouble came when Hank Thomas—the young Howard student from St. Augustine, Florida—sat down at a whites-only lunch counter. Accompanied by Peck, who later recalled that they had hardly settled in their seats when "the restaurant owner dashed away from the counter to call the police," Thomas soon found himself in a conversation with a brawny "police officer who was a stereotype for such a role in Hollywood." "Come with me, boy," the officer drawled. At this point Peck tried to explain that Thomas had a constitutional right to eat lunch wherever he pleased. But this did not seem to faze the policeman, who promptly arrested both men. Within minutes the two Freedom Riders were behind bars in the city jail—in separate Jim Crow cells. After several hours of confusion and indecision, local officials charged Thomas with trespassing and Peck with "interfering with arrest." By this time the rest of the riders—with the exception of Frances Bergman, who was the designated observer for the Winnsboro lunch counter test—had gone on to Sumter, where they were scheduled to spend the night. For several hours Bergman, as a grateful Peck later put it, "braved the hate-filled town alone trying to find out what the authorities intended to do" with the two arrestees. But she got little cooperation from the local police, who seemed pleased that Winnsboro's unwelcome visitors had gotten more than they had bargained for in the heart of Dixie. One officer, after calling her a "nigger lover" and an "outside agitator," told her "to get out of town," adding, "We have no use for your kind here."

Following a CORE policy agreed upon at the beginning of the ride, Farmer left Thomas, Peck, and Bergman behind, hoping that they would be able to rejoin the ride in Sumter. But he did so reluctantly. Farmer knew from his conversations with CORE's South Carolina field secretary, Jim McCain, that Winnsboro—like Rock Hill—was a dangerous town, especially for an assertive young black man such as Thomas. As a white woman, Bergman, despite her lack of experience in the South, would probably be all right, and Peck—a veteran civil disobedient who had served three years in prison as a young man—could probably take care of himself. But Thomas was young and full of pent-up emotion left over from a troubled boyhood. A last-minute replacement for his roommate, he was an unknown quantity compared to most of the other riders. With some justification Farmer worried that the untried recruit might not be able to hold his tongue or his fists if provoked. Fortunately while Farmer was still mulling over his options, the Winnsboro police dropped all charges against Thomas, releasing him around midnight.

While Peck was still languishing in his cell, two policemen drove Thomas to Winnsboro's partially closed and virtually empty bus station. Waiting in the parking lot was a band of tough-looking white men, one of whom ordered Thomas to "go in the nigger waiting room." By this time the police had sped off, leaving the young Freedom Rider at the mercy of what looked like a lynch mob. Somehow he summoned up enough courage to enter the white waiting room, purchase a candy bar, and stroll past "the gaping segregationists," who seemed stunned by his defiance. Before the whites could react, a local black minister whom Bergman had called earlier in the day drove by the bus station and screamed at Thomas. "He told me to get in the car and stay down," Thomas recalled years later. "We expected gunshots, but they didn't come. He saved my life that night, because they were going to kill me." After the rescue the minister drove Thomas twenty-five miles south to Columbia, where he found refuge in the home of a local NAACP leader. The next day he took a bus to Sumter, where he rejoined the other riders—including Peck, who had his own tale to tell.

The Winnsboro police had planned to release Peck and Thomas at roughly the same time. But after dropping the original arrest interference charge against Peck, local officials immediately rearrested him for violating a state liquor law. Though unsure of their legal standing on the matter of segregation, they found a way to extend Peck's ordeal by turning to an obscure South Carolina statute that prohibited the importation of untaxed liquor into the state. Two days earlier, just prior to crossing the South Carolina line, Peck and the Trailways group had stopped for a few minutes at a small terminal attached to a liquor store. Thinking that some alcoholic sustenance might come in handy during the difficult days ahead, Peck purchased a bottle of imported brandy that he promised to share with his fellow riders. This produced a few wry comments from Farmer and others familiar with Peck's fondness for hard liquor, but no one realized that he was about to violate South Carolina law. Later, as he was about to be released from the Winnsboro jail, a police officer spied his bottle of whiskey and proudly informed his superiors that the bottle lacked the required South Carolina state liquor stamp. Within minutes Peck was back in jail, charged with illegal possession of untaxed alcohol. Several hours later, after learning of Peck's second arrest, Farmer and a carload of CORE supporters—including Jim McCain and a local black attorney, Ernest Finney Jr.—drove from Sumter to Winnsboro, arriving just before dawn. After securing Peck's release with a fifty-dollar bail bond, Farmer and McCain whisked their old friend back to Sumter, knowing full well that they could not afford to wait for his day in court. Although jumping bail violated CORE policy, Peck, for once, was in no mood to argue the finer points of legal and organizational responsibility. When Peck and the rescue party arrived safely at McCain's house—CORE's unofficial headquarters in Sumter— everyone was relieved to be back in the fold. Thomas and Bergman's reappearance later in the day completed the reunion, as the returnees swapped jail stories and regaled the other riders with tales of "friendly" Winnsboro.[11]

The safe return of Thomas, Peck, and Bergman buoyed the spirits of the riders, all of whom were thankful that the schedule called for two days of rest in Sumter. Aside from a brief test of a bus terminal waiting room—the small Sumter terminal had no restaurant—the stay in Sumter afforded them a chance to relax, reflect upon the experiences of their first week on the road, and gather their strength for the expected challenges to come. At a mass meeting on Thursday evening at the Emmanuel A. M. E. Church, Farmer talked about the significance of the Freedom Ride, and Peck and Thomas recounted their harrowing experiences in Winnsboro. But the highlight of the meeting, according to Moses Newson of the *Baltimore Afro-American,* was a testimonial by Bergman, who "hushed" the audience with a moving account of her rude introduction to the Deep South. "For the first time I felt that I had a glimpse of what it would be like to be colored," she confessed. "This thing made me realize what it is to be scorned, humiliated and made to feel like dirt. . . . The whole thing was such an eye-opener for me. . . . It left me so filled with admiration for the colored people who have to live with this all their lives. It seems to me that anything I can do now, day or night, would not be enough. . . . Somehow you feel there is a new urgency at this time. You see the courage all about you." Rededicating herself to the cause of racial justice, she praised the activism of young black students but warned that "older persons" should not "sit back and wait for them to do it." Despite its air of presumption, this admonition struck a responsive chord in the crowd, which included a number of students from nearby Morris College, a black Baptist institution that had been a hotbed of sit-in and boycott activity since the establishment of a campus CORE chapter in March 1960. Here, as in many other southern communities, student activists had fashioned a militant local movement that went far beyond anything that their parents or most other black community leaders were willing to endorse.

Jim McCain was justifiably proud of the Morris College CORE chapter, especially after several of the chapter's stalwarts volunteered to join the Freedom Ride. Earlier in the week Farmer had politely brushed off such offers, but that was before the ride faced a temporary personnel crisis. Soon after the riders' arrival in Sumter, Cox took a leave of absence to return to High Point, where he was obliged to deliver a Mother's Day sermon on Sunday morning. Thus, with Lewis already gone, the number of riders was suddenly down to eleven, only four of whom were black. Both Lewis and Cox planned to rejoin the ride in Birmingham on Monday morning. But CORE needed at least two substitute riders for the pivotal four-day journey from Sumter to Birmingham. Fortunately, with McCain's help, Farmer not only found replacements for Lewis and Cox but also added two extra recruits for good measure. One of the four new Freedom Riders was Ike Reynolds, a twenty-seven-year-old, black CORE activist and Wayne State University sophomore who had been awakened on Wednesday morning by a 7:00 A.M. phone call from CORE's national field director, Gordon Carey. The next thing Reynolds knew, he was on a mid-morning plane from Detroit to Atlanta, where he was picked up and driven to Sumter. The other recruits—Ivor Moore, Herman Harris, and Mae Francis Moultrie—were students at Morris College. Moultrie was a twenty-five-year old senior from Sumter, and Harris and Moore, both twenty-one, were northern transplants—Harris from Englewood, New Jersey, and Moore from the Bronx. Harris was president of the local CORE chapter and a campus football star, and Moultrie and Moore had been actively involved in several sit-ins and marches. Trained by McCain, all three were seasoned veterans of the southern freedom struggle.

With the new recruits in hand, Farmer, McCain, and the other CORE staff members spent most of the second day in Sumter assessing the experiences of the previous week and refining the plan for the remainder of the ride. In gauging the future they had to deal with a number of unknowns, including the attitudes of black leaders and citizens in Deep South communities that would inevitably be affected by the ride. Would the Freedom Riders be welcomed as liberators? Or was it just as likely that they would be shunned as foolhardy provocateurs by black southerners, who knew how dangerous it was to provoke the forces of white supremacy? How many black adults were ready to embrace the direct action movement that their children had initiated? And how would the student activists themselves respond to an initiative directed by an organization associated with white northern intellectuals and an exotic and secular nonviolent philosophy? CORE leaders were hopeful, but after a week on the road they still regarded the black South as something of a puzzle.

Equally perplexing, and far more threatening, was the unpredictability of white officials in the Deep South—and in Washington. What would the police do if the Freedom Riders were physically attacked by segregationist thugs? Would the mayors of Augusta, Atlanta, and Birmingham set aside their avowed segregationist beliefs and instruct their police chiefs to uphold the law? Would southern officials enforce the *Morgan* and *Boynton* decisions, now that they knew that at least some members of the public were aware of the Freedom Ride? And perhaps most importantly, what would the Kennedy administration do if white southerners brazenly violated the law as interpreted by the Supreme Court? How far would the Justice Department go to protect the Freedom Riders' constitutional rights, knowing that direct intervention would be politically costly for the administration? The probable answers to all of these questions remained murky as the riders set out on the second week of their southward journey. But with each passing day CORE leaders felt they were getting a better grasp of what they were up against, and of what they could expect from friends and foes alike.[12]

On Friday morning, May 12, the CORE Freedom Riders said goodbye to McCain and their other movement friends in Sumter and headed southward toward Georgia and the challenges of the Deep South. Their next overnight stop was Augusta, and the 120-mile trip from Sumter to the state line took them through the historic midsection of South Carolina—east across the Wateree River to the capital city of Columbia, then southwest through the heart of agrarian Lexington and Aiken counties, and finally to the banks of the Savannah River. Along the way they skirted the edge of notorious Edgefield County— reputed to be the most violent county in the South and celebrated in southern political lore as the spawning ground of such notables as the antebellum Fire Eater James Henry Hammond, the late-nineteenth and early-twentieth-century white supremacist demagogue "Pitchfork Ben" Tillman, and the 1948 Dixiecrat standard-bearer Strom Thurmond. Fortunately for the Freedom Riders, the bombastic Senator Thurmond was in Washington when they passed through, and they were able to slip into Georgia without incident. But later in the week, following several incidents of Klan-inspired violence in Alabama, Thurmond joined other conservative southern senators in denouncing the Freedom Riders as provocateurs and "outside agitators," suggesting they were allied with a Communist-led conspiracy to subvert the "Southern way of life." Not to be outdone, South Carolina's senior senator, Olin D. Johnston, sent a public letter to his constituents on May 29 insisting that "the Freedom Riders are part of the cold war propaganda program of the Communists." Appealing to his northern colleagues for help, Johnston declared that the Freedom Riders "should be stopped in their tracks at the place of origin and not allowed to prey upon the religious, racial, and social differences of our people."[13]

Despite Johnston's plea, the Freedom Rides continued throughout the summer of 1961—though almost all of the later rides took place in Mississippi,

Louisiana, Tennessee, and Arkansas. The only follow-up rides in the Carolinas took place in mid-June, when two groups of CORE-sponsored riders passed through on their way to Florida. As with the original CORE Freedom Ride, the June rides began in Washington. On Monday, June 12, exactly one month after the original riders rolled across the South Carolina border into Georgia, CORE field secretary Genevieve Hughes, held a Washington news conference to introduce two groups of volunteers sporting large blue and white buttons identifying themselves as "Freedom Riders." Both groups, Hughes announced, were scheduled to depart on Tuesday morning. The first, consisting of fourteen Protestant ministers (half of whom were black) and four rabbis, had agreed to undertake an "Interfaith Freedom Ride" from Washington to Tallahassee, Florida. The second, numbering fifteen, represented an eclectic assortment of teachers, students, doctors, and representatives of organized labor. Taking a more easterly route than the interfaith ride, they planned to conduct tests along the Atlantic seaboard, stopping in Wilmington, North Carolina, Charleston, South Carolina, and Jacksonville, Florida, and ending up in the Gulf Coast city of St. Petersburg. It had been more than five weeks since the original CORE Freedom Ride had left Washington, but now the southeastern states would get a second chance to demonstrate compliance with federal law. Flashing her effervescent smile, Hughes predicted that the new riders would "be given service at all stops but Tallahassee and Tampa."

On Tuesday both groups did indeed reach their first-night stopovers in North Carolina without any major problems. The interfaith group spent the night at Shaw University in Raleigh, where SNCC had been founded fourteen months earlier, and the second group stayed at a black hotel in the coastal city of Wilmington. "We have been treated with the utmost courtesy," the Reverend Gordon Negren, pastor of Manhattan's Christian Reformed Church, told reporters in Raleigh, adding: "We hope it will be that way all the way." When the second group arrived in Wilmington, there was a surly crowd of 150 whites waiting outside the local bus station. But a strong police presence kept the crowd at bay. On Wednesday morning the Wilmington riders split into two groups that planned to reunite in Charleston after conducting tests in Myrtle Beach and other lowcountry communities. In Charleston, and elsewhere in South Carolina, the riders received what one reporter called "a cool but orderly reception," and they spent the night in the city of Fort Sumter and secession without incident.[14]

Meanwhile, the interfaith riders made their way to Sumter, South Carolina, where they were greeted by several local CORE stalwarts, including the veteran Freedom Rider Herman Harris. Before arriving in Sumter the riders were warned that the town was fraught with tension stemming from Harris's claim that he had been abducted by four white Klansmen after returning from New Orleans. Blindfolded and taken to an isolated clearing in the woods, he was subjected to a night of terror. After forcing him to strip, his assailants carved crosses and the letters *KKK* into his legs and chest and threatened to castrate him for challenging white supremacist orthodoxy. Even though his abductors vowed to kill him if he reported what had happened, Harris eventually asked the Justice Department to conduct an investigation. When the interfaith riders arrived in Sumter on Wednesday, June 14, the matter was still pending. But a dismissive response from state and local officials—Governor Fritz Hollings called Harris's story "a hoax"—had all but invited local white supremacists to stand guard against any additional civil rights agitation. In this atmosphere some form of confrontation was virtually inevitable, as the riders' first stop in Sumter demonstrated. Stopping for lunch at the Evans Motor Court a few miles north of town, the riders encountered "twenty or thirty toughs" and an angry proprietor who blocked their path. Informing them that he had "no contract with Greyhound" and that he was "not subject" to any Supreme Court decisions, he drawled: "We been segregated, and that's the way we gonna stay." Moments later the local sheriff stepped forward to back him up, literally shouting, "You heard the man. Now move along. I'm ready to die before I let you cross this door." As the stunned riders quickly considered their options, another local man bragged: "I got a snake in my truck over there I'm just dyin' to let loose among them nigger lovin' Northerners." Even this threat did not faze some members of the interfaith group, but the majority prevailed, and all eighteen riders reboarded the bus. Later, at the Sumter bus terminal, the riders had no trouble desegregating the white waiting room and restrooms, and their spirits were further renewed at an extended mass meeting at the same black church that had welcomed the original CORE riders in mid-May. Nevertheless, the earlier retreat continued to bother many in the group, including one minister who vowed to return someday to complete the unfinished business at the motor court.[15]

Just before midnight the riders left Sumter behind and pressed on to Savannah and Jacksonville, where they found the local bus terminals fully integrated, confirming the unpredictability of freedom riding in the South. The riders went on to further adventures and surprises in Tallahassee and Ocala, where several activists were arrested. But the Carolina phase of the Freedom Rides was over. Later in the year, following the ICC desegregation order, local activists in the Carolinas tested compliance in bus and train terminals from Raleigh and Asheville to Greenville and Charleston, and for the most part they encountered nearly universal, if often grudging, compliance on the part of corporate and public officials. For some, old ways died hard, and moving to the front of the bus or sitting at an integrated lunch counter was not always an easy form of freedom to grasp. But in the Carolinas, as elsewhere, the formal and legal constraints of segregated transit were on the way out by the end of 1961. Thanks to the Freedom Riders, who put their bodies on the line, courageously pushing a reluctant region and nation to accept a rising movement's agenda of social and racial justice, the "whites only" and "colored only" signs that had symbolized and sustained the Jim Crow South for three-quarters of a century were finally gone, never to return.[16]

Notes

1. *Morgan v. Virginia*, 328 U.S. 373 (1946); *Boynton v. Virginia*, 364 U.S. 454 (1960). On the Journey of Reconciliation, see Raymond Arsenault, "'You Don't Have to Ride Jim Crow': CORE and the 1947 Journey of Reconciliation," in *Before Brown: Civil Rights and White Backlash in the Modern South*, ed. Glenn Feldman (Tuscaloosa: University of Alabama Press, 2004), 21–67.

2. For an overview of the 1961 Freedom Rides, see James Peck, *Freedom Ride* (New York: Harper and Row, 1962); John Lewis, with Michael D'Orso, *Walking with the Wind: A Memoir of the Movement* (New York: Simon & Schuster, 1998), 121–86; Taylor Branch, *Parting the Waters: America in the King Years 1954–63* (New York: Simon and Schuster, 1988), 412–561; and David Niven, *The Politics of Injustice: The Kennedys, the Freedom Rides, and the Electoral Consequences of a Moral Compromise* (Knoxville: University of Tennessee Press, 2003). On the philosophical, religious, and psychological motivations of nonviolent civil rights activists during the 1960s, see Richard H. King, *Civil Rights and the Idea of Freedom* (New York: Oxford University Press, 1992); and David L. Chappell, *A Stone of Hope: Prophetic Religion and the Death of Jim Crow* (Chapel Hill: University of North Carolina Press, 2004). For a case study of the Freedom Riders' motivations, see David J. Mussatt, "Journey for Justice: A Religious Analysis of the Ethics of the 1961 Albany Freedom Ride" (Ph.D. thesis, Temple University, 2001).

3. See Harvard Sitkoff, *The Struggle for Black Equality, 1954–1992* (New York: Hill and Wang, 1993), 37–117; and James H. Laue, *Direct Action and Desegregation, 1960–1962: Toward a Theory of the Rationalization of Protest* (Brooklyn, N.Y.: Carlson, 1989), 57–132.

4. Peck, *Freedom Ride*, 114–17; Lewis, *Walking with the Wind*, 135–41.

5. Ed Blankenheim, interview by author, April 6, 2001; Blankenheim, "Freedom Ride," unpublished manuscript in author's possession, 3; *Baltimore Afro-American*, May 20, 1961; Peck, *Freedom Ride*, 117 (quotation); Jim Peck, "Freedom Ride," *CORE-lator*, May 1961, 2; Branch, *Parting the Waters*, 413, 822, 834. On Danville, see David C. Roller and Robert W. Twyman, eds., *The Encyclopedia of Southern History* (Baton Rouge: Louisiana State University Press, 1979), 329; W. Thomas Mainwaring, "Community in Danville, Virginia, 1880–1963" (Ph.D. thesis, University of North Carolina, Chapel Hill, 1988); and Jane E. Dailey, "Deference and Violence in the Postbellum Urban South: Manners and Massacres in Danville, Virginia," *Journal of Southern History* 63 (August 1991): 554–90. Danville was the scene of major SCLC demonstrations in the summer and fall of 1963. See Adam Fairclough, *To Redeem the Soul of America: The Southern Christian Leadership Conference and Martin Luther King, Jr.* (Athens: University of Georgia Press, 1987), 145–47, 161; James W. Ely Jr., "Negro Demonstrations and the Law: Danville as a Test Case," *Vanderbilt Law Review* (October 1974): 931–43; Sally Belfrage, "Danville on Trial," *New Republic*, November 2, 1963; and Peggy Thompson, "A Visit to Danville," *Progressive*, November 1963, 28.

6. Peck, *Freedom Ride*, 117 (first and second quotations), 118; Peck, "Freedom Ride," 2; *Baltimore Afro-American*, May 20, 1961; *Greensboro Daily News*, May 7, 8, 1961 (Farmer quotations); *Winston-Salem Journal*, May 8, 1961; *Raleigh News and Observer*, May 7, 1961; William H. Chafe, *Civilities and Civil Rights: Greensboro, North Carolina, and the Black Struggle for Freedom* (New York: Oxford University Press, 1980), 57–141, 155–56; August Meier and Elliott Rudwick, *CORE: A Study in the Civil Rights Movement* (Urbana: University of Illinois Press, 1975), 136; Thomas Gaither field reports, March and April 1961, reel

36, CORE Papers; Benjamin Elton Cox, interview by author, April 6, 2001; John Lewis, interview by author, January 31, 2001; Moses Newson, interview by author, March 2, 2002.

7. Peck, *Freedom Ride,* 118; Peck, "Freedom Ride," 2; Twyman and Roller, *Encyclopedia of Southern History,* 1075–76; Cox interview. The local newspaper, the *Salisbury Evening Post,* ran Associated Press stories on the Freedom Ride on May 9, 10, and 11 but made no mention of the stop in Salisbury.

8. Peck, *Freedom Ride,* 118 (first quotation); Peck, "Freedom Ride," 2; *Charlotte Observer,* May 9, 1961, and May 6, 2001; *Charlotte News,* May 8–10, 1961; *Washington Afro-American,* May 13, 1961; *Baltimore Afro-American,* May 20, 27, 1961; *Salisbury Saturday Evening Post,* May 9, 1961; *Sumter Daily Item,* May 10–11, 1961; *Rock Hill Evening Herald,* May 10–11, 1961; Lewis, *Walking with the Wind,* 141; Joseph Perkins, "My 291 Days With CORE," CORE Papers; David Halberstam, *The Children* (New York: Random House, 1998), 255; Howell Raines, ed., *My Soul Is Rested: Movement Days in the Deep South Remembered* (New York: Putnam, 1977), 111; Blankenheim, "Freedom Ride," 3 (second quotation); Charles Person, interview by author, May 12, 2001; Blankenheim and Newson interviews; Simeon Booker, "Alabama Mob Ambush Bus, Beat Biracial Group and Burn Bus," *Jet,* May 25, 1961, 14; Booker and Theodore Gaffney, "Eyewitness Report on Dixie 'Freedom Ride,'" *Jet,* June 1, 1961, 14. A decade later, Charlotte and surrounding Mecklenburg County became the backdrop of a precedent-setting legal struggle over the use of countywide busing for the purpose of school desegregation. In *Swann v. Charlotte-Mecklenburg Board of Education* (1971), the U.S. Supreme Court unanimously upheld federal district judge James B. McMillan's countywide busing order. See Bernard Schwartz, *Swann's Way: The School Busing Case and the Supreme Court* (New York: Oxford University Press, 1986).

9. James Farmer, "Jail-Inners Resume Struggle," *CORE-lator,* April 1961, 3–4; Gaither reports, March and April 1961; Tom Gaither, interview by author, November 8–10, 2001; *Rock Hill Evening Herald,* May 10–11, 1961, January 29, 2001, and March 18, 2001; *Baltimore Afro-American,* May 27, 1961; *Charlotte Observer,* May 6, 2001; Peck, *Freedom Ride,* 118; Peck, "Freedom Ride," 2; Lewis, *Walking with the Wind,* 141 (quotation). On Tillman, Blease, and Smith, see Francis Butler Simkins, *Pitchfork Ben Tillman: South Carolinian* (Baton Rouge: Louisiana State University Press, 1944); David Carlton, *Mill and Town in South Carolina, 1880–1920* (Baton Rouge: Louisiana State University Press, 1982); Stephen Kantrowitz, *Ben Tillman and the Reconstruction of White Supremacy* (Chapel Hill: University of North Carolina Press, 2000); Bryant Simon, *Fabric of Defeat: The Politics of South Carolina Millhands, 1910–1948* (Chapel Hill: University of North Carolina Press, 1998); Ronald D. Burnside, "The Governorship of Coleman L. Blease of South Carolina, 1911–1915" (Ph.D. thesis, Indiana University, 1963); and W. J. Cash, *The Mind of the South* (New York: Knopf, 1941), 250–59. On Rock Hill, see Work Projects Administration, *South Carolina: A Guide to the Palmetto State* (New York: Oxford University Press, 1941), 253–57.

10. Lewis, *Walking with the Wind,* 142 (first and second quotations), 143–44; Lewis and Newson interviews; *Charlotte Observer,* May 10–11, 1961, and May 6, 2001; *Rock Hill Evening Herald,* May 10, 1961; *Washington Afro-American,* May 13, 1961; *Baltimore Afro-American,* May 20, 1961; *Salisbury Evening Post,* May 10, 1961; *High Point Enterprise,* May 10, 1961; James Farmer, *Lay Bare the Heart: An Autobiography of the Civil Rights Movement* (New York: New American Library, 1985), 199; Peck, *Freedom Ride,* 118–20 (third and fourth quotations); Peck, "Freedom Ride," 2; Blankenheim, "Freedom Ride," 4; Branch, *Parting the Waters,* 415–16; Halberstam, *Children,* 255–57; Raines, *My Soul Is Rested,* 111; Milton Viorst, *Fire in the Streets: America in the 1960's* (New York: Simon and Schuster, 1979), 143–44; Work Projects Administration, *South Carolina,* 315 (fifth quotation) See also the interviews of Moses Newson, James Farmer, Hank Thomas, and John Lewis in the

documentary film *Down Freedom's Main Line* (Washington, D.C.: George Washington University Institute for Historical Documentary Filmmaking, 1998).

11. Work Projects Administration, *South Carolina*, 316–17; U.S. Department of Commerce, *County and City Data Book, 1961* (Washington, D.C.: Government Printing Office, 1961), table 4; *New York Times*, May 10–11, 1961; *Sumter Daily Item*, May 11–12, 1961; *Rock Hill Evening Herald*, May 11, 1961; *Charlotte Observer*, May 6, 2001; Peck, *Freedom Ride*, 120–22 (first and second quotations); Peck, "Freedom Ride," 2; *Baltimore Afro-American*, May 20, 1961 (third quotation); *Atlanta Constitution*, May 10, 2001 (fourth quotation); Blankenheim, "Freedom Ride," 4–5; Hank Thomas, interview by author, April 6, 2001. Halberstam, *The Children*, 257–58, provides a detailed description of Thomas's ordeal but mistakenly identifies the location as Rock Hill.

12. *Sumter Daily Item*, May 10–12, 1961; *Baltimore Afro-American*, May 20, 27 (quotations), 1961; Cox, Blankenheim, and Newson interviews; Peck, *Freedom Ride*, 122–23; Peck, "Freedom Ride," 2; "Freedom Ride Itinerary," reel 25, CORE Papers; Isaac Reynolds, interview by James Mosby Jr., November 5, 1969, Ralph Bunche Oral History Collection, Howard University, Washington, D.C.; Meier and Rudwick, *CORE*, 106, 116–17; *Birmingham Post-Herald*, May 15, 1961; *Montgomery Advertiser*, May 15, 1961; "James T. McCain: A Quiet Hero" (Sumter, S.C., 2002), commemorative pamphlet in author's possession. On Sumter, see Work Projects Administration, *South Carolina*, 265–67. On the legal tangle precipitated by the Morris College sit-ins, see the *Charlotte Observer*, March 3, 1961.

13. *New York Times*, May 26, 30 (quotation), 1961. On the political and social history of Edgefield, see Orville Vernon Burton, *In My Father's House Are Many Mansions: Family and Community in Edgefield, South Carolina* (Chapel Hill: University of North Carolina Press, 1985); Drew Gilpin Faust, *James Henry Hammond and the Old South: A Design for Mastery* (Baton Rouge: Louisiana State University Press, 1982); Fox Butterfield, *All God's Children: The Bosket Family and the American Tradition of Violence* (New York: Knopf, 1995); Simkins, *Pitchfork Ben Tillman*; Kantrowitz, *Ben Tillman and the Reconstruction of White Supremacy*; Nadine Cohodas, *Strom Thurmond and the Politics of Southern Change* (New York: Simon and Schuster, 1993); and Jack Bass, *Ol' Strom: An Unauthorized Biography of Strom Thurmond* (Atlanta: Longstreet, 1998).

14. Israel Dresner, interview by author, November 9–10, 1961; Martin Freedman, interview by author, November 8, 1961; Ralph Roy, interview by author, November 9, 1961; Ralph Roy, "A Freedom Rider's Report from Jail," *New York Amsterdam News*, ca. June 20, 1961; Ralph Roy, "Freedom Ride," unpublished ms. in author's possession, 2001; Robert McAfee Brown, "I Was a Freedom Rider," *Presbyterian Life*, August 1, 1961, 10–11, 32–33; *New York Times*, June 13–15, 1961 (quotations); *Washington Evening Star*, June 13–15, 1961.

15. Brown, "I Was a Freedom Rider," 11 (quotations); Dresner and Freedman interviews; Roy, "Freedom Rider's Report from Jail"; Roy, "Freedom Ride," 3. On the Harris incident, see *Pittsburgh Courier*, June 10, 1961; *Washington Evening Star*, May 30, June 7 (first quotation),1961; and *Baltimore Afro-American*, June 10, 1961. When the interfaith riders arrived in Sumter, Jim McCain was apparently in New Orleans recruiting and training prospective Freedom Riders. Meier and Rudwick, *CORE*, 139–40.

16. Brown, "I Was a Freedom Rider," 32; Roy, "Freedom Ride," 3–4; Dresner and Freedman interviews; *Washington Evening Star*, June 15, 1961; *New York Times*, June 15, November 1–11, 1961; *St. Petersburg Times*, June 15, 1961; Glenda Alice Rabby, *The Pain and the Promise: The Struggle for Civil Rights in Tallahassee, Florida* (Athens: University of Georgia Press, 1999), 135; *Charlotte Observer*, November 1961; *State*, November 1961. On the November 1961 tests of compliance with the ICC order, see the correspondence and reports in reels 44 and 46, CORE Papers.

The Developmental Leadership of Septima Clark, 1954–1967

Stephen L. Preskill

Leadership, for many people, has negative connotations. It is frequently associated with top-down organizations, with "power-over" styles of authority. Leaders, according to this view, dominate discussion and offer little or no room for their subordinates to deliberate or make decisions. Leaders accordingly squelch participation, because dialogue is a waste of time. They already know what course is best. They are furthermore reluctant to promote change, as it is rarely in their interests to do so.

Understanding Developmental Leadership

In this essay the assumptions about leadership are quite different. Leadership is a relational process in which collaboration and shared understanding are the bases for getting things done and exercising influence. Septima Clark stood out as a leader in this sense, as someone who practiced democratic, collaborative, relational leadership. Additionally she was a lifelong learner who not only exemplified in her own thought and action the principles of adult learning, but also led by virtue of her ability to furnish the conditions necessary for others to grow and to learn.

The view of leadership favored here has been influenced by and is drawn from the concept and practice of developmental leadership as explored and expounded by Charles Payne and by Mary Belenky, Lynne A. Bond, and Jacqueline S. Weinstock.[1] This particular leadership practice is based in the experience of mothers and other female nurturers and focuses on quietly and self-effacingly developing the leadership potential in others. It is a form of leadership that seeks to target the silenced and overlooked members of communities, to help them find their voice, and to support them taking a more active role in shaping their individual and collective destinies. Leaders in this developmental tradition care deeply about nurturing each person's individual growth while also building communities of people where each member feels strong ties to some larger whole. They want to know each person as an individual and to help them articulate values and goals that they can hold in common with others. They emphasize each person's special abilities while also building on cultural traditions that provide a foundation for strengthening the whole community. Belenky and her coauthors also found that such leaders "ask good questions and draw out people's thinking. They listen with care. To better understand what they are hearing they try to step into the people's shoes and see the world through their eyes. Then they look for ways to mirror what they have seen, giving people a chance to take a new look at themselves and see the strengths that have not been well recognized or articulated. Because these leaders open themselves so fully to others, we think of them as connected leaders. We also talk about them as midwife leaders because they enable the community to give birth to fledgling ideas and nurture the ideas along until they have become powerful ways of knowing."[2]

Charles Payne, whose work precedes that of the authors of *A Tradition That Has No Name,* introduces the notion of developmental leadership in his book about the Mississippi freedom struggle, *I've Got the Light of Freedom.* He puts special emphasis on the contributions of Ella Baker, Septima Clark, and Myles Horton. He says that all three "espoused a non-bureaucratic style of work, focusing on local problems, sensitive to the social structure of local communities, appreciative of the culture of those communities."[3] Intent on showing that it was a relational, collaborative style of leadership that animated the civil rights movement, Payne writes that the approach Baker, Clark, and Horton took was developmental in that they sought to instill "efficacy in those most affected by a problem." That is, they believed, above all, that local community members fighting for change must "see themselves as having the right and the capacity to have some say-so in their own lives."[4] Developmental leaders thus reject the category of the "other." There are no outsiders or inferior beings. Everyone is included, and each is supported as a learner and as a person capable of unending growth. Each as well is viewed as a potential contributor to improving and enhancing the community at large.

Developmental leaders assume that new knowledge and deepened understanding are constructed most effectively and lastingly in collaborative groups. Developmental leaders are skilled facilitators of group processes and work tirelessly to make groups as inclusive and as fully participatory as possible. As Payne has noted with respect to the leadership exercised at the Highlander Folk School, Horton, Clark, and their allies were "guided by the belief that the oppressed themselves, collectively, already have much of the knowledge needed to produce change."[5] Payne also quotes Clark to the same effect. She concurred that "creative leadership is present in any community and only awaits discovery and development."[6]

Open to the ideas and perspectives of others, especially those who have been repeatedly silenced, developmental leaders are disciplined learners, eager to reexamine old assumptions and to reconsider ingrained practices. They take the lead in questioning, reevaluating, and trying to see things from new vantage points, and they work tirelessly "to get others to do the same. They are such good listeners, because they see themselves learning from everyone, no matter how young, inexperienced or silenced a person might be."[7]

Payne adds another important dimension to the view of developmental leadership that emerges from his study of the Mississippi freedom struggle organizing tradition. He says of Septima Clark, as well as Ella Baker and Myles Horton, that she was a radical democrat by virtue of her insistence on the right of "people to have a voice in the decisions affecting their lives," her confidence in "the capacity of ordinary men and women to develop" a strong and meaningful voice, and her rejection of hierarchically structured organizations in which attention-starved leaders too often held sway. Furthermore, like other leaders, Clark held strong beliefs and took strong stands, but remained surprisingly "open to learning from new experiences" and from the wisdom of those both older and younger than she. She was a leader who constantly learned and who led effectively because of her complete commitment to her own learning and to creating those conditions necessary to support everyone's continuous growth.[8]

Getting Fired

In 1956, just two years after the United States Supreme Court declared segregated schools unconstitutional under its 1954 *Brown v. Board of Education* decision, the Charleston, South Carolina, Board of Education retaliated by firing those local teachers who had been strong advocates for integration. One of the most prominent of these was Septima Clark, widely known for being an outstanding teacher and for devoting her entire forty-year career to South Carolina's schools. From her first years as a teacher, when she was a teenager on the South Carolina Sea Islands, she had developed a reputation for creative, even ingenious instruction. She grew especially effective with those students who rarely succeeded in school and most needed her attention and support. Over time she taught in many places, including long stints in Columbia and Charleston, as her renown for aiding the most resistant learners continued to spread. As a black woman teaching in the Deep South, however, she suffered from one particularly glaring handicap. She was a disciplined and tireless laborer for racial justice who allied herself again and again with the National Association for the Advancement of Colored People (NAACP) in the fight against racism. This connection to the NAACP came to haunt her in 1956 when state governments all over the South cracked down on the association for sponsoring the lawsuits that had culminated two years earlier in the *Brown* decision. In South Carolina the hostile state legislature passed a law that allowed school districts to remove teachers who belonged to the NAACP. Clark, a teacher widely recognized for instructional excellence, was deprived of her livelihood because of her lifelong NAACP membership.[9]

After the *Brown* decision, which declared segregated schools inherently unequal and thus unconstitutional, school districts all over South Carolina distributed questionnaires requiring teachers to list their organizational affiliations. Many teachers omitted their memberships in the NAACP, knowing that declaring this connection could end their careers. Clark knew this as well, but she was too proud of her involvement with the NAACP to exclude it. It probably did not help her cause that she was already working closely with Myles and Zilphia Horton of the Highlander Folk School. Highlander had been founded in 1932 in a rural section of Tennessee to help the least privileged members of society work more effectively to battle economic and social oppression and to secure their constitutionally guaranteed rights. Clark had stayed at Highlander a number of times and was playing an increasingly large role in facilitating some of their workshops. The Hortons, who were white, also journeyed to Charleston and immediately challenged a standard taboo by lodging with Clark in her home. The Hortons' stay in Charleston had further repercussions. At one of the workshops that they and Clark staged together, pamphlets about Highlander and the NAACP were distributed, and school desegregation was strongly and unapologetically

16. Septima Clark (center) teaching at a "citizenship school" on Johns Island, South Carolina, 1956. Photograph courtesy of the Avery Research Center for African American History and Culture at the College of Charleston

promoted. Clark, in particular, spoke frankly and honestly about the importance of desegregation. She knew even then that such outspokenness could jeopardize her teaching career, but she was trying, as she had throughout her life, "to contribute something to the advancement of our southern community by helping elevate the lives of a large segment of it."[10]

The publicity sparked by her association with the Hortons and her continuing involvement with the NAACP induced whites to brand Clark derisively as "a champion of integration." Not long afterward and with no explanation, Clark received a letter from the Charleston Board of Education that her teaching contract would not be renewed. Proud of the work she had done to promote integration and unwilling to accept the board's decision without a fight, Clark gathered together local and state officials of the NAACP to plan a strategy to get the school board to reverse its decision. Despite their efforts, the board took no further action, and Clark's dismissal remained in effect. To add insult to injury, Clark also lost all of the retirement funds that the state had invested on her behalf. For the next twenty years she tirelessly petitioned the state retirement system until this portion of her pension was restored.[11] Someone asked her why she didn't resign when it became clear that her days were numbered. Clark explained that she remained on principle. She knew the school board was in the wrong, and she would not make their work easier by resigning. Also, she believed that by forcing the board to dismiss her she would be in a stronger position "to fight back."[12]

Unfortunately Clark never again taught as a teacher in the South Carolina schools. She remained proud, however, that she had refused to let the Charleston school board intimidate her. She took the principled stand and lost, but she stayed true to her ideals and in some larger sense prevailed over her less principled adversaries. She never forgot the importance of this searing lesson. Furthermore, her dismissal led directly to her greatest triumphs as an educator. Upon hearing of her misfortune, Myles Horton immediately appointed her the director of workshops at the Highlander Folk School, an appointment that soon led to the creation of the Citizenship Education Project and one of the civil rights movement's most memorable achievements.

Highlander and the Citizenship Schools

When Clark joined Highlander as director of workshops in 1956, she was already familiar with the school's educational philosophy and its method for helping workshop participants to learn from their experience. From the start she had found Highlander's philosophy to be highly congenial and a good fit with her own efforts to organize and empower the black community. But her experiences at Highlander also stretched her thinking and gave her a more expansive view of what could be accomplished in the South, despite the persistence of white supremacy.

As Horton has said, Highlander provided opportunities for participants to analyze their experience and to begin to make sense of real problems that existed back home in their own communities. It was this "mining of the experience that the students bring with them" that was the key to Highlander's success.[13] Horton was a true constructivist who believed that no one other than those actually confronted with a problem can solve it, and that the knowledge needed to address that problem must be created in the process of struggling with it. Horton therefore had a great deal of faith in the ability of people to solve their own problems and was convinced that people have much more knowledge about how to solve these problems than they realize. He also knew that when people toiled with others to search out viable solutions to their social predicaments these solutions not only had more meaning for them, they also became an integral part of their mindset and their practice as activists. "Highlander gives them a chance," Horton claimed, "to explore what they know and what some people we bring in as resources can share with them. Then they have to go back home and test what they learn in action. If they have learned anything useful they can teach others because it is now part of their knowledge, not something merely handed to them."[14]

Highlander's open, adaptable approach, which can be summed up as helping "people learn to solve their own problems in their own way," was governed by one inviolable principle: respect for persons.[15] This meant in practice that minority rights were protected with great vigilance and that social equality and freedom of speech were scrupulously preserved. Horton interpreted this to mean that no decisions could be reached before all disagreements and objections were allowed to surface. This furthermore entailed the responsibility of making decisions that would apply equally to everyone. No discrimination on the basis of race, class, or religion was permitted. Highlander gained notoriety in the thirties and forties for practicing what it espoused. It was one of the few places in the entire South where blacks and whites could meet freely to talk, work, and solve problems together.[16]

Finally Horton believed that Highlander must also be a place that stretched the minds of its guests. For him this meant vigorously practicing his "two-eye" theory of education. With one eye he observed how people view themselves and what they think is currently most needed in their communities. He used the information he gathered with this eye to begin the process of guiding the sharing and analyzing of experience. With the other eye, however, Horton saw not what is but what could be, and even what ought to be. He envisioned goals for participants that they themselves had not yet conceived, but which could eventually help them to take their leadership and activism to a new level. He focused on their present level of experience and understanding but also challenged them to aim for something bolder. It was in carrying out this two-eye theory that Horton believed he had the largest role to play in helping workshop participants to grow.[17]

There were many things that Clark learned from Horton as she proceeded with her work at Highlander, but the two-eye theory of education may have been the most important. It is also true that Clark had never been complacent about what she had accomplished with learners and was always looking to extend their thinking to help them grow and to benefit the larger community. In many ways she had as much to teach Horton as Horton had to teach her—which, after all, explains why he was so delighted when she agreed to become Highlander's director of workshops and launch the Citizen Education Project. When Clark arrived at Highlander, Horton had only a vague sense of how to initiate a literacy program. Clark had accumulated many years of experience assisting illiterate children and adults and possessed a deep understanding of the theory and practice of enhancing literacy. She personally knew and understood the most oppressed and least privileged of African Americans. She appreciated the complexities of their culture and was familiar with the intellectual and cultural resources within this community that would help learners succeed. She was also a dogged learner herself, who had great faith in ordinary people's abilities. When she encountered obstacles or difficulties, she refused to give in. Somehow, though, she also practiced a serene forbearance that served her well when progress was slow. She kept right on teaching and encouraging, but she carried out these duties with a light touch that belied her sense of urgency about the educational and political crisis then overshadowing the South. Horton, who shared little of this knowledge or experience, greatly admired Clark's unique constellation of qualities and talents. It is thus probably accurate to say that they both learned a great deal from each other, and that together they led.[18]

This was never truer than when they carried out their plan for developing community leadership on Johns Island. This transforming chain of events began when Clark invited Esau Jenkins, one of the pillars of the Johns Island community, to a Highlander workshop. Although only modestly educated, Jenkins was a gifted, hard-working entrepreneur who became a successful businessman on the island and assumed a major leadership role in local politics. He felt overwhelmed, however, by the burdens he and his neighbors faced in challenging racism and in overcoming their lack of education to become active citizens. One day, a longtime Johns Island resident, Alice Wine, asked for his help in learning to read and write so that she could pass the South Carolina literacy test required for voter registration. He was delighted to be of assistance but wanted to do more. Quickly realizing that he lacked the background to turn this simple request for tutoring into a mass campaign to promote literacy, he sought help through Highlander. When he attended his first Highlander workshop he painted a powerful picture of the need for effective adult education on Johns Island and wanted to know how to achieve this goal. Highlander provided some financing and technical assistance but most importantly gave Clark, an old friend, the job of working directly with Jenkins.[19]

With financial help from Highlander, Clark and Jenkins purchased a small building where a school for illiterate adults could be launched. At the front part of the building a small grocery was set up to deceive whites into thinking that this was nothing more than a modest commercial establishment. Even in the mid-fifties southern whites resisted these attempts by African American adults to educate themselves. They viewed such efforts as "uppity" and dangerously radical. (As it turned out, the grocery made a small profit that helped finance additional schools.) Clark also made arrangements for selecting a teacher. She and Horton sought someone who was respected and had leadership potential but was not a professional teacher. They wanted an instructor who would be open to new methods and strategies, who would not be constrained by old, ingrained habits, and who would not act condescendingly toward her inexperienced students. Bernice Robinson, a beautician and dressmaker, was their choice. She had a high school education, was active in the Charleston NAACP, and understood Highlander's approach to adult education. At first Robinson declined the offer, citing her lack of teaching experience. But Clark persisted and convinced her that she possessed the capacity to inspire the trust of the islanders and had, above all, "the ability to listen to people."[20]

On January 7, 1957, fourteen Johns Island adults showed up outside a building that appeared to be nothing more than a grocery store. Robinson conducted them into the grocery's back rooms and commenced instruction in reading and writing. The first citizenship school had quietly and unceremoniously begun. Robinson brought with her a variety of materials geared toward elementary students, but she realized on the spot that these would be inappropriate for her adult students. She turned to them and asked them what they wanted to learn. As John Glen described in his history of the Highlander Folk School, "It was an inspired question, for the subsequent success of Highlander's Citizenship School program stemmed from its ability to respond to the expressed needs of its students."[21] What the islanders most wanted was to be able to write their names. They sought next to gain the skills needed to read the newspaper and the Bible, and those portions of the South Carolina constitution that must be decoded to qualify for voter registration. They also asked to learn how to fill out mail-order catalog forms and money orders. A few of the men requested instruction in arithmetic. Finally Robinson herself proposed, perhaps with the two-eye theory of education in mind, that by the end of their two months together the students be able to read and understand the United Nations Universal Declaration of Human Rights that she had tacked up on the wall of their classroom.[22]

Clark worked closely with Robinson in planning and evolving the curriculum for this first citizenship school, although, as Aimee Horton has noted in her history of Highlander, it "came about almost entirely from its fourteen adult students."[23] Robinson began, with Clark's support and advice, by writing the names of the students in large letters on pieces of cardboard. They also recorded the occupations of the islanders in the same way. Additionally they prepared oversized examples of money order forms and invited the students to fill in the blanks. The most intense activity, at least at first, entailed learning to write their signatures. At Clark's suggestion, Robinson had them do this kinesthetically—tracing prepared signatures again and again until they could write their names in cursive without a prompt.[24] Using many of the ideas that Clark had developed forty years earlier during her first years on Johns Island, Robinson also had the islanders write stories about their daily routines that they then read aloud to the whole group. The words that caused difficulty were set aside for further practice and were also used to teach spelling.[25] Robinson on her own initiative also found newspaper advertisements that could be used to supplement reading instruction and teach simple arithmetic.

Clark was responsible for one of the most enduring innovations. She prepared a special workbook that "discussed such subjects as the South Carolina election laws, particularly those setting forth the requirements for registering and voting, the laws concerning social security, laws relating to taxes, and various other topics of current importance."[26] As Clark has stated, this booklet was prepared in part to give the students materials that would be appropriate and helpful to them in learning to read. Just as important, though, she wanted to move beyond simple literacy and teach them things they would need to become more informed and active citizens. Because the readings were often difficult, Clark carefully abridged most selections to allow students to experience the gist of these pieces without being overwhelmed by their length or complexity. She also punctuated the booklet with guiding questions that helped students to grasp the main ideas and key supporting details.

The first test of the program's effectiveness was the ability of the students to become registered voters. All of them, without exception, passed that test. They read the required passages and signed their names so flawlessly that they could hardly be denied their registration certificates. They "were so happy about it that they came back to school fairly shouting."[27] It was a great triumph for Clark and Robinson and a landmark in the history of the civil rights movement. What stood out for Clark and Robinson, however, was how much they themselves had learned from the experience. Robinson commented enthusiastically how eagerly the students learned and how satisfying it was, given their thirst for knowledge, to teach them. Working with adults in this way became Robinson's new career path. Clark noted that the students themselves must guide what is learned. "You don't tell people what to do," she observed. "You let them tell you what they want done."[28] Or, as she said on another occasion: "We had to let them talk to us and say to us whatever they wanted to say."[29] The experience reaffirmed one of Clark's lifelong convictions—that a good teacher is, above all, a good listener, intent on "always learning herself."[30] One of the hard-won results of all this learning and listening and assertive action was a fourfold increase in the number of Johns Island residents registered to vote by the early 1960s.

The success at Johns Island spawned many new citizenship schools, first on other islands along the South Carolina coast and later in communities such as Huntsville, Alabama; Savannah, Georgia; and Somerville, Tennessee. As Robinson and Clark refined their methods, the ability of these schools to teach increasingly large numbers of students also expanded. They grew proficient at using the specific, local experiences of their students as the basis for reading instruction, even as they also developed additional collections of readings in skillfully edited, highly accessible versions that presented useful facts about voting and a variety of social services. On Edisto Island, at least eighty participants from the local citizenship school qualified to vote between 1959 and 1960. The instruction they received focused on basic literacy but also included arithmetic, citizenship, sewing, and African American history. Clark was particularly proud to see that, as these programs expanded, it became apparent that islanders were also becoming more astute politically. Graduates were "speaking better, beginning to read other materials, becoming more willing to take places on committees, to serve as poll watchers or secretaries of voters' leagues."[31]

As Carl Tjerandsen points out in his discussion of citizenship education at Highlander, the work that had to be done to produce such changes could be incredibly fatiguing. He recounts the numerous visits Clark made to various schools, cooperatives, and private residences in one five-day week. On each of these visits she spoke or distributed literature or simply affirmed the good work that was being done.[32] Additionally, she maintained a busy workshop schedule at Highlander and continued to recruit new, eager participants for Highlander's all-important residential program. Giving people a taste of the freedom that was lived at Highlander, of the mutual respect that was practiced there, and of the support the staff so unstintingly supplied was almost always an important first step toward imagining new possibilities back home. Despite her wearying schedule, Clark felt revitalized every time she returned to Highlander to witness the energizing effects democratic living could have on beleaguered southern blacks.

Unfortunately, however, Highlander itself was feeling increasingly beleaguered as Tennessee's attacks on the school's progressive and integrationist policies grew even more intense. On July 31, 1959, state law enforcement officers, desperate to contrive a reason to put Highlander out of business, raided the school and charged it with illegal possession of liquor. They arrested Clark on the same charge, though she was a lifelong teetotaler. The trumped-up accusations led to a series of lawsuits that culminated in the decision by the Tennessee Supreme Court to revoke Highlander's charter. When the United States Supreme Court refused to review the case in October 1961, Highlander legally ceased to exist. Although Highlander would soon be reborn as a center for education and research in Knoxville, it was no longer a viable site for citizenship education.

The SCLC and the Citizenship Education Project

In the meantime, Septima Clark had been successful in transferring responsibility for the citizenship education programs begun by Highlander to the Southern Christian Leadership Conference (SCLC). When Clark first brought these programs to the attention of Martin Luther King in 1959, he was so consumed by his commitment to direct, nonviolent resistance through demonstrations, marches, and sit-ins that he could not see the immediate value of Clark's ideas. But as the citizenship programs spread and enjoyed success in a wide range of communities in Georgia, Alabama, and Tennessee, King eventually succumbed to Clark's lobbying. He conceded that despite the enormous effort put into direct action, there was little to show for it. To paraphrase Tjerandsen, King admitted that demonstrations rarely resulted in oppressive laws being taken off the books or new power being gained by blacks. Citizenship education might be a way to reach out to more people, King reasoned, and to build enduring political alliances through the ballot. Thus was the Citizenship Education Project (CEP) born.[33]

It was not an easy birth, however. The organizational unwieldiness of the SCLC and the absence of a galvanizing crisis in 1961 stalled the progress of the CEP. Slowly, thanks to Clark's recruiting energy and imaginative teaching, as well as the mounting tension emerging from a civil rights clash in Albany, Georgia, the CEP began to advance. Clark's chief responsibility was training the teachers, who would then fan out to a variety of different communities to teach literacy, excite political awareness, and spur organized action. Most of the workshops to provide this training were held in Liberty County, Georgia, at the Dorchester Cooperative Community Center, which was associated with the United Church of Christ. Andrew Young, who had ties to this church, made the arrangements for securing the center and was responsible for overseeing the CEP, but he deferred to Clark as the center's "undisputed schoolmistress."[34]

The workshops that Clark led tended to follow a format similar to the one she had learned at Highlander. The people whom Clark, Young, and their colleague Dorothy Cotton carefully recruited were invited to spend four weekdays and an evening at the Dorchester Center. On the opening evening, time was spent getting acquainted and figuring out how the workshop could best serve the needs of those in attendance. The following day teaching sessions began in earnest. Music was used to warm up the participants and enliven the proceedings, and then a variety of strategies for teaching reading and introducing basic math were explored. As Taylor Branch has noted, Clark "taught her pupils how to figure out seed and fertilizer allotments" and, when focusing on literacy, "worked upward from street signs and newspapers to the portions of the state constitutions required for voter registration."[35] According to Tjerandsen, Clark also used the Socratic method effectively. She asked numerous questions, painstakingly tracked responses that seemed contradictory, and patiently used the colloquy that ensued to impart skills and to deepen understanding of the Citizenship Education Project's larger implications. It was not enough for her that participants learn the processes for teaching literacy and arithmetic; they also had to increase their political awareness, learn to think more critically, and gain appreciation for the new leadership role they would be assuming in their communities.[36]

But Clark's real gift, as Branch has also pointed out, was in "recognizing natural leaders among the poorly educated yeomanry" and passing on to them the skills, confidence, and leadership they would need to be effective back in their home communities.[37] Like Ella Baker, she was a developmental leader of the first rank who saw ability in the most ordinary of people and who did all she could to develop this ability to expand the base of black voters and promote social justice. Clark always insisted that workshops must end with participants demonstrating in specific ways how they proposed to use the knowledge they had gained and what they planned to do to make a difference back home. Like Myles Horton, Clark believed that workshop participants should not return to their communities without a clear sense of what they had learned and what they intended to do with it.

Despite Clark's best efforts, however, a feeling prevailed that the citizenship schools had lost something in the transfer from Highlander to the SCLC. Apparently King and the other male leaders never fully appreciated the impact of the citizenship education movement. The SCLC failed to provide the funding that Clark always believed was necessary to fully capitalize on the value of the workshops. The number of trainees to be accommodated continued to balloon, and sessions were frequently cut short, leaving little time for the all-important "What will we do back home?" sessions. Additionally, procedures for following up on participants after they had begun to serve their communities were never clearly established. Clark also believed that because the CEP was run largely by women, it never received the respect it deserved. She has said quite bluntly that the men on the executive staff of the SCLC "didn't have any faith in women, none whatsoever."[38] Reverend Ralph Abernathy repeatedly complained about the presence of Clark on the SCLC's executive council, and King himself never took Clark as seriously as she would have liked. At one point she wrote King a letter expressing concern about his tendency to dominate the movement, willingly accepting invitations to lead every march or keynote every meeting. She proposed, like the dedicated developmental leader that she was, that he commit himself to developing more leaders who could lead major marches and deliver the necessary speeches at public demonstrations. According to Clark, when King read the letter to his staff, they laughed derisively, believing that no one but King could spearhead the civil rights movement. Clark's view was that "you develop leaders as you go along, and as you develop these people let them show forth their development by leading."[39] She knew from experience that when you give ordinary people a chance to lead, when you build their confidence and impart a few skills along the way, there is no limit to what they can accomplish. Her lifelong quest was to develop such leaders wherever she found them and to instill in them the habit of learning—that for her was the hallmark of great leadership.

Despite the CEP's limitations, it nevertheless accomplished a great deal. By 1967 the SCLC had trained at least three thousand citizenship teachers. Clark estimated that these teachers had taught at least forty-two thousand others. As a result of the SCLC programs voter registration had more than doubled in Alabama, and more than tripled in Clark's native Charleston, by 1967.[40] The subsequent impact on voting and, over time, on law and social policy was incalculable. Clark was able to retire in 1970 knowing that her contribution to the struggle for social justice had been enormous.

Clark as Developmental Leader

Septima Clark stood out as a developmental leader. She was a devoted and unceasing learner. She listened more than she declaimed, witnessed more than she professed, and responded to the expressed needs of her students more often than she advanced her own personal perspective. Throughout her life as a teacher and leader she strove to establish the conditions for learners to tell their own stories, to reflect critically on their own experience, to grapple with their own problems, and to work out their own solutions. Even in her teens she was doing these things. There is no question, however, that her involvement at Highlander helped her to develop a philosophy of teaching and leadership that was consistent with these established practices and that also aided her in evolving new methods that were even more democratic than anything she had tried before.

In particular what she learned from Myles Horton and picked up during the many residential workshops that she attended at Highlander was that African Americans themselves had the capacity to bring about the transformation of their own communities. What Highlander could do is give them a taste of the emancipatory possibilities inherent in every local community and provide a few human and financial resources to begin to foster change back home. What Clark added to all of this was a talent for identifying, encouraging, and developing potential leaders. Her willingness to open herself up to the wisdom of others also sensitized her to what ordinary people could teach her and what they might need from her to develop their potential as leaders. The relationship that she cultivated with workshop participants was thus thoroughly mutual. She had much to learn from them, just as they had a great deal to learn from her. But Clark's faith in their ability, in their unique capacity to exert leadership in their own local communities, provided the basis for everything else that transpired between them.

Clark hated artifice of any kind. She refrained from flattering the powerful male leaders who surrounded her, and she refused to put herself above anyone else, despite her extensive education and breadth of organizing experience. She was happiest working directly with the ordinary people who needed her leadership most. As a leader who was also a teacher she endeavored to provide conditions that would support continued learning and spur concerted action. She understood the pedagogy of leadership. That is, she recognized there are ways to approach people and to collaborate with them on tasks that ensure success and that can then be used as a basis for further action and future growth.

Perhaps most important, Clark was genuine; she did not put on airs in an attempt to impress others. She practiced simple virtues such as humility, gentleness, simplicity, and courage. And whatever she asked others to do she was always willing to do herself. Finally, unlike SCLC leaders like King and Abernathy, who often showed little faith in her ability or in the value of the programs she proposed, her own faith in the people she worked with was unbounded, often allowing them to accomplish things that they thought were beyond their capabilities.

Clark's brand of developmental leadership is similar to what Robert Greenleaf has called servant leadership. Greenleaf stressed that one of the defining qualities of a servant leader is to be a listener first. Certainly Clark met this criterion.[41] She gradually realized as she traveled through eleven different southern states, trying to impart basic reading and writing skills to simple working people, that "I could say nothing . . . and no teacher as a rule could speak to them. We had to let them talk to us and say to us whatever they wanted to say."[42] She learned that the more she listened and came to understand what different groups were going through, the more she could then earn the right to speak up as well and perhaps introduce the groups that she met to some new ideas worth hearing. But her turn to speak had to be earned, and it had to be built on an authentic desire to listen and to learn from those around her.

Servant leaders, of course, are willing to do almost anything in order to serve their constituents better. Clark as a young teacher collected dry-cleaner bags so that she would have a writing surface upon which to record her students' stories and to compile their key words. Somewhat later, while attempting to overturn the South Carolina ban on black teachers being employed in public schools, she almost single-handedly gathered twenty thousand signatures for petitions supporting a new, more progressive statute. As the chief organizer of Highlander's citizenships schools, Clark never hesitated to do whatever was necessary to support Bernice Robinson and other teachers. If this meant ordering needed supplies, she would take care of it. If it meant distracting whites suspicious of what was going on in the back of a grocery store on Johns Island, she would do that,

17. Esau Jenkins (at lectern) introducing the Reverend Martin Luther King Jr. (seated third from left) at Emanuel AME Church in Charleston, April 13, 1962. Photograph courtesy of the Avery Research Center for African American History and Culture at the College of Charleston

too. Her goal was always to further the movement for civil rights, never to go out of her way to make herself look good.

Author Belinda Robnett writes about Clark explicitly as an important professional bridge leader, a view of leadership closely aligned with developmental leadership. By "bridge leader," Robnett means someone who leads informally and with little fanfare, but who does this work as part of their livelihood. Robnett particularly highlights Clark's work with the Citizen Education Project and her ability to connect with the rural black masses. When institutional networks failed and national associations performed poorly in attracting the working poor to the civil rights movement, Clark and others used their interpersonal skills and their direct knowledge of local communities to awaken broad interest in literacy, the franchise, and civil rights.

Clark's genius as a bridge leader entailed her ability to translate the somewhat erudite goals of Martin Luther King's SCLC into language and practices that made sense to rural and working-class blacks. She did this literally by providing the people who sought literacy instruction with readable accounts of civil rights movement activity and of the laws that posed barriers for her students. She also did this more informally by talking with people honestly and directly and by exhorting them to give time and effort to a movement that she believed would enhance their freedom and strengthen their rights.

Additionally Clark stood out as a bridge leader because her initial efforts to further black literacy and thus fortify African American voting power were carried out largely on her own, with little or no support from national organizations or broad social movements. The Citizenship Education Project, which eventually gained renown as an arm of the SCLC, linked ordinary people struggling to secure their basic rights with a well-funded national movement. Clark's leadership made that connection possible.

In the end Clark was the kind of leader who, as she herself said, completely identified "with the people in the localities where they live and work."[43] Over time she developed a commitment to democracy that was reflected in everything she did as a teacher and leader. This was not simply an espoused commitment, but one she struggled to enact in every aspect of her professional and personal life. The conclusion of the statement that she wrote about her faith in democracy while in residence at Highlander is a fitting way to end this essay: "An army of democracy deeply rooted in the lives, struggles and traditions of the American people must be created. By broadening the scope of democracy to include everyone, and deepening the concept to include every relationship, the army of democracy would be so vast and so determined that nothing undemocratic could stand in its way."[44]

Notes

1. Charles Payne, *I've Got the Light of Freedom: The Organizing Tradition and the Mississippi Freedom Struggle* (Berkeley: University of California Press, 1995); Mary Belenky, Lynne A. Bond, and Jacqueline S. Weinstock, *A Tradition That Has No Name: Nurturing the Development of People, Families, and Communities* (New York: BasicBooks, 1997).

2. Belenky, Bond, and Weinstock, *Tradition That Has No Name*, 14.

3. Payne, *I've Got the Light of Freedom*, 68.

4. Ibid.

5. Ibid., 70.

6. Ibid.

7. Belenky, Bond, and Weinstock, *Tradition That Has No Name*, 272.

8. Payne, *I've Got the Light of Freedom*, 101.

9. Septima Clark, *Echo in My Soul* (New York: Dutton, 1962).

10. Ibid., 114.

11. Donna Langston, "The Women of Highlander," in *Women in the Civil Rights Movement: Trailblazers and Torchbearers, 1941–1965,* ed. Vicki L. Crawford, Jacqueline Anne Rouse, and Barbara Woods (Brooklyn, N.Y.: Carlson, 1990), 163–64.

12. Clark, *Echo in My Soul,* 117.

13. Myles Horton, *The Long Haul* (New York: Doubleday, 1990), 148.

14. Ibid.

15. Carl Tjerandsen, *Education for Citizenship: A Foundation's Experience* (Santa Cruz, Cal.: Emil Schwartzhaupt Foundation, 1980), 139.

16. Frank Adams with Myles Horton, *Unearthing Seeds of Fire: The Idea of Highlander* (Winston-Salem, N.C.: Blair, 1975), 99–103; Langston, "Women of Highlander," 151–53.

17. Adams and Horton, *Unearthing Seeds of Fire,* 131–32.

18. Cynthia Stokes Brown, *Ready from Within: Septima Clark and the Civil Rights Movement* (Trenton, N.J.: Africa World Press, 1990), 51–54; Clark, *Echo in my Soul,* 131–34.

19. Guy and Candie Carawan, *Ain't You Got a Right to the Tree of Life? The People of Johns Island, South Carolina—Their Faces, Their Words, and Their Songs* (New York: Simon and Schuster, 1966), 167–69, 46–47.

20. Ibid., 49.

21. John Glen, *Highlander: No Ordinary School, 1932–1962* (Lexington: University Press of Kentucky, 1988), 162.

22. Aimee Horton, *The Highlander Folk School: A History of Its Major Programs, 1932–1961* (Brooklyn, N.Y.: Carlson, 1989), 224.

23. Ibid., 223.

24. Clark, *Echo in My Soul,* 147–48.

25. Brown, *Ready from Within,* 50.

26. Clark, *Echo in My Soul,* 150.

27. Ibid., 153.

28. Eliot Wigginton, ed., *Refuse to Stand Silently By: An Oral History of Grass Roots Social Activism in America, 1921–64* (New York: Doubleday, 1991), 243.

29. Brown, *Ready from Within,* 53.

30. Clark, *Echo in My Soul,* 152.

31. Tjerandsen, *Education for Citizenship,* 169.

32. Ibid.

33. Ibid., 181.

34. Taylor Branch, *Parting the Waters: America in the King Years, 1954–63* (New York: Simon and Schuster, 1988), 576.

35. Ibid.

36. Tjerandsen, *Education for Citizenship,* 192.

37. Branch, *Parting the Waters,* 576.

38. Brown, *Ready from Within,* 77.

39. Ibid., 78.

40. Tjerandsen, *Education for Citizenship,* 196.

41. Robert Greenleaf, *Servant Leadership: A Journey into the Nature of Legitimate Power and Greatness* (New York: Paulist Press, 1977), 7–23.

42. Belinda Robnett, *How Long? How Long? African-American Women in the Struggle for Civil Rights* (New York: Oxford University Press, 1997), 90.

43. Clark, *Echo in My Soul,* 238.

44. Ibid., 198.

Part 4 ∽ Resisters

The ways in which the state's white citizens responded to black demands for reform during the "Second Reconstruction" is the focus of part 4, "Resisters." South Carolina has largely enjoyed a reputation as a state that achieved racial equality without major incident. "Integration with Dignity" and integration with "grace and style" are phrases that are frequently used to describe South Carolina's response to the civil rights movement, especially for the years after the integration of Clemson University in 1963. The essays in this section, however, reveal that, far from embracing African American demands for equal protection, white South Carolinians resisted them at every turn. Their response may have been far less violent and headline-grabbing than that of Alabama and Mississippi, but it was no less embedded in an absolute commitment to the principles of white supremacy.

In the years following the Civil War, African Americans in South Carolina enjoyed unprecedented access to the political process, using their newfound equality at the voting booth to reframe the state's constitution so as to eliminate voting restrictions and facilitate the election of African Americans to political office for the first time in the state's history. Such progress was short-lived, however, and after 1876 white politicians began to implement voting qualifications, such as literacy tests and property ownership requirements, in a brazen program designed to limit access to the ballot. Perhaps most insidious, though, was the creation of the Democratic Party's all-white primary, a move that in states such as South Carolina—where an overwhelming majority of votes were cast for the Democratic candidate in the actual election—made the votes of even those few African Americans who were able to vote irrelevant. Although the Supreme Court began as early as the 1920s to end some of the barriers to an equal franchise, it was not until 1944 that it finally outlawed these all-white primaries, declaring that the primary was itself an integral part of the election process, requiring the same protections as the main election. James O. Farmer elaborates in "Memories and Forebodings: The Fight to Preserve the White Democratic Primary in South Carolina, 1944–1950." There, the author traces how the state's white political leaders fought with every procedural weapon they could devise against the first federal initiatives to restore meaning to the Fifteenth Amendment to the Constitution.

In "Could History Repeat Itself?: The Prospects for a Second Reconstruction in Post–World War II South Carolina," Robert Korstad traces how, in 1946, a biracial group of Charlestonians hosted a "New South Lecture Series" aimed at promoting racial equality, unionization of labor, a massive education program for the poor, economic growth, and democratic reform of the political apparatus of the Palmetto State. The lectures grew out of the desire of former New Dealers to continue the progressive policies of the Roosevelt era. Their only hope of success in this endeavor was to "break the stranglehold of conservative southern Democrats," by mobilizing African Americans and poor whites to form a solid voting bloc on their behalf. For inspiration, they self-consciously looked to the original period of African American enfranchisement, the first Reconstruction, with the stated intent of helping "history repeat itself." These efforts, however, were met with broad condemnation from the ruling white establishment of South Carolina, who clearly recognized their true purpose. Perhaps most vitriolic in its response was the Charleston *News and Courier,* which unleashed a withering editorial fire that set forth the basic arguments—and strategies—for the "massive resistance" campaign of the following decade.

That campaign, John White demonstrates in "The White Citizens' Councils of Orangeburg County, South Carolina," grew rapidly as "an outlet for white rage" in the wake of the NAACP's demand for immediate integration of public schools. One of the most visible and aggressive of the organizations formed to defend segregation was found in the series of so-called White Citizens' Councils that began to appear across the South almost as soon as the *Brown* decision was handed down. The first of these groups to organize in South Carolina did so in the county of Orangeburg, an area that was 60 percent African American and in which desegregation was a crucial issue. The councils quickly spread throughout the rest of the state. Receiving open and unapologetic support from white community's leaders, the Orangeburg White Citizens' Council embarked upon a propaganda campaign designed to discredit the NAACP and other African American leaders. It did so, in part, by claiming that ordinary black citizens were being duped by a nefarious foreign group intent on taking their hard-earned money, and in part by playing on white fears of miscegenation to rally support for their cause. African Americans who were members of the NAACP or who signed petitions asking that the county comply with the Supreme Court's instruction to desegregate its schools were especially targeted. They faced economic intimidation that included the calling in of bank loans, a refusal of business at white-run stores, and a loss of jobs. Local civil rights organizations did all they could to alleviate these hardships, distributing food and other supplies and raising money to loan to those most in need. Finally the local chapter of the NAACP organized its own, highly effective, boycott of white businesses in Orangeburg, weakening the resolve of the Citizen's Council and causing a decline in its membership levels, although the underlying white resistance to desegregation remained.

Given the shocking violence that accompanied James Meredith's desegregation of the University of Mississippi in the fall of 1962, it was with some trepidation that many South Carolinians viewed Harvey Gantt's attempts to gain admission to Clemson University the following January. That Gantt was enrolled peacefully and without major incident stood in marked contrast to recent national events and the general sentiment of whites within the state, producing a wave of self-congratulatory articles. Chief among them was one written by George McMillan, which has—with its description of previously staunch white supremacists putting aside their own prejudices to preserve the image of their state—come to be the dominant framework by which the integration of South Carolina's universities is understood. In "'Integration With [Relative] Dignity'—Clemson's Desegregation and George McMillan's Article at Forty," however, Ron Cox shows that the state's leaders were not as uniformly cooperative as the traditional historiography suggests and that Harvey Gantt's reception was not as warm as the first round of reporting led people to believe. Indeed, the article was immediately greeted with strong denials from some of the more prominent politicians that it quoted and with many other commentators grudgingly accepting the inevitability of Gantt's acceptance, but denying that South Carolinians were proud of it. Far from being a sign that race relations within South Carolina were embarking on a new era of equality, therefore, the integration of Clemson University instead indicated that the state's future remained uncertain.

This sentiment was only confirmed by the events surrounding the desegregation of nearby Greenville, arguably South Carolina's most modern city. As with Harvey Gantt's admission to Clemson, the popular account of these events recalls a relatively peaceful process in which the city's white establishment voluntarily demolished its Jim Crow past with "grace and dignity." In "Memory, History, and the Desegregation of Greenville, South Carolina," however, Stephen O'Neill paints a revisionist portrait of the people and events surrounding the city's desegregation. Although Greenville's business leaders had long viewed their home as a progressive city, it in fact had a long history of race- and class-based conflict. Many working class whites viewed the growing African American community as a threat to their livelihoods, while white business leaders feared that their growing activism would provoke ever-escalating levels of violence and consequently sought to undermine and control their activities. Following the *Brown* decision, civil rights organizations increasingly campaigned for the desegregation of Greenville's public accommodations, holding protest marches, student sit-ins, and filing lawsuits. Far from being a voluntary process, Greenville's white community fought long and hard to preserve their racial hierarchy, even in the wake of a 1963 Supreme Court ruling that specifically challenged the constitutionality of segregated lunch-counters in the city. Indeed, it was not until 1970, and faced with the threat of economic sanctions against the city, that Greenville grudgingly gave up the fight against segregation.

But even as explicitly racial discrimination waned and African Americans finally saw improvements in their political rights and access to public accommodations, white Carolinians found other (and often no less effective) ways to limit their advancement. One of them, as R. Scott Baker explains in "A New Racial Order in Education: South Carolina's Response to the African American Struggle for Equality and Access, 1945–1975," was the widespread adoption of standardized tests to rationalize old restrictions that could no longer be sanctioned by law. Although these tests were taken by whites and blacks alike, and therefore seemed on the surface to be color-blind in their design, they were in fact intended for use specifically against African American attempts for equality within the education system, extending from admissions to teacher salaries. By exploiting "racial differences in educational achievement that were a product of generations of economic and educational discrimination," whites were able to retain the edifice of segregation without its most explicit elements. Many of the old battles, in other words, continued to be fought albeit on new grounds.

Memories and Forebodings

*The Fight to Preserve the White Democratic Primary
in South Carolina, 1944–1950*

JAMES O. FARMER

The quest for full participation in our democracy by South Carolina's African Americans entered its final chapter with the fall of the state's white Democratic Party primary in 1948. That victory was long in coming, for the state's white political leaders fought a four-year battle to block black voting following the United States Supreme Court's epochal decision in *Smith v. Allwright* in April 1944. Even after *Brown v. Baskin* dealt the final blow to the white primary in the state, almost two more decades would pass before blacks became full participants in Palmetto State politics. That story is one of tenacity in the face of powerful and determined opposition from whites and complacency and fear among blacks themselves. Its heroes are people such as John Henry McCray, James Hinton, Osceola McKaine, George A. Elmore, Modjeska Simkins, and Thurgood Marshall. Its milestones include the formation of the Progressive Democratic Party of South Carolina and the founding of its mouthpiece, the *Lighthouse and Informer*, which John McCray edited.[1] Both of these events occurred in 1944, inspired by the court ruling in *Smith v. Allwright*. But this is not that story. Rather, it is the story of the efforts by the opponents of these untiring champions of democracy to block their path.

South Carolina governor Olin D. Johnston was a skilled politician. In 1944 he was serving his second, nonconsecutive, term as the state's chief executive. He won a seat in the United States Senate that year, sending Ellison "Cotton Ed" Smith into retirement, and six years later he would solidify his hold on that seat by defeating the outgoing governor, Strom Thurmond, in a hotly contested race. He would hold the seat until his death in 1965. Apparently he had his finger on the pulse of the state's citizenry. When it became necessary, he proved capable of shifting with the changing times, noting late in his career that the vote of African Americans "counts just as much as anybody else's."[2] But as a student of history Johnston left something to be desired. He and his generation of white South Carolinians were reared during the "nadir" of African American history—the era of

18. George Elmore, plaintiff in Elmore v. Rice *(1947). Courtesy of the South Caroliniana Library, University of South Carolina, Columbia*

Tillman and Blease, of legalized Jim Crow and constitutional disenfranchisement. That era also gave the state its white-only Democratic Party primary, and with it the distinction of having "the most complete" system for excluding blacks from its political process.[3] The history lesson learned by that generation, and passed on to Johnston and his contemporaries, was clear. Ben Tillman, as usual, put it most colorfully, when he warned of the possibility that "this black snake" could be warmed back to life and reenter the political arena.[4] Johnston's generation and their successors learned that lesson so well that they could not leave any avenue untried in their determined but increasingly futile efforts to preserve the Tillman legacy. They were still operating in that mode when South Carolina became the first state to challenge the constitutionality of the Voting Rights Act of 1965. Chief Justice Earl Warren, after listening to the state's attorneys' denial of intentional discrimination, noted South Carolina's long history of violations of the Fifteenth Amendment and called it "an insidious and pervasive evil."[5] The rearguard strategy employed to preserve the white Democratic primary from judicial challenge is but one chapter in that sad record.

African Americans had been barred from voting in Democratic primaries throughout the South for decades, but when the "Roosevelt revolution" brought most of them into the Democratic camp beginning with the 1936 election, their interest in the primary, and their sense of justice, led to challenges. Texas had made its white primary vulnerable to attack in 1923 by making it a matter of law. Twice over the next ten years, El Paso physician A. L. Nixon sued election officials, claiming that Texas was violating the Fifteenth Amendment by racially discriminating in what were for all practical purposes its real elections. The Supreme Court based its rulings on the Fourteenth Amendment, and since "state action" was involved, ruled for the plaintiff but evaded the question Nixon sought answer to. In 1935 Texas was again taken to court, but this time it had found a loophole—the party had made its own "white only" rule without state sanction. Still relying on the Fourteenth Amendment, the Supreme Court unanimously ruled that in the absence of "state action," there was no violation of the Fourteenth Amendment.[6]

By 1941, however, the Court had several new faces and a more activist philosophy, and the Justice Department was also more aggressive in providing evidence of vote tampering. Thus the Court ruled that the primary, in a one-party state (Louisiana this time), was an integral part of the election process and thus subject to constitutional protections. The case, *U.S. v Classic,* did not involve black voting rights, but it set the stage for the victory that came on April 3, 1944, with *Smith v Allwright.* Here, NAACP lawyers Thurgood Marshall and William Hastie convinced eight of the justices that the *Classic* case established grounds for overturning the Texas white primary. Applying the Fifteenth Amendment to a primary for the first time, the Court found that Texas was implicated in the Democratic primary by requiring party officials to deny ballots to those not qualified under party rules, and thus in allowing the party to bar blacks Texas was participating in their disenfranchisement. Chief Justice Harlan Stone brought several uncertain brethren around by stressing that the case involved "not all primaries but this primary."[7]

Although he had not heard those words, they would be the grounds for the hope that Governor Johnston acted upon when he called the South Carolina General Assembly into special session on April 14. Hindsight, which David Donald called the historian's best friend and greatest liability, has told students of the civil rights struggle that only the myopic could have missed the message that *Smith v Allwright* was a death sentence for South Carolina's white primary.[8] Legalistically speaking, this was true; in fact the final blow came sooner than its defenders expected, since it was delivered, shockingly, not by the Supreme Court but by federal district judge J. Waties Waring, a Charlestonian with an impeccable pedigree. But rumors of the white primary's death were highly exaggerated, as the voting statistics of the next twenty years would show. For the same determination that characterized South Carolina's white leadership in 1944 continued to place barriers in the paths of black voters for the next two decades. Only the more aggressive among them would cast ballots prior to the passage of the Voting Rights Act of 1965, and only once before that pivotal event, in 1960, did their votes determine the results of the state's vote.[9]

In April 1944 the long shadows of history darkened the chambers of the South Carolina statehouse as the members of the General Assembly gathered to add another chapter in that decade's biggest civil rights battle. Governor Johnston delivered to the special legislative session on April 14, 1944, a history lesson that would inspire them, if inspiration was needed, to stand in the way of history repeating itself. Acting on the advice of his legal staff, Johnston urged the legislature to remove all references in the state statutes to the Democratic primary, leaving the government no role in this crucial contest and thereby risking vote fraud but bolstering the claim that the Democratic Party was merely a private club, which in denying membership and ballots to blacks was not acting in behalf of the state.[10]

Governor Johnston's history lesson said in part: "I need not remind you that ... where you now sit, there once sat a majority of Negroes. What kind of government did they give South Carolina when they were in power? The records will bear me out that fraud, corruption, immorality and graft existed during that regime that has never been paralleled in the history of our State. The representatives of these agitators, scalawags and unscrupulous politicians that called themselves white men ... are in our midst today, and history will repeat itself unless we protect ourselves against this new crop of carpet-baggers and scalawags. ..." Echoing the tone of his predecessor Ben Tillman in another hour of crisis for South Carolina, the governor continued: "After these statutes are repealed, in my opinion, we will have done everything in our power to guarantee white supremacy in our primaries ... so far as legislation is concerned. Should this prove inadequate, we South Carolinians will use the necessary methods to preserve white supremacy in our primaries and to safeguard the homes and happiness of our people. White supremacy will be maintained in our primaries. Let the chips fall where they may!"[11]

Following Johnston's lead, the legislature went to work to remove all references to the primary from the statute books. The result was described in a *Newsweek* article titled "Killbillies": "It probably set some kind of legislative record: a six-day special session, 200 laws repealed and no new ones enacted. But—no matter what the rest of the South might do, South Carolina was determined not to let the 8–1 decision of the United States Supreme Court ... interfere with white control of the Palmetto State." The *Newsweek* reporter might have had even more fun with the piece had he known that the solons, in their anxiety not to overlook any laws, had enacted a "catch-all" bill suggested by

Solicitor Robert Figg, which nullified any statutes that might have been over-looked in the hasty survey of the books.[12]

The chips fell against Johnston and his demagogic strategy. He knew his history well enough to recall that once, in the late 1860s and early 1870s, a combination of northern Republicans, native blacks, and a few native whites, using the power of the ballot—backed by the Fourteenth and Fifteenth Amendments, the state constitution of 1868, and the United States Army—had imposed "Negro rule" on the state. He no doubt knew that history well enough to recall that the odiousness of that "Negro rule" was compounded for whites by the regimented bloc voting of the freedmen, and no doubt he also recalled that at that time, and until the 1920s, his state had a black majority. But if he had been a better student he might have realized that, white hysteria notwithstanding, the temple of white political supremacy would not fall just because blacks were admitted to the Democratic primary. As southern whites have done on more than one occasion, he and the legislators conjured up images that were beyond the capacity, if not the intention, of blacks to realize. One thinks of the many slave conspiracy scares of the antebellum era, the rumors of black riots that bedeviled whites in cities outside as well as within the South, the fear of black rapists that created a regime of perpetual intimidation backed by violence, and the sometimes hysterical warnings in the 1950s and 1960s of the fate that awaited the white race if the schools were desegregated.

In all of those cases, before and after 1944, white fears were exaggerated, and I would suggest that they were this time as well. The black majority that had dictated the state's racial policy for so long had been reduced by the Great Migration to a not-so-frightening 42 percent of the state's population in 1940. By 1950 whites would outnumber blacks by some 470,000.[13] The black exodus was a mixed blessing for southern whites, since it created a growing black presence in northern cities whose votes would help drive the federal government to more liberal policies on race. It also helped Harry Truman weather the attack from southern dissidents led by Thurmond in the 1948 election. Too, the impact of this demographic shift should not be overstated, for about half of the counties in South Carolina still had black majorities in 1950.[14] But with relatively few exceptions, that shrinking percentage of African Americans, victims for generations of woefully underfunded education and almost nonexistent health care and facing limited vocational opportunities, was still far from developing the political consciousness and mustering the courage needed for an all-out assault on the registration books and voting places. They could not, in Johnston's day, hope for the support provided during Reconstruction by the idealism and partisanship of the national political leadership.

Without that support, Johnston might have reflected, perhaps only half of the potential black voters were capable of seeing the ballot as a priority and confident enough to register and vote in the Democratic primaries. South Carolina awarded only some 1,000 high school diplomas to African Americans in 1940, less than one-tenth the number awarded to whites. Ten years earlier blacks had earned only 104 diplomas of a total of 5,646.[15] Perhaps half of them dropped out of school by the seventh grade. The typical African American was a sharecropper who earned less than four hundred dollars a year.[16] Northern blacks visiting the state, especially NAACP officials, were disappointed by what they saw as the complacency of the Palmetto State's African Americans. Most, it seemed, were willing to rely on the old way of appealing to whites for fairness and favors within the status quo. Benjamin Mays described the heralded "New Negro" of the 1940s in his region as only "less conservative" than his old counterpart.[17] Gunnar Myrdal found blacks in the rural South who were so beaten down by their poverty and negative experience that they manifested "a psychopathological form of apathy."[18] Despite the growing assertiveness of the black elite, then, it would be some time before the majority of the state's blacks were armed with the ability to take advantage of the ballot. Estimates of black ballots cast grew from three thousand in 1940 to fifty thousand in 1948, when, for the first time, large numbers voted in the primary. But then the numbers leveled off, and when a new registration was required in 1958, only some fifty-eight thousand blacks registered. On the eve of the Voting Rights Bill, in 1964, only about one-third of them were registered.[19]

Another fact, had they been perceptive enough to see it, might have calmed Johnston and the legislature somewhat as well. At the end of the nineteenth century Walter Hines Page, reflecting on the strength of white prejudice, had written that he would rather be "an imp in hades than a darkie in South Carolina."[20] But as they neared the mid-twentieth century, South Carolina whites, whose ranks still held many with racial attitudes that were unchanged for decades, were beginning to soften their hostility to change in the racial climate. One astute white observer, John Rice, wrote in 1942 that "the Southerner's attitude toward the Negro is incredibly more humane than it was in the South I knew as a child [around the turn of the century]."[21] World War II helped in this regard, as blacks served effectively in the cause of liberty against fascist racism and military spending removed some of the economic anxieties that had driven white racist behavior. The 1944 book *What the Negro Wants* expressed strong determination not to let the opportunities of that moment pass, quoting the historic 1943 Richmond, Virginia, biracial Collaboration Conference's announcement that current conditions presented "a rare challenge to the white leadership [of the South] to find new ways of cooperation and to justify increased confidence of Negro leadership in the white South. . . . " Summarizing the conference, black writer Gordon B. Hancock noted optimistically that the "ground work for some constructive developments in race relations has been laid."[22] The victorious end of World War II in 1945 would usher in a moment of optimism and tolerance. "Here, surely, was a rare and momentous turning point in . . . the checkered history of the South: . . . a hinge of time swinging shut on a constricted past and opening to an expansive future," John Egerton wrote.[23]

Of course we cannot overlook the postwar racial tensions that flared when black soldiers returned with more confidence to challenge Jim Crow, and the cold war that would add the fear of Communist plots of racial unrest to the picture, but the issue of black voting was considerably less volatile than that of the social mixing of the races. Johnston and the legislators need not have acted so hastily and drastically. Further, a calmer response from them might have smoothed the way into the future for South Carolinians of both races. But it would have been out of character in light of their history, a history that taught them that anything less than full vigilance against the black peril put them at risk of being "out niggered" in upcoming elections. Other southern states' political leaders were responding more moderately to the threat posed by *Smith v. Allwright*. But South Carolina's "leaders" were not yet there, and would not be for at least a generation. Ironically Governor Johnston's history lesson and the legislature's hurried response to it, though intended to preserve the traditions of white supremacy, would contribute to the beginnings of the "second reconstruction." For in reading the past as they did, and devising a response based on that reading, they triggered reactions, both from their black victims and from an unlikely source, Judge J. Waties Waring. His subsequent response to his state's history of repression, rendered in his minority opinion in the desegregation case of *Briggs v. Elliott*, would help launch the racial revolution that Johnston and his legislative audience so feared.[24]

19. Black Charlestonians waiting to cast their first ballots in a South Carolina Democratic primary, 1948. Photograph courtesy of the Avery Research Center for African American History and Culture at the College of Charleston

Waring's *Elmore v. Rice* decision, reaffirming *Smith v. Allwright*, was, John McCray told the 1947 convention of the Progressive Democratic Party of South Carolina, "the most eventful act in our history since Lincoln signed the emancipation proclamation." He added, more accurately than he perhaps realized, that "the actual victory has yet to be won."[25] As Steven Lawson has noted, the faith of blacks and their white friends in the power of the ballot was too sanguine.[26] The franchise did not become the panacea for the Palmetto State's racial ills. A cynic might note that it has failed to bring the millennium even as it has polarized the state's politics and ghettoized the political voice of its African Americans. Yet, as the South was transformed by industrial and urban growth, things might have been worse, for as W. E. B. Du Bois wrote in 1930, "a disfranchised working class in modern industrial civilization is worse than helpless. It is a menace, not simply to itself, but to every other group in the community. . . . it will be ignorant; it will be the plaything of mobs; and it will be insulted by caste restrictions." The fall of the white primary in the late 1940s helped avoid Du Bois's frightening prospect, for it encouraged hope and established "a pattern of black pressure and white response" that would define race relations in South Carolina and achieve progress in the decades to follow.[27]

Notes

1. John Henry McCray Papers, South Caroliniana Library, University of South Carolina; Modjeska Monteith Simkins Papers, South Caroliniana Library, University of South Carolina.

2. Lewis P. Jones, *South Carolina: One of the Fifty States* (Orangeburg, S.C.: Sandlapper, 1985), 668.

3. George B. Tindall, *South Carolina Negroes, 1877–1900* (Baton Rouge: Louisiana State University Press, 1952), 89. An excellent summary of South Carolina's racially exclusionary practices is in Orville Vernon Burton, Terence R. Finnegan, Peyton McCrary, and James W. Loewen, "South Carolina," in *Quiet Revolution in the South: The Impact of the Voting Rights Act, 1965–1990*, ed. Chandler Davidson and Bernard Grofman, 191–232 (Princeton, N.J.: Princeton University Press, 1994).

4. Michael Perman, *The Struggle for Mastery: Disfranchisement in the South, 1888–1908* (Chapel Hill: University of North Carolina Press, 2001), 96.

5. Burton et al., "South Carolina," 191.

6. Steven F. Lawson, *Black Ballots: Voting Rights in the South, 1944–1969* (New York: Columbia University Press, 1976), 28–35.

7. Ibid., 44.

8. See, for example, Donald R. Matthews and James W. Prothro, *Negroes and the New Southern Politics* (New York: Harcourt, Brace, and World, 1966), 16–17.

9. The black vote has been credited with putting South Carolina in the Kennedy column in the presidential election of 1960. See *New York Times*, November 9, 1960, 1, 12.

10. Robert M. Figg, interview with the author, March 1969, University of South Carolina. Figg told me that in his opinion *Smith v. Allwright* left open the possibility that complete separation of the primary from state law might save it from further judicial attack.

11. *Journal of the South Carolina House of Representatives*, Second Session, 85th General Assembly, 1155–57. Johnston was referring to the period of "black rule" during Radical

Reconstruction, when African Americans held a majority of the seats in the House. He was ignoring the corruption that continued after the end of "black rule" and the general level of corruption in national government during the Gilded Age. Tillman, who played a minor role in the overthrow of the Radical government, later boasted that whites would resort to any means necessary to maintain their dominance. See Francis B. Simkins, *Pitchfork Ben Tillman, South Carolinian* (Baton Rouge: Louisiana State University Press, 1944), chap. 26.

12. *Newsweek*, May 1, 1944; Figg interview.

13. George C. Rogers Jr. and C. James Taylor, *A South Carolina Chronology, 1497–1992* (Columbia: University of South Carolina Press, 1994), 132, 135.

14. Numan V. Bartley and Hugh D. Graham, *Southern Politics and the Second Reconstruction* (Baltimore: Johns Hopkins University Press, 1975), 28 (map).

15. Walter B. Edgar, *South Carolina: A History* (Columbia: University of South Carolina Press, 1998), 490.

16. John Egerton, *Speak Now against the Day: The Generation before the Civil Rights Movement in the South* (New York: Knopf, 1994), 4.

17. I. A. Newby, *Black Carolinians: A History of Blacks in South Carolina from 1895 to 1968* (Columbia: University of South Carolina Press, 1993), 230, 233–34.

18. Gunnar Myrdal, *An American Dilemma: The Negro Problem and Modern Democracy* (New York: Harper and Row, 1944), 490.

19. Alexander Heard, *A Two-Party South?* (Chapel Hill: University of North Carolina Press, 1952), 302; *Report of the Secretary of State to the General Assembly of South Carolina, 1958* (Columbia: State Budget and Control Board, 1958), 194; *Columbia Record*, March 16, 1965, 1; estimate by the state NAACP, cited in Mickie Ray Cline, "The South Carolina Negro Vote in the Presidential Elections of 1952 through 1964" (M.A. thesis, University of South Carolina, 1966), 30.

20. Burton K. Hendrick, *The Training of an American: The Earlier Life and Letters of Walter H. Page, 1855–1913* (Boston: Houghton Mifflin, 1928), 305.

21. John Andrew Rice, *I Came Out of the Eighteenth Century* (New York: Harper, 1942), 195.

22. Paul D. Escott and David R. Goldfield, eds., *Major Problems in the History of the American South*, vol. 2 (Lexington, Mass.: Heath, 1990), 426–28.

23. Egerton, *Speak Now against the Day*, 5.

24. In *Elmore v. Rice* and *Brown v. Baskin* Judge Waring thwarted the state's attempt to preserve its white Democratic Party primary elections. Soon after these cases were decided, he dissented from the ruling of a three-judge federal panel in the case of *Briggs v. Elliott*. When appealed, that decision, coming out of Clarendon County, joined others under the heading of *Brown v. the Board of Education, Topeka, Kansas*, which resulted in the legal overthrow of segregation.

25. Newby, *Black Carolinians*, 285.

26. Lawson, *Black Ballots*, 352.

27. Myrdal, *American Dilemma*, 512 (Du Bois quotation); Newby, *Black Carolinians*, 287.

Could History Repeat Itself?

The Prospects for a Second Reconstruction in Post–World War II South Carolina

ROBERT R. KORSTAD

On the evening of November 26, 1945, several hundred white and black Charlestonians gathered at the Morris Street Baptist Church to hear Aubrey Williams, former director of the New Deal's National Youth Administration and, at the time, publisher of the *Southern Farmer*. Williams's presentation inaugurated the "New South Lecture Series," five talks by prominent southern progressives on the critical issues facing the region in the postwar world. In addition to Williams, the series featured Charles S. Johnson, the noted African American sociologist and soon to be president of Fisk University; Clifford Durr, an Alabama lawyer and a member of the Federal Communications Commission; Clark Foreman, chairman of the Southern Conference for Human Welfare; and Kelley Barnett, a minister from Chapel Hill who represented University of North Carolina president Frank Porter Graham.[1]

The speakers were members of a well-positioned group of southern New Dealers (scholars, politicians, labor leaders, and civil rights activists) who, at the end of World War II, articulated a vision of a more democratic and prosperous New South. Historians such as Patricia Sullivan, John Egerton, and John Salmond have documented the important role such men and women played in the fight to extend the New Deal. But less attention has been paid to the details of their vision and the particular public policies they advocated.[2]

The New South Lecture Series grew out of an unlikely alliance between members of Local 15 of the Food, Tobacco, Agricultural, and Allied Workers, Congress of Industrial Organization (FTA-CIO) and a group of GIs stationed at Stark General Hospital. Workers at the American Tobacco Company, virtually all of whom were women and a large majority of whom were African Americans, had organized Local 15 in 1943. In the spring of 1945 my father, Karl Korstad, and a few of his army buddies began working with Local 15 as volunteers. They helped around the office, wrote leaflets and press releases, and taught literacy classes for union members. In the fall they planned the lecture series.[3]

On October 22, five weeks before the series was scheduled to begin, over one thousand black and white members of Local 15 walked off their jobs, demanding wage increases, a union shop, paid sick leave, and better working conditions. FTA members at American plants in Philadelphia had struck the week before, and a week later workers at Trenton, New Jersey, would also walk out. The Charleston struggle is most remembered as the birthplace for the civil rights anthem "We Shall Overcome." But the strike was also notable for the degree of interracial cooperation it engendered between black and white women.[4]

Although caught up in a swirl of strike activities, union leaders decided to go ahead with the lecture series, hoping it could mobilize additional support for striking workers in both the black and white communities. Toward that end they recruited three cosponsors: the National Maritime Workers Union; the Citizens' Political Action Committee, the local chapter of the National Citizens' PAC, created in 1944 for middle-class supporters of the CIO's political program; and the Cosmopolitan Civic League, an organization of politically minded African Americans.[5]

After the first lecture Karl was transferred to Alabama in preparation for his discharge from the army. My mother, Frances, a Charleston native, and an ad hoc committee of union leaders, black ministers, and black teachers took over the arrangements and publicity. Their big challenge was to get people to attend the lectures, and here the committee drew primarily on the organizational infrastructure of Charleston's African American community. They distributed blocs of tickets (one dollar for the series, fifty cents for a single lecture) to the ministers of local black churches, the teachers at the Avery Institute (a private high school for African Americans), and the leaders of the local chapter of the NAACP, who in turn sold the tickets to their members and, in the process, discussed the goals of the lecture series. The sponsoring organizations did the same.[6]

Although held at an African American church, the lecture series drew an interracial audience that numbered from a few hundred to more than one thousand for Dr. Johnson, and without fanfare organizers encouraged seating on a nonsegregated basis. These gatherings were remarkable in part because of the class composition of the audiences. Tobacco workers, merchant seamen, ministers, teachers, small shop owners, and a smattering of white-collar professionals sat side by side in the church pews.[7]

Speakers took the occasion to carry their message to an even larger Charleston audience. All met with the Youth Interracial Fellowship at the Avery Institute. Clifford Durr spoke at a luncheon meeting of the Lions Club. Clark Foreman addressed the staff of the white YWCA. Several of the lectures were carried on local radio stations.[8]

In conjunction with the lecture series, Aubrey Williams and Karl planned an edited volume of essays titled "New South." Much like the controversial collection *What the Negro Wants*, published a few years earlier, "New South" aimed to bring together a broad group of southern progressives to outline an agenda for social and economic development in the region. Although the two men never published the volume, they worked out a detailed outline and selected writers for each topic. These same people published articles that year in the *Southern Patriot, Survey Graphic,* and the *Southern Packet,* so the ideas they would have brought to the volume are clear.[9]

By the 1940s the South had emerged as the critical battleground in the effort to maintain the momentum of the New Deal. The region was home to the country's largest bloc of unorganized workers, and the long-term success of the CIO depended on its ability to bring southern workers into the house of labor. Likewise, two out of three African Americans lived below the Mason-Dixon line, and the vast majority of these were working class. To survive and expand, New Dealers had to break the stranglehold of conservative southern Democrats, who owed their seniority and thus their domination of congressional committees to the South's constricted electorate and one-party rule. To do so they had to enfranchise millions of African Americans and mobilize the region's poor whites.[10]

"That's why we need the lecture series," Karl wrote Frances that winter, "and more and more education. We've got to try to change the membership of Congress in the next elections, or we're likely to go into another Harding return to normalcy period. We might go anyway . . . but labor and progressives must this time make their case known, and make it known that they oppose such action, and why they oppose it."[11]

Along with the "normalcy" that followed World War I had come an upsurge of racial violence and antiradical repression. The progressives and laborites of the 1940s feared a similar backlash, which could destroy what the movements of the 1930s had won. All in all, however, they were remarkably optimistic—and their optimism tells us much about the tenor of the times. The pessimists, Karl claimed, had forgotten "that the strikes of the twenties and thirties, the depression, the New Deal, the birth and growth of our great industrial unions and the character of the present war have educated millions of our people. They forget that the complexion of things has changed. . . . There is a strong progressive element in the South," he continued, "an element which is attempting to better labor conditions, to improve the educational and economic and social and political conditions of the poor whites and the Negro. The people of the South like any other people, once they have been given the facts and the opportunity to understand their economic and political plight, will make the right decision. But up to now, most of them haven't had that opportunity." Karl saw the essays and the lecture series as part of an educational campaign to win broader support for progressive goals.[12]

Charleston may seem like an odd place to fire some of the first shots in the postwar battle to change the composition of the southern congressional delegation and ultimately dislodge the planter/banker/industrial oligarchy that had ruled the South since the turn of the century. For no town better represented the Old South, and no state was more tethered to the myths of the past than South Carolina. Yet in the winter of 1945–46, no place better represented the remarkable changes of the past decade and the heightened expectations for the future. The New Deal and World War II had reshaped the social and economic geography of the city and the state. Thousands of new jobs had materialized. Military bases in Charleston and at Fort Jackson outside Columbia brought sailors and soldiers from around the country to the Palmetto State. Most important, workers and African Americans had begun to organize.[13]

Perhaps the most notable of these democratic stirrings was the formation of the Progressive Democratic Party, a mostly middle-class African American challenge to the lily-white Democratic Party. NAACP membership had grown rapidly during the war, and by 1945 the state had a remarkable forty chapters with more than ten thousand members. Organized labor had a more tenuous toehold. The American Federation of Labor had scattered locals in printing, the building trades, and among longshoremen. The most dynamic unions were those affiliated with the CIO: FTA Local 15; the National Martine Union; a local of the Mine, Mill, and Smelter Workers in North Charleston; and a number of upstate outposts of the Textile Workers Union. Also critical were the individual efforts of while liberals in places such as Charleston and Columbia. Judge J. Waties Waring, whose rulings on the white primary and school segregation helped bolster the judicial challenges to Jim Crow, had already begun his attack on the bastions of white supremacy by the end of the war. Women such as Harriet Simmons were deeply involved in social welfare and interracial issues.[14]

South Carolinians were not alone in these efforts to extend the reach of the New Deal. Similar mobilizations were occurring in other places, and in every southern state a network of capable leaders had sprung up that crossed class lines and included blacks and whites, men and women. Regional organizations such as the Southern Regional Council, Highlander Folk School, and the Southern Conference for Human Welfare brought activists together to share experiences and strategies.[15]

Each of the speakers at the New South Lecture Series had played key roles in these regional organizations, and each continued to play a part in national politics, trying to influence Truman's Fair Deal as they had FDR's New Deal. In all those capacities they spoke for what we might call the Southern Front, a loose coalition of labor unionists, civil rights activists, and southern New Dealers who saw a strong labor movement and the enfranchisement of the southern poor as the key to reforming the South and a reformed South as central to the survival and expansion of the New Deal. The only chance progressives had to overcome the "poison and hate of native fascists," as Karl put it, was to put forth a platform for political liberalization and economic modernization that would resonate with the hopes and fears of the mass of southerners. That was the intention of the New South Lecture Series and the proposed essays, and they provide a useful framework for examining the progressive agenda.[16]

The political, social, and economic policies advocated by southern progressives had five main objectives. The first was to extend citizenship rights to African Americans, as well as poor and working-class whites who had effectively been disfranchised for much of the century. The second was to end the racial discrimination that so constrained the talents and aspirations of ten million African Americans. A third goal was to institute a massive education program that would raise literacy rates as well as better prepare people for jobs in industry. A forth goal was to continue the organization of industrial workers that skyrocketed during the war and then to extend that organizational effort to small farmers and farmworkers. The fifth goal was to spur growth in agriculture and industry. In all of these areas progressives saw federal intervention as key.[17]

Aubrey Williams devoted the first lecture to the crisis in southern agriculture, emphasizing especially the lack of effective organization among small farmers and the South's continued reliance on King Cotton. Small farmers, Williams insisted, needed organization as much as did industrial workers. "Fifty farmers, united, marketing their produce together can demand and receive much higher prices than can fifty farmers, divided," he said, echoing the rallying cry of the Populists. "And fifty farmers, united, buying their feed and gas and fertilizer . . . can demand and get a much lower price than can fifty farmers, divided." Williams warned small farmers not to view unions of industrial workers as enemies, which was the position of the Farm Bureau, an organization Williams claimed represented the interests of merchants, bankers, and large farmers but not the small and medium farmers. Unions meant higher wages, and higher wages meant more purchasing power for workers, and that meant greater demand for farm products. Williams also petitioned small farmers to abandon cotton, because they could not compete with the low prices of cotton from other parts of the world. "We must move toward cattle, peanuts, soybeans—in fact, reach a legume basis of agriculture." This was the only way, Williams argued, for small farmers to gain independence from the merchants and bankers who controlled access to credit.[18]

Clifford Durr's December address focused on how to make the South "the nation's number one economic opportunity," instead of, as FDR had called it, the nation's number-one economic problem. The solution, according to Durr, lay in the better use of the region's human as well as natural resources. Arguing a variant of the colonial economy thesis, he said, "We have sought to hold our own in a competitive national economy by mining our farm lands as well as our mineral deposits, by mining our human resources through substandard wages rates and by exporting raw materials instead of finished products." Substandard wages and salaries made it impossible for many southerners to afford the goods they helped produce. Underconsumption was at the heart of poverty in the region, Durr claimed. True to his New Deal affinities, Durr lauded the role that government could play in economic and social development. He cited the Tennessee Valley Authority and the Rural Electrification Administration as two examples of how government could provide the infrastructure for economic development.[19]

Clark Foreman emphasized the role of electoral politics in fashioning a new South. Overthrowing the oligarchy that had ruled the region since the turn of the century required not only opening up the electorate to disfranchised African Americans, but also mobilizing the middle- and working-class voters who too often stayed away from the polls. Foreman also spoke about the importance of cross-class, interracial organizations such as the SCHW, a chapter of which had been organized in Charleston the day before.[20]

Charles Johnson's lecture was the best attended, as African Americans in large numbers turned out to see the noted sociologist. Johnson stressed the need to address the South's social problems, particularly as they affected African Americans. For Johnson, improvements in housing, health care, and education had to be at the top of the progressive agenda.[21]

When South Carolina's Progressive Democratic Party was formed in 1944, its vice-chairman, Osceola McKaine, evoked Reconstruction to describe what he believed was at stake in the years after World War II. "We are here," he said, "to help history repeat itself." But opponents of regional regeneration looked back to Reconstruction as well. They were determined not to let the past repeat itself, to forestall a "Second Reconstruction." William Watts Ball, editor of the *Charleston News and Courier,* was one of the most outspoken defenders of conservative rule. While his vitriolic polemics sometimes made him an embarrassment to his allies, his views on labor, African Americans, and the New Deal were in line with those of the major power brokers in the South: the plutocrats of North Carolina; the plantation owners and industrialists of Alabama; and the oilmen of Louisiana and Texas.[22]

In the turbulent days at the end of the war Ball's editorial page fired daily shots at each and every effort at change. And he closely followed the New South Lecture Series, honing in especially on what he—rightly—saw as the speakers' core message: the need to expand democratic citizenship in the South. "The ailment of South Carolina and of the whole United States is over-dosage of democracy," Ball editorialized in December 1945. "The infatuation for democracy is a disease. It is now epidemic." To state legislators who were at the time contemplating repeal of the poll tax, Ball recommended instead a "constitutional amendment that would reduce the potential negro vote by 90 percent and the potential white vote by a percentage that would shock the democrats." "It is possible," he continued, "that South Carolinians may some day have sense enough to return to the limited democracy that they had 86 years ago [before the Civil War] when government was good, decent, economical, and competent."[23]

Ball was no less extreme in his denunciation of African Americans. "In our part of the country, the Southern United States, the white people have been more the victims of negro exploitation than the negroes have been of whites." In language that we have heard recently in the reparations debates, Ball continued, "Negroes were brought to the South when slavery was common throughout the world, a great proportion of them brought out of slavery in Africa, and the negro population has been on the whole an economic burden on the Southern white people. Had never a negro landed in the South it would this day be not 'the nation's economic problem number one' but one of the richest regions of the globe."[24]

It was, however, the New Deal that took pride of place in Ball's pantheon of progressive horrors. Within weeks of Roosevelt's inauguration, Ball denounced the president and the federal government's intervention in the economy. Over the next decade he never lost a chance to excoriate each New Deal program as a further step on the road to "state socialism." Convinced by the political realignments that brought Roosevelt to power that the national Democratic Party was not his true home, Ball supported the Dixiecrat revolt in 1948. This effort, led by South Carolina's own governor, Strom Thurmond, to unseat President Truman and reclaim southern control of the Democratic Party had limited success at the polls. But it laid the groundwork for massive resistance to desegregation in the 1950s and set the tenor for southern politics for years to come.[25]

Faced with such opposition, what chance did progressives have of achieving a second reconstruction at the end of World War II? Could they mobilize the political support, both North and South, to defeat conservative congressmen, organize southern workers, and enfranchise African Americans? Could they persuade policy makers and elected officials to embrace an agenda of political and economic reform? They were under no illusions about how hard the struggle would be. Karl's letters that winter were filled with apprehension. But the men and women who walked the picket line at the American Tobacco Company that cold winter of 1945–46, the speakers at the New South Lecture Series, the ordinary citizens who attended the gathering did have reason to hope that change would come.

Southerners such as Aubrey Williams, Charles Johnson, Clifford Durr, and Clark Foreman stood ready to assume the mantle of leadership for the South. They had years of experience in regional and national politics; they were members of influential organizations with a growing and diverse membership; and they had well-conceived plans for making the South the engine of postwar prosperity. They were, moreover, in touch with the grassroots, quite ready and willing, for instance, to show up in Charleston in response to the call of a few unknown GIs in league with tobacco workers on strike at a local plant.

In those heady days at the end of World War II, neither the speakers, nor the GIs, nor the tobacco workers could imagine what we know now: that

Republicans and conservative southern Democrats would win control of the House and Senate in 1946 and forestall plans for Truman's Fair Deal; that the CIO's Operation Dixie would fizzle out in less than two years after it started; and that the whole nation would embrace a hysterical anticommunism reminiscent of the late-nineteenth-century white supremacy campaigns.

The politics of polarization that was in place by the 1948 presidential campaign happened quickly, and it was both a response to and a result of the progressive push at the end of the war. The window of opportunity that was opened at the end of the war slammed shut. Karl's fears that without progressive leadership the nation would plunge into another depression proved unfounded, thanks in part to American expansion overseas. Nor did the region by any means succumb to fascism. Nevertheless, it would be safe to say that the history that was repeating itself was not Reconstruction but the mobilization of forces that cut short that grand experiment and made the dream of justice, equality, and prosperity once again a distant dream.

Notes

1. On Williams's lecture, see the *Charleston News and Courier,* November 27, 1945, and O. E. McKaine, "The Palmetto State," *Norfolk Journal and Guide,* December 8, 1945. On plans for the lecture series see McKaine, "The Palmetto State," *Norfolk Journal and Guide,* October 20, 1945. For more on the lives of the individual speakers, see John A. Salmond, *The Conscience of a Lawyer: Clifford J. Durr and American Civil Liberties, 1899–1975* (Tuscaloosa: University of Alabama Press, 1990); Salmond, *A Southern Rebel: The Life and Times of Aubrey Willis Williams, 1890–1965* (Chapel Hill: University of North Carolina Press, 1983); Patrick J. Gilpin, *Charles S. Johnson: Leadership beyond the Veil in the Age of Jim Crow* (Albany: State University of New York Press, 2003); Richard Robbins, *Sidelines Activist: Charles S. Johnson and the Struggle for Civil Rights* (Jackson: University Press of Mississippi, 1996).

2. John Egerton, *Speak Now against the Day: The Generation before the Civil Right Movement in the South* (New York: Knopf, 1994); Patricia Sullivan, *Days of Hope: Race and Democracy in the New Deal Era* (Chapel Hill: University of North Carolina Press, 1996); Salmond, *Conscience of a Lawyer;* Salmond, *Southern Rebel;* John A. Salmond, *Miss Lucy of the CIO: The Life and Times of Lucy Randolph Mason, 1882–1959* (Athens: University of Georgia Press, 1988).

3. Karl Korstad, "Black and White Together: Organizing in the South with the Food, Tobacco, Agricultural and Allied Workers Union (FTA-CIO), 1946–1952," in *The CIO's Left-Led Unions,* ed. Steve Rosswurm (New Brunswick, N.J.: Rutgers University Press, 1992), 72–73.

4. McKaine, "The Palmetto State," *Norfolk Journal and Guide,* November 10, 1945; Karl Korstad, "Tobacco Road, Union Style," *New Masses* 59 (1946): 13–15; Peter Lau, "Freedom Road Territory: The Politics of Civil Rights Struggle in South Carolina during the Jim Crow Era" (Ph.D. dissertation, Rutgers University, 2002).

5. Steve Fraser, *Labor Will Rule: Sidney Hillman and the Rise of American Labor* (New York: Free Press, 1991), 510.

6. Frances R. Korstad to Karl Korstad, December 6, 1945, and December 7, 1945, letters in possession of author.

7. *Charleston News and Courier,* November 27, 1945; McKaine, "The Palmetto State," *Norfolk Journal and Guide,* December 8, 1945. See also Korstad, "Tobacco Road, Union Style," 15.

8. *Charleston News and Courier,* November 27, 1945 and February 20, 1946; Frances R. Korstad to Karl Korstad, December 11, 1945.

9. Egerton, *Speak Now against the Day,* 417–18; Karl Korstad, "Chapter Headings for the 'New South,'" second draft, undated, in possession of author.

10. Robert Rodgers Korstad, *Civil Rights Unionism: Tobacco Workers and the Struggle for Democracy in the Mid-Twentieth-Century South* (Chapel Hill: University of North Carolina Press, 2003), 4.

11. Karl Korstad to Frances R. Korstad, December 7, 1945, in possession of author.

12. Karl Korstad, "Introduction to 'New South'" (n.d.), in possession of the author. John Egerton estimated that at the end of the war, roughly 75 to 80 percent of southerners were undecided about whether the region should continue the New Deal road to reintegration as part of a national economy. Egerton, *Speak Now against the Day,* 338.

13. Lau, "Freedom Road Territory," 238.

14. Sullivan, *Days of Hope,* 142, 169–71, 189–91; Egerton, *Speak Now against the Day,* 407–9.

15. Egerton, *Speak Now against the Day,* 345–532.

16. Robert Korstad, *Civil Rights Unionism,* 5; Karl Korstad to Frances R. Korstad, undated, in possession of author.

17. For an articulation of these goals, see the 1945–1946 issues of the *Southern Patriot,* published by the Southern Conference for Human Welfare.

18. *Charleston News and Courier,* November 27, 1945; McKaine, "The Palmetto State," *Norfolk Journal and Guide,* December 8, 1945.

19. *Charleston News and Courier,* December 16, 1945.

20. McKaine, "The Palmetto State," *Norfolk Journal and Guide,* March 2, 1946; *Charleston News and Courier,* February 21, 1946.

21. Korstad, "Tobacco Road, Union Style," 15.

22. O. E. McKaine, "Keynote Speech," Box 8, A. J. Clement Papers, South Caroliniana Library, University of South Carolina; Charles J. Holden, *In the Great Maelstrom: Conservatives in Post–Civil War South Carolina* (Columbia: University of South Carolina Press, 2002), 87–110. For more on Osceola McKaine, see Miles S. Richards, "Osceola E. McKaine and the Struggle for Black Civil Rights, 1917–1946" (Ph.D. dissertation, University of South Carolina, 1994).

23. *Charleston News and Courier,* December 30, 1946.

24. *Charleston News and Courier,* January 22, 1946.

25. Holden, *In the Great Maelstrom,* 104, 110.

The White Citizens' Councils of Orangeburg County, South Carolina

John W. White

The Supreme Court's decision in *Brown v. Board of Education* (1954), which called for the desegregation of all public schools, ignited a firestorm of southern attacks on the federal court system.[1] Across the South, localities formed groups to combat forced integration. The most notable of these organizations were the White Citizens' Councils (WCC), which developed in Mississippi and quickly spread to every state in the South. The groups formed a loose confederation called the Citizens' Councils of America (CCA). For a short time no resistance group was more powerful or better known than the councils.[2]

The wave of council organization reached South Carolina in August 1955. At that time the state National Association for the Advancement of Colored People (NAACP) initiated a petition in Orangeburg County School District 5 demanding the immediate integration of the public education system. The group argued that, in accordance with the Supreme Court decision in the *Brown* case, the school districts were required to end their policy of segregation.[3]

Shortly after the filing of the petition, the Palmetto State's first citizens' councils were born in Elloree and Orangeburg. The first two WCC chapters sought to preserve a segregated school system and to "oppose the use of force by radicals and reactionaries" who were attempting to "disrupt the peace and good relations among the races." They were quickly joined by a host of other groups under the council banner. Within a month nearly every community in Orangeburg County had formed its own council. There were WCC units in Cope, Eutawville, Holly Hill, North, Norway, and Cordova.[4]

Each Orangeburg group obtained a state incorporation charter, based on the doctrines of the Mississippi WCC. The document declared that the organization's purpose was to defend segregation while maintaining "good relations among the members of all races."[5]

The Orangeburg council immediately received a strong endorsement from local whites, with much of its support coming from local businesses and community "leaders." Atlanta journalist William Gordon claimed that Orangeburg council members were "elite, church going, club and business-minded folk who also claim to be God-fearing." Several business owners demonstrated their support by purchasing advertisements in the *Orangeburg Times and Democrat* to support the WCC. Needless to say, the issue of desegregation quickly dominated the daily life of Orangeburg County's roughly seventy thousand inhabitants. Since more than 60 percent of the county was black, it was a particularly pressing matter for the white minority. On at least one occasion the Orangeburg Citizens' Council placed a recruitment advertisement on the front page of the local newspaper. An August 29, 1955, council meeting attracted more than three thousand local whites. At that meeting South Carolina state senator Marshall Williams encouraged "every white man in the area" to join the WCC.[6]

The Elloree chapter received the endorsement of the town's mayor, W. J. Deer. He proclaimed, "We will fight the leaders of the NAACP from ditches to fence posts to keep Negroes out of white schools." Less than a day after the NAACP petition was filed in Elloree, the WCC claimed 225 mostly middle-class members. Just over a week later, the group had grown to more than 800 members.[7]

Following the formation of the first WCC chapter in Elloree, the group quickly spread throughout South Carolina. By July 1, 1956, fifty-five separate councils had formed. Most of the groups were based in the lowcountry. Charleston County alone boasted over six WCC chapters. Nevertheless, Orangeburg County remained the most organized, with eight active councils.[8]

Council meetings typically attracted hundreds of participants. For example, the first meeting of the Kingstree WCC drew 225 attendees. The second, which was held a week later, drew more than 300 and claimed a membership of nearly 500. In Bowman more than 100 people met to establish a council chapter. The organizational meeting of the Winnsboro Citizens' Council attracted 300 members.[9]

Even areas that were not directly affected by desegregation petitions were motivated by the possibility of integration in their own counties. At the first meeting of the North Citizens' Council, an anonymous speaker declared: "The North schools have not been petitioned by the National Association for the Advancement of Colored People, but the people of that area have had definite leads that the Negro organization has one prepared and ready to serve on their Board of Trustees in the near future."[10]

The rapid spread of the WCC throughout South Carolina eventually led to the creation of the Association of Citizens' Councils of South Carolina. The ACCSC represented the state in regional meetings of citizens' councils and other anti-integration groups. It also participated in the formation of the Citizens' Councils of America and aided the regional organization in the dissemination of propaganda to the local and state councils.[11]

THE ORANGEBURG
CITIZENS COUNCIL

VOL. 1—NO. 2   ORANGEBURG, SOUTH CAROLINA   APRIL 2, 1956

NAACP USING TWO COLLEGES
★   ★   ★   ★   ★
Intermarriage Is Ultimate NAACP Aim

Misguided Negroes Duped By Leaders

Every time a so-called "Negro Leader" opens his mouth before an audience it becomes more evident that the National Association For The Advancement of Colored People is seeking more than integration of the schools.

The ultimate aim of the organization is intermarriage and mongrelization of the white races.

Roosevelt Williams, professor at Howard University in Washington, D.C., drove this fact home with plain and vulgar talk recently while addressing an NAACP rally in Mississippi. A portion of his speech, taken from a recording, follows just to give white citizens an idea of what the NAACP is teaching the misinformed Negroes of the South:

"NAACP is affording you the leadership. . . emancipation is now at hand. White and Methodist women have approved our demand for equality. When our demands have become an actuality. . . .we will honor the leaders of Mississippi with blunt persecution. We demand that the War and Navy departments eliminate Jim Crow. Our good friend Marshall Zukov reported to Stalin that he could never understand why the American Negro fought for America that so long as the U.s. had those splendid Negro soldiers they could never whip America The Negro is the white man's superior. The Negro has always excelled. There has never been a white man who could compete with Jackie Robinson, Nat King Cole, Ralph Bunche, Duke Ellington. . .We demand the abolition of all state laws which forbid interrace marriage of the different races. We demand the removal of the last vestige of barriers. The whole world knows that the white man prefers the Negro woman. The white woman have been subjected to persecution and restriction. The recent announcement by white women's church organizations serves notice they intend to strike their own shackles. It is well known that the white woman is dissatisfied with the white man, and they a l o n g with us demand the right to win and love the Negro men of their choice, so they can proudly tell the world he is my man. . .a man in every respect. The average Negro man has adopted the attitude that why buy a cow when he can get plenty of mountain butter for nothing. We demand the right for every Negro man or woman to marry the white of his or her choice, if he can find one fit to marry. I am proud of my Negro heritage. . . and I will not mix that Negro blood with the stock of an inferior race.

"And now allow me to bring you the good news of Arkansas Wise.

(Continued on Page 4)

Aesop's Fable By NAACP

Once upon a time there was a monstrous, ugly Ogre named Naacp who set himself up as king over the fair land of Texiamissalagasneflatennark. His Vice-ogre was named I· , and Icc called Naacp Nap because he couldn't pronounce Naacp.

Old Nap and Icc decided they didn't like the peoples color nor their happy faces and decided to change both. First they passed a decree saying "black was white" and "white was black." Next Nap had his high priest declare it was a sin to be white and against the law to be black. He passed a law of the land making everything illegal. He then sent Icc ·nt to remove all the white and colored signs from waiting rooms throughout the land which Icc did, with gusto!

But, lo and behold, every morning neatly painted colored and white signs were back on the doors. The station master reported to the police that something was painting signs on his doors at night. The police tried to find out what made the signs pop back every time old Icc erased them. No reliable clues, evidence, or witnesses were ever found and no suspects were ever convicted of painting signs on doors.

The law caught one man with a paint brush and paint in his hands, but it was proven beyond a doubt that he was merely killing flies by painting their tails with a white insecticide. It was finally established by a prominent scientist that a strange bird, known as the White Throated Brusher, which is a member of the Oriole family, was doing the painting.

Colored and white signs stayed up, and of course, all the happy peaceful people used the same waiting rooms they always had. Bad people who used the wrong rooms got into fights and were arrested.

The moral of this story is that the White Throated Brusher is a remarkable bird, and he helped save a nation from the wicked Ogre Nap. Since that time the White Throated Brusher has increased by the billion. They thrive in warm climates.

Discrimination In Chicago

CHICAGO, Ill. — Negroes are complaining that the promised land of integration isn't what its cracked-up to be. For one thing, White Chicagoans object to giving up their homes to the black invaders. But the Negroes just move in and take them over anyway. The main complaint the blights have as they pour in from the South is that by law relief recipients must be residents of the city for one year. The Negroes feel they are being "discriminated against" because they can't get on the relief rolls the first day they arrive.

Letter, Tells Of Activity Of Student Organizations

For those who are not convinced that the National Association For The Advancement of Colored People has set the ground work for active chapters on the campuses of State and Claflin colleges we can offer proof.

Students at the two colleges are being urged to join Youth Chapters of the NAACP. Letters to prospective members and members are handed out. There is little doubt that college officials know (and some are sympathetic to) of the chapters.

Printed below is a copy of a letter mailed to students of Claflin:

> Youth Chapter NAACP
> Claflin College
> Orangeburg, South Carolina
>
> "Dear Member:
> "This is to call your attention to the fact that on the last meeting night the motion was raised and carried out that all members being missing two consecutive meetings without reasonable excuse will have no voice in the business transaction of the organization (no voting power).
> "It has been heard by the organization that some who can . . . . .ing. Don't let this continue for we now have much to do and need your co-operation.
>
> Yours Very Truly
> W. S. Goodwin
> The Executive Committee

It is easy to see from the above letter that all of the students are not supporting the Red-sponsored NAACP. Some were duped into signing and later found out that the organization was not beneficial to the Negro race. They obviously dropped from the chapter, much to the alarm of those who are using it to stir up racial hatred.

There are probably many good Negro students at both of the colleges who know that the NAACP is foreign led, organized only to bleed Southern, and northern Negroes of money to line the leaders own pockets. They have seen Thurgood Marshall, in tailored suits, $50 shoes and $15 shirts. They have heard him say he is not making a dime from the NAACP. He could not fool them, however, and But the evidence that NAACP chapters are active on the t w o

(Continued on Page 4)

Roosevelt Boys Worst Race Mixers

Next to the 3 Negro Congressmen, the worse race mixers in Congress are the Roosevelt boys, Jimmie and Frankie. Eleanor still gallavants around the world advocating racial integration. Of course, none of her children ever tried it. When one of Jimmie's ex-wives read love letters from 11 women she charged he had been carrying on with during the time he was married to her, not one of them was black.

However, Eleanor is all for racial integration— for other peoples' children. She does not even favor integration among her own children. When she found that the Hoovers had integrated the servants, Eleanor immediately unscrambled the staff and commented: "A staff solid in one color works in better understanding and maintains a smoother running establishment.

First in 1928 and again in 1933 after he became President, Franklin Roosevelt caused the deeds to tracts of land he owned in Warm Springs, Ga., to include the following covenant: "Fifth: Neither said land, or any part thereof, shall be sold, rented or otherwise disposed of to any Negro or other persons of African descent, or to a corporation or association owned or controlled by Negroes..." These deeds may be examined in the office of the Clerk of the Superior Court of Meriweather County, Ga. The first is in Book 24, page 188, and the other in Book 20, page 411.

The only way Jimmie and Frankie could get elected to Congress was by moving into Negro districts. Naturally, they don't live with their "colored brothers," but just have voting addresses there. Jimmie and Frankie are exploiting the Negroes for all they are worth. Remember this the next time you hear Eleanor's boys shouting for "civil rights."

Truth Cannot Be Denied By Negro Press

Though the Negro press bitterly complains about action being taken by an increasing number of white citizens, it does not deny any of the charges made against the NAACP and the UL. For nearly five years the National Citizens Protective Association has carried on an active campaign to expose these organizations and t h e i r supporters.

Through its publications, leaflets, meetings and all means at its disposal,' the Association has sought to awaken America to the danger of the NAACP-Urban League assault on White America.

THAT'S WHERE THEIR MONEY GOES—An unidentified Negro soldier is shown making his contribution to the NAACP at a recent meeting. Accepting the offering" is the Rev. Henry Parker, Episcopal minister in Orangeburg. Thurgood Marshall, who spoke to the NAACP rally at Claflin College urged the Negroes to give generously. Wonder who went away with the money?

20. Orangeburg White Citizens' Council newspaper. Photograph by Cecil J. Williams

Even after the formation of the ACCSC, the citizens' councils in South Carolina remained loosely organized. Each local chapter was an autonomous organization and utilized a variety of methods to sharpen white resolve. Most of the
member councils lobbied political leaders, disseminated segregationist propaganda, and criticized African Americans and civil rights leaders who lobbied for
an end to the state's Jim Crow policies. The state organization functioned merely
as a co-coordinating agency. Essentially the local groups gained only advice and
propaganda from the ACCSC.[12]

Most of the citizens' councils in South Carolina focused their efforts on
political organization and lobbying. They rallied voters and warned against the
dangers of integration. Leaders in the movement publicized the political and
legal defense of segregation, and even revived John C. Calhoun's doctrines of
interposition and nullification.[13]

Like the councils throughout the state, the Orangeburg WCC launched a
propaganda campaign aimed at discrediting civil rights leaders and solidifying
white support. The organization published a segregationist newspaper, the
Orangeburg Citizens Council, and maintained an office that provided pro-
council literature to local whites. The *Orangeburg Citizens Council* warned that
the NAACP had "tricked" local blacks into supporting the desegregation movement. Only "good Negroes," the newspaper concluded, "know that the NAACP
is foreign led, organized only to bleed Southern, and northern Negroes of money
to line the leaders' own pockets."[14]

The propaganda piece also warned members about the "disaster" of integration in the North. One editorial insisted that the "inevitable result of integration"
was that either blacks or whites would be forced to leave because "there is no
room" for both races to live together. The unnamed author warned, "The white
people in many cities in the North and East, like the city of Washington, are
getting a belly full of the mixing of the races and they are getting tired of being
run over by the NAACP and vote-seeking politicians. . . . If the race mixing
efforts continue some day the white people will become so nauseated they will
realize the suckers they have been and have nerve enough to stand up and
demand their rights."[15]

Citizens' council propaganda frequently utilized gendered language to play
on white fear of miscegenation. The *Orangeburg Citizens Council* reported that
"millions of decent, self-respecting Americans are at last awake to the true objective of the NAACP and its sinister, alien philosophy, which many people believe
to be marriage of whites and Negroes." The paper quoted Walter White, the
executive secretary of the NAACP, as favoring interracial marriage. The WCC
tabloid also reprinted a statement that NAACP lawyer Albert A. Kennedy made
to the *Orangeburg Times and Democrat.* Kennedy said that "integration will
result in white girls being associated with Negro boys. . . . Naturally, intermarriage would result."[16]

In another issue of the *Orangeburg Citizens Council,* a headline warned: "Intermarriage Is the Ultimate NAACP Aim." The ensuing article reported incorrectly that Roosevelt Williams, a professor at Howard University, had ostensibly claimed that African Americans were superior to whites and that "it is well known that the white woman is dissatisfied with the white man, and they along with us demand the right to win and love the Negro men of their choice."[17] The false reports were widely circulated by various CCA chapters.

Labor unions were also a frequent target of council attacks. The *Orangeburg Citizens Council* called CIO leader Walter Reuther a "Negrophile." The propaganda paper also accused the labor organization of funding a significant portion of the NAACP's "Free by Sixty-Three" program, which hoped to end segregated education by 1963. Furthermore, the paper claimed that CIO funds were paying for NAACP attempts "to move Negroes into white housing projects and into white neighborhoods."[18]

Although the constitutional arguments against forced integration and attempts to lobby public opinion were powerful statements of white supremacy, they were not the most extreme measure adopted by the WCC. With racial animosity running high, the councils in Orangeburg County launched a protracted campaign of economic retaliation against the petitioners and members of the NAACP. The *Orangeburg Times and Democrat* printed the names of each petitioner, and local whites sought to pressure them into backing down. For example, the employer of one of the petition signers asked that the employee withdraw his name and make a public statement rejecting the NAACP cause. When the worker refused, he was immediately fired. Numerous other African Americans lost their jobs, local banks recalled loans, area retailers refused to sell to black clients, and milk firms stopped delivering to the homes of signers.[19]

Even prosperous African Americans were not spared. A black contractor claimed, "I once had more business than I could handle during the height of the season. But now, I'm lucky to get three decent jobs a month." That same contractor pointed out that he had employed as many as twelve full-time workers, but could no longer afford to maintain a large staff. Likewise, an Orangeburg minister who also owned a gas station was denied credit for gasoline products and forced out of business.[20]

Jim Sulton, another black service station owner, believed that "the Negroes in Orangeburg overestimated the white man's integrity when they petitioned the school board." Sulton, whose establishment catered to both black and white clients, claimed that the WCC pressure nearly drove him out of business. He alleged, in an April 1956 interview: "They cut off all my credit. They have tried to squeeze Negroes economically. The man came in and took the ice cream box away from my station. I haven't had Cokes in the station since July."[21]

These retaliations did not go unnoticed by South Carolina civil rights leaders. James M. Hinton, the president of the South Carolina branch of the NAACP, reported the firing of one of the petition signers in Elloree by his white employer.[22] Hinton responded by organizing efforts to limit the impact of the economic reprisals. Some of the assistance was distributed through official NAACP channels. Other aid was raised locally. For example, Hinton secured a loan of $1,053 from the Victory Savings Bank for a petitioner who had his mortgage called in. A rally in Orangeburg for victims of economic reprisals raised more than $3,000, and black leaders reached out to African American communities in Columbia and Charleston to elicit more support.[23]

Sulton received cooperation from Standard Oil Company, which refused to bow to council requests that it cease supplying Sulton's Esso station. He began buying supplies from firms in Charleston and hired an African American worker who was fired from a local appliance store for signing the NAACP petition. Sulton also organized a drive to raise money, clothing, food, and other necessities for the victims of the councils. Local leaders arranged to buy goods in bulk from Charleston and Columbia and rationed out necessities to the most needy.[24]

The NAACP was also able to assist other petitioners who challenged the white power structure in Orangeburg County. In a letter to Roy Wilkins, the executive secretary of the NAACP, Hinton wrote, "I am proud to day [sic] that we have taken care of each person who signed a petition and who have had reprisals." Several petitioners were relocated, the NAACP paid the rent for four signers, and numerous others were given seed and fertilizer when local merchants refused to offer them credit. In January 1956 alone the NAACP donated $2,331.63 to Elloree members who were affected by economic reprisals.[25]

The local NAACP also mobilized to end the economic intimidation. According to an internal memorandum, "Firms holding franchise from 'Coca-Cola, Sunbeam Bread—and Paradise Ice Cream, and several other products decided thru 'Citizens' Councils' not to deliver any products to Negro Merchants, if those merchants signed the petition for Desegregation." In retaliation to the white economic intimidation, the local black leadership initiated a boycott of its own.[26]

The African American counter-boycott began at the area's two African American colleges. When students at Orangeburg's Claflin and State A&M colleges learned that Coca-Cola and Sunbeam bread had stopped supplying black merchants, the students ceased purchasing these products. At the behest of a local civil rights leader, the Reverend Matthew McCollom, and South Carolina State student Fred Moore, they also refused to patronize an Orangeburg apparel store whose owner was a council member. One local student activist pointed out that Orangeburg college students "learned how easy it was to do without Cokes" and even became skilled at baking their own bread.[27]

Although the African American community of Orangeburg County was able to alleviate some of the effects of council activity, it was unwilling simply to wait for white resolve to deteriorate and quickly joined the students at Claflin and State A&M in protest. The state conference of the NAACP called a meeting at the

Trinity Methodist Church to organize the boycott. Black leaders gathered the names of white merchants who were members of the citizens' councils, and singled out twenty-three businesses to boycott. The list of merchants was handed out at local churches and meetings. African Americans were discouraged from patronizing Bryant's Drug Store, Becker's, Coble Dairy, Coca-Cola, Curtis Candy Company, Duncan Supply, Edisto Theater, Holmon Grocery, Horne Motors, Kirkland Laundry, Lance Crackers, Lay's Potato Chips, Lane's Television, Limehouse Men's, Orange Cut-Rate, Paradise Ice Cream, Smoak Hardware, Sunbeam Bread, Shell Oil, Tom's Toasted Peanuts, Taylor Biscuit Co., Waltz Grocery, and Fersner's 5&10.[28]

Hinton, who was impressed by the effort in Orangeburg, wrote:

> Negroes in the south can do great harm to businesses operated by these who would try economic reprisals against Negroes. The $16,000,000 market of Negroes can be the difference between success and failure in this fight for desegregation. Negroes must spend their money with their friends, whether those friends be White or Negroes. All of the enemies are not White, for some Negroes who are in business have taken the side of White Citizens Councils, and those Negroes must be denied trade for the same reason that White Merchants are denied Negro Trade.
>
> We are not angry with any one, but we are fully determined to spend our money with those who believe in FIRST CLASS CITIZENSHIP FOR EVERY ONE, White or Black. I SAY AGAIN, "ORANGEBURG TEACHES A LESSON," one that it will do well for other communities to follow.[29]

21. Signs of the times: a segregated gas station in Calhoun County, 1959. Photograph by Cecil J. Williams

Council leaders disputed the effects of the NAACP counter-boycott. The *Orangeburg Citizens Council* informed its readers that the "local firms, many with a large volume of Negro business in the past, have come out publicly and strongly in favor of striking back at the integrationists." Furthermore, the WCC declared, "The amount of money they are losing is being offset by a picked-up, white trade, although all were, and still are willing to absorb the loss and maintain their integrity." The paper urged its readers to frequent the affected establishments. However, less than three weeks after local blacks initiated the counter-boycott, most of the area's white-owned holding companies and distributors denied any knowledge of any organized economic retaliation of African American merchants and began delivering goods to black-owned businesses. Also, the call for white solidarity failed to rescue a branch of a local laundry company located near State A&M that was forced to close when students stopped patronizing the facility.[30]

The change initiated by the counter-boycott was reflected in a WCC memo from December 1956. The memorandum declared, "race relations are getting better. . . . We do not expect to fan the fire as long as the NAACP stays out of Orangeburg." The Orangeburg WCC decided not to meet because the organization feared a meeting of the council would "stir-up" the NAACP. The letter also reflected a loss of financial support for the citizens' council. WCC leaders declared that they were attempting to convince the ACCSC to take over publishing a regular newspaper and encouraged members to submit council dues immediately.[31]

The NAACP counter-boycott also affected the citizens' council in Elloree. African American leaders reported that blacks in the small South Carolina hamlet were more united than ever. Assistance from the NAACP had helped victims of economic retaliation, and rumors of white fiscal hardship circulated throughout the African American community. Black newspaperman and political activist John H. McCray reported that, even though whites still zealously collected debts and mortgages in African American neighborhoods, "the WCC campaign" and NAACP unity had brought economic hardship to many whites as well.[32]

The lack of white resolve following the counter-boycott demonstrated an end to the power of the citizens' councils as formal organizations in Orangeburg County. A number of white businesses quietly attempted to bring back African American customers without losing their standing in the white community. Also, several unnamed white lawyers supported local blacks with legal advice. The 1957 WCC membership application included the names of several white-owned businesses whose owners were not affiliated with the councils. The document urged WCC members to recruit all white nonmembers into the organization. Clearly the form was an attempt to pressure local whites into joining the citizens' councils.[33]

By 1957 most Orangeburg whites seem to have come to the conclusion that the economic costs of continuing the intimidation campaign were hardly worth the benefits of the reprisals. The loss of economic intimidation as a tool of white resistance left few options for Orangeburg segregationists. Few South Carolinians felt that open violence was an effective means of resisting the move toward integration. Even the state's citizens' councils publicly renounced violence and openly resisted "infiltration" by members of the Ku Klux Klan. Many council members felt that their best options were the continuation of the group's propaganda campaign against the NAACP and a sustained effort to support segregationist candidates at the polls.[34]

Like the Orangeburg groups, the ACCSC faded from the public eye after 1957 in South Carolina. After peaking at forty thousand members in the state in the summer of 1956, the citizens' councils began to decline in South Carolina in 1957.[35] The most the organization could do was briefly command the attention of the state. By July 1958 the *News and Courier* declared the organization was on a "siesta." Several abortive efforts to renew support for the councils characterized the activity of the next few years, but for the most part, the South Carolina councils' main activity was inactivity.[36]

By 1963 council membership had declined to less than one thousand members in the state. Farley Smith, a council member, argued, "when the council was first organized, thousands of persons flocked to join because of the emotional appeal to be in an organization that was doing something." Once people realized that the goals of the organization did not require a large membership, numbers declined to a manageable level, according to Smith. Instead of a mass movement, the citizens' councils had become a small group of true believers who published pro-segregation propaganda in an attempt to sway public opinion.

In a sense Smith was right. After initially providing an outlet for white rage, the councils were left with little to do. The African American boycott had strengthened black resolve and limited the ability of segregationists to intimidate the black community. Without the power of economic retaliation, the WCC was left with few options to combat integration. The group could have turned to violent intimidation, but most of its members were disinclined to leave behind the "respectable" image of the councils. Therefore, it was left with little more than the ability to rally its members with political slogans and anti–civil rights rhetoric.

Of course the decline of the councils did not mean the wholesale abandonment of white resistance in South Carolina. Between January and March 1956, as the limits of extralegal resistance were being exposed in Orangeburg, state legislators worked to reenergize the white resistance movement and maintain the illusion of white unity. In response to the student activism in Orangeburg, South Carolina lawmakers formed a committee to investigate NAACP activity at South Carolina State and passed a law that forbade any state, county, or municipal agency from employing any member of the NAACP. Under the auspices of the new law, Governor George Bell Timmerman Jr., ordered the State Law Enforcement Division (SLED) to investigate "subversive" activity at the school.[37]

Under the direction of Fred Moore and other student leaders, nearly all the school's 1,500 students walked out of class and refused to return until SLED halted its investigation. White officials threatened to close the school, and President Turner announced that students who did not return would face expulsion. Students responded with a list of grievances, and 176 of the school's 190 faculty members signed a petition defending their right to join or support the NAACP. After six days of protests, the students finally acquiesced rather than face expulsion. Nonetheless the all-white board of trustees expelled Fred Moore immediately and informed eleven female and three male students that they could not return for the fall semester. Several faculty members were also fired, and several more resigned in protest. Although they had been instrumental in limiting the effectiveness of economic reprisals, Moore and his fellow student activists paid a high price.[38]

In spite of this new round of state-sanctioned intimidation, the Orangeburg activists were no doubt encouraged by the decline of the White Citizens' Council and the successes of the nationwide civil rights movement. By the end of 1957 black leaders had witnessed the accomplishments of the Montgomery Bus Boycott, the passage of the Civil Rights Act of 1957, and the forced integration of Central High School in Little Rock, Arkansas. As the 1960s approached, many whites also observed these events and began to lose confidence in their ability to stem the tide of black activism in the South. Instead, white leaders focused their efforts on slowing the pace of change and controlling the process of integration.[39]

The inability of the citizens' councils to withstand the counter-boycott clearly demonstrated the resolve of local black activists, but it is incorrect to assume that the councils had no lasting effect in Orangeburg or in South Carolina as a whole. As Kari Frederickson has suggested, southern protest movements allowed conservative whites to gain valuable experience in political organization outside of the Democratic Party. According to Frederickson, the Dixiecrat revolt, the Democrats for Eisenhower movement, and the Independent Electors for Harry F. Byrd were important steps in the breakdown of the solid South. Likewise, the citizens' councils were also important experiments in political organization.[40]

Although they left most of the racially charged rhetoric behind, council members carried on with criticisms of communism, social welfare spending, and other aspects of post–New Deal government. Like the Dixiecrats before them, the citizens' councils championed local control and criticized the unrestrained growth of federal power. The council, much like the Democrats for Eisenhower, was a momentary protest movement, but former members did not lose their interest in political activism after the WCC disappeared from the state. Many former citizens' council supporters found a new voice in the conservative wing of the Republican Party in the 1970s and 1980s. For example, Micah Jenkins, the chairman of the ACCSC and of the Charleston WCC; reporter and council backer William D. Workman; Orangeburg council leader W. T. C. Bates; state congressman and gubernatorial candidate Joseph O. Rogers; Charleston attorney William Gimbal; and numerous others ran for public office as Republicans after supporting the council movement in South Carolina. It is likely that each of these individuals relied on their experience organizing the WCC in their pursuit of political offices. Others continued to support segregated education through the creation of all-white private schools. For instance prominent council supporters Frank Best and T. Elliot Wannamaker were instrumental in the establishment of Wade Hampton Academy in Orangeburg.[41]

Notes

1. Much of the research for this paper was conducted with the assistance of the Ellison Durant Smith Research Award from the Modern Political Collections (now South Carolina Political Collections), University of South Carolina. For a more thorough discussion of the nature of white resistance to desegregation in South Carolina, see John White, "Managed Compliance: White Resistance and Desegregation in South Carolina, 1950–1970" (Ph.D. dissertation, University of Florida, 2006).

2. Numan V. Bartley, *The Rise of Massive Resistance: Race and Politics in the South during the 1950s* (Baton Rouge: Louisiana State University Press, 1969), 82–107; Neil R. McMillen, *The Citizens' Council: Organized Resistance to the Second Reconstruction, 1954–64* (Chicago: University of Illinois Press, 1971), 15–40, 116–20; Pete Daniel, *Lost Revolutions: The South in the 1950s* (Chapel Hill: University of North Carolina Press, 2000), 209–27. It should also be noted that the citizens' councils never referred to themselves as the white citizens' councils. The designation was used by the AFL-CIO, the NAACP, several other activist groups, and the national press.

3. For a discussion the efforts to desegregate the school system in South Carolina, see Marcia Synnott, "Desegregation in South Carolina, 1950–1963: Sometime between 'Now' and 'Never,'" in *Looking South: Chapters in the Story of an American Region*, ed. Winfred B. Moore Jr. and Joseph F. Tripp (New York: Greenwood Press, 1989), 51–64.

4. *Charleston News and Courier*, September 13, 1955; McMillen, *Citizens' Council*, 73–79; Howard H. Quint, *Profile in Black and White: A Frank Portrait of South Carolina* (Washington, D.C.: Public Affairs Press, 1958), 40–53; *Orangeburg Citizens Council*, February 13, 1956.

5. *Charleston News and Courier*, September 13, 1955; Quint, *Profile in Black and White*, 46–49; McMillen, *Citizens' Council*, 73–79.

6. *Orangeburg Times and Democrat*, October 15, 1955; September 1, 1955; *Charleston News and Courier*, August 16, 1955; William Gordon, "Boycotts Can Cut Two Ways," *New South* (April 1956): 5–10; Report on the Census of 1950 for South Carolina, Burnett R. Maybank Papers, Special Collections, Robert Scott Small Library, College of Charleston, Charleston, South Carolina.

7. *Charleston News and Courier*, August 16, 18, 1955.

8. *Charleston News and Courier*, September 2, 1955; McMillen, *Citizens' Council*, 73–77; *Charleston News and Courier*, September 18, 1955; *Charleston News and Courier*, September

17, 1960; William D. Workman Jr., *The Case for the South* (New York: Devin-Adair, 1960); *Charleston News and Courier*, July 1, 1956.

9. *Charleston News and Courier*, August 20, 24, 27, 1955; *State*, August 26, 1955.

10. *Orangeburg Times and Democrat*, August 31, 1955; August 24, 1955; August 25, 1955.

11. *Charleston News and Courier*, January 18, 1957; *New York Times*, February 26, 1956.

12. *Charleston News and Courier*, September 15, 1955; November 16, 17, 1955; Quint, *Profile in Black and White*, 46–49.

13. For some examples, see *Charleston News and Courier*, December 29, 1955; January 26, 1956; February 7, 1956.

14. *Orangeburg Citizens Council*, April 2, 1956.

15. *Orangeburg Citizens Council*, February 13, 1956.

16. Ibid.

17. *Orangeburg Citizens Council*, April 2, 1956. The Williams quotation was widely circulated by white supremacists as a means to discredit the NAACP leader. The controversy is discussed in Alex Lubi, *Romance and Rights: The Politics of Interracial Intimacy, 1945–1954* (Jackson: University Press of Mississippi, 2005), 66.

18. *Orangeburg Citizens Council*, February 13, 1956.

19. Gordon, "Boycotts Can Cut Two Ways," 5–6. James M. Hinton to Roy Wilkins, Executive Secretary, NAACP, August 16, 1955, NAACP Papers, Manuscripts Division, Library of Congress, Washington, D.C. (hereafter NAACP Papers).

20. Gordon, "Boycotts Can Cut Two Ways," 6.

21. Ibid., 6–7.

22. Ibid., 5–6. James M. Hinton to Roy Wilkins, Executive Secretary, NAACP, August 16, 1955, NAACP Papers.

23. "Miss Black" to Roy Wilkins, Executive Secretary, NAACP, October 26, 1956, NAACP Papers; James M. Hinton to Roy Wilkins, Executive Secretary, NAACP, August 16, 1955, NAACP Papers.

24. Gordon, "Boycotts Can Cut Two Ways," 6–7.

25. James M. Hinton to Roy Wilkins, Executive Secretary, NAACP, January 23, 1956, NAACP Papers.

26. James M. Hinton, "Orangeburg, South Carolina Teaches a Lesson Thru Economic Boycott" (flyer), October 13, 1955, NAACP Papers.

27. Ibid.; Gordon, "Boycotts Can Cut Two Ways," 7–8. Also, for a discussion of activism at South Carolina colleges, see William C. Hine, "Civil Rights and Campus Wrongs: South Carolina State College Students Protest, 1955–1968," *South Carolina Historical Magazine* 97 (October 1996): 310–31.

28. Gordon, "Boycotts Can Cut Two Ways," 7.

29. Hinton, "Orangeburg, South Carolina Teaches a Lesson."

30. Hinton, "Orangeburg, South Carolina Teaches a Lesson"; *Orangeburg Citizens Council*, February 13, 1956; Gordon, "Boycotts Can Cut Two Ways," 8–9.

31. "To the Members of the Orangeburg Citizens Council," December 1, 1956, William D. Workman Papers, South Carolina Collections, University of South Carolina (hereafter Workman Papers).

32. John H. McCray, "Council 'Pressure' Unites Elloree Squeeze Victims," *Baltimore Afro-American*, December 15, 1956, NAACP Papers.

33. Gordon, "Boycotts Can Cut Two Ways," 8–9; Orangeburg Citizens' Council membership form, Workman Papers.

34. *Southern School News*, January 1959, 11. For examples of the influence of economic concerns on the tenor of white resistance, see Paul S. Lofton, "Calm and Exemplary:

Desegregation in Columbia, South Carolina," in *Southern Businessmen and Desegregation,* ed. Elizabeth Jacoway and David R. Colburn (Baton Rouge: Louisiana State University Press, 1982), 70–81; Maxie Myron Cox Jr., "1963—The Year of Decision: Desegregation in South Carolina" (Ph.D. dissertation, University of South Carolina, 1996); John G. Sproat, "'Firm Flexibility': Perspectives on Desegregation in South Carolina," in *New Perspectives on Race and Slavery in America: Essays in Honor of Kenneth M. Stampp,* ed. Robert H. Abzug and Stephen E. Maizlish (Lexington: University of Kentucky Press, 1987), 164–84. The ACCSC also condemned the attack of singer Nat King Cole by members of the Alabama WCC: *Charleston News and Courier,* April 12, 1956.

35. McMillen, *Citizens' Council,* 70–130.

36. Ibid., 73–79; *Charleston News and Courier,* January 18, 1957; January 30, 1960.

37. Hine, "Civil Rights and Campus Wrongs," 318–20. "Students Hit Surveillance," April 10, 1956, clipping from the Papers of the NAACP. Septima P. Clark to Roy Wilkins, June 6, 1956, Papers of the NAACP. *Southern School News,* January 1956, 1.

38. *Southern School News,* January 1956, 1.

39. *Southern School News,* April 1965, 8. *Southern Education Report* (November 1966): 22, (November 1967): 15. T. E. Wannamaker, "Private Schools: Developments in South Carolina," *Annual Leadership Conference, January 7–8, 1966, Read House, Chattanooga, Tennessee,* audio recording, reel 1, Mississippi State University. The text of this recording was printed in the *Citizen: Official Journal of the Citizens' Councils of America* (January/ February 1966).

39. Francis Wilhoit, *The Politics of Massive Resistance* (New York: Braziller, 1973), 45; Brian Ward, "The Cole Incident of 1956," in *Race and Class in the American South since 1890,* ed. Melvyn Stokes and Rick Halpern (Providence, R.I.: Berg, 1994), 187–88; Tony Badger, "Fatalism, Not Gradualism: Race and the Crisis of Southern Liberalism, 1945–1965," in *The Making of Martin Luther King and the Civil Rights Movement,* ed. Brian Ward and Badger (New York: New York University Press, 1996), 67–95. For examples specific to South Carolina, see Sproat, "Firm Flexibility," and Lofton, "Calm and Exemplary."

40. Kari Frederickson, *The Dixiecrat Revolt and the End of the Solid South, 1932–1968* (Chapel Hill: University of North Carolina Press, 2001).

41. For a discussion of the growth of the Republican Party from almost nonexistent to highly competitive in South Carolina, see Gregory B. Sampson, "The Rise of the 'New' Republican Party in South Carolina, 1948–1974: A Case Study of Political Change in a Deep South State" (Ph.D. dissertation, University of North Carolina, 1984).

"Integration with [Relative] Dignity"

The Desegregation of Clemson College and George McMillan's Article at Forty

M. RON COX JR.

Within the study of civil rights history, South Carolina's story has, for the most part, been overlooked or ignored because of the state's self-proclaimed and generally accepted reputation for racial "moderation," particularly in contrast to the violent episodes that occurred elsewhere. The origins of this reputation can in many ways be traced back to a single event and a single publication. Forty years ago, in its March 16, 1963, issue, the *Saturday Evening Post* published George McMillan's "Integration with Dignity—The Inside Story of How South Carolina Kept the Peace." The article's focus, of course, was the orderly, peaceful, and uneventful enrollment of Harvey Gantt as a student at Clemson College on January 28, 1963—or, as McMillan described him, "the first Negro student to enroll in a white school in South Carolina."[1]

From a purely historical standpoint, McMillan was wrong. Gantt's achievement made him a "first" in many ways—the first black student admitted to Clemson; the first black student to enroll in a "white school" in South Carolina in the twentieth century. But he was not the first black student ever to have done so. From 1873 to 1877, during the age of so-called Radical Reconstruction, black South Carolinians had enrolled in and attended the University of South Carolina.[2] Undoubtedly, few readers were aware of this, nor likely would it have made much difference if they were. Then as now, perception is reality, and based on extensive national media coverage of the Clemson desegregation story as it unfolded, as well as their own life experiences of twentieth-century South Carolina, for the readers of McMillan's article Harvey Gantt was the first black man to successfully cross the Palmetto State's Jim Crow barrier in higher education.

Four decades later the story of Clemson's desegregation remains conspicuously absent from most historical accounts. Chapters, books, and documentary films on the American civil rights movement almost always include the stories of Rosa Parks in Montgomery, James Meredith at Ole Miss, and Autherine Lucy at Alabama. Rarely, however, are Gantt and Clemson mentioned, even in passing.

Nor is this oversight strictly a historical phenomenon. By the time McMillan's article appeared—less than two months after Gantt's arrival—the Clemson story had all but disappeared from the national media's scope, aside from an occasional newspaper "update" article, usually tucked neatly among the back pages.

The omission, while regrettable, is easily explained. News, like much of written history, often tends to focus on tragedy, on the stories of human failure. In the fall of 1962 national attention had focused on the violence and bloodshed that accompanied Meredith's court-ordered admission at the University of Mississippi. Coming on the heels of that story, the Gantt case generated so much interest and attention in the media in the months and days before his arrival on the Clemson campus because people across the country expected a repeat performance in yet another Deep South state. As McMillan put it, "The logic of South Carolina's history and the force of her traditions argued that Clemson would be another Oxford, Mississippi."[3] Indeed, if Clemson had turned into another Ole Miss, its place in national civil rights history today would no doubt be elevated to the forefront.

Of course, it did not happen that way. Gantt enrolled peacefully at Clemson and completed the spring semester with little incident. National interest in the Carolina Piedmont quickly faded and turned to more newsworthy civil rights hot spots such as Birmingham, Alabama. McMillan's article is somewhat unique, then, not only because it reveals what happened at Clemson College on January 28, 1963, but rather because it explains what did not happen. It is the "inside story" of a nonevent. One can almost discern disappointment in the voice of a New York reporter covering the story, who was overheard to say, "I expected blood. All I got was a cream puff."[4]

Appearing only about six weeks after the events it described, McMillan's article carefully explained that the calm that had prevailed at Clemson "was no mere lucky happenstance."[5] Rather, it was the result of nearly two years of groundwork that had prepared the college and the state for the inevitability of racial change, and of intensive planning for the dealing with the specific moment when the change actually occurred. McMillan's account is all the more interesting because he presented it to his readers in terms of a covert effort, a "conspiracy for peace," a "plot . . . to avert violence" by a "loose, informal coalition" of six key individuals in various parts of the state's power structure—Greenville businessman (and Clemson trustee) Charles Daniel; businessman (and S.C. Textile Manufacturers Association executive vice president) John K. Cauthen; Clemson president Robert C. Edwards; state senate president pro tempore Edgar Brown of Barnwell; *Greenville News* editor Wayne Freeman (also a member of the South Carolina School Committee, a legislatively created body that had spearheaded the state's official resistance to racial change for nearly a decade); and Governor Ernest F. Hollings. Beginning in 1961, McMillan asserted, these men worked quietly to begin assessing public attitudes in South Carolina, and by the end of that year had concluded that there existed "an important body of opinion in the state that firmly believed in law and order at all costs."[6] Putting aside personal opinion about desegregation, these men focused their efforts on one overriding goal: Should Clemson (or any other state institution) be ordered to desegregate, violence must not occur.

Presenting the whole event as a cabal orchestrated by responsible leaders dedicated to "maintaining law and order" is key to McMillan's thesis. By planning secretly, by quietly lining up business and political support for their position, and by making sure that the South Carolina's major newspapers were also in support, they were able to catch the potential opposition largely off guard. As McMillan explained, "The kind of people who might favor making a 'protest' had taken it for granted that everyone in South Carolina would agree with them when the time came. They were not organized, not prepared."[7]

Secrecy could not guarantee success, however. McMillan acknowledged three men in South Carolina capable of rallying the opposition and thwarting the plans for peaceful compliance at Clemson: former governor (and still Clemson trustee) James F. Byrnes; state representative A. W. "Red" Bethea of Dillon; and state senator Marion Gressette of Calhoun County, the number-two man in the senate and chairman of the S.C. School Committee (which was commonly referred to as the "Gressette Committee"). Little could be done to stop an independent statement from the octogenarian Byrnes, although McMillan asserted that by 1963 many South Carolinians had come to view the former governor as "bitter." Bethea was a loose cannon with a well-deserved reputation for fiery and bombastic speeches. He reportedly had threatened to go to Clemson himself and lead a protest, but his poor performance in the previous year's gubernatorial race indicated a lack of widespread support. Gressette, on the other hand, was different. McMillan described him as "a man whose sincerity and integrity have never been questioned in the legislature," a man who so held the confidence of opposition groups such as the white citizens' councils that they felt little need to get directly involved. "If Gressette came out publicly against admitting Gantt," McMillan wrote, "all the hitherto latent forces of disorder in the state would come alive."[8]

Accordingly Clemson president Robert Edwards spent extra time and attention on the senator from Calhoun County. McMillan relayed the story of a "very serious" meeting between Edwards and members of Gressette's committee on January 3. According to the account, Edwards threatened to resign if he were not supported in admitting Gantt peacefully. He then "got down to brass tacks with Gressette about the effect of violence." Knowing that a major manufacturer had expressed interest in building a large plant near Gressette's home, Edwards supposedly said bluntly, "Senator, if there's a ruckus at Clemson those people won't even plant scrub oak in Calhoun County."[9]

The relative success of the cabal's covert efforts was confirmed on January 22, the day that U.S. district judge C. C. Wyche signed the order admitting Gantt to Clemson. On the floor of the state senate, John D. Long of Union County and Herbert H. Jessen of Dorchester County heatedly denounced the decision, using words such as *cowardly* and *tyranny* and urging that South Carolina "not lie down and let itself be walked over." Then, as McMillan reported, "The time had come for Gressette to take his stand. He rose and began to speak slowly, sadly. 'A lot of things happen in life,' he said. 'We have disappointments. Sometimes I feel like making a speech like my two friends made. We have lost this battle but we are engaged in a war. But this war cannot be won by violence or inflammatory speeches. I have preached peace and good order too long to change my thinking.'"[10]

From there, McMillan's article incorporates a statement released by former governor Byrnes, stating only that a court ruling could not force the men and women of Clemson to welcome Gantt, as well as statements from three carefully timed press conferences on January 24 by South Carolina governor Donald Russell, Senator Gressette, and President Edwards, all expressing support for "peace and good order." He further noted that although Representative Bethea was present during Gressette's statement ("hunched deep down in an upholstered chair"), reporters "did not have time to stop and ask him for a comment."[11] The article concludes with a conversation between Edgar Brown and John Cauthen in which the latter says, "I think everything's going to be all right now," to which McMillan added his own summation: "And it was all right."[12]

Written as a contemporary account, McMillan's article is a useful starting point for anyone seeking to understand this generally overlooked event in the civil rights movement. Documentary evidence available to the modern historian does not contradict his account, aside from an occasional misquote or some minor confusion about specific dates. In the end McMillan provides his reader not only with a fascinating explanation of how South Carolina avoided violence during Clemson's desegregation, but also some revealing insight into the nature of state politics and power in the early 1960s.

Since the article's publication, the phrase "integration with dignity" has often been employed to describe South Carolina's official response to a challenging period in its recent history—not only during the Clemson episode but also throughout the rest of the 1960s and even into the 1970s. Gantt's peaceful enrollment at Clemson, proponents claim, demonstrated South Carolina's racial "moderation" and set the stage for generally passive accommodation to racial change throughout the remainder of the decade. The appearance of McMillan's article, they assert, is an indication of the nation's recognition of this "moderation."

However, for an article often cited as a positive portrayal of South Carolina, "Integration with Dignity" stirred up considerable controversy in the Palmetto

State when it first appeared. On March 12, shortly after the *Saturday Evening Post* appeared on newsstands, Senator John Long addressed his colleagues and referred to McMillan's handiwork, commenting that he resented the use of the words *dignity* and *integration* in the same article. Senator Gressette took the floor and pronounced the article's account of his meeting with President Edwards on January 3 "a malicious lie—a bald-faced falsehood," and said that he intended to force McMillan (who lived in Aiken) to name his source for that story.[13]

Long and Gressette were not the only ones angry about the McMillan article. On March 13, Representative Bethea made the latest of many personal privilege speeches to the S.C. House of Representatives criticizing not only the article, but also the whole Clemson episode. Claiming that he represented "the thinking of 90 percent" of South Carolinians, he charged that Charles Daniel and other state businessmen had "sold their way of life for a few measly industries" by calling for peaceful compliance at Clemson. He then produced a copy of the *Saturday Evening Post* and waved it in the air, challenging McMillan's assertion that he had threatened to lead a march on Clemson: "I went home when it was the hardest thing I ever had to do," he said, adding that if he had wanted to hold such a march, he easily could have done so and would have received fantastic support. "Are you proud of what the nation thinks about who did what at Clemson?" he asked his fellow legislators. "I'm not." The state, he concluded, "has lost more prestige in the past six months than it will gain in the next ten years. . . . I wouldn't sell my birthright in South Carolina for every industry in the world. We're Southerners, for God's sake let's act like it."[14]

Critics of McMillan's article were not limited to the die-hard segregationists, either. At least one South Carolinian believed the author had overlooked an important factor that made peaceful desegregation possible—Clemson's students, most of whom did not favor desegregation but had accepted it peacefully: "I just want the people of the United States to know that the students of Clemson College were the real reason for the success of integration that was carried out peacefully in South Carolina. I might add that I am proud to be a member of Clemson's student body that was responsible for 'Integration With Dignity.'"[15] In an editorial titled "The Post Article—in Perspective," the *Greenville News* commented that overall McMillan had provided favorable press for South Carolina as an example for other states, both North and South, but noted that "certain things must be corrected or placed in perspective." First, it denied that President Edwards had made the "scrub oak" threat to Marion Gressette, asserting that anyone who knew the senator realized such a threat "would have evoked a storm of righteous wrath which would have rocked the state." Secondly, the editorial took exception to McMillan's description of former governor Byrnes as "embittered." Conceding that Byrnes had been "disappointed" by many of the U.S. Supreme Court's recent decisions against segregation, it asserted that he never would have considered doing anything to encourage violence or disorder at Clemson. Finally the editorial noted that some people had inferred from the article that there had been a conspiracy of state business and political leaders to get Gantt into Clemson. No such conspiracy existed, the *News* maintained, "unless an unspoken agreement among all of the leading citizens of South Carolina to keep the peace constitutes a conspiracy." Clemson deserved much praise, and credit should also go to "the law abiding people of South Carolina," but the paper further stressed that no one should believe that the state welcomed the event. Nor should anyone infer that support for law and order meant support for racial desegregation. "Our policy has been to oppose integration and is to continue to oppose it," the article concluded. "We shall oppose just as strongly those who either thoughtlessly or deliberately, maliciously or with misguided intentions, say or do anything which might tend to turn South Carolina into a racial battleground."[16]

This last statement makes an important distinction, one that calls into question the definitions of *dignity* and *moderation*. In essence all the editorial did was to restate the public position of every "law and order" advocate mentioned in the McMillan article—a grudging acceptance of the inevitability of desegregation and a desire to avoid violence without ever conceding that segregation was legally or morally wrong. Indeed, documentary evidence exists that strongly suggests that the racial "moderation" exhibited by South Carolina during Clemson's desegregation, although perhaps accurately described as such in relation to states such as Mississippi or Alabama, was at best a thin veneer that required constant attention and precaution to maintain.

State and college officials clearly realized this at the time, and admitted as much. Their detailed and precise preparations for Gantt's arrival was carefully choreographed and directed in order to limit the opportunities for violence to occur, although it is evident from their correspondence and records that the real possibility of violence was never far from their minds. Most importantly, perhaps, they attempted to learn from mistakes made elsewhere. McMillan notes that in September 1962 Governor Hollings sent State Law Enforcement Division (SLED) chief J. P. Strom and state legal counsel Harry Walker to Oxford, Mississippi, to observe events and to devise a security plan for Clemson that the state could implement without the need for federal marshals. The result was a seven-page confidential outline, approved in its final version on January 12, 1963. Section 1 (four pages) established an overall plan for law enforcement—including college officials, campus security, State Highway Patrol, and other SLED officials—before, during and after registration. Section 2 (two pages) outlined a plan for establishing and maintaining student discipline on campus. Section 3 (one page) detailed arrangements for controlling the media.[17]

McMillan's assertion that everything "was all right" after Gantt's enrollment was perhaps overly optimistic, for it is evident that white resentment to his presence there was still quite strong. Governor Donald Russell—who had been in office less than a month when Gantt arrived on the Clemson campus—received hundreds of letters critical of the state's decision to comply without resistance. One woman wrote that she was appalled by the thought of "the Negro entering Climpsone [*sic*]. My blond girls will not go to school [with] Negroes. . . . I did not vote for the man who I knew did want negroes [in] white schools."[18] Nor was such criticism limited to South Carolinians. A Georgia man encouraged Russell to follow the example of Mississippi governor Ross Barnett, because, he said, "Our nation's survival depends on it."[19] Other critics referred to integrationists as "tools of Satan" and claimed that the mixing of the races in schools went "against God's plan for purity." Still others claimed that the entire desegregation movement was a "Communist conspiracy" inflicted upon the South by the "anti-American, anti-Christ traitors of the Supreme Court."[20] Senator Edgar Brown's files indicate that he received similar amounts of critical mail.[21] In late January a group calling itself the Concerned Clemson Alumni sent a mass mailing to Clemson students, suggesting that with Gantt at Clemson, they "should ignore him, should offer him no assistance and should ostracize both him and any student who may offer him association. . . . He should be treated with cold, silent contempt which he has earned."[22]

With Clemson officials threatening expulsion of anyone causing trouble, student opposition had to be waged covertly. In February one group began printing a crudely typed monthly newsletter, the *Rebel Underground*. Its March edition claimed that more than two thousand copies of the first issue had been printed and placed around campus but mysteriously had disappeared. The authors attributed this to "the police state methods of some people on campus." They further accused Clemson's administration of lying to the press when it said no incidents had occurred. Referring to Harvey Gantt as "the Negro" or "the black boy" (never by name), the authors alleged that on two occasions between fifteen and thirty students had gathered in the cafeteria and tried to "stare him down," but campus security had dispersed the group. There were also reports of students marching past his room waving Confederate flags, groups of boys yelling at him from their windows, and several students throwing fireworks at his room. Calling on Clemson students to write opposition letters to the *Tiger,* to give the silent treatment to anyone who favored desegregation, and to boycott any restaurant willing to serve "our unwanted guest," the letter ended with an exhortation: "Make no mistake about it, *we are in a battle!* A battle for our Country and for our Race. . . . Integration will inevitably bring about intermarriage between the two races. . . . FORCED INTEGRATION IS NOT INTEGRATION AT ALL. Refuse to accept it in your heart, and it will never be a fact."[23] Publication of the *Rebel Underground* continued well into the spring semester, and the paper's rhetoric grew increasingly vitriolic. In their April edition the authors reported "several cases where little do-good students gathered up some of our issues and carried them to the master Gestapo agent, Dean [of Students Walter] Cox," to whom they awarded the title of "Honorary Nigger."[24]

Back in the state capital, Representative Bethea and Senator Long continued to bluster against the Clemson decision. By accepting Gantt peacefully, Long charged, South Carolina had earned for itself "the reputation of a quitter—a big talker but no action." He referred to former governor Hollings as "a distinguished integrationist" and charged that recent complimentary remarks from President Edwards about Gantt's academic performance at Clemson were nothing more than "propaganda for integrating colleges of this state." Now fired up by his own indignation, he proposed an amendment requiring any racially integrated school in the state to be resegregated by gender. "Now, you brave South Carolina protectors of womanhood," he contemptuously challenged his colleagues, "I'm asking you to place a barrier between our white women and colored men to keep them from being insulted. The plan I propose would take the heart out of the integration movement. They want to amalgamate the races and this would stop that." Rising in opposition, Senator Gressette calmly remarked that his committee had considered this idea but had decided it was unnecessary at present. However, he added, this did not necessarily rule out the need for such a policy in the future, should massive desegregation occur. When Long's motion failed on a voice vote, he proposed a revised version calling for single-gender facilities in *all* South Carolina schools, with no mention of race. This motion failed as well, by a vote of thirty-eight to five.[25]

The defeat of Senator Long's motions is in itself indicative of South Carolina's refusal to act radically in opposition to desegregation, but their introduction into the senate and the manner in which they were offered do tarnish somewhat the state's carefully molded reputation for racial moderation, for having met "integration with dignity." It is evident that many tempers ran short in the weeks and months after Gantt's arrival at Clemson, and that the "law and order" supporters had to continue to work to prevent them from boiling over into violence. In hindsight, perhaps the best they accomplished was a delay. Five years later, South Carolina's thin veneer of moderation wore off, and the simmering tension of racial violence erupted and led to bloodshed in Orangeburg. That event is mentioned in many of the history books and documentaries.

Perhaps it is, then, that "dignity" must be viewed as a relative concept, subject to the social conventions of the time and the overall context within which it occurs. When Gantt enrolled at Clemson in late January 1963, the violent images of Oxford and Ole Miss were still fresh in the national mind, and attention was already being focused on Alabama, where newly elected governor George Wallace was filling newspaper headlines and television news time with his proclamation to preserve in his state "segregation now, segregation tomorrow, and segregation forever." Comparisons between these events and these three Deep South states were inevitable, and South Carolina, relatively speaking, came out smelling like the proverbial rose. A *New York Times* editorial proclaimed "Bravo, Clemson!" and congratulated the state for its "encouraging display of order and self-restraint" in contrast to the earlier episode at Ole Miss.[26] The *San Francisco Chronicle* wrote: "Too much cannot be said in praise of Governor Donald Russell of South Carolina and all who cooperated with him to guarantee that the shameful events of Oxford, Mississippi, were not repeated, and that the outrageous demagogic defiance of Alabama's Governor [George Wallace] was not emulated. . . . [The state's actions have] already gained great and widespread admiration and support for South Carolina and Clemson College."[27]

In the *Pittsburgh Courier,* native South Carolinian Benjamin Mays also explained the difference between Clemson and Ole Miss in terms of leadership rather than racial moderation. "We might have had the same thing at Clemson," the article read. "The white people of South Carolina are perhaps just as much segregationists as the white people of Mississippi. But in Mississippi we had a Barnett; in South Carolina we had Hollings and Russell. . . . Mississippi had no responsible leadership. South Carolina has. I salute my native state."[28]

The *Washington Daily News* credited "months of careful planning by the state's business civic and political leaders" and the overall "quality of South Carolina's leadership." It further gave credit to Gantt, praising his "great poise at Clemson" and noting that he "has shunned publicity. Reportedly Gantt turned down $10,000 to write a magazine article."[29] The *Washington Post* credited moderate leadership as well as economic interests but tied these factors together in what it called the state's "Liberal Heritage." South Carolina's history and traditions, it said, put it more in tune with North Carolina and Virginia, both of which had accommodated to desegregation, than to Alabama and Mississippi, which did not. "It has been said that Mississippi was conceived in sin while South Carolina fell into it," wrote the author. The violence at Ole Miss, he continued, helped South Carolina prepare itself, providing the "final shock therapy that restored complete sanity. . . . South Carolina, it appeared, had turned the corner nicely."[30] Editorial cartoons in papers throughout the nation praised Clemson's peaceful desegregation, especially in contrast with the violence at Oxford.

South Carolina's newspapers also tried to explain what had made Clemson so different from Ole Miss. The *Greenville Piedmont* gave the credit to Gantt himself. On February 1 it published an editorial contrasting him with Meredith, the student whose forced enrollment at Ole Miss had led to federal intervention and violence. During his enrollment, it claimed, Meredith "tried to keep the spotlight of publicity on himself by issuing frequent press statements after his arrival, and by meeting with Bobby Kennedy." The paper further criticized him for having exhibited a negative regard for his schoolwork. The article concluded, "Meredith, in short, is a professional Negro." In contrast, Clemson had enrolled Gantt, whose demeanor, youth, academic ability, and desire to be treated as any other student made him "an ideal choice to be hand-picked to become the first member of his race to attend Clemson" and "mark him as a credit to his State."[31] In an editorial titled "Why South Carolina Was Calm," the *Columbia Record* rejected economic interests as the motivating factor and even discounted the role played by the state's newspapers, which, it claimed, "only reflected the general feeling of the people." Law and order prevailed, it claimed, because of "the Stoicism of South Carolina [which] far antedates either the industrialization of the State or the modern newspapers. . . . [South Carolina's] tradition of calm courage, so magnificent in the 1860s, was the heritage of the generation of the 1960s."[32]

The state's black press was much more reserved in coverage and praise of Gantt's accomplishment. Columbia's *Palmetto Times* referred to the event as "a great victory," and an editorial proclaimed simply, "It Was Worth It"; but there were no full-page headlines, no announcements that Joshua's trumpets had blown, causing segregation's walls to come a-tumblin' down, and no proclamations that this marked the beginning of additional desegregation efforts in the state.[33] For his part, Gantt offered his own explanation for the lack of violence at Clemson: "If you can't appeal to the morals of a South Carolinian," he said, "you can appeal to his manners."[34]

When George McMillan's article appeared in print in March 1963, South Carolina had indeed turned an important corner and had achieved integration at Clemson with relative dignity. By stressing law and order, the state emerged from the episode with a national reputation for racial moderation, a reputation that most business and political leaders were anxious to protect and foster. Admittedly this was an important first step, and when compared to similar events in Alabama and Mississippi, it was done with a degree of relative dignity.

If "dignity" is taken to mean, however, doing the right thing for the right reason, then South Carolina's claim to having achieved "integration with dignity" falls short. As historian Selden Smith quipped at this conference, "Can you imagine a newspaper reporting a story about a wife-beater who changes his ways, using the headline 'WIFE BEATER SMITH STOPS BEATING WIFE . . . WITH DIGNITY?'" For it seems safe to say that although South Carolina avoided much of the outward violence seen in other Deep South states, among white South Carolinians, most hearts and minds were slow to change; opposition to desegregation in principle was still strong and determined. As other colleges, schools, and towns across South Carolina faced the difficult issue of racial change, it was by no means clear if Clemson's experience had established a pattern for peaceful compliance, or whether, like Fort Sumter over a century earlier, it would prove to have been merely a bloodless battle followed by a long, bloody, and costly tragedy.

Notes

1. George McMillan, "Integration with Dignity: The Inside Story of How South Carolina Kept the Peace," *Saturday Evening Post,* March 16, 1963, 16.

2. Maxie Myron Cox Jr., "1963—The Year of Decision: Desegregation in South Carolina" (Ph.D. dissertation, University of South Carolina, 1996), 3. During its so-called Radical period, the University of South Carolina also had black faculty as well as board of trustees members. The university was closed and reorganized as an all-white institution at the end of Reconstruction.

3. McMillan, "Integration with Dignity," 16.

4. *Charleston News and Courier,* January 30, 1963.

5. McMillan, "Integration with Dignity," 16.

6. Ibid., 16–17. The S.C. School Committee was commonly referred to as the "Gressette Committee," after its chairman, state senator Marion Gressette of Calhoun County.

7. Ibid., 19.

8. Ibid., 20. Bethea won only 5.3 percent of the vote (17,251 votes) in the 1962 S.C. Democratic Primary.

9. Ibid.

10. Ibid.

11. Ibid., 21. Byrnes's statement was less vitriolic than the McMillan quote might indicate. According to other sources, the former governor specifically professed his disagreement with the court's ruling but added, "However, I am convinced there will be no violence against him [Gantt] by the splendid students of Clemson." See *Charleston Evening Post,* January 24, 1963.

12. McMillan, "Integration with Dignity," 21.

13. *State,* March 13, 1963. Although the McMillan article appeared in the March 16 issue of the *Post,* that magazine, like many others, is postdated. Gressette repeated his protests in April, challenging both Charles Daniel and Edgar Brown to deny publicly that they were the source of the story. Brown did so immediately, but there is no record in the state's press that Daniel made any comment. See the *State,* April 11, 1963, and *Greenville News,* April 11, 1963.

14. *State,* March 14, 1963.

15. James W. Hawkes to W. D. Workman Jr., March 14, 1963, William D. Workman Papers, South Carolina Political Collections, University of South Carolina (hereafter Workman Papers).

16. *Greenville News,* March 19, 1963.

17. McMillan, "Integration with Dignity," 17–18; "Confidential—Outline of the Advanced Plan of Law Enforcement, Maintenance of Student Discipline, and Arrangements for the Press for Implementation by Clemson Officials and the Respective State Law Enforcement Agencies in the Event the Federal Courts Order Harvey Gantt's Admission to Clemson College," January 12, 1963, folder 191, Robert C. Edwards Papers, Special Collections, Robert Muldrow Cooper Library, Clemson University.

18. Mrs. H. B. Mincy to Donald S. Russell, January 22, 1963, Integration subject file, Russell Papers, South Carolina State Archives, Columbia (hereafter Russell Papers).

19. C. C. Perkins to Russell, January 22, 1963, Integration subject file, Russell Papers.

20. Quotes from various letters, January 1963, Integration subject file, Russell Papers.

21. *Charleston News and Courier,* December 31, 1962. A similar story on Senator Brown ran in the *Augusta Chronicle* under the headline "Clemson Won't Tolerate Violence—Brown." An anonymous critic sent the clipping to Brown, with the following note attached: "I am quite sure that the motion would be carries [*sic*] unanimously if the votes were by

whites only if I were to nominate you as South Carolina's all-time number one son of a bitch. . . . If integration must come to South Carolina, as evidently you desire it to, then I hope it comes to your house in a big way, by some one of your immediate family, dearly beloved by you, marrying a negro." See folder 271–B ("Crackpot Letters"), Brown Papers, Special Collections, Robert Muldrow Cooper Library, Clemson University.

22. Concerned Clemson Alumni form letter to Clemson students, January 1963, Integration subject file, Russell Papers. In November 1962 the same group had sent a form letter to Clemson students urging them to resist integration through ostracism, not violence. See the *Tiger* (Clemson College), November 9, 1962.

23. *Rebel Underground* (Clemson College), March 1963, in Integration/Clemson subject file, Workman Papers. Gantt has denied that these incidents occurred.

24. *Rebel Underground*, April 1963, Integration/Clemson subject file, Workman Papers. This same article challenged the favorable impression of Gantt vis-à-vis James Meredith: "We have heard a few misled students say that the black boy here at Clemson is a nice boy and not at all like the black one at Ole Miss. This is pure hogwash! He is here for the same reason the other partially domesticated, semi-literate member of a cannibalistic race is at Ole Miss, and that is to break the race barrier. Russia is much nicer than Red China, but both have the same end results planned for the free world."

25. *State* (Columbia), April 26, 1963. The yea votes came from senators Long, J. B. Lawson (Anderson County), Roger Scott (Dillon County), Wilbur Grant (Chester County), and Herbert Jessen (Dorchester County).

26. *New York Times*, January 30, 1963.

27. *San Francisco Chronicle*, January 30, 1963, quoted in *Progress*, a report of the South Carolina Council on Human Relations, n.d., SCCHR Papers, Manuscripts Division, South Caroliniana Library, University of South Carolina, Columbia.

28. *Pittsburgh Courier*, February 16, 1963.

29. *Washington* (D.C.) *Daily News*, June 4, 1963, Clippings/Civil Rights/South Carolina—1963 subject file, Olin D. Johnston Papers, South Carolina Political Collections, University of South Carolina, Columbia (hereafter Johnston Papers).

30. *Washington Post*, February 3, 1963, Clippings/Civil Rights/South Carolina—1963 subject file, Johnston Papers.

31. *Greenville Piedmont*, January 1, 1963, clipping in Integration subject file, Johnston Papers.

32. *Columbia Record*, February 7, 1963.

33. *Palmetto Times* (Columbia), February 7, 1963. This edition of the newspaper was vol. 1, no. 19. Because this was clearly a new publication, it may be that the paper lacked the experience or the staff to carry its reporting any further. The paper also contained several advertisements by white merchants and businesses, and lack of coverage may indicate a simple desire to avoid antagonizing and risk losing its sponsors.

34. Jack Nelson and Jack Bass, *The Orangeburg Massacre* (New York: World, 1970), 16.

Memory, History, and the Desegregation of Greenville, South Carolina

Stephen O'Neill

Communities, like individuals, remember the past selectively. What a community remembers and what it chooses not to remember often reflect that community's self-identity in the present and its aspirations for the future.[1] The historical memory of the civil rights years in Greenville, South Carolina, recalls desegregation of public facilities and schools undertaken voluntarily on the part of the establishment, "integration with dignity," integration carried out carried out with "grace and style."[2] However, events reveal a different and more complex picture. Contrary to prevailing memories, the fight for equal rights was fraught with indignities for Greenville's blacks; and whites did not concede integration voluntarily. Racial change came to Greenville only at the insistence of local black protesters and under the coercion of federal courts. Only when every reasonable avenue of resistance was rendered hopeless did white civic leaders associated with the chamber of commerce enlist the support of their counterparts in the black community to protect Greenville's image and to try to assure a peaceful transition to a desegregated society. Greenville's white leaders were not always successful in their efforts to keep the peace; their efforts to protect the city's image as racially progressive, despite facts to the contrary, have fared better. Greenville was desegregated not by blacks and whites "working together for integration," as the title of a 1992 article by a participant in the chamber's biracial committee asserted. Rather, six lawsuits filed by local attorneys Willie T. Smith and Donald Sampson from 1960 to 1964 left white Greenville no choice but to bow to the inevitable.

On the eve of the civil rights movement, Greenville was a proud New South city that touted itself as the "Textile Capital of the World." In 1960 textiles made up more than one-half of the total value of products made in Greenville County, and textiles factories ringing the city employed twenty-one thousand when the total city population was a little more than fifty-eight thousand.[3] Greenville's textile industry shaped not only the economy but also the values and attitudes of the city's civic, business, and political elite. Optimistic, energetic leaders took civic boosterism, common in many textile towns, to new heights. Although this boosterism often led businessmen to treat civic affairs as corporate enterprise, there is evidence to suggest that in doing so business leaders sincerely believed they could benefit all who lived in the community and at the same time improve their own prospects for wealth.[4] The merger of civic improvement with economic gain was augmented by a business leadership tied tightly together by interlocking directorates in the largest textile, banking, insurance, utility, and real estate companies in the county; and by a strong chamber of commerce that had served as the most powerful voice in civic matters since the early twentieth century.

During the first half of the twentieth century, race and class tensions had, at times, threatened the business elite's vision of Greenville as a progressive New South city and a smart place to invest. These pre–civil rights decades had also established the racial and social dynamic that further unfolded during the 1960s. Before the fight for desegregation began in earnest, a black population roughly one-third of the total in the city and less than 20 percent in the county confronted political and economic impoverishment with efforts that were game for the fight but ultimately overmatched.[5] In 1930 J. A. Brier and William Anderson established an NAACP branch that by the end of the decade had made some progress with a voter registration drive.[6] Two other institutions worked within the segregated and white-dominated system to improve education and cultural life for blacks. Sterling Industrial School, founded by D. M. Minus in 1902, was dedicated to "the intellectual, industrial and religious training of the boys and girls of the Negro race." The Phillis Wheatley Association, established by Hattie Logan Duckett in 1919, served as a community center for blacks.[7]

A white population that was strictly divided by class reacted to black efforts at uplift and self-improvement in two different ways. Mill workers, threatened in their social standing by every advance made by blacks, resorted to violence or threats of violence against blacks.[8] Klan demonstrations swelled in the 1920s in Greenville, and in the 1930s the Klan struck violently against interracial labor groups and against the NAACP voter registration campaign.[9] Greenville's reputation was also stained by five lynchings between 1905 and 1933.[10] At the other end of the economic ladder, the white establishment, fearing these violent reactions to black efforts at advancement but also embracing black uplift as beneficial to the New South economy, sought to control black efforts and coopt black institutions. In 1923 Thomas F. Parker, owner of sixteen cotton mills and the South's foremost advocate of corporate-run welfare programs for workers, cited the dangerous "fears and prejudices" of the "unthinking white population" when he persuaded the chamber of commerce to take over the Phillis Wheatley Association. The chamber replaced the all-black board of trustees with a mixed board

having, according to the bylaws, "a majority of white members and white officers." Immediately the association published a revised statement of its aims,
including the assertion, "We do not believe in the social equality of the races, as
possible or desirable."[11] In 1929 Sterling Industrial School also lost its independence when the city board of education took over its operation, reflecting a
statewide trend of converting private black schools to public.[12]

The Willie Earle lynching in 1947 seemed to confirm the powerlessness of
blacks in Greenville and the divided racial attitudes of Greenville's white citizens.
In February a white mob lynched Earle, a black suspected of murdering a white
cabdriver. Thirty-one men confessed and were indicted. In May a jury of twelve
white males—nine mill workers, one farmer, and two salesmen—acquitted the
defendants on all counts. Prominent Greenville citizens reacted with dismay,
although years later Schaefer Kendrick, at the time a young lawyer observing the
case, admitted that "the real concern, deep down, of the white group, of which I
was a part, was the effect the Earle lynching and resulting trial would have on
Greenville's image as a progressive, cultural, growing city of the New South."[13]

In the 1950s the *Brown* decision and South Carolina's massive resistance
forcefully and continuously pushed race to the forefront of Greenville's attention. Throughout the decade the city's morning daily, the *Greenville News,*
mounted vigorous opposition to the *Brown* decision and racial change in general. The *News* had been founded by textile pioneer Ellison A. Smyth in 1874 and
remained closely associated with the textile industry. In 1954 the *News's* editor,
Wayne C. Freeman, accepted the position of secretary of the South Carolina Segregation Committee, unofficially known as the Gressette Committee after state
senator Marion Gressette, who chaired the group. Freeman remained in both
positions throughout the civil rights years.[14] As editor Freeman defended segregation "as morally right, legally right, and necessary for the preservation of peace
and good order."[15] The *News* also urged only "substantial citizens" and "business and professional men" to lead the state's resistance to integration while
warning of the dangers of the Klan's tendency toward violence.[16] In light of later
developments it is important to note that Freeman's editorials also rejected
President Dwight Eisenhower's recommendation that southern states and cities
establish biracial committees to solve the region's racial problems. The *News*
called such committees "useless" because agitation had narrowed any middle
ground "to the point of disappearance."[17]

Despite the heightened rhetoric in the *News,* Greenville in the 1950s managed to deflect negative publicity over racial issues. In 1956 the nation's most
popular magazine, *Life,* published a collection of articles on race relations in five
southern cities. The article on Greenville, titled "No Trouble Here Unless . . . ,"
was generally positive. It quoted Mayor Kenneth Cass: "there's always been a
good feeling in the race situation." The mayor did not expect that to change
"unless an agitator comes in and stirs it up."[18]

Economic growth seemed to confirm the mayor's optimism. In the 1950s Greenville experienced strong industrial growth, prompting Charles E. Daniel, a construction magnate and Greenville's leading proponent of economic development, to call reports to the contrary "substantially propaganda" from northern competitors.[19] Meanwhile, Klan activity and racial violence in the area rose precipitously in 1956 and 1957.[20]

In 1959 an episode at the airport in Greenville initiated a series of direct action protests and federal lawsuits that chased Jim Crow from Greenville. Over the course of the next eleven years the white establishment in Greenville moved from vocal and massive opposition to quiet but ineffective resistance, and finally, to self-interested and begrudging compliance. With each new episode, the Greenville establishment steadfastly refused to acknowledge any justice behind civil rights changes, citing only practicality and the need to maintain law and order.

The airport incident involved Richard Henry, a civilian employee of the Air Force from Michigan, who was forcibly removed from the "white" waiting room at the airport in February 1959. Henry retained attorneys Lincoln Jenkins of Columbia and Willie T. Smith of Greenville to sue the Municipal Airport Authority. While the Henry case was pending, in October 1959, baseball star Jackie Robinson, visiting Greenville to speak at a national NAACP conference, encountered similar treatment, drawing national attention to Greenville's Jim Crow system. On January 1, 1960, Greenville's branch of the NAACP organized a march of 250 people at the airport to protest the "stigma, the inconvenience, and the stupidity of racial segregation." The plaintiff Henry suffered an initial setback in the federal court of Judge George Bell Timmerman, where the judge ruled "the right to equality before the law . . . invests no one with the authority to require others to accept him as a companion or social equal." However, Henry won his case on appeal, and the Greenville Airport desegregated under court order on February 20, 1961.[21]

Although the march at the airport had been organized and led by adults, students and recent graduates from Sterling High School carried out direct action protests over the course of the next two years. The arrests of the students by Greenville authorities and successful court challenges to those arrests would be the chief force in desegregating Greenville. In March 1960, inspired by Jackie Robinson's example, the airport march, and lunch counter sit-ins then sweeping the South, black students from Sterling attempted to use Greenville's main library. On their second "study-in," seven were arrested. By July local lawyers Willie T. Smith and Donald Sampson had filed suit against the city of Greenville and the library board of trustees. Joining Smith and Sampson were the high-powered and high-profile duo of Jack Greenberg and Thurgood Marshall of the NAACP Legal Defense Fund as well as Matthew J. Perry, state counsel for the NAACP.[22]

On September 2, after the attorneys for the plaintiffs filed for a temporary injunction to allow blacks to use the library, the board voted to close all branches of the library system. On September 15 Federal Judge C. C. Wyche then used the closings as a basis to deny the plaintiffs' request for the temporary injunction. Within a week, however, the library reopened on a nondiscriminatory basis, and Wyche declared the case moot.[23] By the time the threat of federal action had forced the desegregation of the library, sit-in protesters had begun to target downtown lunch counters, and racial violence broke out on Greenville's streets. On July 21, 1960, a brawl erupted following a sit-in at Kress's lunch counter. The melee involved more than thirty white and black teenagers and ranged over an entire block. Over the course of the next week blacks and whites clashed, exchanging gunfire, rocks, and bottles.[24] The city council responded with a 9:00 P.M. curfew on persons under twenty years of age. The sit-ins continued into August, when the first lunch counter arrests were made.[25] Early in 1961 youthful demonstrators targeted the whites-only skating rink operated by the city's Parks and Recreation Department. Again protesters were arrested. As a result of the arrests at the lunch counter and the skating rink, attorneys Smith and Sampson defended those charged with violating Greenville's segregation ordinance and sought to overturn the laws on constitutional grounds.[26]

In 1961, as the cases were pending, the threat of economic sanctions by the executive branch of the federal government pushed Greenville's business elite to weigh profits against the continuation of segregation. In April 1961 the President's Committee on Equal Employment announced that it would suspend contracts to South Carolina textile plants practicing segregation, and Vice President Lyndon Johnson announced that every future federal contract would contain a nondiscrimination clause.[27] A few months later, on July 1, 1961, at the Watermelon Festival in Hampton, South Carolina, Charles Daniel made what would become perhaps the most influential speech of the civil rights era in South Carolina. Daniel, a Greenville resident, was the most powerful economic voice in the state and a major influence in politics as well. A former U.S. senator and a current member of the State Development Board, Daniel was chiefly responsible for recruiting business and investment to the state from the north and overseas. His company, Daniel Construction, had built more than 400 industrial facilities, more than 240 in South Carolina. His widely publicized speech was titled "South Carolina's Economic Challenge" but quickly came to be known as the "Watermelon Speech."[28]

Daniel asserted that economic circumstances demanded white South Carolinians "forsake some of our ways." He urged economic and political leaders to "handle [the desegregation issue] ourselves . . . or it will be forced upon us in the harshest way. Either we act on our own terms, or we forfeit the right to act." He reminded listeners of the new antidiscrimination laws written into federal contracts and emphasized that the time had come for whites to abandon past "pattern[s] of inaction."[29] Daniel's speech, in the words of one Greenville textile man, "gave the blessing of the establishment to desegregation."[30]

That may well have been true, but in 1961 with two pending court cases seeking the desegregation of lunch counters and city parks and with local schools still completely segregated more than seven years after the *Brown* decision, the white establishment took no practical steps toward racial change. In the fall of 1962 the explosion of violence at Ole Miss over the enrollment of James Meredith prompted Greenville's civic leaders to take the first tentative steps to follow Daniel's advice of abandoning their "pattern of inaction." In the wake of the rioting and death at Ole Miss, the Reverend John Haley of Westminster Presbyterian Church approached textile magnate Arthur Magill and remarked, "We can't allow Greenville to burn like Mississippi." "No, we can't," answered Magill.[31] In the fall of 1962 the two men organized a meeting of some one hundred white bankers, lawyers, textile executives, and other businessmen to formulate a plan of coping with racial changes facing Greenville. That group decided to form a biracial committee under sponsorship of the chamber of commerce, with an equal number of black and white members chosen by the chamber.[32]

As the biracial committee was being organized, however, three court decisions forced sweeping changes on Greenville. First, on October 19, 1962, Federal District Judge C. C. Wyche ruled on the skating rink case. "It is, of course, now well settled that enforced racial segregation in the public parks of a city is unconstitutional. . . . the plaintiffs had the right to use both skating rinks on an equal basis with white citizens." However, since both skating rinks had been permanently closed by the city council, the case was declared moot.[33] In 1963 the city quietly dropped its policy of segregation in parks, but it never reopened its skating rinks. Next, in January 1963 a state circuit court declared unconstitutional a city law prohibiting blacks from living on residential city blocks deemed "white." That case began in June 1962, when a black man, Noigra Yarn, was arrested twice in his own house for violating the law. He had been convicted in city court before his appeal.[34] The third decision in this seven-month span was Greenville's most significant civil rights case. On May 20, 1963, the United States Supreme Court struck down lunch counter segregation in Greenville and throughout the South. *Peterson v. Greenville* originated in August 1960, when fourteen Sterling High students, including James R. Peterson, had been arrested at the Kress lunch counter on Main Street. Their convictions in city court were upheld upon appeal in both state circuit court and the South Carolina Supreme Court. Lawyers Perry and Smith had argued the case before the nation's high court in November 1962.[35] At the time of the *Peterson* decision, the issue of lunch counter segregation had been before the city's politicians and its business establishment for three years, and, since November Supreme Court arguments in the case, white Greenville had faced the likelihood that desegregation would once again be forced upon the city by the federal government. Still, white Greenville maintained its "pattern of inaction."

Only in the wake of *Peterson*, the fifth court case in three years forcing desegregation specifically in Greenville, did the city government and white business leaders react. The city council rescinded Greenville's segregation laws, and the chamber's biracial committee carefully arranged for black and white diners to eat together at selected restaurants, working behind the scenes to prepare proprietors and to minimize disruptions.[36] In the spring of 1964 the biracial committee targeted theaters and motels. Black patrons chosen by the committee carried out a gradual desegregation plan over the course of six weeks at preselected establishments. The plan nearly came unhinged when fifteen blacks not affiliated with the chamber sought lodging in the Downtowner Motor Inn. When they were denied rooms, one of the group demanded, "Why don't you people go ahead and cooperate with us instead of waiting and letting the government put a gun to your head." Greenville's Innkeepers' Association, offended by the episode, threatened to back out of ongoing discussions with the biracial committee. Negotiations resulted in the innkeepers agreeing to accept blacks on a limited basis only. The committee assented.[37] Two months after the agreement was reached, the federal Civil Rights Act of 1964 effectively outlawed discrimination in public accommodations. The committee's focus for the rest of the year and in 1965 would be on employment opportunities for blacks and on removing offensive Jim Crow signs in public places.[38]

The biracial committee helped to ease Greenville's transition to a desegregated society; however, two of its ground rules guaranteed that the group would not act as an agent of real change. First, it operated under a strict "no publicity rule." This policy reflected the argument that more progress could be made working behind the scenes and that a low profile would avoid "chaos and discord" that might threaten "law and order and the good name of the community."[39] However, the policy also assured that the chamber of commerce, one of the most traditionally influential voices in Greenville civic affairs, an organization comprising the city's most powerful citizens, would be unable to affect attitudes or shape public opinion. The second operating procedure that undermined the committee's effectiveness was the decision to take the issue of school desegregation off the table for discussion.[40] Since the *Brown* decision, school desegregation had been the South's most volatile civil rights issue. By the time, the Biracial Committee had formed, every southern state but South Carolina had desegregated its schools. Moreover, by 1964 desegregation in nearly every other phase of public life was a fait accompli in Greenville. The school issue was looming and demanded the best efforts of the best people in the community. The biracial committee's inactivity helped assure that the last phase of desegregation in Greenville, the most difficult one, would yet again be carried out under federal compulsion.

Greenville County schools were desegregated over a six-year period, from 1964 to 1970, as a result of a locally initiated federal lawsuit and two sweeping Supreme Court decisions that originated elsewhere. During this period the all-white school board, with the overwhelming support of the city and county politicians, businesspeople, and the *Greenville News,* fought to keep blacks out of white schools. When that proved futile, the board sought to limit black student transfers to the minimum that would satisfy federal mandates. However, in that effort the board miscalculated, and in 1970 a Fourth Circuit Court of Appeals ruling forced a midyear dismantling of Greenville's dual system of schools for blacks and whites.

On August 19, 1963, A. J. Whittenberg, a black gas station owner, filed suit to desegregate Greenville's schools after the superintendent of schools denied transfer requests for his daughter Elaine and five other black children to attend white schools. Just three days later, federal judge Robert Martin Jr., a native Greenvillian, ordered the desegregation of Charleston's schools in *Brown v. School District 20,* a case with similar facts to those in Greenville. Nevertheless, the Greenville County School District contested Whittenberg's suit, seeking a dismissal. In March 1964 Judge Martin denied that motion and offered the school district's lawyers thirty days to reconsider the transfer requests and to formulate a policy on future applications.[41] A month later Martin issued a consent order admitting the students and accepting the school board's new policy for "enrollment, assignment, and transfer of pupils without regard to race, creed, or color."[42]

Judge Martin's consent decree came to be known as the "freedom-of-choice" plan. It was used in Greenville County and throughout the state until 1970.[43] In practice the freedom-of-choice plan maintained the dual racial school system and gave the school board control over the pace of desegregation. Freedom of choice also placed the burden for desegregation on black parents and children. Every summer black parents who wanted their children to transfer to white-majority schools would have to apply to the board, which would then accept or reject the request. In the first year, 1964, 55 of 75 applications were approved.[44] For the 1965–1966 school year, 146 black student transfers were granted out of 260 requests.[45] In 1967 the United States Department of Health Education and Welfare, acting under the authority of Title IV of the Civil Rights Act of 1964, declared that Greenville's school board was moving too slowly and threatened to cut off federal funds.[46] White citizens reacted by drawing up a list of complaints concerning the consequences of forced integration.[47] Before the school board could effectively respond to the HEW's demands, in May 1968 the Supreme Court, in *Green v. New Kent County,* found freedom of choice an ineffective means of integrating schools and demanded that school boards immediately create plans to dismantle dual racial school systems where they existed.[48]

In light of the *Green* ruling, Greenville's school board was required to submit a revised plan of desegregation to Judge Martin. It proposed maintaining freedom of choice through the 1969–1970 school year and creating a unitary, nonracial system beginning with the 1970–1971 school year, a full two years after the Supreme Court in *Green* ordered school districts to act "now."[49] Nevertheless, in July 1969 Judge Martin accepted the revised plan.[50] Within three months, however, the school board's plan was effectively rendered unconstitutional. In *Alexander v. Holmes County Board of Education,* a unanimous Supreme Court proclaimed, "The obligation of every school district is to terminate dual systems at once and to operate now and hereafter only unitary systems." That case involved thirty-three school districts in Mississippi that, like Greenville, had postponed compliance with the *Green* decision.[51] Now in light of the *Alexander* decision, attorneys for Whittenberg appealed Judge Martin's acceptance of the school board's plan for delay. On January 19, 1970, Clement Furman Haynesworth, a Greenville native and presiding judge in the Fourth Circuit Court of Appeals in Richmond, was "left with no discretion" and therefore ordered Greenville's dual system dismantled by February 16, 1970. The school system could devise its own plan or accept one imposed by the court or HEW.[52] Greenville's fight to contain desegregation was over.

The school board had delayed integration for seven years since the *Whittenberg* case had first been filed (or sixteen if one counts back to *Brown*), but now chafed that the law "could be imposed with such brutal unconcern for the consequences." Nevertheless, the school board submitted, and the court accepted, a plan that would transfer twelve thousand of the fifty-eight thousand pupils in the system and five hundred faculty in seeking to achieve an 80/20 white to black ratio in all schools.[53] It was a logistical challenge of epic proportions in one of the largest school districts in the nation. The reaction of the community to the court order and the plan was mixed. The chamber's biracial committee, though still in operation, had atrophied; and in the 1970 crisis it stayed true to its policy of noninvolvement in school desegregation.[54] The *News* denounced the courts' orders as "absurd" but urged compliance to maintain the peace.[55] Leading Greenville's efforts for peaceful compliance with the federal mandate was the citizens' committee of the Greenville County School District, a group of thirty black and white men and women, who took the lead tackling both logistical matters and public relations involved in the transition. Ernest E. Harrill, a political science professor at Furman University, chaired the citizens' committee. Adopting the slogan "Education Is the Important Thing," Harrill's committee enlisted the support of the chamber of commerce, and a number of members of the citizens' committee were former or current members of the chamber's biracial committee.[56] The crisis spawned opposition as well. The Citizens for Freedom of Choice, led by R. L Eskew, raised $2,500 and organized a rally of three thousand people.[57] The Citizens' Committee to Prevent Busing, led by Carroll Campbell (future governor of South Carolina), organized a motorcade to the statehouse in Columbia on January 25. Campbell claimed more than three thousand cars participated in the protest.[58]

As the court-imposed deadline approached, the national media attention grew intense; however, except for a few minor glitches, the transition day itself, February 17, 1970, went off with little trouble. *The CBS Evening News*, UPI, the *New York Times*, the *Philadelphia Inquirer*, the *Washington Post*, *Newsweek*, the *Mexico City Daily Bulletin*, the *Charlotte Observer*, and a host of other media outlets covered the story, generally applauding Greenville as a city whose "compliance [with the law] contrasted sharply" with other southern cities.[59] CBS anchor Walter Cronkite, as well as many of the newspaper journalists, quoted Ernest Harrill to characterize the desegregation of Greenville's schools: "we did what we had to do but the people have done it with grace and style."[60]

Unfortunately the "grace and style" of February 17 contrasted sharply with underlying aspects of the school district's desegregation plan. Most of the formerly all-black schools were closed or demoted from high schools to junior highs. For example, Sterling High and Lincoln High, the flagship schools of black Greenville, were both shut down in 1970. Blacks also bore the brunt of transfers and busing. Sixty percent of the district's 11,600 blacks were reassigned, but only 10 percent of the 46,400 whites were transferred. Blacks also shouldered 75 percent of the busing burden.[61] Black principals and head coaches were forced into assistant roles much more frequently than their white counterparts.[62]

In the fall of 1970, once the spotlight of the national media had dimmed, unresolved complaints and festering discontent exploded in racial fights and riots in several schools. Shots were fired at one, and tear gas and state troopers were required at two more. More than three hundred students were eventually suspended, and several were arrested.[63] *U.S. News and World Report* was one of the few national media outlets to return to Greenville to examine what had gone wrong. It reported that "stunned school officials are groping for answers." For Ernest Harrill, the man who had the coined the phrase "integration with grace and style," the answer was not hard to discern. He explained the unrest simply: "Sad to say, we've been moved only by the law and not by our own spirit."[64]

Moved by law, Greenville's white leadership was indeed moved by law: law challenged by the civil disobedience of young protestors; law argued by attorneys Smith and Sampson, Perry, Marshall, and Greenberg; law overturned in federal courts. White Greenville was also moved by sincere concern for the community and its reputation. And because reputation was closely tied to an inviting climate for business investment, Greenville was moved by a concern for money. White Greenville was not moved by a desire for justice or a spirit of equality.

Since 1970 participants in the desegregation of Greenville have recounted these events in oral histories, for newspaper retrospectives, in masters' theses, in unpublished memoirs, in widely circulated articles for the general public, in public forums sponsored by civic organizations, and no doubt in hundreds if not thousands of personal conversations.[65] These memories reflect a great divide in the recollections of black and white Greenvillians. Blacks recall the arrests, the resistance of the white establishment, the court victories, the indignities they faced in fighting for rights guaranteed by the Constitution. Whites usually remember "working together for integration," the interracial cooperation of the chamber of commerce committee, the "grace and style" of the enormous effort to dismantle peacefully an old system of racially divided schools in order to build a new racially unified system. These memories of white Greenville and especially the memories of chamber's biracial committee have formed the basis for most written accounts of the events. For whites looking back there is a feeling of self-congratulation that is incomprehensible to blacks who lived through that period. Perhaps Greenville's tradition of civic boosterism compels whites to remember selectively and to mythologize those events in ways that continue to enhance Greenville's reputation as a good place to live and invest. On the other hand, ongoing racial tensions in Greenville during the post–civil rights years remind us that selective memories and self-serving myths are a poor foundation on which to build a community of justice and equality.[66]

Notes

1. For an insightful examination of collective memory and southern history, see W. Fitzhugh Brundage, ed., *Where These Memories Grow: History, Memory, and Southern Identity* (Chapel Hill: University of North Carolina Press, 2000).

2. Both of these phrases originated contemporaneously with events; however, each has been employed multiple times since then to characterize civil rights in Greenville, the Upstate, and, inexplicably, the entire state. The former phrase was first used by George McMillan in "Integration with Dignity: The Inside Story of How South Carolina Kept the Peace," *Saturday Evening Post,* March 16, 1963, 16–21. McMillan's article described the efforts by state and college officials to desegregate peacefully Clemson College in January 1963. Dr. Ernest E. Harrill, faculty member at Furman University and a leader in the effort to dismantle peacefully Greenville's dual school system, coined the latter phrase. The phrase was repeated by Walter Cronkite in his report on *The CBS Evening News* on February 17, 1970, and subsequently by the *New York Times,* the *Philadelphia Inquirer,* the *Washington Post,* and *Newsweek.* For historical accounts that have used those terms or asserted the interpretation that Greenville desegregated voluntarily, see Keith Morris, "Desegregation with Dignity: Those Who Made It Work in Greenville—in Their Own Words," *Upcountry Review* (Fall 1999): 28–51; Betty Stall, "With Grace and Style: The Desegregation of the Greenville County Schools in 1970," *Proceedings and Papers of the Greenville County Historical Society* 9 (1990–1991): 80–92; Robert Hart, "Amend or Defend: The End of Jim Crow in Greenville and Charleston" (M.A. thesis, Clemson University, 1997); Alfred L. Burgess, "Working Together for Integration," *Carologue: Bulletin of the South Carolina Historical Society* 8 (Winter 1992) 7, 14. For a similar interpretation of the desegregation of the state as a whole, see John Sproat, "'Firm Flexibility': Perspectives on Desegregation in South Carolina," in *New Perspectives on Race and Slavery in America: Essays in Honor of Kenneth M. Stampp,* ed. Robert H. Abzug and Stephen E. Maizlish (Lexington: University of Kentucky Press, 1986), 164–84; and Walter B. Edgar, *South Carolina: A History* (Columbia: University of South

Carolina Press, 1998), 538–41. For a less sanguine view of events see Archie Vernon Huff Jr., *Greenville: The History of the City and County in the South Carolina Piedmont* (Columbia: University of South Carolina Press, 1995), 401–6. Tomiko Brown Hall's "'Moved by Law and Not by Spirit': Public School Desegregation in Greenville, S.C." (independent study, Furman University, 1990), which is in my possession, argues persuasively that whites conceded little voluntarily on civil rights in Greenville and the state. The ideas behind the present work first started germinating for me when I moderated a symposium titled "'We Were There' . . . Integration of Greenville County Schools," sponsored by the Historic Greenville Foundation on March 19, 2002. I was struck by the very different viewpoints that black and white panelists held concerning the desegregation of Greenville's schools.

3. Cliff Sloan and Bob Hall, "'It's Good to be Home in Greenville' . . . but It's Better If You Hate Unions," *Southern Exposure* 7 (Spring 1979): 88.

4. See Broadus Mitchell, *Rise of Cotton Mills in the South* (Baltimore: Johns Hopkins University Press, 1921); David Carlton, *Mill and Town in South Carolina* (Baton Rouge: Louisiana State University Press, 1982), 33–38, 61–74.

5. U.S. Census, 1950, charts 40–23 and 40–25.

6. Edwin D. Hoffman, "The Genesis of the Modern Movement for Equal Rights in South Carolina, 1930–1939," *Journal of Negro History* 44 (October 1959): 356, 366–367.

7. Sterling High Clipping File, South Carolina Room, Greenville County Library; Huff, *Greenville*, 257, 272; I. A. Newby, *Black Carolinians: A History of Blacks in South Carolina from 1895 to 1968* (Columbia: University of South Carolina Press, 1973), 229–32.

8. See Bryant Simon, *A Fabric of Defeat: The Politics of South Carolina Millhands, 1910–1948* (Chapel Hill: University of North Carolina Press, 1998), 4–35. Simon offers a more complex explanation of the nature of threats that black advancement represented to white mill workers. He argues that black initiatives threatened white workers' masculinity and sense of independence as well as white supremacy and economic standing.

9. Huff, *Greenville*, 323–25; Hoffman, "Genesis of the Modern Movement," 353, 355–56, 361, 366, 368; *Greenville News*, April 3, 1925; May 6, 1926; June 16, 1931; July 7, 1939.

10. Huff, *Greenville*, 356; *Greenville News*, November 30, 1933.

11. *Greenville News*, December 30, 1923.

12. Sterling High Clipping File; Huff, *Greenville*, 356.

13. Schaefer Kendrick, "What Kind of Place Was Greenville in 1947?," *Carologue: Bulletin of the South Carolina Historical Society* 8 (Winter 1992): 14.

14. Andrew M. Secrest, "In Black and White: Press Opinions and Race Relations in South Carolina, 1954–1964" (Ph.D. dissertation, Duke University, 1974), 33–39.

15. *Greenville News*, June 7, 1960.

16. *Greenville News*, August 9, 17, 1955.

17. *Greenville News*, January 23, 1955; September 20, 1955.

18. "No Trouble Here Unless . . .," *Life*, September 17, 1956, 109–10.

19. *Southern School News*, May 1956, 14.

20. *Greenville News*, January 22, 1956; March 3, 1956; June 16, 1956; August 19, 1956; July 27, 1957.

21. Samuel L. Zimmerman, *Negroes in Greenville, 1970: An Exploratory Approach* (Greenville: South Carolina Tricentennial, 1970), 31–32; *State*, January 2, 1960; Huff, *Greenville*, 400–402; *Henry v. Greenville Airport Commission*, 175 F. Supp. 343 (D.C. W.D.S.C. 1959).

22. *Greenville News*, March 2, 1960; *Greenville Piedmont*, July 16, 1960; Zimmerman, *Negroes in Greenville*, 25–26.

23. *Greenville News*, September 3, 19, 1960.

24. *Greenville News,* July 19, 22, 26, 1960.

25. *Greenville News,* August 3, 10, 12, 1960.

26. Zimmerman, *Negroes in Greenville,* 25–26; *Peterson v. Greenville,* 239 S.C. 298 (S.C. Sup. Ct. 1961).

27. *Greenville News,* April 14, 26, 1961.

28. C. R. Canup and W. D. Workman Jr., *Charles E. Daniel: His Philosophy and Legacy* (Columbia: R. L. Bryan, 1981), 75; Hart, "Amend of Defend," 35–36; McMillan, "Integration with Dignity," 16–19.

29. Canup and Workman, *Charles E. Daniel,* 182–83.

30. The quote is from Yancey Gilkerson, interview with Robert Hart, January 15, 1997; Hart, "Amend or Defend," 36.

31. Hart, "Amend or Defend," 41; Morris, "Desegregation with Dignity," 28.

32. Yancey Gilkerson, "The Greater Greenville Chamber of Commerce Biracial Committee, 1961–1969" (Unpublished manuscript in File Box: "Chamber of Commerce Biracial Committee," South Carolina Room, Greenville County Library); Morris, "Desegregation with Dignity," 28–44; Burgess, "Working Together for Integration," 14–15.

33. *Walker v. Shaw,* 209 F. Supp. 569 (1962); *Greenville News,* October 20, 1962.

34. *Greenville News,* January 16, 1963.

35. *Greenville News,* June 21, 28, 1963; Zimmerman, *Negroes in Greenville,* 29–30; *Peterson v. Greenville,* 373 U.S. 244 (1963).

36. *Greenville News,* May 29, 1963; June 4, 1963; Gilkerson, "Greater Greenville Chamber of Commerce," 7–9.

37. Gilkerson, "Greater Greenville Chamber of Commerce," 9.

38. Ibid., 11.

39. "Policy Statement of Greater Greenville Chamber of Commerce Biracial Committee," July 1, 1963, File Box: Chamber of Commerce Biracial Committee, South Carolina Room, Greenville County Library.

40. Gilkerson, "Greater Greenville Chamber of Commerce," 6.

41. *Greenville News,* March 20, 1964.

42. Ibid., April 14, 28, 1964.

43. Paul Wesley McNeill, "School Desegregation in South Carolina, 1963–1970" (EdD thesis, University of Kentucky, 1979), 50–56; William Bagwell, *School Desegregation in the Carolinas: Two Case Studies* (Columbia: University of South Carolina Press, 1972), 175–84.

44. *Southern School News,* July–August 1964.

45. Bagwell, *School Desegregation in the Carolinas,* 183–84.

46. *New York Times,* March 12, 1967.

47. *Greenville Piedmont,* March 22, 1967.

48. *Green v. New Kent County,* 391 U.S. 430 (1968); James T. Patterson, Brown v. Board of Education: *A Civil Rights Milestone and Its Troubled Legacy* (New York: Oxford University Press, 2001), 146–48.

49. The decision read in part, "The burden is on a school board to provide a plan that promises realistically to work *now,* and a plan that at this late date fails to provide meaningful assurance of prompt and effective disestablishment of a dual system is intolerable" (emphasis in the original document). *Green v. New Kent County,* 391 U.S. 430 (1968).

50. *Greenville News,* July 1969.

51. *Alexander v. Holmes County Board of Education,* 396 U.S. 19 (1969).

52. *Whittenberg v. Greenville,* 424 F.2d 195 (1970).

53. "Proposed Plan," School District of Greenville South Carolina, January 23, 1970. Copy at the school district office.

54. Gilkerson, "Greater Greenville Chamber of Commerce," 25–27.

55. *Greenville News,* February 7, 1970.

56. Gilkerson, "Greater Greenville Chamber of Commerce," 5–20; *Greenville Piedmont,* January 31, 1970.

57. Donald Gordon and William Lavery, "Timeline of Greenville's School Desegregation" (n.d.). Dr. Ernest E. Harrill Private Papers (hereafter Harrill Papers).

58. "All Desegregation Orders Obeyed—Then, School Chaos in Greenville, S.C.," *U.S. News and World Report,* December 7, 1970, 26; *Greenville News,* January 26, 1970.

59. The list of media coverage comes from Stall, "With Grace and Style," 90. The quote is from the *New York Times,* February 18, 1970.

60. Ernest Harrill, letter to Greenville community on behalf of the Citizens' Committee thanking Greenville for peace during February desegregation, Harrill Papers.

61. Zimmerman, *Negroes in Greenville,* 11; *Greenville News,* February 17, 1980; Stall, "With Grace and Style," 83.

62. "Grievances from Black Educators," Harrill Papers.

63. "All Desegregation Orders Obeyed," 26; *Greenville News,* November 7, 18, 19, 1970.

64. Hall, "Moved by Law," 35; Harrill's quote originally published in John Egerton, *The Americanization of Dixie: The Southernization of America* (New York: *Harper's Magazine* Press, 1974), 87.

65. In addition to the publications listed in note 1, I am also referring to interviews in an ongoing oral history project by the History Museum of the Upcountry. Those transcripts will be available to the public when the history museum opens. The white attitude of voluntary integration through cooperation is also reflected in many of the more than a dozen interviews with participants in Greenville's civil rights events conducted by Furman students in the fall of 1999. Those tapes are in my possession. Conflicting points of view are also reflected in a series of *Greenville News* articles published in May 2000. The series was titled "Lost Dreams: Desegregation Thirty Years Later," May 28–30, 2000. Dueling perspectives on Greenville's civil rights history were also reflected in a panel, "The History of Integration at Furman in Context," during the symposium "Race, Religion, and the Liberal Arts: The History of Furman in Context." The symposium was held at Furman University, April 29–May 1, 2002. A symposium titled "'We Were There' . . . Integration of Greenville County Schools" sponsored by the Historic Greenville Foundation on March 19, 2002, reflected considerable disagreement along the lines I have described. Civil rights events were also depicted in an exhibition at the Greenville Cultural Exchange Center, "Civil Rights Movement in Greenville," which ran from September 2000 through January 2001. Finally, for some recent opinions or assertions that reiterate the "grace and style" interpretation, see David Shi, "Greenville Risks Setback on Race," *Greenville News,* February 22, 2003; Dale Perry, "From Indian Hunting Grounds to Textile Center, Greenville Goes International," *Greenville News,* May 5, 2002. Clemson English professor Keith Morris's "Desegregation with Dignity: Those Who Made It Work in Greenville—in Their Own Words," published in the *Upcountry Review* in 1999 (see endnote 1), is the most comprehensive report of how whites remember their roles in civil rights.

66. Racial tensions in the post–civil rights years are seen most clearly in NAACP complaints and petitions concerning pupil assignment plans in the 1980s; in controversies over where new schools would be built in the 1990s and the early 2000s; and especially in the long, contentious, and nationally prominent battle to persuade the Greenville County Council to establish a holiday to honor Martin Luther King Jr. Greenville was the last county in South Carolina and one of the last in the nation to adopt the holiday, which it did in 2004.

Schooling and White Supremacy

The African American Struggle for Educational Equality and Access in South Carolina, 1945–1970

R. Scott Baker

"No southern state," Robert Coles wrote in 1968, "can match South Carolina's ability to resist the claims of black people without becoming an object of national scorn." While Orval Faubus, Ross Barnett, and George Wallace incited violence, defied the courts, and invited federal intervention, "South Carolina remained relatively untouched and unnoticed, an island, managed and run, though, by exceptionally clever and cool political leaders who long ago learned how to dress up the rankest kind of exploitation in those lovely, old, 'fine-appearing' clothes that go under the name of 'southern gentility.'" As Timothy Tyson argues, violence intimidated, but what deserves scrutiny in South Carolina is not so much the massive resistance that ultimately collapsed but the more rational and legally defensible evasions that endured. In South Carolina educational and political authorities responded to African American demands for educational access and equality by rationalizing restrictions that could no longer be sanctioned by law, creating a new, higher stage of white supremacy in education.[1]

South Carolina was a key battleground in the struggle for African American equality, the site of NAACP-sponsored campaigns to equalize teacher salaries, desegregate higher education, and eliminate state-imposed segregation in public schools. The NAACP and local African American activists won a series of victories that forced educational authorities to eliminate legalized discrimination. These campaigns accelerated the institutional development in African American schools and colleges, where teachers and professors prepared a generation of students who challenged caste constraints and segregation laws.

As African Americans pressed for access, educational and political authorities adopted new barriers to black equality. The architects of this new racial order in education, like those who promoted segregation as a solution to the region's racial problem in the beginning of the twentieth century, were not extremists but moderates. Beginning in the early 1940s, they saw how standardized tests could be used to rationalize restrictions. Seeking legally defensible solutions to the problem of desegregation, they adopted tests that were used to limit African American access to the professions, colleges and universities, and the public schools. The sophisticated and still largely unnoticed barriers that the state's clever educational and political leadership institutionalized after 1945 illustrate that white resistance to black access and equality, what Michael Klarman calls the backlash, did not begin or crystallize after *Brown*. In South Carolina, at least, the backlash began in the 1940s and was developed, refined, and institutionalized in the decades that followed.[2]

Unlike the caste constraints they replaced, these new, more durable educational policies and practices did not restrict the access of advantaged African Americans, heirs of the state's black elite, but they did limit opportunity for most blacks. The outlines of this new order first emerged in the 1940s, after educational authorities in South Carolina adopted the National Teacher Examinations (NTE) in response to African American demands for the equalization of white and black teacher salaries. The NTE, like the standardized tests adopted to limit black access to universities and the professions in the 1950s and to track students in elementary and secondary schools during the 1960s, heightened class divisions among African Americans even as race remained significant. As new, more rational restrictions replaced those once required by law, the legacies of caste— and the class divisions that developed within the black caste—shaped educational opportunities and outcomes. While advantaged blacks entered schools, colleges, and universities, most African Americans, handicapped by generations of segregation and discrimination, were not prepared to compete educationally with whites and remained cloistered in predominately African American institutions that lost vitality as they became segregated by class as well as race.

"There are," Gunnar Myrdal wrote in 1944, "few major cases of racial discrimination so clear-cut and so pronounced as that found in the teaching profession in the South." In South Carolina, as elsewhere, school officials maintained separate and unequal salary schedules that prevented the best African American teacher from earning as much as the worst white and kept the average annual salary of blacks at a fraction of that of whites. This practice was a cornerstone of the caste system and an ideal target for NAACP legal attacks. Beginning in Maryland in 1936, Thurgood Marshall and courageous African American teachers challenged this practice, winning legal victories in every southern state that forced educational authorities to eliminate caste constraints, but left the door open to new forms of discrimination. Officials in South Carolina responded to litigation by adopting the NTE and using these standardized tests to maintain pay differentials that could no longer be based on race. Advantaged African Americans earned NTE scores and salaries that exceeded those of many whites, but most black teachers continued to make considerably less than whites.[3]

Anticipating legal action, the legislature appointed a special committee to investigate the salary issue in 1940. Chaired by David W. Robinson, a Harvard-educated lawyer who was a key architect of the new racial order in education, the committee enlisted the help of testing and measurement specialist Ben Wood. After meeting with Wood on several occasions in the early 1940s, the committee recommended that the legislature adopt "a steeply scaled" salary system that based pay in large measure on an "objective system of examinations." When Robinson and W.C. McCall, a testing specialist at the University of South Carolina, tried to sell the plan, they encountered stiff opposition from legislators and superintendents, who worried that the exams might allow African Americans to "prove themselves superior to whites." Using data from a pretest administered to a sample group of white and black teachers in the fall of 1944, the committee pointed out that "the average score of blacks was at the lower fifth percentile of whites." Test results convinced a legislature that the political scientist V. O. Key called "the defender of the status quo" to adopt the new salary plan in January 1945.[4]

22. Judge J. Waties Waring (seated at left) being honored by the Charleston NAACP for his landmark rulings in Elmore v. Rice *and* Briggs v. Elliott, *November 1954. Photograph by Boags Modern Arts Photo Studio, courtesy of the Ethelyn Parker Collection, Avery Research Center for African American History and Culture at the College of Charleston*

A month after the legislature established the new salary system, Judge J. Waties Waring upheld its constitutionality. Waring was one of the NAACP's most important allies on the federal bench, but his rulings in teacher equalization cases in Charleston and Columbia are notable for their deference to local authorities. Waring found that school officials discriminated against black teachers "solely on the basis of race," but drawing on precedents established in Maryland, he held that officials were free to determine "the respective amounts to be paid to individual teachers on the basis of individual qualifications, capabilities, and abilities." While no evidence was presented that showed that the NTE predicted performance in the classroom, Waring wrote that the exam was a "proper yardstick by which to measure the stature of a teacher and pay him accordingly." Waring did not see the injustice of judging whites and blacks against the same test norm in a state that maintained five institutions of higher education for whites and only one for blacks, that spent more than four times as much on white as black postsecondary education, and that made no provision for the graduate or professional education of African Americans even though the new salary schedule offered higher pay to those with master's degrees. "The question before this court," he concluded, is whether the new salary and certification system "is free of the tinge of racial prejudice, and I find it to be so." Edgar Brown, the legislative leader who sponsored the salary plan, praised Waring for his "masterful understanding of the issue." It is "comforting to have your judicial conclusion, that the program as written is free from the tinge of race prejudice."[5]

Rather than eliminating racism, the NTE provided a new form through which it was institutionalized and expressed. As new more rational restrictions replaced those once sanctioned by law, the legacies of caste, and the class differences that had developed within the black caste shaped educational outcomes. By 1947 almost all of the state's thirteen thousand teachers had taken the NTE. While 6 percent of the state's black educators earned A's (compared to 44 percent of the whites), more than 66 percent of black teachers received C's or D's (compared to 5 percent of the whites) and the average annual salary of blacks was still only 67 percent of that of whites. Most of those who did earn A's were members of the state's black elite. In Charleston, for example, 10 percent of the black teachers, graduates of private schools and colleges, earned scores and salaries that exceeded those of almost one-half of the city's white teachers. The performance of these advantaged African Americans lent legitimacy to the new salary system and confirmed what Robinson's committee told the legislature in the early 1940s, that "at least a few of the lower salary group will clearly qualify for increases so that increases can be publicized to show the absence of discrimination." When an African American became the highest paid principal in Charleston in 1948, the *Charleston News and Courier* published a profile to show "the absence of discrimination." By allowing advantaged African Americans to earn higher pay without changing the subordinate status of most black teachers, the new salary system did not so much repudiate white supremacy as raise it to a higher, more sophisticated level.[6]

As educational authorities institutionalized new, more legally defensible restrictions to equality, African Americans drew upon resources generated by the legal campaign and postwar prosperity to improve African American schools and promote educational advancement. Although the average salary of African American teachers remained below that of whites, black teachers did win pay increases that many used to finance more-advanced training. "By their improved economic status," recalls Eugene Hunt who taught at Burke Industrial School in Charleston during the 1940s, "many teachers were able to further their own education." More-advanced training helped teachers at Burke strengthen the school's academic curriculum. Building on the groundwork laid in the early 1940s, teachers also improved the school's extra curriculum, training an increasing racially conscious and politically active student leadership. Pushed forward by a network of PTAs, churches, and clubs that promoted advancement inside and outside the schools, growing numbers of students from Burke and other black high schools graduated. G.I. Bill benefits helped unprecedented numbers enroll in college. By mid-century, more than thirteen thousand African Americans were graduating from college each year, three times as many as in 1940. In South Carolina and other southern states these college graduates challenged segregation and exclusion in graduate and professional education, reviving the NAACP's legal campaign to desegregate higher education.[7]

As African Americans pressed for access to higher education and the professions, whites adopted new restrictions. South Carolina, like other southern states, offered African Americans no opportunities for graduate or professional study until the late 1940s. In 1946 John Wrighten, a graduate of South Carolina's African American land grant college in Orangeburg and a World War II veteran, applied for admission to the University of South Carolina law school in Columbia. After university officials rejected his application, the NAACP filed suit. State officials responded by creating a separate law school for African Americans at State College in Orangeburg. Although Waring found it "almost impossible to intellectually compare" the new law school to the program at the University of South Carolina, he nonetheless ruled that the state had complied with the Court's 1938 *Gaines* decision.[8]

At the same time the legislature established new requirements for admission to the state bar that limited black access. During the early 1950s university officials extended these restrictions to the undergraduate level and began requiring for the first time that applicants to the state's white public colleges take entrance examinations. In higher education as in teacher salaries, these new, more legally defensible and durable barriers created patterns of access that were increasingly based on class as well as race.

Before the legislature established the law school at South Carolina State, graduates of the University of South Carolina law school enjoyed the diploma privilege that guaranteed admission to the state bar without examination. In the early twentieth century the American Bar Association launched a campaign to limit the access of "socially undesirable elements" by replacing the diploma privilege with written examinations. By 1947, however, the privilege still existed in Alabama, Arkansas, Florida, Louisiana, Mississippi, South Carolina, and West Virginia, as well as Montana, South Dakota, and Wisconsin. An account in the *State* illustrates how graduates of the University of South Carolina law school were admitted to the bar during the 1940s. Law school graduates participated in "a double ceremony" that was held in the Supreme Court room at the statehouse. After receiving their diplomas from university president Norman Smith, they were "presented to the court" by law school dean Samuel L. Prince, and were "duly sworn in" as members of the bar, before being addressed by Associate Justice E. Ladsen Fishburne.[9]

Faced with the prospect of African American law school graduates participating in the "double ceremony" at the statehouse, gaining admission to the bar, and joining the NAACP's campaign against segregation, authorities turned to other means to restrict black access to the practice of law. Led by David W. Robinson, the South Carolina Bar Association persuaded the legislature to revoke the diploma privilege, and in April 1948 it was repealed. Graduates of the state's law schools were now required to pass a bar examination to practice law. Matthew Perry, who graduated from South Carolina State in 1951, recalls that once African Americans gained access to legal training, "they changed the rules, and announced that hereafter everybody would have to take the exam." John Wrighten believed that the new requirement was an attempt to "punish African Americans." The legislator who introduced the bill that established the new requirement announced that it was designed to "bar Negroes and some undesirable whites." Like the NTE, the bar exam requirement limited African American access. Between 1950 and 1973 only 15 percent of the African Americans who took the bar exam in South Carolina passed, compared to 90 percent of the whites.[10]

While these new, more rational and legally defensible restrictions limited African American access, unlike the caste barriers they replaced they did not restrict it completely. South Carolina State trained many African American attorneys, including John Wrighten and Matthew Perry, who drafted school desegregation petitions, sued for access to libraries and parks, arranged for the release of young people who staged sit-ins, and represented students who desegregated the state's schools, colleges, and universities in the early 1960s. "Without southern black lawyers," most of whom were trained at African American law schools such as South Carolina State, writes the NAACP's Jack Greenberg, "we could never have accomplished what we did." Lawyers trained at the law school in Orangeburg, Perry recalls, "changed the direction of the state."[11]

Political and educational authorities responded to the Supreme Court's 1950 ruling in *Sweatt v. Painter* and the NAACP's challenge to South Carolina's segregation laws in *Briggs v. Elliott* by adopting new requirements that restricted African American access to colleges and universities. While officials considered new requirements in the early 1950s, they did not adopt them until after *Brown*. In 1953 W. C. McCall, director of the examination's bureau at the University of South Carolina, encouraged President Donald Russell to send a representative to Princeton to meet with officials at the Educational Testing Service (ETS). Eager to expand use of entrance exams in a region where almost no college applicants took them, ETS told McCall that it was interested in helping South Carolina "become the very first state" in the South "to require the full program of the College Board." Less than two weeks after *Brown,* Russell secured faculty and board approval of the new requirements. During discussion at a faculty meeting on May 27, 1954, one professor, echoing the sentiments of colleagues on other southern campuses, asked: "Is it not true that these entrance examinations are, in reality, being introduced as a means of keeping out Negro applicants?" The next day the board approved the new requirement that "the admission of all new students to the university shall be by examination." Russell acknowledged that the new admissions policy would allow the university to "legally exclude students. We feel we must establish a system of entrance examinations that are not based on racial standards. This can be avoided if we do not admit anyone without examination." During his 1958 gubernatorial campaign, Russell asserted that the university had "pioneered in protecting our southern way of life and in taking a necessary precautionary step." State universities in North Carolina, Georgia, Florida, Tennessee, and Mississippi followed suit and began requiring that applicants submit standardized test scores.[12]

Like the NTE and the bar exam, these new policies could only limit access; they could not deny it completely. Although more than a dozen African Americans tried to gain access to the university in the late 1950s, the new restrictions forestalled desegregation until 1963, when South Carolina became the last southern state to admit black students to its flagship university. Nine months after Harvey Gantt ended segregation at Clemson, Henrie Monteith, Robert Anderson, and James Solomon crossed the color line and became the first African Americans to attend USC since 1877. While the number of African Americans at the university grew to 279 by 1970, more rational restrictions that had been adopted in the wake of *Brown* limited admission to advantaged African Americans. As the "old-style southern segregation" gave way to a "new-style class segregation," Christopher Jencks and David Riesman found in the late 1960s, access to southern universities was limited to the "abler children of college educated Negroes," who were "often well enough schooled and well enough heeled" to compete on equal terms with white college applicants.[13]

The new college entrance requirements that limited access to "well-heeled" African Americans were only one of the policies that educational and political leaders institutionalized in the wake of the Supreme Court's *Brown* decision. The Court's landmark ruling created new educational possibilities, and defining what those possibilities were became the central issue in the state and the region during the late 1950s. After African American activists in ten South Carolina cities and towns petitioned for desegregation, whites organized citizens' councils and, with the help of the legislature, repressed the NAACP. As significant as massive resistance was in deferring desegregation, it was only part of a broader, more sophisticated effort to block black access to educational institutions. Unlike governors in Arkansas, Alabama, and Mississippi, whose defiance of court-ordered desegregation brought federal intervention, South Carolina's stable, close-knit, and clever educational and political leadership found more legally defensible and durable solutions to the challenges posed by *Brown.* Drawing upon and refining educational policies and practices that had been adopted in the 1940s and early 1950s, David W. Robinson encouraged school boards to expand testing and tracking in the public schools. Well before massive resistance collapsed and the courts and the federal government forced school boards in the state to desegregate the public schools, educational authorities institutionalized more rational restrictions that limited access to advantaged African Americans.[14]

The architect of these evasions was David W. Robinson, who designed the state's response to African American demands for salary equalization and access to universities and the professions in the 1940s and early 1950s. In 1956 Robinson was appointed chief counsel of the state's Segregation Committee, chaired by state senator L. Marion Gressette. Robinson supervised a staff of the state's ablest attorneys, who were charged with conducting "research to determine the nature of school problems, [determining] how they can be met within the law, and advis[ing] school boards on the administration of school laws." While the Court's 1954 decision struck down state-enforced segregation, the 1955 implementation decree, *Brown II,* gave local educational authorities "primary responsibility for elucidating, assessing, and solving" the problems of desegregation. After the Court remanded the *Briggs* case to South Carolina in May 1955, Judge John J. Parker affirmed these prerogatives, ruling that the Court "has not decided that the federal courts are to take over or regulate the public schools of the states."[15]

Calling for "calm and considered thinking," Robinson outlined a strategy for rationalizing, limiting, and controlling the process of desegregation. "The best chance of evolving something satisfactory," Robinson told Byrnes in July 1954, "is to leave the problem in local hands." As Parker interpreted *Brown,* local authorities were not required to "mix persons of different races in the public schools. What it [the Supreme Court] has decided, and all that it has decided," he wrote, "is that a state may not deny any person on account of race the right to attend any school that it maintains." If parents chose different schools, Parker held, "no violation of the constitution is involved." Parker's ruling was the most significant decision to emerge from the district court's reconsideration of the five school segregation cases, and it governed desegregation in the state and the region for more than a decade.[16]

To entice blacks to remain in segregated schools, Robinson urged local officials to equalize school facilities, because "newer, more modern building[s] will tend to keep the Negroes in Negro schools." As much as Robinson hoped that blacks would choose to remain in all-black institutions, he recognized that many African Americans wanted to desegregate schools, and he helped secure passage of laws that strengthened the power and authority of local officials over student assignment. "One of the first things the staff recommended," Robinson recalls, was passage of legislation that gave "local school boards the discretion and power to assign pupils in the best interests of education." South Carolina's pupil placement law, like those adopted in nine other southern states, used ostensibly neutral criteria to limit desegregation. Robinson encouraged school officials to exploit racial differences in educational achievement that were a product of generations of economic and educational discrimination. "There are very few Negroes educationally qualified to go to school with similarly aged white children." Most blacks, he wrote, "can be disqualified by the board of trustees for educational reasons." Like other proponents of tokenism, Robinson believed that standardized tests could be used to prevent the "mixing" of large numbers of whites and blacks and preserve "standards." He recognized that some African Americans would qualify for admission, but he believed that "a few Negroes in white schools would not create severe problems." Following the *Brown* and *Briggs* decisions, Robinson designed a higher stage of white supremacy in education that limited black access to schools, colleges, and universities.[17]

Because *Brown* stiffened white resistance and deprived the NAACP of the momentum and support needed to mount an effective campaign for school desegregation, the direct action demonstrations of African American students were required to end the practice of segregation in the public schools. Sit-ins and demonstrations in Charleston during the early 1960s were a product of a generation of institutional development in the schools. Students from Burke High School played a particularly important role. "Teachers gave us high ideals and ambition," recalls James Blake, who led the movement in Charleston. "They taught us we were first-class citizens." Most of the Burke students who participated in the sit-ins were on the honor roll. Many were deeply involved in the school's extracurricular program that had been created in the 1940s to train student leaders. Searching for a way to express what classes and extracurricular activities taught them, Blake and other students turned to two respected teachers, Eugene Hunt and J. Michael Graves, for advice and guidance. "There was nothing we couldn't talk to them about," recalls Blake. "What should we do? What would you do? Would you stage a sit-in at Woolworth's?" Graves remembers them asking. "I told them that I would probably go and sit down and be served. We encouraged them to do the kind of thing they did." Inspired by their teachers and by students at South Carolina State College, Burke students staged sit-ins during the spring of 1960 that provided Charleston's black community with new ways to realize the rights expressed in *Brown* and stirred the local NAACP, which renewed its efforts to desegregate the schools.[18]

As attorneys prepared for the desegregation case to come to trial in August 1963, student leaders planned a direct action campaign that created the kind of disorder and instability that forced whites to accept court-ordered desegregation. During the summer of 1963, hundreds of African American young people demonstrated in the streets and assembled at night for mass meetings in one of the city's black churches. It was in this context of continuing demonstrations that Judge Robert Martin ordered the Charleston School Board to admit eleven African American students to white schools in August 1963. Facing pressure from local black demonstrators, the NAACP, the courts, and the Justice Department, the board had little choice but to comply with the ruling. *News and Courier* editor Thomas Waring wrote that the board decided to accept the ruling "in order to avoid chaos."[19]

The board's compliance with Martin's desegregation order was based on its desire to maintain control of the public schools. Drawing upon policies and practices developed and refined in the 1940s and 1950s, the board rationalized restrictions that could no longer be sanctioned by law. It expanded testing and tracking in the public schools and created new forms of interdistrict segregation based on class and residence rather than caste and race.

Martin rejected the board's contention that genetic differences "were a rational basis for segregation of the races in schools," but within days Gressette Committee lawyers sent a memo titled "A Plan in Regard to the Integration Push in the Public Schools" to officials throughout the state. "Our fight since 1954" has been to "limit the federal court's responsibility to racial matters," Robinson wrote. As advisers to school boards, Robinson and his colleagues "tried to obtain decrees that recognize [the] board's responsibility to assign pupils to further the best educational interests of the pupil." In December 1963 Robinson told Marion Gressette that "we need to press for a state-wide I.Q. and achievement test administered in all of our schools. This difference in achievement between the two races may be our last line of defense."[20]

In spite of the objections of the NAACP, the school board crafted a desegregation plan that was based in part on Robinson's argument that student's educational needs could be used to maintain segregation. The board used student's scores on the Iowa Tests of Educational Development to deny transfers, arguing that students' "educational needs" could be best met in segregated schools. Hampered by generations of educational exclusion, segregation, and discrimination, the educational achievement of African American students lagged behind that of whites, and acting on Robinson's advice, the board used standardized tests to exploit this lag and limit African American access. By 1964 only seventy-nine African Americans, less than 1 percent of the city's total black enrollment, attended desegregated schools. Persistent legal and political pressure tried to end this isolation, but in Charleston, as elsewhere, legal remedies were undercut by educational and economic realities.[21]

The African American students who desegregated Rivers High School in Charleston found that isolation was the price of access. Charleston school officials created a "very demanding track" for "more able students," and when the schools were desegregated in 1963, Millicent Brown, the daughter of state NAACP leader J. Arthur Brown, was the only African American student in the college preparatory track at Rivers. Like other heirs of the state's African American elite, Brown's class background and schooling prepared her to compete with—and outperform—white students. Her English teacher described Brown as "enchanted with literature. She is the bright light in the class." Solomon Breibart, who taught her history, remembers her as "a very good student, critical and informed about what was going on." Fellow students, however, resented her "fine" work and harassed her inside and outside of class. When Brown appeared in the corridor, other students would clear the hall and cling to the wall, forcing her to walk alone. When she entered a bathroom, students would chant "2–4–6–8 we don't want to integrate," and "go back to your own school, jigaboo." Another African American student, Jacqueline Ford, who joined Brown at Rivers in 1964, recalls feeling that "I didn't belong." Most students would not associate with either Ford or Brown, leaving both isolated, caught between whites that ignored them and blacks that rejected them for "trying to act white." The problems they faced discouraged other students from seeking access to Rivers and left those who did isolated in what black students found to be lonely, hostile, and harmful educational environments.[22]

As increasing numbers of whites and advantaged blacks left Charleston for the suburbs, desegregation became increasingly difficult to achieve in the city. In 1969 the NAACP sought to join the predominately black and white districts in a metropolitan desegregation suit. By the 1960s the racial typography of the Charleston County School District resembled a series of concentric circles. The predominately black city schools were surrounded by a ring of largely white suburban districts that were in turn encircled by mostly black rural districts. Before the suit was filed, the state legislature passed a consolidation act that stymied the NAACP's attempts to achieve interdistrict desegregation. Passed in 1968, this legislation created a consolidated school district that equalized educational expenditures between constituent districts at the same time that it preserved constituent district boundaries that remained the chief obstacle to desegregation. Just as the state's leadership limited the educational impact of previous legal challenges, in the late 1960s it created a new school district that allowed whites to comply with constitutional requirements in a way that preserved and perpetuated high levels of interdistrict segregation, making class, not caste, and residence, not race, the chief arbiters of educational opportunity. Consolidation in Charleston County was a fitting conclusion to a quarter century of sophisticated white resistance, another example of how educational and political leaders rationalized restrictions that had once rested on race. Like earlier responses to African American demands for equality and access, this legislation withstood judicial scrutiny in the federal courts, which held that consolidation was enacted "to equalize funding throughout the county" and not for any discriminatory purpose.[23]

African Americans won significant victories in the campaign for equality and access in South Carolina, but educational and political authorities responded by creating a new, higher stage of white supremacy in education. The elimination of caste constraints, the improvement of African American educational institutions, the repudiation of segregation laws, and the desegregation of schools, colleges, and universities created the possibility that black and white educational cultures, traditions, and institutions might be merged. That possibility, the possibility of whites and blacks sharing power in educational institutions, was foreclosed by policies and practices that limited access to advantaged African Americans and kept most African Americans in predominately black educational institutions. What the NAACP and local African American activists did not anticipate was the strength and sophistication of white resistance to educational equality that emerged as caste restrictions and segregation laws were eliminated. A generation of NAACP litigation and African American activism swept away state-sanctioned segregation, but educational and political authorities in South Carolina created a higher, more sophisticated system of white supremacy in education, which was institutionalized in other southern states in the quarter century after 1945. The durability of these policies suggests that segregation may not be the highest stage of white supremacy.

Notes

1. Robert Coles, *Farewell to the South* (Boston: Little, Brown, 1972), 83–84; Timothy B. Tyson, "Dynamite and 'The Silent South': A Story from the Second Reconstruction in South Carolina," in *Jumpin' Jim Crow: Southern Politics from Civil War to Civil Rights*, ed. Jane Dailey, Glenda Elizabeth Gilmore, and Bryant Simon (Princeton, N.J.: Princeton University Press, 2000), 275–97.

2. John W. Cell, *The Highest Stage of White Supremacy* (New York: Oxford University Press, 1982); Michael J. Klarman, *From Jim Crow to Civil Rights* (New York: Oxford University Press, 2003).

3. Gunnar Myrdal, *An American Dilemma: The Negro Problem and Modern Democracy* (New York: Harper, 1944), 320; Thurgood Marshall, Memorandum to Branch Presidents, September 13, 1937, box I-C-290, NAACP Papers, Manuscripts Division, Library of Congress, Washington, D.C. (hereafter NAACP Papers); "Teachers Salaries in Black and White," box II-B- 89, NAACP Papers; Thurgood Marshall, interview by Ed Erwin, February 15, 1977, Columbia University Oral History Collection, Butler Library, Columbia University, New York; *Mills v. Board of Trustees of Anne Arundel County,* 30 F. Supp. 245 (1939).

4. Louise Jones DuBose, *The Palmetto Who's Who* (Hopkinsville, Ky.: Historical Record Association, 1963); Office of the State Superintendent of Education, June 11, 1941, *U.S. v. Charleston County School District,* case number 81–50–6, plaintiff's exhibit, 101, Charleston Federal Court, Charleston, South Carolina; Ben Wood, interview by Gary Saretsky, November 7, 1977, Princeton, N.J., vol. 2, 35, Ben Wood Papers, Educational Testing Service Archives, Princeton, N.J. (hereafter Wood Papers); Excerpts of Special Committee to Investigate State Laws Dealing with Education, 1–2, file 149, reel 18, Wood papers; W. C. McCall to Ben Wood, November 15, 1940; Ben Wood to D. W. Robinson, March 24, 1941, file 149, reel 18, Wood Papers; V. O. Key, *Southern Politics in State and Nation* (New York: Random House, 1949), 154; Deficiency Appropriation Act, 1945–1946, Section 76, 86, box 110–34, J. Waties Waring Papers, Moorland Spingarn Library, Howard University, Washington, D.C.

5. Tinsley E. Yarbrough, *A Passion for Justice: J. Waties Waring and Civil Rights* (New York: Oxford University Press, 1987), 45–6; *Thompson v. Gibbes,* 60 F. Supp. 872 at 875, 876; Frank A. Decosta, "The Education of Negroes in South Carolina," *Journal of Negro Education* 17 (Summer 1948): 350–60; Edgar Brown to J. Waties Waring, June 6, 1945, quoted in Yarbrough, *Passion for Justice,* 46.

6. *Seventy-Eighth Annual Report of the State Superintendent of Education of the State of South Carolina* (Columbia: South Carolina General Assembly, 1946), 174; *Biennial Survey of Education in the United States, 1946–1948* (Washington, D.C.: Government Printing Office, 1954), 41; Charleston Board of School Commissioners Minute Books (CBSCMB), March 18, 1948, Office of Archives and Records (OAR), Charleston County School District (CCSD), North Charleston, South Carolina; Wood to Robinson, letter, March 24, 1941, file 149, reel 18, Wood Papers; *Charleston News and Courier,* undated clipping, Teacher Salaries Comparative, Box 896, OAR, CCSD.

7. Eugene Hunt, interview by the author, Charleston, South Carolina, July 11, 1990; Henry Hutchinson, interview by the author, Charleston, South Carolina, July 18, 1990; Lois Simms, *A Chalk and Chalkboard Career in Carolina* (New York: Vantage, 1995), 21–35; George Peabody College for Teachers, *The Public Schools of Charleston, South Carolina* (Nashville: Division of Surveys and Field Services, 1949), 36; Septima Clark, *Echo in My Soul* (New York: Dutton, 1962), 80–88; Patrick McCauley and Edward Ball, eds., *Southern Schools: Progress and Problems* (Nashville: Southern Education Reporting Service, 1959), 44, 132, 152; Harry Ashmore, *The Negro and the Schools* (Chapel Hill: University of North Carolina Press, 1954), 152–157; Ambrose Caliver, "Certain Significant Developments in the Education of Negroes During the Past Generation," *Journal of Negro History* 35 (April 1950): 118; Martin Jenkins, "Enrollment in Institutions of Higher Education of Negroes, 1950–51," *Journal of Negro Education* 20 (Spring 1951): 208.

8. *Missouri ex. rel. Gaines v. Canada,* 305 U.S. 337 (1938); Wrighten to Dean of the Law School, letter, June 30, 1946; James Hinton to Thurgood Marshall, n.d.; Robert Carter to Harold Boulware, letter, October 25, 1946; Hinton to Marshall, November 29, 1946, NAACP Papers, box II-B-204; *Wrighten v. Board of Trustees of University of South Carolina,* 72 F. Supp 948 (1947).

9. Jerold S. Auerbach, *Unequal Justice: Lawyers and Social Change in Modern America* (New York: Oxford University Press, 1976), 293–94; Robert Stevens, *Law School: Legal Education in America from the 1850s to the 1980s* (Chapel Hill: University of North Carolina Press, 1983), 182; "Law Graduates Get Diplomas; Admissions," *State*, undated clipping, University of South Carolina Law School Archives, University of South Carolina, Columbia.

10. George C. Rogers Jr., *Generations of Lawyers* (Columbia: South Carolina Bar Foundation, 1992), 205, 208; Transactions of the Fifty-Third Annual Meeting of the South Carolina Bar Association, 1947, 24, Law School Archives, University of South Carolina. "Transactions of the Fifty-Fourth Annual Meeting of the South Carolina Bar Association," *Law Quarterly* 1 (September 1948): 15; *Journal of the Senate, 1948* (Columbia: South Carolina General Assembly, 1948), 1472; *Richardson v. McFadden*, 540 F. 2d 744 (1976); Matthew Perry, interview by Grace J. McFadden, August 18, 1980, quoted in "The Quest for Civil Rights," University of South Carolina Film Library; Jay Bender, "One Week That Changed the State," *South Carolina Lawyer* 11 (November–December 1999), 37; Matthew Perry, interview by William Hine, June 19, 1995, South Carolina State University Historical Collection, Miller F. Whittaker Library, South Carolina State University, Orangeburg; William Peters, "A Southern Success Story," *Redbook* 115 (June 1960): 104; *Richardson v. McFadden*, case number 73–2512, trial transcript, vol. I, 10; National Archives, Philadelphia, Pennsylvania; Frank Edward Cain to President Norman O. Smith, January 9, 1952, Negro Problem file, Smith Papers, University Archives, Caroliniana Library, University of South Carolina, Columbia, South Carolina.

11. Jack Greenberg, *Crusaders in the Courts: How a Dedicated Band of Lawyers Fought the Civil Rights Revolution* (New York: BasicBooks, 1994), 38; *Richardson v. McFadden*, trial transcript, vol. II, 543; Peters, "Southern Success Story," 104.

12. *Sweatt v. Painter*, 339 U.S. 629 (1950); *Briggs v. Elliott*, 98 F. Supp. 529 (U.S. Dist. Ct. 1951); W. C. McCall to Dr. Bowles and Dr. Fels, October 23, 1953; Donald Russell to Dr. R.F. Poole, May 14, 1954; W. L. Williams to Donald Russell, November 10, 1953, Russell Exams and Counseling file, 1953–1954, University Archives; University of South Carolina, Faculty Minutes, May 27, 1954; Board of Trustees of the University of South Carolina, Minutes, May 28, 1954, Caroliniana Library, Manuscripts Department; Chester C. Travelstead, "I Was There," Travelstead, topical file, University Archives; Committee on Entrance Examinations, Minutes, December 6, 1955, Russell Exams and Counseling file, 1955–1956, University Archives; South Carolina College Entrance Examination Program Committee, Minutes, February 6, 1958, Sumwalt, Examination and Counseling Bureau file, 1957–1958, University Archives; Earl Black, *Southern Governors and Civil Rights: Race, Segregation and Campaign Issues in the Second Reconstruction* (Cambridge, Mass.: Harvard University Press, 1976), 82; Robert A. Pratt, *We Shall Not Be Moved: The Desegregation of the University of Georgia* (Athens: University of Georgia Press, 2002), 17; S. Donald Karl, *The College Handbook* (New York: College Entrance Examination Board, 1959–1965); *Ayers v. Allain*, 893 F. 2d 732 (1990) examines the history of desegregation at the University of Mississippi.

13. *State*, January, 16, 17, 18, 1958; "Application for Entrance Examination to Enter the University of South Carolina," Cornell Franklin and James Jones, February 11, 1958, Sumwalt Papers, University Archives; Meeting of the Board of Trustees, October 24, 1951, Sumwalt Papers; *Papers of the NAACP, Part 3: The Campaign for Educational Equality. Series D: Central Office Records, 1956–1965. Group III, Series A, General Office File, Desegregation-Schools, South Carolina*, ed. John H. Bracey Jr. and August Meier (Bethesda, Md.: University Publications of America, 1995), reel 8, frames 0296–0377; *Papers of the NAACP, Part 22: Legal Department Administrative Files, 1956–1965. Group V, Series B Administrative Files. General Office File-Schools South Carolina*, ed. John H. Bracey Jr. and August Meier

(Bethesda, Md.: University Publications of America, 1995), reel 26, frames 22–34; *State*, July 12, 1970; Maxie Myron Cox Jr., "1963–The Year of Decision: Desegregation in South Carolina" (Ph.D. dissertation, University of South Carolina, 1996), 93–101; Christopher Jencks and David Riesman, *The Academic Revolution* (Garden City, N.Y.: Doubleday, 1968), 411, 448.

14. *Brown v. the Board of Education*, 347 U.S. 483 (1954); for accounts of school and university desegregation in other southern states, see especially Tony Freyer, *The Little Rock Crisis* (Westport, Conn.: Greenwood, 1984); Taylor Branch, *Parting the Waters: America in the King Years, 1954–63* (New York: Simon and Schuster, 1988), 647–72; William Doyle, *An American Insurrection: The Battle of Oxford, Mississippi, 1962* (New York: Doubleday, 2001); Mark V. Tushnet, *Making Civil Rights Law* (New York: Oxford, 1994); Amilcar Shabazz, *Advancing Democracy: African Americans and the Struggle for Access and Equity in Higher Education in Texas* (Chapel Hill: University of North Carolina Press, 2004); Robert J. Norrell, *Reaping the Whirlwind: The Civil Rights Movement in Tuskegee* (New York: Random House, 1985); E. Culpepper Clark, *The Schoolhouse Door: Segregation's Stand at the University of Alabama* (New York: Oxford University Press, 1993).

15. The South Carolina School Committee, May 5, 1983, Desegregation files, David W. Robinson Papers, South Carolina State Archives, Columbia; Gressette Committee, "Statement," August 3, 1955, William D. Workman Jr. Collection, Box 20, Integration, Civil Rights file, South Carolina Political Collections, University of South Carolina; *Charleston News and Courier*, August 18, 1955; *Brown v. the Board of Education*, 349 U.S. 294 (1955), in *Argument: Oral Arguments before the Supreme Court*, ed. Leon Friedman (New York: Chelsea House, 1983), 534; *Briggs v. Elliott*, 132 F. Supp. 776 (U.S. Dist. Ct. 1955), 777.

16. David W. Robinson to James Byrnes, July 13, 1954, Correspondence, Robinson Papers; *Briggs* at 777.

17. David W. Robinson to T. C. Callison and Robert McC. Figg, June 5, 1954, Correspondence, Robinson Papers; Undated Memorandum, Legal Memoranda, 1954–1972; Memorandum, May 5, 1983, Desegregation files, Robinson Papers.

18. William Henry Chafe, *Civilities and Civil Rights: Greensboro, North Carolina, and the Black Struggle for Freedom* (New York: Oxford University Press, 1980), 17–34; James Blake, interview by author, Charleston, South Carolina, July 17, 1990; R. Scott Baker, "Ambiguous Legacies: The NAACP's Legal Campaign against Segregation in Charleston, South Carolina, 1935–1975" (Ph.D. dissertation, Columbia University, 1993); Hunt interview; J. Michael Graves, interview by author, Charleston, South Carolina, July 16, 1990; Burke *Parvenue*, March 1960, Burke High School Library, Charleston, South Carolina.

19. *State*, June 6, 1963; "The Charleston Movement," n.d., Record Group 1–III-28, Civil Rights-South Carolina, Highlander Research Center, New Market, Tennessee; *Charleston Inquirer*, June 21, 1963; Blake interview; *Brown v. School District Number 20*, 226 F. Supp. 819 (1963); CBSCMB, August 22, 24, 1963; *Charleston News and Courier*, August 24, 1963.

20. "A Plan in Regard to the Integration Push in the Public Schools of South Carolina," August 22, 1963, plaintiff's exhibit 923, *U.S. v. Charleston County*, case number 81–50–6; David W. Robinson to Senator L. Marion Gressette, December 10, 1963, plaintiff's exhibit 927; Augustus T. Graydon to D. W. Robinson, August 22, 1963, Correspondence, Robinson Papers; *U.S. v. Charleston County*, plaintiff's exhibits 1403 and 1406.

21. CBSCMB, February 10, 1965; December 11, 1963; March 11, 1964; October 14, 1964; October 13, 1965; Information for the Board, number 1868, n.d., box 862, OAR, CCSD; Plaintiff's Motions, *Brown v. School District Number 20*, May 20, 1966.

22. Millicent Brown, interview by author, Charleston, South Carolina, August 9, 1989; November 3, 1989; July 6, 1990; July 1, 1990; Jacqueline Ford, interview by author, Charleston, South Carolina, September 12, 1991; Soloman Briebart, interview by author, Charleston,

South Carolina, September 11, 1991; Robert Rosen, interview by author, Charleston, South Carolina, July 17, 1990; Information for the Board, number 1868, OAR, CCSD.

23. *U.S. v. Charleston County*, trial transcript, day 10, 9, 41–42; Joseph Dardeen, deposition, *U. S. v. Charleston County*, 115; Thomas Carrere, Memo, Major Reservations Concerning Gibson Bill, Box 862, OAR, CCSD; *U.S. v. Charleston County*, trial transcript, day 25, 32–41; day 13, 142–3; day 6, 89; *U.S. v. Charleston County School District*, 758 Fed. Supp. 1513 (1990); *U. S. v. Charleston County School District*, 960 F. 2d 1227 (1992).

Part 5 ∽ Retrospectives

This fifth section of the book contains transcriptions of the autobiographical remarks delivered at the conference by some of the most prominent figures in the civil rights movement in South Carolina. Taken as a whole, their personal reflections provide a unique insight into the state's response to the civil rights movement and remind us of the numerous sacrifices, both personal and professional, that these brave men and women were prepared to make in pursuit of the right to live as equal citizens.

The first group of reflections focuses on the years from the filing of the first case to desegregate public schools (*Briggs v. Elliott* in Clarendon County) to the admission of the first black student (Harvey Gantt) to a state university (Clemson). John Hope Franklin, the dean of American historians, begins with his memories of the role he played in conducting the historical research for the NAACP's first legal briefs against racially segregated schools. He is followed by Joseph A. De Laine Jr., son of the original leader in the landmark *Briggs* case, and Beatrice Brown Rivers, one of the original *Briggs* plaintiffs, who discuss the hardships their families faced. Following their comments, a question and answer session was held, in which all three participants amplified their remarks to comment on a number of subjects concerning race relations in the state, from the original cases that made up *Brown v. Board of Education* to the issue of paying reparations to the descendants of slaves. This is followed by comments from Charles McDew, first chairman of the Student Nonviolent Coordinating Committee, and Constance Curry, leader of the National Student Association, who both reflect on the people they met and the perils they encountered as student organizers in rural South Carolina during the early 1960s. Closing this section are Matthew J. Perry Jr. and Harvey B. Gantt, who discuss the challenges they faced, as the lead attorney and the plaintiff, respectively, in the campaign to desegregate Clemson College.

By 1965 the legal edifice of South Carolina's Jim Crow regime had been destroyed, but there remained the task of implementing equal rights and promoting mutual respect within the new framework. If there were any doubts about how difficult those tasks would be, they were removed on the night of February 8, 1968, when at the climax of demonstrations against the continuation of de facto segregation in Orangeburg, state law enforcement officers fired on a crowd of students from South Carolina State College—killing three people and wounding at least twenty-seven.

The second group of reflections in this section come from persons who were involved in that most violent, tragic, and controversial racial confrontation in modern South Carolina history. Cleveland Sellers, the most visible student leader on that fateful evening, opens it with his memories of the terror that occurred and the ways in which official accounts misrepresented what actually happened. Jordan Simmons concurs in a moving account of what it felt like to be one of the surviving victims. They are followed by Jack Bass, coauthor with Jack Nelson of *The Orangeburg Massacre*—the under-publicized but definitive account of this still-controversial incident, originally published in 1970—who provides a summary of the events that led to the confrontation and a detailed account of the eight seconds of gunfire that produced the casualties. William C. Hine, a professor of history at Orangeburg's South Carolina State University, closes the section with his essay "'We're Not There Yet': Orangeburg, 1968–2003," a meditative analysis of the different perspectives that the state's black and white citizens had on the incident and the ways in which the gap between them has only partially narrowed in the intervening years.

Briggs v. Elliott a Half Century Later

John Hope Franklin

Thank you very much. It's a very great honor to be here this evening. I remember so well the first Citadel conference that I came to some years ago and Bo, I don't remember how long ago it was, but I remember so well that I spoke there on "Pursuing Southern History, A Strange Career," which was in the proceedings of that conference. And I was thinking about that this evening as I came onto the campus and as I saw some change in the campus since the first time that I was here; and I want to commend the president and all the others who are responsible for the changes. I was moved also by the mayor's comment about the courage that it took to stand up at that particular time, and I was thinking as he talked about the courage that it took 1965 when we marched from Selma to Montgomery, and you can call it courage if you want to, but I was as scared as I could be! I never have been so afraid in my life as I was that day marching through the narrow streets of Montgomery and not knowing who, as the mayor said, on the other side was going to mow me down as it were. And it came home to me when I saw the director of the University of Chicago Press, who is an old and dear friend and who had persuaded me in 1946 to write *From Slavery to Freedom*. He was marching too and he was white, and he was so thirsty that he went into some refreshment stand there on the streets of Montgomery to get some kind of cold Coke or soda of some kind, and he was refused service. He said that for the first time he realized—he'd never been denied anything before in his life—for the first time he realized what it meant to be ostracized or to be segregated against or to be discriminated against. And that was for him the most sobering experience of his life up to that time. So that it takes all kinds and it takes all kinds of experiences to stand up for what is right and just.

The struggle to free the children of South Carolina goes back a long way, but even as they were suffering discrimination in the public schools of South Carolina, there were those who were trying to lay the groundwork for the struggle that was to come, to lay the groundwork quite some distance away. And it was in Kentucky in 1947 and 1948 that some of the groundwork was laid for *Briggs*

v. Elliott, Brown v. Board of Education and the other school desegregation cases
that came up to the court in 1952. In 1948 I had been teaching at Howard University for one year, and the word was getting around that I had written a few
things. And I met Thurgood Marshall in the spring of 1948, and he said to me,
"You look like you might be able to help us in our case." I said, "What is the
case?" He said, "Well, we've got a man who is applying to the University of Kentucky to study history and he has been denied admission. And we think that you
can prove that the University of Kentucky is a place that he ought to be permitted to go because it's argued that he can get what he wants at the Kentucky State
College for Negroes at Frankfort." And he said, "We know he can't, but we have
to prove that he cannot." And so he asked me if I would go out to Kentucky
and study the library resources of the University of Kentucky and the library
resources of Kentucky State College for Negroes and do the same thing with
respect to faculty and with respect to curriculum, and I did. And then we all went
out there, that is, Thurgood Marshall and James Nabret and I went out to Frankfort, and I was going to be the expert witness in the case. And I was more than
anxious to be a witness in the case not merely because I was anxious to do justice for Lyman Johnson and get him into the University of Kentucky, but also
because my father was a lawyer and I had at one point wanted to be a lawyer and
then was spellbound by a young white professor at Fisk University and forgot the
practice of the law altogether. And this was my chance to vindicate my waywardness by showing my father that I could contribute to the sound interpretation of
the law. And so I was more than diligent in my study of the problems of the University of Kentucky, the Kentucky State College for Negroes, and I was very much
prepared to take the stand and strike a blow for justice.

As we went to the university, to the federal court in Frankfort, the president
of the University of Kentucky was asked to come to the witness stand, and the
counsel for the defendant asked him a few questions, and the burden of the effort
of the president of the University of Kentucky was to show how ordinary and
common and unprepared the University of Kentucky was compared to Kentucky
State College for Negroes. And he argued that there was nothing that they had at
the University of Kentucky that Lyman Johnson couldn't get at the Kentucky
State College for Negroes. And he made quite a splash, and as he was making that
splash, I watched Thurgood Marshall, who was downcast. I said, "Oh my goodness what's wrong?" And after the testimony of the president of the University of
Kentucky, Thurgood asked the judge, Judge H. Church Ford, if he could have a
recess, and the judge said yes. And we all went out, and Thurgood said, "They
don't have a case." He said if this is the best they could do, they don't have a case.
"I'm going to ask the judge to dismiss this case and rule in favor of our client."
And the other lawyers, not nearly as brazen and as confident as Thurgood Marshall was, said, "Are you sure you want to do that?" He said, "I know what I'm
doing. Yes, this is what I want to do."

When we went back into court, Thurgood arose and said, "May it please the Court, I would like to suggest, your Honor, that in view of the fact that the University of Kentucky does not have a case, cannot make a case, that you rule in favor of our client and command the University of Kentucky to admit him forthwith." Silence in the courtroom. And the judge said, "I'm going to do just that." And he said, "I rule that Lyman Johnson be admitted to the University of Kentucky forthwith." And then he gave the president of the University a lecture. He said, "You ought to be ashamed to come in here and to claim that you are—that the Kentucky State College for Negroes is on a base of equality with the University of Kentucky." And with that he pounded his gavel and dismissed us all. I suppose I was the only person really dejected about the decision. I'm all dressed up and nowhere to go. And I was not able to vindicate my waywardness by showing my father at long last that I could handle a legal matter. And so I was somewhat dejected, and I remained not only dejected, but at least somewhat disappointed until I was awarded an honorary degree about five or six years ago from the University of Kentucky, and among the things that they praised me for was the fact that I had been a participant, not a litigant, but a participant in the case against the University of Kentucky that was brought in behalf of Lyman Johnson. And that was one of the things for which they cited me as deserving of an honorary degree from the University of Kentucky, and I thought that was sort of an odd way to get into the good graces of the university, but there I was.

And so we had that kind of experience in 1948, that was the way it was until we began to bring suits against the boards of education and county school boards throughout the South. You remember that there had been a long and interesting and successful drive to get students admitted to graduate and professional schools throughout the South. There had been the case of *Sweatt v. Painter* in Texas. There was the case of *McLaurin v. Oklahoma,* and then there was the civil rights transportation case of *Morgan v. Virginia,* which of course outlawed segregation in transportation, but we had not had any real strike at where it was most important, that is in the precollegiate level of public education.

The great fight, then, was to get this task accomplished. It was extraordinarily difficult, and one can only sense the difficulty if one could witness the various obstructions that were placed in the paths of people who wanted to bring cases, bring suits against the various lower schools in various parts of the South. And yet at long last, there were those courageous people in South Carolina who were willing to stand up. There were those people in the District of Columbia who stood up. There were those in the state of Delaware who were willing to stand up, and those in the state of Kansas who were willing to stand up. And the courage that these people displayed is the courage that is unmatched, I think, by any people who have entered into military battle or any other kind of battle. And one shudders merely to think of the dangers that they faced every day of their lives, and one feels nothing but sorrow for the way in which one after one was picked off and fired. All you had to do was to appear at a mass meeting where the case was being planned or to put one's name as a participating plaintiff—well, that's all one had to do in order to lose one's job or be blacklisted. We speak of the blacklist of the Hollywood Ten and that crowd out there, but the blacklist in South Carolina, the blacklist in Maryland, in Delaware, the blacklist in the District of Columbia, and the blacklist in Kansas were indescribable when you think of what it meant to the people who were the victims of these blacklists. And yet, there they were. But they stood their ground. They found other ways to make a living, and they were at times the beneficiaries of the largess of those who had not lost their jobs but who were willing to share with these people whatever they had so they could feed their children and clothe them and to make it possible for them to continue to live a decent, upstanding life.

When these cases finally went to the United States Supreme Court, after having made their way up through the district and the circuit courts, there they were in the United States Supreme Court. And in 1952 they were argued before the Court, and in 1953 the Court, I personally believe, was bidding for more time in order to do something and yet was afraid to do the right thing. In 1953 the Court merely remanded the cases back to the courts of origin and raised certain other questions. The questions had to do with the intent of the framers of the Fourteenth Amendment in 1867 and 1868. What was the intent of the framers of the Fourteenth Amendment with respect to the whole question of the segregation of schools? What was the intent of those who ratified the Fourteenth Amendment with respect to their view of segregation in schools and so on and on? And they asked the litigants to come up with answers, and they asked their lawyers to prepare briefs containing these arguments and to come back and argue them in the fall of 1953. These were historical questions, pure and simple, and the people on both sides were simply petrified as to what they could do. How can they answer these questions? They were not historians. They didn't know how to gather even the evidence that would prove these points one way or the other. And so they began to cast around for people who might be able to answer these questions.

I was teaching that summer, the summer of 1953, I was teaching at Cornell University in Ithaca, New York. I was on what I called my missionary circuits. I had given to several universities by this time a sense of smug satisfaction that they were on the right side. Harvard University invited me in 1950 to teach in the summer school. Never mind that I had two degrees from Harvard University, never mind that I had published several books; they just wanted me there for a few weeks, and so I agreed to go. At the end of one summer they asked me if I would teach again. I said, "No, I've done it one time. I know better now. Why should I come back here? I'll go somewhere else and let someone else salve their conscience." So I went the next winter of 1953 to the University of Wisconsin to teach one semester. And there was some discussion among the students as to whether they could persuade the faculty, the Department of History, to invite me to teach on a more stable and more extended basis, and there was no favorable response on the part of the history department of that.

I went on from Wisconsin to teach at Cornell University. I was teaching there in the summer of 1953 when one day I came into the classroom before they were settled for class and I saw them passing around a letter or what seemed to be a letter, and I didn't know what it was and I didn't express any great curiosity although I *did* want to know what was in the letter that was circulating. And so one student came to me at the end of class and said we just want you to know that we're writing a letter to the Department of History asking them to invite you to be a professor in the department. I said, "Well, good luck to you." That was the last I heard of that, and the conscience of Cornell University along with others was salved by that experience. But when I was getting ready to leave Ithaca, New York, in August 1953, I got a call from Thurgood Marshall. And Thurgood asked me, "Have you been keeping up with what's going on in the cases?" I said, "Yes." He said, "Well, you know what I want you to do?" I said, "No." He said, "I want you to come and work for me this fall." I said, "Man, I've got to go back to the university. I've got to go back to my job at Howard University." He said, and I cannot quote him here. He said, "If you don't show up in New York on the first of August," and then he told me what he would do to me. Thurgood Marshall was a man of many words if he wanted to be, but he was a man of very direct action when he wanted to be. And so I simply said, "Yes sir, I'll be there." And so he wanted me to come to—I went up to see him and he said, "Look, we've got to answer these questions that the court has asked, and so I want you to sort of head the team of historians, and I want you to get to work and find some answers for us."

I began to travel every week to New York City from Washington. It became so routine that I could do it almost impulsively without any preparation. I would go on Thursday about noon, get to New York City about 4:30 or 5:00, and this is before the air shuttles. You're not shuttling up to New York, you've got to get on the train and go there. They always had a room for me at the Algonquin Hotel, and that was almost worth going to New York for; and I would go and check in at my hotel and go around the corner, just two blocks, to the Legal Defense Fund office, and Thurgood would be there. I never went to that office that he wasn't there. He was there sitting, working, working, working. There were others whom he had enlisted, other nonlegal researchers. There was Rayford Logan from Howard University, my colleague there. There was C. Vann Woodward, by this time at Yale. There was Al Kelly from Wayne State University, the great constitutional historian, and there were others: some psychologists, some sociologists, and others. Also there was Kenneth Clark, who had developed the experiment with the dolls that were used in the arguments here in South Carolina. And not only were we there for resources that the lawyers could use when they felt they needed us, but we were asked to do a number of things including preparing working papers for the lawyers and answering questions that they raised and participating in the seminars, which Thurgood organized.

Among the lawyers associated with Marshall there were Spottiswood Robinson from Richmond and George E. C. Hayes from Washington and Louis Redding from Delaware sometimes Harold Boulware from Columbia, South Carolina, and others. Other lawyers would come up and provide information about the local scene. And we worked, we worked hard and at length doing this and trying to provide the kind of information that we thought would help the lawyers write their briefs. I never saw anyone, anyone, who wants to read about what I had to say—Richard Kluger, his book *Simple Justice*, quotes me a number of times in which I said that I had never seen anyone, anytime, anywhere, work as hard as Thurgood Marshall worked. I don't know how he got the energy or the will or the resources to carry on as he did day after day after day. Remember I was there on Thursday, Friday, and Saturday, all day long, and whenever I got to the office he was there. He was there poring over his papers and working. And sometimes he would take time out to have a bite to eat; sometimes he did not.

I did not know until later that Thurgood's wife was incurably ill at that very time, and he very seldom even indicated that there was anything wrong with her or that he was having personal problems such as that. And around midnight or one or two, I would say about midnight or one, I was not there at two, he said, "I think maybe we should take a fifteen-minute break." Then I would break for the Algonquin, but when I would come back the next morning he would be there, and as I said he worked all the time, permitting no speculation. We sometimes would say, "Well they can't do this." He would say, "They can. . . . That's not your problem. You say what you think we ought to say and stop worrying about what they ought to do." Now, I can only say that there was one bad area, which I think he knew about, we didn't discuss it with him, but we had some young people doing the research in these places working on the minutes and the journals of the state conventions that ratified the Fourteenth Amendment and the proceedings of the legislatures in these various states, and one of the things we did was to make certain that these materials out of which the opposition might be able to get their answers were misplaced in the stacks or if they could be loaned or borrowed then we would borrow them for an indefinite period of time. We did not know then that John W. Davis, the principal lawyer for the other side, was not doing any research and was not interested in that. He was interested only in making his oration and his peroration before the Supreme Court. But we thought if we just misplaced enough of these journals and proceedings, it might have some salutary effect on the arguments that our side could make. In any case, that's what we did. Not too much of, but we did enough so that we thought that that might contribute to the ongoing effort of the plaintiffs. So when we ended our work in the early part of December 1953, we fancied ourselves as having answered the questions which the court had propounded and which had been passed on to us by counsel for plaintiffs. We did not know how effective or successful we were until the 17th of May, 1954. My wife called me from Spingarn High School, where she was the librarian, and said, "Have you heard the news?" I said, "What news?" She said, "Then you have not heard the news." And she told me, and I heaved a sigh of relief and said, "At long last maybe I've vindicated my waywardness of not becoming a lawyer because maybe I contributed just a little, a tiny bit, to turning the tide in this case." At the time we thought that we had done everything for counsel for plaintiffs, but as time has receded, we have concluded several things. One was that we didn't really do very much and that the plaintiffs were favored by the good will and good wishes of the Supreme Court that had made its decision perhaps earlier but were stalling for time. Trying to prepare the country for the stupendous historic decision that they would hand down on the 17th of May, but that in any case the counsel for plaintiffs had done a magnificent job, and we could bask in their glory so to speak and enjoy the fruits that came down from it. And as all of us celebrated that night, it was a sort of premature celebration as we, looking back, now can realize. For there were people in many parts of the South, certainly in South Carolina, who were not celebrating, instead were counseling and thinking about what they could do to nullify and make ineffectual the Supreme Court decision. But in the long, long run, the long run of history and of time, they would fail, and this meeting this evening is proof to some extent of their failure.

Joseph A. De Laine Jr.

I will take a few moments to talk about the genesis of the *Briggs v. Elliott* lawsuit originating in Clarendon County, South Carolina.

Very often people assume that the *Brown v. Board* Supreme Court decision of May 1954 was based primarily on the case that originated in Topeka, Kansas. This is not true. There were a total of five cases heard under the umbrella of *Brown* and covered in that decision. *Briggs v. Elliott* was the first of the five cases to be filed in federal courts. It was also the first of the cases to reach the Supreme Court on appeal. *Briggs* was returned to the lower court for review of the progress South Carolina had recently made. This progress related to the fact that South Carolina had initiated a $75 million bond and instituted a 3 percent sales tax intended to equalize its separate school systems. When *Briggs* was returned to the Supreme Court, it was joined by the four other cases. The Supreme Court consolidated these cases and rendered its decision under the umbrella of *Brown v. Board of Education et al.* It is said that Justice Tom Clark suggested *Brown v. Board of Topeka* be first so that the whole question would not smack of being a purely southern one.

What happened in Clarendon County that caused the genesis of *Briggs*? The movement began with the denial of a simple request for bus transportation for

23. The Reverend Joseph A. De Laine (left) and his family standing amid the charred ruins of their home, destroyed by arsonists. Photograph by Cecil J. Williams

African American students who had to walk as much as up to nine miles, one way, to get to school. When the request for transportation was denied, the parents' efforts metamorphosed into a community demand for improved educational opportunities for its children.

At the request of my father, the Reverend J. A. De Laine, a meeting was scheduled (March 1949) with Mr. Thurgood Marshall to solicit the NAACP's assistance for an improved educational environment for African Americans. Accompanying Reverend De Laine were several other individuals (including five from the Levi Pearson extended family) who represented the Davis Station community in Clarendon County. It was perceived that Mr. Marshall's plans were to inform the group that the NAACP was not prepared to take a case from Clarendon County at that time. The reason was believed to be that Clarendon County, not a widely known location, would probably fail to attract sufficient funds to underwrite a case. The NAACP was totally dependent on fund-raising to support the organization's ability to perform its mission. Before the meeting concluded Mr. Marshall did agree to sponsor litigation. After the six petitions were filed with the Clarendon County Board of Education and the district board of trustees with 107 signatures, the plaintiff's list was apparently narrowed to 20 when the attorneys filed in the federal district court. That case, known as *Briggs v. Elliott,* was filed in federal district court for the "Equalization of Educational Opportunity for Negro Children" on May 16, 1950.

During the district court prehearing on November 17, 1950, Judge J. Waties Waring questioned the NAACP attorneys very closely on the intent and outcome expected from this lawsuit. Judge Waring then indicated that, based on the responses given, the outcome of the case would simply be reaffirmation of the established "separate but equal" doctrine. Mr. Marshall quickly realized the need for change in the wording so that the segregation issue could come directly under the recent Supreme Court ruling in the *Sweatt, McLaurin,* and *Anderson* cases. At the request of Mr. Marshall the case was immediately dismissed, without prejudice. *Briggs v. Elliott,* now modified to challenge state law on the separate but equal requirement, was resigned by the twenty plaintiffs on December 18, 1950, and filed in federal district court on December 22, 1950.

It is interesting to note that the case in Farmville, Virginia, was initiated because of the action of school students. Only after students rebelled, without knowledge of their parents, was the community action initiated that resulted in the *Davis et al. v. County School Board of Prince Edward County Virginia* case. After the Clarendon County efforts were specifically focused on the then School District 22 in Summerton, it was the student activism at Scott's Branch High School that made a difference in the activism of their parents. I credit the senior class of 1949 at Scott's Branch, because of their activism, to have been a unifying force for those in Summerton who previously demonstrated timidity in the support for the *Briggs* lawsuit.

Immediately after the *Briggs* case was submitted to the Clarendon County Board of Education and the district board of trustees, retribution began. Individuals were fired from their menial job positions, and many were threatened in subtle ways as a method of frightening them into submission. Among the plaintiffs, Mr. Willie "Bo" Stukes accidentally lost his life, after being terminated by his employer, while attempting to earn a livelihood using unsafe equipment. Another individual who has been overlooked by history was murdered in early 1950. He was thought to have been a plaintiff. I ran across some documents in my father's FBI files about this case. My father had written to the FBI requesting an investigation. The FBI responded that they had no jurisdiction and that the reports provided them indicated that this was a situation of a disorderly black man who happened to have gotten in a struggle with a white man. The murderer was never prosecuted! Our home in Summerton was destroyed by arson, with the fire department refusing to extinguish the blaze because the house was twenty feet outside the town limits.

After the Supreme Court rendered its decision in May 1955, retaliation on African Americans appeared to escalate in Clarendon County. This was especially true with the advent of the White Citizens' Council. Blacks had difficulty selling their crops at local markets and difficulty in purchasing food products locally. Individuals were terminated from their employment because of suspicions that they or a family relative were suspected of being supporters of the cause. Many other ruses were designed and used.

There were white individuals who sympathized with the plight of these African Americans, but they could not openly act for fear of jeopardizing their personal situations.

My father's bishop transferred him, against his wishes, in 1950 to a church in Lake City, fifty miles from Summerton and outside of Clarendon County. Despite the church-assigned relocation, Reverend De Laine continued his leadership role in Clarendon County until 1955. After the Supreme Court ruling of May 1955, the one referred to as "With All Deliberate Speed," an open solicitation of members by the White Citizens' Council began in the Lake City area. The South Carolina secretary of that organization reputed to have brought to the attention of his listeners that they were harboring the individual that started the desegregation problem. Shortly afterward, vandalism of the De Laines' residence, a church parsonage, began to occur. A letter, delivered by the U.S. Postal Service, gave Reverend De Laine "ten days to leave town or die." A reference in that letter reminded him of the fate of the black Lake City postmaster who was burned to death in 1898. About six or seven days later, the church that my father pastored, St. James AME Church, was destroyed by arson. On the tenth day after the letter, around midnight, gunfire aimed at the parsonage became a reality. Reverend De Laine ultimately responded with gunfire to protect himself and his wife. He immediately escaped, fleeing the state for his personal safety. The news media indicated that Reverend De Laine injured three individuals, the grand jury records claimed he injured five people and the rumor mill was rife with stories that a police officer was fatally wounded. The truth is not known. A warrant for Reverend De Laine's arrest remained in effect until the year 2000, forty-five years after the event and twenty-three years after his death.

BEATRICE BROWN RIVERS

In 1949, when the petition was being signed that led to *Briggs v. Elliott,* I was a thirteen-year-old kid whose only interests were in trying to be the smartest kid in my class, winning the spelling bee every year, participating in sports, and pretending that I was good enough to sing solo at school activities. I had no idea that I would be thrown into something as important as this at that age. However, we had to grow up pretty quickly after the petition was signed, because life as we knew it no longer existed. People were being threatened, people were losing their jobs, they were losing their homes, and people were being thrown off land that they were sharecropping. Everything was in turmoil. My parents and I am sure other parents did everything they could to protect us from the craziness that was going on.

Some of the businesses would not deal with the people that were involved in the case. So it was decided that we would boycott the businesses in Summerton as well. Families that had cars would take those who did not to Columbia, Sumter, and other places to shop.

As children we had no idea how dangerous it was for our parents. Whenever I think about it, I always ask myself why did they do it? Why did these people stand up to change the system? Keep in mind, these were basically uneducated people who knew why they were denied an education. They also knew that their parents had been denied the opportunity to get an education. Therefore, they knew that if they did not take a stand we would be relegated to an inferior education or no education at all. I thank God that our parents were our heroes who fought to make life better for us.

As we go through life doing things that our parents could only dream of, we should always remember the sacrifices these brave men and women made for to us to have the opportunities we enjoy today.

Questions and Answers

Isaac Williams: My question is for Mr. Franklin. What was the climate in the other states with reference to their suits, and did you note that there were similar circumstances in all of the companion cases in *Brown v. the Board of Education*? Was the climate similar in each of the five states where suits were filed? My name is Isaac Williams. I'm a former state field director of NAACP, and I work for Congressman Clyburn. . . . I also wanted to bring greetings from the Congressman who happens to be in Washington, and he shook his head early this afternoon, he said, "Ike, I wish I was here to participate." And he may get down here before it's all over Saturday, but this is a tremendous opportunity to set the record straight and open up some fields of thought for a lot of people.

John Hope Franklin: I think that it would be fair to say that of the states involved, you know you have them all the way from a so-called northern state like Kansas to sort of a lower southern state like South Carolina. I think it would be fair to say that the more extreme positions would be taken in the South Carolina. The more extreme positions with respect to the status of blacks in the community. The willingness of people, employers, to fire employees who were veering from the straight and narrow path would be here, first of all, and as you move up the ladder, up toward the north it would be better. I'm not though inclined to make that contrast nearly so great as you might think I'm inclined to make it. I would not suggest for a moment that those blacks who brought suit in Delaware were home free because they were in Delaware or even in Kansas, no, no, no. It was entirely possible for them to suffer reprisals and retributions and recriminations of every conceivable kind even in those communities. Don't forget that there's a great vested interest in segregation wherever it existed and even where it did not exist. When they were fighting for the right to go to school on an equal basis in South Carolina, I moved to New York, and I had the worst time that I have ever had in my life in Brooklyn, New York, trying to protect my family, trying to buy a home when no real estate dealer in Brooklyn would show me a home. No bank in the city of New York including the Carver National Bank in Harlem would lend me the money to buy the home when I found it. And my wife had to give up her career to stay at home and protect our son from our neighbors when we moved into their neighborhood. So climate—ha. Let me tell you about it. It was stormy weather everywhere, and maybe the storm was a little more obvious in South Carolina, but it was everywhere, and that's what we can't forget. I'll never forget when I was a first-year graduate student at Harvard, and Juanita Jackson before she married Clarence Mitchell was up there to set up a youth branch of the NAACP, and I had the temerity to go to her meeting that she called. She asked me to come and I went, and she asked me to make some remarks and I said, "Well, we do need this youth branch. We do need a strong NAACP in Boston because," and then I enumerated some of my own experiences, not at Harvard, but in the community, like not being waited on for an hour or an hour and a half in a restaurant and that sort of thing. I said, "We need an NAACP, strong chapter for adults and a good chapter for young people." And how can I tell you that it was one of the black women dowagers in Boston who stood up and told me that I came from the wilds of Oklahoma and I had no business coming up there telling them how to live. And then she turned to all the young people in the audience and said, "I hope you ostracize him. Don't even speak to him," she said. "Because he doesn't know how good Massachusetts is." Well, I didn't want to know if it would make me like she was. So climate—it's not good. There's stormy weather everywhere.

Joseph A. De Laine Jr.: The case from South Carolina and the case from Virginia were challenging state constitutional law. The case from Washington, D.C., was challenging federal law and practice. *Brown v. Board* in Kansas was a situation where there was no state law demanding it, but there was an option given to the local areas that they could either segregate or have integration, and I believe I'm not sure about Delaware, but I think they had a similar situation up there as Kansas. I just wanted to add that.

Franklin: They did.

De Laine: Yes, that means it is true that Delaware did have a similar situation to Kansas. I might also add that the Washington, D.C., case was argued under the Fifth Amendment of the Constitution. The other four cases were argued under the Fourteenth Amendment of the U.S. Constitution.

Jim Felder: I'm Jim Felder, president of the South Carolina Voter Education Project, followed Ike Williams at the NAACP and in 1970, Herbert Fielding and I. S. Leevy Johnson and myself added color to the legislature. Question for Ms. Rivers. Ms. Rivers, as I understand it, your father during this period of time, worked as the custodian at the white high school. How did he manage to keep his job when others were being fired and so forth?

Beatrice Brown Rivers: Yeah, my father was the janitor at the white school at that time, but my father was also more than the janitor at that school. My father played the piano, so they had him play for their school dances and other activities, and the superintendent of the school resisted firing my father. And as a matter of fact, my father kept his job until 1956 when the White Citizens' Council forced the superintendent to fire him.

Sylvester Rod: Yes, my name is Sylvester Rod from Charleston, South Carolina, [and I] wanted to ask Dr. Franklin how was the question answered as far as when the Supreme Court sent asking what was the intention of the framers of the Fourteenth Amendment. I understood that the Davis people felt confident that you couldn't find anything in the record because the D.C. school systems maintained, Congress maintained, that the D.C. school system would remain segregated. So how was that question finally answered?

Franklin: I was hoping you wouldn't ask that question, because frankly it reflects on us. The pickings were very thin, very slender, and we could not answer that question. We could not answer those questions. We scraped and scrounged and went through the records, and we would see comments by people like Thaddeus Stevens in the House who would rail against segregation, but there's not a great deal of conscious opposition to segregation in 1868 at the time they were debating the ratification of the Fourteenth Amendment. And so the pickings were pretty slim at that point, and it's sobering for us to realize that we didn't make that much contribution to the arguments of counsel for plaintiff. And so I'm sorry you showed us up like that.

Robert Ross: My name is Robert Ross, and my question is since all this terrorism was going on in Summerton and Clarendon County, you know, African Americans losing their jobs, man, woman, and child. Mr. John Hope Franklin, my question is what is your feeling about reparations for African American man, woman and child?

Franklin: I think you ought to know that a suit was filed in the city of Tulsa on Monday, this past Monday, in favor of the survivors and the descendants of the survivors of the race riot in 1921, and I had a friend who called me the next morning to ask me if I would remember him in my will since I am a presumed beneficiary of that litigation if it is successful. Now so I'm in favor of reparations. But to answer your question more seriously, when you think of what these African Americans have done for this country, they have cleared the forests, tilled the soil, mined the coal, and built the buildings including the Capitol. And much of this was with the sanction first of the British, secondly of the colonists, thirdly of the United States government itself forcing this kind of activity on the part of your ancestors and my ancestors, and when I look at what they have as Wall Street, as this kind of street and that kind of street and there's relief for many of us, there's no limit to what I think they owe. One man told me one day, "I don't owe you anything. My people came over here in 1900 from Europe and I got an education and I made my way up." I said, "Do you know that in 1900 my father was paying taxes in the State of Oklahoma for you to go to school where I could not go to school.

The law prevented me from going to school there, and I was exiled to Harvard. And you mean to tell me that you don't owe me something?" You see. No, I would say—I've got sense enough to know that I'm barking up a tree 'cause they're not going to do anything. If they—if you get this loud outcry against something so innocent as affirmative action, which is a tiny, tiny, tiny kind of reparation, where the president of the United States takes a powerful stand against affirmative action when he was born on third base and thought he hit a home run when he got home. What can we do, you see? So I've got sense enough to know that they're not going to do anything, but I've got enough sense to keep on saying that they owe me a lot. And I'll keep on saying it.

Unidentified Speaker: I would just like to make an observation [that] our panelists have had a very profound effect on me this evening and I give sincere appreciation. And I would like to comment on some of the times that we were all laughing and the stories were very sad, some of them were funny, but some of the stories were very sad, and yet all of us laughed in response and I think it was not because they were funny. Sad stories are not funny, but because we feel funny today. We still feel funny today, and I hope we can transform that into some positive action.

Ted Phillips: . . . I'm Ted Phillips. Mr. De Laine, I grew up near Summerton and spent a lot of time there and know that overt racism is still a real problem around there, but I was wondering if you could tell us, I know you might not be able to, who the murder victim and who the murderer was that you spoke of earlier.

De Laine: The murder victim was James McKnight. The murder took place on highway 301 north of Summerton. He was a member of Reverend De Laine's church and resided in the Rimini community. I will not name the murderer. I am aware of his name, but I prefer not to identify him at this time.

Peter Lau: My name is Peter Lau. Hi, Mr. De Laine, and I was wondering if Mr. Rivers and Mr. De Laine could talk about the kind of work that is going on to commemorate the fiftieth anniversary of *Brown v. Board* coming up in Clarendon. I know both of you had wanted everybody to know about the foundation, but you know I would like to know more about what is going on, and I'm sure the people would be enlightened by it as well.

De Laine: There is a foundation in Summerton, which is named the Briggs, De Laine, Pearson Foundation, and it's been in existence since 1993. It hasn't been very active or progressive over the years with programs. Several of us, Ms. Rivers and I, became deeply involved with this last year. We started with a program of searching out descendants of the *Briggs* case, most of whom don't live in Summerton or in South Carolina any longer. We had a program there in May, and we brought people from thirty states to Summerton, mostly descendants. As a part of that effort, we did a social studies teachers' guide on the *Briggs* case, which was donated to the Department of Education of South Carolina to use as they see fit. We also did a booklet on the case. In addition to that, we tried to do something that was culturally of benefit to the county, and that was a pictorial history of the county. We went back at least 50 years, from 50 to 150 years, with pictures that we could find, and developed a book on it. That's what's been done there in the past. Presently our organization is looking at several other programs. One is a possibility of developing some type of training program to create more of an ownership and interest on the part of parents in the school system and support to the school system. In addition to that, the federal—due to the fiftieth anniversary of *Briggs,* there are a number of programs coming about from universities and several I am involved with, and I think here this evening would be some representatives from the Levine Museum in Charlotte, who are doing a story on the Carolina connection, which is specifically Clarendon County for 2004.

Unidentified Speaker: Scott's Branch, can you tell me the status of integration. . . . I'm thinking it's not that great or much integration there at this time.

Rivers: Well, at this time Scott's Branch High School has a population of about 1,275 students. That's all of the schools, that's from pre-K to the twelfth grade, and it's 97 percent black, 3 percent white and other, which include[s] Hispanic and Asian; that's the way it stands right now. Now as to why it is so slow to integrate is because the people don't want to integrate. They opened a private school there during the '60s, and 97 percent of the white kids go to the private school, which has two black students in the private school. So they don't want integration, not ready. Two black students. Okay.

Roberta Tracy: I'm Roberta Tracy, and I work at the Citadel, but I want to say one of the things that I thought was most important that you brought up from Clarendon County was the fact that young people were used and that young people took a stand for civil rights and justice. I think that one of the things that isn't said enough about any of the movements, even if you take the student movement that directly followed in '55 through the '60s, they don't emphasize enough that young people and students got out on the line and fought for the rights that they believe people—and that even though Martin Luther King or someone else was leading a movement that most of the participants were young people who thought about issues and moved to do something about it. I'm to say that I feel that maybe we haven't done our jobs enough when we ask a question as to what should we do because the simple thing is if you just remember Paul Dunbar, I think he told us all, "Just keep a-plugging away." Because there was always a understanding as to who you are and what you have to go for, so I'm very concerned that we've slipped somewhere when black folks have to ask the question "what can we do?" Because we have got to continue the work that has to be done, and we've got to always try to bring somebody up with us because we're not alone and the struggle involves all of us. Because I say one thing about the education issues is if the least of us is not educated, then none of us are. And as long as we sit and as long as South Carolina can boast being fiftieth and forty-ninth in education then somebody hasn't done their job and that we have to do it. And so education's got to be a primary focus, and until we're ready to die for something that we believe in, and get involved, nothing will change. And I say to young people, "If you haven't got balls now; you're not going to get them later." So try.

Sid Stuart: . . . my name is Sid Stuart, and I'm from Summerton. I was born— I've lived in the same house there my entire life. . . . I can see the Summerton High School out from my bedroom window. I just wanted to know, in the rest of the county in Manning and Turbeville and up there, what was going on there during this time? Was it the same kind of stuff going on?

De Laine: The movement in Clarendon County was generally felt by most African Americans within the county. The first to speak out were the people from the Davis Station and Jordan communities regarding bus transportation to Scott's Branch High School and the Manning High School. The reason that the case focused its attention on Summerton was because Mr. Marshall and his staff preferred to narrow their attention on one school district and preferred that to be District 22, which is the Summerton area. However, there was evidence of strong support on the part of African Americans from all areas of the county.

Armand Derfner: I'm Armand Derfner from Charleston here. I've got a question for Professor Franklin. Were the defendants also working on this history? Did they have professors? Can you tell us something about what they were doing, and did you have any contact with them?

Franklin: I don't know. I don't know the extent to which they did have people working on it. We couldn't find them. And in those instances where we found them I indicated what we did. What we tried to do was to hide the material from them so it wouldn't be prepared. But Mr. Davis wasn't interested in that sort of thing. He was interested only in oratory, which he thought would be quite effective. And so our impression is, the impression we got from the people who worked out in the field and were doing the research at various archives and the obvious places like the Library of Congress and so forth, that they just weren't working. They weren't doing what we were doing. We couldn't find any evidence that they were doing the kind of research that we were trying to do.

Vernon Burton: The University of Illinois is planning a fifty year [event], and they originally called it a celebration of *Brown v. Board of Education,* and I was on the committee and pointed out that perhaps *celebration* is the wrong word. In fact, *Brown v. Board of Education* for its fifty year in 1954 a lot of people suffered and still suffer from right here in South Carolina throughout the nation in this. It was not until 1964, which is of course the Civil Rights Act, that there was some way to make this happen, and that's the thirtieth-year celebration to me or fortieth-year celebration. It's of extraordinary importance. I've always argued there are two things that changed the American South for the better, and that's the Voting Rights Act, which followed the next year, which is so important. Important to vote and air conditioning. And in American education, in American education we understand better how air conditioning worked because we get that in science education, but in history and in our social studies and what we used to call I guess different things we aren't learning why in fact you had to have a 1964 Civil Rights Act; a 1965 Voting Rights Act, and why in fact things that are so important today people have turned their backs on and rolling back, trying to roll back some of the gains we've come. So that's just my answer. Be careful about *Brown v. Board of Education*. It wasn't until 1964, that we began to sort of see desegregation begin and really after that, '71 or so in many places in South Carolina.

Voices from the Civil Rights Movement in South Carolina

Charles F. McDew

It was sort of fascinating for me to come back here and to see so many people from my life from down here over the years. I was thinking as I came in last night, damn, the last time I saw that guy, he was having me thrown in jail. And now he's the champion of the liberal causes—that's Fritz Hollings.

We had gone from South Carolina State to Columbia to present a petition asking that at least there be the signs of segregation be taken down in public places. And at the time we had gone we had made two mistakes. One, it was a noncolored day. Colored people, we were colored back then. Colored people could go to the Capitol on Sundays. We thought, damn, we didn't think that would do much good since you couldn't pursue any business, and we questioned whether Governor Hollings would be there on a Sunday afternoon, so we went on a Monday, a noncolored day, and that was the first punishable offense. Because once again it was the breaking of the laws of segregation of the state of South Carolina, and we were arrested then. But before that happened we were taken in to see the governor, and there was this discussion of our local blacks, good little blacks, the governor was saying until all these outside agitators came in, and I know you're one of the biggest of those agitators. He always had this marvelous senatorial deep voice, and I said this guy really sounds like a leader of the great state of South Carolina. So he went on and said our local blacks were good blacks until y'all came down, you outside agitators came down here and started bringing them Communist ideas. When I talk to my students now about that there even used to be an organization called the House Un-American Activities Committee, they are flabbergasted and they react with disbelief. "Don't be so disbelieving, you'll see it again soon, you know from the next few weeks or months." And my students always ask me why, you know, "Professor, why did you come to Minnesota?" Well, it's simple really. Minnesota shares a border with Canada. Next time my fellow Americans get crazy I can walk. You know I don't need a visa or anything else. I can make it out safely. I said, "And that time may be sooner than you want to imagine."

But coming here yesterday, I haven't been back to South Carolina. When I left I said, "Lord, let me out of here. I'm gone." And at the point the last time I left there were certain places I could say, "I'm not going there anymore." And one I said to the Lord, I was in prison in Louisiana charged with criminal anarchy, highest treason against the sovereign state of Louisiana, and I said, "Lord, if you get me out of here, I will never, ever again in life as long as I am black come back to the state of Louisiana or Texas." Those are two places that they can—there's got as Emmett Till's grandfather used to say "You can take my part of the South, I'm gone. I'm done with it." And I didn't come back. I mean I left, got on a plane when I got out of prison, and headed for the furthest place I could get to away from our country and ended up in Finland. And so I really held to that for a long time. And then when I met Vernon a few years ago and he was talking about this conference, and I was saying "The Citadel? You're kidding?" And when Vernon was saying, "No, they're going to give me an appointment now." I said, "It is a topsy turvy world. If they're going to give you, Vernon, an appointment to work

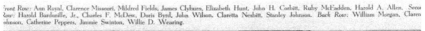

24. *South Carolina State students of 1960, including Charles McDew and James Clyburn (first African American elected to the U.S. House of Representatives from South Carolina during the twentieth century). Photograph courtesy of the South Carolina State University Historical Collection, Miller F. Whittaker Library, South Carolina State University*

at the Citadel things have changed." I said, "Don't you know the Citadel was one of those places that if we came within a couple of blocks, you were subject to be arrested back in the '60s. The Citadel was the symbol and sign of white dominance and rule. When Mathew Perry was mentioning preparing to get Harvey Gantt into Clemson, there were all these memories that came back for me.

I remember the speech that Governor [Ross] Barnett made that day when he told the citizens of Mississippi that no, Ole Miss would never be integrated. And there would be segregation now, segregation tomorrow, and segregation forever. It was at the halftime of the football game between Ole Miss and the University of Alabama. The Alabama attorney general was in prison and so was Richmond Flowers Sr. for not turning over the list of the NAACP to the governor of Alabama, then George Wallace. But I had said right along all along that South Carolina was no better than Mississippi. All y'all sitting out there talking about—you're patting yourselves on the back and praising how civil the good citizens of South Carolina were, they didn't impress me as that way.

When I came here and when I went to Mississippi that opinion never really changed. So this is one of the few times I've been back, and when Vernon—I said, "What, they're going to let Vernon in?" Then by all means I'm going. If he can get me there even for a day or two, I'll do that, because after I left I just didn't come back. And as I said there were all these memories of things that there were occasioned by seeing many of you and being here.

I was raised in Ohio. My father had gone to South Carolina State, and I was raised in a place called Massillon, Ohio. And in Massillon, Massillon is a big football city, and I was one of them hotshot football players. And my life was all set for me; by the time I was fifteen I knew what I was going to do. In my family the boys split between Ohio State and Michigan, and that's what I was going to do. I was going to finish high school and go to Michigan, play ball, go into the pros, play pro ball, marry a good-looking woman, have bright children, and, you know, retire and buy a liquor store or whatever they do. Liquor store or used car lot—live out the American dream. So I had never—but my father felt that it was important for us, me, my brothers, my sister, to go spend some time at a historically black university, so he chose for me South Carolina State. At that time I had never been further south than Columbus, Ohio. When I first came—when I was brought down to South Carolina, and it was just strange. I remember my classmates at Lowmam Hall at South Carolina State were asking me, were saying, you know how you carry yearbooks and things. and they were saying, "You went to an integrated school? How many of you were in your class?" I said, "Well, I don't know. I mean, I had never counted them." And then I found—you know I counted there were 12 black students out of a class of about 470. And at first when I first came down here, it was sort of wonderful because at South Carolina State I saw more black girls in one day than I had seen in my entire life in

Massillon, Ohio. And all these girls were not my cousins, and that was just wonderful. I thought my father was a bright fellow.

. . . insisting on us going to these black—he's a fine man and a bright fellow. And to myself I was thinking about if this ain't the fox throwing the fox in the henhouse; that's where my father was smart, I think. This is a wonderful place to be, and I was sent initially because he wanted me to have black role models where in my town you know there was the black doctor, the black lawyer, the black undertaker, and four or five black preachers. Those were the professionals. They didn't have black teachers. My sister was the first black teacher in Massillon, Ohio, and they didn't generally have black teachers in public schools until after the '54 decision. So I had never had a black teacher until I went to South Carolina State. So this was good. This was all good. And I was seeing a black environment, and that was wonderful until the first time I had to leave campus, and that was Thanksgiving of my freshmen year. I went to Sumter, South Carolina, with my roommate, and we went to a party and they drank and I didn't; so I was like the designated driver after the party. As we were driving back to the house, the police pulled me over, and we were talking—you know the guy—what's the problem officer? Do we have a problem here? Blah, blah, blah. Them cops said, "Where you from, boy?" I said, "Ohio, why? Why? You've got the license; look. You can read, can't you? It says these are Ohio license." "Didn't they ever teach you how to say 'yes, sir' and 'no, sir' to white men up there?" I said, "You've got to be jiving. Are you kidding?" "Yes, sir" and "no, sir" to white men up there? Now remember, this is 1959, I'm a sixteen-year-old freshman, newly licensed driver, in fact, and had done nothing wrong, so I could talk to this cop just like another person. And I said, "What do you mean, 'yes, sir' and 'no, sir' up there to white men? You've got to be jiving." And he hit me; the cop hit me. And being from Massillon, Ohio, which is a rather tough steel-mill town, I hit him back before he ever got his fist out of my face and was proceeding to stomp on his head when his partner grabbed me. That was my introduction to the other side of the world. They beat me bloody in Sumter, South Carolina, and as they were beating me I was saying to the guys in the car, "I'm going to get you for this," because where I came from, you don't allow a friend, a partner, to be beaten without helping. What I didn't understand that in 1959, November, in Sumter, South Carolina, it could have cost them their lives to hit a white cop. And so they beat me, broke my jaw, busted my arm, and I was arrested for disturbing the peace by screaming as they were administering the beating.

When I got out of jail, I went to get on the train to go back to the campus, and the conductor said, "All right, get on back to the baggage car." I said, "Hey, sport, where—?" He says, "Back to the baggage car." What I didn't know was the old rule when the colored car was filled, you rode in the baggage car. I hadn't been on a train in the South ever. So I said to the conductor, "I'm sorry, sport, you know, not for my little $8.20 do I ride with, you know, smelly cats and mangy dogs. There are seats right here, and I'm having one of them." I was back in jail for violating the law of segregating the races. I came to understand that in South Carolina it was a very simple rule that if it said open to the public, it meant it was closed to black people.

So by the time I got home for Christmas, I had been arrested six times, I had my jaw wired shut, I had a busted arm, and my father is saying, "Okay, forget it. You know, the great experiment ends. We can't keep you down there; they're going to kill you." And by then, too, I was fired. He was saying, so you have to come home. I was saying, "Cool, that's wonderful. My year of penitence had ended." It was over, and I had only been there for two months, three months. I was so glad when my father said I could come home, but fate sort of took a hand at that point. My father said, "Okay, I'm going to drive you back to campus. You stay here on campus until I come and get you." I said, "Fine." It so happened that we were on semesters. The semester ended at the end of February and on February 1, 1960, three students from A&T College in Greensboro went to a lunch counter, sat down, and were arrested, thus starting the modern sit-in movement. The group of students on my campus came to me and said, "Chuck, you heard about what's happening in Greensboro didn't you?" I said, "Yes, of course I have." Said, well, we want to do that here; my response was go ahead, do it. What's that got to do with me? And they wanted me to be the spokesman. By that time I had gained a reputation of being somewhat crazy. And they asked me to be the—I said, "No, no, no. I'm not, there's nothing wrong with me, but what y'all have to understand these white people are collectively insane. I mean they're just a mass of crazy white people." Said, "I don't know what happened. I don't need to figure this out, but I do know what the end result is. A society of insane people, and y'all ain't wrapped too tight either for putting up with them. So here y'all are down here in the asylum together, a bunch of crazy white people and a bunch of crazy black people. Well, I don't have to be here much longer. I will soon be going back home in another three weeks, and after that I will never go any further South than Cincinnati as long as God's sun shines on this earth. I don't have to be in the South. I won't be in it. I'm out of it. So Au revoir, Au revoir, you know it's French you know for 'Bye, y'all; I'm gone.'" Well, later I was reading the Talmud. In the Talmud the words of Rabbi Hillel pointed out—gave the thought if I'm not for myself who will be for me? If I am for myself only what am I? If not now, when? And I thought about that and I thought about that all night, and I thought that this place is as it is because my father went here and he didn't do what he should have done. And if I don't do what I should do, then my children will have to face this, and so if there is ever going to be a change in the way this is, it should be now. . . .

So I went back and apologized to these people who had asked me to join them, and I joined the movement. . . .

So I joined the movement and changed my life, changed this country because what I thought would be a commitment for a few days that summer grew into a commitment for a lifetime. It wasn't long after that, you know, that we started having—attacking the symbols and the ways of segregation in Orangeburg. So the first time I met Matthew Perry was as my lawyer coming to get me out of jail. The first time I ever went close to Clemson was, you know, I told you I came from a big football town, and I knew the coach here was famous. And Clemson back then had good football teams, and I wanted to go to—I was going to go to a game to watch the Clemson Tigers play. And the kids around me said, "Are you crazy? We don't go up there." I said, "Why not?" Said, "Because they don't want us up there," and then they went through the whole thing of segregated football and segregated this and segregated that. And I remember I used to—. . . . these people are sick. They used to watch the Washington Redskins. I used to call them the Washington Paleskins. It was an all white team with an owner who said they would never have black players on the team, and in fact the first black player they got came under court order. And I thought, "How can you black men stand up here and cheer these little white boys?," and the same was true of Clemson, the University of South Carolina, the Citadel, and all. And I'm saying how can y'all do that? You're crazy, that's why. I can answer my own question. But yet that you are mental, that they're all crazy. I don't know if I've completely given up that idea, but it grew, but as time went on and I was in on the founding of SNCC and later became SNCC's chairman and became very involved in hammering out the strategy that we could get and employ in voting and other ways to change the way this place was.

It's nice and it's good to be back, because it has changed and it's changed a lot. I often hear young students say there ain't nothing changed. I say, if you say nothing's changed it's only because you don't know what used to be and what it was like.

So, though reluctant at first to come back when Vernon said he could get me into the Citadel for a few days, I said that's something I want to see. To the citizens of the Citadel and one of the old cadets, fine, silver-haired gentleman, and, lo and behold, the last one I saw when I left South Carolina, was the first one I saw last night— the Honorable Governor Fritz Hollings—but it was good. And you know, we have chatted. We chatted last evening, and it's marvelous being back here with you all.

Constance Curry

Let me begin by saying that I have known Chuck McDew, Hayes Mizell, and Charles Joyner—all three of these men up here on the stage—for over forty years. I grew up in Greensboro, North Carolina, and I must say my first contact with South Carolina in the '40s and '50s was going to the pavilion at Myrtle Beach to do the shag. Anyone remember that great dance? Secondly, you could get married in South Carolina without a blood test, which was big for North Carolina, and then the third thing was good peaches. My neighbor would go down and always bring back these wonderful peaches from South Carolina.

Now back then I don't know who could have dreamed that in February 1961—not too many years later (forgive me for pulling out this archival newspaper story), one of the guest speakers at a black church in Rock Hill, South Carolina, was a white woman, Connie Curry, of NSA [National Student Association], who said to the group, "We lost our finest hour last year during mass arrests resulting from demonstrations, but perhaps the students in Rock Hill have given us or will give us a second finest hour." To explain—by 1961 I was the first white woman on the executive committee of the Student Nonviolent Coordinating Committee, based in Atlanta. I had met Chuck and a lot of the other leaders in SNCC, and we were constantly planning and strategizing for the follow-up activities to the sit-in movement, which had started in 1960. SNCC decided when the nine students from Friendship Junior College went to the chain gang in Rock Hill in 1961, to have a different strategy, which was to fill the jails. That's when a lot of the students from Atlanta and all over came to Rock Hill, to demonstrate and be arrested, with the policy of "jail, no bail." It's funny the little personal things you remember from those times. Ruby Doris Smith, who was one of the leaders from Spelman who came to help fill the jails, wouldn't go downtown for the demonstrations until her hair was curled. Ella Baker, Reverend Ivory, everybody sat in the living room and waited because Ruby Doris would not remove her curlers until her hair was appropriate for the jail stay. Then we went downtown for the demonstration. I was the designated observer and remember the anger of the white people, who jeered and cursed the students.

The summer of 1960, Will Campbell and I ran a human relations seminar in Ohio, and Chuck McDew was one of the student leaders who came up for that meeting. Later on Chuck wrote to Valerie, another student at the seminar. I haven't told him I was going to read this, but I assume it's all right:

> Please excuse my stationery. (It was written on brown paper towels from the Orangeburg jail.)
>
> I was arrested about an hour ago with three students. We sat down at the SH Kress and Company lunch counter and asked to be served. I can hear singing outside the jail. They are singing "We Shall Overcome," and it sounds so wonderful that I kind of want to cry. Dot, the girl in the next cell, can see them, and there are nearly four hundred students out there all singing. Now they're singing "The Star Spangled Banner," and then I feel a kind of bitter feeling deep inside. I know that those singing as well as we

25. *"Breaking the Ties That Bind": a Charleston Movement poster, 1963.*
Photograph courtesy of the Avery Research Center for African American History
and Culture at the College of Charleston

who are in here do believe that we shall overcome and the truth will make
us free, and I'm trying very, very hard also to believe that this is the home
of the brave and the free. I keep asking myself just how brave are the people who put me here. Oh God, why must it be that way? Why can't we be a
world of blind men and then we would all be free and equal. Or would a
group of blind bigots start discriminating on the basis of tone quality?
Would all people with high voices have to live in filthy ghettos and be sec-
ond-class citizens? Would the children of high-voiced people have to fight
mobs to get into school? Would their Braille tablets say that they aren't as
good as the low-voiced and that they smell bad, have VD, and live from day

to day with one dream in their dark world, to sleep with a low-voiced woman? Oh sickness, oh hate, go and leave the hearts of men. Let me be me, Charles Fredrick McDew, man, student, lover of life. I don't want to be that nigger with no personality, no being, just a dark blob. I want to be me with my color that I love, with my eyes, my body, my dreams and aspirations. I'll close now. It's been a very trying day and we have a trial in the morning. Pray for us, Val. Pray for us all. Chuck, or as the fellows call me— from the cell—Number 247771.

Pretty profound for a twenty-one-year-old. I want to point out something else interesting about South Carolina. Following Rock Hill there was an enormous organizing effort pushed by the South Carolina Human Relations Council. They formed a Student Human Relations Council as an affiliate of the adult group. Marcia Synnott was telling you the other day about the role that Alice Spearman and Libby Levine took in that, and to the best of my knowledge it was the only southern state that formed an interracial statewide student organization. It was very active, and the group held meetings for the next several years in Columbia and also at Penn Center on the coast. Again, I remember a funny incident. Casey Haden, another white woman in the movement, and I were riding up to Columbia to a meeting of the South Carolina student council, and Reggie Robinson, who was with SNCC was with us, and we needed gas. We were going to pull into a station in a small town and were debating whether Reggie, who is black, and Casey and I were going to pull into this small-town filling station. Should Reggie get on the floor and let Casey and I get in front, or should Casey and I get on the floor in back and Reggie drive in? So Reggie said, "Well, I've solved all that," and he put on a chauffeur's cap he had brought with him, and Casey and I got in back and we played *Driving Miss Daisy* all the way into Columbia. Somewhere in that period I also met Matthew Perry, who was helping get people out of the jail, and Fred Reese, the head of the Adult South Carolina Council on Human Relations, and Hayes Mizell, and Dan Carter, and Charles Joyner, and Selden Smith. I went to the apartment that they shared, and it is so great that they are here today—still in the battle and still good friends. Three of them are totally brilliant historians who are preserving the history of South Carolina and the freedom movement. It's unusual to find four men who have kept the faith this long. Hayes is coming back to South Carolina and will continue his work in public education and foundation work.

Now I want to read you a piece that I found on the South Carolina Student Human Relations Council from November 1961: "The theme of our student conference is the role of the southern student in a democracy. There will be four workshops. One: 'The Meaning of Democracy'; Two: 'The Radical Right as a Threat to Democracy'; Three: 'The Role of the Student in the Changing Politics of the South'; and Four: 'The Role of the Student in Changing the Economics of the South.'"

Pretty prescient topics considering politics today. At that meeting in '61 there were students from Allen, Benedict, Claflin, Clemson, Columbia, Converse, Erskine, Lutheran Theological Seminary, Lander College, Morris, Newberry, South Carolina State, University of South Carolina, Voorhees, Winthrop, and Wofford. That's a lot of South Carolina student support for that time. Following that conference I got a memo from Casey about developments at South Carolina State: "Although South Carolina is a state university and has been a leader in the movement in Orangeburg, Claflin has really given a majority of the people. The state of South Carolina through the university administration is working to destroy the longstanding relationship between Claflin and South Carolina State. The first move was to put up a ten-foot high hurricane fence with barbed wire."

Now these are two black colleges and both very active, but of course South Carolina State was afraid of losing their funding. There was a law or rule saying no meetings could be held on the state campus without two faculty members

26. *Charleston chief of police William Kelly attempting to disperse picketers on King Street, June 1963. UPI photograph, courtesy of the Avery Research Center for African American History and Culture at the College of Charleston*

present. Benedict College is another black college, and students were not allowed to meet with a Freedom Rider nor schedule meetings related to the movement, and other campus meetings were moved to conflict with any movement meeting. You could not belong to a protest group if you were under twenty-one or unless you had your parents' permission.

I read this to you just to give you some idea the difficulties students increasingly faced for their continued participation in the movement. I found a lot of this material in going back through my own archives and in the archives at the King Center. It became more fascinating as Harvey Gantt attempted to enroll as the first black student at Clemson University. I read in the files that the South Carolina movement, student and adult, was focusing on getting black students admitted to the state universities. News clippings from the *Washington Post* in February of '63 reported:

> It has been said that Mississippi was conceived in sin, while South Carolina fell into it. This is a reference to the birth of Mississippi as a frontier state in the early nineteenth century just at a time that the economy was making slavery profitable. By then, South Carolina was already generations old. A cosmopolitan state with a gentle aristocracy born and nurtured in the liberalism that helped forge the nation. This comparison is used today to explain why the enrollment of a Negro in Clemson last Monday was accomplished with calm and dignity. One writer recently pointed out that South Carolina's tradition and heritage make it akin to North Carolina and Virginia which have accommodated themselves to racial desegregation where Alabama and Mississippi haven't.

The article points out that South Carolina has a certain class or style that would avoid the panic and shambles that occurred at Ole Miss at the attempted enrollment of James Meredith. I say this to point out to you that several years later South Carolina had the Orangeburg Massacre. So much for the image of class and gentility and the aristocracy.

I'm going to end here, but point out to you that right after Harvey Gantt's admission, a newspaper commented, "although South Carolina should take great pride in what happened in Clemson, it should be regarded as one step and should encourage us to work harder on our problems. There are more than eight hundred thousand African Americans in South Carolina who desperately need job opportunities. Our schools need improving. We need more technical education, more of our citizens need to register and vote." And they go on to talk about the need to make black public education open with more emphasis on quality. I would add that my own work and my feeling about South Carolina and all of the southern states show the enormous need to work on the issue of public education. Public schools everywhere are resegregating with dropouts, expulsions, and suspensions helping to create a fast track to prison, particularly for youth of color. More state money is being spent on incarceration rather than on education. This country has the highest prison rate in the world, with over two million people incarcerated, with a vast majority of black men. There are more black men in prison in the United States than in college.

We must look to that and to the other issue mentioned this morning in one of the sessions. Chuck and I are working on St. Simons and some of the other islands along the coast, where land that has belonged to black people is literally being stolen away by developers and builders. We talked to a woman at Hilton Head who said, "I live on the mainland now. I catch a bus every day over to Hilton Head and work in a house that had belonged to my father since the end of slavery." So that's at least three issues that we must work on. I guess what I'm saying is that it's not over.

MATTHEW J. PERRY JR.

It's such a pleasure to be here and I have followed the events during this conference for the last several days, and let me tell you, it's so very, very impressive.

27. Matthew J. Perry Jr., South Carolina's foremost civil rights litigator, 1963. Photograph by Cecil J. Williams

Unfortunately I was not able to get here—just before the luncheon hour, and I'm very glad that I arrived in time for lunch, because there was the most magnificent presentation by Dr. Joyner over lunch. Let me tell you, the speech was superb. And while you talked about things of which most of us are already aware, you collected them and organized them and put them forth in such a wonderful fashion. I hope, of course, that the speech is available such that we may reference it from time to time.

I'm very pleased to be here, and I'm told that this part of the program involves some personal testimonies. And I was also told that it would be very useful if the audience were given a chance to interact, ask questions, and give us, help us to focus upon things that you are vitally interested in. And now, of course, a part of my name recognition is attached to my—certainly one of my, and I think actually my most, famous client. The young man who sits to my immediate left, Harvey Gantt, who of course has become a nationally known person and of whom I am certainly proud and who has my eternal admiration. So it would be in my view the best way to start off this discussion by having you focus your attention upon the person who I think really is the star of that period.

He is of course the young man I met back in the early 1960s. Perhaps it was around 1962, I think, when he was just a senior at Burke High School and was at that point involved, he and several of his young high school colleagues had been involved in a racial protest, much of the same sort that Dr. Joyner told us about over lunch. They had sat in down at I believe Kress Five and Dime, and they decided they wanted a hamburger or whatever, but that was not to be. And so they got arrested, and it became necessary that they be defended. Well, at that point in time I was somewhat of a young whippersnapper of a lawyer who was widely known as the go-to person. And so I and my several colleagues, including Judge Bernard Fielding, who is sitting right here with you today, went to the aid of these young people and provided their defense. Well, of course, I met my young clients and I interacted with them, and by the way, we ultimately prevailed in their behalf, but during the course of the trial of that case, I met more pointedly my young, famous client. And he came over to me and—now he may not remember the events as pointedly as I do, or he may remember some aspects about it that I do not remember—but it went sort of like this. And of course I'm very careful, I don't want to do any revisionist history here.

He came over to me. He was indeed—he was a very, very intelligent, bright, upbeat young man. And he came over, and he said, "Hello, I'm Harvey Gantt." Or "My name is Harvey Gantt." And he said, "I'm a senior at Burke High School, and I'm going to be an architect." Fine, you know. And he said something like this, now he—as he and I have discussed this, his memory is not exactly the same as mine, but this is by my recollection. He said, "And I want to go to Clemson, which I understand is one of the better schools of architecture in the country, but I understand there might be a problem." He, of course, had already applied, and I believe had been accepted at Iowa State University's School of Architecture, but he was still focusing upon Clemson, which, as he pointed out, was considered one of the premier schools of architecture. And so he was keenly aware, of course, of the racial climate of that period. After all, one of my purposes of being in Charleston on this occasion and the occasion on which I had met him was—came about because of his involvement in an effort at breaking down racial barriers in terms of the availability of service at a restaurant in Charleston. So he wanted to know if I would guide him and possibly offer—provide whatever legal assistance might be involved in his effort at entering Clemson, if indeed that should come about. And he needed to make the decision on whether to honor the commitment or his acceptance at Iowa State University.

All right, my recollections still—he may not remember it this way—is that I was very impressed with him, and I wanted to know initially whether he had discussed his desires with his parents. And of course, might I have the pleasure of meeting his parents, which I did in fact meet his parents. Whether I met them that very afternoon or during the following days or weeks, my memory has faded on that point, but in any event I considered that a rather crucial portion of the scenario. And of course, as it developed, we outlined an approach. The suggestion was that he go ahead and submit his application to Clemson, but meanwhile I knew that there might be problems also.

You see, at that time South Carolina's racial climate—you've already heard about it during the course of this entire conference. It was pretty well known. Now, of course there were provisions in the South Carolina Constitution that I suppose had been placed there in fairly recent times, but they had outlined the University of South Carolina and Clemson and other institutions like Winthrop, the Citadel, and the various other schools of the state as reserved for the attendance of young white people. And South Carolina State College, I beg your pardon, the school then known as "the colored normal agricultural and mechanical college at Orangeburg," now South Carolina State University, was reserved for young black persons. And should any person present himself or herself at either the University of South Carolina or Clemson or the Citadel or the Medical University at Charleston or Winthrop or any of the other schools, such school was to immediately close its doors and simultaneously, so too was the colored normal agricultural and mechanical college at Orangeburg required to close its doors.

Well, you know, also the same scenario governed our elementary and secondary schools, but coming back to the universities, that was the climate. Now I mention that because we have heard in more recent times that there were people at Clemson and at the University of South Carolina and at perhaps some of the other state-supported colleges and universities who were open to accepting persons of color. But who of course simply could not do so because the laws prohibited them from doing so, and moreover, you know, our presiding governors, the members of our state General Assembly, and all of the public officials were committed to maintaining adherence to racially separate schools and racially separate everything.

In any event, in order to address my young, famous client's desires, I had to contemplate how to get around this legislative scheme and indeed the scheme set forth in our state constitution. And so I associated myself with the NAACP legal defense fund and interacted with the lawyers, all of whom were then well known and who have since become well known to all of you.

And so we decided young Mr. Gantt ought to go ahead and honor his commitment, lest he interrupt his educational sojourn, and enter the University of Iowa's Law School—I'm sorry, School of Architecture—while we fashioned out the submission of his application for admission to Clemson, which we did. And so, without belaboring you with all of the approaches, he applied, and of course he was required to submit follow-up data. By the way, another young man also applied. I believe he and Harvey Gantt were friends. And so Harvey Gantt went ahead and began his schooling at Iowa. The other young man began his over in Georgia, and we fashioned both of those applications simultaneously. I point that out because the other young man did not follow through. But as Harvey Gantt was later on the witness stand in connection with his application, in connection with our lawsuit, one of the attorneys for Clemson armed with the knowledge that the president had been receiving letters practically simultaneously, identically written, seemingly written on the same typewriter, you know, following through on various stages of the application process and of the delay and tactics that we encountered. They wanted to know how does it happen that you wrote a letter from Ames, Iowa, on thus and such date, which is identical, identically worded to a letter that came from a student over in Georgia. And of course we stipulated that I, of course, had written the letters and indeed that I was representing both of these young men in their desire to enter. In any event, without taking too much further time, you will recognize that there came a time when we prevailed and the courts finally ordered that Harvey Gantt be admitted. This came of course after quite a legal battle and a pronouncement finally by the United States Supreme Court denying an application by Clemson's authorities to stay the order, and of course the result is now well known.

You heard yesterday Governor West's recollection of the speech that then outgoing governor Fritz Hollings made to the South Carolina General Assembly at that point in time, which was—and I agree with Governor West—it was an outstanding, it was a very dramatic moment. And it set the stage for the events that then unfolded.

Harvey Gantt. . . . —by the way we had urged Mr. Gantt to withdraw from Ames, Iowa, at the end of the first quarter—the first quarter of his second year. Iowa is on the quarter system; Clemson is on the semester system. And Iowa's second quarter would have overlapped the beginning of Clemson's second semester, and we wanted our client to be ready to enter Clemson as we fully anticipated that we would complete the legal work and bring about his admission by the beginning of Clemson's second semester. So we had him to withdraw, so he withdrew and returned to his home in Charleston and awaited the final stages of the legal skirmishes. And then of course our predictions were correct and the time came. The rest is history. There's a great deal of background that you will need to know about it, and if time permits I'm going to be pleased to share with you that part of it that I know. I know Mr. Gantt is going to be able to tell you, and I know you're anxious now to hear from Mr. Harvey Gantt, who I consider my most famous client, for whom I have great admiration and pride.

HARVEY B. GANTT

Well, it's always great to be at a gathering with folks who write the history of what happened in our world. And I understood coming out of the dining hall after Mr. Joyner's great speech, and I didn't get to hear that, unfortunately, and perhaps I'll get a copy of the tape. We were talking about some revisionist history

28. Harvey Gantt (third from left) and family seeking the racial desegregation of Clemson University, 1960. Photograph by Cecil J. Williams

that's gone on and some of the great myths and tales that have been told about some of the civil rights events that occurred, many of them forty, fifty years ago. And there were a number of events that surrounded my entrance that have become legend, and often times I've had to sit and say, well, did that really happen to me? The great football story that Frank Howard tells about my coming out to practice and his stacking the line so that I would be discouraged after getting the ball a couple of times. And in two cases he passed the—he had the quarterback give me the ball to go to the right, and the defense was stacked in that direction. And they gave me the ball on the one-yard line, and I ended up in the end zone about nine seconds later with a touchdown. The coach, the assistant coach, came over to Frank and said, "Frank, what are we going to do about this nigger? He got away from a hundred-yard touchdown." He says, "Well, pass the ball to him out in the flat on the left, and we'll make sure that the quarterback will be in position to get him this time." They passed the ball out on the flat. I caught it on the five-yard line, and about eight seconds later I was in the end zone with a touchdown. They said, "Well, Coach, what are we going to do about this nigger?" He says, "I don't see any nigger out there. I see my next halfback is what's. . . . " A legend, a myth, never happened, trust me, and there were numerous other stories I've heard over the last forty-some years—almost forty years now about my going there.

And while I'm flattered in a way that this has become a legend. I thought you might want to hear just a few stories about some of the things that led up to my going to Clemson. And I think these are true, but as the Judge just pointed out, there are some things that we remember a little bit more clearly than other events. I will say about his story that, yes, as a young student, a number of us admired this very dashing attorney from Columbia by way of Spartanburg who just impressed us with his fearlessness at that time and opened up a lot of possibilities for us. And when I first met him I indeed told him I wanted to be an architect and Clemson was a possibility. Now he got the story a little wrong when he said '62. It was 1960 when we graduated from [Burke High School]. He didn't meet my parents right away, but ultimately got to meet them, and we were very influenced by that. I had decided at that time to go to Iowa State, but always felt that Clemson might be a possibility one day. What really ran me back to have him manage our case, and he did in fact write all those letters, was that the forty-two-degree-below-zero weather in Iowa made my stay there much, much shorter. And my inclination then to want to go to one of the better schools of architecture in the country—a more pressing reason to get back home. And the logical person to turn to, of course, as he said, was him, and we have been lifelong friends from that point on as he shepherded my case very skillfully through the federal courts.

I want to talk a little bit more about how a kid from a salt-of-the-earth, working-class family, growing up in the '40s and the '50s, ultimately ends up making this kind of a momentous decision and not even recognizing that that decision would be written in history. We don't grow up—we didn't grow up in the South in the '40s and early '50s deciding that we were going to be the first student to go to this institution or the first mayor or whatever. Those things don't happen—it doesn't happen that way. And often times when I see history written it seems as if these people come full-blown to these rather special occasions.

My childhood—my life was influenced in the early years by a very nurturing family. I saw my dad go off to work everyday. He was fortunate enough to be working in an industry that did not feel the direct economic pressures that a lot of other people felt 'cause he worked in the Charleston Naval Shipyard, which no longer exists. I was impressed by his strong leadership of our family and the fact that every night we came home, we ate as a family together. And we little ones, and I had four other sisters, would listen to the banter and the discussion back and forth that my mother and father had and on occasion an uncle or aunt would have about what was happening around us. On the other hand, while I listened to the politics at the moment spoken by my parents and their adult guests, I grew up in a South that was very segregated, and we were, shall we say, benign to that segregation, not accepting of it one way or the other. It was just the way things were, and our parents said when you get on the bus there was a certain decorum that was expected and you did go in fact to the back of the bus. But we were little kids, you know, we were nurtured. We had teachers that loved us. We did ask questions about why we would pass Mitchell Elementary School to go to A. B. Rhett Elementary School. The white kids went one way, and we went—but that was the way it was. It was not until 1954; the young lady who is a researcher brought me the newspaper article because I told her in a previous interview that that was a life-changing experience for me as an individual.

The *Charleston Evening Post* carried a story that said "Supreme Court rules that segregation is unconstitutional." I was eleven years old, and all of a sudden I was going to be a party to the discussion at the dinner table tonight and, as it turned out, forever and ever after. It changed my life. It had a great impact on me, because now I wanted to understand what the word *segregation* meant. And then I wanted to read everything I could about it, and I did as an eleven-year-old student. There was a library called Dart Hall Library for colored children a few blocks from my house, and the librarian will tell you that I spent every afternoon trying to read everything I could in *Ebony, Jet,* the newspapers, and the periodicals she guided me to. And every article written about, so I knew about, the White Citizens' Councils, and I understood a little bit about the politicians who were making decisions on those kinds of things. And as an eleven-year-old I became politicized and then ultimately became an activist. My dad was a member of the NAACP. It was of course a subversive organization, but he was about to lose his job. And as I listen to him talk, I became a member of the NAACP

Youth Council. But I should say that I never was a firebrand activist in that sense. More a scholar, like many of you are, I suppose, at least interested in all these different movements that were going on, but not an activist. So I saw Autherine M. Lucy in 1955 at the University of Alabama, and I watched the 1957 Little Rock trial and read everything I could, voraciously grabbing any magazine that dealt with it. And I started to know clearly the civil rights luminaries in the movement, Roy Wilkins, Thurgood Marshall, and so forth and so on. And if they ever came to Charleston, I'd find a way to tag along with my father to go to that meeting wherever it was being held. Fascinated, and saw all the possibilities for my life, and the bottom line was I became the activist when four guys sat down at a lunch counter in Greensboro and then they did something that was real. It didn't require going through a court. It didn't require finding a lawyer. It just required having the courage to go sit down, and twenty-seven of us at Burke High School didn't tell our parents, just decided that it was probably better not to ruffle the feathers of the family. My father would have been very supportive of that, but my mother would have said, "No, no, no." And Judge Perry will tell you that even in the latest days of the Clemson trial she had reservations about her son subjecting himself to the possible dangers that would be there by entering that school. But we pulled off that sit-in movement and we were fortunate, even then, as I said much later about South Carolina, you could appeal to the manners of these who managed South Carolina's policy-making whether it was the police chief and mayor in Charleston or the governor and certain members of the legislature. They didn't want us sitting down, but they weren't going to treat us too badly.

So while we had prepared for ketchup to be poured over our heads and for all kinds of terrible things to happen to us, nothing happened to the twenty-seven of us. We got herded off not to a jail but to a courtroom while the chief went and called our parents and told them we had gotten into trouble and therefore come get your kids. Oh yes, they have been arrested and they trespassed and they violated laws, but we're going to let them go home if you will post the bond, and of course that was arranged. I'm not sure how, but they—and of course we got our tongue-lashing from our parents. But I became an activist at that point and met this gentleman and others and all other kinds of possibilities opened up to us. Opened up to me and to my friends and Camellias Flood, who was the person you were referring to, and to a child growing up in the South in 1960 who was aware of what was happening, this massive amount of social change. Of course we didn't say "massive social change," but we were thinking we have an opportunity to change some things. And what's more it seemed like the right and logical thing to do. What's even more is that the other side as big and as powerful as they were seemed a little bit jittery about whether they were right about it, you know. And sometimes kids can pick that up, and we did. So that generation of activists back then all the way down to those students in Orangeburg saw the possibilities for change, and change did happen.

So I wanted to share that little piece of how we sort of arrived at the moment. Now I want to close out by mentioning just a few vignettes about the Clemson experience. I'm not going to talk about the legal aspects of it except to say that—well, let me say three things about that period.

There was the buildup to going to Clemson. What I call the buildup is the first time that I saw a headline, and I believe it was June of 1962, that said, "Negro applies to enter Clemson"—that's the *Charleston Evening Post*. We got the *Charleston Evening Post* in Charleston because the afternoon newspaper is what my daddy read. He didn't read the *News and Courier* in the morning. Those of you from Charleston will understand that. So we always got the evening paper. And the evening paper said I was going to Clemson, and my sister got the paper off the front porch and she ran in the house and she said, "Oh my gosh, we're in trouble. You're on the front page." I said, "Yep, yep, logically it was going to happen. Mr. Perry filed the lawsuit that said we're going to go to Clemson." And so my sister started to look at me a little bit differently. I was a little bit handsomer now and a little bit taller and little bit more—you know because her brother had the courage to go to Clemson.

I went back to Iowa for the fall semester in 1962, and the guys I used to play bridge with in the college lounge picked up on the newspaper story that said "Iowa State student now applies to go to school in the South." And they asked me, "You really going to do that?" I said, "Yes, I am." And then the six o'clock news would come on, Huntley-Brinkley, and you'd see the story about this fellow James Meredith down at the University of Mississippi and there were federal troops and all, and I'd be just getting ready to put my bid in in the bridge game and somebody would stop and say, "Harvey, are you crazy? Are you crazy? You're going to school in a very benign and conducive environment for learning. Look at that guy. Look at all those people. They kill folks down there. Those folk in the South are crazy." But, you know, for the strangest reasons, I never felt that fear about South Carolina. I was telling someone earlier perhaps it has to do with the fact that South Carolina was one of the thirteen original colonies. Perhaps it had something to do with the fact that I grew up in Charleston. Perhaps it has something to do with the fact that Charlestonians always felt that they dominated policy-making in South Carolina. Perhaps it had something to do with the fact that they always felt that they were a cut above—aristocratic, maybe morally as challenged as Mississippi, but from a main standpoint they were going to try to do it the right way. I never felt fear, because I, being the voracious reader that I was, made sure that I got copies of newspapers across the state while at Iowa, kept up with what was going on from the legal perspective from Mathew Perry, but read everything. Particularly read the *Clemson Tiger Daily* newspaper and read the editorial pages to see how the editor, Frank Gentry, who became a major figure in the merger of Bank of America living in Charlotte—and we talk about this even now—was a very levelheaded editor who kept saying, "We've got to do the right thing here." But listening to the student comments, the letters that they wrote. How are we going to act when Harvey comes to school? How are we going to do this, that, and the other? They themselves had this air of inevitability. It's going to happen. We might as well get ready for it. So maybe I had a comfort level about going to school there. It was suggested that if the students were left to their own devices, maybe things wouldn't change. Now of course there were the—the negative side to that was that somebody named Gressette that was running a committee in the General Assembly and the racists and others who suggested ostracizing Harvey Gantt would be the best policy. Don't talk to him; don't do anything, and then he'll leave very soon. Architecture is a tough, tough curriculum. The fellow will flunk out if he even gets in, and I was amused by that. I was just amused by some of that, but my sense was that things would be okay.

The trials were interesting. I didn't understand all the legal ins and outs, but I was comfortable with the leadership of Mathew Perry and Connie Motley and other folks who worked on that. And also amazed at the degree of civility between the attorneys. And I was a nineteen-year-old kid watching the attorneys for the state of South Carolina fraternizing with the attorneys for the plaintiff, and they had an air of inevitability about them. They knew this guy was right and that even though—in fact it was like a play being played out for the benefit of citizens of South Carolina. I thought that was wrong. Politically I thought that was wrong for politicians to extend the resources of the state to fight a battle that they knew they were going to lose. That they didn't trust their citizens to say, "look, the right thing to do is to admit this guy and let's not go through all this," but to exhaust every legal and administrative remedy at their disposal was in fact the way they had to fight this case. And everybody understood what the end result was going to be. Just curious for a nineteen-year-old kid who ultimately ended up in the political arena to observe sometimes the kinds of things we go through to get to where we are.

Finally a lot's been said about the first day that I entered school there. The drama of driving down the highway with Matthew Perry and myself alone in his great big black Buick—lawyers were very impressive even back then and drove wonderful-looking cars. And the gravity of the moment was that I didn't realize, probably didn't dawn on me, I had now just turned twenty years old. I had to stop and get something out of my briefcase about ten or fifteen miles from Clemson. And in stopping that car, I thought we were moving down the highway alone. We knew we were going to be protected when we got to Clemson, I stopped, got out of the car and looked behind, and everything else stops above and below and it hit me that this was different. This was special. This was special.

I signed in to the university, but the thing that really stays with me to this day is the first time I went to the dining hall to eat. I knew I had to do that at some point. The newsmen had all gone. Matthew Perry was driving back to Columbia or holding a news conference somewhere. All of these conferences were over. I was sitting in my room, and the decision was made that—by me, by my stomach I suppose—I've got to go eat. And so I've got to go through this ordeal, and the flashback came to James Meredith's situation of the kids beating on the table in the dining hall and things being really rough. But I set out for the dining hall, which was just a few steps away from my dorm, and when I hit the door of the dining room, there stood all these people, my people, black people. I had forgotten that they serviced the university; that they provide all the domestic services, the janitorial services. They cooked all the food and had been there all along since the university was opened, I suppose, but I had forgotten that. All of us had forgotten that. People wondered how I was going to exist at this school; I was going to be taken care of. They gave me the biggest portion of meat. They gave me the best desserts, but more important than that for the first time I understood. Here was a young man seeking an education, and I said that over and over and I was serious about that, but for the first time it really hit me what this meant, because I could see their chests, their collective chest swell with pride. 'Cause now they could see their children, their uncles and their nieces, their nephews, their cousins could be in that line, too. And yes, they would serve those descendants, but it would be a different day and a different time, and I understood why I had done what I had done.

The Orangeburg Massacre

Cleveland L. Sellers Jr.

As I begin my presentation, I want to share how unexpected consequences will happen as a result of this historically significant conference at the Citadel. There will be many positive consequences for South Carolinians as a result of this Citadel conference, some more profound than others. One major contribution will be the further establishment of the fact that there was a civil rights / freedom struggle in South Carolina. Second, it will be determined that this movement was made up of ordinary citizens, local men, women, and youth; black, white, and native. Third, we will find that the movement was not sporadic or an aberration but instead a well-organized resistance to racial prejudice, violence, discrimination, and poverty. A few days before I came to this conference I received a phone call from two former South Carolina State College (SCSC) students who were very much involved as student activists there back in the mid-1950s. They wanted to make sure that when we talk about SCSC that we did not forget that there was a very rich student protest tradition in Orangeburg and at SCSC beginning even before the 1960s sit-ins and the Freedom Rides. That tradition was begun by male and female youth and students and in collaboration with students at neighboring Claflin College.

In 1956 Charles Brown and Fred Moore led SCSC students in protest against segregated businesses that had economic interests with the college. Then-president Dr. B. C. Turner forcefully ended the protest with the expulsion of nine students, including Moore, the SGA [Student Government Association] president (a senior who was one month away from graduation), Alice Pyatt, Alvin Anderson, and Barbara Brown. This legacy would stay intact as race leaders worked to find ways to implement the 1954 *Brown v. Board of Education* decision desegregating the public schools "with all deliberate speed."

More students would come and raise the banner for change. In 1959 Charles McDew, Ohio native, football player, and son of an SCSC alumnus, enrolled as a freshman. He was swept up by the actions taken by the Greensboro Four, when they launched the February 1, 1960, sit-ins in Greensboro,

N.C., suffering beatings and being arrested several times. Later, McDew withdrew from SCSC to work full time in the freedom struggle and served as the chairman of the Student Nonviolent Coordinating Committee, the largest and most effective group of young organizers in the civil rights / freedom struggle. As Fred Moore reminds us, it is within this historical context of the protest tradition that we must talk about the tragic 1968 event known as the Orangeburg Massacre.

The Orangeburg Massacre was not an aberration. The city of Orangeburg had experienced protest demonstration by both the black community and the student community before, and there had been excessive and abusive use of force such as fire hoses, beatings, and arrests, but never the use of lethal force. There was rhyme and reason to what happened in this city over the course of two decades, and the state very well could have prevented the tragedy if it had not blindly linked itself with the FBI's COINTELPRO [Counter Intelligence Program], "Law 'n' Order," disinformation, character assassination, extralegal and unconstitutional initiatives.

The tragic event which became known as the Orangeburg Massacre was so named because of its similarity to the South African Sharpeville Massacre. In the South African town of Sharpeville, black demonstrators assembled in an open field and peacefully protested apartheid, a vicious system of racial segregation in that country. The Sharpeville demonstration was in protest of black South Africans being mandated to carry national identity cards. The all-white police force opened fire, savagely slaughtering seventy-two Africans and seriously wounding two hundred more. Just as the Sharpeville tragedy was an important event in the struggle to overthrow the South African apartheid system, the Orangeburg Massacre was a significant event to South Carolinians in their efforts to overthrow America's version of apartheid that was still very real in South Carolina.

The Orangeburg Massacre and the facts surrounding the tragedy were, from the outset, marked by suspicion and confusion. Much of the confusion can be attributed to several factors. First, at the time of the tragedy, accurate information was deliberately withheld by the state. Also, the initial reports were distorted, deliberately or otherwise. Third, the collective consciousness of America no longer held the moral suasion of the civil rights movement as an urgent and universal concern. By 1968 the coalition of church, labor, liberal, and civil rights groups had dissolved. On the other side, a reactionary agenda, which emphasized law and order, the new "southern strategy," and a so-called moral majority was emerging under the leadership of Richard Milhous Nixon and the Republican Party. George Wallace had become an active force for nationwide reaction against the movement by running as a third-party candidate for president in 1968. Fourth, there was never a statewide investigation, local investigation, or inquest. There was however an FBI investigation, but it was self-serving and superficial at best. Frank Beacham, a freelance writer and cub reporter for a Columbia television station on the night of the shooting, was quoted as saying, "FBI officials friendly with the South Carolina officers did a superficial investigation obscuring the truth." When U.S. Attorney General Ramsey Clark attempted to investigate, the FBI compromised key evidence and the local U.S. attorneys would not cooperate. Beacham stated that he unquestionably accepted the distorted version of the tragedy.

Initially this smokescreen was an attempt to maintain South Carolina's racially moderate image. Later, it would become the state's sense of denial that kept the truth behind a haze of half-truths and lies—a veil of secrecy. The critical issue surrounding the tragedy remains: why the use of deadly force? The students were unarmed and on their campus. The officers used lethal weapons, double-ought buckshot, which is used for killing large animals like deer, not riot control. The use of deadly force was sanctioned by the FBI for use by state and local police in response to the urban disturbances, rebellions that began in the Harlem section of New York during the summer of 1964. Beacham explains that state authorities claim the deaths were the result of two-way gun battles between students and lawmen. The highway patrolmen insisted that their shooting was done in self-defense to protect themselves from an attacking mob of students. To bolster their claim and deflect responsibility from its own actions, the state hastily devised a media campaign to blame the riot on outside agitators, using a tactic of blame the victim. Henry Lake, a former highway patrolman and official spokesman for the governor, on the night of the shooting accused me of throwing a banister that struck a highway patrolman in the face. Lake insisted, "Sellers, he's the main man. He is the biggest nigger in the crowd."

One day after the shooting the Reverend I. DeQuincey Newman, the state NAACP field secretary, stated, "The fact that such a thing could happen and did happen is an indication that despite all that might be considered progress in terms of interracial cooperation beneath the surface South Carolina—is just about in the same boat as Alabama and Mississippi. The perpetrators of the tragedy and those who have covered it up for them have rendered a great disservice to sometimes heroic efforts that have been made in race relations and interracial cooperation." Many of the students were politically conscious and understood what was happening and who was responsible for the police riot. Dr. Martin Luther King, with whom I had worked on numerous other southern protest activities and campaigns (March on Washington, Selma March, Mississippi Summer Project, and Mississippi Meredith March) was horrified by the shooting. In a statement regarding the Orangeburg Massacre he stated, "The death and wounding of these students lies on the conscience of J. P. Strom, the officer in charge, in his capacity as chief of the South Carolina Law Enforcement Division, the governor of South Carolina to whom Strom is directly answerable and the conscience of all men of good will. We demand the U.S. attorney general act now to bring justice to the perpetrators of the largest armed assault under-taken under cover of law in recent southern history. No further delay or insensi-tivity to this destructive use of police force is conscionable."[1]

South Carolina had touted a pretentious form of pseudo-civility, but what appeared to be a resolution of the civil rights wars came shattering down on top of the empty rhetoric when armed patrolmen were allowed to career out of con-trol and brutally gun down innocent young people.

The state officials believed that if they could maintain a semblance of no con-flict, they could avoid the trouble of other southern states while maintaining their status quo. They miscalculated the pervasive problem by equating quiet with resolve and peace. It was assumed the problem of discrimination and racial prejudice would just go away. Time and again it has been proven that conflict is necessary if change is to occur. Problems cannot solve themselves. Social issues do not simply disappear. We must publicly and relentlessly confront racial prej-udice, racism, and oppression. Peace is not merely the absence of conflict. It is the presence of truth and justice. For more than thirty years, the effort to ignore, distort, and conceal the truth about this tragedy in Orangeburg has continued because state officials have refused to discuss the case or have a review commis-sion. The conspiracy of silence has helped to obstruct the massacre's documen-tation and delayed its entry into the annals of civil rights movement history.

Several factors influenced this treatment of the Orangeburg Massacre. One, the victims were African American students. The timing, 1968, marked for many writers what they considered the end of the civil rights era, and the indigenous student participants were not sponsored by a national civil rights organization. (The protest at the Allstar Bowling Lanes was organized by the college chapter of the NAACP—a fact most seem to forget) However, the Orangeburg movement was truly "of the people," so the idea of blocking its historical reality is as absurd as it is disheartening and pathetic. [Thomas] Carlyle was correct when he stated no lie can live forever.

Since the 1960s a few books have been published and critiqued the idea of the indigenous nature of the freedom movement. Most of the early civil rights literature used the traditional narrative to analyze the freedom struggle. That approach was flawed because it framed the movement around major leaders, national organizations, especially men's involvement and leadership. More recently scholars have moved away from the traditional narrative to recognize that any critical analysis of the civil rights / freedom movement must include the significance of not only race but also class and gender. The new literature exam-ines local movement operations from the bottom to the top using an indigenous grassroots / local people perspective.

In the case of Orangeburg, two astute journalists, Jack Bass and Jack Nelson, became sufficiently determined to confront the silence and disinformation that they wrote the only definitive record of the events surrounding the Orangeburg shooting, in the book *Orangeburg Massacre.* Their effort was courageous and exemplary and utilized the local organizing perspective. This book is the most definitive, scholarly, and documented book on the events of February 1968. Surely there are some S.C. officials who have still refused to read the book because it will shed some light on their complicity in the Orangeburg Massacre.

The book clears up many misconceptions. State government officials stated that there was a confrontation between the students and law enforcement officers. They claim that the patrolmen were in imminent danger and only shot the students because they said the students were charging the officers. They also stated that the troopers were trained by the FBI for riot duty. None of these statements were true. There was no confrontation and no exchange of gunfire.

As an eyewitness myself, and as was discovered by Bass and Nelson, it just did not happen that way. The students who were shot suffered wounds in the back or the bottom of their feet, which indicated clearly that the students were in retreat. National guardsmen who were adjacent to the state police were never ordered to load their weapons. No lock-and-load order meant that the National Guard did not feel or see any imminent danger. There were five police agencies on the scene the night of the tragedy, including army intelligence representatives and three hundred law enforcement officers. Of that total only nine claim that they felt threatened, and the others did not see the imminent danger. Even now, some thirty-plus years later, there has never been an unbiased or objective investigation of any of this tragedy on the part of the state of South Carolina. Ramsey Clark, U.S. attorney general at the time of the massacre, stated later that "in a generalized sense the thought at Orangeburg was the thought of the nation and the people. Our failure to right grievous wrongs permitting conditions to arise in statutory rights and of their opportunity for personal fulfillment in our society. In a specific sense, the shooting was a failure of discipline and professionalism in law enforcement and the leadership's racist attitudes. I think people in charge of law enforcement contingencies that are working in these highly volatile areas must recognize their responsibility and realize that the men will be under a lot of pressure and the risks of shooting people are real and present."[2]

The Orangeburg Massacre remains an example of how government officials, segregationists, and much of the mainstream press did on some occasions collaborate to protect their interests and cover up police brutality and the carnage that characterized the Orangeburg student movement and the student movement in general.

The South Carolina Council on Human Relations and the state chapter of the American Association of University Professors called on the governor, Robert McNair, to appoint a blue-ribbon commission to carry out a complete investigation into the case and circumstances surrounding the tragedy and disclose its finding and recommendation.

The governor stated, "A full disclosure of the facts is essential because of concerns and confusion over the tragedy and because of the pressing urgency that the facts be made public." A University of South Carolina sociologist submitted a proposal to the governor to investigate, but the governor rejected the request, and no state agency ever investigated the tragedy.

Roy Wilkins, executive director of the NAACP, called upon Governor McNair to "rise up above the usual politics and posture of South Carolina and acknowledge that the patrolmen made a mistake. That they shot without any gunfire coming from the campus. That it was a tragic error and that South Carolina wants to start over again," but all efforts by outside agencies and groups to secure an apology or admission of guilt were for naught.[3]

Without an honest and objective assessment of the cause of the police riot in Orangeburg, the perimeter of the killing grounds expanded, increasing the numbers of victims to include Kent State, in Ohio, Jeff Miller, Sandy Scheurer, Bill Schroeder, and Allison Krause; Jackson Mississippi—Jackson State, Jim Hill, Phillip Gibbs, and James Green; North Carolina A&T State—Willie Grimes and the many who were critically wounded. Some of the victims were wounded emotionally, some lost faith in law enforcement, government, democracy, and their ability to secure justice. Some were crushed by the indifference and lack of respect for human decency.

The common threads woven through these tragedies include racism, classism, sexism, and the overzealous and undertrained lawmen of the FBI's COINTELPRO and army intelligence. The real question then and now is what is happening in a society when it becomes unconscionable, sinister, and inhumane to the point that it destroys its young under the pretext of law and order. How can a nation expect young citizens to believe in justice and democracy when they observe lawmen trampling on the ideals of freedom, justice, and peace? Because the Orangeburg Massacre was state-sponsored terror and because there has not been an effort by the state to unveil the truth, the list of victims goes beyond the students wounded or killed and goes beyond their families and loved ones.

I was the *only* person arrested. The only person tried. The only person found guilty and sentenced. I did not commit a crime, and the date on the indictment was changed from the night of the shooting to two nights prior to the shooting (the change of dates created case law). The S.C. attorney did not want to proceed with a trial, because there was not any evidence, but Governor McNair insisted that the state go forward. All of the original charges were dropped, and in two of the three Riot Act charges the judge ruled a "directed verdict" because of lack of evidence. All of the people who testified against me were white law enforcement officers. In the only testimony or evidence that could be used to secure a guilty verdict against me, a white South Carolina Law Enforcement Division officer lied and testified that he saw me on top of a fire truck on the night of February 6, 1968, saying, "Burn, baby, burn." I was found guilty of a "one-man riot" and sentenced to one year hard labor. There was no justice. It was a legal sham. I was summoned to serve the time while my wife was pregnant with our first baby daughter. My daughter was born while her father was away doing time for a crime he did not commit. We named her Nosizwe (Child of the Nation) Abedemi (Born While Father Is Away) Sellers.

Apart from those killed and wounded, who are the victims of the Orangeburg Massacre?

The first victim is justice. The second victim is truth. The third victims are many ordinary citizens who have waited for those responsible to admit their complicity in the cover-up and in the atrocities against humanities. An admission of truth and contrition would allow healing and reconciliation to take place. The denial and distortion continue to place a heavy burden on all citizens, black and white. The denial prevents closure and healing.

In my travels across the state of South Carolina, older men and women who supported the movement in their own ways, some with what little money they could spare, others with quiet dignity, and still others who attended the rallies, marches, and demonstrations, have told me how they prayed for me during my Orangeburg ordeal. I have also had young whites, Orangeburg natives who were children and/or students in 1968, still trying to reconcile the tragic set of circumstances surrounding the Orangeburg Massacre.

Each year families of the slain students, college administrators, and people of good will along with current students commemorate the tragedy, although some critics argue with the effort to continue to commemorate the death and the wounding. A memorial cross with a granite monument is located in the campus center, and a health and physical education building is named Smith, Hammond, and Middleton in memory of the three who lost their lives.

I can understand all of the tears and mourning. Lord knows, I have shed many tears for all who were killed and those whose bodies or minds, and in some cases, both, were broken in the freedom struggle. In some instances they were friends and coworkers; sometimes I asked myself if I could be responsible for their fate by my introducing them to the freedom movement, but that is a moral question that I can never answer. I am proud of the fact that I helped some people to develop a social consciousness that led to their empowerment. They could then gain control over their lives and help bring about change. I always focused on the overall goal to create a better world for all of humanity. In the case of Orangeburg I was a local boy doing exactly what I was supposed to be doing. I didn't hurt or threaten anyone. I was home. This focus, plus the responsibility of family and an understanding of the American protest tradition, forced me to deal with the ugliness, bitterness, and anger that had built up inside me, a result of numerous persecutions.

I wanted to continue to be relevant and rational. I wanted to be a good father figure, not just to my children but to all children. I maintain an abiding faith and a deep spirituality. I also maintain hope for reconciliation. I want to grow, love, and live. Having control over my life requires me to make important adjustments, so I will continue to remember those in the freedom struggles who suffered and who were killed. The memory of being shot down like dogs, seeing students die while using segregated facilities, and grudgingly being provided medical attention remains vivid and horrific. I will constantly purge myself of the enmity while never giving up the fight for equality, truth, and justice, the overall objective of the freedom struggle and the student movement. We live in a broken world, so we must maintain a level of mutual trust just to survive. Maintaining that requisite level of mutual trust requires that I continue to struggle and resist. Struggle and resistance were the two concepts that kept me alive and able to focus on equality, justice, and truth.

I like to use this analogy. There is a man in a damaged boat. The boat has a hole in its bottom. The boat is away from the dock. If the man bales the water, he keeps the boat from sinking, but if the boat is out in the bay it serves no purpose. If he paddles the boat to the dock, it will fill up with water before it gets to the dock. What does the man do to resolve his dilemma? He must do both. He must paddle and bale. Patience and vigilance are very vital characteristics to possess, but one must struggle in order to resist; and one must resist in order to struggle.

As I close, let us not forget that more than thirty-five years after the S.C. state troopers went onto the campus of SCSC, at 10:30 P.M. at night, opened fire and used lethal force on unarmed high school and college students, killing three and wounding many more than the twenty-seven, there is no blue-ribbon review/investigation. Nor is there any sign of contrition, reconciliation, truth, or justice. The massacre remains the litmus test for race relations in South Carolina. A veil of secrecy and silence has been draped over the massacre as if it never happened. State officials from 1968 as well as many current members of the state legislature have a collective sense of denial. I often wonder if that disorder would exist if the dead and wounded had been Clemson students. Governor McNair's original distortion of the truth about what really happened, and his dogged determination to live with the sense of denial, have prevented traction by those who would like to see some investigation to find the truth, an apology, contrition, justice, and restitution.

As time passes the freedom fighters must pass the torch and the legacy of what we have learned. Hegel concluded "it is solely by risking life that freedom is obtained. The individual who has not staked his or her life may no doubt be recognized as a person, but he or she has not obtained the truth of this recognition as an independent self-consciousness." Knowledge of the freedom struggle and the role of students will create the consciousness and give force to the next generation of organizers, student activists, and field secretaries. They will pick up the torch and step onto the stages of history, bringing humanity even closer to the ideals of freedom, justice, and peace. They will carry the banner for the Orangeburg student movement and assure that justice prevails. This group will insist that South Carolina will embrace diversity and equal opportunity for all citizens and create an environment where students, black or white, can never again get caught in the crosshairs.

Notes

1. Jack Bass and Jack Nelson, *The Orangeburg Massacre*, 2nd ed., revised (Macon, Ga.: Mercer University Press, 1984), 197, 150.
2. Ibid., 190.
3. Ibid., 85

JORDON M. SIMMONS III

On the eighth night I remember I went to class, and that afternoon, like I normally would do almost every day, I made my way over to Claflin, where my fiancée was attending school, and I spent time with her that evening. And upon leaving, just prior to leaving, we heard the noise, and I think the students were coming in saying that, you know, there were things going on at the front of the campus, in front of State's campus. And she turned to me and she said, "Well, please don't go off campus." I said, "Well, I'm not going to go off campus." And I told her I would not go off campus. And walking through, I crossed over into State's from Claflin's campus, I ran into Dean Henry Hammond . . . and he was walking up there. He was just walking to campus, you know, patrolling, so to speak, and he was headed up there. And I said if he's going, I'm going to see what's going on also. I think we heard sirens going over. It was not long before the shooting itself, I do know that.

Immediately, instinctively, I dropped to the ground, and within a second, within two or three seconds I began to hear rounds going past my ears. I felt my coat like it was being—somebody was trying to pull it off, you know, with—what it really was, was rounds hitting my coat, and then I got hit. Prior to being hit, just before—prior to being hit I heard some people, you know, people started yelling. In fact, I remember hearing somebody laugh just before we realized we were being shot at. We thought they were shooting in the air. It entered right here and just missed my spine.

I didn't see much, really. I remember running, getting up and moving. I think the coat that I had on probably formed, functioned as a compress, maybe. I don't know; I had a large overcoat on. I remember asking him, I said, "Joe, can you see? Am I just nicked?" I was hoping that it just—that I just got grazed, you know. And he said, "No, it looked like there was a hole there, Jordon." I said, "Oh gollylee." You know, and we got on to the infirmary, and there was blood all over the place. I mean, people were lying around yelling and screaming, and the poor nurse on duty, she was—she was a mess. She—I mean she had never seen anything—it was worse than any combat situation. Let's put it this way. It was probably . . . [similar] to a combat situation in the war. The official count was twenty-seven plus three, actually. Three died and twenty-seven injured.

I recall being awakened by my mother, probably at about two or three o'clock in the morning. She was told that I had about a fifty-fifty chance of making it, you know, based on, I don't know how they came up with those statistics, but they did tell her that. And her driving goal at that point was to get up there and to talk to me and to make certain that if I was to die that I did not harbor any hatred or anger towards the people—towards the people. And she said that she talked to me about that, and she told me that while I was going and passing in and out subconsciously that probably burned into my mind. I've never, you know, if those guys, any—the guy that shot me was to walk into here today, I would not harbor any hard feelings towards him. In all probability he felt that he was doing what he felt was right, but he was scared. But she was fearful, she did not want me to stay here. She did not want me to be operated on. She didn't want them to touch me. So she got me out as soon as she could, and I was taken to a hospital in Charleston. And I was operated on a day or two, within the next day or so.

Jack Bass

I'm Jack Bass, and I'm from North. For those of you who do not know where North is in South Carolina, North is ninety miles southeast of Due West. By geography.

I first really want to thank Vernon Burton and Bo Moore for putting this whole conference together and providing this much larger context to discuss this extremely important episode in South Carolina history, in South Carolina civil rights history. And it's especially timely now, because what is really happening today is we're having a situation in which history is colliding with the present. And it is timely because of the events on the campus of S.C. State, its oral history, and Governor Hodges's apology and presentation, and Governor Sanford this year made a formal apology. And which then resulted in Senator Robert Ford calling for reparations and Senator Darrell Jackson of Richland County and Senator Ford in separate pieces of legislation calling for an official state investigation, and so that is now in play, I guess we can say. I'm going to come back at the end to why the screen is up.

But first let me just give you the facts of what actually happened that week, and I'll try and summarize it quickly. Students protested the segregationist policy of the only bowling alley in Orangeburg. This is in 1968, four years after passage of the 1964 Civil Rights Act, which outlawed discrimination in public accommodations. And . . . there were some questions [about whether] a bowling alley [was] covered, and in the end the courts said, yes, this bowling alley was covered because it had a snack bar in which a substantial amount of food moved in interstate commerce, and I won't get into the legal history, but maybe I should with legal historians here. But—well, maybe I should. It was covered under the Interstate Commerce Clause of the Constitution because the U.S. Supreme Court in 1883 ruled unconstitutional the Civil Rights Act that had passed earlier under the Fourteenth Amendment, and that was the reason.

And so, when students protested and came back the second night there was a confrontation at the bowling alley, and students were arrested in order that they might have the legal challenge made. And then the police chief, who was new to Orangeburg, he was a good police chief. He had closed the bowling alley the first night, but for reasons not very clear he called in a fire truck for precautionary reasons. When the fire truck comes in with—you know, with red lights and so forth, just after students had been released from jail and when—after the arrest that night some of the students who weren't arrested went back to the campus as a movie was letting out, and several hundred students came down five blocks to see what was going on. They were beginning to head back toward the campus when the fire truck came. The police chief did not realize that several years earlier in Orangeburg, a fire truck was used in 1960 to hose down students who were protesting at South Carolina State. So the appearance of the fire truck changed the dynamics of the situation. And let me just say bowling never stopped that night, inside the bowling alley. But as students there was a surge toward the bowling alley and someone broke a side panel to the front door, cracked it, you know, fairly severely, and a police officer grabbed the student and others said he didn't do it. And then someone reportedly threw some liquid in a highway patrolman's face. Now, highway patrol had been brought in because of the events the night before and the bowling owner said he wanted protection and called the governor's mansion.

When the patrolman then supposedly swung his riot baton and hit someone and violence just erupted. By the end of the evening you had one police officer and ten students hospitalized with injuries. Other students treated at the infirmary. At least two instances, and there were faculty and staff of the college there observing, at least two instances in which a highway patrolman held a female student while another clubbed her.

So not surprisingly, when students returned toward the campus they were angry. They passed by a construction site, some picked up rocks, bricks, broke some windshields on automobiles, some windows in buildings along the way, broke four windows at a automobile dealer showcase, and the state of South Carolina response was as though this were the Detroit riot. In fact, the total insurance claims for all the damages that night amounted to less than five thousand dollars.

So National Guard was called in the next day. More highway patrolmen were called in. I had been on the campus earlier and covered some things. I had met Cleveland Sellers the previous fall and done a story on him. He was organizing what were then black awareness groups. It was the beginning of African American studies programs really around the country. He was the quiet member of the trio that then was leading SNCC and thoughtful. He did have a large afro at the time, which to some people in Orangeburg looked like a fright wig. And I met members of the Black Awareness Coordinating Committee, and they had a meeting on the campus Wednesday morning. I got a call from a faculty member at home on Tuesday night, and the shooting occurs on Thursday.

The mayor came and the city manager and the chairman of Black Awareness Coordinating Committee had the microphone. He had an afro himself, a young man from New Jersey, and the city manager insisted that was Cleveland Sellers, who was present, and he was among the people who were rather laughing in response to the inadequate answers they were getting from city officials. And frustration was just sort of building on the campus, and the governor went on television and talked about the outside agitator, meaning Cleveland, who grew up twenty miles away and his mother is a graduate of South Carolina State.

You could—the tension kept building up, and some rocks were thrown at passing automobiles. The highway was blocked in front of the campus. The next day it was more of the same. The acting president, Maceo Nance, who was a tower of strength that week, in my opinion, sent word out students to remain on campus. I went by Cleveland Sellers's house that afternoon and interviewed him, and he said, "Everybody is looking for a scapegoat," which was sort of the headline on my story in the *Charlotte Observer* the next morning. That afternoon—that evening again—highway 601 in front of the campus was closed because of the rocks and so forth thrown. Also on Wednesday night, two white teenagers, who happened to be from North, came on the campus firing a pistol and got—went down a dead-end road, and finally the campus police chased them off campus and shot out a tire. They were never prosecuted.

There was a bonfire built, this was February 8. It was a cold night on a street just in front of the campus. Some boards were taken from a vacant house, a house that had been unoccupied for ten months, and about nine o'clock there were a few gunshots, .22 caliber pistol shots, fired from the Claflin campus over the head of some patrolmen. Another reporter and I went to look at that, and then we heard what sounded like an explosion. And asked the patrolman—the patrolman fired a riot gun in the air, and everything got quiet. Meantime, all of downtown Orangeburg was cordoned off.

Let me give you an example of how tense the situation was, because the other reporter and I went by the National Guard Armory and they were putting out a news release. It took a half hour, you know, I mean the sergeant typing and the corporal correcting and the lieutenant editing and the captain looking at it, and finally the major releases it. And it was about one sentence each of the two—myself and another reporter—could add to our story, and we had a foot race to a pay telephone booth a block away, and I won. And as soon as I picked up the phone, you know this city police car comes roaring up, slams on brakes, and officers jump out on both sides with guns drawn. And I wasn't trying to be cute, I mean, I was just sort of spontaneous. I said, "Do you want to use the phone?" But that's how tense things were, and by the time we got back to what had been Check Point Charlie the shooting had occurred.

And here's what happened. You had five, as Cleveland said, you had five different law enforcement agencies, SLED, the Highway Patrol, National Guard, city police, and the sheriff's department, operating on five different radio frequencies. All the crowd control, riot control manuals at that time, I'm talking about the National Guard, the Army, the FBI, 'cause Jack Nelson and I looked at all of them, had a couple of provisions. One is, nobody fires a weapon unless a senior officer gives an order. Now the National Guard that night was operating that way, and they never loaded weapons. Highway patrolmen were instructed, each officer to decide for himself whether or not his life or a fellow officer's life might be in danger. Direct violation of procedures. They were armed with riot guns, short-barrel shotguns, which by dictionary definition are weapons used to disburse a crowd or mob and not intended to maim or kill. Now for those of you who are hunters will understand the distinction easily between bird shot and buckshot. But a shotgun shell, they all look alike on the outside. On the base of them there is a number, it goes anywhere from zero-zero, a double-ought, to nine, and number nine is what you use for clay pigeons, very tiny pellets. Number eight is slightly larger, for small birds, you know. Number four might for duck hunters. Double-ought, as Cleveland said, is for deer hunting. Each shell contains nine to twelve pellets each the size of a .32 caliber pistol slug, and when it is shot they disburse out. They're lethal, and that's what was issued to the patrolmen.

And when the bonfire reached a certain height, chief of SLED thought, you know, it might endanger some overhead wires, so they called in a fire truck, and then policemen moved to protect the firemen. They moved—you had sixty-six patrolmen moved to the edge of the campus, there were also a few city policemen in there. And as one of the policemen came to the edge, someone, the students then retreated to the interior, someone threw into the air a banister rail about this big taken off the house. As a patrolman looked up, it hit him right in the face, had teeth marks on it. It knocked him down with a bloody face, some people thought he'd been shot. The ambulance was called in. Now the official reaction the next morning, the explanation was, that's what caused the shooting.

What actually happened is the officer was placed in a patrol car and taken to the hospital. By the time the ambulance driver got there he'd already been moved. The ambulance driver had gotten out and had walked around several minutes before the shooting began, so at least five minutes had lapsed.

Here's what actually happened. The students retreated. They came back toward the patrolmen, who were behind the embankment, and as they got about twenty feet away, now a couple were throwing a few small things. And people in front were saying, "Don't throw things." One officer fired what he thought were warning shots, bang, bang, bang, and as soon as those shots were fired, eight- to ten-second fusillade of shotguns, pistols, followed. Now this is eight seconds. Boom, boom, boom, boom, boom, boom, boom, boom, boom, boom, boom, boom. That's what eight seconds of gunfire would sound like. The sky lit up, and of course as soon as, you know, when the first shot went out people thought they were firing blanks or in the air and immediately realized they weren't. Now the— when it was all over, and you'll see this on the video, but what Cleveland I don't think fully explained was he ended up being convicted of riot. He was shot that night and served seven months of a one-year sentence in state prison. And I think what I've described is a level of confusion that existed. They had a bullhorn. They had tear gas. None of that was used.

The video that you're about to see is based on—before I get to that just a couple other things. In terms of—when Cleveland Sellers got pardoned ten years ago by the state Pardon, Probation, and Parole Board. Seven-member board unanimously voted for a pardon after an investigation, and then this video you're about to see a couple of weeks ago, I thought, you know, we should have some excerpts from this oral history just to demonstrate. And I went down to my office eight o'clock one night and had gotten from Marvin Dulaney the transcripts of eight of the people who had returned who had been shot. And after reading them all, I realized that within those transcripts you could pull out excerpts in which they would tell the story of what happened that night. And this what you're going to see is a rough cut. It's not really a documentary. It has a similar format, but it's very much a rough cut in terms of what video people would call production there as it has its flaws. In terms of content, I think it's very powerful.

"We're Not There Yet"

Orangeburg, 1968–2003

WILLIAM C. HINE

Forty years ago, on January 23, 1963, Harvey Gantt enrolled as the first black student at Clemson College, an episode characterized by the *Saturday Evening Post* as "integration with dignity." Thirty-five years ago, on February 8, 1968, three students were killed and twenty-seven young men were injured in the Orangeburg Massacre, an event no one associates with dignity—not to mention nonviolence or peaceful change.

Though—and unlike Kent State—the Orangeburg Massacre has been all but ignored by American historians, it has endured in South Carolina's past as one

29. Waiting for "equal justice under law": Orangeburg County courthouse, 1959. Photograph by Cecil J. Williams

30. *South Carolina State and Claflin students marching against segregation, 1960. Photograph by Cecil J. Williams*

31. *A Ku Klux Klan march in Orangeburg, 1962. Photograph by Cecil J. Williams*

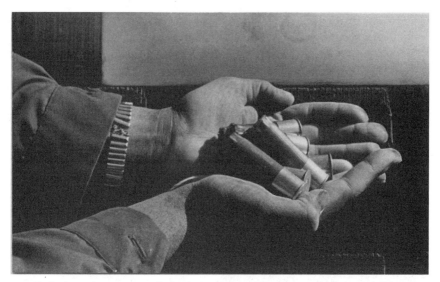

32. Shells from shotgun rounds fired at South Carolina State students, February 1968. Photograph by Cecil J. Williams

33. Samuel Hammond Jr., 1949–1968. Photograph by Cecil J. Williams

34. Delano Middleton, 1950–1968.
Photograph by Cecil J. Williams

35. Henry Smith, 1948–1968.
Photograph by Cecil J. Williams

of the genuine tragedies of the twentieth century. For three decades the massacre has been an open and festering wound that has deeply divided the black and white communities in Orangeburg. There have been two primary reasons why this racial animosity has persisted for so long.

First, South Carolina State University has held a memorial service every February 8 since 1969. That ceremony has usually attracted newspaper and television coverage that has laid bare diametrically opposed views of what happened in 1968. Most people in the black community regarded it as fitting and proper that there be an annual tribute to those whose lives were sacrificed in a fusillade of gunfire from untrained and racist highway patrolmen. To the contrary, more than a few people in the white community considered the young men not martyrs but angry and dangerous black militants, incited by outside agitators, who were bent on mayhem and violence. Only the heroic efforts of the highway patrolmen saved Orangeburg from destruction and devastation.

Second, many white people in Orangeburg regard the book written by Jack Bass and Jack Nelson and published in 1970 as no more than a series of misrepresentations and inaccuracies that utterly fails to explain what really happened in Orangeburg. The book has remained in print and thus has continued to be a disagreeable reminder of a past that many do not believe happened.

On the thirtieth anniversary of the massacre in 1998 an especially unpleasant series of exchanges were published in the local newspaper, the *Orangeburg Times and Democrat,* that finally prompted many black and white people to join together in 1999 to begin the slow process of reconciliation. The first letter published on February 8, 1998, came from a black woman and graduate of Claflin University.

Nellie C. Bradley lived near the campuses and, as she recounted the fears and apprehensions that she and her two children experienced in 1968, she blamed the students. "This tragedy could have been avoided, if those students who were breaking the law had been disciplined. The best discipline that I can think of would be to have sent them home. Demonstrations are all right, but breaking the law is something else."[1]

Bradley's letter enabled white correspondents to unleash years of pent-up anger at the veneration of the protesting students and to complain that the events of those days and nights in February 1968 had been grossly misrepresented. W. W. Dukes, one of Orangeburg's prominent businessmen—the founder and CEO of Applied Engineering Co.—and a former Orangeburg Citizen of the Year, composed a long letter praising Bradley and excoriating those responsible for misleading the public about the event. "Jack Bass's book was wrong when it was published and each year it is exaggerated, distorted, and added to. We, who lived here at the time, are seeing history literally rewritten before our eyes and yet no one speaks out for fear of being called a racist." Dukes added that the demonstrating students, who had already destroyed property,

were urged on by "outside agitators sent in by civil rights leaders" who were
determined to foment racial division and who wanted to destroy Orangeburg:
"they passed the word that they were going to burn the town." Dukes insisted
that the students opened fire first on law enforcement personnel. He claimed
that a friend who "was on the scene at the time" had told him. "I know for a fact
that the first shots came from the students' side."

Dukes then advised black people that if they quit complaining about history
their lives would improve. "If blacks would stop living in the past and stop
dwelling on the terrible injustices their ancestors endured—by being sold into
slavery by their own people and suffering many years of it under my ancestors as
well as the discrimination they have been subjected to since—then they will be
better off."

Dukes proffered still more wisdom, recommending that people of color dis-
criminate more carefully in who they choose to admire and honor. "They need
to portray Clarence Thomas as a role model rather than an 'Uncle Tom.'" He suggested that they pay heed to distinguished writers Dr. Thomas Sowell and Armstrong Williams.

Finally Dukes lamented his own past—"the injustices done to my ancestors
by the North and Sherman's inhuman march." His family endured the burning
of Orangeburg and the destruction of a plantation in Darlington at the hands of
Sherman's troops in 1865. He finally concluded by asking readers to "beat this
racial discrimination" and to come together so that "there are no African, Hispanic, Oriental, White, etc. Americans—just plain Americans."[2]

The Dukes letter inspired others to take pen in hand. Eugene R. Walter Jr.
wrote to commend both Dukes and Bradley for speaking the truth. "I completely agree with Mr. Dukes' advice to both blacks and whites to put the past
to bed and concentrate on the future." A retiree from the North, Charlene A.
Baker, responded diplomatically: "I think Mr. Dukes has very good intentions,
but some of his thoughts are just a little off." She explained that she thought
black people could select their own role models. "I may be mistaken, but I
never heard a black person tell white people who their role models should be."
She added that she considered Thurgood Marshall more worthy of emulation
than Clarence Thomas.[3]

Samuel T. Fogle, the longtime manager of the Orangeburg County Fair,
returned to the source of the controversy. "For far too many days the pages of the
T&D have been filled with garbage entitled 'The Orangeburg Massacre.'" "Why
should we," he asked, "be expected to believe or expect much from a scalawag
author, Jack Bass, a native of North (near where I reside)? But we do expect more
from our local newspaper." He went on to absolve the highway patrolmen and to
blame the students. "Logic proves that rioters provoked troopers to return fire in
self defense." He ended by appealing for people to put the past behind them and

"to move forward in harmony. Orangeburg is too nice a town to be constantly bombarded with negative publicity."[4]

James Sulton, an Orangeburg leader for nearly a half century and prominent black businessman, responded to Dukes with a long letter. "I happen to know that Bill Dukes is not a bad person, but what he says is very, very bad." Sulton acknowledged that perhaps Bass (Nelson is never mentioned) may not have written a perfect book, "but Dukes would do well to take the author to task on the facts rather than ask us to deem the entire work a distortion just because he says so. Dukes himself brings no contrary facts to the table. He backs up his bodacious claim that students fired the first shot with the flimsy evidence that a friend told him so. That is fine if such hearsay convinces Dukes, but he should not expect the rest of the world to buy such a crock." Sulton wondered about the consistency of Dukes's argument. "Dukes also criticizes black people for their victimization complex. Then he goes into great detail about his own family's travails before, during and after the Civil War. Dukes does not only delve into it, he waddles in it."

Sulton finished on a positive note. He commended Dukes for expressing his views: Dukes "takes an important step in the direction of open, honest communication. I believe we need a lot more of that. It is not important that he adopt my point of view or I subscribe to his. It remains important, though, for everyone to freely express their views on the delicate matters of history without expecting to impose those views on others as 'the truth.' Only then can we approach the elusive unity that Dukes says he advocates."[5]

Sulton was prophetic. People in Orangeburg—weary of the annual vituperation that accompanied the anniversary of the massacre and genuinely disturbed at the ugly tenor of the 1998 comments—took action to foster a measure of reconciliation in 1999. Twelve local leaders—"concerned with the broken relationships in Orangeburg"—drew up a statement: "Orangeburg, let us heal ourselves. . . ." Among those twelve leaders were Dean Livingston, the publisher of the *Times and Democrat,* and M. Maceo Nance Jr., the retired president of South Carolina State University. "History cannot be rewritten," they declared, "but it can and should be used to move forward and rebuild racial relations." They acknowledged the importance of the yearly commemoration of the tragedy. "The annual memorial service must continue to be the foundation for better relations among the races, not the root of increased tension in the Orangeburg community." More than 250 people signed the statement, published on a full page of the *Times and Democrat* on Sunday, February 8, 1999. It was a singular achievement for a city not renowned for its racial harmony.

The process of reconciliation took another step forward in 2001. With funding provided in part by the South Carolina Humanities Council, South Carolina State University collaborated with the University of South Carolina and the College of Charleston to conduct an oral history of some of the survivors and people directly involved in the massacre. There were, however, unintended consequences of what simply began as an effort to expand the historical record of what had happened in 1968.

The participants in the oral history project were also invited to take part in a public program on the thirty-third anniversary of the event, and it became a profoundly moving moment of remembrance and reconciliation as hundreds of people assembled on the campus of South Carolina State. The committee responsible for initiating the oral history asked South Carolina State University president Leroy Davis (who was a student at the time of the massacre) to invite Governor Jim Hodges. Davis did, and Hodges accepted.

Hodges proceeded to apologize: "We deeply regret what happened on the night of February 8, 1968. The Orangeburg Massacre was a great tragedy to our state. Even today, the state of South Carolina bows its head, bends its knee, and begins the search for reconciliation."[6] Perhaps the most astonishing development occurred days earlier when Captain David Deering, commander of district 7 of the South Carolina Highway Patrol, asked President Davis if a delegation of highway patrolmen could attend the ceremony. Six patrolmen—three white men and three black men—did attend and were recognized during the program. As much as anything else, the voluntary participation of a younger generation of highway patrolmen eliminated the ugly and mean-spirited rhetoric that erupted around previous observances.

No one who lives in Orangeburg in 2003 would contend that the community has freed itself of racial rancor and division. It has not. But neither is it the same community that it was in 1968 or even in 1998. With the willingness and commitment of local citizens to take a public stand for racial healing in 1999, with the governor's apology in 2001, and with the presence of the six highway patrolmen at the same ceremony, Orangeburg has exorcized some of its racial demons. But the process is far from finished. Will that dedication to strengthening bonds and ties among all the community's residents continue or will it falter?

Notes

1. *Orangeburg Times and Democrat,* February 8, 1998.
2. Ibid., February 10, 1998.
3. Ibid., February 15, 1968.
4. Ibid.
5. Ibid.
6. Ibid., February 8, 2001.

Part 6 ᥱᎇ Crosscurrents at Century's End

In this closing section of the volume, three of the region's best historians reflect, as professional observers and as citizens, on the legacy of the civil rights movement in South Carolina at the beginning of the twenty-first century.

Economic historian Gavin Wright in "The Economics of the Civil Rights Revolution," provides one of the first overviews of the subject. Arguing that the civil rights movement was an economic as well as a political and social revolution, Wright shows that, contrary to popular thought, African Americans won real benefits from their activism, not simply limited access to the white world at the cost of losing many vibrant black institutions. Its effects, in fact, included economic gains for blacks in the South that were tangible and enduring, encouraging a resurgence in African American communities and a corresponding increase in the number of black-owned businesses. More than that, however, the movement had a profound impact on the southern regional economy as a whole, creating a substantial African American presence in its economic as well as political life, a development that continues to be a distinguishing feature of the South.

In his autobiographical essay "Civil Rights and Politics in South Carolina: The Perspective of One Lifetime, 1940–2003," Dan Carter evocatively describes the web of racial customs that bound him as a boy growing up in Florence, South Carolina, in the early 1950s and that made him believe that normal white South Carolinians, including himself and his own family, were the "innocent victims of a ruthless conspiracy led by that infamous NAACP." Carter then goes on to explain the whirlwind of social ferment that tore him away from the traditions of his upbringing as a college student in Columbia in the early 1960s. The subsequent changes in the state's racial affairs were great and have helped

make great advances for the state's African American population, he acknowledges. But, Carter argues, sharp racial differences persist and continue to
shape—more than any other single factor—the lives of the people of the Palmetto State, leading him to caution that there remains much work to do before
the society of justice and equal opportunity that inspired the civil rights movement is reached.

Carter's fellow South Carolinian and college roommate, Charles Joyner,
expands on those themes in the volume's concluding essay, "How Far We Have
Come—How Far We Still Have to Go." Joyner describes in equally evocative
fashion the policies of South Carolina that he encountered as a young man.
Describing the state as being run by men who did not understand the word
democracy in the way the rest of the world did, he denounces their blatant
racism and resistance to demands for equality. Joyner goes on to recall the
activists who worked in the state to achieve social justice, praising their courage
but lamenting their inability to remove all the barriers that separate black and
white Carolinians and, thereby, promote a fuller brotherhood between them.
What is worse, Joyner suggests, is that this failure allowed the opponents of
progress to regain much of the ground they lost in the mid-twentieth century
and to implement policies that seemed to be designed to return the nation
to the days of "separate but equal." He believes, however, that a basis for
achieving the dream of full brotherhood still exists within the rich folk culture
that black and white South Carolinians have historically shared. The key now,
as always, is whether or not they are willing to continue to try.

The Economics of the
Civil Rights Revolution

GAVIN WRIGHT

Economics and economic history are usually neglected stepchildren at sessions on civil rights history. This neglect is unfortunate, because expanding economic opportunity was an important motivation for the civil rights movement from its earliest days. And the perception of failure on the economic front is generally the main reason for pessimistic assessments of the movement's overall success. Glenn Eskew concludes his book on Birmingham: "Clearly the civil rights movement failed to solve the problems experienced by many black people. The movement . . . gained access for a few while never challenging the structure of the system."[1] After telling the story of the movement in Tuskegee, Alabama, Robert Norrell reports: "The attainment of political rights in the 1960s had raised the hopes of poor blacks for material advancement. . . Most of the hopes for economic advancement were disappointed, however."[2] One often hears that integration inflicted heavy losses on black business communities, leaving the overall balance unclear. Peter Applebome writes that the civil rights revolution was "a mixed blessing for southern blacks, who won a measure of integration into a white world at the expense of some of the enduring and nurturing institutions of the old black one." Applebome reports that black nostalgia for the era of segregation has become "a common theme throughout the South."[3] According to Robert E. Weems Jr., "White-owned businesses, rather than unfettered black consumers, were the primary beneficiaries of the Civil Rights Act of 1964."[4]

Are these appraisals accurate? We will not know until the full economic history of the civil rights revolution has been written, and this project has barely begun. As Zhou Enlai is reported to have replied when asked in the 1970s about the historical effect of the French Revolution, "It's too early to say." This presentation attempts a modest beginning by surveying the record of the movement from an economic perspective. South Carolina evidence is highlighted where possible, but perhaps the core propositions pertain to the regional as a whole.

I argue, first, that the civil rights revolution was an economic as well as a political and social revolution, and that its effects included economic gains for blacks in the South that were tangible and enduring; second, that the civil rights revolution was a liberating economic breakthrough for the southern regional economy as well as for its black population; and third, that the black presence in economic as well as political life continues to be a distinguishing feature of the South, another lasting consequence of the civil rights revolution of the 1960s.

Economic Goals of the Civil Rights Movement

Although one may read many historical accounts without realizing it, demands for economic justice were an important feature of the grassroots mobilizations that we now know as the civil rights movement. Clearly there was an economic dimension to the campaigns for equal treatment of blacks as consumers—at lunch counters, movie theaters, hotels, amusement parks—which were the immediate objects of pressure in boycotts of downtown business districts. But just as prominent were the demands for "responsible jobs" that had long been denied to blacks, no matter how large the black share in the local population or consumer base. A flyer from Warrenton, North Carolina, in the summer of 1963, uses traditional American political rhetoric ("Citizens Who Truly Believe in Real Democracy") in support of both consumer rights and employment rights: "Why Spend Your Dollars in Any Store Where They Do Not Hire Any Negroes in Responsible Jobs?"

Similar examples can be found throughout the South. In Birmingham pickets wore sandwich boards that read: "Don't buy where you cannot be a salesman," and continued their pressure until each of the five downtown department stores had hired at least one black clerk.[5] Calls for equity in municipal hiring were also prominent.

In industrial settings black workers had long struggled against segregated promotion lines that denied them access to higher-paying skilled and supervisory positions—if indeed they were not excluded entirely from the industry, as was virtually true in the case of textiles. For those inclined to believe in the power of economic incentives, it is chilling to acknowledge how readily southern employers acquiesced in these discriminatory policies, including northern firms with southern plants such as the Scott Paper Company.[6] In Alabama, with one of the longest industrial histories in the South, a survey of firms in all major branches of the economy found not a single case before the 1960s where management "drawing on cost calculations, business norms, or some abstract concept of justice, chose to desegregate the work place or break down job discrimination. . . . Even in retrospect, off the record, within the confines of their own offices, businessmen did not recall that the racial order created any 'impediments' or 'difficulties' for their enterprises."[7] African American workers struggled

CITIZENS!

ALL CITIZENS WHO TRULY BELIEVE IN A REAL DEMOCRACY:

Wherein All Citizens Have An Equal Opportunity To Employment And Full Enjoyment Of All Services Of Any Store.

PLEASE READ THIS!

Why Spend Your Dollars In Any Store Where They Do Not Hire Any Negroes In Responsible Jobs? Why Spend Your Dollars For Drugs And Cosmetics And Not Be Offered Fountain Service In The Same Store? Any Self Respecting Negro Who Desires First Class Citizenship Will Not Support Such Stores And Businesses.

Your Full Cooperation Is Needed In This Drive.

DO NOT BUY IN WARRENTON, NORTH CAROLINA

36. *Business boycott flyer, 1963*

against these barriers for years with little success. But they were keenly aware of the relevance of the movement for their objectives.

Taking a longer view, civil rights goals of integrated schools and access to higher education constituted demands for participation in career opportunities that white southerners had long enjoyed. In the wake of agricultural mechanization, economic prospects for blacks in the South grew steadily bleaker throughout the 1950s. The out-migration of four million African Americans between

1940 and 1965 reflects the absence of realistic hopes for advancement within the region.

The Civil Rights Revolution and the Labor Market

The federal legislative breakthroughs of 1964 and 1965 had a dramatic effect on this situation. Let me concentrate here on the textiles industry, the most extreme example of segregation and the most discontinuous break with historical practice. Southern textiles had been virtually all-white for one hundred years until the 1960s. But the share of black employees in South Carolina textiles jumped from less than 5 percent in 1963 to more than 20 percent in 1970, rising to more than one-third by 1980 (fig. 37).

A detailed case study by economists James Heckman and Bruce Payner confirms the close association between integration in textiles and the passage of the Civil Rights Act of 1964, effects largely driven by federal pressure exercised through government contracts.[8] Similar patterns were observed in all the southern textiles states.

This breakthrough was an authentic part of the civil rights movement, not just through "top-down" channels from Washington but in the minds of the participants. Floyd Harris, one of the first black textile workers in West Point, Georgia, recalled, "I was active in the social revolution that went on from the fifties, through the sixties and early seventies, so I was aware of what the black leaders were talking about. We wrote the laws and they passed the Civil Rights bill, and I knew that if the federal government made it a law it'd have to be followed. Our management here is smart, and they knew it too. Besides, that was the only way they could survive."[9] According to oral histories, blacks in textile areas referred to integration as "the Change" and associated it with the reversal of black regional migration between the 1960s and the 1970s.

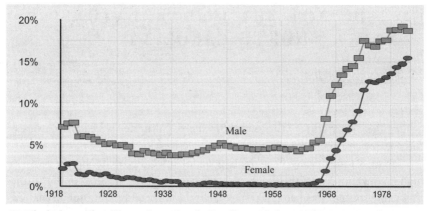

37. *Black share of textile workers, South Carolina, 1918–1981. Source: South Carolina Department of Labor,* Annual Reports

Several aspects of the textiles story deserve closer scrutiny. One is the allegation sometimes heard that employment of blacks did not represent a change of heart on the part of the companies but was merely a lifesaving response to labor-market conditions during the boom years of the 1960s. Is this what Floyd Harris meant in saying "that was the only way they could survive"? Indeed, there is something in this view. Textile firms did have a self-interest in employing black workers, a consideration that may help to explain the puzzle of how a small, underfunded agency such as the Equal Employment Opportunity Commission could have such a powerful impact with such limited resources devoted to overt enforcement. One mill executive wrote in 1968 that the Civil Rights Act was "a blessing in disguise for us," because it allowed them to blame the federal government in justifying integration to resistant white workers. Timothy Minchin quotes the personnel manager of another firm: "The government gave us a nice way to facilitate it and if anybody wanted to complain about it, white people who would say 'hey why are you hiring all of these black people,' you'd say 'because the government forces us to do this,' you could place the blame on the government."[10]

But the element of employer self-interest does not diminish the central role of the civil rights movement—both the legislation and the broader change in atmosphere—in promoting "the Change." Sixty to seventy years before, textile firms faced strong incentives to hire black workers, and numerous "experiments" were conducted in Georgia and North and South Carolina. In that early case of "market-driven integration," all of the experiments failed. When blacks were introduced into existing plants, white workers rebelled. All-black mills failed because of a lack of skills and capital—which is to say, because of a lack of patience on the part of investors—perversely confirming the prevailing prejudice that blacks could not handle factory work. Evidently employer self-interest and tight labor markets in themselves were not enough.

Minchin also stresses that it would be quite mistaken to say that there was just one breakthrough historical moment in 1964–65, after which integration was all downhill, propelled by market forces. Although some firms were ready to jump at the first legal excuse, many others made their move only after charges were filed by the Equal Employment Opportunity Commission or under the threat of litigation. The J. P. Stevens plant in Abbeville, South Carolina, for example, rapidly increased its hiring of African Americans after the filing of a case in 1972. Between 1971 and 1972 the share of female hires who were black tripled, from 10 to 30 percent. The proportion of black doffers jumped from 3.8 to 28.6, spinners from 9.6 to 24.5, and warper and creel tenders from 0 to 16.7 percent.[11]

Even with the backing of the federal government and the law of supply and demand, the first pioneer black textile workers often had to cope with hostile reactions from white workers and doubts about their competence on the part of supervisors. Minchin tells the story of a personnel manager at Dan River Mills, who in 1969 was genuinely astonished to read a newspaper article in which a textile executive claimed that blacks had proven to be good textile workers. The manager wrote to a colleague: "When I read [this] comment . . . , I was curious because, from all I have heard, the Negroes we are employing are shiftless, lazy, don't want to work and leave as soon as they are hired." So a Dan River team undertook a systematic study of comparative worker performance in their own company, the results of which showed conclusively that blacks had lower turnover rates and absenteeism than whites and "no discernible difference in productivity," except that black workers scored marginally higher than whites in certain job classifications.[12]

Exactly as an economist would predict in a case of complete racial exclusion, the first cohorts of black textile workers were better qualified and performed better on the job than the average for whites; and because they had fewer outside employment opportunities, they displayed greater attachment to their textile jobs. In at least some cases relations between the races on the shop floor were reported to have improved over time, as stereotypes on both sides were undermined by experience.[13]

Producing textiles was the largest southern industry, but not the only one to be integrated as the result of civil rights legislation and litigation. For South Carolina we actually have rather good data on the racial employment, because of annual state labor reports established in the 1930s to enforce the segregation laws. Figure 38 displays the remarkable fact that between 1940 and 1964, 90 percent of new manufacturing jobs in South Carolina went to whites. Within fifteen years of the Civil Rights Act, more than one-third of these jobs were held by blacks, a share nearly equal to their representation in the state population.

Figure 38 actually understates the significance of integration for black job opportunities, because in contrast to textiles, other southern industries employed blacks but restricted their potential for advancement by means of segregated progression lines or seniority ladders. In the paper industry, a prime growth sector in the twentieth-century "second wave" of southern industrialization, blacks were consigned from the beginning to heavy, low-paying, laboring jobs. Skilled positions were controlled by segregated (all-white) unions, which the companies preferred not to challenge. This racial structure showed no signs of moderating over time, but was if anything more entrenched during the 1950s than before World War II.[14] In oral history recollections, both black and white workers agreed that industrial segregation would have persisted indefinitely if it had not been for the Civil Rights Act of 1964.[15]

As with textiles, the Civil Rights Act itself was only the beginning, a landmark that gave black workers the confidence to launch a series of lawsuits against companies and unions. The breakthrough in the paper industry was the 1968 decision against the Crown-Zellerbach Company of Bogalusa, Louisiana, which determined that a superficially neutral seniority system could be illegal if it

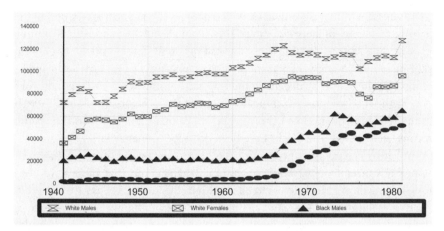

38. *Employment in South Carolina manufacturing, 1940–1980. Source: South Carolina Department of Labor,* Annual Reports

impeded rectification of historical restrictions on black workers to less desirable jobs. The decision led in turn to the Jackson Memorandum of 1968, in which International Paper and its southern unions accepted the principle that blacks advance to their "rightful place" on the company-wide seniority ladder. Under this system, black representation in industry blue-collar jobs increased from 15 to nearly 30 percent by the 1990s, including many of the higher-paying, machine-tending jobs they had previously been denied.[16] In the Alabama pulp and paper industry, minority representation in clerical and sales jobs increased from less than 1 percent in 1966 to 15 percent by 1981.[17]

Overall, national figures show a sharp upward shift in relative black incomes between 1965 and 1975. On closer examination, these gains were almost entirely attributable to black workers in the South.[18] Careful econometric studies confirm the striking mid-1960s southern discontinuity in relative black wages.[19] Similar discontinuities occurred in black infant mortality and other indicators of basic living standards.[20] Pulling the picture together, the notion that the civil rights revolution had little impact on ordinary people should be emphatically rejected.

Moving Up in the Labor Market

The onetime breakthroughs in previously segregated industries would not be enough to make the case for an enduring civil rights economic revolution. There have been many economic downs as well as ups since the 1960s, in the South as in the rest of the nation. If integrating the textiles industry was the biggest success of the movement, this would not be much of a rock on which to stand for the long haul. Employment in American manufacturing has been declining since the 1950s, especially in labor-intensive, import-competing industries such as textiles. Much of the disillusionment with the movement is traceable to broad trends in the national labor market, which have resulted in near stagnation in the average real wages of labor since the 1970s, despite the continuation of economic growth. The reasons for this trend are still debated: slow productivity growth, skill-biased technology, immigration, and yes, political factors such as the weakening of unions and the decline in the real minimum wage. Although in history everything is related to everything else, most of these factors should not be seen as indirect consequences of the civil rights movement. But the South has by no means been spared, and blacks have been disproportionately affected.

What we can say is that education has become increasingly essential for economic advancement in twentieth-century America, and that there have been long-term gains in black access to education in the South. The positive trend in relative spending on black students and educational attainment long predates the modern civil rights movement. From the disastrous setback that accompanied disfranchisement at the turn of the twentieth century, there was a long, slow improvement in the relative quality of black schools, propelled by agitation, litigation, and private philanthropy—in short, by the forerunners of the civil rights movement, broadly construed.[21] For the era in which we can clearly assign resources to students by race—the era of segregated schools—we know that by such indicators as pupil-teacher ratios, term length, and relative teacher pay, black schools had progressed to near equality with whites by the late 1950s.[22] The first substantial progress in desegregation came only in the late 1960s, impelled by financial penalties for noncompliance contained in the Civil Rights Act and the Elementary and Secondary Education Act of 1965. The proportion of southern black students in schools more than 90 percent black declined from 77.8 percent in 1968 to 24.7 percent in 1972, ushering in an era in which the South has had the most desegregated classrooms in the nation. School integration brought measurable benefits in educational attainment and earnings to black students enrolling after the policy shift.[23] Indeed, some economists attribute virtually the entire gain in relative black incomes to this long-term increase in black human capital.[24]

The problem with this reductionist perspective is that it neglects the feedback effects from the labor market on the value of black schooling. This relationship is an old story in southern economic history. Why educate the black, the planter wanted to know, "when as soon as one of the younger class gets so he can read and write and cipher, he wants to go to town. It is rare to find one who can read and write and cipher in the field at work."[25] Ostensibly sympathetic whites, even philanthropic northerners, believed "that it is a crime for any teacher, white or black, to educate the negro for positions which are not open to him," and that the purpose of black schools should be to "educate [blacks] for their environment and not out of it."[26] When the Rosenwald Fund sought to encourage black high schools in the 1920s and 1930s, the fund sponsored surveys of "Negro jobs" in various cities, so as to adapt the curriculum to the jobs actually available. In place after place the responses indicated that there were no black jobs for which a high school education would be useful. Thus, black schools typically did not offer training in such subjects as stenography, accounting, bookkeeping, printing, or typing. The black high school in Greenville, South Carolina, excluded textiles entirely.[27]

In the face of such disincentives, it is remarkable how much progress was achieved through sheer effort and willpower on the part of the NAACP. But even if resources for black schools were increased, the dampening effects of labor market discrimination on the schools could not be fully overcome in the Jim Crow era. Glaring gaps in curricula between black and white high schools were still present as late as the 1960s. By that time training in auto mechanics was one of the more popular options in vocational education, but with a few exceptions these courses were offered only at white high schools, not black. High school officials defended their programs by saying that their curriculum was a rational response to job availability.[28] Persistent black students who overcame discouragements to complete high school sometimes found that they had to conceal this fact in order to gain employment. James Fields was hired as a laborer at Union Bag in Savannah in the 1940s and was told "they didn't want no smart black man." As Fields recounted: "When I filled my application out . . . I put ninth grade instead of twelfth, because I figured they didn't want . . . no smart black man, in order to get hired. I was hired."[29]

Thus we find that the labor market breakthroughs of the mid-1960s coincided with a sharp increase in the black high school graduation rate in the South, from 35 percent (of the twenty- to twenty-four-year-old population) in 1960 to 57 percent in 1970 and to 71 percent by 1977. Black enrollment in higher education grew even more dramatically, from 84,000 in 1960 (overwhelmingly in historically black institutions) to 426,000 in 1976. Complementarity between higher education and labor market desegregation is suggested by the simultaneous upsurge in recruitment visits by corporate representatives to historically black colleges, from an average of just four per school in 1960 to nearly three hundred per school in 1970. The largest single component of the increased black enrollment, however, was at predominantly white institutions, from virtually 0 in 1960 to 243,000 in 1976.[30]

In recent years, many observers have expressed frustration over the fact that black enrollments in higher education have not increased as a share of the total since the 1970s, in the South as in the rest of the nation.[31] The frustrations are real, as are the concerns for the future of historically black institutions of higher education. But we should place these debates in historical perspective. In essence the civil rights revolution of the 1960s launched an upgrading of black higher education in the South, and these gains have largely been maintained across the intervening years, despite dramatic changes in the political climate.

Economic Liberation for the Whole South?

If southern business interests stood to gain from integration, was their acquiescence essentially an expression of *regional* economic interests? Was the civil rights revolution an economic revolution for the South as a whole, not just for its black population? I believe the answer is yes. Unfortunately for historical methodology, it is difficult to confirm this proposition with a simple before-and-after test. The South began its convergence toward national per capita income levels around the time of World War II, a full generation prior to its emancipation in the 1960s. What we have to argue, therefore, is that the South could not have sustained its rate of economic progress if it had not been for civil rights. But this case can be made.

On one level, postwar regional economic convergence had a basis in long-term trends in the scientific roots of technology, including the falling cost of distance effected by new modes of transportation and communication. Science-based technologies relaxed many of the constraints that implicitly limited the geographic spread of modern practices to the temperate zone—air conditioning being the most popularly cited example, but by no means the only one. The result has been a steady trend toward geographic dispersion in economic activity since World War II, to the western and southwestern parts of the country as well as to the southeast.[32]

As it happened, however, the proximate causes of the southern economic "takeoff" took the form of a series of discrete historical events, beginning with national policy shifts in the 1930s and culminating with the diffusion of mechanical cotton harvesting in the late 1950s. Together, these developments tipped the political balance in southern states toward vigorous efforts to attract business through tax breaks, municipal bonds for plant construction, industrial development corporations, research parks, and expenditures on publicity far beyond those of other regions. James C. Cobb calls the phenomenon itself the "selling of the South."[33] It was reflected not just in business recruitment but in aggressive competition for defense spending and federal transportation funding.[34] One still hears it said that the South has not changed all that much, deep down. But on the economic policy front, the transformation was nearly total. Numan Bartley writes: "In 1940 the raison d'etre of Southern state governments was the protection of white supremacy and social stability; thirty years later their central purpose was the promotion of business and industrial development."[35]

In this first phase of the economic revolution, the South was trying to modernize economically while retaining "white supremacy and social stability." Few of the region's political and economic leaders questioned the viability of this strategy at the time. But their new central purpose had unintended consequences for the race issue, when the forces of boosterism collided with the emerging civil rights movement in the 1950s and 1960s. The leverage of the movement derived from the fact that competition for outside capital required southern leaders to present their towns and cities as safe, civilized communities, with a labor force that was well behaved and eager for work. The most famous case in point was Little Rock, Arkansas, where a promising postwar development program came to a standstill when Orval Faubus called out the National Guard to block court-ordered school integration in 1957. Though the city had attracted eight new plants in 1957, not a single new plant came to Little Rock during the next four years. A widely discussed *Wall Street Journal* headline for May 26, 1961, read: "Business in Dixie: Many Southerners Say Racial Tension Slows Area's Economic Gains." In her systematic review of southern businessmen's response to the desegregation crisis, Elizabeth Jacoway writes: "In the 1950s and 1960s, white businessmen across the South found themselves pushed—by the federal government and civil rights forces as well as by their own economic interests and values—into becoming reluctant advocates of a new departure in southern race relations."[36]

To be sure, more often than not these businessmen favored only the minimum accommodation necessary for an "absence of turmoil," "community stability," "racial harmony." Even in the early 1960s surveys showed that southern community leaders overwhelmingly preferred segregation, balking only at extreme measures that jeopardized their primary goal of promoting economic growth.[37] In a sense they had to be coerced to act in their own economic interest. But as Jacoway goes on to say: "The changes they accepted were the entering wedge for the much greater changes that have since taken place in southern life and race relations."[38] Although few were willing to say so in public, many local leaders and business proprietors were privately grateful for the civil rights legislation of the 1960s, at least after the fact. These measures largely put an end to disputes over public accommodations and employment segregation, while providing managers the ready-made excuse that the matter was no longer in their hands.

Intended or not, the results were liberating for the regional economy as well as for its African American members. Figure 39 tracks the course of South Carolina personal income as a share of the national total, an indicator that reflects population growth as well as relative per capita income—thus representing an approximation to the developer's view of the world. The figure suggests that growth in the state stagnated from the mid-1950s to the early 1960s, and that the greatest expansion occurred only after the civil rights revolution.

Accommodating the civil rights revolution allowed the region to return to an agenda in which support for economic growth has been the highest priority. Much of the region's continuing economic distinctiveness is traceable to this progrowth regime. Relative to the rest of the country, the South in recent decades has been characterized by low corporate taxes; by inattention to the environmental consequences of growth; by low levels of expenditure on public education; and

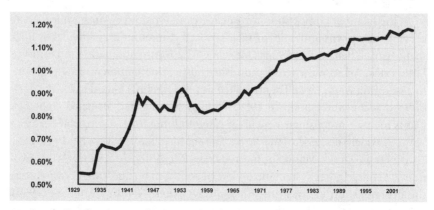

39. *South Carolina personal income, 1929–2004. Source: U.S. Bureau of the Census,* Historical Statistics of the United States, Colonial Times to 1970 *(1976),* 243–45; Statistical Abstract of the United States.

by a favorable "business climate," sometimes taken as a euphemism for an absence of labor unions. Politically appealing or not, pursuit of this agenda has succeeded in attracting capital, enterprise, and affluent migrants into the region over an extended period.

Black Southerners and the New South

Perhaps the most conclusive evidence that the civil rights revolution of the 1960s was real and economic is the reversal of prevailing racial patterns of regional migration. After the political breakthroughs of the 1960s, more than fifty years of net black out-migration came to an end, and blacks have been moving into the region ever since. The timing of the shift was directly related to the opening of new job opportunities. On the basis of her survey of black textile workers, Mary Fredrickson attributed the shift to "the fact that black children no longer have to leave the region to become successful, that a decent education in an integrated public school is attainable for both black and white, and that black workers are not denied industrial jobs on the basis of their race." She quotes a black employment manager: "There is a marked difference now, and people who couldn't get away from here fast enough are coming back comfortably."[39] Evidence from the 2000 Census indicates that this trend was stronger than ever in the 1990s. Demographer William H. Frey reports that net black migration into the South was more than 579,000 during the 1990s, whereas each of the other census regions saw net black out-migration.[40] Figure 40 shows the increase in South Carolina's black population after 1970, though that the state's white population growth has been even faster.

The attraction of the New South for blacks has economic as well as cultural, political, and geographic aspects. Surveys report that as many blacks as whites

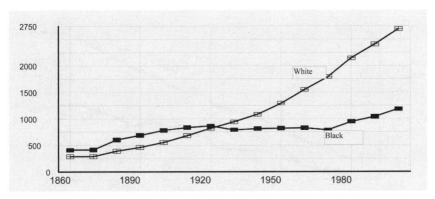

40. *South Carolina population by race, 1860–2000. Source: Susan B. Carter et al.,* Historical Statistics of the United States, *Millennial Edition (Cambridge University Press, 2006), p. 1–337;* Statistical Abstract of the United States.

self-identify as southerners.[41] Although the southern black population is disproportionately poor and rural, regional black immigrants are most likely to reside in the suburbs or burgeoning metropolitan areas. Seven of the ten fastest growing counties for blacks are in the suburbs of metropolitan Atlanta. Other areas of strong black population growth include Charlotte, Raleigh-Durham, and Greensboro in North Carolina; Norfolk and Richmond in Virginia; Miami, Tampa, and Jacksonville in Florida. A story about the spread of affluent suburbanites into rural areas such as Newton County, Georgia, reports: "Many well-educated natives of the county who once assumed they would have to leave to find a good job, like Michael David, the plant scheduler at SKC, now say they are thrilled to be able to work where they grew up."[42] When they self-identify as southerners, likely it is the presence of viable middle-class black communities that they find attractive. Tourist sites in the South now self-consciously cater to black visitors, especially at historic civil rights locales, but also at rediscovered landmarks from earlier eras.[43]

Despite the frustrations of minority representation, the African American presence is apparent in southern politics as well as in economic life. It is not that southern whites are more racially enlightened than American whites elsewhere: Studies recounting the persistence of racially polarized voting and of white efforts to "dilute" the black vote make depressing reading.[44] But the Voting Rights Act of 1965 did bring an end to the extreme racist rhetoric that until that time had been the hallmark of southern politics. Since then, the number of black officeholders in the South has steadily increased. Figure 41 shows the rise for South Carolina, in the two largest categories, county and municipal officials and school board members.

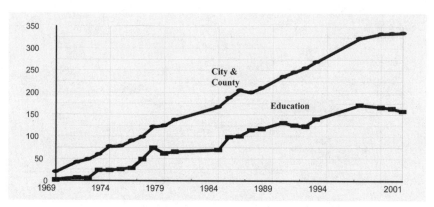

41. *Black elected officials, South Carolina, 1969–2001. Source: Joint Center for Polit-ical and Economic Studies,* Black Elected Officials, *various issues.*

Even if they do not control any one state, the black presence cannot be ignored in the post–civil rights South. Senator Strom Thurmond, who fought all civil rights legislation for forty years, in 1969 became the first southern senator to appoint a black staff aide, and he was the first to sponsor an African Ameri-can for a federal judgeship.[45] Political participation has had at least some posi-tive effect on black access to government services: such things as street paving, garbage collection, recreation facilities, and access to FHA loans and agricultural extension services.[46] After the election of a black mayor in Atlanta, employment of black municipal administrators jumped from 7.1 percent to 32.6 percent of the total, and professionals from 15.2 percent to 42.2 percent. Inevitably this political presence spills over into economics.[47] Although southern white public opinion is strongly opposed to race-based employment policies—a good exam-ple of a dramatic change in prevailing ideology—southern-based corporations are generally comfortable with affirmative action programs.

Black business leaders from the Jim Crow era often complained about the downside of integration, and with good reason. Firms that formerly catered to a semi-captive market found that the liberation of black consumers marked the demise of their competitive niche. Russ Rymer writes: "Integration became the greatest opening of a domestic market in American history, but the windfall went only in one direction. . . . In this way, integration wiped out or humbled an important segment echelon of the black community—the nonclergy leadership class that fought so hard for civil rights and was needed to show the way to prag-matic prosperity."[48]

As real as these losses were in their time, the subsequent resurgence of south-ern African American communities has generated business opportunities as well as a sense of identity. As of 1977 the majority of the nation's black-owned busi-nesses have been in the South. The number of southern black-owned firms grew from 92,838 in 1972 to 330,791 in 1992, and leaped to 435,290 in 1997, keeping pace with the rise of the black population.[49] The share of firms that were black-owned was larger in the southern states than in any other part of the country. To be sure, most of these firms were small, not necessarily evidence of affluence. But the figures refute the myth that African Americans are any less business-minded than other ethnic groups, under favorable conditions.[50]

Political representation, economic and educational gains, and the rise of black-owned businesses have had mutually reinforcing effects in the South. Elections of black mayors have often had a dramatic effect on the allocation of municipal contracts.[51] Atlanta is the best-known and best-documented example. The city had never awarded a procurement contract to a black-owned company until 1973. But by the end of Maynard Jackson's first term of office in 1978, minority firms accounted for about one-third of Atlanta's construction contracts. The H. J. Russell construction and development company (HJR) was founded in 1952, but its propulsion into national prominence dates from Jackson's 1974 "Atlanta Plan" for black business representation, predating federal set-aside programs by at least two years. According to Thomas D. Boston, the significance of municipal affirmative action programs has been to allow black-owned businesses to expand and diversify away from personal services and retail trade into new, desegregated markets.[52]

Can we identify these developments as consequences of the civil rights movement? I believe we can, because in my view the movement was fundamentally a southern regional phenomenon, and these patterns are distinctively regional to this day. Research on the geography of self-employment confirms a strong southern regional effect for black-owned business. The same body of research shows a significant positive association between racial income levels in a metropolitan area and the *returns* to self-employment.[53] This finding suggests that the linkages are essentially positive, no longer symptomatic of economic marginality. Note furthermore that the complementarity between black political representation and black business has persisted in the South even after the 1989 *Richmond v. Croson* decision challenging racial set-aside programs, a ruling that elsewhere in the country had devastating effects on contracts awarded to minority-owned enterprises. To be sure, owners of successful businesses, black or white, constitute a relatively elite group in society. But research clearly shows that black-owned firms are far more likely than their white-owned counterparts to hire black employees, so that the potential impact of these developments reaches well beyond the returns to the owners alone.[54]

Confirming this complementarity, Figure 42 shows that median black income grew faster in the South than in any other region of the country during the 1990s. This remarkable regional trajectory has gone almost unnoticed in the national discussion about race. But by the end of the decade, median black income in the South was virtually equal to that in the Northeast and the Midwest.

Median black income in the West (not shown in the figure) remained somewhat higher. Yet blacks migrated even from the high-income western region in favor of the South during the 1990s. Clearly something was happening in the South that was not happening elsewhere in the country. Identifying the roots and implications of these developments is a challenge for both historians and economists, but it can hardly be doubted that they are outgrowths of the civil rights revolution.

Conclusion

My conclusion is that the civil rights revolution of the 1960s was indeed an economic as well as a political and cultural revolution. In one sense it is quite correct to say that the revolution did not challenge the basic structure of the system, if "the system" refers to the progrowth political regime that has prevailed for the past half century. But it did offer access to the rewards of that regime to substantial numbers of black as well as white southerners, and this is no small matter. Many other countries and regions of the world, immersed in racial, ethnic, or religious conflict, have not made or have not been able to make that kind of collective choice. When mutual suspicion reaches the level where communication is difficult and compromise agreements all but impossible to maintain, the economic costs are extremely high. Instead, the South has followed the American path of boosterism and inclusion, and given the likely alternatives, on the whole we can be grateful for that.

To emphasize the revolutionary economic impact of civil rights for the South is not to minimize the fragility of this legacy. For those at the lower end of the economic scales, the breakthroughs in labor markets and schooling have largely slipped away since the 1970s. Because these effects have fallen disproportionately on blacks, it is understandable that they are often experienced and understood in racial terms. Southern black political leaders have often been criticized

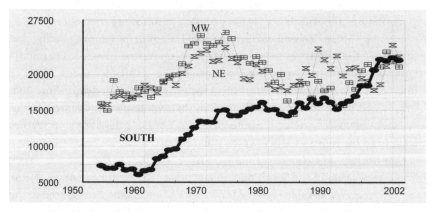

42. Median black male income by region, 1953–2001. Source: U.S. Census Bureau, Historical Income Data, table P-1.

for neglecting the poor, but municipal and county leaders have not been in position to defy the global economic and technological forces that have undermined labor market opportunities for low-income workers. Worse than this, partisan realignment within the South—a phenomenon that may be seen in part as a lagged response to the civil rights revolution—has generated a set of regional representatives who take a reactionary position in national politics, opposing measures that would moderate the impact of market forces and improve the life chances of ordinary people. These are national as much as regional issues, but persistent racial polarization in the South makes escape from this political outcome difficult.

All complex historical events have multiple consequences, mostly unintended and almost always beyond the range of prediction at the time. The adverse reactions just described are neither inevitable nor eternal. We will be in better position to cope with them if we first appreciate the momentous character of the economic changes brought about by the civil rights revolution in the South.

Notes

1. Glenn T. Eskew, *But for Birmingham: The Local and National Movements in the Civil Rights Struggle* (Chapel Hill: University of North Carolina Press, 1997), 331.

2. Robert J. Norrell, *Reaping the Whirlwind: The Civil Rights Movement in Tuskegee* (New York: Knopf, 1985), 206.

3. Peter Applebome, *Dixie Rising: How the South Is Shaping American Values, Politics and Culture* (New York: Times Books, 1996), 17, 215.

4. Robert E. Weems Jr., *Desegregating the Dollar: African American Consumerism in the Twentieth Century* (New York: New York University Press, 1998), 69.

5. Eskew, *But for Birmingham,* 199, 326.

6. Timothy Minchin, *The Color of Work: The Struggle for Civil Rights in the Southern Paper Industry, 1945–1980* (Chapel Hill: University of North Carolina Press, 2001), 8, 17.

7. Stanley Greenberg, *Race and State in Capitalist Development* (New Haven: Yale University Press, 1980): 231–33.

8. James J. Heckman and Bruce Payner, "The Impact of the Economy and the State on the Economic Status of Blacks: A Study of South Carolina," *American Economic Review* 79 (1989): 138–77.

9. From oral history reported by Mary Fredrickson, "Four Decades of Change: Black Workers in Southern Textiles, 1941–1981," *Radical America* 16 (1982): 73.

10. Timothy J. Minchin, *Hiring the Black Worker: The Racial Integration of the Southern Textile Industry, 1960–1980* (Chapel Hill: University of North Carolina Press, 1999), 51; Minchin, "Federal Policy and the Racial Integration of Southern Industry," *Journal of Policy History* 11 (1999): 157–58.

11. Minchin, *Hiring the Black Worker,* 59.

12. Ibid., 266–67

13. Ibid., 116, 182–3.

14. Herbert Northrup, *The Negro in the Paper Industry,* Racial Policies of American Industry, report no. 8 (Philadelphia: University of Pennsylvania Press, 1969), 45.

15. Minchin, "Federal Policy," 151.

16. Minchin, *Color of Work,* 213–14.

17. Conner Bailey, Peter Sinclair, John Bliss, and Karmai Perez, "Segmented Labor Markets in Alabama's Pulp and Paper Industry," *Rural Sociology* 61 (1996): 483.

18. John J. Donahue III and James J. Heckman, "Continuous versus Episodic Change: The Impact of Civil Rights on the Economic Status of Blacks," *Journal of Economic Literature* 29 (1991): 1583–1614.

19. Richard B. Freeman, "Black Economic Progress after 1964: Who Has Gained and Why?," in *Studies in Labor Markets,* ed. Sherwin Rosen (Chicago: University of Chicago Press, 1981); Kenneth Y. Chay,"The Impact of Federal Civil Rights Policy on Black Economic Progress," *Industrial and Labor Relations Review,* 51 (1998): 608–32.

20. Chay and Michael Greenstone, "The Convergence in Black-White Infant Mortality Rates during the 1960s," *American Economic Review* 90 (May 2000): 326–32.

21. John J. Donahue III, James J. Heckman, and Petra Todd, "The Schooling of Southern Blacks: The Roles of Legal Activism and Private Philanthropy, 1910–1960," *Quarterly Journal of Economics* 117 (2002): 225–68.

22. David Card and Alan Krueger, "School Quality and Relative Black/White Earnings," *Quarterly Journal of Economics* 107 (1992): 151–200.

23. Gary Orfield, *Public School Desegregation in the United States, 1968–1980* (Washington, D.C.: Joint Center for Political Studies, 1983). On the beneficial effects of desegregation for black students, see Orley Ashenfelter, William J. Collins, and Albert Yoon, *Evaluating the Role of Brown vs. Board of Education in School Equalization, Desegregation, and the Income of African Americans,* NBER Working Paper, no. 11394 (Cambridge, Mass.: National Bureau of Economic Research, 2005).

24. James Smith, "Race and Human Capital," *American Economic Review* 74 (1984): 685–98; Smith and Finis Welch, "Black Economic Progress after Myrdal," *Journal of Economic Literature* 27 (1989): 519–64.

25. United States, *Final Report of the Industrial Commission* (Washington, D.C.: U.S. Government Printing Office, 1902), 10:497.

26. William H. Baldwin Jr., quoted in James D. Anderson, *The Education of Blacks in the South, 1860–1935* (Chapel Hill: University of North Carolina Press, 1988), 84, 91.

27. Anderson, *Education of Blacks,* 220–30.

28. Southern Regional Council, *The Negro and Employment Opportunities in the South* (Atlanta: Southern Regional Council, 1961–62).

29. Minchin, *Color of Work,* 37–38.

30. James R. Mingle, *Black Enrollment in Higher Education: Trends in the Nation and in the South* (Atlanta: Southern Regional Education Board, 1978). On corporate recruiting visits to predominantly black colleges and universities, see Richard B. Freeman, *Black Elite: The New Market for Highly Educated Black Americans* (New York: McGraw-Hill, 1976), 34–36.

31. Stephen C. Halpern, *On the Limits of the Law: The Ironic Legacy of Title VI of the 1964 Civil Rights Act* (Baltimore: Johns Hopkins University Press, 1995).

32. Sukkoo Kim, "Expansion of Markets and the Geographic Distribution of Economic Activities," *Quarterly Journal of Economics* 110 (November 1995): 881–908.

33. James C. Cobb, *The Selling of the South: The Southern Crusade for Industrial Development, 1936–1980,* 2nd ed. (Chicago: University of Illinois Press, 1993).

34. Bruce J. Schulman, *From Cotton Belt to Sunbelt: Federal Policy, Economic Development, and the Transformation of the South, 1938–1980* (New York: Oxford University Press, 1991), 114–16, 140–42.

35. Numan Bartley, "In Search of the New South: Southern Politics after Reconstruction," in *The Promise of American History,* ed. Stanley I. Kutler and Stanley N. Katz, 150–63 (Baltimore: Johns Hopkins University Press, 1982) (quotation, 160).

36. Elizabeth Jacoway and David R. Colburn, eds., *Southern Businessmen and Desegregation* (Baton Rouge: Louisiana State University Press, 1982), 1.

37. M. Richard Cramer, "School Desegregation and New Industry: The Southern Community Leaders' Viewpoint," *Social Forces* 40 (1963): 384–89.

38. Jacoway and Colburn, *Southern Businessmen,* 5.

39. Mary Fredrickson, "Four Decades of Change," 75.

40. William H. Frey, *Census 2000 Shows Large Black Return to the South,* Population Studies Research Report no. 01–473 (Ann Arbor: University of Michigan, May 2001), fig. 1.

41. James C. Cobb, *Redefining Southern Culture* (Athens: University of Georgia Press, 1999), 41.

42. David Firestone, "As a Region's Economy Booms, So Does Interest in Its Politics," *New York Times,* March 7, 2000.

43. Peter Applebombe, "New South Puts On a New Face for Black Tourists," *New York Times,* September 10, 1990; "Move Afoot to Preserve Historic Black Buildings," *Asheville Citizen-Times,* March 21, 2000.

44. Chandler Davidson and Bernard Grofman, *Quiet Revolution in the South: The Impact of the Voting Rights Act, 1965–1990* (Princeton, N.J.: Princeton University Press, 1994).

45. Nadine Cohodas, *Strom Thurmond and the Politics of Southern Change* (New York: Simon & Schuster, 1993), 412–13, 427–28.

46. William R. Keech, *The Impact of Negro Voting* (Chicago: Rand-McNally, 1968); Lawrence J. Hanks, *The Struggle for Black Political Empowerment in Three Georgia Counties* (Knoxville: University of Tennessee Press, 1987).

47. Peter K. Eisinger, "Black Empowerment in Municipal Jobs: The Impact of Black Political Power," *American Political Science Review* 76 (1982): 385.

48. Russ Rymer, "Integration's Casualties: Segregation Helped Black Business; Civil Rights Helped Destroy It," *New York Times Magazine,* November 1, 1998, 48. The decline of the black insurance industry is traced in Robert E. Weems Jr., "A Crumbling Legacy: The Decline of African American Insurance Companies in Contemporary America," *Review of Black Political Economy* 23 (Fall 1994): 25–37.

49. United States Census Bureau, *1997 Economic Census: Surveys of Minority- and Women-Owned Business Enterprises,* 2002, http://www.census.gov/csd/mwb/.

50. Timothy Bates, *Race, Self-Employment and Upward Mobility: An Illusive American Dream* (Washington, D.C.: Woodrow Wilson Center Press, 1997).

51. Juliet E. K. Walker, *The History of Black Business in America: Capitalism, Race, Entrepreneurship* (New York: MacMillan Library Reference USA, 1998), 318; Bates, *Race, Self-Employment, and Upward Mobility,* 174–87.

52. Thomas D. Boston, *Affirmative Action and Black Entrepreneurship* (London: Routledge, 1999), 2–3, 12–18.

53. Dan Black, Douglas Holtz-Eakin, and Stuart Rosenthal, "Racial Minorities, Economic Scale, and the Geography of Self-Employment," *Brookings-Wharton Papers on Urban Affairs,* no. 2 (2001): 257, 263.

54. Boston, *Affirmative Action,* 25–32; Timothy Bates, *Banking on Black Enterprise* (Washington, D.C.: Joint Center for Political and Economic Studies, 1993), 90–91, 146.

Civil Rights and Politics in South Carolina

The Perspective of One Lifetime, 1940–2003

Dan Carter

In the summer of 1952 I traveled to Charleston on a Greyhound Bus for a week's visit.[1] The attraction was not simply that my aunt and uncle were favorites of many such relatives: they lived on Folly Beach. As we rolled through the flat land just east of Lake City, an older black woman hailed the bus, and from a tightly bound handkerchief she carefully counted out the fare for (I presume) her granddaughter to ride to a small town less than thirty miles away. As we drove away, I watched in surprise as the eight- or nine-year-old girl tentatively sat down on the front seat of the almost empty bus. At first the driver did not see her; when he did, he gruffly mumbled, "Move on back." Either she did not hear, or she simply did not understand the taboo she had violated. Somehow I had the sense that this was the first time she had ridden a public bus. When she remained seated, he suddenly pulled the bus to the side of the road, stood up, and towered over her: "I told you to move to the back of the bus," he shouted. Paralyzed with fear, she remained in her seat, crying softly. From the back of the bus an older and poorly dressed black man moved up the aisle and gently took her hand: "Come on back here with me, honey," he said. Until she got off the bus thirty minutes later, I sat with eyes carefully averted as I heard her sobbing slowly subside. I remember this as vividly as anything from my childhood. I also recall that my indignation was not against a system that allowed such brutalities, but against the driver's bad manners. Even as a twelve-year-old, I knew that we were supposed to be "polite to colored people."

Ten years after that experience, I left the state of my birth and childhood. For the next thirty-eight years, I returned only briefly to visit my family in rural Florence County. But in the summer of 2000 I moved back to South Carolina to accept a position at the University of South Carolina. My next-door neighbors in Columbia were an African American couple who personified the American dream. He was the personnel director for a major international corporation based in Columbia; she a former assistant to the governor. My neighbor across the street was a brilliant young Chinese American attorney; my other next-door neighbor, a Lebanese American cardiologist, was a woman working in a specialty almost exclusively male just two decades ago. Three houses away was an African American neighbor who was a senior budget officer for the state government.

When I graduated from the University of South Carolina in 1962, the only black people on campus were service workers. The faculty of the history department where I gained my degree consisted of sixteen white men. (I do not want to disparage white men; some of my best friends are white men. Still, that faculty was hardly a representative portrait of the state). Today, the student body is—depending upon whose figures you believe—17 to 19 percent African Americans. We white men are hardly an embattled minority in today's USC history department, but we have five black colleagues, nine women, and a commitment, I believe, to making it a department that does reflect the diversity of the people of the state.

When I look back to that morning when I sat on a Greyhound bus and listened to the wracking sobs of a terrified young black girl, the South Carolina of my childhood seems far away.

But not so far. By now, most of us have heard, and reheard, the quote from one of William Faulkner's characters in *Requiem for a Nun:* "The past is never dead. It's not even past." However familiar, the quote was never more relevant than in a discussion of the underlying continuities of race relations in America—and South Carolina—as we move into the twenty-first century. My understanding of those continuities has been shaped by my research as a historian, but also by my own experience as a native of the state.

I was born in 1940 at the tail end of the Great Depression on the eve of World War II and grew up on a tobacco farm ten miles southeast of Florence. As far as race relations were concerned, the world into which I was born seemed little changed from the one created in the 1890s. Segregation was absolute. There were a handful of black voters, but their ballot hardly counted since they were excluded from the Democratic primaries—the only elections that really counted. And any column of social, economic, educational, or health data that distinguished black and white told a horrifying story of two different worlds. To be sure there was poverty, poor health conditions, and inadequate education among whites, but it did not match the desperate conditions that existed for black South Carolinians; a disparity exposed by the draft and wartime mobilization. Between 1940 and 1945 the armed forces rejected 8 percent of the white South Carolinians for reasons of educational deficiencies and poor health. For African Americans, the figure was 44 percent.

All of us are aware of the way in which state and local governments flouted the "equal" part of the "separate but equal" requirement of *Plessy v. Ferguson* (1896). What is hard to grasp is just what a mockery it was. While tax-supported institutions for whites reflected the poverty of the state and were relatively underfunded by national standards, for blacks such institutions were almost nonexistent. African Americans made up a majority of the population in the state during much of the first half of the twentieth century, but in higher education, the Colored Normal, Industrial, Agricultural and Mechanical College of South Carolina (South Carolina State College)—the only state-supported institution for African Americans—received less than 10 percent of the state's higher education appropriations during the first two decades after it was founded in 1896. Conditions worsened in the 1920s, and as late as 1930, 96 percent of the state's appropriations for higher education went to the three white colleges (the University of South Carolina, Winthrop College for Women, and Clemson University). State-supported graduate and professional education in most areas was simply not available for blacks until the 1960s.[2]

Of course most South Carolinians received their final education in public schools, and racial disparities in expenditures reflected the same pattern of discrimination. While the state's schools were generally segregated during the Reconstruction era, per-student expenditures were relatively equal between black and white. With blacks disenfranchised, however, the state began appropriating less and less for black schools. By 1915 several counties in the state were spending nearly ten times as much to educate white as black children, and there was little support for anything beyond the most rudimentary primary education for black students. In 1915 the editor of the *Charleston News and Courier* repeatedly attacked northern philanthropists' support for improving black education as "the most insidious attack that has ever been made upon the sentiment and civilization of the South."[3]

Throughout the 1920s and 1930s the imbalance improved, but very slowly. When I began school in the fall of 1946, 2,689 black South Carolinians graduated from high school—3 percent of the students who had enrolled in the first grade eleven years earlier. In a supplementary report to the General Assembly, South Carolina's superintendent of education estimated that six of every ten African Americans in the state were totally or functionally illiterate.[4]

Conditions were hardly idyllic for many whites in the state. The rural elementary school where I enrolled in the fall of 1946—two grades to the classroom—would be condemned in any western industrial democracy. Even in the 1950s my high school was a ramshackle frame wooden building heated by potbellied coal stoves stoked each morning in a rotation shared by the nine male members of my graduating class. However primitive the physical setting, the education I received ranged from adequate to exceptional. All of my teachers were college graduates; one was taking courses for a M.A. degree in chemistry. In the South of the 1940s and 1950s, teaching was the most prestigious position for a woman who wished to work, and many of the women who taught me were remarkably well educated.

There was often that same commitment in the black community, but the conditions were hardly equal. That same year I started to school in 1946, the state of South Carolina spent ninety dollars for my education—hardly a princely sum. But for black students, it was thirty-three dollars.

While there were improvements in the health and well-being of black South Carolinians in the years between 1920 and 1960, every socioeconomic index of social well-being—health, housing, literacy rates, and education—reflected the enormous distance between the two races. In 1949 the median family income for African Americans in South Carolina was 39 percent of that of whites. Although economic conditions improved in the 1950s for black South Carolinians, the income gap between the two races actually increased as whites saw even more progress. By 1959 black families had incomes of only one-third that of whites.[5]

I lived in the midst of segregation—massive inequality—repression. But as a child—even as an adolescent—I had no reference point to suggest that this was anything other than the natural order of the world.

I began my remarks by describing my first encounter with formal racial segregation; that moment is certainly vivid in my memory, but it was hardly my first encounter with racial issues. Race was everywhere.

While preparing an essay on the career of Judge Matthew Perry, I wandered through the stacks of the University of South Carolina's Thomas Cooper Library and pulled from the shelf my fourth-grade history text: *The Simms Centennial History of South Carolina*. In 1840 the South Carolina novelist and historian William Gilmore Simms had written a school history of the state. A hundred years later, one of his descendants—Mary Simms Oliphant—published another revision of this venerable text.

Just at random—

On slavery: "the planters took pride in seeing that their slaves were well cared for. On . . . many . . . plantations there were hospitals for the slaves, nurseries for the little children and recreations of various kinds." To be sure, there were occasional threats of slave riots brought by "agents from the North working to dissatisfy the slaves," but these were rare. In fact, concluded Oliphant, it was "the slave and not the master who received the real benefits of slavery" (216–17).

Everything, in fact, was idyllic until the North waged its war of aggression against the states in 1861—a war that culminated in the nightmarish and deliberate burning of Columbia. Some folks may debate the actual cause of the firing of Columbia, but not Oliphant. In her words: "Sherman's army set fire to Columbia. The citizens brought out the fire engines, but the soldiers slashed the fire hoses with swords and bayonets. They ran into the houses and set fire to the lace curtains. . . . They snatched ear rings from the women's ears and rings from their fingers" as the city burned to the ground. Simms concludes her account of this dastardly deed by approvingly citing "one little darkey," on getting a close-up look at Sherman's troops: "Why, dey's folks. I tought dey was animals" (250–51).

Or listen to Oliphant's discussion of emancipation that created South Carolina's "Greatest Problem"—the former slaves were ignorant and uneducated, unable to "make a living without the supervision of the white man. They stole cattle and chickens and hogs, burned barns and stables. They were not willing to work. They were like children playing hooky the moment the teacher's back was turned." They had nearly ruined the state during the years they voted, concluded Oliphant. And as for Reconstruction—the words roll by: "scalawags," Carpet Baggers," "lowest and most disreputable," "corrupt," "hordes of thieves and robbers," "an outraged helpless people," "insolent Negroes," "women insulted on the streets." Only with the brave efforts of the Ku Klux Klan, which was able to "frighten the superstitious Negroes into submission," and the actions of the heroic Red Shirts did South Carolina emerge into a new era in which the wise whites of Hampton's generation passed "regulations. . . . which prevented the Negroes from voting, and to this day, South Carolina has a white man's government" (265).

Except in its rather lurid language, the Simms-Oliphant history is, of course, not dramatically different from the interpretation of other historians of the day. But as I read this grade school text, I thought about the thousands of black South Carolinians who read those same pages of their *History of South Carolina.* [6]

No . . . race was everywhere; it was just a problem of sorting it all out.

To a rural South Carolina youngster of the 1940s and the 1950s, few events were more eagerly awaited than the annual county fair. Since I raised cattle and showed them in the livestock exhibition of the Florence County Fair, it meant essentially a week away from school, often sleeping in the barns and slipping away during the afternoons for walks through the carnival booths and rides. At ten or eleven, for a prepubescent adolescent, the highlight of these excursions on the sawdust-covered midway was to move to the edge of the crowd facing one of the two burlesque tents in which a dozen skimpily clad girls paraded across the platform to the constant patter of the barker who promised those who paid their fifty cents ("Men only over the age of eighteen") a far more revealing look inside the tent. I say two burlesque shows, because one was white and the other was black, or "colored," as it was called.

The week afterward, I spent a Saturday afternoon fishing on Lynch's Creek with my cousin and two black teenagers. They were a little older than me; one would say they were "boys" like myself except for the painful twist of meaning that word has come to have for black men. All of us, it turns out, had been to the fair. It did not occur to me that it was peculiar that there was a single "colored day" set aside for my black friends. That too was simply part of the world in which we lived. I began talking about how beautiful I had thought the "colored girls" were at the fair. I did not mean my comments in a predatory way; I thought of it as a compliment. I, as a white boy, was generously recognizing the beauty of an inferior race. I do not remember what my black friends said, but I distinctly remember that both recoiled as though they were physically struck. One stood and simply walked away without saying a word.

Afterward, still bewildered, I told my mother about how upset my friends had seemed. She groped for some way to try and help me understand the taboos I had unknowingly violated. Finally she said: "What if they had started talking about how beautiful the white girls were at the fair?"

By the time I was fifteen or sixteen, these lessons had been absorbed, accepted, and made the basis for my response to the world around me. Much I have forgotten, but—even at age thirteen—I understood the gravity of that morning in the spring of 1954 when the principal of the little school I attended called together the seventh through twelfth graders in the rickety auditorium to announce that the Supreme Court of the United States had passed a decision outlawing the separation of the races in the schools. We were likely to encounter "colored friends" or acquaintances who might be boastful or taunting, he warned, and we must respond with restraint as young ladies and gentlemen— implicitly young white ladies and gentlemen.

But there were no taunts, only silence as a wall of fear and anger divided black from white. And as the first challenges to the racial status quo emerged, I became a part of the white South as it mobilized for massive resistance.

It is difficult to re-create the memories of those special pleasures of oppression. What did they know of us? Why did they taunt and abuse us? Our colored people were happy and contented; it was those hated Yankees, those outside agitators who were creating turmoil and conflict where only peace had prevailed. Why did they seek to turn our tranquil lives upside down? By us, of course, I meant "us" in a tribal sense: the white South.

It seems impossible to believe as we look backward, but somehow we white South Carolinians had convinced ourselves that we were the victims of oppression: this in a state where white mobs had lynched 126 black men between 1880 and 1920.[7] This in a state where—even in the 1950s and 1960s, when attention was focused upon the brutalities in Mississippi, Alabama, and Louisiana—there were dozens of racially motivated shootings, assaults, and dynamite attacks. Among other incidents: a mob savagely beat a white high school band director in Camden for allegedly criticizing segregation; the following week, hooded terrorists shot another white South Carolinian in the chest after he also expressed "liberal" racial views. And in 1957 a group of Klan terrorists dynamited the home of a Gaffney, South Carolina, woman who had written a short essay expressing her religious concerns over segregation.[8]

In my own hometown, Jack O'Dowd, editor of the *Florence Morning News* and a graduate of the Citadel, became one of the most hated white men in the state when he bluntly told his readers that *Brown v. Board of Education* was the law of the land and should be obeyed. Those who promised that segregation could be maintained were living in "self-delusion and false hope." Eighteen months later, gun-wielding Ku Klux Klansmen tried to force O'Dowd off the road as he drove home from work. He managed to outrun his pursuers and take refuge in the apartment of a young Florence attorney named Nick Zeigler. Zeigler is a longtime South Carolina Democratic activist, serving in the state house of representatives as well as the senate before assuming the thankless task of running as the Democratic nominee against Strom Thurmond in 1972. By taking in O'Dowd, Nick and his wife, Ann, made themselves the target of unrelenting abuse and threats. Repeatedly the telephone would ring, to be followed by a string of obscenities or, worse, quiet ominous breathing. On one occasion a caller told Zeigler that "they" had a marksman who was going to kill members of his family if he did not stop his "race" agitation. Zeigler survived, but O'Dowd eventually had to resign the editorship and leave the state.

Even when the weapon was not overt violence, the effects could be felt everywhere. The South Carolina legislature (as in a number of other southern states) pushed through legislation that barred state-employed African Americans (mostly schoolteachers) from membership in the NAACP, while private individuals—with official encouragement—harassed and often fired vulnerable black employees who sought to assert their constitutional rights.[9]

Between 1940 and 1946 the efforts of civil rights activists led to an increase from 1,500 to 50,000 in the number of blacks registered to vote, although this still amounted to less than 15 percent of the state's black voting-age population. From 1946 to 1961, however, white registrars and public officials tenaciously resisted black efforts to increase political participation, and the number of black voters increased by less than 10,000 as the state legislature passed a number of laws including a new literacy test and statewide full-slate and majority-vote requirements for elections, measures that were bluntly designed (as lawmakers openly told reporters) "to control Negro voting in primaries."

And yet white South Carolinians—I among them—convinced themselves that they were innocent victims of a ruthless conspiracy led by that infamous NAACP.

In the fall of 1955 the *Florence Morning News* described the arson of a black church in nearby Lake City. The minister, reported the *News*, claimed that it had been torched because of his political activism. But of course I knew the real story; I had sat in the local general store with my father and listened to a Florence County deputy sheriff as he contemptuously described this "NAACP preacher." This preacher was no victim, said the deputy. He had burned his own church to collect the insurance on the building. And, he added, the FBI agents brought into the case agreed with him.

A short time later I read with that this ruthless troublemaker had brazenly fired without provocation on a group of innocent white men who just happened to be driving by his home. Unfortunately he had managed to flee the state before he could be brought to justice.

That "preacher's" name meant nothing to me at the time.

Only years later did I learn the story of Rev. Joseph A. De Laine and how he had organized the *Briggs v. Elliott* lawsuit in Clarendon County and then moved to Lake City because of threats against his life, only to be terrorized there by local whites. As I read the death-threat letter in his papers at the USC library, the sheer insanity of the decade—and my own complicity—came home to me once again. For in that same collection is his FBI file and several interagency memos by J. Edgar Hoover identifying De Laine as a "a controversial figure in racial segregation matters in South Carolina," and a note to field officers that he would not acknowledge De Laine's complaint in writing "since he might be able to use this to his own advantage at some later date."

That FBI file confirmed what that Florence County deputy had said as we sat around the potbellied stove at McCain's Grocery. The FBI men gave no credence to the threats against Joseph De Laine; they had no concern over the burning of his church. He had either done it himself; or—if not—he had brought it upon himself by acting as a troublemaker.

It seems so far away. White South Carolinians would regain some sense of equilibrium and move—slowly and hesitantly—away from the worst aspects of the hysteria of the 1950s and 1960s. Of course I changed as well. From 1958 to 1960 I attended night classes at what was then the Florence extension of the University of South Carolina while I worked as a reporter at the local *Morning News*. Much of the work was the usual for a rookie reporter: writing obituaries, covering the local tobacco warehousemen's convention and the latest multiple-car accident. But I was aware of the role that the previous editor, Jack O'Dowd, had played. And my two editors, Dew James and Joe Dabney—while mainly intent on teaching me the pitfalls of adjectives and the superiority of active-voice verbs, introduced me to the astonishing possibility that I could be critical of my culture without becoming a traitor to its best values. On the surface, whites in the small town of Florence seemed united in their defense of segregation, but appearances were deceiving. Over endless cups of coffee at a downtown coffee shop, I came to know and to be instructed by men (and a couple of women) who had a vision of a South without racism. In some cases their convictions sprang from deep religious conviction; others had served in the military or lived outside the region at some time in their lives and had a direct experience with black men and women that challenged their early assumptions about white supremacy. Publicly they may have spoken cautiously; privately they peeled away my halfhearted defenses of the "southern way of life."

In the end, there would be no Damascan experience, but in the spring of 1960, as a nineteen-year-old reporter, I stood in a Kress five-and-ten-cent store photographing raucous whites who screamed obscenities at the dozen well-dressed black young men and women sitting quietly at the lunch counter. "Which side are you on?" asks the old union rallying song. As I took those photographs, there was no longer any doubt in my mind about which side I had chosen. In two short years, the racial moorings of a lifetime had been severed.

My next two years at the University of South Carolina in Columbia completed that transformation. Despite the fact that political pressure had led to the firing of two outspoken professors in the late 1950s for condemning segregation, faculty members such as Raymond Moore in international studies and historians Robert Ochs and Bill Foran made little effort to hide their contempt for the state's commitment to maintaining white supremacy. Within months after my arrival at the university I gravitated toward a small group of students who openly challenged segregation, a system that most white South Carolinians still saw as the bedrock of their society. Only later did I realize how fortunate I was to meet and work with an extraordinary group of men and women over the next two years: my three apartment mates, Hayes Mizell, Charles Joyner, and Selden Smith; James McBride Dabbs, the Maysville, South Carolina, planter turned author and civil rights leader; Alice Spearman, the head of the South Carolina Council on Human Relations; Libby Ledeen of the University's YWCA; Mae Gautier, a young university Methodist chaplain; and activists Will Campbell and Connie Curry.

And those were just the white folks! Not long after I arrived at Carolina, I heard Matthew Perry at the Methodist Center on Lady Street inspire a group of black and white college students. I met Ella Baker, John Lewis, Andrew Young, and Julian Bond. . . . I'm doing more than name-dropping here: I'm acknowledging the extraordinary moment in the history of this state and my great good fortune to be there to witness that turning of the wheel of change.

Encouraged by Alice Spearman and Libby Ledeen, we joined with about thirty to forty black and white students from the state's colleges and universities and—rather grandly—called ourselves the "South Carolina Student Council on Human Relations." We elected Charles Joyner as our first president only because he could play the guitar and knew most of the words to the freedom songs. From the fall of 1960 until I went away to graduate school at the University of Wisconsin in 1962, there were a continuous round of Saturday "conferences" and evening meetings in Columbia and civil rights workshops at Monteagle, Tennessee; Dorchester, Georgia; and Penn Community Center near Beaufort, South Carolina. (Penn Center was the only place in the state where integrated groups could safely meet overnight.) It is difficult to recall how daring we felt as we assembled—black and white—to plan for a day when segregation would be only a bitter memory. In truth, there were many meetings, a great deal of talk, constant singing, and little concrete action, but it transformed the lives of those of us who saw another possibility for the South and its place in the nation.

When I left South Carolina in September 1962, USC was still a segregated university; in the Senate campaign that fall, the Republican candidate William Workman was calling voters to arms with the warning that it was do or die: the last-ditch struggle to preserve, as he put it, "the people of South Carolina from a new era of reconstruction sought by radical Democrats." Publicly the state's leadership remained committed to maintaining segregation. But Workman lost decisively to Olin D. Johnston, and outgoing governor Fritz Hollings would soon be throwing in the towel and acknowledging that the state could no longer maintain segregation. In the aftermath of the fall 1962 election, I wrote to a Michigan friend I had met earlier that summer. "It will soon be over," I said, referring to segregation. "South Carolina and Mississippi can't hold out forever, and when the dam breaks, the whole system of Jim Crow will be on the ropes." (I cannot help but quote that letter since I am so seldom right in predicting anything.)

But by then I was gone. It was not that my interest in race relations or my hostility to Jim Crow faded, but I was in another country—in graduate school at Wisconsin; married and completing my Ph.D. at Chapel Hill; starting a new family and a new career, teaching at the University of Maryland. Although there were regular trips back to visit my family in Florence, my connection with the state was more distant with each year. During the years after I left, I recall only snapshots: memories of reading about the peaceful integration of schools in Charleston in the fall of 1963; my concern over the race-baiting Republican state campaign in 1970 and the possibility that Albert Watson might defeat John West. And my depression over the fact that my old friend Nick Zeigler had gone down to defeat at the hands of Thurmond in 1972.

Even when I went to teach at Emory in Atlanta in the mid-1970s, my connection as well as my knowledge of developments in the state was relatively limited. But in the years after I returned to South Carolina in 2000 I have sought to understand the racial changes and what I see as the pernicious and ongoing legacy of the past.

Sociologists and historians have always drawn a distinction between private attitudes and public actions and behaviors and institutional structures that have a racially discriminatory impact. Despite the change in public rhetoric and private behavior, the historical record of the forty years since the end of legal segregation shows that race continues to play a critical role in all aspects of life in our state, as indeed it does throughout the nation. Certainly the changes in the politics of the state should give us pause in weighing the extent of racial progress.

Much of the story of this change (for better and for worse) has been linked with larger forces at work in national and regional politics. Since the days of John C. Calhoun, white South Carolinians have welcomed federal largesse in the form of military bases and spending on domestic programs. But—like most white southerners—they have resisted federal involvement in the life of the region if it involved changes in race relations. From the nomination of South Carolina's governor, J. Strom Thurmond, as standard-bearer for the Dixiecrat Party in 1948, through the 1950s, this hostility increased dramatically as the federal courts slowly but increasingly insisted upon an enforcement of civil rights.

And in the aftermath of the Civil Rights Act of 1964 and the Voting Rights Act of 1965, the Civil Rights Division of the United States Department of Justice struggled to deal with the transition away from a political and legal system recently dominated by racial discrimination. This meant a constant weighing of state and local legislation that was (on its face) race neutral but had a racially discriminatory impact. From election procedures (at-large elections, the full-slate law, the numbered-place rule, etc.), to emotional issues of school desegregation, to questions of employment discrimination, white South Carolinians who had traditionally—and fiercely—resisted federal "interference" on racial issues found their actions under scrutiny to an unprecedented degree.

It is clear that much of the growth of antigovernment sentiment among white South Carolinians is related to the activism of the federal government in protecting the rights of black citizens of the state. Nowhere was this truer than in the response to the federal court mandates for the desegregation of the public schools. (When the Charleston schools were desegregated under court order in 1963, the city's main newspaper, the *Charleston News and Courier*, attacked the district court's decision an example of "alien and hateful regulations imposed by the national government on an unwilling populace.")

In some counties, particularly those in areas where African Americans were a majority or a large minority, the "private academy movement," as it was called, spread rapidly. Columbia attorney Tom Turnipseed was executive director of the South Carolina Independent School Association in the 1960s before he became an adviser to Alabama governor George Wallace. According to Turnipseed, there was a dramatic exodus of whites out of the public schools in the 1960s stemming directly from the fears of integration. Publicly, said Turnipseed, he and other spokesmen for the newly created schools insisted that it was simply a matter of "quality education." Privately, he added, "everyone knew that our purpose was to set up segregated schools.[10] Within five years of court-ordered desegregation, for example, half of the city of Charleston's white students had transferred to private and overwhelmingly segregated schools.[11]

At the same time, national white "backlash" trends interacted with developments in South Carolina and the South. In 1964, over the objection of many members of his own party, Senator Barry Goldwater, the Republican Party's presidential nominee, announced his opposition to the Civil Rights Act of 1964. Publicly he justified his actions on the basis of constitutional objections to the laws; privately he acknowledged the political implications of his action. The Republican Party was "not going to get the Negro vote," he told a group of southern Republicans, "so we ought to go hunting where the ducks are."[12] And that meant angry white southern voters who he believed would give him the southern base he needed to have a chance at winning the election.[13] As historians Numan Bartley and Hugh Davis Graham and political scientists Earl and Merle Black concluded in their respective studies of southern politics during the "second Reconstruction": the Goldwater campaign sought to create a general polarization of southern voters along racial lines.[14]

Although the strategy failed in 1964 in the North (and in the border South), it played a decisive role in establishing the Republican Party at the grassroots level in the Deep South. It may fairly be said that the Goldwater campaign, coupled with the decision of Senator Thurmond to leave the Democratic Party, laid the foundations for the Republican Party in South Carolina. And political scientist Donald Fowler reflects the viewpoint of historians and political scientists in his judicious assessment of presidential voting in South Carolina, arguing that economic conservatism and other issues such as "anticommunism" helped to explain Goldwater's appeal to white South Carolinians, but "dominating these issues was the race question."[15]

Richard Nixon was more subtle in his attempt to exploit the resentment of white southern voters, but he quietly promoted a variation of Senator Goldwater's "southern strategy." In 1970 Kevin Phillips, the Republican Party's main expert on ethnic and racial voting patterns, argued: "The GOP can build a winning coalition without Negro votes." Indeed, he said, "Negro-Democratic mutual identification" was a critical factor in the growth of the Republican Party in the South. With the Democratic Party becoming the "Negro party through most of the South," the Republicans would become the majority party in the region and attract disenchanted white working-class voters in the North as well. After reading Phillips's recommendations, Nixon wrote a memo to his staff. "Use Phillips strategy," he ordered; "don't go for Jews & Blacks."[16]

If the national Democratic Party embraced black political participation and supported civil rights during the Kennedy and Johnson administrations, the state Democratic parties in the South were hardly free from racial considerations. The measures restricting the impact of black voting in South Carolina in the 1960s and 1970s were enacted by an overwhelmingly Democratic state legislature. Former lowcountry Republican congressman Tommy Hartnett vividly recalled the degree to which racial tensions were heightened during his first race for the legislature in 1964 (as a Democrat). Ruth Williamson, a popular incumbent in the legislature, endorsed Lyndon Johnson's presidential candidacy and greeted "Lady Bird" Johnson when she campaigned in Charleston. "The next day," recalled Hartnett, "all I heard at the polls was: 'I'm here to vote against those nigger lovers.'" Goldwater handily carried the county, and Williamson went down to decisive defeat.[17]

By the mid-1970s, however, white Democrats had only two options if they were to remain active in state and local politics: they could join hands with (overwhelmingly) Democratic black voters or they could switch to the Republican Party. Thus, although there were certainly examples of white Democrats giving less than enthusiastic support to fellow Democrats who were black, the political equation seemed to mandate a biracial political coalition, and as early as the 1970 elections, black and white Democratic candidates were linking their campaigns in advertisements and public appearances.

Given the angry racial feelings of many white South Carolinians, the Republican Party, on the other hand, became the home of voters angry with the pace of racial change. State elections in 1970 were particularly bitter examples of the intersection of race and party affiliations.

In Charleston elections took place in the aftermath of the bitter 1969 strike of Charleston's black hospital workers, a strike that had led to more than one thousand arrests and polarized the black and white communities.[18] While white Democrats sought the support of black voters, the Charleston County Republican Party released a series of newspaper and television ads accusing the Democrat Party legislative and county council candidates of being controlled by the "Black bloc vote." One ad warned that the election of Democrats would lead to control of local government by the Political Action Committee of the NAACP. Another headlined in bold capitals: "REMEMBER THE NIGHTMARE OF A HOSPITAL STRIKE? THE NEED FOR ARMED TROOPS? THE CRIPPLING 113 DAY CURFEW? THE THREAT TO BURN THE CITY?" Election of the "bloc controlled Democrat slate" would mean a "formal invitation to [SCLC president Ralph] ABERNATHY and his wrecking crew to return to Charleston, more triumphantly and arrogantly."[19]

Racial tensions also marred the statewide race for the governorship that year as Republican candidate Albert W. Watson staked his campaign on an all-out attack on court-ordered school desegregation. Watson called upon his followers to "stand up and use every means" to fight what he called "illegal" orders of the federal courts, advice that Darlington County supporters followed when they attacked school buses carrying terrified black students. In part because of the reaction to these violent attacks, Lt. Governor John West was able to win 53 percent of the vote and capture the governorship with a coalition of solid black support and more than 35 percent of the state's white voters.[20]

Watson's defeat marked one of the last statewide campaigns based upon explicitly racial issues in the post–civil rights era in South Carolina. Nevertheless, the politics of race have not disappeared from the state's politics. During the 1970s, 1980s, and 1990s, for example, there was persistent conflict over access on the part of African Americans to the polls. While no one would suggest that black South Carolinians were disfranchised in large numbers, the efforts to intimidate and harass black voters was a persistent reminder of the ongoing connection between race and politics.

Despite the increasing tendency of white South Carolinians to vote Republican for congressional and presidential candidates, through the late 1970s and 1980s the coalition of white and black Democrats managed to remain the dominant party.[21] As late as 1988, nearly 220,000 whites voted in the Democratic primary, with less than 75,000 white South Carolinians voting in the Republican primary. (Black voters have never made up more than 5 percent of the vote in

Republican primaries). Between 1988 and 1992, however, two statewide polls showed that the number of white South Carolinians who identified themselves as Democrats had plummeted from 30 to less than 15 percent of the white voting population. By the end of the 1990s whites were nearly twice as likely to identify themselves as Republican and to vote in the Republican primary. In some counties the two parties had come close to the situation predicted in 1990 by First District congressman Arthur Ravenel, who had foreseen the emergence of a virtually all-white Republican Party and a virtually all-black Democratic Party. [22]

These are not simply academic questions concerning racial party affiliation, for such partisan differences reflect the racial polarization on public policy issues that continues to exist between black and white South Carolinians. For example, the Palmetto Project, an independent and nonpartisan attempt to understand racial attitudes in South Carolina, found the following in their 1998 survey: Approximately half of the white respondents agreed that a "white child in South Carolina has a much better chance of achieving financial success in his or her lifetime than a child who is not white," while 80 percent of black respondents agreed with the statement.

In viewing the impact of race upon employment, attitudes were even more polarized. Four out of five white South Carolinians agreed with the statement that a nonwhite job applicant had "as good a chance as a white person of getting a job for which he or she is qualified." By contrast, 70 percent of black South Carolinians rejected that statement. There are other political issues that reflect similar differences. When asked if South Carolina's criminal justice system treated people of color more harshly than whites, 29.5 percent of white respondents agreed, but more than 80 percent of blacks interviewed endorsed that notion.[23]

Of course "race" is a relatively crude way to measure political attitudes; obviously all African Americans do not agree on every subject; neither do all whites. But as these and other surveys show, there are critical political issues that statistically reflect "racial" attitudes. Given the sharp polarization in views that exists along racial lines, it is difficult to defend the notion that "partisanship" between two parties divided along roughly racial lines is somehow an abstract concept divorced from those racial attitudes. Overt racism has declined dramatically over the last fifty years, but black and white South Carolinians still perceive the world in different and conflicting ways.

This is hardly surprising, since black South Carolinians—despite significant progress in the 1960s and 1970s—continue to suffer from severe social and economic disadvantages. The good news from the 1990s was the increasing economic well-being of all South Carolinians.[24] Despite this improvement, black per capita income is still only slightly more than half that of whites, and the level of black poverty is more than one in four. (One in twelve whites lives below the poverty line). In 1990 whites in South Carolina were nearly three times more likely than blacks to have graduated from college and four times more likely to have obtained a professional degree. Other indices of social well-being show similar disparities.[25]

Even more depressing is the fact that—despite the economic boom of the 1990s—the overall number of South Carolina's children living in poverty, black and white, increased from 18 to 20 percent. Despite significant improvement in the 1990s, the infant mortality rate for African Americans in South Carolina in 1997 was two and a half times that of whites. And as the recession deepened in 2001 and 2002, South Carolina was one of only two states in the nation to experience an increase in the number of its citizens living below the poverty line.[26]

As political scientist Glen Broach and *State* newspaper editor Lee Bandy have noted, politicians today seldom emphasize explicitly racial issues, but in a state in which many of African Americans are "clustered near the lower end of the socioeconomic scale and firmly in the Democratic camp," an emphasis on government waste and rising crime has "fit comfortably with white perceptions of black lawlessness and abuse of government largesse funded largely with taxes paid by whites." Inevitably, some of the most contentious public policy issues that divide the two parties, such as welfare reform, crime, taxes, and affirmative action, inevitably take on a "racial context" in the political arena.[27] Everyone is familiar with the racial dimensions of the conflict over the Confederate flag, but it seems difficult to avoid the racial implications of the television ads by white Republican John Chase in the 1992 district congressional campaign. Chase accused James Clyburn, a black Democrat, of supporting a "welfare express card," a charge clearly designed to evoke white voters' linkage of race and welfare. When Charleston Republican state representative John Graham Altman told voters that "I'm standing at the door, guarding your tax dollars," it was a clear and unmistakable echo of Alabama governor George Wallace's 1963 promise to "stand in the schoolhouse door" to block the integration of public schools and an unmistakable effort, in the words of one Charleston political observer, to "trigger a deep-seated set of assumptions by whites that tax dollars are going to blacks who are lazy, shiftless, and intent on relying upon the government to support them."[28]

Most white South Carolinians, like most Americans, would acknowledge the existence of that history of discrimination. But there is an understandable desire to avoid extensive references to the pervasiveness of past racial discrimination, and there is an even stronger tendency to see this discrimination as part of the distant past that has no great relevance to today. In a recent case over the issue of single-district versus at-large representation on the Charleston County Council, a leading member of the council acknowledged that the African American community continues to be characterized by lower socioeconomic conditions. But he added, "I don't think the discrimination of the 1800s and early 1900s and middle 1900s is the cause of these problems."[29]

Such a point of view is based upon the assumption that the end of legal segregation led to an overnight transformation in economic and political opportunities for African Americans in this state. There are many individuals who manage to rise above the handicaps imposed by poverty and poor educational opportunities, but virtually every study of social mobility in American society confirms common sense: statistically, young people who come from homes marked by social stability, economic security, and higher educational levels are more likely to achieve and to function more successfully in the economic and political arena. None of these factors can be attributed, as a whole, to the state's black community as it emerged from two hundred years of slavery and a hundred years of segregation and discrimination.[30]

This has both racial and class implications insofar as the political process is concerned. In their highly regarded study *Who Votes?*, political scientists Raymond Wolfinger and Steven Rosenstone document the strong and direct correlation between political participation and socioeconomic and educational status. Their central conclusion was that "citizens of higher social and economic status participate more in politics." In the South, they conclude, this disparity in turnout between the rich and the poor and between the educated and uneducated is even more pronounced. Southerners with eight years of schooling or less, they note, vote 16 percentage points less than their northern counterparts. All these factors have a disparate racial impact since African Americans remain grouped in the ranks of lower social, educational, and economic status.[31] It is a tribute to the African American community in the state that they have been able to maintain higher than expected levels of voter participation. During the 1980s African American communities in the South mobilized (often energized by the presidential campaign of Jesse Jackson). But in the 1990s registration and turnout numbers of African Americans began to return to the pattern described by Wolfinger and Rosenstone. In their survey of politics in South Carolina in the 1990s, Broach and Bandy described a fall-off in black voter turnout in the state.[32]

These somewhat bleak observations should be tempered with a recognition that much has changed and much has improved in the lives of all South Carolinians—black as well as white—over the lifetime of Matthew Perry. But these statistics remind us that South Carolina remains a state with much unfinished racial and economic business.

Arthur Locke King, a self-educated Georgetown lawyer during the 1940s and 1950s, was one of the white South Carolinians who contributed essays to the 1957 booklet *South Carolinians Speak: A Moderate Approach to Race Relations.* Its publication led to a storm of anger and outrage by most whites in the state even though reading it today, one is tempted to say that most of the authors were so "moderate" that they seldom got around to approaching race relations. But King was one of the exceptions. He praised the NAACP for defending the rights of black folks, he rejected each argument for segregation as nothing more than a "child of blind prejudice . . . , too absurd to command the respect of intelligent citizens." Discrimination in any form, he concluded, was the "work of the devil," "contrary to the law of nature and of nature's God."[33]

But beyond the moral arguments for justice, Arthur King appealed to the people of South Carolina to understand the self-inflicted wounds caused by what he called a "system of practical serfdom toward the Negro." The greatest folly the white people of the South had ever committed, said King, was their failure to create a society in which black people were "deprived of an opportunity to contribute in full measure" toward society. By so doing "the people as a whole were kept in poverty and without the benefits of the good things of life which lay at their very doorsteps."

Segregation and the overall structure of the legal and economic serfdom that King saw in his lifetime as well as the worst of the poverty of that era has passed away. But as long as hundreds of thousands of black and white South Carolinians remain mired in poverty and, in King's words, "deprived of an opportunity to contribute in full measure" to the state of South Carolina,[34] we cannot pause to congratulate ourselves on how far we have come. We have many miles to go before we can claim to have created the society of justice and equal opportunity that inspired the civil rights movement of South Carolina and the nation.

Notes

1. Portions of this essay were first published in "Unfinished Transformation: Matthew J. Perry's South Carolina," in *Matthew J. Perry: The Man, His Times, and His Legacy,* ed. W. Lewis Burke and Belinda F. Gergel, 238–61 (Columbia: University of South Carolina Press, 2004).

2. I. A. Newby, *Black Carolinians: A History of Blacks in South Carolina from 1895 to 1968* (Columbia: University of South Carolina Press, 1973), 260–65; Leon Fink and Brian Greenberg, *Upheaval in the Quiet Zone: A History of the Hospital Worker's Union, Local 1199* (Urbana: University of Illinois Press, 1989), pp. 129–58. In response to a 1938 lawsuit by the NAACP, the state promised to set up a law program for blacks at South Carolina State. Instead, they shipped a few hand-me-down law texts to the college and hired one professor of law. The all-black law school produced a number of outstanding graduates during its brief history, including Judge Matthew M. Perry, but no one would disagree that it was in no way equal in facilities or resources to the University of South Carolina. There was no opportunity for African Americans to obtain even an inferior medical education within the state. Richard Kluger, *Simple Justice: The History of* Brown v. Board of Education *and Black America's Struggle for Equality* (New York: Knopf, 1975), 299.

3. Quoted in Louis R. Harlan's *Separate and Unequal: Public School Campaigns and Racism in the Southern Seaboard States, 1901–1915* (New York: Atheneum, 1968), 185.

4. And the school year was often only three or four months long in many rural schools. Newby, *Black Carolinians,* 308.

5. U.S. Bureau of Census, *U.S. Census of Population, 1950:* Characteristics of the Population, Part 40, South Carolina, l92; U.S. Bureau of the Census, U.S. Census of Population, 1960: Characteristics of the Population, Part 2, South Carolina, 359–60.

6. Oliphant's history went through several editions; by the 1960s some of the more explicit defenses of white supremacy had been softened.

7. Terence Finnegan, "Lynching and Political Power in Mississippi and South Carolina," in *Under Sentence of Death: Lynching in the South,* ed. W. Fitzhugh Brundage (Chapel Hill: University of North Carolina Press, 1997), 193.

8. Police arrested three Klansmen, and one of the men confessed; but he later died under mysterious circumstances before the trial of his fellow Klansmen, and a jury quickly acquitted the two other accused men. Timothy B. Tyson, "Dynamite and 'the Silent South': A Story from the Second Reconstruction in South Carolina," in *Jumpin' Jim Crow: Southern Politics from Civil War to Civil Rights,* ed. Jane Dailey, Glenda Elizabeth Gilmore, and Bryant Simon (Princeton, N.J.: Princeton University Press, 2000), 276–97.

9. Numan Bartley's *The Rise of Massive Resistance* (Baton Rouge: Louisiana State University Press, 1969) and Neil McMillen's *The Citizens' Council: Organized Resistance to the Second Reconstruction, 1954–64* (Urbana: University of Chicago Press, 1971) remain the best accounts of southern white resistance to equal rights for African Americans. Howard H. Quint, a former professor of history at the University of South Carolina in the mid-1950s, describes the many forms of economic and political pressure (and sometimes violence) used to maintain segregation and white supremacy in the state. See *Profile in Black and White: A Frank Portrait of South Carolina* (Washington, D.C.: Public Affairs Press, 1958).

10. According to Turnipseed, the organization attracted families and students that would never have been interested in private schools were it not for the race question. The association tried to work with local churches so that contributions to the new segregated schools could be tax exempt. Tom Turnipseed, interview with the author, August 28, 2001, Columbia, S.C.

11. Maxie Myron Cox Jr., "1963—The Year of Decision: Desegregation in South Carolina" (Ph.D. dissertation, University of South Carolina, 1996), 179–88.

12. Dan T. Carter, *The Politics of Rage: George Wallace, the Origins of the New Conservatism, and the Transformation of American Politics* (New York: Simon & Schuster, 1995), 218.

13. Robert Alan Goldberg, *Barry Goldwater* (New Haven: Yale University Press, 1995), 197.

14. Numan Bartley and Hugh Davis Graham, *Southern Politics during the Second Reconstruction* (Baltimore: Johns Hopkins University Press, 1975), 187; Earl Black and Merle Black, *Politics and Society in the South* (Cambridge, Mass.: Harvard University Press, 1987), 143–44. Four out of five southern Goldwater delegates to the 1964 Republican convention rejected any judicial or legislative action to remedy voter discrimination—even when it could be shown that blacks were denied access to the ballot box. Bernard Cosman and Herbert Huckshorn, eds., *Republican Politics: The 1964 Campaign and Its Aftermath for the Party* (New York Praeger, 1968), 242.

15. Donald L. Fowler, *Presidential Voting in South Carolina, 1948–1964* (Columbia: University of South Carolina Bureau of Governmental Research and Service, 1966), 13.

16. Dan T. Carter, *From George Wallace to Newt Gingrich: Race in the Conservative Counterrevolution, 1963–1994* (Baton Rouge: Louisiana State University Press, 1996), 45; Kenneth O'Reilly, *Nixon's Piano: Presidents and Racial Politics from Washington to Clinton* (New York: Free Press, 1995), 285–86.

17. Thomas Hartnett, interview with the author, August 8, 2001, Charleston, S.C.; *Charleston News and Courier,* November 4, 1964.

18. Fink and Greenberg, *Upheaval in the Quiet Zone,* 129–58. In addition to the impact of the local Charleston strike, the state had been shaken by the violent events in Orangeburg in 1968, when South Carolina State Highway Patrol officers fired on black South Carolina

State students, killing three students and wounding twenty-seven others. Jack Nelson and Jack Bass, *The Orangeburg Massacre* (New York: World, 1970), 98.

19. *Charleston News and Courier,* October 26, November 1, November 2, 1970. In its news headlines, the *News and Courier* used the same phrase repeatedly to describe the participation of black voters.

20. *State,* November 4, 5, 1970; Jack Bass and Walter DeVries, *The Transformation of Southern Politics: Social Change and Political Consequence since 1945* (New York: Basic Books, 1976), 262–63.

21. Beginning in 1984, the state assembled demographic information on registration and voting in primary and general elections by race. It is available on the internet at http://www.scvotes.org/ Although there are no figures for the 1970s, most observers believe the racial composition of the two parties remained relatively stable from 1974 to 1984.

22. *Charleston Evening Post,* February 18, 1990.

23. "Palmetto Project: A Survey of Racial Attitudes, conducted by Information Research Group, Charleston, S.C., February 1998. Copies of the survey are available from the Palmetto Project, 1031 Chuck Dawley Boulevard, Suite 5, Mount Pleasant, SC 29464. The United States leads the world in the number of individuals incarcerated and, in South Carolina (like other states), the racial disparity is extraordinary. One in eight black men in their twenties and thirties were behind bars last year, compared to one in sixty-three white men, a disparity attributed to a variety of factors, including poverty, inferior education, and enforcement and sentencing policies that focus on drug enforcement. *Baltimore Sun,* June 1, 2003.

24. Black per capita income in South Carolina was 48 percent of whites' in 1990 and 53 percent of per capita white income in 2000, although it should be noted that the actual gap between black and white incomes increased from $7,315 to $10,319.

25. *Census of the U.S., 1990,* Summary of Social and Economic Characteristics, South Carolina, table 8, 32, 35; Educational Attainment by Age, Race, and Hispanic Origin, South Carolina, table 3, 398–99.

26. These figures and those from the previous paragraph are taken from the 1990 and 2000 census results and from Gina Smith's "Good Times Didn't Help Poor Kids," in the *State,* March 8, 2002, and James L. Coleman Jr. et al., "Eliminating Health Disparities in African American South Carolinians: A Call for Bold Action," in *The State of Black South Carolina: Millennium Edition,* ed. Kenneth Campbell (Columbia, S.C.: Columbia Urban League, 2000), 109. Moreover, it is not simply that black per capita income is half that of the white community; recent studies point out that because of a number of a factors, including the past history of economic discrimination, black households on the average have less than 10 percent of the wealth held by white households. Melvin L. Oliver and Thomas M. Shapiro, "Race and Wealth," *Review of Black Political Economy* 17 (1989): 5–25.

27. Glen Broach and Lee Bandy, "South Carolina," in *Southern Politics in the 1990s,* ed. Alexander Lamis (Baton Rouge: Louisiana State University Press, 1999), 71; Hartnett, interview.

28. *Charleston Post and Courier,* October 31, 1992. F. Truett Nettles, interview with the author, July 25, 2001, charleston, S.C. The most extensive analysis of such coded messages is in the sociologist Tali Mendelberg's *The Race Card: Campaign Strategy, Implicit Messages, and the Norm of Equality* (Princeton, N.J.: Princeton University Press, 2001).

29. Deposition of Charles Thornwell Wallace, M.D., *USA* v. *Charleston County, SC,* July 12, 2001, 97–99.

30. There is an extensive literature on the intergenerational carryover of income and social status, some of which takes issues of race into consideration. See Neil J. Smelser

and Seymour Martin Lipset, eds., *Social Structure and Mobility in Economic Development* (Chicago: Aldine, 1966); Michael Hout, "Status, Autonomy and Training in Occupational Mobility," *American Journal of Sociology* 30 (1984): 1379–1409; Otis Dudley Duncan, "Inheritance of Poverty or Inheritance of Race?," in *On Understanding Poverty,* ed. Daniel P. Moynihan (New York: Basic Books, 1968), 85–110; Oliver and Shapiro, "Race and Wealth."

31. Raymond E. Wolfinger and Steven J. Rosenstone, *Who Votes?* (New Haven: Yale University Press, 1980), 13, 93.

32. Glen Broach and Lee Bandy, "South Carolina," in *Southern Politics in the 1990s,* ed. Alexander Lamis, 71 (Baton Rouge: Louisiana State University Press, 1999).

33. Arthur Locke King, in Ralph E. Cousins et al., *South Carolinians Speak: A Moderate Approach to Race Relations* (Dillon, S.C.: Privately published, 1957), 51–53.

34. Ibid.

How Far We Have Come—
How Far We Still Have to Go

CHARLES JOYNER

As I was driving to Coastal Carolina University the other day, I listened to an old tape I have of a fascinating conversation among Thurgood Marshall, Reinhold Niebuhr, and Norman Thomas. Marshall told them how he had been interviewed by a newspaper on May 17, 1954, the day the Supreme Court announced its *Brown v. Board of Education* decision. Not wishing to raise hopes too high too soon, he urged people to be patient. Things won't change overnight, he had said. We won't see real integration for years—four, or maybe even five.

When I returned to my native South Carolina in 1960, after nearly two years of unsegregated life in the United States Army, it had already been six years; and the official policy of my state's government was still a white supremacy so comprehensive as to be scarcely believable in retrospect. The caste system of segregation branded all black South Carolinians as racial inferiors. It was reflected in the disfranchisement of black citizens and in the systematic separation of the races in schools, in jobs, and in public accommodations. The only sanctioned associations of blacks and whites were in the roles of subordinate and superior. Black South Carolinians were relegated to Jim Crow schools, to the back of the Jim Crow bus, and to the Jim Crow balcony—the "buzzard's roost"—at the movie theaters. This caste system was the result of an official state commitment to white supremacy and to a pervasive distrust of democracy. Democracy, as the word was understood elsewhere, had not yet been embraced by the government of my native state as late as 1960. And few South Carolinians thought it ever would be. Only twelve years earlier the governor of our state, running for president on the Dixiecrat ticket in 1948, had taunted the United States with the challenge that "there are not enough soldiers in the army" to end the system of segregation.

The Jim Crow laws were unconstitutional on their face. But segregation also involved the inequitable enforcement of other laws and the discriminatory administering of social services as well. As a result, in 1960 black Carolinians had less than half the chance of finishing high school as white Carolinians and less than a third the chance of finishing college or entering a profession. Black Carolinians had the prospect of earning less than half as much as white Carolinians, were twice as likely to be imprisoned or unemployed, and could look forward to a shorter life span.

The governor of our state at that time denied that segregation was discriminatory. He said he did not know anyone who believed in "any prejudice on account of race." Segregation was based on "history, culture, and economic background." It was a "natural thing," preferred not only by whites but also by "a majority of Negroes." The quest for equality was whipped up by anti-southern forces. "If there's one thing against our way of life in the South," he declared, "it's the NAACP. And if the U.S. Supreme Court can declare certain organizations as subversive, I believe South Carolina can declare the NAACP both subversive and illegal."

And according to our junior United States senator, running for his second full term in 1960, the quest for racial equality represented the closest the country had yet come to Communism. It was "made to order for Communists to use in their designs upon National Security." The justices of the United States Supreme Court, he declared, were "not worthy to wear the robes of their high offices." He denounced their 1954 school desegregation decision as "one of the worst ever handed down." Most of the authorities cited by the court in that case, he asserted, "were either members of Communist-front organizations" or their loyalty was "in serious question." He called on South Carolinians to "resist integration by every legal means harder than the integrationists fought to end segregation." Soon he was congratulating the White Citizens' Councils for what he called the "orderly and lawful manner" in which they were approaching the "problem" created by the quest for racial equality.

A significant part of the quest for racial equality was what Jack Bass has called "Judicial Reconstruction." The courage and wisdom of southern judges—white men such as J. Waties Waring in our state—have since received well-earned praise. But in those days, for a white man to take a stand for racial justice was to burn most of his bridges with the white community. When these judges took their stands, they and their families suffered for their actions.

There were other white liberals in South Carolina who took stands for racial justice in the 1950s and 1960s, most of them at great risk and some of them at great cost. And they should not be forgotten. Marion Wright, who, as a young lawyer in Conway, as early as 1919 called for the dismantling of segregation. He became president of the Southern Regional Council in the 1950s. John Bolt Culbertson served as a longtime counsel for the NAACP. Alice Buck Norwood Spearman, granddaughter of a slaveholder, was an effective director of the interracial South Carolina Council on Human Relations. Her friend Eliza-beth Ledeen organized the council's interracial youth programs. Jack Bass, a young editor of the University of South Carolina's student newspaper, the *Game-cock,* wrote eloquent editorials excoriating segregation; courageous young min-isters such as Larry Jackson, Howard McLain, and Lucius DuBose, a Presbyterian pastor in Mullins, who was fired from his pulpit because he preached what Jesus really meant by "all God's children." The editors Mac Seacrest of the *Cheraw Chronicle* and Jack O'Dowd and James Rogers of the *Florence Morning News* educated their readers to both the inevitability and moral necessity of ending segregation. There were many others, perhaps above all James McBride Dabbs, the farmer-writer of Sumter County. Dr. King—in his "Letter from Birmingham Jail"—wrote that Dabbs "grasped the meaning of this social revolution" and "wrote about our struggle in eloquent, prophetic, and understanding terms." But the white conversion narrative is not the whole story. "How the White Folks Got Over" is not even the main story. Tony Badger points out that when race became the acid test of southern liberals of the 1940s and '50s, too many of them flunked.

We must never forget that it was blacks, not whites, who were at the center of the civil rights movement, men and women who risked not only their social standing but their livelihoods, their homes, and indeed their very lives. It was the grassroots black community that furnished the leadership and the largest sup-port base for the movement. It was the grassroots black community that pro-duced people such as the workers from South Carolina who took their great song that we know as "We Shall Overcome" to the Highlander Folk School in the early 1940s. It was the grassroots black community that produced people such as Alice Wine of Johns Island, South Carolina, who in 1956 introduced the song "Keep Your Eyes on the Prize." In the early 1960s Guy and Candie Carawan helped spread these songs to civil rights activists at conferences in Nashville, Raleigh, Atlanta, and at Highlander. Those activists in turn carried them across the South, and they became the great anthems of the civil rights movement.

It was grassroots black leaders such as Benjamin E. Mays, who came out of Ninety-Six, South Carolina, to become "the Benjamin Franklin of Black Amer-ica," the president of Morehouse College, the teacher of Martin Luther King Jr. and the grandfather of the civil rights movement; and the Reverend Joseph De Laine, who was forced out of South Carolina for standing up to the power struc-ture in Clarendon County; and Esau Jenkins, who founded the Progressive Club on Johns Island and devoted his life to improving conditions in the South. It was grassroots black teachers such as Septima Clark, who taught and inspired Esau and who herself went on to a career full of distinguished contributions to civil rights; and Bernice Robinson, who—with no experience in teaching—helped to create the citizenship education schools on Johns Island that would sweep the South as "freedom schools" in the 1960s. It was black men and women such as

James Hinton and Modjeska Simkins who formed the South Carolina Conference of the NAACP; black journalists such as John McCray and Osceola McKaine who kept the flame burning in the 1940s and 1950s; and Jim McCain, who was the first CORE field secretary in South Carolina. It was the brilliance and dedication of black lawyers such as Thurgood Marshall, Matthew Perry, and Lincoln Jenkins who planned the strategies and researched the statutes and precedents; but it was the courage of grassroots black litigants such as George Elmore, David Brown, and Harry Briggs that instigated the suits that made possible such great victories as *Elmore v. Rice, Brown v. Baskins,* and *Briggs v. Elliott.* And it was a handful of young black activists such as Chuck McDew and Cleveland Sellers at South Carolina State, who became founders of SNCC (the Student Nonviolent Coordinating Committee); and Diane Nash and Tom Gaither of CORE in Rock Hill; and David Carter, who led the Columbia movement; and many other unsung black heroes and heroines who launched the nonviolent direct action phase of the movement in the 1960s.

As an idealistic young graduate student, fresh from the army, I became deeply involved in this quest for equality, deeply involved in protests and demonstrations against segregation, deeply involved in organizing a statewide biracial student movement—the South Carolina Student Council on Human Relations. Perhaps because I had learned to play the guitar in the army and knew a lot of freedom songs, I was elected its first president.

I shared an apartment at 1015 Henderson Street in Columbia with three remarkable young southerners—Selden Smith, Dan Carter, and Hayes Mizell. We shared much more than an apartment; we became lifelong friends. We were all graduate students in history, we all shared idealistic visions of a better South Carolina, and we were all involved in the civil rights movement. We played host to various members of SNCC, SCLC (the Southern Christian Leadership Conference), and others as they came through the state. We engaged in earnest dialogues with Andy Young of SCLC, Will Campbell from the Committee of Southern Churchmen, Marion Wright of the Southern Regional Council, and Connie Curry of the National Student Association. And I served as chauffeur to Ella Baker (the first executive director of SCLC and the godmother of SNCC) when she was in Columbia.

As the movement grew, sit-ins and other antisegregation protests were intensified across the state—in Columbia, in Greenville, in Orangeburg, in Rock Hill. The segregationists mobilized for all-out resistance. Red-baiting was organized on a statewide scale by such groups as the citizens' councils, the John Birch Society, and Operation Alert. SLED (the State Law Enforcement Division) was called out to investigate the so-called subversives. A friend who worked in the governor's office told us he had seen our pictures on the governor's desk. Hayes Mizell and I lost our teaching assistantships at the university. Ella Baker urged us not to be cowed by the red-baiting and harassment. She said that our problem in the South was not radical thought, nor even conservative thought, but simply lack of thought. If we were ever going to break the pattern of segregation, we could no longer let the opposition decide who our associates could be.

The opposition did not stop with red-baiting. In Rock Hill Tom Gaither and eight Friendship Junior College students were arrested in a sit-in and sentenced to thirty days on the York County road gang. In Orangeburg police used tear gas and fire hoses on demonstrators. (A year later similar attacks in Birmingham drew national headlines and lead stories on the network news. By then the movement had learned that if it did not happen on TV, it did not happen.) In Columbia my friend Lennie Glover was stabbed in the spleen by a white man while police looked on. The perpetrator was never apprehended. In Rock Hill jail became a badge of honor. "The only thing they had to beat us over the head with was the threat of sending us to jail," Tom Gaither maintained. So when the student demonstrators began to pack the jails, refusing bail, he said, "It upset. . . [the power structure] considerably."

The segregationists in high places and low called for order, as though order without justice were not tyranny. The segregationists called us extremists, but they were the extremists. The civil rights movement offered an alternative to the extremes of insensitive complacency on the one hand and senseless violence on the other, the one a failure of the heart, the other a failure of the mind. The segregationists called us traitors to the South, but the black and white southerners of the movement were the most truly loyal southerners the region has ever had, most loyal to our shared traditions, the truest expression of the South. The racists represented our region at its worst: ignorant of the past, fearful of the future, and dangerous to the South they claimed to love. But we understood the resentment of the racists. We came out of the same folk culture. We understood their hostility and frustration. We understood their need for someone to blame. Diane Nash wrote an eloquent letter from her cell in the York County jail: "We are trying to help focus attention on a moral question. Segregation is immoral. Seek a world where all . . . may be as free as you yourself want to be. Let us truly love one another, and under God, move toward a redeemed community."

The racists hated the movement, because we demanded justice, when few white Americans were prepared to grant justice to black Americans. They persecuted us and they reviled us. They rebuked us and they scorned us. They cursed us, and at Orangeburg they killed some of us. But they never stopped us. We used to sing a lot of the old spirituals. It took only a slight change in the words—usually just substituting the word *freedom* for the word *Heaven*—to make them into freedom songs. One we used to sing was

> Ain't gonna let nobody turn me 'round,
> gonna keep on a-walkin',

keep on a-talkin',
marchin' up to Freedom Land.

Inspired by such songs, we could not be stopped.

I don't think any of us who witnessed or took part in the large mass demonstrations and marches will ever forget them. In August 1963, shortly after our marriage, my wife, Jeannie, and I joined some two hundred thousand others in the March on Washington. Many of us were white, but most of us were black. We marched along, singing innumerable verses of "We Shall Overcome" and a parody of "Amen":

Everybody wants Free-ee-ee-dom.
Everybody wants Free-ee-ee-dom.
Everybody wants Free-ee-dom.
Free-dom. Free-dom.

With each verse, the marchers substituted the name of a state—"Alabama wants free-ee-ee-dom," "Mississippi wants free-ee-ee-dom," "Illinois wants free-ee-eedom," etc. I wanted to hear "South Carolina wants free-ee-ee-dom," but nobody sang that. I mentally resolved that at end of the verse we were singing, before anybody started another state, I was going to heist up "South Carolina wants free-ee-ee-dom." When I did, I noticed that a slender, middle-aged black man walking beside me did exactly the same thing. We started on exactly the same beat. While the marchers took up our chorus, we looked at each other like, "Hey, man, where have you been?" When we had a chance we introduced ourselves to each other. He was Rev. Herbert Williams. He lived in New York but had grown up in Georgetown, thirty miles south of my hometown of Myrtle Beach. Years later, when we both had moved back home, Rev. Williams enrolled in my class on South Carolina history. It is the only time my lectures were ever greeted with "Amens" from the "congregation."

On that day in 1963 we stood across the reflecting pool from the Lincoln Memorial, increasingly pushed back and crushed together as more and more marchers arrived. We heard Mahalia Jackson sing, her rich, pure voice bending and sliding around the notes, occasionally prancing and swaggering like a sanctified preacher—even though we knew she was a Baptist. Her proudly southern singing, in the moaning and growling style of down-home churches, filled all our hearts with bountiful, generous emotions. And all our hopes soared to the sky as we hung on Dr. King's lyrical refrain: "I have a dream!" It must have been the grandest assembly for the redress of grievances Washington had ever witnessed. And after nearly forty years it remains an unforgettable experience.

The courage and effectiveness of the direct action phase of the movement across the South prodded Congress to pass the Civil Rights Act of 1964 and the Voting Rights Act of 1965, effectively demolishing the legal foundations of segregation and disfranchisement.

But menacing signs of resistance were manifest almost immediately. Dan Carter has brilliantly demonstrated in his *From George Wallace to Newt Gingrich* that the conservative counterrevolution adopted and adapted the racial ideology of George Wallace, gave it a cosmetic makeover for greater respectability, and turned back the tide of racial progress. In this endeavor they were abetted by what Paul Gaston calls "an exuberant band of right-wing politicians, pundits, and think tanks." Exemplified in Richard Nixon's shrewd exploitation of the busing issue, Ronald Reagan's amiable assaults on affirmative action, and George Bush's clever employment of the Willie Horton ad, three presidential administrations moved forcefully to delay desegregation under the 1964 Civil Rights Act, to dilute black political gains under the 1965 Voting Rights Act, and to deter federal spending aimed at black advancement. Meanwhile their congressional allies launched determined attacks on the enforcement of existing civil rights statutes.

The Supreme Court appointments of these three presidents turned that body toward resegregation. William Rehnquist, one of four justices appointed to the Court by President Nixon, was already on record that he believed "*Plessy v. Ferguson* was right and should be reaffirmed." He was elevated to chief justice by President Reagan in 1986. President Bush's appointments finally gave the court the majority necessary for a series of landmark opinions in 1991, 1992, and 1995, each favoring resegregation, each chipping away at *Brown v. Board of Education.* The last one, *Missouri v. Jenkins,* went even further in support of separate but unequal rights than *Plessy* a century earlier. It forbade improving inner-city schools as a means of attracting white students from the suburbs.

And the reaction continues. As we speak, affirmative action policies on behalf of blacks—instituted in an effort to redress the effects of three centuries of affirmative action policies on behalf of whites—are under sustained attack. And the current President Bush has already indicated his support for a resegregation decision. Vernon Jordan's question is as relevant today as it was thirty years ago: "Are we today going back to separate and unequal?"

The "Second Reconstruction," as the great historian C. Vann Woodward once dubbed it, has by now turned into a bizarre parody of the first. Once again the region has had its government taken over by Republicans; the old "Solid South" has been replaced by a new "Solid South." But this time it is all turned upside down and inside out. The opportunistic Yankees called carpetbaggers now have names like Gingrich and Bush; and the turncoat natives called scalawags now have names like Thurmond and Helms. And far from being the party of Abraham Lincoln and Frederick Douglass, the latter-day carpetbaggers and scalawags wave the Confederate flag.

So now as I look back over our flawed successes and our magnificent failures, I return to a statement I wrote more than a decade ago. It is still true. "We have come a long way since 1960. Some say there has been no progress, but they have forgotten where we started. Some would stop here, for they cannot see how far we still have to go." Some think we have reached the Promised Land. Others say we are not even out of Egypt yet!

Because we knew the solid rock of brotherhood as well as the quicksand of white supremacy, because we knew the sunlit path of racial justice as well as the dark and desolate thickets of segregation, because we knew the beauty as well as the tragedy of the human spirit, for a brief and shining moment in the early 1960s we shared the dream, we truly believed that we were going to change the world and achieve the redeemed community. We won the battle of the lunch counters. We won the battle of school desegregation. We won the battle of voting rights. But we did not change the world. Perhaps the world changed us. We seem to have lost the dream of a redeemed community. Perhaps that was more radical than any of us were capable of. But I know the dream is not dead when I see black and white schoolchildren playing together, laughing and running like the brothers and sisters they are. I know the dream is not dead when I see black and white coworkers eating together, sitting together at the welcome table, laughing and joking like the friends they are. I know the dream is not dead when I see the thousands of black legislators, and sheriffs, and judges across the South.

But a dream deferred is a dream denied. And I know the dream is deferred when I see the destruction of an ancient and precious black culture in the South Carolina Sea Islands as black landowners are forced into selling out and the islands are "developed" into resorts for rich whites. I know the dream is deferred when I see the continuing concentration of black southerners in low-paying service jobs. I know the dream is deferred when I see the growing army of unemployed black southerners. We are by no means all "Free at Last!"

How long will we allow our state to be symbolized by retrogressive politicians, and irreligious evangelists, and Confederate flags still waving on our capitol grounds? How long will we have to endure the present drift to racial retrogression? I don't know when the tide will turn. But I do know this: our beloved South Carolina will never reach its potential until we can lay down the burden of racism.

Fortunately we in South Carolina have a shared culture to draw upon as we strive to reconcile our divided society. For out of the cultural triangle of Europe, and Africa, and our native Carolina soil has emerged a profound and creative exchange that has given us a distinctive folk culture of great strength and of great beauty, a folk culture that unites all our people, perhaps in deeper ways than we even yet understand.

We are the products not only of the defeats of our history but also of the achievements of our culture, a culture of folk and feeling—the rich and instructive humor of our Buh Rabbit tales; the haunting cadences of our majestic spirituals, our stately ballads, and our doleful but defiant blues; the awesome virtuosity of our jazz and bluegrass artists; the beauty of our prized sweetgrass baskets; our striking wrought-iron gates; and our acclaimed Edgefield and Catawba pottery. These are in themselves serious and significant artistic expressions. But they also reveal the visions and values by which our people have lived. They provide an insight into the essence of South Carolina.

It is the sharing of cultural traditions in South Carolina that is more responsible than any other single factor for the extraordinary richness of our culture. For whether stubbornly denied or acknowledged with pride, every black South Carolinian has a European heritage as well as an African one; and every white South Carolinian has an African heritage as well as a European one. A lot of our people still do not recognize it, but South Carolina was multicultural before multicultural was cool. "The black Southerner and the white Southerner are locked to the land and to history," declares the novelist Maya Angelou. We must now join hands as the brothers and sisters we are to eliminate completely the racism that has held down the state we share so long. As Dr. King put it, "Our destinies are tied together. Somewhere along the way the two must join together, black and white together, we shall overcome, and I still believe it."

Now I can't sing like angels, and I can't preach like Paul. But I know we are brothers and sisters, and I know the worth of all. Facing the rising sun of a new day begun, we're gonna keep on a-walkin', keep on a-talkin', keep on a-keepin' on. Let us make anew the old commitment that still remains to be won. For the torch has been passed—to us. I know the way is hard and progress is slow; but we must not flag in the race until the ideal becomes reality.

A few years ago I was in Brazil, a thousand miles inland at a place called Manaus. A few miles northwest of Manaus, two rivers converge at a place they call "the meeting of the waters." The Rio Solomos, a clearwater river, flows down out of the mountains and intersects the Rio Negro, a blackwater river like the Waccamaw near my home in South Carolina. At first their waters do not mingle but flow along side by side. I have videotape of myself on a boat going back and forth across that line. But after two or three miles the two rivers flow together, and when they do they become the mightiest river in the world—the Amazon. I see that as a metaphor for the people of our beloved South Carolina.

Another revitalized spiritual we used to sing was "We Shall Overcome." Someday. Some day. But how soon is someday? Someday is not a dream to be awaited, it is a goal to be achieved. Someday is not a matter of chance. It is a matter of choice.

Someday we're going to lay down the burden of race, down by the riverside. Someday we shall overcome our racism and our complacency and our violence.

Someday. But how soon is someday? Someday we shall, together, finally achieve the redeemed community. And when we do, the shared traditions that unite us will be among the symbols for which we are best known—and among the symbols of which we South Carolinians will be most proud. But how soon is someday? How soon, my brothers and my sisters, depends on us.

43. *Remembering Harry Briggs (1915–1986): son Nathaniel; wife, Eliza; and* Briggs v. Elliott *petitioner Annie Gibson at Harry Briggs's graveside on the fortieth anniversary of* Brown v. Board of Education. *Photograph by Cecil J. Williams*

Appendix

"Orangeburg, Let Us Heal Ourselves"

Statement

"Physician, heal thyself," Jesus commanded to the Israelites in a time of broken covenants and spiritual unrest. Christ offered this proverbial lesson to the spiritually impaired Jews in hopes that they would examine their relationships with God as well as with each other. Bandaging those torn relationships, or healing themselves, was His cure that would lead to redemption.

Today we must extrapolate Christ's proverbial command to the broken relationships in the Orangeburg community.

The events that took place on the campus of South Carolina State College on February 8, 1968, that led to the deaths of three students and injuries to others are deeply regrettable. More than thirty years later there is no cure, nothing that can be done to erase the fact that Henry Smith, Samuel Hammond, and Delano Middleton were killed while they were in the prime of their lives.

Each year since their deaths, there has been a memorial service in honor of these three young men. This acknowledgment of their deaths is a vital chapter in the civil rights history of Orangeburg, as well as South Carolina and the entire nation.

Today, however, we are concerned with the broken relationships in the Orangeburg community as a result of the misinterpretations of that tragic night. We recognize the right to, as well as the necessity of, a memorial service commemorating the event, but we also feel that it should be kept to the dignity for which it is intended—a solemn observance of that tragic night in 1968. It should not be marred by creating a day of racial hatred in Orangeburg by those of either race who try to rewrite the chronicle of events of that unforgettable incident.

Therefore, as a group of people dedicated to racial harmony in Orangeburg, we ask that the curtain be drawn on the theatrics of this tragedy. History cannot be rewritten, but it can and should be used to move forward and rebuild racial relations. Let us stop recreating, but solemnly recall the untimely deaths of those three young men. The annual memorial service must continue to be a foundation for better relations among the races, not the root of increased tension in the Orangeburg community.

If we do not use this memorial service as a building block for strengthened relationship, it will be detrimental to our community. Unfortunately the middle ground of both races reacts to the actions of the extremists of both races. The result is racial divisiveness, which then leads to more negative publicity in the media whose appetite for the sensational may overshadow any real concern for the well being of the community. Let us heed the age old advice to "heal ourselves" and thereby entice families to make their homes, businesses to locate, students to attend school and couples to retire in our community. Let us show them how far we have come in terms of racial relations since the tragedy of 1968.

Let us be the physicians who bring healing to our broken community,

Ronald R. Afflebach	Janie Cooper	C. A. Fischer, Jr.
James M. Albergotti, II	Steven B. Counts	George F. Flowers
Maude D. Albergotti	Catherine Cox	Gail R. Fogle
Cyrus W. Alexander, III	W. B. Cox	Ozzie Fogle
Henry B. Allen	W. B. Cox, Jr.	Dwight Frierson
Jack Anderson	Austin Cunningham	Henry F. Frierson
Ted Andrae, III	Thomas Dandridge	Alex Gardner
A. O. Anoruo	Harris B. Davis	Bob L. Garrick
W. Eugene Atkinson, II	Leroy Davis	Keith J. Gavin
J. Harvey Atwill	Nancy B. Davis	John B. Gibson
E. J. (Bob) Ayers	Lamar W. Dawkins	Ann O. Glover
George R. Barnes	Geo. R. Dean	James Glover
Joy W. Barnes	C. Parker Dempsey	Georgia Good
Wyman W. Bates	Doris D. Dempsey	Robert C. Gordon
Thomas Bell	E. W. Dickson	David M. Gmerek, Sr.
Eddie A. Bellinger	S. C. Disher, Jr.	Johnny Gramling
Isaac E. Bennett	Harvey Durant	F. Reeves Gressette, Jr.
James R. Bethune	Lula T. Durant	Paul H. Grossman, Jr.
Vance L. Boone	Jesse C. Eargle	Bert V. Gue
Charlie Boswell	Bose Edmonds	Jimmy Guthrie
John T. Bowden, Jr.	Carolyn Emanuel-	J. M. Guthrie
L. M. Bradshaw	McClain	William P. Hamilton
Barbara K. Brewer	Samuel L. Erwin	Kate E. Harper
Bennie H. Brickle	C. F. Evans	Lee Harter
Roy C. Campbell	Johnny Evans	Ray C. Hartzog
Carl A. Carpenter	Alethia H. Everett	Stephen A. Hartzog
Parthelia D. Carpenter	F. G. S. Everett, Jr.	Warren C. Hewett
Martin C. Cheatham	Joe Fairey, III	J. Rob Hibbits
Warren L. Clarke	F. R. Faulling	W. F. Hickson
Gilda Cobb-Hunter	David E. Ferrier	Mr. and Mrs. George Hill
David L. Colman	T. B. Fersner	Donnie L. Hilliard

C. John Hipp III
Robert R. Horger
Bob H. Horton
Mamie G. Howard
Robert E. Howard
Bernice Hubbard
Robert Hubbard
Ronald K. Huber
Cathy Hughes
James C. Hunter, Jr.
Trilvia Hutto
Thomas B. Jackson, Jr.
Broadus J. Jamerson, III
Donnie H. Jameson
Rachelle Jamerson
Annie A. Jamison
Marion W. Jamison, Jr.
Mark A. Jamison
Mr. and Mrs. Ulysses S.
   Jarvis., Jr.
Mary E. Jeffries
Willie Jeffries
Barry L. Jenkins
Frances H. Jennings
R. H. Jennings, III
C. Birnie Johnson
James "Poppa" Johnson
Ted M. Johnson, Jr.
Alan M. C. Johnstone
Jeannine Kees
Joseph L. Keitt
Carl D. Kennerly
Gene R. Kizer
David Lawson
Alba M. Lewis
Alexander C. Lewis
Catherine D. Livington
Clyde B. Livingston
Dean Livingston
Ezra G. Livingston
Heyward Livingston
George F. Manigo, Jr.

Hyman Marcus
Kailash Mathur
Irene W. McCollom
Joe McComb, Jr.
Donald McCurry
Edgar C. McGee
Dwight McMillan, Jr.
Earl M. Middleton
Kenneth E. Middleton
Paul Miller
Rob Miller
Harry M. Mims, Jr.
Edward Mirmow, Jr.
H. Larry Mitchell
Georgia Montgomery
Marion F. Moore
Marion Moultrie
Julie W. Nance
M. Maceo Nance, Jr.
Jeffery R. Olson
J. C. Pace
Julius Page
Jorge Pantaleon
Daniel F. Peck
Michael J. Polewczak
W. Newton Pough
Eddie Reed
George L. (Skip)
   Reynolds
John W. Rheney, III
Joyce W. Rheney
Leonard F. Rice
Richard Richardson
John H. Rickenbacker
John J. Rickenbacker
Maggie Rickenbacker
L. C. Roache
Charles A. Roberts
Herman R. Robertson
Clara B. Robinson
George L. Robinson
Willie Robinson

Jim Roquemore
D. D. Salley
Michael G. Salley, Jr.
W. Everette Salley
Tom Sanchez
Paul E. Sanders
Dow Sanderson
Leonard Sanford
Reginald E. Shaw
John F. Shuler
John Townsend Sifly
Hugo S. Sims, Jr.
Ray K. Smith
Theron W. Smith, Jr.
Melvin Smoak
Randolph Smoak, Jr.
Randy Snell
Frank M. Staley, Jr.
Valeria H. Staley
Samuel D. Stroman
Jim Sutton
Roy Sutton
Ruby Sutton
J. Steve Summers
Brian Szakovits
Kathy Tatum
William T. Taylor
Anthony C. Thompson
Henry N. Tisdale
Walter L. Tobin
D. R. Todd
Zack E. Townsend
Bernice Tribble
R. Donald Tribble
Mark Trimmier
Ron Turnblad
Leo F. Twiggs
Charles W. Underwood
Daniel W. Walker, Jr.
James F. Walsh
W. C. Wannamaker, Jr.
Dewall Waters

Allen S. Way	Carol P. Whisenhunt	Calvin Wright
Richard T. Waymer	Brenda L. Williams	Johnnie Wright, Sr.
Sara A. Waymer	Cecil J. Williams	Shellie E. Wright, Jr.
Clemmie E. Webber	Charles H. Williams	Cathy Yeadon
A. W. Welch	Margaret S. Williams	Hall Yarborough
Ben R. Wetenhall	Mary W. Williams	Henry G. Young, Sr.
L. D. Westbury	Harry F. Wimberly	Eugenia U. Ziegler
Paul Whatley	Michael A. Wolfe	Mr. and Mrs. D. M.
James R. White	John M. Worley, Jr.	Zimmerman
Jerry Whitman	Bernie L. Wright	

Press Release

A group of 250 Orangeburg citizens, in an effort to promote racial harmony, have come together to issue a joint statement asking "Orangeburg, let us heal ourselves. . . ."

The statement,[1] published in a full-page advertisement on Page 9A in today's edition of The Times and Democrat, remembers Feb. 8, 1968 and the three students who died that day on the campus of South Carolina State University: Henry Smith, Samuel Hammond and Delano Middleton.

The three students died when shot by state troopers during a prolonged confrontation centered around the desegregation of an Orangeburg bowling alley. It is often called by the name "Orangeburg Massacre," after the book by journalists Jack Bass and Jack Nelson.

And while the statement published today acknowledges the importance of remembering Smith, Hammond and Middleton, it asks that the remembrances "be kept to the dignity for which it is intended—a solemn observance of that tragic night in 1968."

"It should not be marred by creating a day of racial hatred in Orangeburg by those of either race who try rewrite the chronicle of events of that unforgettable incident," the statement says.

Each year, South Carolina State University and Orangeburg remember the deaths of Smith, Hammond and Middleton with a memorial and rededication ceremony.

But many people remember the events surrounding the deaths of the young men in different ways. Occasionally the different versions of the story clash, as they did under the heavy media coverage marking the 30th anniversary of the event last year. The controversy over the tragedy lingered for weeks on the editorial pages of The T&D and in the community as a whole.

The statement says that "History cannot be rewritten, but it can and should be used to move forward and rebuild racial relations. Let us stop recreating, but solemnly recall the untimely deaths of those three young men."

"The annual memorial service must continue to be a foundation for better relations among the races, not the root of increased tension in the Orangeburg community," the statement says.

Those signing the statement say it was created by a group of friends and acquaintances, black and white, who want to see race relations improve in the community.

Dr. Maceo Nance Jr., interim president of S.C. State on that fateful day in 1968, said he became involved in the project because, "I've been concerned as an individual down through the years about some of the negative comments emanating annually after the memorial service.

"Having harbored this concern for some time and after having expressed it to some friends and acquaintances, it was thought that some effort ought to be put forth to negate such responses. The question remained as to how to approach such an effort to gain the greatest visibility and hopefully the most positive response.

"Thus, the idea of a proclamation was suggested, voluntarily acquiring the names of a representative number of citizens of this community," he said.

Nance continued, "The proclamation, in my opinion, does three things: One, it establishes the right of the university to have a memorial program. Two, it expresses the sorrow of those participating as citizens of this community for the very tragic incident occurring in our community.

"Three, it prayerfully requests this community use this tragedy as a motivating vehicle to pull ourselves together as citizens to improve the relationships of the community and enhance the quality of life for all of us," Nance said.

"The question might arise, 'What does it all mean?' To some of us, it's hard to realize that we're moving into a fourth generation since this tragedy 31 years ago. It's appropriate for us to ask the question whether or not the supreme sacrifice made 31 years ago will go for naught," Nance said.

But, hopefully, it will ensure future generations are enlightened, "which, in turn, might provide some assurance it will not happen again," Nance said.

Dean Livingston, publisher of The T&D and one of those at the forefront of covering the tragedy three decades ago, said he joined the effort because "After 30 years, I don't see how there can be any new facts. I think we have to accept the facts and go on with our lives."

"In my lifetime, and I have been in Orangeburg now for 58 years, this is the most concerted, sincere effort for racial harmony with no ulterior motives" that he has seen.

"We're not here to pass judgment on anything," Livingston said. "We're here to accept an event that happened and make every effort to heal the wounds it caused."

"I think it's a giant step forward for Orangeburg. Our small signature can make a giant statement," he said.

Livingston said organizers are a non-political group acting in an unofficial capacity.

They were "12 people who divided these names and went out personally and got each individual's signature We're not tied to politics or anything, we're just a group of friends."

In gathering endorsements for the statement, "We didn't go to anybody in an official capacity. We just went as citizens," he said. Two anonymous donors paid for the newspaper space the statement covers, he said.

Orangeburg businessman and former legislator Earl Middleton said, "In 1999 there is a racially conciliatory mood in Orangeburg that did not exist in 1968. We must take advantage of this harmony and work together to raise the standard of living and opportunity for all the citizens of our community."

"Are things perfect? No. Have blacks caught up with whites in economic and educational opportunities? No. Do we still need to work for better health care? Yes. The difference in 1999 is that our community leaders now recognize that Orangeburg cannot progress without including everyone," he said.

Middleton continued, "In 1968, three young men—Smith, Hammond and Middleton—lost their lives trying to strengthen the access of blacks to Orangeburg's community resources. Blacks being denied admission to a recreation facility, the only bowling alley in town, ultimately led to their deaths.

"For one, I do not intend to forget their sacrifice. The fitting memorial to these young men would be for us to achieve what they died for—being able to live and work in the community in harmony with all people reaching their potential.

"This is the reason I am supporting the 'Orangeburg, let us heal ourselves . . .' letter appearing in publication this weekend. As we enter the millennium, I believe it is important for us to be open to the changes that it will take to achieve what the three young men would have wished for had they lived," Middleton said.

Businessman Parker Dempsey, an Orangeburg resident since 1953, acknowledged he has been part of the grassroots project which he hopes will help bring better focused racial harmony to Orangeburg.

"We must work to improve race relations and I think this is a great step forward toward creating a better, positive understanding between the races," he said.

"The regrettable, tragic events that took place on February 8, 1968 can't be undone. They happened. The proclamation signed by 250 people in a mixture of blacks and whites, men and women, clearly defines the course of action we must take with our lives from now on," Dempsey continued.

The memorial and rededication program for Henry Smith, Samuel Hammond and Delano Middleton will be held at 7 P.M. Monday in the Martin Luther King Jr. Auditorium on the South Carolina State University campus.

Harold A. Middlebrook, pastor of Canaan Baptist Church of Christ in Knox-ville, Tenn., will deliver the keynote address. A silent march and rededication ceremony will follow.

Note

1. Gene Crider, "'Orangeburg, let us heal ourselves': Citizens Seek Unity," *Orangeburg Times and Democrat*, February 7, 1999.

Contributors

Simon Appleford received his master's degree in modern American history from the University of St Andrews, Scotland, and currently works for the Illinois Center for Computing in Humanities, Arts, and Social Science. His research interests include the urban unrest of the 1960s and the intersection of history and digital technologies.

Raymond Arsenault is the John Hope Franklin Professor of Southern History and codirector of the Florida Studies Program at the University of South Florida, St. Petersburg. A graduate of Princeton and Brandeis universities, he has written widely on race, civil rights, and regional culture. His most recent publications are *Paradise Lost? The Environmental History of Florida* (2005), coedited with Jack E. Davis, and *Freedom Riders: 1961 and the Struggle for Racial Justice* (2006).

Tony Badger, a specialist in post–World War II southern political history, is Paul Mellon Professor of American History at Cambridge University and Master of Clare College. His books include *Prosperity Road: The New Deal, Tobacco, and North Carolina* (1980); *North Carolina and the New Deal* (1981); and *The New Deal and the Depression Years, 1933–1940* (1989). He is presently at work on a biography of Albert Gore Sr.

R. Scott Baker is an associate professor of education at Wake Forest University. He is author of *Paradoxes of Desegregation* (2006).

Jack Bass, professor of humanities and social sciences at the College of Charleston, has a Ph.D. in American studies from Emory University and is author or coauthor of seven books about the American South. They include *Strom: The Complicated Personal and Political Life of Strom Thurmond* (2005); *The Orangeburg Massacre* (1970); *Unlikely Heroes* (1981); *The Transformation of Southern Politics* (1976); and *Taming the Storm* (1993), a biography of Judge Frank M. Johnson Jr. that won the 1994 Robert Kennedy Book Award. Bass served as executive editor for *The American South Comes of Age*, a fourteen-part television course, was twice was named South Carolina journalist of the year, and was a Nieman Fellow at Harvard.

FRANK BEACHAM's latest book is *Whitewash: A Southern Journey through Music, Mayhem and Murder* (2002). Based in New York City, he was executive producer of Tim Robbins's feature film *Cradle Will Rock* (1990). His new play, *Maverick,* is about a year-long collaboration with the late Orson Welles.

BEATRICE BURTON is a Ph.D. candidate studying southern history at the University of Georgia.

ORVILLE VERNON BURTON, a native of Ninety Six, South Carolina, is Burroughs Distinguished Professor of Southern History and Culture at Coastal Carolina University and the author or editor of numerous articles and books, including *In My Father's House Are Many Mansions: Family and Community in Edgefield, South Carolina* (1985) and *The Age of Lincoln* (2007).

DAN CARTER is Educational Foundation Professor of History Emeritus at the University of South Carolina. He is the author and editor of numerous books and articles including *Scottsboro: A Tragedy of the American South* (1969); *When the War Was Over: The Failure of Self-Reconstruction in the South, 1865–1868* (1985); *The Politics of Rage: George Wallace, the Origins of the New Conservatism and the Transformation of American Politics* (1995); and *From George Wallace to Newt Gingrich: Race in the Conservative Counterrevolution, 1963–1994* (1996).

M. RON COX JR., a native of Williamsburg County, attended East Clarendon High School (Turbeville) and graduated summa cum laude from Wofford College (Spartanburg) with a bachelor's degree in history. He completed his master's and Ph.D. at the University of South Carolina working under Dr. Walter Edgar, and his dissertation focused on South Carolina's desegregation efforts in 1963. Ron is associate dean for academic and student affairs at USC Lancaster and also continues to teach courses in U.S., southern, and South Carolina history.

CONSTANCE CURRY is an activist and author of three books about grassroots leaders she met while working in the freedom movement in Mississippi in the 1960s—*Silver Rights* (1995), *Aaron Henry: The Fire Ever Burning* (2000), and *Mississippi Harmony: Memoirs of a Freedom Fighter* (2002)—and coauthor/editor of *Deep in Our Hearts: Nine White Women in the Freedom Movement* (2000). A graduate of Agnes Scott College and Woodrow Wilson College of Law, she lives in Atlanta and is presently involved in work to undo the "schools to prison pipeline" now rampant with public school resegregation and the racism in the criminal justice system.

JOSEPH A. DE LAINE JR. is a retired marketing and advertising executive. He lives in Charlotte, North Carolina, and remains active in civil rights work.

JAMES O. FARMER earned his Ph.D. from the University of South Carolina and holds the June Rainsford Henderson Chair in Southern and Local History at the

University of South Carolina Aiken. He has published on antebellum religious thought, the impact of outside cultures on southern communities, Civil War reenactments, and the woman suffrage movement in the Palmetto State. His current research focuses on the histories of Edgefield and Aiken counties.

TERENCE R. FINNEGAN is an associate professor of history at William Paterson University. He is co-editor of *Charting Advances in Social Sciences Computing* and the author of articles on lynching in Mississippi and South Carolina.

JOHN HOPE FRANKLIN is James B. Duke Professor Emeritus of History at Duke University. His many trailblazing books include *From Slavery to Freedom: A History of African Americans* (1967), *The Militant South, 1800–1861* (1956), and, most recently, *Mirror to America: The Autobiography of John Hope Franklin* (2005). Paralleling his academic career as one of the most influential historians of the past century are his numerous contributions to American public life, including his work on the National Council on the Humanities, on the Advisory Commission on Public Diplomacy, as U.S. delegate to UNESCO, and as chairman of President Bill Clinton's Advisory Board for One America: The President's Initiative on Race.

HARVEY B. GANTT is a cofounder of the firm of Gantt-Huberman Architects and a fellow in the American Institute of Architects. In addition to his architectural career he has held many public positions, including served two terms as mayor of Charlotte, North Carolina.

WILLIAM GRAVELY, a native of Pickens, South Carolina, is a graduate of Wofford College and Duke University. He is Professor Emeritus at the University of Denver, where he taught from 1968 to 2001. He is author of *Gilbert Haven, Methodist Abolitionist* (1973) and of essays on religion and race in U.S. history.

WILLIAM C. HINE has taught history at South Carolina State University for more than thirty years. In 2001 he helped coordinate compilation of oral histories of those who had been involved in the 1968 Orangeburg Massacre. He is also a coauthor (with Darlene Clark Hine and Stanley Harrold) of the widely adopted college textbook *The African-American Odyssey* (2000).

ERNEST F. HOLLINGS recently retired from public life. He served in the United States Army during World War II and practiced law prior to launching a political career in 1948. Among the many offices he has hold are those of governor of South Carolina (1959–1963) and United States senator from South Carolina (1966–2005).

JANET G. HUDSON is assistant professor of history at the University of South Carolina—Continuing Education. Her essay in this volume is part of a larger study in progress about the intersection of race, class, and reform in World

War I–era South Carolina—a society constructed and constrained by the ideology of white supremacy.

CHARLES JOYNER is Burroughs Distinguished Professor Emeritus of Southern History and Culture at Coastal Carolina University. He is the author of *Down by the Riverside: A South Carolina Slave Community* (1984) and *Shared Traditions: Southern History and Folk Culture* (1999), and he has lectured on the South in Europe, Africa, North and South America, Asia, and Australasia. He is currently writing a book titled "A Region in Harmony: Southern Music and the Sound Track of Freedom."

ROBERT R. KORSTAD is associate professor of public policy studies and history at Duke University. His research interests include twentieth-century U. S. history, labor history, African American history, and contemporary social policy. His publications include *Civil Rights Unionism: Tobacco Workers and the Struggle for Democracy in the Mid-Twentieth-Century South* (2003); *Remembering Jim Crow: African Americans Talk About Life in the Segregated South* (2001); *Like a Family: The Making of a Southern Cotton Mill World* (coauthor, revised edition, 2000).

PETER F. LAU teaches history at the Wheeler School and Rhode Island School of Design, both in Providence, Rhode Island. He is the author of *Democracy Rising: South Carolina and the Fight for Black Equality since 1865* (2006) and editor of *From the Grassroots to the Supreme Court: Brown v. Board of Education and American Democracy* (2004). He lives in Rumford, Rhode Island, with his wife and two children.

CHARLES F. McDEW is a professor of African American history and civil rights at Metropolitan State University. He is at work on a book about the civil rights movements of the twentieth century.

JOHN MONK is an award-winning journalist with the *State* newspaper in Columbia, South Carolina.

WINFRED B. MOORE JR. is professor of history at the Citadel. He is the editor of several books including most recently *Warm Ashes: Issues in Southern History at the Dawn of the Twenty-First Century* (2003).

STEPHEN O'NEILL is an associate professor of history at Furman University, where he also serves as director of Furman's Huff Center for Piedmont History. He has also been the chief history consultant for exhibit design and content at the History Museum of the Upcountry in Greenville, South Carolina. He is currently writing an environmental history of the Saluda and Reedy River watersheds, which are located in upstate South Carolina.

MATTHEW J. PERRY JR. is a U.S. district court judge in Columbia, South Carolina. Prior to his appointment to the bench, he was legal counsel for the NAACP in South Carolina, in which capacity he acted as chief litigator in many landmark civil rights cases.

STEPHEN L. PRESKILL is Regent's Professor in the Educational Leadership and Organizational Learning Department in the College of Education at the University of New Mexico. He is the coauthor of *Discussion as a Way of Teaching: Tools and Techniques for Democratic Classrooms* (1999).

BEATRICE BROWN RIVERS resides in Summerton, South Carolina.

ELIZABETH ROBESON is a doctoral candidate in American history at Columbia University specializing in the social and cultural history of early-twentieth-century South Carolina.

WIM ROEFS is a historian and free-lance writer as well as an art dealer, consultant, and curator. He did doctoral work in American history at the University of South Carolina and is the owner of ART Gallery in Columbia, South Carolina.

CLEVELAND L. SELLERS JR. is director of the African American Studies Program at the University of South Carolina. He is the author of *The River of No Return: The Autobiography of a Black Militant and the Life and Death of SNCC* (1973).

JORDAN M. SIMMONS III (Lt. Col, U.S. Army retired) is a veteran of the Vietnam War and of Operation Desert Storm. He currently works for Lockheed Martin in Falls Church, Virginia.

JOHN C. WEST was a veteran of World War II and held many public offices, including governor of South Carolina (1971–1975) and U.S. ambassador to Saudi Arabia (1977–1981).

JOHN W. WHITE is archivist of special collections at the Robert Smalls Library of the College of Charleston. He is at work on a book on the citizens, council movement in South Carolina.

GAVIN WRIGHT is the William Robertson Coe Professor of American Economic History at Stanford University. His publications on southern economic history include *The Political Economy of the Cotton South* (1978); *Old South, New South* (1986); and *Slavery and American Economic Development* (2006). Wright's current research deals with economic aspects of the Civil rights revolution in the South.

Index

Page numbers in italics refer to photographs.